Time Out

Tokyo

timeout.com/tokyo

Penguin Books

PENGUIN BOOKS

Published by the Penguin Group
Penguin Books Ltd, 80 Strand, London WC2R ORL, England
Penguin Books USA Inc., 375 Hudson Street, New York, New York 10014, USA
Penguin Books Australia Ltd, 250 Camberwell Road, Camberwell, Victoria 3124, Australia
Penguin Books Canada Ltd, 10 Alcorn Avenue, Toronto, Ontario, Canada M4V 3B2
Penguin Books (NZ) Ltd, cnr Rosedale and Airborne Roads, Albany, Auckland, New Zealand

Penguin Books Ltd, Registered Offices: Harmondsworth, Middlesex, England

First published 1999
Second edition 2001
Third edition 2003

Third edition 2003
10 9 8 7 6 5 4 3 2 1

Colour reprographics by Icon, Crowne House, 56-58 Southwark Street, London SE1 1UN
Printed and bound by Cayfosa-Quebecor, Ctra. de Caldes, Km 3 08 130 Sta, Perpètua de Mogoda, Barcelona, Spain

Edited and designed by
Time Out Guides Limited
Universal House
251 Tottenham Court Road
London W1T 7AB
Tel + 44 (0)20 7813 3000
Fax + 44 (0)20 7813 6001
Email guides@timeout.com
www.timeout.com

Editorial
Editor Nigel Kendall
Deputy Editor Rosamund Sales
Listings Editor Sonobe Yuka
Proofreader Nicholas Royle
Indexer Anna Raikes

Editorial/Managing Director Peter Fiennes
Series Editor Ruth Jarvis
Deputy Series Editor Lesley McCave
Guides Co-ordinator Anna Norman
Accountant Sarah Bostock

Design
Art Director Mandy Martin
Art Editor Scott Moore
Senior Designer Tracey Ridgewell
Designers Astrid Kogler, Sam Lands
Digital Imaging Dan Conway
Ad Make-up Charlotte Blythe
Picture Editor Kerri Littlefield
Acting Picture Editor Kit Burnet
Acting Deputy Picture Editor Martha Houghton
Picture Desk Trainee Bella Wood
Picture Researcher Alex Ortiz

Advertising
Sales Director Mark Phillips
International Sales Manager Ross Canadé
International Sales Executive James Tuson
Advertising Sales (Toyko) Alexandra Press
Advertising Assistant Sabrina Ancilleri

Marketing
Marketing Manager Mandy Martinez
US Publicity & Marketing Associate Rosella Albanese

Production
Guides Production Director Mark Lamond
Production Controller Samantha Furniss

Time Out Group
Chairman Tony Elliott
Managing Director Mike Hardwick
Group Financial Director Richard Waterlow
Group Commercial Director Lesley Gill
Group Marketing Director Christine Cort
Group General Manager Nichola Coulthard
Group Art Director John Oakey
Online Managing Director David Pepper

Features in this guide were written, updated and researched by:
Introduction Nigel Kendall. **History** Steve Walsh. **Tokyo Today** Victor France. **Architecture** Steve Walsh. **Geography** Steve Walsh. **Sex & the City** Rob Schwartz. **Accommodation** Nigel Kendall. **Sightseeing** Nigel Kendall (general sights, Ginza, Ikebukuro, Roppongi, Shibuya, Ueno, Toyoko Line, Yanaka), John McGee (museums), John Paul Catton (Asakusa, Odaiba, Shimo-Kitazawa), François Trahan (Marunouchi), Rob Schwartz (Harajuku & Omotesando, Shinjuku), James Barrett (Chuo Line). **Eating Out** Nigel Kendall (*Cheap chain gang* Matsuoka Chitose) (*Japanese cuisine* Robbie Swinnerton) (*Street food* Aeve Baldwin) (*Themed dining* Nigel Kendall) (*Menu reader* Hosoe Masami). **Coffee Shops** Steve Walsh. **Shops & Services** John Paul Catton. **Festivals & Events** Steve Walsh. **Children** Obe Mitsuru, Obe Rie. **Film** Kobayashi Mika. **Galleries** John McGee. **Gay & Lesbian** Alex Vega. **Music** François Trahan, Ubukata Mami, Michael Pronko (jazz). **Nightlife** Pip. **Performing Arts** Nigel Kendall. **Sport & Fitness** Steve Walsh. **Trips Out of Town** Nigel Kendall (Yokohama, Hakone), François Trahan (Kamakura, Mountains, Beaches, Nikko). **Directory** Sonobe Yuka (*Getting by in Japanese* Hosoe Masami).

The Editor would like to thank: All contributors to the previous two editions, particularly Robbie Swinnerton and Aeve Baldwin, and Sonobe Yuka, Robb Satterwhite, Charles Spreckley, Nakano Miwako, Hosoe Masami, Matsuoka Chitose, Kate Ryan, Nicholas Royle, Ito Daisuke, Tanaka Yuko and the staff of the Tokyo Convention and Visitors Bureau, and the staff of the Yokohama Convention and Visitors Bureau.

Maps J.S. Graphics (john@jsgraphics.co.uk). Street maps are based on material supplied by the Tokyo Convention and Visitors Bureau.

Photography by Mitchell Coster except: pages 129, 193, 233, 277 Adam Eastland; 12 AFP; 6, 9 AKG London; 253 AP Photo; 118 Buena Vista (now available on DVD); 11 Corbis; 25 Infoterra; 211 John McGee; 262, 265 Nigel Kendall; 13, 249 Popperfoto; 29, 31 Rob Schwartz.
The following images were provided by the featured establishments/artists: pages 18, 199, 244, 271.

Contents

Introduction

Welcome to one of the biggest and most undiscovered cities in the world. It's a curious fact that for all Japan's economic prominence as the world's second largest economy, its capital city remains firmly off the tourist trail.

While this is in no small part due to the Japanese government's longstanding reluctance to promote Japan as a tourist destination, the other factor most often cited is expense. Year after year, Tokyo tops the table of the world's most expensive cities, yet even a cursory glance through our recommendations will reveal that it really isn't that costly at all.

The Japanese recession, which has now been depressing the world's markets for over ten years, may be bad news for banks and shareholders, but it's great news for visitors. Prices here have changed little in a decade, giving other cities such as London and New York time to catch up. Japanese tourists now regularly return from London complaining about the cost of eating out.

So if expense is no longer an issue, what is it that keeps people away? The main problem faced by first-time visitors to Tokyo is the language. Although the situation has improved in recent years, particularly during the World Cup in 2002, many signs in shops and stations remain in Japanese only. At first, this can be utterly bewildering, though it's surprising how quickly one retains regularly seen Chinese characters. If you have time, you will find that learning *katakana*, the syllabary used to spell out foreign words, will boost your enjoyment of Toyko significantly, enabling you to read menus and shop names.

The lucky few who do visit Tokyo will find it one of the most rewarding experiences of their lives. Not only is the city vibrant, its restaurants superb and its bars open all night, the people here are among the friendliest in any major city. Tokyoites are warm, generous and fiercely curious about the world outside their shores. They're undoubtedly the city's greatest asset.

ABOUT THE TIME OUT CITY GUIDES

The *Time Out Tokyo Guide* is one of an expanding series of Time Out City Guides produced by the people behind London and New York's successful listings magazines. Our guides are all written and updated by resident experts who have striven to provide you with all the most up-to-date information you'll need to explore the city, whether you're a local or first-time visitor.

THE LOWDOWN ON THE LISTINGS

Above all, we've tried to make this book as useful as possible. Addresses, telephone numbers, websites, transport information, opening times, admission prices and credit card details are all included in our listings. And, as far as possible, we've given details of facilities, services and events, all checked and correct at the time we went to press. However, in Tokyo, businesses open and close with lightning speed. Furthermore, many restaurants and bars can close unexpectedly for the day at the whim of the owner. Before you go out of your way, we would advise you whenever possible to phone and check opening times. While every effort has been made to ensure the accuracy of the information contained here, the publishers cannot accept responsibility for any errors it may contain.

PRICES AND PAYMENT

Prices throughout this guide are given in Japanese yen (¥). The prices we've supplied should be treated as guidelines, not gospel. If they vary wildly from those we've quoted, please write and let us know. We aim to give the best and most up-to-date advice, so we always want to know if you've been badly treated or overcharged, or if (as we hope) you've been pleasantly surprised.

We have noted whether venues take credit cards but have only listed the major cards – American Express (**AmEx**), Diners Club (**DC**), MasterCard (**MC**) and Visa (**V**). Note that most small businesses tourist sights in Japan do not accept credit cards.

THE LIE OF THE LAND

We have divided the main city area of Tokyo's 23 wards into Central, North, South, East and West. The Sightseeing section, *see p54*, contains maps of the key areas, with all local recommendations clearly marked. The map on page 55 provides an overview of the 23 wards of Tokyo. A map of the entire greater Tokyo area can be found on page 310. All listings contain the name of the nearest railway station and most convenient station exit, and map references are provided where appropriate.

TELEPHONE NUMBERS

The area code for central Tokyo is 03. This is always followed by an eight-digit number. All central telephone numbers given in this guide omit the 03 prefix. The outlying areas of Tokyo have different codes. For such places, the full number is provided. Numbers beginning with the prefix 0120 are freephone numbers, while most mobile phone numbers in Japan begin with the prefix 090. The international dialling code for Japan is 81. For further details of telephone codes and charges, see p289.

Advertisers

We would like to stress that no establishment has been included in this guide because it has advertised in any of our publications and no payment of any kind has influenced any review. The opinions given in this book are those of Time Out writers and entirely independent.

ESSENTIAL INFORMATION

For all the practical information you'll need for visiting the city – including visa and customs information, advice on facilities for the disabled, emergency telephone numbers and medical services, plus a list of useful websites and the full lowdown on Tokyo's vast, amazingly efficient rail and subway networks – turn to the **Directory** chapter. You'll find it at the back of this guide, starting on page 278. A full map of all rail services is on page 314.

LET US KNOW WHAT YOU THINK

We hope you enjoy the *Time Out Tokyo Guide*, and we'd like to know what you think of it. We welcome tips for places that you believe we should include in future editions and take notice of your criticism of our choices. There's a reader's reply card at the back of this book – or you can email us at guides@timeout.com.

There is an online version of this guide at **www.timeout.com**.

In Context

Features

Tokyo blossoms in the Meiji era.

History

From prehistoric uncertainty to modern-day madness.

Archaeological evidence suggests today's metropolitan area was inhabited as long ago as the late Paleolithic period, and stone tools belonging to hunter-gatherers of pre-ceramic culture have been discovered at sites such as Nogawa in western Tokyo Prefecture.

Pottery featuring rope-cord patterns developed in Japan during the so-called Jomon period (10,000-300 BC). Around 6,000 years ago, Tokyo Bay rose as far as the edge of the high ground that makes up the central *yamanote* area of the modern city (*see p26*); its retreat left behind a marshy shoreline that provided a rich food source. The late Jomon shell mounds at Omori, identified in 1877 by US zoologist E S Morse, were the site of Japan's first modern archaeological dig and forerunner to a long line of similar excavations.

The Yayoi period (300 BC-AD 300) is named after the Yayoi-cho district near Tokyo University in Hongo, where in 1884 the Mukogaoka shell mound yielded the first evidence of a more sophisticated form of pottery. Along with other advances such as wet-rice cultivation and the use of iron, this seems to have been introduced from the Asian mainland. Only after arriving on Kyushu did new techniques spread through Honshu.

BACKWATER

Kanto remained a distant outpost as the early Japanese state started to form around the Yamato court, which emerged in the fourth century as a loose confederation of chieftains in what is now Nara Prefecture before slowly extending to other parts of the country. Chinese ideographs and Buddhism both arrived via the Korean peninsula.

Senso-ji Temple (*see p82*) supposedly dates from AD 628, when two fishermen are said to have discovered a gold statue of the *bodhisattva* Kannon in their nets. Under Taika Reform from 645, the land on which Tokyo now stands became part of Musashi province, governed from Kokufu (modern-day Fuchu City). State administration was centralised in emulation of the Tang imperial model and China's advanced civilisation exerted a strong influence.

After the imperial capital was moved to Heian (Kyoto) in 794, a Japanese court culture flourished, and the invention of the *kana* syllabary helped the writing of classics such as Sei Shonagon's *Pillow Book* and Lady Murasaki's *Tale of Genji*. The emperors were largely figureheads, manipulated by powerful regents from the dominant Fujiwara family. But the political power of the Kyoto court nobles went into slow decline as control of the regions fell into the hands of the local military aristocracy.

REBELLION

An early revolt against Kyoto rule was staged by Taira no Masakado, a tenth-century rebel. According to one version, a quarrel over a woman among different members of the 'Eight Bands of Taira from the East' in 931 escalated into full-scale military conflict, during which Masakado won control of all eight provinces of Kanto. He then declared himself emperor of a new autonomous state.

After defeat by central government forces in 940, grisly evidence of Masakado's demise was dispatched to Kyoto. Legend has it that his severed head took to the skies and flew back to be reunited with his other remains in the fishing village of Shibasaki. The site is now in the Otemachi financial district but has remained untouched by generations of city builders, perhaps fearful of Masakado's vengeful spirit (Masakado Kubizuka, Otemachi station, exit C5).

BIRTH OF EDO

Tokyo's original name, Edo ('Rivergate'), is thought to derive from a settlement near where Sumida river enters Tokyo Bay. Its first known use goes back to a minor member of the Taira clan, Edo Shigenaga, who is thought to have adopted it after making his home in the area. In August 1180 Shigenaga attacked the forces of Miura Yoshizumi, an ally of the rival Minamoto clan. He switched sides three months later, though, just as shogun-to-be Minamoto no Yoritomo entered Musashi province.

By the late 12th century, the rise of the warrior clans had developed into a struggle between the Taira and Minamoto families. After Minamoto no Yoritomo wiped out the last of the Tairas in 1185, the emperor dubbed him Seii Tai Shogun ('Barbarian-Subduing Generalissimo'). Yoritomo shunned Kyoto, setting up his government in Kamakura (*see p266*).

This inaugurated a period of military rule that was to last till the 19th century. *Bushido*, 'the way of the warrior', emphasised martial virtues, while the samurai class emerged as a powerful force in feudal society. Nevertheless, attempted Mongol invasions in 1274 and 1281 were only driven back by stormy seas off Kyushu, something attributed to the *kamikaze*, or 'wind of the gods'. Dissatisfaction grew with the Kamakura government, and in 1333 Ashikaga Takauji established a new shogunate in the Muromachi district of Kyoto.

The first castle at Edo was erected in 1457 by Ota Dokan, a *waka* poet known as Ota Sekenaga before taking a monk's tonsure in 1478, now celebrated as Tokyo's founder. Above the Hibiya Inlet, he constructed fortifications overlooking the entrance to the Kanto plain on the Pacific sea road. To improve navigation, he also diverted the Hirakawa east at Kandabashi to form the Nihonbashi river.

In 1486, during a military clash between branches of the locally powerful Uesugi family, Ota was falsely accused of betraying his lord, and met his end at the home of Uesugi Sadamasa in Sagami (modern-day Kanagawa).

Central government authority largely disappeared following the Onin War (1467-77), as regional lords, or *daimyo*, fought for dominance. Only after a century of civil strife did the country begin to regain unity under Oda Nobunaga, although his assassination in 1582 meant that final reunification was left to Toyotomi Hideyoshi. In 1590, Hideyoshi established control of the Kanto region after successfully besieging Odawara Castle, stronghold of the powerful Go-Hojo family.

'In an age when London still had under one million people, Edo was the world's biggest metropolis.'

Hideyoshi ordered his ally Tokugawa Ieyasu to exchange his lands in Shizuoka and Aichi for the former Go-Hojo domains in Kanto. Rather than Odawara, in present-day Kanagawa Prefecture, Ieyasu chose Edo as headquarters. A new castle was built on the site of Ota Dokan's fortifications. After Hideyoshi's death, Ieyasu was victorious in the struggle for national power at the Battle of Sekigahara in 1600, and three years later was named shogun. The emperor remained in Kyoto, but Edo became the government capital of Japan.

EDO ERA (1600-1868)

When Ieyasu arrived in 1590, Edo was little more than a few houses at the edge of Hibiya Inlet. This changed quickly. Equally divided between military and townspeople, the population grew dramatically before levelling off in the early 18th century at around 1.2 million. In an age when London still had under one million people, Edo was probably the world's biggest metropolis. Fifteen successive Tokugawa shoguns ruled for more than 250 years. All roads led to Edo: five highways radiated from the city, communications aided by regular post stations, including Shinagawa, Shinjuku, Itabashi and Senju.

Feudal lords retained local autonomy, but a system of alternate annual residence forced them to divide their time between their own lands and the capital. *Daimyo* finances were drained by the regular journeys with retinues and the need to maintain Edo residences. There was little chance to foment trouble in the provinces, and as a further inducement to loyalty, family members were kept in Edo as permanent hostages.

Although Tokugawa Ieyasu's advisers had included Englishman Will Adams (whose story is fictionalised in the novel *Shogun*), a policy of national seclusion was introduced in 1639. Contact with western countries was restricted to a small Dutch trade mission on the island of Dejima, near Nagasaki in Kyushu, far from Edo.

The layout of Edo reflected the social order, with the *yamanote* high ground the preserve of the military classes, and the townspeople occupying the *shitamachi* ('low city') areas outside the castle walls to the east. There was also an attempt to conform to Chinese principles of geomancy by having the two temples that would hold the Tokugawa family tombs, Kanei-ji and Zojo-ji, in the auspicious north-east and south-west of the city. More problematically, since Mount Fuji lay west rather than north, the traditionally favoured direction for a mountain, Edo Castle's main Ote gate was placed on its east side, instead of the usual south.

Completed in 1638, Edo Castle was the world's largest. Its outer defences extended 16 kilometres (ten miles). The most important of the four sets of fortifications, the *hon-maru* or principal fortress, contained the shogun's residence, the inner chambers for his wife and concubines, and the halls of state. The keep stood on an adjacent hill, overlooking the city. Between the double set of moats, provincial *daimyo* had their mansions arranged in a strict hierarchy of 'dependent' and 'outside' lords.

East of the castle walls, the low-lying *shitamachi* districts were home to merchants, craftsmen, labourers and others attracted to Edo's wealth and power. Less than one-fifth of the land, much of it reclaimed, held around half of the population. Nihonbashi's wooden bridge was the hub of the nation's highways and the spot from which all distances were measured.

Nearby were wealthy merchants' residences and grand shops, the city's prison, and the fish market. Behind grand thoroughfares, the crowded backstreet tenements of Nihonbashi and Kanda were a breeding ground for disease and were in constant danger of flooding. Fires were common in the largely wooden city.

LONG SLEEVES FIRE

The original castle buildings were just one victim of the Long Sleeves Fire of 1657. Over 100,000 people died, around a quarter of Edo's total population, in three days of conflagration across the city. The flames began at a temple, Hommyo-ji in Hongo, where monks had been burning two long-sleeved kimonos belonging to young women who had recently died. By the morning of the fourth day, three-quarters of Edo had been destroyed.

Reconstruction began soon afterwards. Roads were widened and new fire breaks introduced. Many had perished because they couldn't escape across the Sumida river, which, for military reasons, had no bridges: opening up Fukagawa and Honjo for development, a bridge was now built at Ryogoku. There was also a dispersal of temples and shrines to outlying areas such as Yanaka and reclaimed land in Tsukiji. The Yoshiwara pleasure quarters were moved out, too – from Ningyocho to beyond Asakusa and the newly extended city limits.

'By the morning of the fourth day, three-quarters of Edo had been destroyed.'

New residences for *daimyo* were established outside the castle walls, leading to a mix of noble estates and districts for townspeople, although the basic pattern of eastern *shitamachi* areas was retained. *Daimyo* mansions inside the castle were rebuilt in a more restrained style. The innermost section of the reconstructed castle was more subdued, lacking the high tower of its predecessor.

47 RONIN INCIDENT

One by-product of the stability of the Tokugawa regime was that the large number of military personnel stationed in Edo found themselves with relatively little to do. A complex bureaucracy developed, and there were ceremonial duties, but members of the top strata of the feudal system found themselves outstripped economically by the city's wealthy merchants. In these circumstances, a daring vendetta attack staged by the band of masterless samurai known later as the 47 *ronin* caused a sensation. In 1701, provoked by Kira Yoshinaka, the shogun's chief of protocol, Lord Ako had drawn his sword inside Edo Castle, an illegal act for which he was forced to commit ritual suicide.

Two years later, 46 of his former retainers (one dropped out at the last moment) attacked the Edo mansion of the man they blamed for his death. Emerging with Kira's head, they marched through the city to offer it to Lord Ako's grave at Sengaku-ji Temple (*see p80*). Despite public acclaim for their righteous actions, the 46 were themselves now sentenced to ritual suicide.

Over 60 per cent of Tokyo homes were destroyed by the 1923 earthquake. *See p11.*

The incident forms the basis of one of *kabuki*'s most popular plays, *Kanadehon Chushinjura* ('The Treasury of the Loyal Retainers'), written originally for *bunraku* puppet theatre and first staged in 1748. The story was diplomatically relocated to 14th-century Kamakura.

CULTURE CAPITAL

A vibrant new urban culture grew up in Edo's *shitamachi* districts. During the long years of peace and relative prosperity, the pursuit of pleasure provided the populace, particularly the city's wealthy merchants, with welcome relief from the feudal system's stifling social confines. Landscape artists such as Hiroshige (1797-1868) depicted a city of theatres, temples, scenic bridges, festivals and fairs. There were numerous seasonal celebrations, including big firework displays to celebrate the summer opening of the Sumida river, as well as cherry-blossom viewing along its banks in spring.

Kabuki, an Edo favourite, didn't always have the approval of the high city. In 1842 a government edict banished theatres up the Sumida river to Asakusa, where they stayed until after the fall of the shogunate. As the district already boasted Senso-ji Temple, with its fairs and festivals, and the Yoshiwara pleasure quarters lay only a short distance away, the act merely cemented Asakusa's position as Edo's favoured relaxation centre.

BLACK SHIPS

Notice that Japan could no longer isolate itself from the outside world arrived in Edo Bay in 1853 as four US 'black ships' under the command of Commodore Matthew Perry. Hastily prepared defences were helpless, and the treaty signed with Perry the following year proved to be the thin end of the wedge, as western powers forced further concessions. In 1855, Edo suffered a major quake that killed over 7,000 and destroyed large parts of the lower city. In 1859, Townsend Harris, the first US consul-general, arrived to set up a mission at Zenpuku-ji Temple in Azabu (*see p81*).

Voices of discontent had already been raised against the government: there were increasingly frequent famines, and proponents of 'National Learning' called for a return to some purer form of Shinto tradition. The foreign threat now polarised opinion. In 1860, the senior councillor of the shogunate, Ii Naosuke, was assassinated outside Edo Castle. Under the slogan 'expel the barbarian, revere the emperor', a series of incidents took place against foreigners. Power drained from Edo as the government looked to build a unified national policy by securing imperial backing in Kyoto. *Daimyo* residences in Edo were abandoned after the old alternate residence requirement was abolished in 1862.

The Tokugawa regime was finally overthrown early in 1868, when a coalition of forces from the south declared an imperial 'restoration' in Kyoto in the name of the 15-year-old Meiji emperor, then won a military victory at Toba-Fushimi. Edo's population fell to around half its former level as remaining residents of the *yamanote* areas departed. A last stand by shogunate loyalists in Ueno was hopeless, and left in ruins large parts of the Kanei-ji Temple complex, which housed several Tokugawa shoguns' tombs.

MEIJI ERA (1868-1912)

Edo was renamed Tokyo ('Eastern Capital') when the emperor's residence was transferred from Kyoto in 1868. It now became both the political and imperial capital, with the inner section of Edo Castle serving as the new Imperial Palace. The population had reverted to its earlier level by the mid 1880s, but *shitamachi* lost much of its cultural distinctiveness as wealthier residents moved to smarter locations. Industrialisation continued to bring newcomers from the countryside. By the end of the Meiji era, Tokyo housed nearly two million people.

'Rich country, strong army. That was the rallying-cry, but learning from abroad was essential.'

To the south-west of the palace, Nagatacho and Kasumigaseki became the heart of the nation's new government and bureaucratic establishment. 'Rich country, strong army' was the rallying cry, but learning from abroad was recognised to be essential: government missions were dispatched overseas, foreign experts brought in, and radical reforms initiated in everything from education to land ownership.

Laying the foundations of a modern state meant sweeping away much of the old feudal structure. Government was centralised, the *daimyo* pensioned off. The introduction of conscription in 1873 ended the exclusive role of the warrior class. Disaffected elements led by Saigo Takamori rebelled in Satsuma in 1877, but were defeated by government forces. The next year, six former samurai from Satsuma staged a revenge attack and murdered Meiji government leader Okubo Toshimichi.

Ending old social restrictions fuelled economic development. The Bank of Japan was established in 1882, bringing greater fiscal and monetary stability. Industrialisation proceeded apace and factories sprang up near the Sumida river and in areas overlooking Tokyo Bay. After 1894, Marunouchi became the site of a business district called 'London Town' because of its blocks of Victorian-style office buildings.

In 1889, a written constitution declared the emperor 'sacred and inviolable'. Real power remained with existing government leaders but there was a nod to greater popular representation. Elections were held among the top 1.5 per cent of taxpayers, and the first session of the Imperial Diet took place in 1890.

By the early 1890s, the government was making progress on ending the much-hated 'unequal treaties' earlier conceded to the west. Taking a leaf from the imperialists' book, Japan seized Taiwan in 1895 after a war with China. Ten years later its forces defeated Russia. This was the first victory over a western power by an Asian country, but there were riots in Hibiya Park at the perceived leniency of the peace treaty. In 1910, Japan annexed Korea.

EAST MEETS WEST

New goods and ideas from overseas started to pour into Tokyo, especially after Japan's first train line started services between Yokohama and Shinbashi station in 1872. Men abandoned traditional topknots; married women followed the lead of the empress and stopped blackening their teeth. There were gas lights, beer halls, the first public parks and department stores, and even ballroom dancing at Hibiya's glittering Rokumeikan, where the elite gathered in their best foreign finery to display their mastery of the advanced new ways.

The former artisan district of Ginza was redeveloped with around 900 brick buildings after a major fire in 1872, and newspaper offices were the first to flock to what would become Tokyo's most fashionable area. Asakusa kept in touch with popular tastes through attractions such as the Ryounkaku: at 12 storeys, it was Tokyo's tallest building and had the city's first elevator. Asakusa was also home to Japan's first permanent cinema, which opened in 1903, and the cinemas, theatres and music halls of the Rokku district remained popular throughout the early decades of the new century.

TAISHO ERA (1912-26)

The funeral of Emperor Meiji was accompanied by the ritual suicide of General Nogi, a hero of the Russo-Japanese War. The new emperor was in constant poor health and his son, Hirohito, became regent in 1921.

There was a brief flowering of 'Taisho Democracy': in 1918 Hara Takashi became the first prime minister from a political party, an appointment that came after a sudden rise in rice prices prompted national disturbances, including five days of rioting in the capital. Hara was assassinated in 1921 by a right-wing extremist, but universal male suffrage was finally introduced in 1925.

General MacArthur prepares to introduce democracy to Emperor Hirohito. *See p13.*

The city was beginning to spill over its boundaries and part of Shinjuku was brought inside the city limits for the first time in 1920, an early indication of the capital's tendency to drift further westwards following the expansion of suburban train lines. Ginza was enjoying its heyday as a strolling spot for fashionable youth. In nearby Hibiya, a new Imperial Hotel, designed by Frank Lloyd Wright, opened in 1923.

GREAT KANTO EARTHQUAKE

Shortly before noon on 1 September 1923, the Kanto region was hit by a devastating earthquake. High winds fanned the flames of cooking fires and two days of terrible conflagrations swept through Tokyo and the surrounding area, including Yokohama, leaving over 140,000 dead and devastating large areas.

Around 63 per cent of Tokyo homes were destroyed, with the traditional wooden buildings of the old *shitamachi* areas hardest hit. Rumours of well-poisoning and other misdeeds led vigilante groups to massacre several thousand Koreans before martial law was imposed.

Temporary structures were quickly in place and there was a short building boom. The destruction in eastern areas accelerated the population movement to the western suburbs, but plans to remodel the city were largely laid aside because of cost.

SHOWA ERA (1926-89)

The reign of Hirohito, the longest of any Japanese emperor, coincided with a period of extraordinary change and turbulence. Tokyo recovered gradually from the effects of the 1923 quake and continued growing. Post-quake reconstruction was declared officially over in 1930. In 1932, Tokyo's boundaries underwent major revision to take account of changing population patterns, with growing western districts such as Shibuya and Ikebukuro, and the remaining parts of Shinjuku, coming within the city limits. The total number of wards jumped from 15 to 35 (later simplified to the 23 of today) and the city's land area increased sevenfold. At a stroke, the population doubled to over five million, making Tokyo the world's second most populous city after New York. Meanwhile, the country was sliding into dark days of militarism and war (*see p12*). In March 1945, Allied bombing brought huge devastation to the capital once more. Defeat was followed by occupation, but Tokyo was to rise again as Japan entered a new era of peace and unprecedented economic prosperity.

War and peace

In August 2001, prime minister Koizumi Junichiro ignited a storm of protest from neighbouring Korea and China by visiting Yasukuni Shrine in central Tokyo – he was only the third Japanese premier since 1978 to do so.

The name Yasukuni can be translated as 'peaceful country', but for many the shrine stands as a potent symbol of Japan's former militarism. During the war it was a focus of nationalism and state Shinto worship. Today, the spirits of nearly 2.5 million Japanese war dead are enshrined there, the vast majority from the 1930s and 1940s. Controversially, these include 14 top leaders executed by the Allies as Class A war criminals.

Founded in 1869 to honour those killed in service of their country, Yasukuni Shrine takes an unrepentant line on the historical controversies that continue to bedevil Japan's relations with nearby Asian nations. Alongside the main shrine buildings, the newly renovated and extended Yushukan Museum greets visitors with a perfectly preserved Mitsubishi Zero fighter aircraft.

Inside, the first exhibition rooms focus on the period from the arrival of Perry's 'black ships' in 1853 to the outbreak of the Pacific War in 1941. A timeline outlining the various military conflicts, both domestic and international, is helpfully translated into English, although individual exhibits are in Japanese only. The stress is on the threat from the western powers, rather than Japan's own aggression in Korea and China. Events such as the infamous Rape of Nanking in 1937, probably one of the worst massacres of modern times, are barely acknowledged.

Downstairs, the section on the Greater East Asian War revisits old arguments casting Japan in the role of liberator of Asian countries from Western colonial rule. The personal sacrifice of young Japanese soldiers is illustrated in a series of rooms lined with black and white portraits, many accompanied by personal letters or notebooks. But there is absolutely no mention of any non-Japanese victims of the conflict. Finally, an enormous exhibition hall is used to show off a fearsome

MILITARISM AND WAR

The early 20th century era of parliamentary government was not to last. Political stability fell victim to the economic depression that followed a domestic banking collapse in 1927 and the Wall Street crash two years later. Extremist nationalist groups saw expansion overseas as the answer to the nation's problems. In November 1930, after signing a naval disarmament treaty, prime minister Hamaguchi Osachi was killed by a right-wing extremist in Tokyo station.

In 1931, dissident army officers staged a Japanese military takeover of Manchuria, bringing conflict with world opinion. Pre-war party government ended after a shortlived rebellion of younger officers on 15 May 1932; prime minister Inukai Tsuyoshi and other cabinet members were assassinated and a series of national unity governments took over, dependent on military support. A puppet state, Manchukuo, was declared in Manchuria and Japan left the League of Nations. On 26 February 1936, the army's First Division mutinied and attempted a coup. Strategic points were seized in central Tokyo, but the rebellion was put down.

In an atmosphere of increasing nationalist fervour, Japan became involved in a widening international conflict. Full-scale hostilities with

collection of heavy-duty vintage military hardware, including a *kaiten* manned suicide torpedo.

Yasukuni Shrine claims it receives eight million visitors annually, but whether prime ministers will be among future visitors remains unclear. Apart from the international political cost, there's also the tricky question of Japan's constitutional separation of state and religion. Koizumi, though, having broken the initial taboo, seems keen to continue. Despite a government advisory panel looking at a possible new war memorial to provide a less emotive alternative to Yasukuni, he made further visits in both 2002 and 2003.

Yushukan at Yasukuni Jinja

3-1-1 Kudankita, Chiyoda-ku (3261 8346/ www.yasukuni.or.jp/english). Kudanshita station. **Open** *Nov-Feb* 9am-5pm daily. *Mar-Oct* 9am-5.30pm daily. **Admission** ¥800; ¥300-500 concessions. **Map** p62.

China broke out in July 1937, but Japanese forces got bogged down after early advances. Western powers, led by the US, declared a total embargo of Japan in summer 1941. Negotiations between the two sides reached an impasse, and on 7 December 1941, Japan attacked the US Pacific fleet at Pearl Harbor.

After a series of quick successes in the Pacific and South-east Asia, Japanese forces began to be pushed back after the Battle of Midway in June 1942. By late 1944, Tokyo lay within the range of American bombers. Incendiary attacks devastated the capital; the one on 10 March 1945 is estimated to have left 100,000 dead. On 6 August, an atomic bomb was dropped on Hiroshima, followed by another on Nagasaki three days later. Cabinet deadlock left the casting vote to the emperor, whose radio broadcast to the nation on 15 August announced Japan's surrender.

POST-WAR

Much of Tokyo lay in ruins; food and shelter posed immediate problems. As many as one in ten slept in temporary shelters during the first post-war winter. General MacArthur set about demilitarising Japan and promoting democratic reform. The emperor kept his throne, but renounced his divine status. Article nine of the new constitution included strict pacifist provisions and the armed forces were disbanded. In 1948, seven Class A war criminals, including war-time prime minister Tojo Hideki, were executed.

The outbreak of the Korean War in 1950 provided a tremendous boost to the Japanese economy, with large contracts to supply UN forces. Under MacArthur's orders, a limited rearmament took place, leading to the eventual founding of the Self-Defence Forces. Occupation ended in 1952 and there was a new security treaty with the USA.

With national defence left largely in US hands, economic growth was the priority under the long rule of the pro-business Liberal Democratic Party (LDP), formed in 1955. Prosperity started to manifest itself in the shape of large new office buildings in central Tokyo. In 1960, prime minister Ikeda Hayato announced a plan to double national income over a decade – a target achieved with ease in the economic miracle years that followed.

The Olympics were held in Tokyo in 1964, the same year *shinkansen* (bullet trains) started running between the capital and Osaka. Infrastructure improvements were made inside the city. Even after the Olympics, Tokyo's redevelopment continued apace. Frank Lloyd Wright's Imperial Hotel, a survivor of both the 1923 earthquake and the war, was demolished in 1967, the year the city's inner 23 wards achieved their peak population of almost nine million. To the west of Shinjuku station, Tokyo's first concentration of skyscrapers started to take shape during the early 1970s.

Despite the economic progress, there was an undercurrent of social discontent. Hundreds of thousands demonstrated against renewal of the security treaty with the United States in 1960, and the end of the decade saw students in violent revolt. In 1970, novelist Mishima Yukio dramatically ended his life after failing to spark a nationalist uprising at Ichigaya barracks. In Chiba, radical groups from the other end of the political spectrum joined local farmers to battle with riot police, delaying completion of Tokyo's new international airport at Narita from 1971 to 1975 and its opening until 1978.

The post-war fixed exchange rate ended in 1971 and growth came to a temporary halt with the oil crisis of 1974, but the Japanese economy continued to outperform its competitors. Trade friction developed, particularly with the United States. After the Plaza Agreement of 1985, the yen jumped to new highs, inflating the value of Japanese financial assets. Shoppers switched to designer labels as a building frenzy gripped Tokyo, the world's most expensive city. Land values soared and feverish speculation fuelled a 'bubble economy'.

HEISEI ERA (1989-)

The death of Hirohito came at the beginning of the sweeping global changes marking the end of the Cold War. As the 1990s wore on, the system that had served Japan so well in the post-war era stumbled. A collapse in land and stock market prices brought the bubble economy to an end in 1990 and left Japanese banks with a mountain of bad debt. An economy that had been the envy of the world became mired in its deepest recession since the end of the war.

'A sarin gas attack by members of a doomsday cult provoked more horror and much agonised debate.'

Tokyo ushered in a new era in 1991, when the metropolitan government moved to a thrusting new skyscraper in Shinjuku, symbolising the capital's shift away from its traditional centre. In January 1995, however, the Kobe earthquake reminded Tokyo residents of their vulnerability to natural disaster. Soon after, a sarin gas attack on city subways by members of the Aum Shinrikyo doomsday cult provoked more horror and much agonised debate. Discussions about moving the national government to a less quake-prone location continued.

Longstanding demands for an end to 'money politics' finally proved irresistible in 1993, when the LDP lost power for the first time in 38 years. A shortlived nine-party coalition enacted a programme of political reform, but the LDP clawed its way back to power in 1994 through an unlikely partnership with its erstwhile foe, the rapidly declining Socialists. Voter apathy grew as new coalitions came and went.

In a climate of job insecurity and fragile consumer confidence, the 'Heisei recession' proved resilient to the traditional stimulus of public works programmes. In April 1999, attracted by the promise of strong leadership, Tokyo voted hawkish former-LDP independent, Ishihara Shintaro, as their new governor. Two years later, LDP outsider Koizumi Junichiro took over as prime minister from Mori Yoshiro, boasting record popularity ratings and promising reform with 'no sacred cows'.

Nevertheless, the slow pace of political and economic change in Japan continues to frustrate observers. Overseas, hopes raised by a first-ever bilateral summit with North Korea in autumn 2002 gave way to renewed concerns about Pyongyang's nuclear arms and missile programme in a deteriorating international security environment.

Key events

c10,000-300 BC Jomon period.
c300 BC-AD 300 Yayoi period; introduction of wet-rice cultivation, bronze and ironware into Japan from continental Asia.
1st century AD Japan ('land of Wa') first mentioned in Chinese chronicles.
4th century Yamato court exists in Nara area.
538 or 552 Buddhism introduced from Korea.
710 Nara becomes imperial capital.
794 Capital moves to Heian (Kyoto).
1019 Murasaki Shikibu writes *Tale of Genji*.
1180 First recorded use of the name Edo.
1185-1333 Kamakura is site of military government.
1274, 1281 Attempted Mongol invasions.
1457 Ota Dokan builds first castle at Edo.
1590 Edo becomes headquarters of Tokugawa Ieyasu. Construction of Edo Castle.
1592 Hideyoshi invades Korea.
1598 Withdrawal from Korea.
1603 Ieyasu named shogun; Edo becomes seat of national government.
1635 Edicts formalise system of alternate residence in Edo for feudal lords.
1639 National seclusion policy established.
1657 Long Sleeves Fire decimates Edo.
1688-1704 Genroku cultural flowering.
1703 47 *ronin* vendetta carried out.
1707 Mount Fuji erupts, ash falls on Edo.
1720 Ban on import of foreign books lifted.
1742 Floods and storms kill 4,000 in Edo.
1787-93 Kansei reforms; rice granaries set up in Edo after famine and riots.
1804-29 Bunka-Bunsei period; peak of Edo merchant culture.
1825 Government issues 'Order for Repelling of Foreign Ships'.
1841-3 Reforms to strengthen economy.
1853 Arrival of US 'black ships' at Uraga.
1854 Treaty of Kanagawa signed with Commodore Perry.
1855 Earthquake kills over 7,000 in Edo.
1860 Ii Naosuke assassinated.
1862 End of alternate residence system.
1868 Tokugawa shogunate overthrown in Meiji Restoration. Imperial residence moved from Kyoto; Edo renamed Tokyo.
1869 Yasukuni Shrine established to Japan's war dead. Rickshaws appear in Tokyo.
1871-3 Meiji leaders tour US and Europe.
1872 Shinbashi to Yokohama train service.
1874 Tokyo's first gas lights appear in Ginza.
1877 Satsuma rebellion.
1883 Rokumeikan completed in Hibiya.
1889 Meiji constitution promulgated.
1890 Ryounkaku brick tower built in Asakusa.
1894-5 Sino-Japanese War.
1902 Anglo-Japanese alliance signed.
1904-5 Russo-Japanese war.
1910 Korea brought into Japanese Empire.
1912 Emperor Meiji dies; Taisho era begins.
1923 Great Kanto Earthquake.
1925 Universal male suffrage introduced.
1926 Hirohito is emperor; Showa era begins.
1927 Asia's first subway line opens between Asakusa and Ueno.
1930 Post-earthquake reconstruction declared officially complete.
1931 Military takeover of Manchuria.
1932 Prime minister Inukai Tsuyoshi assassinated. Extension of Tokyo boundaries means city's population is doubled.
1933 Japan leaves League of Nations.
1936 Army rebellion in central Tokyo.
1937 Hostilities in China; Rape of Nanking.
1940 Tripartite Pact with Germany and Italy.
1941 Pearl Harbor attack begins Pacific War.
1945 Incendiary bombing of Tokyo. Atom bombs dropped on Hiroshima and Nagasaki. Japan surrenders; occupation begins.
1946 Emperor renounces divinity. New constitution promulgated.
1951 Security treaty signed with US.
1952 Occupation ends.
1954 Release of first *Godzilla* film.
1955 Liberal Democratic Party (LDP) formed, along with Japan Socialist Party.
1960 Demonstrations against renewal of US-Japan security treaty.
1964 Tokyo Olympic Games. First *shinkansen* bullet train runs between Tokyo and Osaka.
1968-9 Student unrest.
1971 Yen revalued from 360 to 308 US$.
1989 Death of Hirohito (Showa Emperor); Heisei era begins.
1990 End of 'bubble economy'.
1993 LDP loses power after 38 years.
1994 Socialist Party's Murayama Tomiichi becomes prime minister in coalition with LDP.
1995 Kobe earthquake. Sarin gas attack on Tokyo subway.
1998 Asian economic crisis spreads.
2000 Mori Yoshiro replaces Obuchi Keizo as LDP leader and prime minister.
2001 Koizumi Junichiro replaces Mori Yoshiro.
2002 Japan co-hosts football World Cup; Koizumi visits North Korea.

Tokyo Today

The future is more uncertain than at any time since the war.

If you're a first-time visitor to Tokyo, and a newspaper reader, you may be forgiven for expecting a city where the cloud of economic stagnation hangs heavy. True, Japan is a different country now than 15 years ago. But those familiar with the cataclysmic recessions of the UK or US will find few immediate signs of the so-called 'lost decade' that followed the bursting of the economic bubble in the early 1990s. With the country mired in deflation, banks technically bankrupt, unemployment at record levels and crime soaring, Tokyo seems remarkably calm. For a people unaccustomed to economic insecurity, many Japanese have little choice but to put the shoulder to the grindstone and pray that things will improve.

DOWN AND OUT

For the worst hit, however, this option no longer exists. Over the past ten years tented communities of homeless people have mushroomed in many of Tokyo's parks – one of the few visible symptoms of recession.

The figures are daunting. The capital's unemployment rate now exceeds six per cent. A March 2003 survey found that of the more than 25,000 people sleeping on Japan's streets, 6,361 were in Tokyo. The average age of those questioned was 55.9 years old, although 15 per cent were at least 65. While 36 per cent said they had ended up on the streets due to redundancy, the same number said they had lost their jobs through company bankruptcies. Many claimed to have found employment, but three-quarters of that was collecting waste materials to sell, an occupation that rarely brings in more than ¥30,000 per month.

Indicative of how much a feature of the urban landscape the down-and-outs have become is the authorities' new-found 'tolerance'. The police have all but tired of the cat-and-mouse game that once saw whole communities evicted from one park, only to reappear overnight in another. Indeed, the English word 'homeless' has now entered the vernacular, a sure sign of acknowledgment of a reality, if nothing else.

Perhaps what is most surprising is how polite and peaceable the homeless are. Panhandling is almost unknown – in fact the presence of an underclass could hardly be

From the first western toilet in Japan (*see p90*) to the multi-function lavatories of today, Japan's development into a world power can be symbolised by its water closets.

described as a noticeable phenomenon. Desperation hasn't led to the predicted jump in serious crime. And alcohol abuse, although prevalent, is mostly a private pastime – much as it is among the employed. In the tent cities, as in Japan's more established communities, neighbourhood peace is cherished and social rules, right down to shoes being removed before entering a tent, are strictly adhered to.

BRICKS AND MORTAR

Above the tented cities, the reshaping of the Tokyo skyline carries on unabated. Ever taller and plusher office and condominium blocks continue to rise on cleared or reclaimed land. We can never know what Tokyo would have looked like if it had escaped the furies of World War II. However, if the disfigurement of Kyoto – where Japanese construction firms have achieved what the American air force was loath to attempt – is any indication, we may assume that it would have been little different from what we see today.

Tokyo is essentially a new city. Historical landmarks are rare, and can be disappointing for anyone hoping to find remnants of Edo among the steel, glass and concrete. Temples and shrines have been rebuilt, renovated, enlarged and asphalted to the extent that they contain very little, if any, of their original materials. Private buildings predating 1960 mostly survive through indifference, and are often no more than decaying structures awaiting demolition. What little pre-20th-century architecture there is lies hidden away.

Sadly, Tokyo also lacks the modern grandeur of such cities as New York. There are few wide boulevards and spacious parks; there is no Downtown. Even the subtleties that differentiate Shinjuku from, say, Ikebukuro may be too fine for a visitor to appreciate. Out with the old, in with the new is Tokyo's philosophy. It is a city striving towards a future that will perhaps never be realised.

FREE AND EASY

As Tokyo continues to evolve, so do its people. Shame and acceptance, two crucial elements of Japanese society, are beginning to loosen their age-old grip. This is especially noticeable among the ever more restless youth.

The coining of the term *fureeta* to describe a freewheeling life of part-time work and cheap housing with the onus on enjoyment has given a name to a social upheaval that has been building for ten years. The babies of the bubble have come of age, and, like the 'me' generation of 1960s America, are turning against the culture that has fed, clothed and educated them.

Parents have become the new anti-role models. Repulsed by the selfless servitude of their fathers, male school-leavers are increasingly shunning the corporate culture. Young women no longer follow their mothers

The long recession has pushed prices way down.

down the path to maternal bliss, having discovered that being single, childless and well-off can be far more gratifying.

What this will mean to a society that is rapidly ageing is still unclear. Already, the economic and political repercussions are beginning to be felt, with the birthrate plummeting and health costs and pensions eating into welfare budgets.

LOVE AND PEACE

The outpouring of anti-war sentiment during the 2003 invasion of Iraq said a lot about the changing attitudes of the Japanese. Tens of thousands marched through Tokyo's shopping districts to denounce the US-led war to remove Saddam Hussein from power. Unlike the violent demonstrations of the 1960s and '70s, when students took to the streets to oppose American hegemony, the rallies were peaceful. The sight of so many young people discovering their political voice was heartwarming to those who had written them off as a spoilt, unthinking lot addled by computer games and designer labels.

With demonstrations taking on a carnival-like appearance, complete with live music, food, and costumes that said little about war and suffering, cynics could argue that exhibitionism and enjoyment had replaced ideology. But if raising awareness and attracting others to the cause were the principal goals, then those who came out on the street clearly succeeded.

Of course, it can be argued with some justification that, fed on a diet of television and the internet, this new generation of peaceniks was simply mimicking demonstrators the world over. But that denies a Japanese reality: the real fear of an attack by their belligerent and unpredictable neighbour, North Korea. The question of how Japan would react to such aggression remains to be answered.

SUPPLY AND DEMAND

Changing values are also evident in the high street, where low price stores are squeezing out businesses unable to satisfy the prevailing appetite for cheaper goods.

Daiso's chain of shops was the first to profit from the economic downturn. Manufacturing its products by the millions in China, Daiso was able to price everything for a mere 100 yen. In doing so, it launched a mini retail revolution. Soon, every mall could boast at least one 100-yen store, leading the press to describe the new style of shopping as a 'game for housewives'.

To survive, established outlets, whose costs are linked to exorbitant rents and the outdated belief that their customers 'want' expensive goods, are being forced to cut prices. Supermarkets crammed full of 99-yen items, restaurants that serve 200-yen meals, bars that charge 300 yen per drink have all become fixtures of the retail landscape.

Tokyo may never shake off its image as the world's most expensive city, but any drop in prices is good news for a society that has for so long been taken for a ride.

THEM AND US

For non-Japanese who choose to make Tokyo their home, the present climate is mixed.

The job market is contracting. Where once casual work, be it teaching English or digging roads, was abundant, Tokyo today offers too few vacancies for too many candidates. A recently advertised position for a part-time proofreader attracted 150 applicants. Unskilled labourers from third world countries must now compete with their Japanese counterparts for jobs that were once deemed *kitanai*, *kitsui* and *kiken* (dirty, hard and dangerous). The murder of British bar hostess Lucy Blackman in 2000 highlighted a sleazier side of Tokyo's nightlife and did little to boost a profession already hit by corporate spending cuts. According to Gaijin Pot, an online job centre, the most important qualifications for the foreign job-seeker are to be 'bilingual, bilingual, and bilingual'.

That said, Tokyoites are slowly, if begrudgingly, accepting that, as in all modern cities, immigrants have a part to play in reshaping the cultural environment. As evidenced by the ease with which Governor Ishihara Shintaro spouts racist one-liners, Tokyo is far from multicultural. But compared to two decades ago, when the sight of a westerner brought giggles and stares, today's climate is much more tolerant and inclusive. Some of the city's most prominent architecture has been designed by local foreign talent. Japanese corporations, such as Nissan, which once defined economic isolationism, are being remodelled by overseas executives. Japan's national football team now has Brazilian-born Zico as its coach. Bilingual television personalities, such as Dave Spector, regularly poke fun at their audience. All are helping to shatter suspicions that have long marred relations between foreigners and their hosts.

Myths and stereotypes still persist, however: blue eyes are weaker than brown eyes; London is shrouded in fog; Russians can't bathe Japanese-style; foreigners can't use chopsticks; the Japanese language is too complex for anyone but the Japanese to master. But these are minor issues that will eventually fade. The growing pains that Tokyo is currently suffering can only lead to a society that is more mature, more diverse, and more open – a better place for citizens and visitors alike.

Traditional buildings are an endangered species.

Architecture

Novelty thrives in a city shaped by natural disasters.

Since it first flung open its doors to the world back in 1868, Tokyo has been a laboratory for the meeting and synthesis of local and western styles that continue to inform the development of Japanese architecture today. Lacking monuments such as the ancient temples of Kyoto and Nara, Tokyo has also been stripped of much of its own architectural heritage by a history of fires, terrible earthquakes and heavy war-time bombing, compounded by break-neck post-war economic development and an unsentimental lack of attachment to the old.

OLD JAPANESE STYLES

Japanese architecture has traditionally been based on the use of wooden materials. Very few original structures remain from the city's former incarnation as Edo, capital of the Tokugawa shoguns, although parts of the imposing pre-modern fortifications of Edo Castle can still be seen when walking around the moat and gardens of the Imperial Palace, built on part of the castle site.

The original wooden houses and shops of Edo-era *shitamachi* (downtown) have now almost completely disappeared. Outside the very heart of the city, recognisably traditional features, such as eaves and tiled roofs, are still widely used on modern suburban housing, while tatami mats and sliding doors are common inside even more western-style apartment blocks.

The city's shrines and temples are overwhelmingly traditional in form. The **Meiji Shrine** (*see p101*) is an impressive example of the austere style and restrained colours typical of Shinto architecture, which is usually quite distinct from that of Buddhist temples, where the greater influence of Chinese and Korean styles is usually apparent, most noticeably in the use of colour. Many present-day buildings of older religious institutions are reconstructions of earlier incarnations; the well-known temples of **Sensoji** (*see p87*) and **Zojoji** are both examples, although in these cases some remnants of earlier structures also survive. The 1605 Sanmon Gate of Zojo-ji Temple and Gokokuji Temple, which dates from 1681, are rare, unreconstructed survivors.

In contrast, when the wooden building of Honganji Temple in Tsukiji burned down for the ninth time in its long history, after the 1923 earthquake, it was rebuilt in sturdier stone. The design, by architect Ito Chuta, earlier responsible for the Meiji Shrine, was also quite different: an eye-catching affair recalling Buddhism's roots in ancient India.

WESTERN INFLUENCES

After the Meiji Restoration of 1868, the twin influences of westernisation and modernisation quickly made themselves felt in Tokyo, the new national capital. Early attempts to combine western and traditional elements by local architects resulted in extraordinary hybrids featuring Japanese-style sloping roofs rising above wooden constructions with ornate front façades of a distinctly western style. Kisuke Shimizu's Hoterukan (1868) at the Foreign Settlement in Tsukiji and his First National Bank (1872) in Nihonbashi were two notable Tokyo examples. Neither survives today.

'The city's first cluster of skyscrapers has been described as resembling a set of urban tombstones.'

Tokyo's earliest buildings of a purely western design were chiefly the work of overseas architects brought to Japan by the new Meiji government. Englishman Thomas Waters oversaw the post-1872 redevelopment of Ginza with around 900 red-brick buildings, thought to be more resilient than wooden Japanese houses. Ironically, none of them made it through the 1923 earthquake.

Waters' fellow-countryman Josiah Conder, who taught at Tokyo Imperial University, was the most influential western architect of the early Meiji period, with important projects in the capital including ministry buildings, the original Imperial Museum at Ueno (1881) and Hibiya's Rokumeikan reception hall (1883). His Furukawa mansion in Komagome (1914) and **Nikolai Cathedral** in Ochanomizu (1891, *see p67*) still exist, although the latter was badly damaged in the 1923 earthquake.

Later Meiji official architecture was often a close reflection of western styles, although it was Japanese architects who increasingly handled the prestige projects. Remaining red-brick structures of the period include the Ministry of Justice (1895), built in Kasumigaseki by the German firm of Ende and Bockman, and the **Crafts Gallery** of the National Museum of Modern Art (1910, *see p65*), which once housed the administrative headquarters of the Imperial Guard. The imposing **Bank of Japan** building (1896, *see p63*) was built by one of Conder's former students, Tatsuno Kingo, who was also responsible for the Marunouchi wing of Tokyo Station (1914), modelled on Centraal Station in Amsterdam. A far more grandiose overseas inspiration, that of Versailles, is said to have been used for **Akasaka Detached Palace** (1909, *see p113*), created by Katayama Tokuma, whose other work includes the **Hyokeikan Building** of the National Museum in Ueno (also completed in 1909, *see p92*).

The era after World War I saw the completion of Frank Lloyd Wright's highly distinctive Imperial Hotel (1922), which famously survived the Tokyo earthquake shortly after its opening, but has since been demolished. The period after the earthquake saw the spread of social housing, and a prominent example now threatened by the relentless march of development is the **Dojunkai Aoyama** tenement apartment blocks (1926) on Omotesando, which were approved for demolition in late 2002 but are still standing at the time of writing.

Another post-quake innovation was the *kanban* (signboard) style, designed to protect buildings against fire by a cloaking of sheet copper. These can often still seen today as the heavily oxidised green mantles of surviving pre-war shops.

The influence of contemporary overseas trends can be discerned in the modernism of Yoshida Tetsuro's **Tokyo Central Post Office** (1931) and the art deco of **Tokyo Metropolitan Teien Art Museum** (1933, *see p108*), built originally as a mansion for Prince Asaka and planned mainly by French designer Henri Rapin. The present-day Diet Building (1936) also shows a strong art deco influence, but its design became a source of heated debate in the increasingly nationalist climate of the period when it was completed.

A reaction against westernisation had already been apparent in the work of Ito Chuta, who had looked towards Asian models. The **Kabuki-za** (1925, *see p243*) harked back to the medieval Momoyama era, a style retained when it was rebuilt after the war.

Demands for a distinctive national look now led to what has been called the 'Imperial Crown' style, usually represented by the main building of the **National Museum** (1938, *see p92*) in Ueno. This was the design of Watanabe Hitoshi, an architect of unusual versatility whose other works include the Hattori Building (1932) of Wako department store at Ginza 4-chome crossing, and the Daiichi Insurance Building (1938). The latter was used by General MacArthur as his Tokyo headquarters during the Occupation, and is now the shorter and older part of the DN Tower 21 complex in Hibiya.

What *was* that building?

Memorable buildings seem to crop up with amazing frequency in the random confusion of the Tokyo cityscape. Even so, hurrying by on your way somewhere else, it's easy not to get around to properly identifying a particular structure. Here's a brief selection of places you might want to put names to.

Aoyama Technical College (1990)

7-9 Uguisudanicho, Shibuya-ku (Shibuya station).
Outlandish post-modernism from Watanabe Sei that throws together strangely haphazard angles, insect-like protrusions, and blocks of eye-catching red on metal. Also widely known as Gundam, after the popular sci-fi anime.

La Collezione (1989)

6-1-3 Minami-aoyama (Omotesando station).
Subtle commercial building in Tokyo's fashion heartland provides one of the capital's most easily accessible works by world-renowned architect Ando Tadao, appointed professor at Tokyo University in 1997.

Former The Wall (1990)

4-2-4 Nishi-Azabu, Minato-ku (Azabu station).
The red-brick façade was given a deliberately aged look by British-born architect Nigel Coates in an apparent attempt to evoke the spirit of Roman ruins. A retro cast-iron frame and external stairways were also thrown into the mix.

St Mary's Cathedral (1963)

16-15-3 Sekiguchi, Bunkyo-ku (Edogawabashi station).
Dazzling in the sunlight, the stainless steel exterior sweeps upward to the sky; inside, the rough concrete finish and subdued lighting provide a stark contrast. Another Tange masterpiece.

Sankyo Tokyo Headquarters (1998)

3-29-14 Shibuya, Shibuya-ku (Shibuya station).
A foreboding lattice encloses an otherwise standard medium-size office building, giving it the illusion of being held in suspension above ground level. Ohe Tadasu came up with the unusual design.

Telecom Center (1996)

2-38 Aomi, Koto-ku (Yurikamome Telecom Center station).
Yet another hard-to-ignore Odaiba landmark, the Telecom Center, the focal point for Tokyo's satellite communications is reminiscent of a huge squared-off arch. The HOK architectural team of St Louis was responsible.

Tokyo Bankers Association (1993)

1-3-1 Marunouchi, Chiyoda-ku (Otemachi station).
Follows the preservation concept of the nearby DN Tower 21 by joining together a restored example of an earlier western style, a red-brick assembly hall in this case, with a noticeably taller update.

Washington Hotel (1983)

3-2-9 Nishi-Shinjuku, Shinjuku-ku (Shinjuku station).
Its cool white modernist exterior makes it a stand-out in the blandness of west Shinjuku's hotel district.

AFTER THE WAR

The priority in the early post-war period was often to provide extra office space for companies trying to cope with the demands of an economy hurtling along at double-digit growth rates, or a rapid answer to the pressing housing needs of the city's growing population. Seismic instability meant that tall buildings were not initially an option, and anonymous, box-like structures proliferated.

While confidence began to grow about new construction techniques, designed for greater protection against earthquakes, many of the early buildings incorporating these techniques were strangely undistinguished. The city's first cluster of skyscrapers, built in west Shinjuku from the early 1970s, has been described as resembling a set of urban tombstones. Even so, a later addition, the twin-tower Tokyo Metropolitan Government complex (1991, *see p113*) by Tange Kenzo, is now among the capital's best-known landmarks.

The dominant figure of post-war Japanese architecture, Tange has embraced both western and traditional Japanese elements in his astonishing variety of high-profile Tokyo projects, which stretch all the way back to the now-demolished metropolitan offices in Yurakucho (1957). Highlights include Yoyogi National Stadium (1964), the Hanae Mori

Building (1978) on Omotesando, Akasaka Prince Hotel (1983), and the UN University (1992) in Aoyama.

Tange's long career also connects completely different generations of Japanese architects. One collaborator was Maekawa Kunio, a pre-war student of Le Corbusier who became one of Japan's foremost modern architects with works such as Tokyo Metropolitan Festival Hall (1961) and the **Tokyo Metropolitan Art Museum** (1975, *see p92*). Another was acclaimed post-modernist Isozaki Arata, responsible for the Ochanomizu Square Building (1987), as well as the Museum of Contemporary Art (1986) in Los Angeles.

Tokyo ordered itself something of a post-modernist make-over as the bubble economy took hold during the 1980s, and this splurge of 'trophy architecture' left the city with a string of new and enjoyably eye-catching landmarks. The landmark **Spiral Building** (1985, *see p214*) in Aoyama is one contribution to the new city look by Maki Fumihiko; another is the strange and low-level **Tokyo Metropolitan Gymnasium** (1990) in Sendagaya. Also difficult to ignore is the Super Dry Hall in Asakusa by Philippe Starck, one of a number of foreign architects to have worked on projects in Tokyo in recent years. These also include Rafael Vinoly, creator of the stunning Tokyo International Forum (1996, *see p229*) on the site of the old Tokyo government building in Yurakucho, and Norman Foster, whose Century Tower (1991) is located near Ochanomizu.

The reclamation of Tokyo Bay has also opened up land for a wide range of projects. On Odaiba (*see p77*), designated as a futuristic showcase back in the bubble era, Tange's Fuji TV headquarters (1996), Watanabe Sei's K-Museum (1996) and Sato Sogokeikau's Tokyo Big Sight (1994) all vie for attention, while the interior of Venus Fort (1999) offers a bizarre Vegas-style take on Ancient Rome. Nearby, on the city side of Rainbow Bridge, an imposing new generation of skyscraper offices continues to thrust upward on the waterfront skyline, defying talk of economic recession.

Meanwhile, over in south Shinjuku, Takashimaya Times Square (1996) and the NTT DoCoMo Building (2000), a scaled-down Empire State clone, suggest a continuing fascination with popular overseas models. Finally, a municipal project that should be mentioned is Kikutake Kiyonori's Edo-Tokyo Museum (1992) in Ryogoku, its alien spacecraft look made up of traditional elements recalling the city's past, and its height of 62 metres (207 feet) exactly matching that of Edo Castle.

Tokyo will continue to rebuild itself, as it has for hundreds of years. What's here today may well be gone tomorrow, to be replaced by something even more unusual or spectacular.

Tokyo Metropolitan Gymnasium.

Geography

In a city of so many millions, where do you draw the lines?

Tokyo has long since slipped the confines of the city's original boundaries around the present-day Imperial Palace area. Today, it lies at one end of the highly developed Pacific belt that runs west along the coast of Japan's main Honshu island to Osaka and holds around half the national population of 126.92 million. In a country where up to two-thirds of the land is mountainous, the greater Tokyo metropolis sprawls relentlessly over much of the Kanto plain, Japan's largest plain and a natural population magnet.

But while distant commuter suburbs and satellite towns continue to spread outwards over the hinterland, the balance inside the capital itself is also constantly shifting. Older districts have lost ground to upstart newcomers as huge development and infrastructure projects continue to remodel the landscape and draw new crowds to different areas of the city.

THE HEART OF THE MATTER

At the heart of Tokyo lie the city's 23 inner wards, or *ku*, covering 616 square kilometres (238 square miles) and currently home to 8.21 million people. Perhaps in reaction to recent land price falls, there seems to be a drift back to the bright lights of the city proper, with the 23 wards registering their first overall population increase for 15 years in the 2000 census. Even so, the current figure still stands below the peak of nearly nine million recorded in the late 1960s.

Visitors to Tokyo are usually advised to orientate themselves by the Yamanote train line that circles the central areas of the city, linking important districts such as Shinjuku, Shibuya, Ikebukuro, Ueno, Tokyo and Shinagawa. The growth of these huge transport hubs, connected to subways and suburban train lines, means Japan's capital lacks the focus of a single central area but instead possesses a whole series of multi-functional sub-centres, each one boasting its own unique flavour.

The name of the Yamanote line recalls an older division between the smarter *yamanote* areas on the higher ground to the west and south of the city and the lower-lying *shitamachi* downtown districts (*see p8*). The comparison is far from exact, however, since the present-day loop runs through both old *yamanote* and old *shitamachi* districts, as well as through western areas that lay outside the official city limits until as late as 1932. Even so, the broad

Quaking

Japan's location on the unstable geological foundations of the Pacific 'rim of fire' has left the city of Tokyo seismically vulnerable. Residents of the capital were given a disturbing reminder that the much-feared Big One could strike at any time by the Kobe earthquake of 1995, which left over 6,000 dead. In 1923, the Great Kanto earthquake destroyed much of Tokyo and around 100,000 people were killed. While the city hasn't suffered a natural catastrophe since then, the chances of a future disaster nevertheless remain high.

Locals tend not to be easily jolted out of their outward calm by the smaller tremors that are relatively common in Tokyo. Nevertheless, with earthquake prediction a notoriously inexact science, excessive complacency is best avoided. The Kobe quake led to reviews of flawed emergency planning procedures and building regulations. Meanwhile, the Tokyo Metropolitan Government holds city-wide exercises every year on 1 September, the anniversary of the 1923 quake.

Preparation will be one of the keys to survival in the event of a major disaster, so Tokyo residents are advised to keep a small bag handy at home containing essentials such as a bottle of water, preserved foodstuffs, some cash and a torch. If you're unlucky enough to experience the Big One, attempt to shut off any stoves and gas mains, secure an exit, and look for a table or similar to protect your body, especially the head.

sweep of the magic Yamanote circle is generally taken to define the central part of the city.

To an extent, this illustrates a general westward shift in Tokyo's centre of gravity, particularly in the post-war era. In the early years of Japan's modernisation, areas to the east of the Imperial Palace in the general vicinity of Tokyo station, such as Ginza, Marunouchi, Otemachi and Nihonbashi, were the focus of commercial and financial activities. Ueno stood almost directly north of them, while further east lay the old *shitamachi* districts, including the popular entertainment area of Asakusa near the Sumida river.

In more recent times, however, the city's growth has been strongest in what were previously considered outposts for suburban train connections along the west side of the Yamanote line, such as Shibuya, Shinjuku and Ikebukuro. The 1964 Olympics provided a boost for Harajuku and the nearby fashionable districts of Omotesando, Aoyama and Roppongi. In 1991 the Tokyo Metropolitan Government recognised the city's new western axis by relocating from its old headquarters in Yurakucho to a gleaming new Gotham City style skyscraper in Shinjuku.

Outside the central part of the city, but still reflecting the same trend, the population has continued to grow in suburban wards west of the Yamanote line, such as Setagaya-ku. Conversely, many of the less wealthy industrial wards are still located in the north and east of the city, clustered around the Sumida, Arakawa and Edogawa rivers, which empty into Tokyo Bay.

CONSTANT CHANGE

The Japanese capital remains capable of unexpected twists and changes of direction. In recent years, the huge waterfront development at Odaiba has turned attention back to the Tokyo Bay area in general, and also continued a long tradition of land reclamation that goes back to the earliest days of the city.

Indeed, Tokyo has never been averse to improving on its own natural endowments. Furiously remodelled over the centuries, many physical features of the city are often scarcely recognisable in their original form, even allowing for the present-day concrete cladding. Hills and valleys have been evened out; lakes and marshes drained; rivers re-routed. What was once a city of canals and waterways is now joined together by networks of overhead trains and highways, with natural greenery at a premium.

Making the best use of every last inch still remains a priority in the central areas, despite the post-bubble crash in real estate prices. Housing conditions throughout the city are still cramped by western standards, while park area per head remains a mere one-tenth that of New York. In a country that prides itself on its closeness to nature, the capital has scarcely a trickling stream without ugly man-made embankments. The headlong rush to development has also raised continuing concerns about air pollution and the urgent need for more recycling.

Over 20 per cent of Japan's 120 million population live within easy reach of Tokyo.

Futuristic west Shinjuku, Tokyo's first high-rise district.

In common with other large Japanese cities, Tokyo has felt the effects of the rapid population shift from countryside to city since the end of the war. But as the rural population came one way, Tokyo itself was heading in the opposite direction. With the height of its buildings traditionally limited by possible earthquakes, the metropolis has tended to grow outward rather than upward, and what were paddy fields have been covered over by concrete. Commuters retreating to distant suburbs pay the price for cheaper housing and more spacious living conditions with famously long journeys to work.

WHERE DOES IT END?

One result of the city's headlong march into the surrounding countryside is that defining just where Tokyo's sprawling metropolis ends sometimes appears to be a matter of arbitrary choice. Official boundaries turn out to be nothing more than lines on a map as the urban landscape stretches seemingly endlessly outwards.

Tokyo Prefecture, the 2,187 square kilometres (844 square miles) administered from the skyscraper offices of the Metropolitan Government in Shinjuku, provides one wider definition. According to figures released in 2002, the prefecture's total population now stands at 12.17 million. As well as the 23 inner wards, this area includes what the authorities classify as 27 cities, five towns and eight villages. These mainly consist of commuter belt and semi-rural districts on the Musashino plain in the western part of the prefecture. Also under metropolitan administration, however, are nine sets of scattered Pacific islands (two towns and seven villages), most of them part of the Izu Islands, but also including the semi-tropical Ogasawara Islands, lying some 1,000 kilometres (625 miles) south of the inner wards.

Meanwhile the UN Department of Economic and Social Affairs Population Division ranks Tokyo as the world's largest urban agglomeration, defined as 'the population contained within the contours of contiguous territory inhabited at urban levels of residential density without regard to administrative boundaries'. By this measure, the 2001 Tokyo population figure was 26.5 million; over 20 per cent of Japan's entire population, all living on less than two per cent of the nation's land. Tokyo thus remains far ahead of Sao Paulo, with an estimated 18.3 million population, as well as Mexico City, New York and Bombay.

Probably the widest measure of the greater Tokyo area is the National Capital Region, which takes in all seven Kanto prefectures plus Yamanashi. Together these have a population of over 40 million, mostly in metropolitan Tokyo and neighbouring Kanagawa, Chiba, and Saitama prefectures. The outlying four prefectures of Tochigi, Gunma, Ibaraki and Yamanashi remain more rural and mountainous, particularly Yamanashi, which contains Mount Fuji on its southern borders.

Kafunsho!

It may not be immediately obvious in the crowded capital, but more than two-thirds of Japan is covered by forest. Indeed, among industrialised countries only Finland and Sweden can boast higher percentages of forestation, and both these nations have far lower population densities. For many Tokyo residents, though, the forests are a mixed blessing.

Every spring, Japanese TV news programmes feature regular pollen count updates for the benefit of the estimated one tenth of the population afflicted by hay fever, or *kafunsho*. Pollen from cedar trees, which make up around 20 per cent of Japan's total forest cover, is the prime cause of the allergy sufferers' misery.

The problem is largely man-made. In the post-war rush to industrial development, the Japanese government embarked on a huge afforestation programme, with the aim of making the country self-sufficient in wood products. This plan focused almost solely on the planting of vast expanses of cedar forests. Decades later, the now-mature trees flower in February and March, dousing the entire nation with their pollen. And air currents ensure that the Tokyo metropolis is far from immune.

Face masks and medications have done little to halt the ever-rising number of sufferers in the face of this annual onslaught. Japanese scientists are making valiant attempts to reduce the amount of pollen that is actually released by the forestation, but so far with few clear results. In the face of cheap hardwood imports, there's also now little prospect the cedar forests will be cut down for lumber and replaced by different types of trees.

For the time being, the pollen count outlook for *kafunsho* sufferers is bleak indeed.

Sex & the City

It may not be out in the open, but there's a lot of it about.

The first-time visitor to Japan often arrives with a host of expectations, from the neon lights of Ginza and Shinjuku, to the temples of Kyoto, or the bullet train that takes you there from Tokyo. What they may not expect in this country that famously trades on its manners is Tokyo's booming sex trade.

Indeed, until recently, your average foreign visitor to Tokyo, unable to read or speak Japanese, would have found little evidence of its existence. The hundreds of clubs, hotels, bars, coffee shops and baths where sexual services are part of the package are hardly discreet, but until the recession they relied almost exclusively on Japanese customers. Now, though, things are very different, and any man walking alone through the Kabuki-cho district of Shinjuku is likely to be approached and offered sex once every 100 yards.

How can this be, in a country that's so famous for its lack of crime, and its love of decorum? The answer, as is so often the case with Japan, is that things are done differently here, and sex is no exception.

First off, there are cultural differences. Japanese people are, by and large, free of the guilt that is forever associated with sex in conventional Judeo-Christian morality, and the country lacks any prominent feminist movement to assert that sex is one of the ways men wield power over women.

The irrelevance of these models to Japanese society has both positive and negative effects. While the sexual atmosphere in Japan is often freer and less guilt-ridden than in the west, it is at the same time less reflective and considered.

Nevertheless – to an even greater extent than in the west – sex is not something that is generally discussed openly in Japan, and an individual's principles or code of conduct remain very much private and personal. This is not just reticence, but is intrinsically connected to the Japanese concept of *tatemae* (face value) and *honne* (real value), which delineates what can be shown in public from what is really going on. Broadly speaking, this psychological model has contributed to a situation where people follow their desires or emotions freely in private but it is taboo to exhibit evidence of them publicly, even to the extent of kissing your loved one in public.

This reluctance to confront things head on extends to the language surrounding sex, too. A foreign film, for instance, may mention genitalia explicitly in the dialogue, but the Japanese subtitles would be more likely use the non-specific word '*are*' (down/over there) as opposed to anything more descriptive. Every adult native speaker of Japanese would know exactly what was being referred to. In fact, in modern Japanese there is really no indigenous word for the sexual act that's used regularly. One can use '*sekusu*', clearly borrowed from English, or the more popular '*echi*', which is thought by many also to be derived from a foreign root. In any case, this latter word can mean horny, sexually hot, sex or simply naughty. It does not have to mean the sexual act.

Such attitudes also extend to much of the media. In September 2001, there was a fatal fire in an unsafe club building in Shinjuku's Kabuki-cho. Here's how the *Daily Mainichi* reported the incident: 'Investigators believe that the Kabuki-cho fire started in front of the elevator near the mahjong parlour on the third floor of the four-storey building. All of the victims were either in the mahjong parlour or in the establishment on the fourth floor.'

The 'establishment on the fourth floor' was a highly dubious hostess club called Superloose, where 27 of the fire's 44 victims perished. Superloose's speciality was providing customers with young women dressed as schoolgirls. The television cameras of state broadcaster NHK, too, went to great pains to get just the right angle to make sure the Superloose sign was invisible, even as they filmed the fight to put the fire out.

Services are specified in euphemistic code.

'The western concept that one should pursue sexual partners near one's own age holds little sway in Japan.'

The message is clear: sex may not be in the open, but there's a lot of it going on. Premarital and teenage sex is a usual (if unacknowledged) occurrence, stretching down into middle school. The big scandal of a few years ago was the discovery that girls as young as 15 were regularly prostituting themselves in order to buy trendier gear. Yet even once the scandal broke, the practice was rarely referred to as what it was, but given the soubriquet of '*enjo-kosai*', or 'assisted dating'. A law was eventually enacted to enhance punishment of the men involved (it says something that the standing regulations weren't sufficient) and the first man caught was a Buddhist priest.

Japanese society has a roaring, behind-closed-doors sexuality, an active sex industry as well as a clear fascination with *rorikon* (Lolita complex) – Japan's expression for its sexual obsession with young, supposedly innocent girls. Japan's gigantic *manga* (comic book) culture (some popular volumes sell five million copies a week) often depict wide-eyed pubescent girls being thrust into sexual situations (significantly, while these scenarios are explicit, the penis cannot be shown, even in comic book form). Paste-up leaflets in public phone booths for all manner of sexual services often depict young girls in suggestive poses.

The fascination with teenage girls also hints at another facet of sexual activity here. The western concept that one should pursue sexual partners near one's own age holds little sway in Japan. A stroll through any 'love hotel' district in Tokyo will reveal elderly gentlemen with much younger companions, or sometimes the reverse. There is an established phenomenon of upper-middle-class and upper-class men and women taking much younger mistresses or lovers – a custom that is accepted but never discussed. Class is key to this practice as it takes money in Tokyo to maintain these relationships, even if they are not based on sex-for-money per se.

The Japanese sex industry also exists with deference to *tatemae*, and actual practices are rarely discussed openly. At the bottom of the industry ladder are hostess clubs, where women simply pour men's drinks and contribute conversation, and any physical contact is frowned upon. Then there are telephone clubs (known as *tere-kura*), where men pay to sit in booths and accept hot phone calls from supposedly frustrated housewives. From here, the services progress to the real thing, where nudity and/or sexual services are provided. These range from fondling to oral or full sex, and the function of each establishment is clearly marked out in a *tatemae* euphemistic code. A 'fashion massage' is code for manual stimulation, while a 'fashion health massage' stands for oral sex. To spice up these categories many establishments go by such names as *gakuen tengoku* (schoolgirl heaven). Additionally, there are places called 'soapland', which offer a hot Japanese bath followed by sex. Formerly called Turkish baths, their current name is rumoured to derive from a diplomatic incident in which the Turkish ambassador to Tokyo asked a taxi driver to take him to a Turkish bath, where he was offered more than he bargained for. Following an official complaint, all such establishments became soaplands overnight.

The appeal of these places, and the average male's frequency of use, are open to question, but the sheer number and breadth of selection are themselves a comment on the sexual universe here. Yet to frame this as pure perversion or the sign of a patriarchy run riot would be a mistake. Tokyo has numerous and energetic sexual subcultures, of which the straight male-oriented sex industry is merely one aspect. Expressions of these erotic dimensions extend to the gay and committed straight couples' worlds.

Tokyo's thriving gay and lesbian community is markedly less observant of the Japanese strictures of *tatemae*. Homosexuality has long been an accepted private pursuit in Japan. Old samurai tales are rife with positive descriptions of gay love. No one batted an eyelash when (now) conservative TV commentator and filmmaker Oshima Nagisa enthusiastically portrayed exactly this in his 1999 movie, *Gohatto*. In addition, some of Japan's earliest literature includes references to lesbianism. The virulent condemnation of homosexual conduct so prevalent in the west has practically never surfaced in Japan.

There is also a relatively visible gay sex industry, mostly centred around 'host' services. In a stunning reversal of common sense, but in keeping with a prostitute's separation of the

professional and private, many suppliers insist their boys actually be straight.

Nor should straight couples feel left on the fringes of Tokyo's sex trade. The couples' *kissaten* (literally 'coffee shop'), or couples' *kissa* for short, is a scene that straddles the line between swinging and exhibitionism. Here couples go into dimly lit clubs that resemble a low-slung living room and engage in sex with their partner, or if consensual, other members at the club. These clubs, and their newer incarnation, the 'happening bar', are surprisingly numerous and inexpensive. Generally admittance is limited to couples, and many who use these places engage in sex only with their own partner but may make friendships with others or simply enjoy watching them.

So, is Tokyo sexually twisted, or a city with an unusually liberal secret side? Is it to be condemned or applauded for its approach? Before you make any swift judgements, make sure your own preconceptions aren't getting in the way.

Accommodation

Features

Accommodation

From budget hostels to luxurious hotels, Tokyo has room for everyone.

Like any major world city, Tokyo offers a plethora of accommodation choices. In Tokyo's case, these range from some of the most exclusive hotels in the world to tiny straw mat rooms without bath or shower. Good news is that budget travellers are sure to find something to suit their wallet.

Because Tokyo is so vast, your choice of accommodation will have a profound effect on the quality of your stay. Before you book, think about the sort of place you want to stay. Is it nightlife you're after? Then think about Shibuya or Roppongi. Culture? Asakusa or Ueno. Something in between? Shinjuku or Ebisu. Do you want all the trappings of a western hotel room, such as a bed, or are you happy to go native and sleep on a futon (a choice that could save you some cash)? The earlier you answer these questions, the better your stay will be.

Below are explanations of some of the terms used in this chapter.

BUSINESS HOTELS

As their name suggests, business hotels are primarily designed with commercial travellers in mind. A step down in quality and service, business hotels offer solid value for money, though rooms are often on the small side.

CAPSULE HOTELS

The last resort of the drunk, desperate and male (most are men-only), a capsule hotel offers a cheap place to put your head down for the night, and not much more. Accommodation is likely to be a small tube barely big enough to sleep in, and extended stays are unheard of.

DELUXE

Most of the top hotels in Tokyo offer western-style accommodation, although some also offer the option of a slightly pricier Japanese-style room. All of these hotels offer every possible comfort and convenience, so we do not list their services separately.

RYOKAN

Staying at a *ryokan*, or Japanese-style inn (*see p38* **Etiquette**), is one of the best ways to enhance your enjoyment of Tokyo. Most *ryokan* offer Japanese-style accommodation – there will be tatami (woven straw mats) on the floor rather than carpet and you will be expected to sleep on a futon. One of the bonuses of the *ryokan*-style room for budget travellers is that most *ryokan* are happy to accommodate several guests in one room, bringing the price per head down. Another plus is that by day the futons are folded away in a cupboard, giving you much more living space than a room with fixed beds. More expensive *ryokan* will usually come with individual bathrooms, but at the cheaper end of the scale you will be expected to bathe Japanese-style in a communal bath. A word of warning: some *ryokan* expect their guests to be back in their room by 11pm. Make sure to check this when booking.

Ginza & Marunouchi

Deluxe

Dai-ichi Hotel Tokyo

1-2-6 Shinbashi, Minato-ku (3501 4411/fax 3595 2634/www.daiichihotels.com). Shinbashi station, Hibiya exit or exit 7. **Rooms** 277. **Rates** ¥27,000-¥34,000 single; ¥31,000-¥45,000 double; ¥80,000-¥350,000 suite. **Credit** AmEx, DC, JCB, MC, V. **Map** p57.

This 1993 tower rises above the relatively low skyline of Shinbashi, a ten-minute walk from Ginza. The interior is a strange mix of styles: the entrance hall is a self-conscious echo of the grand style of old European luxury hotels; the restaurants are a tribute to the designers' ability to cram many different styles of interior decor into one building. Rooms are immaculate, of a good size and beautifully furnished and decorated.

Four Seasons at Marunouchi

Pacific Century Place, 1-11-1 Marunouchi, Chiyoda-ku (5222 7222/fax 5222 1255/ www.fourseasons.com/marunouchi). Tokyo JR station, Yaesu (south) exit. **Rooms** 57. **Rates** ¥55,000-¥65,000 single; ¥60,000-¥70,000 double; ¥85,000-¥400,000 suites. **Credit** AmEx, MC, V. **Map** p62.

The new Four Seasons offers unparalleled luxury and style in the heart of Tokyo's business district. It's decorated in cool modern timber, beautifully lit to exude an atmosphere of serenity. The rooms are among the biggest in any Tokyo hotel, and some of them boast great views across the railway tracks to Tokyo International Forum. Service is multilingual and utterly impeccable, as you're entitled to expect for the price. Each room comes with high-speed internet access, a 42-inch plasma TV screen with surround-sound, and a DVD player.

Hotel Seiyo Ginza

1-11-2 Ginza, Chuo-ku (3535 1111/fax 3535 1110/ www.seiyo-ginza.com). Ginza-Itchome station, exits 7, 10. **Rooms** 77. **Rates** ¥42,000-¥57,000 double; ¥60,000-¥150,000 one-bedroom suite; ¥105,000-¥195,000 two-bedroom suite; ¥200,000 premier suite. **Credit** AmEx, MC, V. **Map** p57.

By Tokyo standards, this is a small hotel, and it plays up its boutique credentials, with European-style decor of the antique drawing room school. Wonderfully located for both business and pleasure in an area that straddles the Marunouchi financial district and Tokyo's premier shopping area, Ginza, the Seiyo combines great service with immaculate accommodation. Business travellers benefit from a personal secretarial service, while all rooms have a stereo, fax machine and video-on-demand service.

Imperial Hotel

1-1-1 Uchisawaicho, Chiyoda-ku (3504 1111/fax 3581 9146/www.imperialhotel.co.jp/cgi-bin/imperial_hp/index_e.cgi). Hibiya station, exits A5, A13 or JR Yurakucho station, Hibiya exit. **Rooms** 1,058. **Rates** ¥34,000-¥48,000 single; ¥39,000-¥53,000 double; ¥60,000-¥170,000 suite. **Credit** AmEx, DC, JCB, MC, V. **Map** p57.

There has been an Imperial Hotel on this site overlooking Hibiya Park since 1890. This 1970 tower block-style replaced the glorious 1923 Frank Lloyd Wright building that famously survived the Great Kanto Earthquake on its opening day. The vast reception area is a popular meeting place for businessmen and couples. Inside, though, the hotel is starting to show its age: the rooms are blandly furnished and the corridors feel cramped. The newer tower annexe has a slightly less dated feel.

Palace Hotel

1-1-1 Marunouchi, Chiyoda-ku (3211 5211/fax 3211 6987/ www.palacehotel.co.jp/english/index.html). Otemachi station, exit C13b or Tokyo JR station, Marunouchi (north) exit. **Rooms** 390. **Rates** ¥23,000-¥29,000 single; ¥32,000-¥60,000 twin; ¥33,000-¥45,000 double; ¥100,000-¥230,000 suite . **Credit** AmEx, DC, JCB, MC, V. **Map** p62.

Despite its position, on the edge of the moat that skirts the Imperial Palace, something about the Palace doesn't quite strike the right chord. The entrance hall has a dingy, faded feel, and while rooms are comfortable and the views potentially spectacular, the slightly depressing ambience takes some of the shine off moving in next door to the emperor. The Crown Bar on the top floor is a good place for a drink with a view.

Expensive

Ginza Renaissance Tobu Hotel

6-14-10 Ginza, Chuo-ku (3546 0111/fax 3546 8990/ www.tobuhotel.co.jp/ginza). Higashi Ginza station, exits A1, A4. **Rooms** 206. **Rates** ¥17,000-¥30,000 single; ¥28,000-¥50,000 double; ¥60,000-¥130,000 suite. **Credit** AmEx, DC, JCB, MC, V. **Map** p57.

A stone's throw from Ginza's Kabuki-za, the Renaissance is an unprepossessing building whose main interior motif is shiny and golden. This may explain its popularity as a venue for young couples to tie the knot. The rooms are comfortable in a functional, bland sort of way, and service is good.

Hotel services *Air-conditioning. Babysitting (by arrangement). Bar. Beauty salon. Business services. Conference facilities. Currency exchange. Disabled: access; toilets. Fax. Laundry. Multilingual staff. Parking (¥1,000/day). Restaurants (3). Safe.* **Room services** *Cable TV. Disabled: adapted rooms. Hairdryer. Minibar. Modem port. Radio. Room service (6.30am-midnight). Tea in room (Japanese). Voicemail.*

Mitsui Urban Hotel

8-6-15 Ginza, Chuo-ku (3572 4131/fax 3572 4254/ www.mitsuikanko.co.jp/english/urban.htm). Shinbashi station, Ginza exit. **Rooms** 265. **Rates** ¥14,000-¥17,500 single; ¥21,000-¥30,000 twin; ¥21,000-¥24,500 double. **Credit** AmEx, DC, JCB, MC, V. **Map** p57.

The Mitsui is an unassuming, practical choice on the edge of Ginza. Rooms are quite small and basically furnished, and the relative lack of facilities is reflected in the price. Reception is on the second floor, with rooms on the third to 11th.

Kimi Ryokan.
See p37.

Hotel services *Air-conditioning. Bar. Currency exchange. Disabled: access. Fax. Laundry. Multilingual staff. No-smoking floor. Parking (¥1,000/day). Restaurants (2). Safe.* **Room services** *Cable/satellite TV. Hairdryer. Ironing facilities (on request). Minibar. Modem port. Radio. Room service (night only). Tea in room (Japanese).*

Moderate

Hotel Ginza Daiei

3-12-1 Ginza, Chuo-ku (3545 1111/fax 3545 1177/ www.ginza-daiei.co.jp). Higashi Ginza station, exit A7. **Rooms** 82. **Rates** ¥11,300 single; ¥13,600-¥20,800 twin; ¥13,600-¥15,300 double. **Credit** AmEx, DC, JCB, MC, V. **Map** p57.

A well-furnished and well-situated hotel that provides a more comforts than you might expect for the price. Modern-looking rooms are of a good size, with plain, functional pine furniture and inoffensive, light decor. If you opt for the top price 'Healthy Twin' room, you'll get the added bonus of a jet bath.

Hotel services *Air-conditioning. Business services. Conference facilities. Currency exchange ($ only). Fax. Laundry. Multilingual staff. Parking (¥1,000/day). Safe.* **Room services** *Cable TV. Hairdryer. Minibar. Radio.*

Ikebukuro

Budget

Kimi Ryokan

2-36-8 Ikebukuro, Toshima-ku (3971 3766/www. kimi-ryokan.jp). Ikebukuro station, exit C6 or west exit. **Rooms** 38. **Rates** ¥4,500 single; ¥6,500-¥7,500 double. **No credit cards. Map** p69.

A *ryokan* that caters almost exclusively for foreign visitors, offering simple, small Japanese-style rooms. Bathing and toilet facilities are communal but very clean; there's even a Japanese bath for use at set times. Downstairs in the communal lounge, backpackers and travellers exchange gossip. Kimi also runs an information and accommodation service for foreigners apartment-hunting in Tokyo (3986 1604), and a telephone answering service for businesspeople (3986 1895). Booking is advised.

Hotel services *Air-conditioning. Fax. Internet. Multilingual staff. Safe. Tea in lounge.* **Room services** *Hairdryer (on request). Ironing facilities (on request). TV.*

Roppongi & Akasaka

Deluxe

Akasaka Prince Hotel

1-2 Kioi-cho, Chiyoda-ku (3234 1111/fax 3262 5163/ www.princehotels.co.jp/english/index1.html). Akasaka-Mitsuke station, exit D or Kojimachi station, Kojimachi exit or Nagatacho station, exits 7, 9A, 9B. **Rooms** 761. **Rates** ¥27,000-¥36,000 single; ¥33,000-¥42,000 twin; ¥37,000-¥45,000 double; ¥80,000-¥130,000 suite/Japanese. **Credit** AmEx, DC, JCB, MC, V.

Designed by award-winning architect Kenzo Tange, the 40-storey Akasaka Prince is part of a complex that includes a convention centre, European-style guesthouse and banqueting building. Inside the main tower, it's all glittering marble and bright lights. The clean lines of the building extend to the furnishings in the rooms, which in their elegant simplicity look like something out of *Star Trek*.

The best Hotels

For being in the lap of luxury at the heart of the action

It simply has to be the spanking new **Grand Hyatt**, *see p38.*

For being cute above and beyond the call

The owner of **Cozy House**, *see p51*, who offers experience along with the accommodation.

For making new friends

The **Kimi Ryokan**, *see p37*, is like an unofficial club for foreign travellers.

For fabulous night-time panoramas

What **Le Meridien Grand Pacific**, *see p40*, lacks in location, It makes up for with eye-popping views of Rainbow Bridge, Odaiba and the waterfront.

For lovable eccentricity

It's great to see the **Hilltop Hotel**, *see p46*, still holding its own against the flashy newcomers.

For being cheap, and very cheerful

The owners of the **Ryokan Sawanoya**, *see p43*, are always ready with a smile and helpful tips.

For the full Japanese experience

Nothing in the heart of Tokyo can offer the same genuine old-world atmosphere as the **Homeikan** buildings, *see p41*.

For wealthy trainspotters

Ask for a room with a view over Tokyo station at the incredibly swish **Four Seasons** at Marunouchi, *see p34*.

Etiquette

If you can bear to forgo a few of the comforts of home, such as a mattress and feather pillow, then staying in a *ryokan* (a traditional Japanese inn) is a great choice, particularly since they tend to be cheaper than western-style hotels. *Ryokan* are also fine for people travelling in groups of more than two, since, as long as the room is big enough, you can have as many futon as you like on the tatami (straw mat floor), for an extra charge significantly less than the price of another room.

There are a few other differences with a *ryokan*. The first is that you take off your shoes when you go in. After that, *ryokan* staff will show you to your room, and introduce you to the waiting flask of hot water and green tea. Decor will include a *shoji* (sliding paper screen) and a *tokonoma* (alcove), which is for decoration, not for storing luggage. Inside the cupboard you will find a *yukata* (dressing gown) and *tanzen* (bed jacket), which you can wear around the *ryokan*, and which double as pyjamas. When putting on a *yukata*, put the left side over the right. Many *ryokan* have communal bathing facilities, so follow the rules of bathing in Japan – wash first in the shower, no soap in the water, and don't immerse your head or wash cloth. The *ryokan* staff will return to make up the futon in your room at around 8pm. They'll be back the following morning at about 8am with breakfast.

Note that because most *ryokan* are family-run businesses, many of them impose a curfew of 11pm. If you're going to be out later, tell your hosts. If a curfew doesn't suit you, check with the individual *ryokan* in advance.

ANA Hotel Tokyo

1-12-33 Akasaka, Minato-ku (3505 1111/fax 3505 1155/www.anahotels.com/tokyo/e/index.html). Tameike-Sanno station, exit 13. **Rooms** 901. **Rates** ¥24,000-¥29,000 single; ¥32,000-¥42,000 twin; ¥32,000-¥59,000 double; ¥70,000-¥280,000 suite; ¥80,000 Japanese. **Credit** AmEx, DC, JCB, MC, V. **Map** p74.

This 13-year-old, 29-storey hotel, owned by All Nippon Airways, is situated in Ark Hills, one of the wealthiest areas of Tokyo, about ten minutes' walk from Roppongi. The entrance hall and lobby are vast, all marble and bright lights; rooms themselves are spacious, comfortable and well equipped. Room rates rise the higher in the hotel you stay, and there are stunning views on a clear day, when, from beside the roof-top open-air pool, you can see Mount Fuji. The lack of 24-hour room service is a curious blemish on an otherwise top-class place.

Capitol Tokyu

2-10-3 Nagatacho, Chiyoda-ku (3581 4511/fax 3581 5822/www.capitoltokyu.com/english/index.html). Kokkaigijido-mae station, exit 5. **Rooms** 459. **Rates** ¥26,000-¥37,500 semi-double; ¥38,000-¥55,000 double/twin; ¥100,000-¥380,000 suite. **Credit** AmEx, DC, JCB, MC, V.

For the first 20 years of its existence, until 1983, the Capitol Tokyu was the Tokyo Hilton. This is where the Beatles stayed in 1966, and more recent guests have included Michael Jackson. One of the attractions is the hotel's location, close enough to the centre to be interesting, isolated enough, overlooking the Hie Shrine, to be quiet and peaceful. Rooms are well furnished with nice Japanese touches such as paper screens in the windows.

Grand Hyatt Tokyo

6-10-3 Roppongi, Minato-ku (4333 8800/fax 4333 8123/grandhyatttokyo.com). Roppongi station, exits 1, 3. **Rooms** 390. **Rates** ¥46,000-¥53,000 single or double; ¥66,000-¥470,000 suites. **Credit** AmEx, MC, V. **Map** p74.

This new top-class hotel in Roppongi Hills, which opened in April 2003, is so posh that it has 'residences' rather than rooms. The look of the hotel – the currently voguish warm woods, rather than the marble that graces Tokyo's older classy establishments – is the result of a collaboration between three top interior design firms. Rooms are spacious, with wonderfully large bathrooms featuring super-size tubs. The top-price presidential suite, incidentally, is the only such suite in Tokyo to feature a private roof-top swimming pool set in a Japanese garden.

Hotel New Otani

4-1 Kioi-cho, Chiyoda-ku (3265 1111/fax 3221 2619/www1.newotani.co.jp/en). Akasaka-Mitsuke station, exit D or Nagatacho station, exit 7. **Rooms** 1,600. **Rates** ¥26,000-¥29,000 single; ¥31,000-¥47,000 double; ¥47,000 triple; ¥75,000-¥220,000 suite; ¥74,000 Japanese. **Credit** AmEx, DC, JCB, MC, V.

The New Otani sprawls over a vast area ten minutes' walk west of the Imperial Palace. From the outside the building bears the unattractive hallmarks of its 1969 construction, but inside the dim lighting and spacious foyers produce the feeling of a luxury cruise ship. To the rear of the hotel there's a beautifully laid-out and tended Japanese garden. Within the garden stands several of the hotel's 34 restaurants. Capacity was increased in 1979 by the addition of a 40-storey tower block.

Hotel Okura

2-10-4 Toranomon, Minato-ku (3582 0111/ fax 3582 3707/www.okura.com). Roppongi-Itchome station, exits 2, 3. **Rooms** 858. **Rates** ¥32,500-¥42,000 single; ¥40,000-¥120,000 double; ¥180,000-¥500,000 suite. **Credit** AmEx, DC, JCB, MC, V. **Map** p74.

The Okura, next door to the US Embassy, oozes opulence. The huge wooden lobby somehow manages to evoke the tranquillity of a Japanese garden, with its rock centrepiece and artfully arranged chairs. To travellers dazzled by the 21st-century chic of Tokyo's more recent hotels, the Okura may appear old fashioned, but only in a reassuring, solid way. This is one of the world's great hotels, and it knows it. The Okura is also justifiably famous for its cuisine, offering everything from Cantonese and Japanese to French haute cuisine.

Expensive

Arca Torre Hotel

6-1-23 Roppongi, Minato-ku (3404 5111/fax 3404 5115/www.arktower.co.jp). Roppongi station, exit 3. **Rooms** 77. **Rates** ¥11,000-¥13,000 single; ¥14,000-¥17,000 double; ¥21,000 twin. **Credit** AmEx, DC, MC, V. **Map** p74.

Arca Torre is a smart, bright high(ish)-rise business hotel sandwiched between the adults' playground of Roppongi and the new Roppongi Hills complex. Rooms here are small and functional; if you want a bigger room, it's best to go for the twin. For nightlife lovers, this hotel's location is hard to beat, but be prepared if you want an early night as the streets can get noisy, and the noise may make it up to your window and keep you awake into the early hours.

Hotel services *Air-conditioning. Business centre. Café.* **Room services** *Hairdryer. Internet access. Plasma TV.*

Roppongi Prince Hotel

3-2-7 Roppongi, Minato-ku (3587 1111/fax 3587 0770/www.princehotels.co.jp/english/index1.html). Roppongi-Itchome station, exit 1. **Rooms** 216. **Rates** ¥18,500 single; ¥24,500-¥26,500 double; ¥23,000-¥26,500 twin; ¥50,000-¥60,000 suite. **Credit** AmEx, DC, JCB, MC, V. **Map** p74.

The best way to view the Roppongi Prince Hotel is to stand on the roof and look down. The hotel was designed by architect Kisho Kurokawa around a Perspex-sided open-air swimming pool heated to 30°C all year round. It's handily located in a quiet back street five minutes from the nightlife of Roppongi. The reception area is so anonymous it's easy to miss it, while the rooms are well furnished, if a little on the small side.

Hotel services *Air-conditioning. Bar. Business services. Conference facilities. Currency exchange. Disabled: access; toilets. Fax. Jacuzzi (outdoor). Multilingual staff. No-smoking floor. Restaurants (4). Safe. Swimming pool (outdoor).* **Room services** *Cable TV. Hairdryer. Modem port. Radio. Room service (7am-midnight).*

Moderate

Hotel Ibis

7-14-4 Roppongi, Minato-ku (3403 4411/fax 3479 0609/www.ibis-hotel.com). Roppongi station, exit 4A. **Rooms** 182. **Rates** ¥11,500-¥16,300 single; ¥14,100-¥23,000 double; ¥36,000 suite. **Credit** AmEx, DC, JCB, MC. **Map** p74.

It seems hard to believe, given the recent burst of building activity in the area, but just three years ago, this was the closest hotel to the centre of Roppongi. Now, with all the new competition, Hotel Ibis is starting to look a little worn, and customers may well be enticed elsewhere. That said, this hotel is always clean, functional and good value.

Hotel services *Air-conditioning. Business services. Conference facilities. Currency exchange. Disabled: access. Fax. Multilingual staff. No-smoking floor. Parking (¥2,100 night). Restaurants (3). Safe.* **Room services** *Cable TV. Hairdryer. Ironing facilities. Minibar. Modem port. Radio. Room service (5am-10.30pm). Tea/coffee free on request.*

Budget

Asia Centre of Japan

8-10-32 Akasaka, Minato-ku (3402 6111/fax 3402 0738/www4.ocn.ne.jp/~asiacntl/main.html). Nogizaka station, exit 3. **Rooms** 71. **Rates** ¥5,100-¥7,500 single; ¥6,800-¥10,500 twin/double; ¥12,300 (adapted for disabled). **Credit** JCB, MC, V. **Map** p74.

Founded by the Ministry of Foreign Affairs in the 1950s as a cheap place for visiting students to stay, this has long since outgrown its origins and offers comfortable, no-frills accommodation to all visitors on a budget. The tiny rooms (the cheapest of which don't have baths) still bear the hallmarks of their institutional beginnings. Rooms in the newer wing have been refurbished and have extras that the older rooms lack. Very convenient for the Aoyama area.

Hotel services *Air-conditioning. Business services. Coffeeshop. Conference facilities. Currency exchange. Disabled: access; toilets. Fax. Laundry. Multilingual staff. Parking. Restaurant. Safe.* **Room services** *Hairdryer (new wing). Ironing facilities. Modem line (on request). Radio. Room adapted for disabled. Tea/coffee in room (new wing). TV.*

Odaiba & area

Deluxe

Hotel Inter-Continental Tokyo Bay

1-16-2 Kaigan, Minato-ku (5404 2222/fax 5404 2111/www.interconti.com). Takeshiba (Tokyo monorail) station or Hamamatsucho station, south exit. **Rooms** 339. **Rates** ¥36,000-¥62,000 double; ¥100,000-¥300,000 suite. **Credit** AmEx, DC, JCB, MC, V.

The Inter-Continental opened in September 1995 in the hitherto little-explored area that fronts Tokyo's Sumida river. Amid the grim industrial surroundings, the luxurious hotel and the adjoining New Pier Takeshiba shopping and dining complex stand out like a diamond in a cow pat. If its location is the hotel's main shortcoming, then its main selling point is the view, over the river and the spectacular Rainbow Bridge, to the island of Odaiba. Those that love a room with a view will be pleased that all rooms, and their bathrooms, have a view of the river.

Le Meridien Grand Pacific

2-6-1 Daiba, Minato-ku (5500 6711/www.htl-pacific.co.jp/english/grand_pacific.html). Daiba station (Yurikamome Line). **Rooms** 884. **Rates** ¥31,000-¥49,000 twin; ¥31,000-¥46,000 double; ¥80,000-¥180,000 suite. **Credit** AmEx, DC, JCB, MC, V. **Map** p78.

Luxury hotels don't come much more luxurious than this. The Meridien opened in 1998 on the island area of Odaiba and boasts spectacular views over Rainbow Bridge and the Tokyo skyline. The only real drawback is its location: Odaiba is great place for a day out but as base for touring Tokyo it's inconvenient. Perhaps aware of the lack of much in the way of local character, the hotel supplies some of its own, in the form of an art gallery on the third floor and, more bizarrely, a museum of music boxes on the second. Even if you don't stay here, it's worth stopping off at the Sky Lounge on the 30th floor for one of the best views over Tokyo and the bay.

Asakusa

Expensive

Asakusa View Hotel

3-17-1 Nishi-Asakusa Taito-ku (3847 1111/fax 3842 2117/www.viewhotels.co.jp/asakusa/english/index.html). Tawaramachi station, exit 3. **Rooms** 338. **Rates** ¥13,000-¥33,000 single; ¥21,000-¥34,000 twin/double; ¥40,000-¥63,000 Japanese style; ¥50,000-¥300,000 suite. **Credit** AmEx, DC, JCB, MC, V. **Map** p83.

Although smaller and more compact than many of Tokyo's high-priced hotels, the Asakusa View boasts a high standard of accommodation and its rates reflect its status as the only luxury hotel in this touristy area. If you want to make the hotel live up to its name, go for a room as high up as you can: the view from the top over Asakusa and the Sumida river is worth catching. If the hotel is beyond your budget, the Belvedere lounge on the 28th floor offers the chance to take in the view over a drink. A nice touch is that the sixth floor is given over to Japanese-style rooms, complete with their own garden.

Hotel services *Air-conditioning. Bars (3). Beauty salon. Conference facilities. Disabled: access. Fax. Fitness centre. Karaoke room. Laundry. Multilingual staff. No-smoking rooms. Parking. Pharmacy. Restaurants (6). Safe. Shopping arcade. Swimming pool.* **Room services** *Hairdryer. Ironing facilities (on request). Minibar. Modem port. Radio. Room service (6am-2am). Satellite TV. Tea in room (Japanese). Voicemail.*

The luxurious **Hotel New Otani**. *See p38.*

Moderate

Hotel Sunroute Asakusa

1-8-5 Kaminarimon, Taito-ku (3847 1511/fax 3847 1509/www.sunroute-asakusa.co.jp/webmaster@sunroute-asakusa.co.jp). Tawaramachi station, exit 3. **Rooms** 120. **Rates** ¥8,500-¥10,500 single; ¥16,500 twin ¥19,000; ¥14,500 double. **Credit** AmEx, DC, MC, V. **Map** p83.

Small rooms and lack of facilities notwithstanding, this business hotel offers reasonable value for money for those determined to sleep in beds rather than on futons. The building itself is so bland and unremarkable there's a danger of walking straight past it without realising – look out for the Jonathan's restaurant sign on the street. American-style Jonathan's is situated on the second floor and doubles as the hotel's restaurant.

Hotel services *Air-conditioning. Disabled: access; toilets. Fax. Laundry. Multilingual staff. Parking (¥1,500/day). Restaurant. Safe.* **Room services** *Hairdryer. Minibar. Modem line. Radio. Rooms adapted for disabled. Satellite TV. Tea (Japanese) in room. Telephone message system.*

Ryokan Shigetsu

1 31 11 Asakusa, Taito-ku (3843 2345/fax 3843 2348/http://shigetsu.com). Asakusa station, exits 1, 3, 6, A4. **Rooms** 23. **Rates** ¥7,300 single; ¥9,000-¥14,000 twin/double; ¥9,000-¥40,000 Japanese (1-5 people). **Credit** AmEx, MC, V. **Map** p83.

Barely 30 seconds' walk from Asakusa's market and temple complex, the Shigetsu offers a choice of comfortable rooms in Japanese and western styles. All rooms have their own bathrooms, although there is a Japanese-style communal bath on the top floor. Booking is recommended and can be made through the Japan Inn Group (*see p52*).

Hotel services *Air-conditioning. Currency exchange ($ only). Disabled: access; toilets. Fax. Laundry. Multilingual staff. No-smoking floors (2). Parking. Restaurant. Safe.* **Room services** *Hairdryer (on request). Internet access. Ironing facilities (on request). Minibar. Radio. Tea (Japanese) in room. TV.*

Sukeroku No Yado Sadachiyo

2-20-1 Asakusa Taito-ku (3842 6431/fax 3842 6433/www.sadachiyo.co.jp). Asakusa station, exits 1, 3, 6, A4 or Tawaramachi station, exit 3. **Rooms** 22. **Rates** ¥12,000-¥15,000 single; ¥17,600-¥36,000 double. **Credit** AmEx, DC, JCB, MC, V. **Map** p83.

This smart modern *ryokan* is wonderfully situated five minutes' walk from Asakusa's temple and pagoda tourist traps. From the outside the building looks oddly like a European chalet, but inside it's pure Japanese, with receptionists shuffling around the desk area dressed in kimono. Staff are obliging but speak only minimal English. All rooms are Japanese-style and come in a variety of sizes, the smallest being just five mats. The communal Japanese baths should help make a stay here a memorable and incredibly relaxing experience.

Hotel services *Air-conditioning. Disabled: access. Fax. Restaurant. Room service (4-10pm). Safe.* **Room services** *Tea (Japanese)/coffee in room. TV.*

Budget

Asakusa Ryokan

2-17-4 Asakusa, Taito-ku (3844 5570). Tawaramachi (Ginza Line) station, exit 3. **Rooms** 6. **Rates** ¥4,000 single; ¥5,000 double. **No credit cards. Map** p83.

A *ryokan* whose best days look to be about 200 years behind it, the Asakusa sneaks in here because of its fabulous location close to the tourist sites. Be prepared to speak Japanese, and to have your bathing etiquette closely monitored.

Hotel services *Air-conditioning. Japanese bath. Japanese & western rooms.* **Room services** *Hairdryer (on request). Tea (Japanese) in room. TV.*

Sakura Ryokan

2-6-2 Iriya, Taito-ku (3876 8118/fax 3873 9456/ www.sakura-ryokan.com). Iriya station, exit 1. **Rooms** 18. **Rates** ¥5,300-¥6,300 single; ¥9,200-¥10,600 twin/double; ¥5,300-¥6,300 Japanese single; ¥9,600-¥10,600 Japanese double. **Credit** AmEx, JCB, MC, V.

Ten minutes' walk from Asakusa's temple complex, in the traditional downtown area of Iriya, the Sakura is a friendly, traditional family-run *ryokan*. Of the Japanese-style rooms, only two have their own bathrooms, while seven western-style rooms have baths. There's a communal bath on each floor.

Hotel services *Air-conditioning. Beer vending machine. Disabled: access. Fax. Japanese & western rooms. Laundry.* **Room services** *Cable TV. Hair dryer (on request). Ironing facilities (on request). Tea/coffee in room.*

Ueno

Expensive

Hotel Sofitel Tokyo

2-1-48 Ikenohata, Taito-ku (5685 7111/fax 5685 6171/www.sofiteltokyo.com). Yushima station, exit 1. **Rooms** 83. **Rates** ¥17,000-¥27,000 single; ¥22,000-¥32,000 double; ¥36,000-¥70,000 suite; ¥24,000-¥90,000 double, twin suite. **Credit** AmEx, DC, JCB, MC, V. **Map** p88.

The Sofitel is, you might say, distinctive. Shaped like an enormous white Christmas tree, it towers over neighbouring Ueno Park. Inside, guest rooms are bigger than average, and the hotel's brilliant white colouring makes it lighter than most.

Hotel services *Air-conditioning. Bar. Beauty salon. Business services. Conference facilities. Currency exchange. Disabled: access. Fax. Laundry. Multilingual staff. No-smoking rooms (12). Parking (¥1,500/day). Restaurants (3). Safe.* **Room services** *Cable/satellite TV. Hairdryer. Ironing facilities (on request). Minibar. Modem line. Room service (24hrs). Tea (Japanese)/coffee in room.*

Moderate

Homeikan Honkan/ Daimachibekkan

5-10-5 Hongo, Bunkyo ku (Honkan 3811 1181/ Daimachibekkan 3811 1186/fax 3811 1764/www1. odn.ne.jp/homeikan/info_j.html). Kasuga station (Toei Mita Line), exits A5, A6 or Hongo-sanchome station, exit 2 or Hongo-nichome exit. **Rooms** *Honkan* 26; *Bekkan* 333. **Rates** ¥6,500-¥7,500 single; ¥11,000-¥13,000 double. Special long-stay rate available. **Credit** AmEx, DC, JCB, MC, V.

This wonderful old *ryokan* looks like a Japanese inn ought to wooden, glass-fronted and an ornamental garden at the front. Some of the furnishings look frayed around the edges, but this only adds to the charm. The *ryokan* is divided into two buildings, which face each other, while the branch is a five-minute walk away. The only drawback is its location, around 20 minutes' walk from the nearest real action around Ueno or Ochanomizu stations.

Branch: **Morikawabekkan** 6-23-5 Hongo, Bunkyo ku (3811 8171/fax 3811 1764).

Hotel services *Air-conditioning. Disabled access. Fax. Parking (3 spaces). Safe.* **Room services** *Hairdryer (on request). Ironing facilities (on request). Tea (Japanese) in room.*

Hotel Park Side

2-11-18 Ueno, Taito-ku (3836 5711/fax 3831 6641/ www.parkside.co.jp). Yushima station, exit 2 or Ueno JR station, Shinobazu exit. **Rooms** 128. **Rates** ¥9,200-¥11,500 single; ¥14,000-¥17,500 twin/double; ¥16,600-¥26,200 Japanese (2-4 people). **Credit** AmEx, DC, JCB, MC, V. **Map** p88.

This hotel's title is something of a misnomer, as it's one street away from the Shinobazu Pond end of Ueno Park, bang in the middle of Ueno's late-night

drinking and entertainment district. Still, if you get a park-facing room on an upper floor, you might just be able to convince yourself you're in the countryside. Western-style rooms are a bit small, so go Japanese and put the futons away in the morning.
Hotel services *Air-conditioning. Bar. Conference facilities. Disabled: access. Fax. Japanese & western rooms. Laundry. Multilingual staff. Parking. Restaurants (4). Safe.* **Room services** *Disabled: adapted rooms. Hairdryer (on request). Minibar. Modem line. Radio. Room service (3-10.30pm). Tea (Japanese) in room. TV. Telephone message system.*

Ueno First City Hotel

1-14-8 Ueno, Taito-ku (3831 8215/fax 3837 8469/ www.uenocity-hotel.com). Yushima station, exit 6. **Rooms** 77. **Rates** ¥8,000-¥8,500 single; ¥14,000-¥16,000 twin; ¥13,000 double; ¥8,000-¥24,000 Japanese (1-6 people). **No credit cards**. **Map** p88.
A cut above the normal business hotel, this place offers comfortable accommodation in a modern red-brick block not far from Ueno Park.
Hotel services *Air-conditioning. Banquet Hall. Bar. Coffeeshop. Conference facilities. Fax. Internet. Japanese & western rooms. Restaurant.* **Room services** *Hairdryer. Massage. Satellite TV. Tea/coffee in room.*

Budget

Hotel Edoya

3-20-3 Yushima, Bunkyo-ku (3833 8751/fax 3541 3263/www2u.biglobe.ne.jp/~edoya/top.htm). Yushima station, exit 5. **Rooms** 49. **Rates** ¥4,300-¥6,800 single; ¥6,900-¥11,200 twin/double; ¥6,000-¥21,300 Japanese (max 7 people). **Credit** AmEx, DC, JCB, MC, V. **Map** p88.
This mainly Japanese-style *ryokan*, not far from Ueno Park, offers a good standard of accommodation at reasonable prices. There's a small Japanese tearoom and garden on the first floor; the roof has an open-air hot bath open to both men and women.

Sawanoya Ryokan. *See p43.*

Hotel services *Air-conditioning. Fax. Multilingual staff. Japanese restaurant. Parking.* **Room services** *Hairdryer. Ironing facilities. Modem line. Tea (Japanese)/coffee in room.*

Ueno Tsukuba Hotel

2-7-8 Moto Asakusa, Taito-ku (3834 2556/ fax 3839 1785/www.hotelink.co.jp). Inaricho station, exit, 2. **Rooms** 111. **Rates** ¥5,000-¥5,500 single; ¥8,000 twin; ¥7,000 double. **No credit cards. Map** p88.
A basic business hotel in Ueno, the Tsukuba is clean and good value for money. Rooms are tiny, so opt for a Japanese-style room, where the futon is cleared away in the morning. Western-style rooms have baths, but if you stay in a Japanese room you'll be expected to bathe Japanese-style in the communal bath on the ground floor. The hotel is two minutes' walk from Inaricho station on the Ginza Line.
Branch: Iriya Station Hotel, 1-25-1 Iriya, Taito-ku (3872 7111/fax 3872 7111).
Hotel services *Air-conditioning. Japanese bath. Japanese & western rooms.* **Room services** *Tea (Japanese) in room. TV (coin).*

Yanaka

Budget

Annex Katsutaro

3-8-4 Yanaka, Taito-ku (3828 2500/fax 3821 5400/ www.katsutaro.com). Sendagi station, exit 2. **Rooms** 17. **Rates** ¥6,000 single; ¥10,000-¥12,000 double. **Credit** AmEx, MC, V. **Map** p94.
A modern concrete *ryokan* that opened in 2001, Annex Katsutaro is located smack in the middle of charmingly old-fashioned Yanaka. The original Katsutaro (*see below*) is a short walk away, but this more modern building has more in the way of facilities. Three or four people can stay in one room, for an additional charge of around ¥5,000 per person.
Hotel services *Air-conditioning. Coin laundry. Free coffee. Ice maker. Internet access. Iron. Parking (space limited).* **Room services** *Internet access.*

Ryokan Katsutaro

4-16-8 Ikenohata, Taito-ku (3821 9808/fax 3821 4789/www.katsutaro.com). Nezu station, exit 2. **Rooms** 7. **Rates** ¥4,500 single (no bath); ¥8,400-¥16,000 (no bath, 2-4 people); ¥9,000-¥17,200 (with bath, 2-4 people). **Credit** AmEx, MC, V. **Map** p94.
In a back-street on the other side of Ueno Park, Katsutaro is a small, friendly *ryokan* with good-sized rooms and the atmosphere of a real family home (which it is). As is the case with many *ryokan*, rooms can be occupied by up to four people, at an extra charge of roughly ¥4,000 per person. The owner speaks a little English, but have a phrasebook handy if you want the conversation to progress. The Annex (*see above*) is more modern.
Hotel services *Air-conditioning. Fax. Internet. Laundry. Safe. Tea/coffee downstairs.* **Room services** *Ironing facilities (on request). TV.*

Ryokan Sawanoya

2-3-11 Yanaka, Taito-ku (3822 2251/fax 3822 2252/www.tctv.ne.jp/members/sawanoya). Nezu station, exit 1. **Rooms** 12. **Rates** ¥4,700-¥5,000 single; ¥8,800-¥9,400 double; ¥12,000-¥13,500 triple. **Credit** AmEx, MC, V. **Map** p94.

One of the few *ryokan* to cater almost exclusively for foreign visitors, Sawanoya has a small library of English-language guidebooks and provides its own map of the old-style Yanaka area. Rooms are small but comfortable, and there are signs in English reminding you how to behave and how to use the bath. More expensive rooms have their own bath, cheaper ones have access to the communal bath and shower. A small coffee lounge provides space to study the guidebooks. The couple who own the place will do everything to make your stay enjoyable.

Hotel services *Air-conditioning. Coffee shop. Internet.* **Room services** *Hairdryer (on request). Ironing facilities. Tea (Japanese) in room. TV.*

Shibuya & Ebisu

Deluxe

Cerulean Tower Tokyu Hotel

26-1 Sakuragaoka-cho, Shibuya-ku (3476 3000/fax 3476 3001/www.ceruleantower-hotel.com). Shibuya JR station, south exit. **Rooms** 414. **Rates** ¥24,000-¥31,000 single; ¥34,000-¥58,000 double/twin; ¥80,000-¥380,000 suites. **Credit** AmEx, MC, V. **Map** p102.

The Shibuya area was bereft of top-class accommodation until this hotel opened in late 2001. Housed on the 19th to 37th floors of the area's tallest building, the Cerulean offers grandstand views. In addition to the usual restaurants and bars (*see p163* **Booze with a view**), the Cerulean also has a Noh theatre (*see p243*), and a jazz club, JZ Brat (*see p225*). Room furnishings may be a step down from the likes of the Grand Hyatt (*see p38*), but so is the price.

Westin Tokyo

1-4-1 Mita, Meguro-ku (5423 7000/fax 5423 7600/www.westin.co.jp/english/index.html). Ebisu station, east exit. **Rooms** 445. **Rates** ¥34,000-¥51,000 single; ¥39,000-¥56,000 twin/double; ¥105,000-¥420,000 suite; ¥52,000 triple. **Credit** AmEx, DC, JCB, MC, V.

The Westin, at the far end of Ebisu's giant Garden Place development, opened in 1994. Its spacious lobby attempts to recreate the feeling of a European palace, while all guest rooms are palatial in size and feature soft lighting and antique-style furniture. A good view is pretty much guaranteed.

Expensive

Arimax

11-15 Kamiyamacho, Shibuya-ku (5454 1122/fax 3460 6513/www.arimaxhotelshibuya.co.jp). Shibuya JR station, Hachiko exit. **Rooms** 23. **Rates** ¥19,000-¥55,000 single; ¥24,000-¥34,000 double; ¥55,000 suite. **Credit** AmEx, MC, V. **Map** p102.

Modelled on European boutique hotels, the Arimax has a choice of English or neo-classical room styles and exudes the atmosphere of a long-established gentlemen's club, with warm, dim lighting and dark wood panelling the dominant decorative themes. All guest rooms include business amenities.

Moderate

Excel Hotel Tokyu

Shibuya Mark City, 1-12-2 Dogenzaka, Shibuya-ku (5457 0109/fax 5457 0309/www.tokyuhotels.co.jp/en/TE/TE_SHIBU/index.shtml). Inside Shibuya station. **Rooms** 408. **Rates** ¥18,500-¥19,000 single; ¥25,000-¥36,000 twin; ¥23,000-¥25,000 double; ¥30,000 triple; ¥36,000 quadruple; ¥100,000 suite. **Credit** AmEx, DC, JCB, MC, V. **Map** p102.

A middle-ranking hotel in the Mark City complex attached to Shibuya station. Pleasant, clean, with good-sized rooms offering good views of the city, this place is remarkable mainly for its location, in an area of the city that once suffered from a shortage of good-quality accommodation. Of note is the fact that the hotel offers women a floor of their own.

Hotel services *Air-conditioning. No-smoking rooms. Restaurants. Women-only floor.* **Room services** *Fax & PC rental. Hairdryer. High-speed internet. Minibar. Modem point. TV.*

Hotel Excellent

1-9-5 Ebisu-Nishi, Shibuya-ku (5458 0087/fax 5458 8787). Ebisu station, west exit. **Rooms** 127. **Rates** ¥8,700 single; ¥12,500 twin; ¥11,000 double. **Credit** MC, V.

A thoroughly basic but phenomenally popular business hotel offering no-frills accommodation in small, functional and intensely unexciting rooms. The main reason for its popularity is its location, one stop away from Shibuya on the Yamanote Line and in the heart of the lively Ebisu area.

Hotel services *Air-conditioning. Restaurant. Coffee shop. Vending machines.* **Room services** *TV (cable).*

Shinjuku

Deluxe

Century Hyatt Tokyo

2-7-2 Nishi-Shinjuku, Shinjuku-ku (3349 0111/fax 3344 5575/http://tokyo.century.hyatt.com/). Shinjuku JR station, west exit or Tochomae station (Toei Oedo Line), exit A7. Free shuttle bus service from bus stop No.35, Shinjuku JR station, west exit. **Rooms** 766. **Rates** ¥23,000-¥26,000 single; ¥32,000-¥36,000 double; ¥36,000 Regency Club twin, double; ¥52,000 grand room; ¥72,000 Japanese room (max 4 people); ¥70,000-¥400,000 suite. **Credit** AmEx, DC, JCB, MC, V. **Map** p109.

A dull, red 28-storey building, in the heart of west Shinjuku, the Century Hyatt is one of Tokyo's most celebrated hotels. The entrance hall, with its huge chandeliers, mirrors and stained glass, is breathtaking, and the standard of accommodation and service are both exceptionally high. A treat.

Keio Plaza Intercontinental

2-2-1 Nishi-Shinjuku, Shinjuku-ku (3344 0111/fax 3345 8269/www.keioplaza.com/index.html). Shinjuku JR station, west exit or Tochomae station (Toei Oedo Line), exits A1, B1. **Rooms** 1,450. **Rates** ¥18,500-¥31,000 single; ¥26,000-¥34,000 double; ¥80,000-¥250,000 suite. **Credit** AmEx, DC, JCB, MC, V. **Map** p109.

The first luxury western hotel to open in west Shinjuku, the Keio Plaza is starting to look a little faded next to its more modern competitors. Service, though, is of a high standard, and the bars on the top floor offer commanding views of the area from their 47th-floor vantage point. This is still one of the tallest buildings in the area.

Park Hyatt

3-7-1-2 Nishi-Shinjuku, Shinjuku-ku (5322 1234/fax 5322 1288/http://tokyo.park.hyatt.com). Shinjuku JR station, west exit or Tochomae station (Toei Oedo line), exit A4. Free shuttle bus from in front of Shinjuku L Tower, Shinjuku JR station, west exit. **Rooms** 178. **Rates** ¥52,000-¥63,000 double/twin; ¥100,000-¥500,000 suite. **Credit** AmEx, DC, JCB, MC, V. **Map** p109.

The Park Hyatt is Tokyo's most decorated hotel, having been the recipient of several 'best hotel in the world' awards since it opened in the early 1990s. By Tokyo standards, it's a small, intimate establishment, a feeling emphasised by the well-lit decor and selection of artworks on display. From the moment you step in you know you've arrived somewhere special: the reception is on the glass-walled 41st floor, with stunning views over the whole of Tokyo. On a clear day you can even see Mount Fuji. Service is attentive but not overly fussy, and the immaculately equipped and tastefully furnished rooms are among the largest in any Tokyo hotel.

Tokyo Hilton

6-6-2 Nishi-Shinjuku, Shinjuku-ku (3344 5111/fax 3342 6094/www.hilton.com). Shinjuku JR station, west exit or Nishi-Shinjuku station, exit C8. Free bus from Keio department store (bus stop No.21), Shinjuku JR station, west exit. **Rooms** 806. **Rates** ¥29,000-¥44,000 single; ¥35,000-¥50,000 double; ¥50,000-¥96,000 Japanese room; ¥70,000-¥240,000 suite. **Credit** AmEx, DC, JCB, MC, V. **Map** p109.

Another west Shinjuku luxury hotel, the Hilton opened in 1984, after vacating its previous premises in Akasaka (now the Capitol Tokyu, *see p38*). Rooms are of a good size, although the views, often blocked by other towers in the area, can be disappointing. As you'd expect, the standard of service is high. For business travellers, the hotel offers five executive floors, with their own separate check-in, a fax in each room and their own guest relations officers, on hand to help out and advise.

Branch: Hilton Tokyo Bay 1-8 Maihama, Urayasu shi, Chiba-ken (047 355 5000).

Expensive

Shinjuku Prince Hotel

1-30-1 Kabuki-cho, Shinjuku-ku (3205 1111/fax 3205 1952/www.princehotels.co.jp/english/index1.html). Above Seibu Shinjuku station. **Rooms** 571. **Rates** ¥16,000 single; ¥18,000-¥32,000 double; ¥28,000-¥32,000 twin. **Credit** AmEx, MC, V. **Map** p109.

The cheapest hotel in the fairly prestigious Prince chain is also the least attractive, a monolith rising above the tracks next to Seibu Shinjuku station. The main attraction is its location, in the centre of Shinjuku, two minutes' walk from the Kabuki-cho entertainment area. Rooms are smallish and minimal but clean. Enjoy great views from the 25th-floor restaurant.

Branches: throughout the city.

Hotel services *Air-conditioning. Bar. Beauty salon. Conference rooms (2). Fax. Fitness centre. Laundry. Multilingual staff. No-smoking floor. Parking. Pool. Restaurants (9). Safe. Shopping centre.* **Room services** *TV (cable with evening video on request). Hairdryer. Minibar. Modem port. Room service (11am-midnight).*

Shinjuku Washington Hotel

3-2-9 Nishi-Shinjuku, Shinjuku-ku (3343 3111/fax 3342 2575/www.wh-rsv.com/english/index.html). Shinjuku JR station, south exit. **Rooms** 1,285. **Rates** ¥11,300-¥13,900 single; ¥17,000-¥24,000 double. **Credit** AmEx, DC, JCB, MC, V. **Map** p109.

A step down in price and luxury from many of the hotels surrounding it in west Shinjuku, the Washington nevertheless offers a high standard of accommodation and service. Its main target market is businessmen, so rooms tend to be small and blandly furnished. For frequent visitors, there's an automatic check-in and -out service.

Branches: **Akihabara Washington Hotel** 1-8-3 Kandasakuma-cho, Chiyoda-ku (3255 3311/fax 3255 7343); **Tokyo Bay Ariake Washington Hotel** 3-1 Ariake, Koto-ku (5564 0111/fax 5564 0525).

Hotel services *Air-conditioning. Bar (2). Beauty salon. Conference facilities. Disabled: access. Fax. Laundry. Multilingual staff. No-smoking rooms. Parking (not free). Pharmacy. Restaurants (7). Safe. Travel agent.* **Room services** *Hairdryer. Minibar. Modem port. Radio. Rooms adapted for disabled (2). Room service (6am-10pm). Tea in room (Japanese). Trouser press. TV (cable). Voicemail.*

Shinjuku

Moderate

New City Hotel

4-31-1 Nishi-Shinjuku, Shinjuku-ku (3375 6511/fax 3375 6535/www.newcityhotel.co.jp/English/index.html). Shinjuku JR station, west exit or Tocho-Mae station (Toei Oedo Line), exit A5. **Rooms** 400. **Rates** ¥9,000-¥11,000 single; ¥12,000-¥16,600 twin; ¥15,000 double; ¥18,000 triple. **Credit** AmEx, DC, JCB, MC, V. **Map** p109.

The **Arimax**: modelled on a European boutique hotel. *See p43.*

The New City has a grand view over Shinjuku central park and the skyscrapers of west Shinjuku, but is definitely a poor relation of the many luxury hotels in the area. The interior has a faded '70s feel, and the rooms, though comfortable, spotlessly clean and quite spacious, are furnished in the same style. Next door there's a hot spring bath and sauna, an amazingly popular feature with Japanese customers.
Hotel services *Air-conditioning. Bar. Conference facilities. Fax. Hot spring bath. Laundry. Multilingual staff. No-smoking rooms. Parking (¥1,500/24hrs). Restaurant. Safe. Station shuttle bus.* **Room services** *Hairdryer. Ironing facilities. Modem line. Radio. Room service (5-11pm). Tea (Japanese) in room. TV.*

Star Hotel Tokyo

7-10-5 Nishi-Shinjuku, Shinjuku-ku (3361 1111/ fax 3369 4216/www.starhotel.co.jp/city/tokyo.html). Shinjuku JR station, west exit. **Rooms** 214. **Rates** ¥11,000-¥11,500 singles; ¥17,000-¥26,000 twin; ¥17,000-¥18,000 double. **Credit** AmEx, JCB, MC, V. **Map** p109.
In terms of position, the Star offers everything its more expensive west Shinjuku rivals do; in fact it's closer to the station than most of them. It has the sort of decor you expect from a business hotel coupled with the standard of service and facilities offered by a tourist hotel. The rather gaudy bars and restaurants may not be the sort of places you'd want to hang around in for long, but this really doesn't matter when five minutes' walk away are the many restaurants and bars of east Shinjuku. A great location to base your explorations of Tokyo.
Hotel services *Air-conditioning. Bars (2). Conference facilities. Fax. Karaoke room. Multilingual staff. No-smoking rooms. Parking (¥1,500/night). Restaurant.* **Room services** *Hairdryer. Minibar. Room service (5-11pm). Trouser press. TV (cable).*

Budget

Shinjuku Palace Hotel

2-8-12 Kabuki-cho, Shinjuku-ku (3209 1231). Shinjuku JR station, east exit. **Rooms** 34. **Rates** ¥7,000-¥7,200 single; ¥10,300-¥11,500 double. **No credit cards. Map** p109.
A palace in name only, this business hotel in the heart of Shinjuku's nightlife centre, Kabuki-cho, offers basic, no-frills accommodation aimed primarily at local businessmen or salarymen who've stayed one drink too long and missed the last train home. Still, it's clean and friendly; just don't expect to be able to make much meaningful communication in English. Rooms are small, but how much time are you going to spend here anyway?
Hotel services *Air-conditioning. Fax. Japanese-style rooms on request.* **Room services** *Hairdyer. Radio. Tea (Japanese) in room.*

Elsewhere

Deluxe

Agnes Hotel & Apartments

2-10-1 Kagurazaka, Shinjuku-ku (3267 5505/fax 3267 5513/www.agneshotel.com). Iidabashi station, west exit or exit B3. **Rooms** 61. **Rates** ¥25,000-¥48,000 single; ¥28,000-¥48,000 double; ¥58,000-¥150,000 suite. **Credit** AmEx, DC, JCB, MC, V.
An upmarket low-rise boutique hotel in the unfashionable but enjoyable Kagurazaka area, the Agnes offers a choice of superior hotel rooms or apartment-style accommodation with self-catering facilities. The hotel prides itself on its attention to its guests. Decor is designed to relax rather than impress, and the quality of the bars and restaurants is high. Rooms all have jacuzzis and are internet-ready.

Four Seasons at Chinzan-so

2-10-8 Sekiguchi, Bunkyo-ku (3943 2222/fax 3943 2300/www.fourseasons.com/tokyo/index.html). Mejiro station, then 61 bus or Edogawabashi station, exit 1A. **Rooms** 283. **Rates** ¥43,000-¥45,000 single; ¥48,000-¥70,000 double; ¥120,000-¥150,000 suite. **Credit** AmEx, DC, JCB, MC, V.

Inconveniently located out in the wilds of northern Tokyo, this is a breathtakingly opulent and beautiful hotel. Take a stroll around the Japanese garden, littered with ancient statues from Nara and Kamakura, then enjoy the wide open spaces of the lobby area: the one complements the other perfectly. Everything is immaculate, from the service to the size and decor of the rooms, in a mixture of old Japanese and European styles. Attention to detail is so great that iced tea comes with ice cubes made of tea, so as not to dilute the drink.

Royal Park Hotel

2-1-1 Nihonbashi-Kakigara-cho, Chuo-ku (3667 1111/fax 3667 1115/www.royalparkhotels.co.jp/index-e.html). Suitengu-mae station, exits 1B, 4. **Rooms** 449. **Rates** ¥22,000-¥45,000 single; ¥30,000-¥49,000 twin/double; ¥80,000-¥250,000 suite; ¥40,000 Japanese. **Credit** AmEx, DC, JCB, MC, V.

A glorious hotel ingloriously located next to the Shuto expressway in the business district of Nihonbashi. The clientele reflects the location: suits do deals in the impressive lobby, which somehow contrives to have a view of a waterfall. Rooms are spacious and well equipped, and executives can pay a ¥4,000 premium to upgrade their accommodation to executive standard, which includes in-room fax and free translation and interpretation.

Expensive

Hilltop Hotel

1-1 Kanda Surugadai, Chiyoda-ku (3293 2311/fax 3233 4567/www.yamanoue-hotel.co.jp). Ochanomizu station, Ochanomizubashi exit. **Rooms** 75. **Rates** ¥15,000-¥18,000 single; ¥22,000-¥25,000 double; ¥22,000-¥32,000 twin; ¥40,000-¥50,000 suite. **Credit** AmEx, DC, JCB, MC, V.

Not many hotels in Tokyo can be said to exude genuine charm, so the Hilltop deserves some credit for retaining its old-fashioned traditions, with an antique writing desk in every room and small private gardens for the more expensive suites. Known throughout Tokyo as a literary hangout, the Hilltop tries to boost the concentration of blocked writers by pumping ionised air into every room. Slightly shabby, but ever so appealing, with a great wine bar.

Hotel services *Air-conditioning. Babysitting (by arrangement). Bars (3). Beauty salon. Conference facilities. Currency exchange. Fax. Japanese & western rooms. Laundry. Multilingual staff. Parking (¥1,000/day). Restaurants (7). Safe.* **Room services** *Hairdryer. Ironing facilities (on request). Minibar. Modem port. Radio. Room service (7am-2am). Tea (Japanese)/coffee in room. TV (cable/satellite).*

Le Meridien Pacific Tokyo

3-13-3 Takanawa, Minato-ku (3445 6711/fax 3445 5733/www.htl-pacific.co.jp/english/grand_pacific.html). Shinagawa station, Takanawa exit. **Rooms** 954. **Rates** ¥21,000-¥35,000 single; ¥25,000-¥38,000 double; ¥50,000, ¥100,000 suite. **Credit** AmEx, DC, JCB, MC, V.

This 1971 monolith benefits from an extensive, pleasant garden that gives it a sense of space that many Tokyo hotels lack. It might look its age from the outside, but within it is immaculate. Rooms are of a good size and are kept bang up-to-date thanks to what appears to be a constant proces of renovation and redecoration. The Sky lounge on the 30th floor offers international cabaret and spectacular views over the city, although the Shinagawa area hasn't got much to recommend it. This is another of the hotels frequently used by travel companies for package tours and stopovers.

Hotel services *Air-conditioning. Babysitting (by arrangement). Bars (3). Beauty salon. Business services. Conference facilities. Currency exchange. Fax. Laundry. Multilingual staff. No-smoking rooms. Parking. Restaurants (6). Safe. Swimming pool (summer only).* **Room services** *Hairdryer. Ironing facilities (on request). Minibar. Modem line. Radio. Room service (6.30am-1am). Tea/coffee in room. TV (cable).*

New Takanawa Prince Hotel

3-13-1 Takanawa, Minato-ku (3442 1111/fax 3444 1234/www.princehotels.co.jp/english/index1.html). Shinagawa station, Takanawa exit. **Rooms** 946 (New Takanawa Prince); 299 (Sakura Tower); 414 (Takanawa Prince). **Rates** ¥25,000 single; ¥28,000-¥32,000 twin; ¥31,000-¥36,000 double; ¥65,000-¥80,000 suite. **Credit** AmEx, DC, JCB, MC, V.

The Takanawa Prince, The Sakura Tower and the New Takanawa Prince – all part of the same chain – operate as separate hotels, with separate tariffs, but are linked by glorious landscaped grounds, and guests at one hotel are free to use the facilities of the other two. The oldest of the three, the Takanawa Prince, has a solid, reassuring elegance. The New Takanawa Prince is gaudy from the outside, but impressive within, while the Sakura Tower, a pink monster of a building, offers the most up-to-date facilities and most expensive accommodation. Service in all three is impeccable, although the Shinagawa area will be a disappointment to those seeking nightlife. Facilities below are for all three hotels combined.

Hotel services *Air-conditioning. Babysitting (by arrangement). Bars (6). Beauty salons (3). Bridal salon. Business services. Conference facilities. Convenience store. Currency exchange. Disabled: access; toilets. Fax. Fitness centre. Japanese & western rooms. Laundry. Multilingual staff. No-smoking rooms. Parking. Restaurants (13). Safe. Station shuttle bus. Swimming pool (summer only).* **Room services** *Hairdryer. Ironing facilities (on request). Minibar. Modem line. Radio. Room service (24 hours). Rooms adapted for disabled (2). Tea/coffee in room. TV (cable). Voicemail.*

Moderate

Hotel Bellegrande

2-19-1 Ryogoku, Sumida-ku (3631 8111/fax 3631 8112/www.hotel-bellegrande.co.jp). Ryogoku station, west exit. **Rooms** 150. **Rates** ¥9,000-¥16,000 single; ¥16,000-¥40,000 twin; ¥14,000-¥16,000 double; ¥80,000 suite. **Credit** AmEx, DC, JCB, V.

A modern business-style hotel barely a wrestler's stride from the sumo stadium in Ryogoku, a quiet, traditional area of Tokyo that comes alive during the three annual Tokyo sumo tournaments. Its unglamorous location, ten minutes by train from Tokyo station and across the river from nearby Akihabara, is reflected in the prices of the rooms, which are small but comfortable. Booking is recommended for any visit during a sumo tournament.

Hotel services *Air-conditioning. Bar. Conference facilities (2). Fax. Japanese & western rooms. Parking (paid). Restaurant (3).* **Room services** *Hairdryer. Radio. Tea (Japanese) in room. TV.*

Hotel Kazusaya

4-7-15 Nihonbashi-Honcho, Chuo-ku (3241 1045/ fax 3241 1077/www.h-kazusaya.co.jp). Shin-Nihonbashi station (Sobu Kaisoku Line) or Mitsukoshi-mae station, exit A10. **Rooms** 71. **Rates** ¥8,500-¥9,500 single; ¥14,000 twin; ¥10,000-¥12,000 double; ¥18,000 triple; ¥21,000 Japanese room (sleeps 3); ¥24,000 Japanese room (sleeps 4). **Credit** AmEx, DC, JCB, MC, V.

There has been a Hotel Kazusaya in Nihonbashi since 1891, but you'd be hard-pushed to know this from the modern exterior of the current building, in one of the last *shitamachi* areas in the heart of Tokyo's business district. Inside, the Kazusaya offers good-sized, functionally furnished rooms. Service is obliging, although only minimal English is spoken. If you're not in Tokyo on business, you might find the area just a little too restful.

Hotel services *Air-conditioning. Bar. Conference facilities. Disabled: access; toilets. Fax. Japanese & western rooms. Laundry. Parking (¥2,000/day). Restaurant. Safe.* **Room services** *Hairdryer (on request). Ironing facilities. Tea (Japanese) in room. TV (cable/satellite).*

Kayabacho Pearl Hotel

1-2-5 Shinkawa, Chuo-ku (3553 8080/fax 3555 1849/www.pearlhotel.co.jp/kayabacho/). Kayabacho station (Tozai & Hibiya lines), exit 4B. **Rooms** 268. **Rates** ¥7,900-¥9,000 single; ¥11,200-¥20,000 twin. **Credit** AmEx, DC, JCB, MC, V.

An upscale business hotel in the heart of the business district, the Pearl has good-sized, well-furnished rooms and a reasonable level of service. Staff speak some English. One unexpected plus is the canalside location.

Hotel services *Air-conditioning. Bar. Business services. Conference facilities. Currency exchange ($ only). Disabled: access. Fax. Laundry. Multilingual staff. Parking (¥1,500/day). Restaurant. Safe.* **Room services** *Hairdryer. Ironing facilities (on request). Modem port. Tea (Japanese) in room. TV.*

River Hotel

2-13-8 Ryogoku, Sumida-ku (3634 1711/www2.ocn.ne.jp/~river.h/top.html). Ryogoku station, west exit. **Rooms** 97. **Rates** ¥6,600-¥7,200 single; ¥11,000-¥12,000 twin; ¥7,000-¥12,000 Japanese (1-2 people). **Credit** AmEx, DC, JCB, MC, V.

Offers tiny, slightly shabby western- or Japanese-style rooms (the latter are much better value). Booking recommendedduring a sumo tournament.

Hotel services *Air-conditioning. Fax. Conference room. Parking. Restaurant (Japanese).* **Room services** *Hairdryer. Ironing facilities. Radio. Tea/coffee in room. TV.*

Ryokan Ryumeikan Honten

3-4 Kanda Surugadai, Chiyoda-ku (3251 1135/ fax 3251 0270/http://stay.dlinx.co.jp/stays/ ryumeikan/index.html). Ochanomizu station, Hijiribashi exit. **Rooms** 12. **Rates** ¥9,000 single; ¥15,000 double. **Credit** AmEx, DC, JCB, MC, V.

Just south of Ochanomizu's Russian cathedral, this *ryokan* is modern and clean, with helpful staff and good-sized Japanese rooms. Architecturally, though, it's a nightmare, occupying part of a modern office building that blends so well into the surrounding bank buildings and skyscrapers as to be virtually invisible. The interior is a testament to how ingeniously the Japanese can disguise the shortcomings of a building to produce a pleasant atmosphere, but you still might find yourself wishing you'd stayed somewhere a little more traditional. The branch, in Nihonbashi, is slightly cheaper and more imposing.

Branch: **Hotel Yaesu Ryumeikan** 1-3-22 Yaesu Chuo-ku (3271 0971/fax 3271 0977).

Four Seasons at Chinzan-so. *See p46.*

Love hotels

How well do you think you might sleep on a vibrating bed? Tokyo's legions of love hotels offer you the chance to find out. Although not strictly designed for overnight stays, and not particularly economical, love hotels are such a quintessentially Japanese experience that any couple travelling to Tokyo should try one out, if only for the afternoon.

Although the system varies from hotel to hotel, here are the basic rules. Love hotels are open all day and (mostly) all night, and offer bargain rates for 'breaks' of two or three hours. Overnight rates are steeper, and most hotels will not admit overnight guests until 10pm, in order to maximise the profit from the day trade. On entry to a hotel, you will be faced by a panel of pictures of the rooms, each with their prices beneath – the cheaper price for a break, the higher for an overnight stay. Only the illuminated rooms are unoccupied. Push a button on the room of your choice, then go to the front desk to pick up the key. Some hotels are totally automatic, and have machines that print out room numbers, so as to avoid the potential embarrassment of seeing another human face. Go up to your room, lock the door and the rest is up to you.

As with any hotel, the more you're prepared to pay for a love hotel, the more you're likely to get. Prices for a two-hour break range from around ¥3,500 for a room with a bed, TV, bathroom and nothing more, to ¥15,000 or more for a room with its own swimming pool, swings, or bondage paraphernalia. All love hotels have immaculate bathrooms, some with jacuzzi or sauna, since Japanese people like to wash before jumping in the sack. At check-out time, pay the person on the desk, or in automatic hotels, feed your money into the talking machine by the door.

The highest concentrations of love hotels in Tokyo are to be found in Shinjuku's Kabuki-cho district, Shibuya's Dogenzaka and by the railway tracks near Ikebukuro station, although many other areas, such as Ebisu, have a sprinkling.

Hotel Listo

2-36-1 Kabuki-cho, Shinjuku-ku (5155 9255). Shinjuku JR station, east exit. **Rates** ¥5,800-¥8,000 break; ¥9,500-¥15,000 stay. **Credit** AmEx, DC, MC, V. **Map** p109.

One of the newest love hotels in Kabuki-cho, this one is surrounded by fir trees so discretion is assured.

Villa Giulia

2-27-8 Dogenzaka, Shibuya ku (3770 7781) Shibuya JR station, Hachiko exit. **Rates** ¥5,500-¥9,500 break; ¥9,500-¥18,000 stay. **Credit** AmEx, DC, MC, V. **Map** p102.

From the outside Villa Giulia looks something like an Italian restaurant. Inside, it's clean and fully automatic. Push a button, take

Hotel Services *Air-conditioning. Conference facilities. Fax. Laundry. Multilingual staff. Parking. Restaurant. Safe.* **Room services** *Hairdryer. Ironing facilities. Room service (7.30am-10pm). Tea (Japanese) in room. TV (cable/satellite).*

Sumisho Hotel

9-14 Nihonbashi-Kobunacho (3661 4603/fax 3661 4639/www.sumisho-hotel.co.jp/Sumisho@po.teleway.ne.jp). Ningyocho station (Toei Asakusa, Hibiya Line), exit A5. **Rooms** 86. **Rates** ¥8,200-¥8,400 single; ¥12,000-¥14,800 twin; ¥13,200 double; ¥13,200-¥20,800 Japanese-style (2-4 people). **Credit** AmEx, DC, JCB, MC, V.

A little tricky to find, this charming Japanese-style hotel manages to take an ugly modern Tokyo building and imbue it with something quintessentially Japanese, in this case a small pond, which you need to cross to get to the foyer. This is a pleasant enough place to stay, with good facilities and a high level of service, although non-Japanese speakers may find it difficult to make themselves understood.

Hotel services *Air-conditioning. Conference facilities. Disabled: access; toilets. Fax. Japanese & western rooms. Laundry. Pets by prior arrangement. Restaurant.* **Room services** *Hairdryer (on request). Ironing facilities (on request). Modem line (on request). Tea (Japanese) in room. TV (cable/satellite).*

Budget

Economy Hotel New Koyo

2-26-13 Nihonzutumi, Taito-ku (3873 0343/fax 3873 1358/www.newkoyo.jp). Minowa station, exit 3. **Rooms** 75. **Rates** ¥2,500-¥2,700 single; ¥4,800 double. **Credit** AmEx, MC, V.

Clean and friendly, with facilities that put more expensive places to shame, the New Koyo may be the cheapest overnight stay in Tokyo. Rooms are tiny, and the place is slightly out of the way, though central Tokyo is easily accessible from the nearby Hibiya Line station. The New Koyo has proved so popular that the owners opened a more traditional

a slip for your room, and then follow the spoken (in Japanese) instructions for automatic payment.

Bron Mode

2-29-7 Kabuki-cho, Shinjuku-ku (3208 6211/ www.sankei-hotel.co.jp/hotel/boutique/ bronmode/shinjuku/shinjuku.htm). Shinjuku JR station, east exit. **Rates** ¥6,000-¥9,800 break; ¥11,000-¥19,800 stay. **Credit** AmEx, MC, V. **Map** p109.

Very flashy and futuristic looking, the Bron Mode fancies itself as a little bit upmarket. Rooms all have karaoke, jet bath/jacuzzi and sauna, and gay and lesbian couples are welcome.

Meguro Club Sekitei

2-1-6 Shimo-Meguro, Meguro-ku (3494 1211/ www.gs-net.ne.jp/hotels/meguro.html). Meguro station, west exit. **Rates** ¥8,000-¥13,000 break; ¥12,000-¥22,000 stay. **Credit** AmEx, MC, V.

A famous Tokyo love hotel, standing on its own like a fairytale palace. Check in and pay in the foyer via machine. Rooms are huge and well-furnished, with free drinks provided. Karaoke, jet bath and sauna are standard, as are microwave ovens. Don't ask.

P&A Plaza

1-17-9 Dogenzaka, Shibuya-ku (3780 5211/ www.p-aplaza.com). Shibuya JR station, south, central exit. **Rates** ¥5,420-¥15,010 break; ¥10,510-¥28,870 stay. **Credit** AmEx, MC, V. **Map** p102.

One of the most famous love hotels in Tokyo, the P&A's top-priced suite contains a swimming pool. Jet bath or Jaccuzzi standard in all rooms.

and upmarket Japanese-style *ryokan*, the Andon (www.andon.co.jp), in the same area in June 2003.
Hotel services *Air-conditioning. Bicycle hire. Coin laundry. Internet access. Japanese & western rooms. Kitchen.Showers.* **Room services** TV.

Hotel Nihonbashi Saibo

3-3-16 Nihonbashi-Ningyocho, Chuo-ku (3668 2323/fax 3668 1669/www.hotel-saibo.co.jp). Ningyocho station, exit A4. **Rooms** 126. **Rates** ¥7,600-¥9,900 single; ¥12,000 twin; ¥10,000 double. **No credit cards**.

This hotel's double room price is something of a bargain. The downside is that rooms are quite small, and are western-style, with beds rather than futons. That said, some business hotels charge more for similar accommodation. Don't expect to get across anything but the most basic requests in English.
Hotel services *Air-conditioning. Conference facilities. Fax. Restaurants (2). Safe.* **Room services** *Ironing facilities (on request). Free internet access. Radio. Tea (Japanese) in room. TV.*

Juyoh Hotel

2-15-3 Kiyokawa, Taito-ku (3875 5362/fax 5603 5775/www.juyoh.co.jp). Minami-Senju station, south exit. **Rooms** 76. **Rates** ¥3,200 single; ¥6,000 double. **No credit cards**.

Another cheap option in Taito-ku, the Juyoh caters almost exclusively for foreigners. The rooms are tiny, and since only three of them are doubles, early booking is essential, via the well-designed website. Doors close at 1am and reopen at 5am.
Hotel services *Air-conditioning. Coin laundry. Internet access.* **Room services** *TV.*

Sakura Hotel

2-21-4 Kanda-Jinbocho, Chiyoda-ku (3261 3939/ fax 3264 2777/www.sakura-hotel.co.jp/sakusaku@ po.iijnet.or.jp). Jinbocho station, exits A1, A6. **Rooms** 41. **Rates** ¥5,800-¥6,800 single; ¥7,500; twin ¥8,000. **Credit** AmEx, DC, JCB, MC, V.

Of all the budget hotels and *ryokan* in Tokyo, this is the most central, occupying a site in the Jinbocho district, just a mile or so north of the Imperial Palace.

Desperate measures

There may be a time, for whatever reason, when you find yourself in need of a room in a hurry, or you may just be too skint to stay in a regular Tokyo hotel or *ryokan*. In such an emergency, there is a small street in Shinjuku, opposite the Virgin Megastore, that might just be able to accommodate you. On this street are a dozen or so small business hotels, all of them well past their prime, offering a bed for the night from ¥2,100. The most pleasant-looking among them is called Suehiro (4-4-14 Shinjuku, Shinjuku-ku, 3341 3181, rooms ¥4,100). The hotels on this street are in no way recommended, but in dire straits it's good to know they're there.

For small groups, Sakura offers the option of shared rooms sleeping six people for ¥3,600 per person per night. Staff are on duty 24 hours and all speak good English. Rooms are tiny but clean, and all are no-smoking. Book well in advance.
Hotel services *Air-conditioning. Bar. Coffeeshop. Disabled: access. Fax. Laundry. Multilingual staff. No-smoking rooms. Safe.* **Room services** *Hairdryer. Ironing facilities. Modem line (1 room). Tea (Japanese) in room.. TV.*

Tokyo International Youth Hostel

Central Plaza 18F, 1-1, Kaguragashi, Shinjuku-ku (3235 1107/fax 3267 4000/www.tokyo-yh.jp/eng/e_top.html). Iidabashi station, west exit or exit 2B. **Rooms** 33. **Rates** ¥3,500 per person per night; ¥2,000 children. **No credit cards**.
Shared rooms are the order of the day at this hostel, which occupies the 18th and 19th floors of a skyscraper above Iidabashi station. All rooms are spotlessly clean. Men and women sleep in separate rooms, the entire place is no-smoking and guests are not allowed access to the building between 10am and 3pm daily. The excellent website is regularly updated with room availability information, and weekends tend to be booked up weeks in advance. Watch out for the 11pm curfew.
Hotel services *Air-conditioning. Coin laundry. Disabled: access; rooms. Meeting room. Multi-lingual staff. Self-catering facilities.*

YMCA Asia Youth Center

2-5-5 Sarugaku-cho, Chiyoda-ku (3233 0611/fax 3233 0633/www.ymcajapan.org/ayc/jp). Suidobashi station, east exit. **Rooms** 55. **Rates** *Non-members* ¥4,800-¥6,000 single; ¥8,800-¥11,000 twin; ¥11,040-¥13,800 triple. *Members* ¥4,200-¥5,400 single; ¥7,700-¥9,900 twin; ¥9,660-¥12,420 triple. **Credit** JCB, MC, V.
This offers many of the same facilities and services you'd expect at a regular hotel, a fact reflected in its relatively high prices. In terms of location, it shares many advantages with the nearby Hilltop Hotel (*see p46*). The smallish rooms are western-style with their own bathrooms.
Hotel services *Air-conditioning. Conference facilities. Disabled: access. Fax. Laundry. Multilingual staff. Restaurant. Safe.* **Room services** *Tea (Japanese) in room. TV.*

Other accommodation

Minshuku

A *minshuku* is the Japanese equivalent of bed and breakfast accommodation, offering visitors the chance to stay in a real family environment for around ¥5,000 per night. Reservations should be made at least two days in advance.

Japan Minshuku Association

302 Shinjuku Eiko Bldg, 7-17-14 Nishi-Shinjuku, Shinjuku-ku (3364 1855/www.minshukukyokai.com). Shinjuku JR station, west exit. **Open** 10am-4pm Mon-Fri. **Map** p109.

Japan Minshuku Centre

Kotsu Kaikan Bldg B1F, 2-10-1 Yurakucho, Chiyoda-ku (3216 6556/fax 3216 6557/www.koyado.net). Yurakucho station, exit A8, Ginza exit. **Open** 10am-7pm Mon-Sat. **Map** p57.

Capsule hotels

Business Inn Shinbashi & Annex

4-12-11 Shinbashi, Minato-ku, 4-12-10 Shinbashi, Minato-ku (3431 1391/annex 3431 1020/www.rikkyo.com/bis/). Shinbashi JR station, Karasumori exit. **Capsules** 88 (56 annex). **Rates** ¥4,300 Mon-Fri; ¥3,950 Sat, Sun. Closed 31 Dec-3 Jan. **No credit cards**. **Map** p57.
Air-conditioning. Alarm. Daytime shower & siesta service. Men only. Radio. Reading lamp. TV. Video.

Capsule Hotel Azuma

3-15-1 Higashi-Ueno, Taito-ku (3831 4047/fax 3831 7103/www2.famille.ne.jp/~uenoyado/azuma.html). Ueno JR station, Asakusa or Hirokoji exit. **Capsules** 144. **Rates** ¥3,500. **No credit cards**. **Map** p88.
Alarm. Bath. Fax. Intercom. Japanese restaurant. Men only. Sauna. Satellite TV (paid). Radio. Toothbrush (free). Towel. TV.

Central Land Shibuya

1-19-14 Dogenzaka, Shibuya-ku (3464 1777). Shibuya JR station, Hachiko exit. **Capsules** 140. **Rates** ¥3,700. **No credit cards**. **Map** p102.
Bath (public). Men only. Shower.

Shinjuku Kuyakusyo-Mae Capsule Hotel

1-2-5 Kabuki-cho, Shinjuku-ku (3232 1110/www.toyo-bldg.ne.jp/hotel/index.html). Shinjuku JR station, east exit. **Capsules** 460. **Rates** from ¥4,200. **No credit cards. Map** p109.
Japanese restaurant. Massage. Men only. Sauna.

Long-term accommodation

For foreigners, finding long-term accommodation in Tokyo can be a nightmare. Firstly, many Japanese landlords refuse to deal with non-Japanese. This has led to a growth in companies specialising in letting to foreigners, some of which let apartment space by the week. Secondly, you need a lot of money. When you find an apartment, you will be required to pay a damage deposit (*shikikin*), usually equivalent to between one and three months' rent, a brokerage fee (*chukairyo*) to the agent, usually another month's rent, and finally key money (*reikin*), usually one or two months' rent – a non-refundable way of saying thank you to the landlord for having you. You then have to find a month's rent in advance.

Understandably deterred by the cost of finding somewhere of their own, many foreigners fall back on so-called *gaijin* houses – apartment buildings full of foreigners who share bathrooms, cooking facilities and, in some cases, rooms. All the places listed below are used to dealing with foreigners and offer a full range of accommodation.

Asahi Homes

3-2-19 Roppongi, Minato-ku (3583 7544/fax 3583 7587/www.asahihomes.co.jp). Roppongi-Itchome station, exit 1. **Credit** AmEx, DC, MC, V.
Upmarket agency offering fully serviced apartments in well-chosen locations, with a minimum stay of one week. Weekly rent starts from ¥140,000 for a studio, rising to ¥210,000 for a two-bedroom apartment.

Bamboo House

3-31-3 Kami-Takada, Nakano-ku (Central reservations 3645 4028/www.bamboo-house.com/nakano.html). Arai-Yakushimae station (Seibu Shinjuku Line), south exit. **Rooms** 16. **Rates** ¥4,000-¥6,000 per night or ¥62,000-¥78,000 per mth. **Credit** AmEx, MC, V.
One of a chain of eight rooming blocks dotted all over the less fashionable parts of Tokyo. For your money you get a four-mat (very small) or eight-mat tatami room, with shared kitchen and bathroom.

Cozy House

3-15-11 Ichikawa, Ichikawa-city, Chiba (047 379 1539/www.cozyhouse.net). Konodai station (Keisei Main Line), then a 10min walk. **Rooms** 7. **Rates** *Daily* ¥2,500-¥3,000 shared; ¥3,500 private. *Monthly* ¥34,000-¥40,800 shared; ¥69,000 private. **Credit** AmEx, MC, V.
Cozy House has two locations, one within Tokyo's central 23 wards, in Kita-ku, and this main branch, slightly out of the way in Chiba. Its mission is to bring foreigners in Japan together and make them feel at home, to which end the incredibly friendly owner lays on demonstrations of Japanese crafts and traditions. A 15-minute train ride from Tokyo station.
Branch: 15-1 Sakae-cho, Kita-ku (090 8176 0764).
Hotel services *Air conditioning. Bicycle loan (free). Microwave. TV & VCR. Lounge.*

Crystal Village

1-2-10 Arai, Nakano-ku (3388 7625/fax 3388 7627). Nakano station, north exit. **Credit** AmEx, MC, V.
Offers private rooms with shared bathroom and kitchen for ¥21,500 per week, or ¥75,000 per month. Studio apartments cost ¥44,000 per week or ¥130,000 per month (¥30,000 deposit required). Bad experiences with Spanish speakers mean that they're no longer welcome.

Fontana

3-31-5 Chuo, Nakano-ku (3382 0151/fax 3382 0018/fontana@gol.com). Shin-Nakano station, Nabeyayokocho exit. **Open** 9.30am-7pm daily. **No credit cards.**
A bona fide estate agent with a section devoted to English-speaking clients, Fontana can also find medium-term accommodation. Studio apartments are ¥39,000-¥45,000 per week (¥50,000 deposit), family-sized apartments ¥120,000-¥500,000 a month (¥100,000 deposit; terms of three months or longer require one month's deposit).

Hoyo Tokyo

4-19-7 Kita-Shinjuku, Shinjuku (3362 0658/fax 3362 9438/www.hoyotokyo.jp). Okubo station, north exit. **No credit cards.**
Studio apartments cost from ¥42,000 per week (¥50,000 deposit) or ¥135,000 per month, family apartments range from ¥300,000-¥500,000 a month (¥100,000 deposit; terms of three months or longer require one month's deposit).

Hilltop Hotel. *See p46.*

Taxing questions

The more expensive the hotel you choose to stay at, the more unpleasantly surprised you are likely to be when you receive your bill. Although most top hotels include a standard service charge of 10-15% in their room rates, some do not. Ask when booking. All room rates are subject to Japan's usual five per cent purchase tax, but if your bill climbs to the equivalent of over ¥15,000 per night (including service charges), you will be liable to an additional three per cent tax. Finally, there's a flat-rate tax, introduced in Tokyo only in October 2002. This ¥100 surcharge applies only to rooms costing ¥10,000 or more per night. If the room costs more than ¥15,000, the surcharge rises to ¥200. The money goes to help the metropolitan government promote Tokyo as a tourist destination. On the plus side, no tipping is expected in any Tokyo hotel.

Oak House

4-30-3 Takashimadaira, Itabashi-ku (3979 8810/ www.whatsuptokyo.com/). Shin-Takashimadaira station (Mita Line). **No credit cards**.

In the middle of nowhere, closer to Tokyo's neighbouring prefecture of Saitama than Shinjuku, this has shared dorm-style rooms for ¥35,000 a week, with private rooms (shared bathroom and kitchen) for ¥33,000 per month. Deposits of ¥30,000 for single rooms or ¥10,000 for shared rooms are required. Deposits refundable.

Sakura House

K-1 Bldg 9F, 7-2-6 Nishi-Shinjuku, Shinjuku-ku (5330 5250/fax 5330 5251/www.sakura-house.com). Shinjuku JR station, west exit. **Credit** MC, V.

Owned by the people who operate the Sakura hotel (*see p49*), which is in itself a guarantee of quality. A room in a guest house with shared bathroom and kitchen costs ¥48,000 a month, apartments run from ¥75,000 to ¥160,000 per month. A ¥30,000 deposit is required. Deposits refundable. A pleasant enough area to stay in, convenient for all of Shinjuku's amenities and good for transportation.

Tokyo Apartment

4-16-12 Kita-Shinjuku, Shinjuku-ku (3367-7117/ fax 3367 1661/www.tokyoapt.com). Okubo station, north exit. **Credit** MC, V.

An agency that deals exclusively with foreigners, and offers everything from one-night backpacker deals to fully fledged long-term apartment contracts. Apartments basically start at ¥100,000 per month, but the longer you stay, the cheaper they are. The website is updated regularly.

Tokyu Stay

8-14, Shinsen-cho, Shibuya-ku (3477 1091/fax (3477 1092/www.tokyustay.co.jp). Shinsen station (Keio Inokashira Line). **Credit** AmEx, MC, V.

Offers apartment-type accommodation in a modern block close to NHK headquarters. Stay length starts at a single night, but the longer you stay the less it costs per night, the single studio rate falling to ¥7,500 from ¥8,900 for stays of 30 nights or more. The most expensive apartment-type accommodation starts at ¥22,000 on a single-night basis, falling to ¥18,000 for a stay of 30 nights or more. There are a further eight branches in less lively areas, including Shinbashi, Nihonbashi and Yotsuya.

Town House

508, 2-7-6 Yoyogi, Shibuya-ku (3320 3201/ fax 3320 3202). Shinjuku JR station, south exit.
No credit cards.

A private room with a shared bathroom and kitchen is ¥40,000-¥70,000 per month, apartments are ¥55,000-¥200,000 per month. The deposit depends on individual landlords.

Weekly Centre

Central reservations 5950 1111/www.weeklycenter.co.jp. **Rates** ¥25,000-¥60,00 per week.
No credit cards.

This budget chain has a dozen locations dotted around Tokyo, offering the chance to stay for a week for around the same price as top hotels charge for one night. Monthly rates are also available. Don't expect to stay in the lap of luxury, but rooms are clean. Prices vary with location, the cheapest central branch being in Ochanomizu.

Booking organisations

Hotel Finder

www.japanhotelfinder.com.

An internet-only booking service that offers substantial discounts on stays at many of Tokyo's top hotels, including the Cerulean Tower (*see p43*) and the Westin Tokyo (*see p43*).

Japan City Hotel Association

www.jcha.or.jp/english/.

Like the Japan Inn Group (*see below*), this is a collective of owners of mid-priced hotels. The website offers direct links to each member hotel, which can then be contacted individually.

Japan Inn Group

www.jpinn.com.

A collective organisation founded and run by *ryokan* owners across Japan, it offers direct links to its members' premises via the website. You then contact the *ryokan* of your choice by fax, phone or email.

Japan Youth Hostels

www.jyh.or.jp/english/index.html.

Comprehensive listing and booking service for all youth hostels in Japan.

Sightseeing

Maps

Introduction

Time to get out and explore the mixed-up Japanese capital.

Let's not beat about the bush here. Tokyo is not one of the world's great sightseeing cities. This is, after all, a city that was razed to the ground twice in the twentieth century, once by earthquake and once by wartime bombing raids. On each occasion, Tokyo has risen from the ashes, but precious little of true historical value survives. Even the most historic centre of Asakusa consists largely of concrete post-war reconstructions. That's not to say that it's not worth the trip, but simply that historical sightseeing in Tokyo, and Japan as a whole, can feel like something of a hollow experience.

Yet despite this, Tokyo still has the power to make you go 'Wow!'. The sense that nothing here is permanent and could disappear at any moment has produced a city – or rather a collection of mini-cities – that renews itself at a speed unimaginable in the west. From the futuristic new cityscapes of Odaiba (*see p77*) or Roppongi Hills (*see p73*) to the bustling shopping and entertainment centres of Shibuya and Shinjuku, all are fully functioning self-contained areas where the first-time visitor runs the risk of neck-ache from craning up to see the neon signs, or the summit of a skyscraper.

Away from the trophy architecture, bright lights and bustling streets, Tokyo offers smaller scale attractions, too. On a fine spring or autumn day, a stroll round one of the city's many traditional Japanese gardens is an unbeatable restorative, while a trip to one of the tight-knit communities in the older areas, such as Yanaka (*see p93*), offers a glimpse into a lifestyle that is fast disappearing.

You want culture? Tokyo's got it, in spades. The city as a whole boasts over 200 museums, dedicated to everything from salt to swords and all points in between. Ueno Park (*see p89*) is home to the world's highest concentrations of top-class museums, and dotted throughout the city are scores of smaller independent museums, often the extension of an individual's passion or obsession.

Art galleries, too, are thriving, with new spaces opening seemingly on a daily basis, while established bigger galleries are increasingly playing host to travelling blockbuster exhibitions from abroad.

The general rules for museum and gallery visiting are as follows: entrance fees are paid in cash, ID is required for discount admission, museum admission ends 30 minutes before the museum closes, lockers are free (with a refundable key deposit of ¥100), photography is forbidden, there is little disabled access. Most museums offer little or no explanation in English. Where they do, we say so.

Some museums are closed on national holidays (e.g. Golden Week and O-bon) while others are open. Those that are open on holidays are usually closed the following day. Nearly all museums shut over the New Year's holidays, around 28 Dec-3 Jan. Finally, some of the museums that hold temporary exhibitions are open only sporadically.

Back in the city, meanwhile, everybody who has ever spent some time here has their own favourite districts, and the key areas we highlight over the following pages are merely a starting point for any thorough exploration. The great thing about Tokyo for visitors is not only that public transport is so utterly reliable, but that the city as a whole is so safe. Crime is virtually unknown, and it's not only possible, but very enjoyable to wander through the streets of the centre at the dead of night. It's the only time you'll ever be alone there.

Another plus for visitors is the slightly surprising fact that for such a famously modern city, Tokyo is bursting with old-fashioned character. Just off the highways of any major area are tiny local streets where family-run businesses still ply their trades, even though their wooden premises now stand in the shadow of a 60-storey skyscraper. It's this contrast between ancient and super-modern that gives the city its defining energy. This energy, perhaps more than any individual sight, is most likely to leave a lasting impression.

All in all, Tokyo is a fantastic place to visit, a city destination like no other in the world, and if you find your appetite whetted for more by our guide to sights in the centre, we've also included suggestions for worthwhile destinations outside the city's defining Yamanote Line train loop. Out here, on the city's suburban commuter railway lines, life is lived at a more relaxed pace, and locals are friendlier and eager to chat.

Perhaps in the end, Tokyo's best-kept secret is that it's so massive, with so many things to see and do, that it can become any kind of city you want it to be. Grab a camera and a train ticket and make it yours.

The 23 wards (ku) of central Tokyo

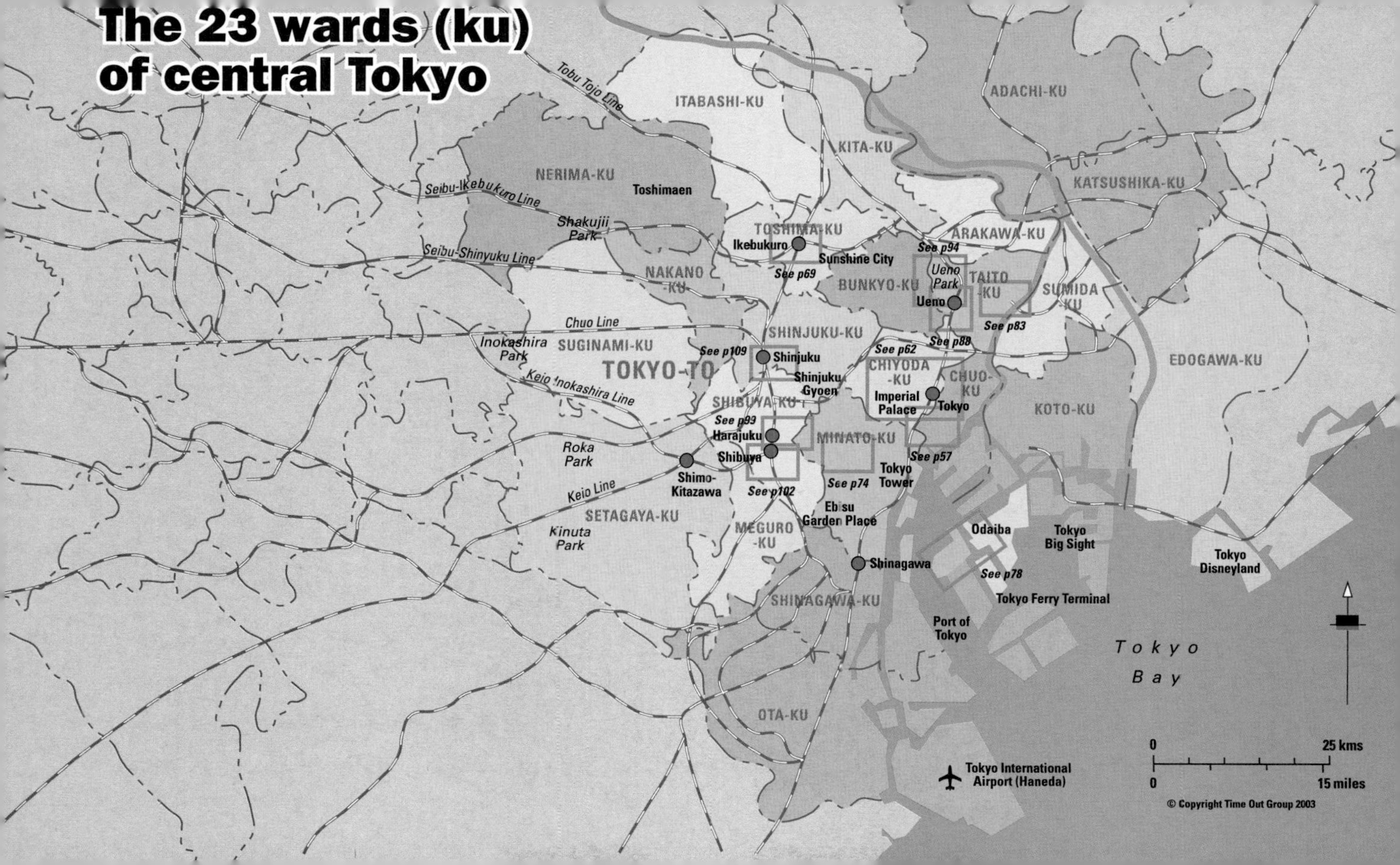

Central City

The geographical centre of the city is home to the emperor, a world-famous shopping district and the business hub that keeps Japan Limited ticking (or not).

Ginza

Map p57

If Tokyo has one area that is famous the world over, Ginza is it. Crammed into its eight main blocks are over 10,000 stores, many of them selling goods at prices most people can only dream of being able to afford.

The area's reputation for exclusivity stretches right back to the 19th-century Meiji period, when Ginza became the first part of Tokyo to be rebuilt in red brick, rather than wood. Red brick was thought to offer greater protection from natural disasters, a theory that was disproved in 1923, when the area was razed by the great Kanto earthquake. Unfortunately, not one single red brick from Ginza's first golden era survives today.

What does survive, though, is the Tokyo pastime of Ginbura, or Ginza strolling. For Tokyo, the area has unusually wide pavements, which lend themselves to window-shopping and aimless strolling. On Sundays from noon cars are banned from Ginza Dori to create what is known as *hokosha tengoku* (pedestrian heaven), and cafés spill out on to the Tarmac, lending the area a positively European feel.

This is the only part of Tokyo where older fashions mix easily with the latest trends. There are elegant department stores such as **Mitsukoshi** (*see p168*) and **Matsuya** (*see p168*), wooden shops selling traditional items, brand-name boutiques, small old galleries exhibiting avant-garde art, showrooms where you can touch and test the latest high-tech products and a huge number of coffee shops and Japanese tea rooms. Foreign retail chains choose to have their first Japanese outlets in prestigious Ginza before opening up elsewhere.

The latest big name to be lured by the Ginza name is Apple Computer, which is scheduled to open its first direct retail outlet in Japan in Ginza in late 2003.

The reputation of the area for elegance and class is fiercely guarded by local shopkeepers. After the closure of the Sogo department store near Yurakucho station in 2001, they mounted strong resistance to the arrival of discount electronics superstore Bic Camera – which took over the Sogo building, giving the company its first presence in designer-label land.

Elsewhere, despite Japan's much-discussed recession, business has continued as normal in Ginza. When French fashion house Hermès

Accommodation
1 Daiichi Hotel, p34.
2 Seiyo Ginza, p35.
3 Imperial Hotel, p35.
4 Ginza Renaissance Tobu, p35.
5 Mitsui Urban, p35.
6 Ginza Daiei, p37.
7 Japan Minshuku Centre, p50.
8 Business Inn Shinbashi&Annex, p50.

Sightseeing
9 Bridgestone Museum, p63.
10 Hibiya Park, p60.
11 Metropolitan Police Museum, p60.
12 National Film Centre, National Museum of Modern Art, p60
13 Old Shinbashi Station, p60.
14 Sake Plaza, p60.
15 Sony Building, p60.

Restaurants
16 Afternoon Tea, p124.
17 Birdland, p125.
18 Daidaiya, p125.
19 Edogin, p125.
20 Kihachi China, p127.
21 Little Okinawa, p127.
22 Ohmatsuya, p127.
23 Oshima, p127.
24 Robata, p127.
25 Shichirinya, p127.
26 Ten-Ichi, p127.
27 Ten-Ichi deux, p127.
28 Yurakucho under the Tracks, p128.

Coffee Shops
29 Le Café Doutor Espresso, p152.
30 Café Fontana, p153.
31 Football Café, p154.
32 Ki no Hana, p154.
33 Kissa Hibiya, p154.

Bars
34 Kagaya, p156.
35 Lion Beer Hall, p156.
36 Pop Inn 2, p157.

Shops and Services
37 H2 Sukiyabashi Hankyu, p167.
38 Matsuya, p168.
39 Matsuzakaya, p168.
40 Akebono, p174.
41 Kimuraya, p174.
42 Hasegawa Ginza, p182.
43 Hayashi Kimono, p182.
44 Ito-ya, p182.
45 Tanogokoro, p184.
46 Mujirushi Ryohin, p185.
47 Meidi-ya, p185.
48 Sanmi Discount Store, p186.
49 4 degrees C, p186
50 Ginza Diamond Shiraishi, p187.
51 Mikimoto, p187.
52 Tasaki Shinju, p187.
53 Wako, p187.
54 American Pharmacy, p192.

Children
46 Mujirushi Ryohin, p185.
55 Royal Baby Salon, p191.

Film
56 Cine La Sept, p207.
57 Cine Pathos, p207.
58 Cine Switch Ginza, p208.
59 Ginza Théâtre, p208.
60 Hibiya Chanter, p208.
12 National Film Centre, National Museum of Modern Art, p60.

Galleries
61 Base Gallery, p212.
62 Creation Gallery-G8, p212.
63 Dai-ichi Seimei Minami Gallery, p212.
64 Forum Art Shop, p212.
65 Galleria Grafica, p212.
66 Gallery Koyanagi, p212.
67 Ginza Graphic Gallery, p212.
68 Guardian Garden, p212.
69 INAX Gallery, p212.
70 Leica Gallery Tokyo, p212.
71 Kobayashi Gallery, p212.
72 Kodak Photo Salon, p212.
73 Maison Hermes, p213.
74 Moris Gallery, p213.
75 Nishimura Gallery, p213.
76 Okuno Building, p213.
77 Shiseido Gallery, p213.
78 Tokyo Gallery, p213.
79 Gallery Yamaguchi, p212
80 Wacoal Ginza Art Space, p213.

Music
81 Someday, p226.
82 Hibiya Kokaido, p226.
83 Hibiya Outdoor Theatre, p228.
84 Tokyo International Forum, p229.

Performing Arts
85 Kabuki-za, p243.
86 Shinbashi Embujo, p244.
87 Tokyo Takarazuka Gekijo, p245.
83 Hibiya Outdoor Theatre, p228.

Ginza
0
150 m
0
150 yds
Hibiya Park
Theatre
Idemitsu Museum of Art
Tokyo International Forum
Yurakucho Station
MARUNOUCHI-NAKA DORI
Yurakucho Station
Tokyo Kotsukaikan Bldg.
Hibiya Station
YURAKUCHO
Seibu
Tokyo Takarazuka Theatre
Nissei Theatre
Hibiya Chanter
Yurakucko Hankyu
H2 Sukiyabashi Hankyu
Imperial Hotel
Mitsuo Aida Museum
Sony Building
Ginza Station
Hibiya Public Hall
UCHIBORI-DORI
Mizuho Bank
UCHISAIWAICHO
HIBIYA-DORI
Hibiya Hospital
Dai-Ichi Hotel Annex
Daiichi Hotel Tokyo
SOTOBORI-DORI
NAMIKI DORI
CHUO DORI
Shiseido Boutique
Yamaha Hall
Hakuhinkan
© Copyright Time Out Group 2003
SHINBASHI
Shinbashi Station
Kyobashi Station
National Film Centre, National Museum of Modern Art
CHUO-DORI
TOKYO EXPRESSWAY
Ginza-Itchome Station
Meidi-ya
Printemps Ginza
Tiffany & Co.
Matsuya
SHOWA-DORI
HARUMI-DORI
Wako
Mitsukoshi
San-ai Building
Nissan Gallery
Matsuzakaya
GINZA
Higashi-Ginza Station
Kabuki-za
Ginza Tobu Hotel (Renaissance Tokyo)
HARUMI-DORI
TSUKIJI
Tsukiji Station

opened its flagship outlet in Ginza in June 2001, over 1,000 customers queued outside on the first day to pick up a special commemorative handbag – a snip at ¥50,000.

However, there are bargains to be had here, even for those on a budget. As elsewhere in Tokyo, most restaurants in Ginza offer special set-lunch deals, the difference here being that you have a chance to eat food for around ¥1,000 that might cost ten times as much in the evening. Most restaurants in the area are off the main drag, many of them in basements, so take a walk around the back streets and check out the prices, which are usually posted on boards outside. Alternatively, if you fancy a picnic in nearby Hibiya Park, the food halls of department stores offer top-quality food at reasonable prices to take away. In the run-up to closing time, around 7.30pm, many items go for as little as half the regular price.

Ginza by night is the haunt of the exceedingly wealthy, or politicians on bottomless expense accounts. Look for the lines of black, chauffeur-driven limos to see where they hang out. Hidden in the back streets are many small traditional Japanese restaurants, where basic meals start from around ¥15,000. Unless you want to terrify your bank manager, do not go anywhere that does not have a price list clearly displayed. If you need to ask the price, as the old saying goes, you probably can't afford it.

There are many ways to explore Ginza on foot, but setting off from Yurakucho station is best. Take the exit for Ginza and walk down the narrow street with the Ciné La Sept cinema (*see p207*) on the corner. Continue straight through the arcade running inside the Mullion complex – home to the **Hankyu** and **Seibu** department stores (*see p167* and *p169*) and several cinemas – and you come out at the multi-directional zebra crossings of Sukiyabashi (Sukiya Bridge). Confusingly, there is no bridge. There used to be one going from the present-day Sukiyabashi Hankyu department store towards Hibiya, across the old outer moat of Edo Castle (now the Imperial Palace), but both bridge and waterway were casualties of 1960s road construction. Today, a small monument marks the spot where the bridge stood.

Standing with Sukiyabashi Hankyu department store on your right, you will see a large Sony sign on the other side of the crossing. The tall, slim **Sony Building** offers eight floors of entertainment. Technology and games fans can easily spend hours here, but even non-obsessives find it an enjoyable place to kill time. Sounds, visuals, computers – all the latest Sony models are on display and can be tried out. The sixth floor is dedicated to PlayStation and you can request games to play. This section is packed with kids at weekends, so try to be there during the week.

If you carry on up Harumi Dori away from Yurakucho, you come to Ginza 4-chome crossing. Walk down Sotobori Dori (Outer Moat Avenue, once part of Edo Castle's waterway defences), towards Ginza 8-chome and Shinbashi. Ginza streets are named and laid out in a grid, so it's difficult to get lost. On your way down to 8-chome, stop off at some of the small galleries, most of which are free to enter. When you reach the boundary of Ginza at Gomon Dori, turn left towards Ginza Dori and the narrower streets of Sony Dori, Namiki Dori, Nishi Gobangai Dori and Suzuran Dori.

Whichever route you take back to Harumi Dori, the atmospheric streets between Ginza Dori and Sotobori Dori are the best pottering area in Ginza. Zigzag towards 4-chome crossing, enjoying the back streets and Ginza-dori window-shopping on on the way. When you reach the 4-chome crossing, you will see Le Café Doutor Espresso (*see p152*), of the Doutor coffee shop chain. On the other side of the crossing is **Wako** (*see p187*), a watch and jewellery department store famous for its dazzling window displays; its mini clock-tower is the popular symbol of Ginza. In Ozu's *Tokyo Story* (1953), two women are chauffeur-driven past Wako, the store representing the high-class, modern face of Tokyo. 'Outside Wako at 4-chome crossing' is a common meeting spot.

Another meeting place is the **Nissan Gallery**, also on the corner of the crossing. Latest models are exhibited on the ground floor. Since admission is free, the ground floor gets busy on rainy days.

Further down Harumi Dori is the **Kabuki-za** theatre (*see p243*), home of *kabuki*. Reserved seats are pricey, but a single act of the day-long programme can be enjoyed for around ¥1,000. You have to queue for tickets, and opera glasses are essential, but it's a good way to get a taste of traditional performing arts. Another way of seeing Ginza is to begin the day here (performances start at 11am), then head off and sample the delights listed above. Alternatively, visit **World Magazine Gallery** (*see chapter* **Directory: Media**), behind Kabuki-za, where you can browse 800 titles for free.

Away to the southern limits of Ginza. towards the Shinbashi area, you may notice a collection of skyscrapers gleaming in the distance. This is the brand new mini-centre of **Shiodome**, built on the site of a former Japan Railways goods yard and fully opened in mid 2003. It's a futuristic city with wide-open plazas, crisscrossed by aerial walkways and a monorail designed to accommodate 60,000

The **Nissan Gallery**, a prime Ginza meeting point. *See p58.*

workers and residents. As recently at 2000, it was Tokyo's biggest patch of waste ground. The area is now home to the headquarters of Dentsu, Japan's biggest advertising agency, and houses the **ADMT Advertising Museum Tokyo**, the **Old Shinbashi Station** (a reconstruction of the original) and a theatre, as well as a shopping complex and scores of restaurants and cafés.

Also in the Ginza area is the **Tokyo Disneyland Ticket Centre** (Hibiya Mitsui Bldg, 1-1-2 Yurakucho, Chiyoda-ku, 3595 1777). The theme park is out of town, but this foreigner-friendly ticket office (staff speak English) is open from 10am until 7pm daily. The office can be reached from Hibiya Station, exit A11.

GETTING THERE

Ginza station is on the Ginza, Hibiya and Marunouchi subway lines. The best way to tour the area is to start at Yurakucho station, Ginza exit, on the JR Yamanote line, and walk down.

Shiodome can be reached from exit 2 of Shinbashi station, or from Shiodome station on the Toei Oedo and Yurikamome lines.

Sights

ADMT Advertising Museum Tokyo

Caretta Shiodome, 1-8-2 Higashi-Shinbashi, Minato-ku (6218 2500/www.admt.jp). Shinbashi station, exit 2 or Shidome station (Toei Oedo/Yurikamome lines). **Open** 11am-6.30pm Tue-Fri; 11am-4.30 pm Sat. **Admission** free.

It's new! Check it out! This petite museum, sponsored by Japan's largest ad agency, Dentsu, opened in December 2002 in the stylish mall next to the company's new Jean Nouvel-designed headquarters in the Shiodome development. Interactive and other displays trace the history of Japanese advertising from 17th-century woodblock prints through to 20th-century posters and on to the latest TV advertisements. And if this isn't enough, visitors can also peruse over 100,000 digitised images from the company's database and library via some amazing touch-screen technology.

English pamphlet. Café. Gift shop.

Hama-Rikyu Detached Garden

1-1 Hama-Rikyu Teien, Chuo-ku (3541 0200). Shiodome station, exit 5 or 6 (Toei Oedo/Yurikamome lines). **Open** 9am-5pm daily. **Admission** ¥300; free over-65s.

This large garden, once a hunting ground for the Tokugawa shogunate, now cowers in the giant shadow of the new Shiodome development. The park's main appeal lies in the abundance of water in and around it and the fact that it feels deceptively large, thanks to its beautiful landscaping. Situated on an island, the park is surrounded by an ancient walled moat with only one entrance, over the Nanmon Bridge (it's also possible to reach Hama-Rikyu by boat from Asakusa; *see p87*). The park's focal points are its huge Shiori Pond, which has two islands of its own, and is connected to the shore by charming wooden bridges, and a photogenic 300-year-old pine tree. Access to the garden has been much improved since the opening of nearby Shiodome station in 2002.

Hibiya Park

1-6 Hibiya Koen, Chiyoda-ku (3501 6428). Hibiya station, exit A10 or Kasumigaseki station, exit A5. **Open** 24hrs daily.

Next to the Imperial Palace and five minutes' walk from Ginza, Hibiya Park was once the parade ground for the Japanese army, but was turned into Japan's first western-style park in 1903, complete with rose gardens, bandstand and open-air theatre.

Metropolitan Police Department Museum

3-5-1 Kyobashi, Chuo-ku (3581 4321/www.keishicho.metro.tokyo.jp/index.htm). Kyobashi station, exit 2. **Open** 10am-6pm Tue-Sun. **Admission** free.

Learn to love the Man in this short stop-off. Out front, you can sit on a Kawasaki police motorcycle with flashing lights. Inside, peer into a helicopter or mock Pipo-kun, the force's mousy mascot. Just be sure to keep your hands where they can see them.

NAIS

1-5-1 Higashi-Shinbashi Minato-ku (6218 0010). Shinbashi station, exit A4, or Shiodome station, exit 3 (Toei Oedo or Yurikamome lines). **Open** 10am-8pm daily. **Admission** free.

Opened in April 2003, this brand-new showroom in brand-new Shiodome, for Matsushita Electric's world-famous National Panasonic brand, gleams like a new toy. But it isn't half as much fun as the old showroom in Shinjuku was. Over three floors, you can inspect the latest in bathroom, toilet (always good fun in Japan) and kitchen technology, but it appears that the days when you could sit for hours and play with the massage chairs have gone.

National Film Centre, National Museum of Modern Art

3-7-6 Kyobashi, Chuo-ku (3561 0823/www.momat.go.jp/FC/fc.html). Kyobashi station, exit 1. **Open** 10.30am-6pm Tue-Fri. *Library* 10am-6pm Tue-Fri. **Admission** ¥200; ¥70 concessions; additional charge for special exhibitions. **No credit cards**.

Japanese and foreign films – 19,000 of them – star at the country's only national facility devoted to the preservation and study of cinema. Fans throng to its two cinemas for series focusing on, for example, DW Griffith or Korean films from the 1960s. Visitors can also check out the film-book library on the fourth floor or exhibitions of photographs, graphic design and film-related items (often drawn from its own collection) in the seventh-floor gallery.

Café. English pamphlet.

Old Shinbashi Station

1-5-3 Shinbashi, Minato-ku (3572 1872). Shinbashi station, exit 2, or Shiodome station, exit 3 (Toei Oedo or Yurikamome lines). **Open** 11am-6pm Tue-Sun. **Admission** free.

Part of the newly redeveloped Shiodome area just east of the present Shinbashi station, this is a painstaking reconstruction of the original Shinbashi passenger terminus, part of the first railway in Japan, which opened in 1872 and ran from here to Yokohama. The present building, which opened in April 2003, stands on the original foundations of the old one. They were uncovered during archaeological excavations, and can be viewed through a glass floor in the basement. Those of ironic bent may notice that Londoners still use stations every day that would be considered archaeological treasures in Tokyo, but such quibbles aside, this is a brilliant small-scale project, with a permanent railway history exhibition hall and full labelling of items in English. There's a pleasant café on the ground floor.

English pamphlet and labelling. Café.

Sake Plaza

Nihon Syuzo Centre Bldg 1F, 4F, 1-1-21 Nishi-Shinbashi, Minato-ku (3519 2091/www.japansake.or.jp/sake/english/index.html). Toranomon station, exit 9 or 10, or Kasumigaseki station, exit A11a, B2, C3, C4. **Open** 10am-6pm Mon-Fri. **Admission** free.

The recession, and too many freeloaders, seem to have struck Sake Plaza, where the former free tasting of Japan's national brew has now transmogrified into a ¥550 charge for a five-cup sample. It's still a bargain, though, compared with bar prices, and you no longer have to try and identify your drinks by region, which is a relief.

Sony Building

5-3-1 Ginza, Chuo-ku (3573 2371/www.sonybuilding.jp/). Ginza station, exit B9. **Open** 11am-7pm daily. **Admission** free.

Play to your heart's content with seven floors of Sony products at this high-tech mecca. One floor is devoted to PlayStation, where you can request games to play on the giant screens, while another floor shows you the insides of many of Sony's best-selling products.

Marunouchi

Map p62

Like Wall Street or the City of London, Tokyo's central business district has traditionally been a sedate area, especially at weekends, but the last few years have seen a major effort to liven things up a bit. The ambitious vision of transforming it into an appealing centre is paying off and, though Marunouchi has yet to regain a strong identity, there's more to do around here than ever before.

Marunouchi is officially only a small section around Tokyo station, but is historically linked to the **Imperial Palace** a few hundred metres away. Nothing of what's currently known as Marunouchi really lives up to its name as the word means 'within the moat or castle walls'. But the world that was once within the walls was the most influential in Japan.

Edo came to life in 1457 as Ota Dokan settled where the Palace now stands. Once the shogun decided to rule from here too, his castle became the centre of the city. The Marunouchi area was created as he decreed that all *daimyo* (feudal lords) must live in Edo for half of the year. This set in motion the reclaiming of land from the sea to make room for the compounds and residences of each daimyo. These were huge projects, built to house anything from 500 to 5,000 people.

The palace grew and the walls expanded to include more of the area around it. But eventually the process was reversed and the castle grounds shrank as the city took on a life of its own. Meanwhile, the palace became isolated, closing its doors to the outside world. But even today, the Imperial Palace and Marunouchi remain the centre of Tokyo in many senses – political, imperial, economic and geographical.

Although people do come to shop and play here, most visitors make a beeline for the **Imperial Park**. It's directly in front of Tokyo station's central exit, across Hibiya Dori, about 500 metres (160 feet) away.

The moat and walls still divide it from the city, as they did long ago. Entry through either gate (Kikyomon and Otemon) leads to **Kokyo Higashi Gyoen** (East Gardens), but not the Imperial Palace. It's out of bounds, except on 2 January and 23 December, the emperor's birthday. There are few historical features in the manicured park, save for two old watch-houses, the remains of the old dungeon at the northern end (near Kita-Hanebashi-mon), and at the exit into the next area, the wall of hand-carved stones dropping a great height into the water.

Across the main road is another park, Kitanomaru. This one has an unkempt feel and other than the **Nippon Budokan** (*see p229*), the main attraction is again where the wall and the water meet, at Chidorigafuchi. This moat is surrounded by cherry trees and makes a postcard-perfect sight at blossom time in April.

Marunouchi went through a second heyday in the Meiji era (1868-1912), when it became the economic centre of the country. The army sold the land to Mitsubishi after the Emperor's restoration and the area became famous for its buildings, a showcase of foreign architecture then dubbed London Town. They were not only the pride of the city but also a sign that the country had opened to the world. The main remaining example is **Tokyo Station**, built to resemble Amsterdam's Centraal Station. One storey was removed and the roof replaced due to bomb damage after the war, although Japan Railways currently has plan to restore it to its former glory by 2006.

Nearby Otemachi is still the financial centre, but the action on the streets long ago moved to the new centres of Tokyo, and Marunouchi went into a steady decline. With visitors failing to venture even from neighbouring Ginza, Hibiya and Yurakucho, it became a dead area, especially once the thousands of local workers had gone. Now, though, the construction boom has hit Marunochi again, and there's as much building going on here as anywhere else in the city, with several new blocks due to open in 2004.

The Imperial Palace remains the main draw, but the focal point of the area's renewal and facelift is the new 36-storey **Marunouchi Building** (*see p171*). Opened to great fanfare in September 2002, and still drawing the crowds nearly a year later, it leads the promotion of the area, with its own website (www.marubiru.jp) and small newspaper, highlighting the changes that are going on in the area.

The biggest transformation yet has happened on Naka Dori (Centre Street), which was recently repaved and lined with trees to create a pedestrian-friendly feel. Most new shops and restaurants are found around here. Retail is mainly upmarket international brands, but others are starting to appear.

The modern highlight of the area is the **Tokyo International Forum** (*see p229*), along the train tracks. Divided in two buildings, the most striking is the ship-shaped Glass Hall Building designed by Rafael Vinoly and opened in 1996. The glass roof and a 60-metre glass wall make it one of the architectural wonders of the city. The adjacent building is far less impressive but hides an interior bustling with people attending conventions and other social events. The three main halls are increasingly used for concerts, film premieres and festivals.

Going under the tracks leads to Yaesu and Kyobashi, the other main exit of Tokyo station. At the crossing stands the new **Pacific Century Place**, opened in 2001, which contains Tokyo's second Four Seasons hotel (*see pp34-52*), and the requisite number of restaurants and coffee bars. The backstreets of Kyobashi retain the feel of a smaller, more intimate neighbourhood with many small stores, restaurants and coffee shops still thriving. This area and the adjacent Nihonbashi are the most populous around Tokyo station, especially at night.

Nihonbashi also has an important place in the history of Tokyo, as depicted by several *ukiyo-e* artists of the 19th-century. There's not much left now. Even the renowned Nihombashi bridge – where all distances to and from Tokyo used to be calculated – is in the shadow of an elevated highway, retaining none of the character it must once have had.

GETTING THERE

Tokyo station is the terminus of the JR Chuo line and is on the JR Yamanote and Keihin Tohoku lines, as well as the Eidan Marunouchi subway line. It is also the main terminus for *shinkansen* bullet trains.

Marunouchi
Akihabara Station
Jinbocho Station
Kudanshita Station
YASUKUNI-DORI
Awajicho Station
Kanda Station
Kanda JR Station
KITANOMARU PARK
KANDA-NISHIKICHO
HONGO-DORI
CHUO-DORI
Kodenmacho Station
UCHIKANDA
Takebashi Station
SANBANCHO
UCHIBORI-DORI
CHIYODA-KU
Hanzomon Station
Otemachi Station
OTEMACHI
Ote-mon Gate
Ningyocho Station
Mitsukoshi
Mitsukoshimae Station
Imperial Palace
Tokyo Station
Nihonbashi Station
MARUNOUCHI
Daimaru
Maruzen Bookstore
NIHONBASHI-KABUTOCHO
KOKYO-GAIEN
Takashimaya
UCHIBORI-DORI AVE
HIBYIA-DORI
MARUNOUCHI-NAKA DORI AVE
SOTOBORI-DORI AVE
Pokemon Center
NIHONBASHI
Kayabacho Station
Chuo Police Station
Central Post Office
YAESU
CHUO-DORI AVE
SHOWA-DORI AVE
Bridgestone Museum of Art
SHIN-OHASHI-DORI AVE
Nagatacho Station
AOYAMA-DORI
Sakuradamon Station
Imperial Theatre
Idemitsu Museum of Art
Yurakucho Station
Tokyo International Forum
CHUO-KU
Kyobashi Station
KYOBASHI
National Film Centre,
Hatchobori
NIHONBASHI-KAYABACHO
0
300 m
0
300 yds
© Copyright Time Out Group 2003

Sights

Bank of Japan

2-1-1 Nihonbashi Hongoku-cho, Chuo-ku (English tour reservations 3279 1111/www.boj.or.jp). Mitsukoshi-mae station, exits A5, A8, B1, B3. **Tours** 9.45am-3pm Mon Fri. Tours must be booked 1wk in advance. **Admission** free.

The Bank of Japan was the first western-style building to be built by Japanese people. It's modelled on the Bank of England in London.

Bridgestone Museum of Art

1-10-1 Kyobashi, Chuo-ku (3563 0241/www.bridgestone-museum.gr.jp). Tokyo station, Yaesu central exit. **Open** 10am-8pm Tue-Fri; 10am-6pm Sat, Sun. **Admission** ¥700; free-¥600 concessions.

Ishibashi Shojiro, founder of the giant Bridgestone Corporation, wheeled his private collection into this museum back in 1952. Impressionism, European modernism and Japanese western-style paintings form the core holdings, but exhibitions can cover genres ranging from Ancient Greek to 20th-century abstraction. In 2002, the building underwent earthquake retrofitting and a new tearoom was added to the first floor. For a taste of what's inside the galleries, stroll past the artworks displayed in the street-level front windows.

Communications Museum

2-3-1 Otemachi, Chiyoda-ku (3244 6811/www.iptp.go.jp/museum). Otemachi station, exit A5. **Open** 9am-4.30pm Tue-Sun; 9am-6.30pm Fri. **Admission** ¥110; ¥50 concessions.

This massive, three-floor museum relays the stories and technological histories of national public broadcasting company NHK, telecoms giant NTT, and the now defunct Post and Telecommunications Ministry. Philatelists can peruse 280,000 old and new stamps (including the world's first, an 1840 English Penny Black) from Afghanistan to Zimbabwe. Kids can race post office motor bikes in a video game, compare international post boxes and ogle a room-sized mail sorter. On the telecommunications floor, ample interactive displays teach how the phone works. Their full range of historic public payphones – from pink to yellow to green – is sealed behind glass. The gift shop sells vintage postcards (for example, of Frank Lloyd Wright's now demolished Imperial Hotel) and collectible stamps.

Gift shop. Lounge.

Currency Museum

1-3-1 Nihonbashi Hongokucho, Chuo-ku (3277 3037/www.imes.boj.or.jp/cm/english_htmls/index.htm). Mitsukoshimae station, exits A5, A8, B1, B3. **Open** 9.30am-4.30pm Tue-Sun. Guided tours (1hr) 1.30pm Tue, Thur. **Admission** free.

Run by the Bank of Japan, this museum traces the long history of money in this country, from the use of imported Chinese coins in the late Heian period (12th century) to the creation of the yen and the central bank in the second half of the 19th century. See beautiful Edo-period calligraphy-inscribed gold oblongs, Occupation-era notes from Indonesia and the Philippines, Siberian leather money and Thai leech coins. Or try raising some easy cash by lifting ¥100 million yen (about the size of two phone books), safely stored inside a plexiglas box.

English pamphlet.

Idemitsu Museum of Arts

Tei Geki Bldg 9F, 3-1-1 Marunouchi, Chiyoda-ku (5777 8600/www.idemitsu.co.jp/museum). Hibiya station, exit B4. **Open** 10am-5pm Tue-Sun. **Admission** ¥800; free-¥500 concessions.

Idemitsu Sazo, founder of Idemitsu Kosan Co, collected traditional Chinese and Japanese art for more than 70 years. The museum, opened in 1966, has a variety of exhibitions drawn from the respected permanent collection of ceramics, calligraphy and painting (for example, Rimpa-style irises painted by Sakai Hoitsu on a six-fold screen). The museum has a good view of the Imperial Palace grounds.

Gift shop.

Imperial Palace

1 Chiyoda, Chiyoda-ku. Otemachi station, exits C10, C13B.

Tokyo has been home to the Japanese royal family since 1868 and the Imperial Palace occupies a chunk of prime real estate in the geographical

Accommodation
1 Four Seasons, p34.
2 Palace Hotel, p35

Sightseeing
3 Bank of Japan, p63.
4 Communications Museum, p63.
5 Currency Museum, p63.
6 Idemitsu Museum, p63.
7 Imperial Palace, p63.
8 Imperial Palace East Garden, p64.
9 Japan Science Foundation Science Museum, p64.
10 Kitanomaru Park, p64.
11 Kite Museum, p65.
12 National Museum of Modern Art, Tokyo, p65.
13 National Museum of Modern Art, Crafts Gallery, p65.
14 Tokyo Station Gallery, p65.
15 Tokyo Stock Exchange, p65.
16 Japanese War-Dead Memorial, p66
17 JC II Camera Museum, p66.
18 Bridgestone Museum, p63.
19 Map Museum, p66.
20 Nikolai Cathedral, p67.
21 Transportation Museum, p67.
22 Yamatane Museum, p67.
23 Yasukuni Shirine, p67.
24 Yushima Seido, p72.

Restaurants
25 Botan, p124.
26 Isegen, p124.
27 Izumo Soba, p124.
28 Kandagawa Honten, p124.
29 Kanda Yabu Soba, p124.

Coffee Shops
30 Marunouchi Café, p155.
31 Mironga, p155.
32 Rihaku, p155.
33 Sabouru, p155.

Bars
34 Ieyasu Hon-jin, p157.

Shops and Services
35 Daimaru, p167.
36 Mitsukoshi, p168.
37 Marunouchi Bldg, p171.
38 Maruzen, p174.
39 Hara Shobo, p182.
40 Ohya Shobo, p183.
41 Pokemon Centre, p188.
42 American Pharmacy, p192.

Children
9 Japan Science Foundation Science Museum, p204.
21 Transportation Museum, p204.

Film
43 Iwanami Hall,p208.

Galleries
44 Zeit-Foto Salon, p213.

Music
45 Nippon Budokan,p229.

Performing Arts
46 National Theatre Large Hall, p244.
47 National Theatre Small Hall, p244.
48 National Engei Hall, p246.

Sports
45 Nippon Budokan, p250.
49 Chiyoda Kuritsu Sogo Taiikukan Pool, p254.

The **Imperial Palace**. *See p63.*

centre of the city, on part of the former site of Edo Castle, seat of the Tokugawa shogun. The non-Imperial masses are graciously allowed into some of the Imperial Palace grounds twice a year (2 January and the emperor's birthday on 23 December, *see p194*). Otherwise, it's a matter of walking around the outside, visiting the Imperial East and Outer Gardens, and maybe stopping off to admire the scenic view and to take a photograph or two from Nijubashi Bridge. The path that follows the course around the moat is Tokyo's most popular route for joggers.

Imperial Palace East Garden (Kokyo Higashi Gyoen)

Chiyoda, Chiyoda-ku. Tokyo station, Marunouchi exit, then a 5min walk to Ote-mon gate. **Open** 9am-4.30pm daily. Closed 29 Dec-3 Jan. **Admission** free (token collected at gate to be submitted on leaving).

This is the main park of the Imperial Palace, accessible through three old gates: Ote-mon, Hirakawa-mon (close to Takebashi Bridge) and Kita-Hanebashi-mon (near Kitanomaru Park). The park dates from the early days of Tokyo (or Edo, as it was then known) and is mostly landscaped. Inside is the Museum of Imperial Collections, as well as two old watch-houses and the remains of a dungeon dating from the days of Edo Castle.

Japan Science Foundation Science Museum

2-1 Kitanomaru Koen, Chiyoda-ku (3212 8544/ www.jsf.or.jp/index_e.html). Takebashi station, exit 1B or Kudanshita station, exit 2. **Open** 9.30am-4.50pm daily. **Admission** ¥600; ¥250-¥400 concessions.

This museum takes to extremes the maxim 'learning by doing'. The unique five-spoke building, in a corner of Kitanomaru Park, consists of five floors of interactive exhibits. Its drab, dated entrance belies the fun displays inside. Children can learn the rudiments of scientific priniciples while standing inside a huge soap bubble, lifting a small car using pulleys and generating electricity by shouting. There's not a lot of English used, but much of the interaction needs no translation.

Gift shop.

Kitanomaru Koen

1-1 Kitanomaru Koen, Chiyoda-ku (3213 0095). Kudanshita station, exit 2. **Open** 24hrs daily.

Part of the Imperial Palace grounds till 1969, when it became a public park. The park is home to several museums, including the National Museum of Modern Art (*see p65*) and the Japan Science Foundation Science Museum (*see above*).

Kite Museum

Taimeiken 5F, 1-12-10 Nihonbashi, Chuo-ku (3275 2704/www.tako.gr.jp/eng/index_e.html). Nihonbashi station, exit C5. **Open** 11am-5pm Mon-Sat. **Admission** ¥200; ¥100 concessions.

This uplifting museum is a cornucopia of kites, including Indonesian dried leaves, giant woodblock-print samurai, and a 1.5m-long styrofoam iron. The former owner of the first-floor restaurant (one of Tokyo's earliest forays into western-style dining) spent a lifetime collecting the 2,000 kites now layering the walls, packing display cases and crowding the ceiling. The museum is not well marked, but is in the only building on the street with a big sign out front. Don't come here expecting detailed explanations of the exhibits or interactivity. This is more of a space for putting a private hobby on public display, as often happens in Tokyo.

Gift shop.

National Museum of Modern Art, Crafts Gallery (Bijutsukan Kogeikan)

1-1 Kitanomaru Koen, Chiyoda-ku (5777 8600/ www.momat.go.jp/CG/cg.html). Takebashi station, exit 1b. **Open** 10am-5pm Tue-Sun. **Admission** ¥420; free-¥130 concessions.

This impressive 1910 European-style brick building was once the base for the legions of guards who patrolled the Imperial Palace. Now it exhibits work from its permanent collection of more than 2,400 pieces of Japanese and foreign handicrafts, from dating the Meiji era to the present. Temporary exhibitions are enhanced with artist demonstration videos and regular talks.

Gift shop. Lockers.

National Museum of Modern Art, Tokyo (Tokyo Kokuritsu Kindai Bijutsukan)

3-1 Kitanomaru Koen, Chiyoda-ku (5777 8600/ www.momat.go.jp/honkan/honkan.html). Takebashi station, exit 1b. **Open** 10am-5pm Tue-Thur, Sat, Sun; 10am-8pm Fri. **Admission** ¥420; free-¥130 concessions. Additional fee for special exhibitions.

This is an alternative-history MOMA, one consisting mostly of Japanese art from the turn of the 20th century on. Noteworthy features of the permanent collection are portraits by early Japanese modernist Kishida Ryusei and grim war-time paintings by Fujita Tsuguharu. The first floor is devoted to temporary exhibitions organised both internally (for example, on contemporary Japanese photography) and borrowed from top-flight institutions abroad (for example, recent Kandinsky and Wolfgang Laib shows). The 1969 building, designed by Taniguchi Yoshiro (father of architect Taniguchi Yoshio) reopened in January 2002, following a two-and-a-half-year, ¥ 7.8 billion renovation. Its location next to the moat and walls of the Imperial Palace make it a prime stop for seeing spring cherry blossoms and autumn foliage.

Gift shop. Lockers. Restaurant. English pamphlet.

Tokyo Station Gallery

Tokyo Station, 1-9-1 Marunouchi, Chiyoda-ku (3212 2485/www.ejrcf.or.jp). Tokyo station, Marunouchi, Chuo (central) exit. **Open** 10am-7pm Tue-Fri, 10am-6pm Sat, Sun. **Admission** ¥800; ¥400-¥600 concessions; children free Sat.

Your JR train ticket helps support this small museum; it's run by East Japan Railways. Though the aged, interior brick walls of the old station may not be the best background for paintings, they do give a look deep into its past. The museum has no permanent collection but brings in shows from around Japan and the world. Recent exhibitions have included modern Mongolian painting, 19th-century Scandinavian landscape painting, and a survey of architect Ando Tadao.

Gift shop, café.

Tokyo Stock Exchange

2-1 Nihonbashi-Kabuto-cho, Chuo-ku (3665 1881/ www.tse.or.jp/english/index.shtml). Kayaba-cho station, exit 10. **Open** 9am-4.30pm Mon-Fri. **English tour** 1.30 pm daily. **Admission** free.

Come and watch the Japanese economy collapse for yourselves. In 2003, the Nikkei average (Japan's equivalent of the FTSE) plummeted to all-time lows, taking a host of companies down with it. Sadly, you won't be able to witness much wailing and gnashing of teeth, since the TSE, home to global giants such as Toyota and Sony, abolished its trading floor in April 1999. The stock market of the world's second largest economy is now run (or should that be 'ruined'?) almost entirely by sophisticated computers, which means the building is eerily quiet, the former trading floor taken over by a huge glass cylinder with the names and real-time stock prices of listed companies revolving at the top. Apart from the cylinder, there is very little movement. If you want to catch what little action there is left, head for the Stock Exchange on a weekday between 9-11am, or 12.30-3pm. The English-language guided tour lasts approximately 40 minutes and includes a 20-minute video explaining the history and function of the TSE. On the way out, don't forget to invest in a souvenir T-shirt, mug or golf balls.

Other sights in central Tokyo

Archaeological, Commodity, and Criminology Museums at Meiji University

University Hall 3F-4F, 1-1 Kanda Surugadai, Chiyoda-ku (3296 4432/ www.meiji.ac.jp/museum/ index.html). Ochanomizu station. **Open** 10am-4.30pm Mon-Fri, 10am-12.30pm Sat. **Admission** free.

Just one building on Meiji University's campus houses these three small but interesting (and free) museums. The Archaeological Museum, opened in 1952, features objects found on digs around Japan such as clay *haniwa* (tomb figures shaped like houses and horses), Jomon and Yayoi pots, obsidian scrapers, and the lower jawbone of a Naumann's elephant.

Bear in mind that the Japanese archaeological community has been thrown into turmoil following revelations in 2000 that one of Japan's preeminent archaeologists, Fujimura Shinichi, was actually burying artefacts before miraculously finding them. The Commodity Museum is a small room dedicated to Japanese handicrafts and tourist trinkets. Models and photos depict the step-by-step process involved in making lacquerware – from carving the wood to applying the layers of lacquer and polish – as well as other items. Meiji University was founded in 1881 as the Meiji Judicial School, so its Criminology Museum, the only one in Japan, somehow makes sense. A small selection of the school's 250,000 Edo period and Meiji era crime-related objects capture vintage crime and punishment. Enlarged woodblock prints show kimono kleptos getting their just deserts. Life-size replicas of torture devices vividly depict burnings, decapitations and other punishments. One book details the best way to torture Christians (force them to kneel on a jagged-edged platform with a large stone in their laps).
English pamphlets. Gift shop.

Button Museum

Iris Bldg 4F, 1-11-8 Nihonbashi-Hamacho, Chuo-ku (3864 6537/www.iris.co.jp). Hamacho station (Toei Shinjuku Line). **Open** 10am-noon, 1-5pm Mon-Fri. Visits by appointment preferred. **Admission** ¥300.
The museum of button-maker Iris, holed up on the fourth-floor of its headquarters, looks out over the Sumida river. But we aren't here for the view. A 15-minute video introduces the extensive collection of animal horn, enamel, porcelain, mosaic, gold, glass and other buttons. Apparently Egyptians were the first to begin using them, around 4000 BC. Japan didn't start until the Edo period, with imports from Portugal. Look out for Halley's Comet, lion's head Chanel and Betty Boop designs.
English pamphlet. Gift shop.

Hie Jinja

2-10-15 Nagatacho, Chiyoda-ku (3581 2471/www.hiejinja.net/eindex.htm). Kokkaidogijido-mae station, exits 1, 5 or Akasaka-Mitsuke station, Belle Vie Akasaka exit or Nagatacho station, exit 8. **Open** *Apr-Sept* 5am-6pm daily. *Oct-Mar* 6am-5pm daily.
Nicknamed 'Sanno-sama' (Mountain god), the Hie Shrine was originally established in the grounds of Edo Castle, to protect it from its enemies. It moved here in 1659, its role as protector of Edo Castle (now the Imperial Palace) unchanged. Every two years, in June, the shrine hosts one of Tokyo's biggest *matsuri* (*see p197*), and participants have the rare privilege of entering the castle gates.

Japanese War-Dead Memorial Museum

Yasukuni Shrine, 3-1-1 Kudankita, Chiyoda-ku (3261 8326/www.yasukuni.or.jp). Kudanshita station, exits 1, 3. **Open** *Nov-Feb* 9am-5pm daily. *Mar-Oct* 9am-5.30pm daily. **Admission** ¥800; ¥300-¥500 concessions. Group discounts.
One of Japan's most controversial sites is a Shinto shrine. Yasukuni ('peaceful country') hits the headlines every 15 August – the anniversary of Japan's World War II surrender – when the prime minister or another high-ranking politician visits to pay respects to the 2.5 million spirits of Japan's war dead enshrined here. Because the list of the dead dates back to the Meiji Restoration (1868) and includes convicted war criminals such as the notorious General Tojo, each visit reopens wounds from Japan's war-mongering past (*see p12* **War and peace**). A fascinating array of soldiers' personal effects from conflicts such as the Sino-Japanese War (1894-95), the Russo-Japanese War (1904-05) and World War II covers two floors. There's also one of Japan's human torpedoes, found in Hawaii, on loan from the US army. For shrine details, *see p67*.

JCII Camera Museum

JCII Ichibancho Bldg B1, 25 Ichibancho, Chiyoda-ku (3263 7110/www.jcii-cameramuseum.jp/index_e.htm). Hanzomon station, exit 4. **Open** 10am-5pm Tue-Sun. **Admission** ¥300; free-¥100 concessions.
Operated by the organisation that tests and inspects Japanese cameras, the JCII Camera Museum displays over 500 cameras from around the world. Among the collection is an original 1839 Giroux Daguerrotype, the first camera ever made: it's a surprisingly compact wooden box. Other early models include a decorated Photosphere, an Escopette, and a Sutton Panoramic Camera. APS and digital cameras show recent evolutions.
Gift shop.

Kanda Myojin Shrine

2-16-2 Soto-Kanda, Chiyoda-ku (3254 0753/www.kandamyoujin.or.jp). Ochanomizu station, Hijiribashi exit. **Open** *Shrine* 9am-4pm daily. *Grounds* 24hrs daily.
This shrine is said to have been established in Otemachi in 730, but was moved here in the 17th century. One legend connected with it is that the head of an executed rebel leader flew back to Kanda Myojin in 935 to rejoin his body. The original 17th-century building was destroyed in the Great Kanto Earthquake of 1923, and the building that stands here today, surrounded by a host of smaller shrines, is a concrete replica built in 1924. A two-stop ride on the Chuo Line from Tokyo station.

Map Museum

2-1-36 Kudan-Minami, Chiyoda-ku (3261 0075/www.senshu-bunko.or.jp). Kudanshita station, exit 2. **Open** 10am-4pm Mon-Sat. **Admission** ¥300; ¥150-¥200 concessions. Japanese only.
When the Satakes, a powerful *daimyo* family living in Hitachi, remained neutral in the 1600 Battle of Sekigahara, they were punished: their fiefdom was halved and they were forced to move to the northern prefecture of Akita. They built a castle and thrived, ruling for 12 generations until the 1868 Meiji restoration placed the land and people in the emperor's hands. Satake Yoshiharu (34th generation)

Tokyo station contains an art gallery. *See p65.*

founded this museum on the site of Lord Satake's Edo residence, bequeathing finely detailed Edo period maps of the shogun's holdings, ancient documents, paintings, personal seals, and other effects used by his family for hundreds of years. Compare old maps to current ones to see how Tokyo was able to build highways for the 1964 Olympics – by covering most of its canals.
Gift shop.

Nikolai Cathedral

4-1 Kanda-Surugadai, Chiyoda-ku (3291 1885). Ochanomizu station. **Open** *Visitors* 1-4pm Tue-Fri. *Service* (in Japanese) 10am-12.30pm Sun.
This cruciform Russian Orthodox church, complete with an onion dome, was designed by the British architect Josiah Conder (*see p22*) and completed in 1891. The original, larger, dome was destroyed in the 1923 earthquake.

Transportation Museum

1-25 Kanda-Sudacho, Chiyoda-ku (3251 8481/www. kouhaku.or.jp). Akihabara station, Electric Town exit. **Open** 9.30am-5pm Tue-Sun. **Admission** ¥310; ¥150 concessions.
From rickshaws to rockets, this large museum is a compendium of land, sea, air and space transport. But it started as a railway museum in 1921 and the exhaustive and exhausting train section is where you'll still find the kids. See how Tokyo's JR lines start their day in a massive model railway set-up. Virtually drive a Yamanote line train through Tokyo in a real conductor car or change antique switching lights from red to green. The museum has the first train used in Japan – an 1872 steam locomotive made in England that travelled between Shinbashi and Yokohama – and the latest, an experimental maglev system. The gift shop is stocked with every conceivable Japanese model train, unique transportation paraphernalia and unusual souvenirs.
Café. Gift shop. Lockers.

Yamatane Museum of Art

Sanbancho KS Bldg 1F, 2 Sanbancho, Chiyoda-ku (3239 5911/www.yamatane-museum.or.jp). Kudanshita station, exit 2. **Open** 10am-5pm Tue-Sun. **Admission** ¥500, free-¥400 concessions. **Credit** (shop only) DC.
Yamatane Museum of Art, opened in 1966, takes its name from Yamatane Securities. Curators select from the company's 1,800-strong collection of modern and contemporary *nihonga* (Japanese-style painting) for the frequently changing, often seasonally themed, shows.
Gift shop.

Yasukuni Shrine (Yasukuni Jinja)

3-1-1 Kudankita, Chiyoda-ku (3261 8326/www. yasukuni.or.jp/english/index.html). Kudanshita station, exits 1,3 or Ichigaya station exits A3, A4. **Open** *grounds* 6am-7pm daily.
Yasukuni annually invites controversy when a high-ranking politician visits on 15 August, the anniversary of Japan's World War II defeat (*see p12*).

North City

Laid-back Ikebukuro is the undisputed capital of the north for bargain shopping.

Ikebukuro station is so big that even locals get lost.

Ikebukuro

Map p69

Ikebukuro, which ranks third behind Shinjuku and Shibuya as one of the main sub-centres of Tokyo, has a resolutely uncool reputation that actually works in its favour. Ikebukuro lacks the cutting-edge style of its bigger siblings, but the resulting lack of pretension gives the whole area a freer, more laid-back atmosphere. Indeed, it has something of a homey feel, because many who come to Ikebukuro live in the area, and the atmosphere is comparable to that found in Japan's provincial cities.

Don't go to Ikebukuro expecting wide vistas and empty streets, however. As the recession bites and more upmarket places feel the pinch, Ikebukuro has been quietly thriving, luring people with its promise of discount shopping and a cheaper night out.

Most of the major chain department stores have a branch here, and every available square inch of the area is crammed with shops, bars, restaurants, karaoke rooms, love hotels and other 'entertainment' establishments.

So how did a one-time collection of ponds and little farming villages become one of the largest commercial centres of one of the largest cities in the world? In the early 1900s, the region was served by the Tobu and Musashino lines (now the Tobu Tojo and Seibu Ikebukuro lines), but as the population grew and the sleepy villages became one very large town, more train and subway lines were built, resulting in a major junction. Yasujiro Tsutsumi and Kaichiro Nezu, the arch-rivals responsible for developing the Seibu and Tobu lines respectively, encouraged expansion of the area by each building a department store by the station. Both stores grew to enormous proportions, and until recently, **Tobu** enjoyed the status of largest department store in the world. Other department stores saw the success of the two empires, and wanted part of the action. Small shops offering goods at discount prices came along to fill the gaps. Cafés and restaurants appeared to feed the throngs of shoppers, and bars, clubs, and other entertainment venues came along to satisfy the needs of those who wanted to stay on into the night.

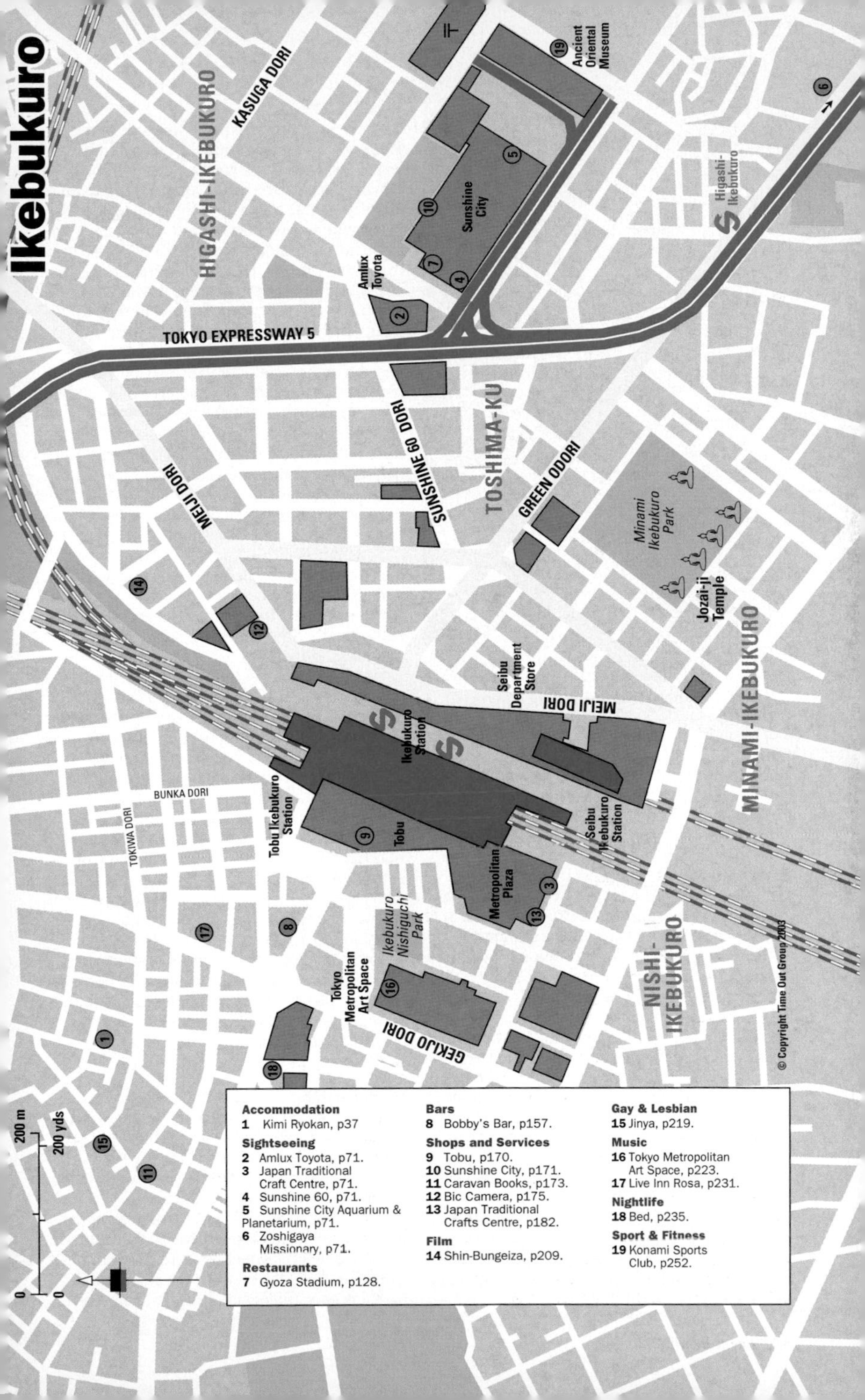
Ikebukuro
HIGASHI-IKEBUKURO
KASUGA DORI
Ancient Oriental Museum
Sunshine City
Amlux Toyota
TOKYO EXPRESSWAY 5
Higashi-Ikebukuro
SUNSHINE 60 DORI
TOSHIMA-KU
MEIJI DORI
GREEN ODORI
Minami Ikebukuro Park
Jozai-ji Temple
Seibu Department Store
MINAMI-IKEBUKURO
Ikebukuro Station
BUNKA DORI
TOKIWA DORI
Tobu Ikebukuro Station
Tobu
Seibu Ikebukuro Station
Metropolitan Plaza
Ikebukuro Nishiguchi Park
Tokyo Metropolitan Art Space
GEKIJO DORI
NISHI-IKEBUKURO
© Copyright Time Out Group 2003
0
200 m
0
200 yds
Accommodation
1 Kimi Ryokan, p37
Sightseeing
2 Amlux Toyota, p71.
3 Japan Traditional Craft Centre, p71.
4 Sunshine 60, p71.
5 Sunshine City Aquarium & Planetarium, p71.
6 Zoshigaya Missionary, p71.
Restaurants
7 Gyoza Stadium, p128.
Bars
8 Bobby's Bar, p157.
Shops and Services
9 Tobu, p170.
10 Sunshine City, p171.
11 Caravan Books, p173.
12 Bic Camera, p175.
13 Japan Traditional Crafts Centre, p182.
Film
14 Shin-Bungeiza, p209.
Gay & Lesbian
15 Jinya, p219.
Music
16 Tokyo Metropolitan Art Space, p223.
17 Live Inn Rosa, p231.
Nightlife
18 Bed, p235.
Sport & Fitness
19 Konami Sports Club, p252.

View from **Sunshine 60 Building**. *See p71.*

The major obstacle to exploring Ikebukuro is the station, which even locals find confusing. The subterranean warren of pedestrian walkways stretches for miles, has over 40 exits, and few maps. The main exits are clearly signposted, however, and it is often easiest to get out at the nearest one and navigate by the department stores. The most popular place to meet up in Ikebukuro is the statue of an owl (the Japanese for owl is *fukuro*, so the statue is a sort of 3-D pun) that stands inside the station.

In keeping with Tokyo's tradition of contradictions, the **Seibu** store (*see p169* for branch address) – whose name originates from 'west area railway line' – is located at the east side of the station, and Tobu – the 'east area railway line' – has the west side covered, quite literally. The areas around the two are the main starting points for visitors to Ikebukuro. Before leaving the station, check the two stores out. It's advisable to pick up a store map, as there's a danger of getting very lost. If you fancy trying out some of the local cuisine but don't feel in need of a whole meal, do what the locals do – trot down to the food hall and help yourself to the free samples. The Seibu supermarket is especially worth a visit, offering Japanese food as well as one of the best selections of imported food and ingredients in the city.

EAST SIDE

There are two main exits on this side of the station – the east exit and the Seibu exit. Turn left out of either, and you will come to **Parco**, which is part of the Seibu complex. **P'Parco** is slightly further along, and the clothes on sale here make you wonder if those youngsters who frequent the trendier areas of Tokyo come here in disguise to buy their fashion creations.

If you think the areas to the left and right of Seibu are mobbed, try making your way to the main centre of Ikebukuro – **Sunshine 60 Street**. Upon leaving the station, it's almost possible to be swept there directly by the crowds. Just head up the wide tree-lined street. You can always tell the busiest corners of Tokyo by the concentration of tissue distributors and karaoke touts; the corner just before the entrance to Sunshine 60 Street is so packed with them that by the time you've made it to the crossing, you'll have acquired enough tissues to open your own shop.

Sunshine 60 Street is packed with tiny stores – most offering discount clothing – as well as restaurants and cinemas. The Sanrio shop is worth a giggle – two whole floors offering Hello Kitty goods, all of which are cooed over by seemingly grown women.

Sunshine 60 Street is so called because it ultimately leads to the **Sunshine 60 Building**, part of the Sunshine City complex. In the building's massive marble mall are all kinds of fashion shops and restaurants, and within the complex, an observatory, an aquarium, a planetarium, a theme park, and the **Ancient Orient Museum**, among other attractions. Behind Sunshine City you will find a wide selection of love hotels, along with offers of entertainment from scantily clad young ladies who happen to be strolling in the area. Some of the sex establishments are advertised in Sunshine 60 Street itself, by shady-looking characters holding rather graphic placards.

After a long day's sightseeing and shopping, there are plenty of clubs and bars to relax in on this side of the station. Or head across to the other side of the station. The other half of Ikebukuro awaits…

WEST SIDE

This side of the station is considerably quieter than the east, especially during the day. The number of little shops and bars, however, is still mind-boggling, and you will wonder how it's possible they all stay in business.

Aside from Tobu (*see p170*), the only other major department store is **Marui**, which is directly down the street perpendicular to the west exit. The area between the station and Marui is choc-full of small shops, clubs, bars and restaurants. All other main shopping action is towards the south. The **Metropolitan Plaza**, home to the **Japan Traditional Craft Center**, is right next to Tobu, and can be reached by the Metropolitan exit of the station, which is the evening venue of choice for a couple of groups of die-hard breakdancers – a chance to see Japanese youth in action.

Directly opposite the Metropolitan exit is **Tobu Spice**, yet another building full of restaurants. In the basement of the next building behind it is **The Dubliners** (*see p161*) – a bar that attracts long-time foreign residents and Japanese regulars, as well as musicians keen on Celtic music.

Further along, the **Tokyo Metropolitan Art Space** (*see p223*) houses the world's largest pipe organ, which costs around five million yen a year to maintain. An extremely long escalator takes you to the fifth floor, where an art gallery offers free exhibitions.

Walking across the tiny park from there towards the north side, tiny discount clothes stores, generally catering to the reggae/rap/ska/grunge crowd.

GETTING THERE

Ikebukuro is on the JR Yamanote and Saikyo lines, the Eidan Subway Marunouchi and Yurakucho lines, the Seibu Ikebukuro Line and the Tobu Tojo Line. The Narita Express also stops here on a limited service.

Sights

Amlux Toyota Auto Salon

3-3-5 Higashi-Ikebukuro, Toshima-ku (5391 5900/www.amlux.jp/Tokyo/english/index.html). Ikebukuro station, exit 35. **Open** 11am-7pm Tue-Sun (B1F, 1F open until 9pm). **Admission** free.

Toyota used to claim this was the world's biggest car showroom, but just to make sure, it opened an even bigger one in MegaWeb (*see p79*). But there's more to this place than cars. As well as being able to sit and fiddle with the controls in all of Toyota's range, you can watch free 20-minute films in the Amlux Theatre, on chairs that vibrate in time with what's on screen. There's also a virtual driving experience that's so realistic that you're not allowed to have a go without a valid driving licence.

Japan Traditional Craft Centre

Metropolitan Plaza 1-2 F, 1-11-1 Nishi-Ikebukuro, Toshima-ku (5954 6066/www.kougei.or.jp/english/center.html). Ikebukuro JR station, Metropolitan exit or via Tobu Department Store Plaza Hall 2F. **Open** 11am-7pm daily (11am-5pm every other Tue; closed occasional Wed). **Credit** AmEx, MC, V. **Admission** free.

Learn about, then shop for, a broad cross-section of Japanese traditional crafts (lacquer, ceramics, paper, kimono, knives, and so on) at this showroom-cum-museum. It has permanent and temporary exhibitions, a reference library and even classes. The gift shop sells the work of living craftspeople (who sometimes give demonstrations) from across the country. Look for their big crafts fairs held periodically throughout the city.

Gift shop.

Sunshine City

World Import Mart Bldg 10F, 3-1-3 Higashi-Ikebukuro, Toshima-ku (3989 3466/www.sunshinecity.co.jp). Ikebukuro station, exits 35, 41. **Open** *Aquarium* 10am-6pm Mon-Fri; 10am-6.30pm Sat, Sun. *Planetarium* noon-6pm Mon-Fri; 11am-7pm Sat, Sun. **Admission** *Aquarium* ¥1,600. *Planetarium* ¥800.

The first aquarium in the world to be located in a high-rise building is here. It hosts over 20,000 fish from 400 different species, swimming around at high altitudes. The planetarium is, appropriately enough, also located in the sky, on the same floor.

Sunshine 60 Building

3-1-1 Higashi-Ikebukuro, Toshima-ku (3989 3331/www.sunshinecity.co.jp). Ikebukuro station, exits 35, 41. **Open** *Observatory* 10am-8.30pm daily. *Namjatown* 10am-10pm daily. **Admission** *Observatory* ¥620; ¥310 concessions. *Namjatown* ¥300; ¥200 concessions. Passport ¥3,900; ¥3,300 concessions. **No credit cards.**

One of the fastest lifts in the world will whisk you to the top of one of the tallest buildings in Asia in around 35 seconds. The building is the centre of a complex of four buildings that occupies the former site of Sugamo Prison, where General Tojo Hideki and six other class-A war criminals were hanged in December 1948. Other attractions here include shopping mall World Import Mart, a planetarium, an aquarium (*see below*), a theatre, museum and Namjatown, an indoor amusement park.

Zoshigaya Missionary Museum

1-25-5 Zoshigaya, Toshima-ku (3985 4081). Higashi Ikebukuro station, exit 5. **Open** 9am-4.30pm Tue-Sun (closed 3rd Sun of mth). **Admission** free.

Very few homes of early foreign residents have escaped the ravages of time and development. This one, built in 1907, belonged to American missionary J M McCaleb. When it was threatened with demolition a few years ago, residents campaigned to save it. Now restored and open to visitors, the two-storey building is strangely displaced, time-warped from old America to the hubbub of modern Tokyo.

Other sights in north Tokyo

Joren-ji Temple

5-28-3 Akatsuka, Itabashi-ku (3975 3326). Narimasu station (Tobu Tojo Line), north exit, then bus or 20min walk. **Open** 9am-4pm daily.

A hillside temple way out in northern Tokyo that was once a favourite resting point for travellers. Home to the third largest Buddha in Japan.

Koishikawa Botanical Garden (Koishikawa Shokubutsuen)

3-7-1 Hakusan, Bunkyo-ku (3814 0138/www.bg.s.u-tokyo.ac.jp). Hakusan station (Toei Mita Line), then a 10min walk. **Open** 9am-4.30pm Tue-Sun. **Admission** ¥330 (tickets from Yoneda Food Shop across the road).

A botanical garden with a history stretching back over 300 years, Koishikawa was once a herbal garden attached to a paupers' hospital. It is now beautifully landscaped in a mixture of Japanese and Chinese styles, with bridges, stone monuments and ponds teeming with carp.

Koishikawa Korakuen

1-6-6 Koraku, Bunkyo-ku (3811 3015). Iidabashi station, exit A1 or Korakuen station, exit 2. **Open** 9am-5pm (last admission 4.30pm) daily. **Admission** ¥300.

The oldest garden in Tokyo, Koishikawa Korakuen was first laid out in 1629. Redevelopment, earthquake and war damage have reduced it to a quarter of its original size but it's still beautiful, with a range of walks, bridges, hills and vistas (often the miniatures of more famous originals) that encourage quiet contemplation. The entrance, tucked away down a side street, can be a little difficult to find.

Kyu Furukawa Gardens

1-27-39 Nishigahara, Kita-ku (3910 0394/www.tokyo-park.or.jp/english/jpgarden2.html#Furukawa). Komagome station, north exit. **Open** 9am-5pm daily. Closed Dec 29-Jan 3. **Admission** ¥150.

The spacious grounds of the former home of the Furukawa family spread down an Italian-style terrace, featuring rose and azalea gardens, to a traditional Japanese garden set around a pond. Overlooking the garden, from the top of a hill, is a stone mansion built in traditional English style by British architect Josiah Conder in 1914. There is a tearoom inside, but reservations may be necessary.

Paper Museum

1-1-3 Oji, Kita-ku (3916 2320/www.papermuseum.jp). Oji station, south exit. **Open** 10am-5pm Tue-Sun. **Admission** ¥300; ¥150 concessions.

Founded in 1950 on the site of the first production of western-style paper in Japan (Horifune, Kita-ku), the museum moved to its present parkside location in 1997. The collection comprises over 38,000 items, with displays on the making and use of modern paper and the history of paper around the world, including Japanese *washi*.

English pamphlet.

Rikugien

6-16-3 Hon-Komagome, Bunkyo-ku (3941 2222). Komagome station, exit 2 or Sengoku station, exit A3. **Open** 9am-5pm (last entrance 4.30pm) daily. **Admission** ¥300.

A relatively small but attractive place that combines landscaped gardens and islands in a large pond with trails in the woods around it. Rikugien was established in 1702 and the water, landscapes and flora create 88 scenes described in famous poems. It's hard to see the literary connection, but it is peaceful.

Tokyo Dome City

1-3-61 Koraku, Bunkyo-ku (5800 9999/www.tokyo-dome.co.jp/e/). Suidobashi JR station, west exit or Korakuen station, exit 2. **Open** 10am-10pm daily. *LaQua spa* 11am-9am daily. **Admission** free. *Rides* ¥200-¥1,000. *Premium value multi-ride ticket* ¥3,000. *LaQua spa* ¥2,800; ¥3,100 Sat, Sun; ¥4,600 midnight-6am.

After a two-year refurbishment, the amusement park formerly known as Korakuen opened with a fanfare in May 2003, as part of an urban theme park with baseball stadium Tokyo Dome at its centre. On a newly developed section of land behind the original, and small, funfair there's now an ultra-modern section, called LaQua, comprising a shopping centre, restaurants, the world's first spokeless big wheel and a hot mineral bath theme park with its own cafés and restaurants, where spring water is pumped up from 1,700m (5,670ft) below.

Toshimaen

3-25-1 Koyama, Nerima-ku (3990 8800/www.toshimaen.co.jp/index.html). Toshimaen station (Toei Oedo or Seibu Toshima lines), exit A2. **Open** varies. *Toshimaen Garden Spa* 10am-11pm daily. **Admission** *Entry only* ¥1,000. *Entry & ride pass* ¥3,800. *Toshimaen Garden Spa* ¥2,000; ¥1,200 after 9pm.

The opening of the Oedo line in 2000 made this out-of-the-way entertainment complex more accessible to all. The jewel in its crown is Hydropolis, a waterpark that includes a surf pool and a very elaborate set of waterslides. For the more sedate, there's also a restored turn-of-the-century carousel. Next door, in what is becoming a trend in Tokyo, an *onsen* natural mineral water spa opened in June 2003, offering, among other things, a bath made with salt from the Dead Sea.

Yushima Seido Shrine

1-4-25 Yushima, Bunkyo-ku (3251 4606). Ochanomizu JR station, Hijiribashi exit. **Open** *Hall* 10am-5pm Sat, Sun. *Grounds* 9.30am-5pm daily. **Map** p62.

Founded in Ueno Park in 1631, this shrine, dedicated to Confucius, moved here 60 years later and evolved into an academy for the study of the classics. The hall itself was rebuilt in the 1930s. A statue of Confucius stands in the grounds.

Yushima Tenjin Shrine

3-30-1 Yushima, Bunkyo-ku (3836 0753/www.yushimatenjin.or.jp/pc/eng-page/english.htm). Yushima station, exit 3. **Open** 6am-8pm daily.

This shrine was founded in the 14th century, in honour of ninth-century poet and statesman Sugawara Michizane, who was given the title *tenjin* ('heavenly god') after his death. At exam time, thousands of students come to pray for success, hanging handwritten messages on *ema*, small wooden tablets.

South City

Roppongi and Odaiba are the highlights of this area: the first for 24-hour party people, the second for lovers of outrageous modern architecture.

Roppongi

Map p74

Traditionally, there are two places in Tokyo that concerned parents warn their virtuous daughters to stay clear of, one being Shinjuku's Kabuki-cho, the other Roppongi. For years, Roppongi has enjoyed a reputation as Tokyo's wildest frontier, a playground where anything goes and where foreign residents and visitors cavort with locals like nowhere else.

Remarkably for Tokyo, Roppongi remained underdeveloped for years and was left very much to its own devices. All this changed in spring 2003, thanks to the efforts of local property magnate Mori Minoru. At the end of April, his construction company finished work on the biggest development in inner Tokyo, **Roppongi Hills** (*see p171*), an expanse of concrete and glass that contains some 200 upmarket restaurants and shops, an art gallery and a multiplex cinema.

Instantly, Roppongi was flooded with people who would never normally venture here, the new complex drawing over one million visitors on its opening weekend. Pre-opening targets of 100,000 visitors per day are still being comfortably exceeded, and the apparent success of the venture has led another company to announce plans to build Japan's second tallest skyscraper on an empty Roppongi plot of land.

Just how fast, and how far, the upmarket businesses of Roppongi Hills will start to spread into the centre of Roppongi is still uncertain, but it's a sure thing that there will be a ripple effect. The next few years, therefore, may be the last stand of old Roppongi. Make the most of it while you can.

The best way to attack Roppongi is from the central crossing near the subway station exits. Hidden in the streets that radiate off from here are more bars, clubs and restaurants than anyone has ever bothered to count, although around 5,000 would be a safe ball-park figure.

For the first-time visitor, Roppongi is a bewildering experience, with its flashing neon lights, street hawkers, giant video screens and seemingly never-ending procession of places offering food (of varying quality), drink and dancing, all crammed into the six blocks, or *chome*, that make up the area.

The people who come here are from all nations and all walks of life, from salarymen to curious schoolgirls, to international pop stars. It says something that Roppongi has something that can satisfy all of them.

Incongruously, the name 'Roppongi' means 'six trees' in Japanese, thought to be a reference to six ancient gingko trees that once stood in the area, the last of which was destroyed, along with the rest of Roppongi, by allied firebombing raids in World War II. Nowadays the only forest in the area is composed entirely of neon lights. In the mid 18th century, however, the place was a village of 500 or so inhabitants, where badgers roamed free and inhabitants of the nearby village of Shibuya would come to catch insects. The *shogun* would use the main road (which passes behind the present-day police station) as a route to go hawk hunting.

The pattern for today's Roppongi was first set at the end of the 19th century, when it was decided that the Imperial Guard would move its barracks to the area from Marunouchi. The presence of soldiers brought money, and businesses flourished. More people flooded in after the 1923 Kanto earthquake spared the area of fire. After the allied firebombings, history repeated itself as the American occupying forces chose to station the First Cavalry and Signal Corps in Roppongi. With the Americans came food, and a demand for the type of bar and services that had previously barely existed in Japan. Modern-day Roppongi was born.

It's a strange location for such a centre to be created. Until 2000, only one subway line served Roppongi, which is slightly away from the all-powerful loop of the JR Yamanote Line. Yet its isolation has served it well, insulating it from the mad crowds of squealing teenagers that infest Shibuya or Shinjuku. Coming to Roppongi for a night out is making a statement; you've made a choice, you're here for the duration, and you can take whatever's coming.

And what's coming usually involves eating, drinking and clubbing – to excess. The legacy of the 1950s American soldiers lives on, and although this is one of the most cosmopolitan areas of Tokyo, it's also the only area where you sometimes need to be on your guard. A quick look at the relevant sections elsewhere in this book will give some idea of the variety of

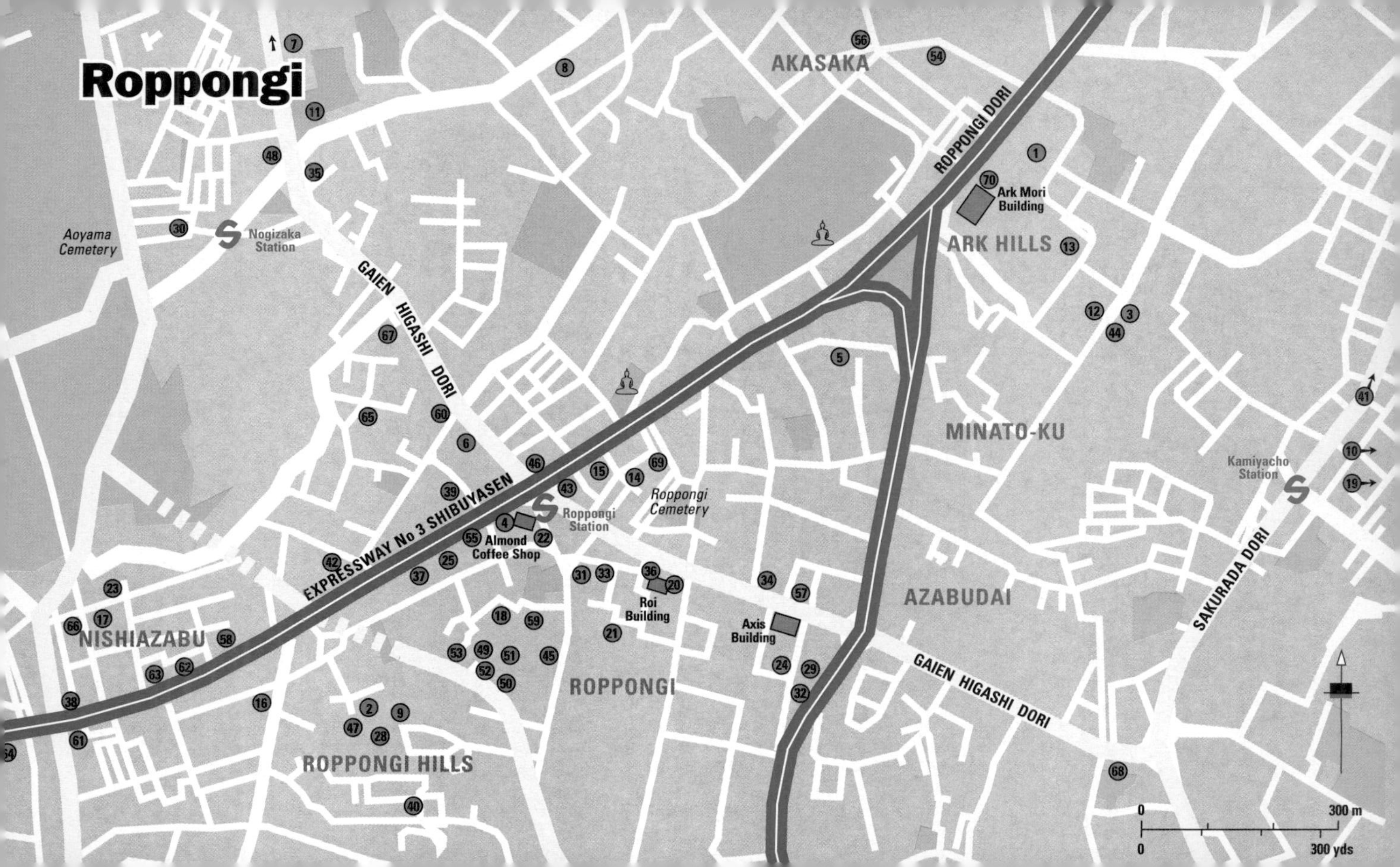

Roppongi
Aoyama Cemetery
Nogizaka Station
AKASAKA
ROPPONGI DORI
Ark Mori Building
ARK HILLS
GAIEN HIGASHI DORI
MINATO-KU
Kamiyacho Station
EXPRESSWAY No 3 SHIBUYASEN
Roppongi Station
Roppongi Cemetery
Almond Coffee Shop
Roi Building
Axis Building
AZABUDAI
SAKURADA DORI
NISHIAZABU
ROPPONGI
ROPPONGI HILLS
GAIEN HIGASHI DORI
0
300 m
0
300 yds

Tokyo Tower. See p77.

Accommodation
1 ANA Hotel, p38.
2 Grand Hyatt, p38.
3 Hotel Okura, p39.
4 Arca Torre, p39.
5 Roppongi Prince, p39.
6 Hotel Ibis, p39.
7 Asia Centre, p39.
8 Capsule Inn.

Sightseeing
9 Mori Art Museum, p75.
10 NHK Museum, p76.
11 Nogi Shrine, p76.
12 Okura Shukokan, p76.
13 Suntory Museum, p77.

Restaurants
14 Bangkok, p128.
15 Bincho, p128.
16 Brendan's Pizzakaya, p128.
17 Coriander, p128.
18 Vietnamese Cyclo, p131.
19 Daigo, p128.
20 Erawan, p129.
21 Fukuzushi, p129.
22 Hassan Hinazushi, p129.
23 Ken's Dining, p129.
24 Kisso, p129.
25 Moti, p130.
26 Nodaiwa, p130.
27 Noodles, p130.
28 Olives, p130.
29 Phothai Down Under, p130.
30 Chez Pierre, p128.

Bars
31 Bauhaus, p157.
32 Bernd's Bar, p157.
33 Cavern Club, p158.
34 Gas Panic, p158.
35 George's Bar, p158.
36 Paddy Foley's Irish Pub, p158.
37 Shanghai Bar, p158.
38 These, p158.
39 Tokyo Sports Café, p158.

Shops and Services
40 Roppongi Hills, p171.
41 Japan Sword, p182.
42 C'bon Biyu Body Salon, p191.
43 Nail Bee, p191.
44 Koyasu Drug Store Hotel Okura, p192.
45 Poppongi Pharmacy, p192.

Film
46 Haiyu-za, p208.
47 Virgin Cinemas, p209.

Galleries
48 Gallery MA, p211.
49 Gallery Min Min, p211.
50 Hiromi Yoshii+, p211.
51 Ota Fine Arts, p211.
52 Roentgenwerke, p211.
53 Taro Nasu Gallery, p211.
54 Gallery Side 2, p211.

Music
55 Alfie, p224.
56 B Flat, p224.
57 Roppongi Pit Inn, p226.
58 Bullet's, p229.
59 STB139, p232.
60 Y2K, p232.
70 Suntory Hall, p222.

Nightlife
61 328 (San Ni Hachi), p234.
62 Alife, p234.
63 Bullet's, p235.
64 ClubJamaica, p237.
65 Core, p237.
66 Space Lab Yellow, p241.
67 Velfarre, p241

Performing Arts
68 Tokyo International Players, p245.
69 Tokyo Comedy Store, p247.

nightlife that's on offer here, but if you're in no hurry, then take the time to walk around, first by heading down **Gaien Higashi Dori** in the direction of **Tokyo Tower**. Follow this by spreading your net to the right and left of the main drag. If you head right and follow the main roads down, you'll end up in Nishi-Azabu, a Roppongi satellite area that has its own lively bars, clubs and restaurants. When you get tired with the south side, head north of the crossing you started from and follow the same routine. Head too far north and you'll be at Aoyama-Itchome. Then follow the same routine for west and east. West eventually leads to Aoyama and Shibuya, while east takes you into lively Akasaka. Not many people resist Roppongi's temptations for long enough to find this out.

GETTING THERE

Roppongi is on the Hibiya and Toei Oedo lines.

Sights

Mori Art Museum

Roppongi Hills Mori Tower 52-53 F, 6-10-1 Roppongi, Minato-ku (6406 6100/www.mori.art.museum/english/index.html). Roppongi station, exit 1. **Open** 10am-10pm Mon-Wed, Sun; 10am-midnight Thur-Sat. **Admission** varies.

The private Mori Art Museum is draped in superlatives: the world's highest museum of contemporary art (on the 52nd and 53rd floors of the landmark tower in the new Roppongi Hills development); the first Japanese art museum to hire a non-Japanese as director (Englishman David Elliot); and the city's best, unobstructed view. Opening on 18 October 2003, the Mori will be dedicated to promoting contemporary art through world-class exhibitions and an educational programme to match. It will also be open the latest, until midnight at weekends.

Gift shop. Cafe. English pamphlet.

Stream of Starlight big wheel at **Mega Web**. *See p79.*

New Otani Museum

Hotel New Otani, The Garden Court 6F, 4-1 Kioicho, Chiyoda-ku (3221 4111/www.newotani.co.jp/museum). Akasaka-Mitsuke station, exit D. **Open** 10am-6pm Tue-Sun. **Admission** ¥200-¥500 concessions; free hotel guests.

One of Tokyo's grand dame hotels, the New Otani houses a collection of Japanese and Japanese-inspired woodblock prints plus a selection of traditional Japanese and modern European paintings (including works by Vlaminck and School of Paris artists). The museum is small, consisting of two rooms near the hotel reception, but often has shows not seen elsewhere.

Gift shop. English pamphlet.

NHK Broadcast Museum

2-1-1 Atago, Minato-ku (5400 6900/www.nhk.or.jp/bunken/museum-en/index.html). Kamiyacho station, exit 3. **Open** 9.30am-4.30pm Tue-Sun. **Admission** free.

This museum, run by the national public broadcasting company, tunes you into the history of radio and TV in Japan. The nation's first radio station began broadcasting in July 1925 from this location (NHK has since moved to bigger digs in Shibuya). There are two floors of early equipment, and vintage TV shows and news broadcasts play throughout the museum and can also be viewed in the video library.

Gift shop.

Nogi Shrine

8-11-27 Akasaka, Minato-ku (3478 3001/house enquiries 3583 4151/www.nogijinja.or.jp). Nogizaka station, exit 1. **Open** 8.30am-5pm daily. *House* 12-13 Sept 9.30am-5pm.

The Nogi Shrine is dedicated to the memory of General Nogi Maresuke, whose house and stables are adjacent to the site where the shrine now stands. When the Meiji Emperor died, on 13 September 1912, the general and his wife proved their loyalty by joining him in death; he killed himself by *seppuku*, she by slitting her throat with a knife. The house in which they did away with themselves is open only two days a year, on the eve and anniversary of their deaths, but an elevated walkway allows you to peek in through the windows, one of which affords you a glimpse of Nogi's bloodstained shirt.

Okura Shukokan Museum of Fine Art

2-10-3 Toranomon, Minato-ku (3583 0781/www.okura.com/tokyo/info/shukokan.html). Roppongi-Itchome station, exits 2, 3. **Open** 10am-4.30pm Tue-Sun. **Admission** ¥700; free-¥500 concessions; free hotel guests. Additional fee for special exhibitions.

This two-storey Chinese-style building sits in front of the retro-modern Hotel Okura, one of Tokyo's finest. Inside there's a small mix of Asian antiquities: paintings, calligraphy, Buddhist sculpture, textiles, ceramics, swords, archaeological artefacts, lacquerware and metalwork. The exhibitions change five or six times a year.

Gift shop.

Sogetsu Art Museum

Sogetsu Kaikan 6F, 7-2-21 Akasaka, Minato-ku (3408 9112/www.sogetsu.or.jp/museum/home.html). Aoyama-Itchome station, exit 4. **Open** varies with exhibition. **Admission** varies.

This small museum holds irregular shows, mostly of modern arts and crafts. Japanese-American artist Isamu Noguchi created the expansive, multi-level cut-stone waterfall in the entrance lobby of the mirrored glass building designed by Tange Kenzo.

Suntory Museum of Art

Tokyo Suntory Bldg 11 F, 1-2-3 Akasaka, Minato-ku (3470 1073/www.suntory.co.jp/sma). Akasaka-Mitsuke station, exit B. **Open** 10am-5pm Tue-Thur, Sun; 10am-7pm Fri. **Admission** varies.

Founded in 1961 by Keizo Saji, former president of the alcohol distiller, Suntory Museum has a collection of some 3,000 works of traditional Japanese art and crafts, focused mainly on objects used in daily life (including paintings, ceramics, textiles, glass, and the like). The regularly changing temporary exhibitions usually draw from the collection.

Tokyo Photographic Culture Centre

Kiyou Bldg 4F, 5F, 3-9-1 Akasaka, Minato-ku (3505 2335/www.tpcc-akasaka.com). Akasaka-Mitsuke station, exit A. **Open** 11am-7pm Tue-Fri, 11am-6pm Sat, Sun. **Admission** ¥650; free-¥600 concessions.

The TPCC holds exhibitions focusing on contemporary Japanese and international photographers.

Tokyo Tower

4-2-8 Shiba-Koen, Minato-ku (3433 5111/2/www.tokyotower.co.jp/web2003/english/index.html). Kamiyacho station, exit 1. **Open** *Tower* 9am-10pm daily. *Other attractions* 10am-9pm daily. **Admission** *Main observatory* ¥820; ¥310-¥460 concessions. *Special observatory* (additional charge) ¥600; ¥350-¥400 concessions. *Waxwork museum* ¥870; ¥460 concessions. *Mysterious Walking Zone* ¥410; ¥300 concessions. *Trick Art Gallery* ¥400; ¥300 concessions. **No credit cards**.

When it was built, in 1958, the Tokyo Tower must have been a monster, its 333m (1093ft) – by design 13m (43ft) more than the Eiffel Tower – looming over Tokyo's low-rise skyline. Since then, a great deal of the tower's original magic has been lost, as a succession of increasingly tall skyscrapers and high rises has blunted the novelty of high buildings, and taken the edge off the view from the top. The tower itself was designed as a television and radio mast, and still performs this function to this day. But it was also intended to echo the more famous tower in Paris – a comparison that Tokyo Tower's current owners are still fond of making. A more apt comparison, however, might be with Britain's Blackpool Tower, since the attractions inside – a waxwork museum (3F), aquarium (1F, opening times vary, call 3434 8833 to check), Hollywood Collection (1F), Trick Art Gallery (4F); Mysterious Walking World (3F) and hologram gallery – mean there's a lot more tat than class about the tower these days. Still, it looks undeniably lovely when illuminated at night.

Odaiba

Map p78

The seafront area of Odaiba has established itself as part of modern Tokyo's cultural identity, and the most potent symbol of this is the gleaming, futuristic sphere at the top of the **Fuji TV building**. Odaiba started out as a Bubble-era project to develop Tokyo Bay on reclaimed land, with the name being taken from the cannons placed offshore by the Tokugawa Shogunate in the late Edo period to protect Japan from invasion. Two of the islands housing those gun emplacements are still here, and one is open to the public. In the same place where these guns were stationed to ward off foreign barbarians, there now stands a scale replica of the Statue of Liberty. To compound the irony, the figure's contemplative gaze is directed inland, the opposite of Ellis Island.

Odaiba is immensely popular with courting couples, and on Christmas Eve, the most romantic day for couples in Japan, you can't move here for people walking arm in arm. It's also home to **Tokyo Big Sight** (3-21-1 Ariake, Koto-ku, www.bigsight.jp), one of Japan's biggest venues for business fairs and exhibitions and **Zepp Tokyo** (*see p229*), a top music venue for big-name bands and DJs.

A trip to Odaiba begins by taking the Yurikamome Line from Shinbashi station; sit at the front of the driverless train and watch the view unfold. The track crosses the spectacular Rainbow Bridge, opened in 1993. Get off at Odaiba-Kaihin Koen station (¥310 from Shinbashi), and a five-minute walk will take you to **Decks** (*see p171*), a shopping mall and entertainment centre. The nautical theme is quickly evident – the wooden planks underfoot, portholes for windows, walkways and gantries overhead, palm trees in unlikely places. Inside, you'll find the Island and Seaside Malls, the Joypolis Game Centre and several restaurants on the sixth floor. The Decks Tokyo Brewery, on the fifth floor, is notable for the Daiba brand micro-beer that it brews on the premises.

Follow the signs to Daiba-Itchome Shotengai, on the fourth floor, and you'll find one of Odaiba's most intriguing attractions; a loving recreation of 1960s Japan and China. Corridors as dark and twisty as the streets of old Shanghai, shopfronts covered in old movie posters selling food and toys from the hazily remembered post-war days. All this is a prelude to Little Hong Kong on the floor above, a cluster of Chinese restaurants surrounded by mock-ups of 1940s railway stations, complete with sound-effects.

Opposite Decks is another shopping mall, **Aqua City**, which contains the vast Mediage multiplex cinema. Strolling along

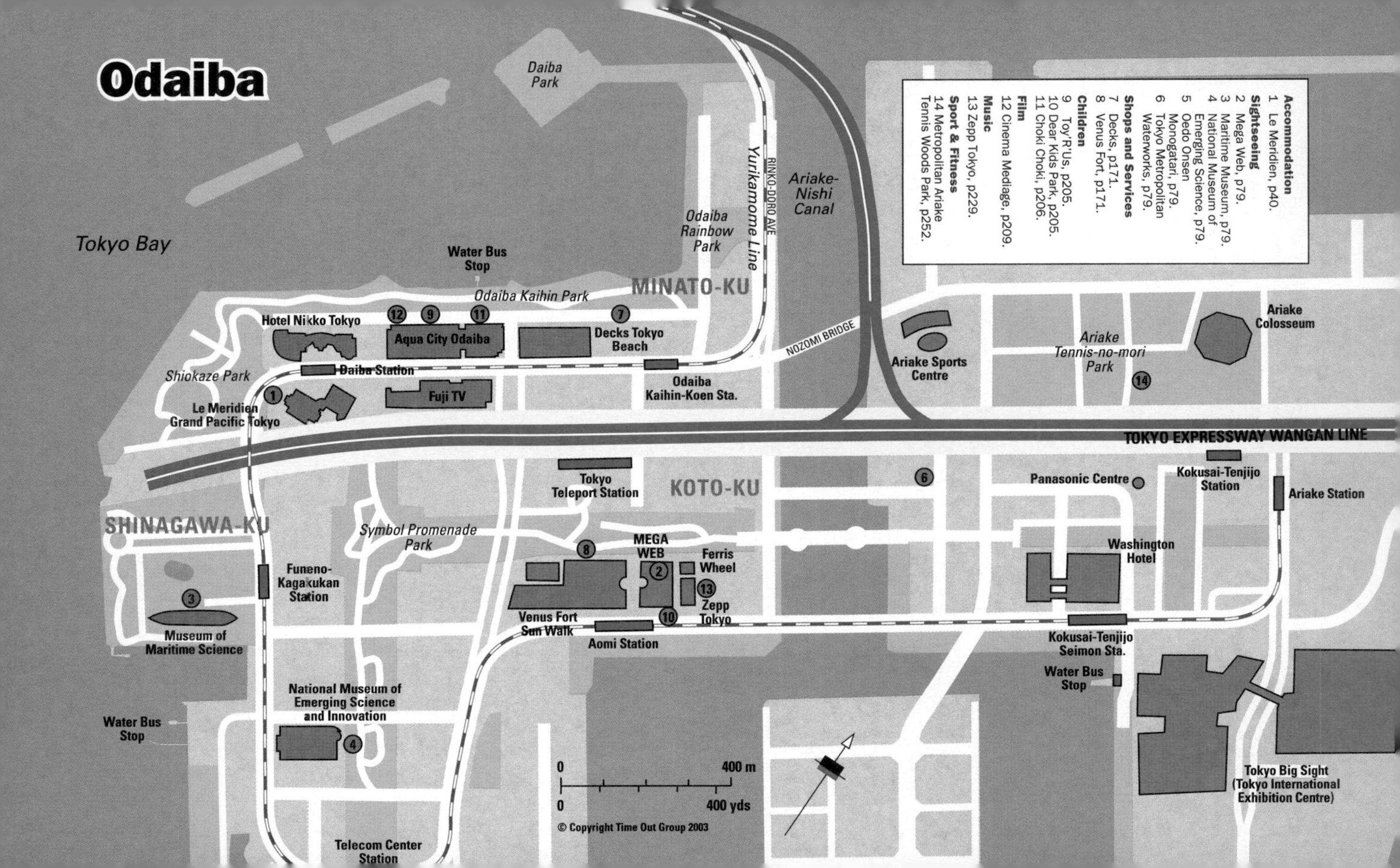
Odaiba
Accommodation
1 Le Meridien, p40.
Sightseeing
2 Mega Web, p79.
3 Maritime Museum, p79.
4 National Museum of Emerging Science, p79.
5 Oedo Onsen Monogatari, p79.
6 Tokyo Metropolitan Waterworks, p79.
Shops and Services
7 Decks, p171.
8 Venus Fort, p171.
Children
9 Toy'R'Us, p205.
10 Dear Kids Park, p205.
11 Choki Choki, p206.
Film
12 Cinema Mediage, p209.
Music
13 Zepp Tokyo, p229.
Sport & Fitness
14 Metropolitan Ariake Tennis Woods Park, p252.
Daiba Park
Tokyo Bay
Water Bus Stop
Odaiba Kaihin Park
Odaiba Rainbow Park
Yurikamome Line
RINKO-DORO AVE
Ariake-Nishi Canal
MINATO-KU
Hotel Nikko Tokyo
Aqua City Odaiba
Decks Tokyo Beach
NOZOMI BRIDGE
Ariake Sports Centre
Ariake Tennis-no-mori Park
Ariake Colosseum
Shiokaze Park
Daiba Station
Fuji TV
Odaiba Kaihin-Koen Sta.
Le Meridien Grand Pacific Tokyo
TOKYO EXPRESSWAY WANGAN LINE
Tokyo Teleport Station
KOTO-KU
Panasonic Centre
Kokusai-Tenjijo Station
Ariake Station
SHINAGAWA-KU
Symbol Promenade Park
MEGA WEB
Ferris Wheel
Zepp Tokyo
Washington Hotel
Funeno-Kagakukan Station
Venus Fort Sun Walk
Aomi Station
Kokusai-Tenjijo Seimon Sta.
Museum of Maritime Science
Water Bus Stop
National Museum of Emerging Science and Innovation
Water Bus Stop
0
400 m
0
400 yds
© Copyright Time Out Group 2003
Tokyo Big Sight (Tokyo International Exhibition Centre)
Telecom Center Station

the promenade beside Aqua City will give you a view of Tokyo Bay and the Rainbow Bridge, as well as the aforementioned Statue of Liberty. At the end of the promenade, you'll come to a central plaza where looms the **Fuji TV building**. The observation deck on the 25th floor – inside the huge metal sphere – gives a clear view over Tokyo as far as Mount Fuji.

A wide avenue behind the Fuji TV building will take you to the picturesque **Wildflower Park**, and from there the path straight ahead leads to the Aomi-Itchome area, with **Telecom Centre** in the distance. This towering building resembles the Arc de Triomphe redesigned by a *manga* artist and houses several restaurants. On the way there, you'll pass the **Museum of Maritime Science**, and the must-see **National Museum of Emerging Science and Innovation**, located in a futuristic precinct that'll make you wonder which half of the 21st century you're in. A few steps past the Telecom Centre, however, and you'll experience a severe case of time-slippage, because you'll be facing **Oedo Onsen Monogatari**, a hot-spring theme park with visitors in *yukata* (dressing gowns) strolling past traditional wooden bathhouses.

Back at the Wildflower Park, the path to the left will take you over the 'Dream Bridge' to **Palette Town**, home of **Mega Web**, one of Tokyo's newest amusement parks.

It's even possible to walk back to the rest of Tokyo across the Rainbow Bridge; it'll seem like walking off the set of a science-fiction film, and back into the 'real' world.

GETTING THERE

Odaiba is on the Yurikamome line. A one-day Yurikamome travel pass costs ¥800.

Sights

Mega Web

1 Aomi, Koto-ku (3599 0808/www.megaweb.gr.jp/English/index.html). Odaiba Kaihin Koen station (Yurikamome line). **Open** *Futureworld* 11am-11pm daily. *Toyota City Showcase* 11am-9pm daily. *History Garage* 11am-10pm daily. **Admission** free.

Part of the huge Palette Town development that opened on the island of Odaiba in 1999, Mega Web certainly lives up to its name; its giant Stream of Starlight ferris wheel – at 115m (383ft) the tallest in the world – is visible for miles, and brightly illuminated at night. Beneath it is the world's largest car showroom, the Toyota City Showcase. Here you can sit in the newest models, take a virtual drive (¥600), or be ferried around in the company's self-driving electric town-car prototypes (E-com ride, ¥200). Expect a queue for tickets, especially at weekends. There's also Futureworld, a virtual-reality rollercoaster, and History Garage, a motor museum.

Museum of Maritime Science (Fune-no-kagakukan)

3-1 Higashi-Yashio (Odaiba), Shinagawa-ku (5500 1111/www.funenokagakukan.or.jp). Fune-no-kagakukan station (Yurikamome line). **Open** *Winter* 10am-5pm Mon-Fri; 10am-6pm Sat, Sun. *Summer* 10am-6pm daily. **Admission** ¥700 main building only; ¥1,000 all areas; ¥400-¥600 concessions. **Credit** V (restaurant only).

The main building is ship-shaped. Outside there's a lighthouse, a seaplane, a bathysphere and a floating cruise liner with a so-called 'Magical Vision' theatre.
Restaurant.

National Museum of Emerging Science and Innovation (Nihon Kagaku Miraikan)

2-41 Aomi (Odaiba), Koto-ku (3570 9151/www.miraikan.jst.go.jp). Telecom Centre or Fune-no-kagakukan station (Yurikamome line). **Open** 10am-5pm Mon, Wed-Sun. **Admission** ¥500; ¥200 concessions; children free Sat.

Opened in 2001, this up-to-the-minute museum educates and entertains with the latest developments in science and technology. Robots, maglev, and micromachines – it's got the lot. A globe 6.5m (22ft) in diameter hangs in the central open space, the 851,000 LEDs on its surface showing real time global climatic changes.
English pamphlet. Gift shop. Restaurant.

Oedo Onsen Monogatari

2-57, Omi, Koto-ku (5500 1126/www.ooedoonsen.jp). Telecom Centre station (Yurikamome line). **Open** 11am-9am daily (last entry 2am). **Admission** ¥2,700; ¥800-¥1,500 concessions. Extra charge of ¥1,500 after midnight. **No credit cards**.

This extraordinary new theme park opened in March 2003, and aims to bring the current boom in hot-spring bathing into the city, along with a touch of nostalgia. There is something paradoxical about soaking in a hot tub in a traditionally constructed bathhouse, while at the same time contemplating the futuristic buildings of the rest of Odaiba through the windows. The price of admission includes *yukata* (dressing gown) and towels. As well as the expected hot tub, there's also an outdoor tub, hot sand baths and saunas. The foot massage bath and healing sauna are mixed, otherwise the sexes are segregated. Drunkenness or tattoos result in an instant ban.

Tokyo Metropolitan Waterworks Science Museum

2-4-1 Ariake, Koto-ku (3528 2366/www.waterworks.metro.tokyo.jp/pp/kagakukan/kagaku.htm). Kokusai Tenjijo-Seimon station (Yurikamome line). **Open** 9.30am-5pm Tue-Sun. **Admission** free.
No credit cards.

This museum channels a fundamental ingredient of life, water, into exciting displays and interactive games. Witness the cutting power of a high-pressure stream of water and marvel at an enormous underground pump. Take a virtual ride down a river with

sound effects, movement and all. If the scientific displays saturate your brain, chill out watching big bubbles pass through huge tubes in a dimly lit room.
English pamphlet.

Other sights in south Tokyo

Funasei Yakatabune

1-16-8 Kita-Shinagawa, Shinagawa-ku (5479 2731/ www.funasei.com). Kita-Shinagawa station (Keihin Kyuko line). **Open** 10am-7pm for reservations. **Average** incl food ¥10,000.

This is one of the few covered dining boats on the Sumida river that accepts bookings from individuals as well as parties. Choose between traditional Japanese meals of sushi and sashimi or western-style dishes, especially created for visitors. The booking number is operated in Japanese only, so get someone to call for you. Book early for the best view of the Sumida fireworks in July (*see p198*).

Hara Museum of Contemporary Art

4-7-25 Kita-Shinagawa, Shinagawa-ku (3445 0651/ www.haramuseum.or.jp). Shinagawa station Takanawa exit, then a 15-min walk. **Open** 11am-5pm Tue-Sun; 11am-8pm Wed. **Admission** ¥1,000; ¥500-¥700 concessions; free high school students 2nd & 4th Sat of mth. **Credit** AmEx, DC, MC, V.

Housed in a converted 1938 Bauhaus-style home built by art collector Hara Toshio, the museum hosts some of the best contemporary art shows in Tokyo. Several pieces from the permanent collection are dedicated installations, while temporary exhibitions often feature new work by international stars, but also take chances with emerging artists, lesser-knowns, and design. The tranquil grounds are a remnant of an all-but-extinct central Tokyo lifestyle.
Café. Gift shop. English pamphlet.

Hatakeyama Memorial Museum

2-20-12 Shirokanedai, Minato-ku (3447 5787/www. ebara.co.jp/culture/hatakeyama). Shirokanedai or Takanawadai station (Toei Asakusa Line). **Open** *Oct-Mar* 10am-4.30pm Tue-Sun. *Apr-Sept* 10am-5pm Tue-Sun. **Admission** ¥500; ¥350 concessions.

Hatakeyama Issei was a man of many talents. He founded the Ebara Corporation, makers of industrial pumps and waste incinerators. He assembled a small but exquisite collection of Chinese, Korean and Japanese traditional arts (with an emphasis on Noh and tea ceremony-related objects). And he designed this museum, in the quiet backstreets of residential Shirokanedai. Exhibitions change seasonally.
Gift shop.

Kyu Shiba-Rikyu Garden

1-4-1 Kaigan, Minato-ku (3434 4029). Hamamatsucho station, north exit or Daimon station, exit B2. **Open** 9am-5pm (last entry 4.30pm) daily. **Admission** ¥150.

Another beautiful landscaped garden, not far from the larger Hama-Rikyu Detached Garden (*see p59*). This one is laid out around a central pond, with an island connected by a stone walkway (a miniature of an ancient Chinese original) on one side and a bridge on the other. There's also an archery range, which costs an additional ¥140 per hour to use.

Mukai Junkichi Annex, Setagaya Art Museum

2-5-1 Tsurumaki, Setagaya-ku (5450 9581/www. setagayaartmuseum.or.jp). Komazawa Daigaku station (Tokyu Denentoshi Line), west exit. **Open** 10am-6pm Tue-Sun. **Admission** ¥200; ¥100-¥150 concessions.

Born in 1901, painter Mukai Junichi made his home and studio in this traditional Japanese house. He donated the house and 500 paintings to the Setagaya Art Museum (*see below*) in July 1993. Mukai's lifelong mission was to capture Japan's disappearing thatched farmhouses in his work. The garden's carefully maintained oaks hark back to the Tsurumaki area's past as part of the Musashino forest.
Gift shop.

Sea Line Tokyo Company Ltd

2-7-104 Kaigan, Minato-ku (reservations 3798 8101/www.symphony-cruise.co.jp). Hamamatsucho station.

If you want to take in Tokyo Bay in style, Sea Line offers four departures a day from Hinode Pier, at 11.50am, 3pm, 4.30pm and 7.10pm. At lunch and dinner there's a choice of Italian or French meals in the ship's plush restaurant (bookings required, average ¥13,000), though you're free just to take in the scenery of the Bay, which will include Rainbow Bridge, the Disney Resort and a glimpse of the open sea. Cruises last 50, 120 or 150 minutes, depending on the time of day.

Sengaku-ji Temple

2-11-1 Takanawa, Minato-ku (3441 5560/www. sengakuji.or.jp). Sengaku-ji station (Toei Asakusa Line), exit A2. **Open** *Temple* 7am-6pm daily. *Museum* 9am-4pm daily. **Admission** free.

The most interesting thing about this temple is its connection with one of Japan's most famous stories – that of 47 samurai attached to Lord Ako (*see p8*). After he drew his sword on a rival, Kira Yoshinaka, in Edo Castle (a serious breach of protocol), Ako was ordered to commit *seppuku* (death by ritual disembowelment). He was buried here. His 47 loyal followers then became *ronin*, or samurai without a master, bent on avenging their master's death. They killed Kira and were then themselves permitted to die in the same manner as their master, and to be buried close to him, here at Sengaku-ji. Their tombs are at the top of a flight of steps. Follow the smoke trails from the incense left by well-wishers.

Setagaya Art Museum

1-2 Kinuta Koen, Setagaya-ku (3415 6011/www. setagayaartmuseum.or.jp). Denenchofu station (Tokyu Toyoko line), then bus bound for Chitose Funabashi. Alight at Bijutsukan Iriguchi stop. **Open** 10am-6pm Tue-Sun. **Admission** ¥200; ¥100-¥150 concessions; children free Sat. Additional fee for special exhibitions.

Odaiba's landmark **Telecom Centre** building. *See p79.*

This ward-owned museum, set in a beautiful Kinuta Park, compares favourably with Tokyo's better private museums. Though its once edgy, international exhibitions have become more conservative since curator Yuko Hasegawa left, the museum still produces interesting shows, such as a recent Miró retrospective that focused on the Spanish painter's innovative early work. Regardless of the show, the attractive Frank Lloyd Wright-inspired building and surrounding grounds are reason enough to visit.
Gift shop. Lockers. Restaurant.

Shiba Park

4-10-17 Shiba Koen, Minato-ku (3431 4359). Shiba Koen station (Toei Mita Line), exit A4. **Open** 24hrs daily.

Situated near Tokyo Tower (*see p77*), this park is the spot for great memorial photos of your trip, with the Tower and Zojo-ji Temple (*see below*) framed in a classic Tokyo shot. In the summer several pools are open to the public and there are playgrounds, a bowling alley and other attractions, all of which are within walking distance.

Shinagawa Aquarium

3-2-1 Katsushima, Shinagawa-ku (3762 3433/www.aquarium.gr.jp/home.html). Omorikaigan station (Keihin Kyuko Line). **Open** 10am-5pm Mon, Wed-Sun. **Admission** ¥1,100; ¥300-¥600 concessions.

Divided into sea surface and sea floor levels, Shinagawa Aquarium (which is actually some distance from Shinagawa station) covers most aspects of marine life. The main attractions are the dolphin and sea lion shows (four or five times a day) as well as the tunnel water tank, in which you walk through a tank of fish. Other displays include freshwater fish and river life, corals, fish that make sounds, unusual sea life and the sea at Shinagawa. To get there, take the train from Shinagawa.

Sony the Museum

Sony Headquarters Bldg, 6-7-35 Kita Shinagawa, Shinagawa-ku (5448 4455/www.sony.co.jp/SonyInfo/Environment/ecoplaza/museum.html). Shinagawa, Gotanda, or Osaki stations. **Open** 10am-5pm Mon-Fri. 50-min tour available by appointment. **Admission** free.

A range of products from Sony's early days to the latest innovations are on display here. The most interesting part of the museum, however, is the interactive Environmental Exhibition Room. You can see how old electronic equipment is recycled and how Sony uses an ingredient derived from oranges to harmlessly break down Styrofoam.

Zenpuku-ji Temple

1-6-21 Moto-Azabu, Minato-ku (3451 7402/www.azabu-san.or.jp). Azabu-Juban station, exit 1. **Open** 9am-5pm daily.

This temple, founded in 832, has been repeatedly destroyed by fire, most recently in World War II. Rebuilt after the war, its main claim to fame is as the site of the first American legation to Japan under the leadership of Townsend Harris, from 1859 to 1875.

Zojo-ji Temple

4-7-35 Shiba Koen, Minato-ku (3432 1431). Shiba Koen station (Toei Mita Line), exit A4. **Open** *Temple* 6am-5.30pm daily. *Grounds* 24hrs daily.

Today, Zojo-ji is something of a disappointment: it's hard to imagine that in the 17th century, 48 temples stood on this site. The main hall has been destroyed three times by fire in the last century, the current building being a post-World War II reconstruction. The most interesting thing in the temple grounds is the historic Sanmon gate, which in each of its three sections represents three of the stages that are necessary to attain nirvana. The gate, which dates back to 1605, is the oldest wooden structure in Tokyo.

East City

The historic eastern part of Tokyo enchants with its ancient temples, marvellous museums and quaint, old-fashioned neighbourhoods.

Nakamise Dori, the heart of Asakusa.

Asakusa

Map p83

If a city can be said to have a heart and soul, then Tokyo's soul has to be Asakusa, and the heart of Asakusa itself is **Senso-ji Temple**. Every year millions of visitors stand before the three-metre-high red lantern that hangs above Kaminarimon (Thunder Gate), the portal to the inner sanctum guarded by likenesses of Raijin, god of thunder, and Fujin, god of wind. Asakusa is Tokyo's biggest tourist attraction, one of its most ancient districts, a bridge between the city of skyscrapers and old Edo.

Asakusa is in one of Tokyo's *shitamachi* (downtown) neighbourhoods, and Senso-ji Temple has been an integral part of it from the very beginning. Established in 645, Senso-ji is the oldest temple in Tokyo, and is dedicated to Kannon, the Buddhist goddess of mercy.

When Senso-ji became the shogunate's main place of prayer, and the nearby Sumida river became one of Edo's important transportation routes, Asakusa began to grow in influence. The merchant class, despite having social positions rigidly defined by the constantly suspicious shogunate, nevertheless acquired considerable financial power and prestige.

Asakusa also began to acquire a reputation as an entertainment district. The new art forms of *kabuki* and *bunraku* (puppet theatre) were brought from Kyoto in the early Edo era – their dramatic storytelling and costumes greatly appealing to the moneyed merchant class. Despite official disapproval, the hedonistic atmosphere of the *ukiyo-e* ('floating world') found its home in Asakusa and the nearby 'licensed pleasure-quarters' of Yoshiwara.

The area continued to grow during the Meiji and Taisho periods, with Tokyo's first subway route opening between Asakusa and Ueno in 1927. However, the narrow mazes of wooden buildings were under constant threat from fire. During World War II large parts of Tokyo were levelled by bombing raids, the *shitamachi* area suffering heavily, and in March 1945 Asakusa was almost completely destroyed by the heaviest air raid inflicted upon Tokyo.

After the war the rebuilding began, but the atmosphere had changed; prostitution was officially outlawed in the 1950s, and the Yoshiwara area declined to the stage where it no longer appears on maps. The swaggering merchants and delicate kimono-clad ladies faded into memory – with the exception of Mukoujima, across the river, one of Tokyo's oldest surviving geisha houses. Other areas, Shinjuku and Marunouchi, were swiftly built up as new commercial and social centres. Asakusa was overtaken by progress – until recently, when the Japanese rediscovered Asakusa as a place that contains all the qualities that make Tokyo what it is, was, and might one day be.

Asakusa is approached by the Ginza or Toei Asakusa lines, and is square on the banks of the Sumida river, where it's possible to take a cruise boat for a leisurely tour of Tokyo by waterbus or *yakata-bune* boat. The waterbus cruise takes approximately 40 minutes from Asakusa to Hinode Pier near Odaiba, travelling under 12 bridges and passing rows of old

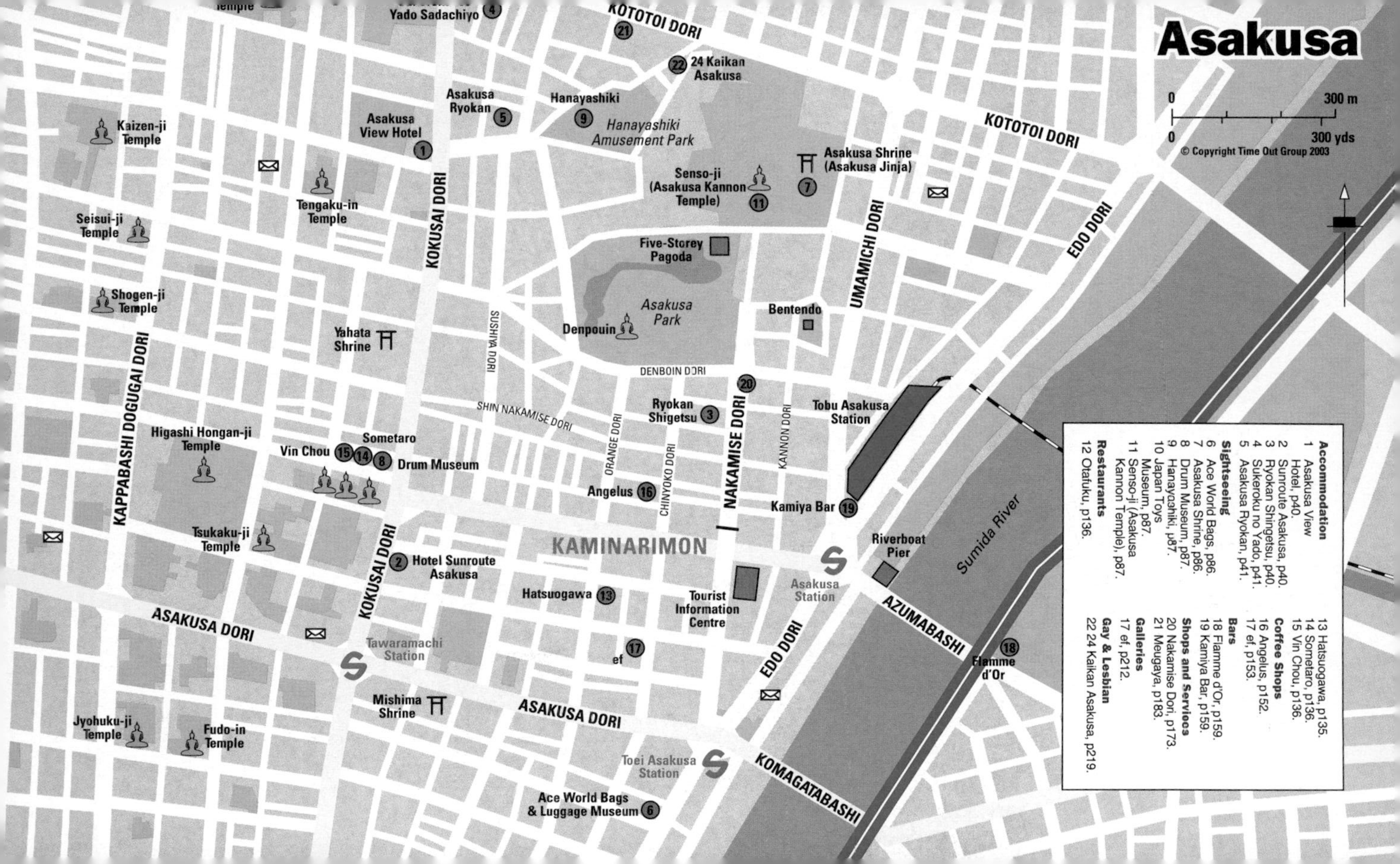
Asakusa
0
300 m
0
300 yds
© Copyright Time Out Group 2003
Accommodation
1 Asakusa View Hotel, p40.
2 Sunroute Asakusa, p40.
3 Ryokan Shingetsu, p40.
4 Sukeroku no Yado, p41.
5 Asakusa Ryokan, p41.
Sightseeing
6 Ace World Bags, p86.
7 Asakusa Shrine, p86.
8 Drum Museum, p87.
9 Hanayashiki, p87.
10 Japan Toys Museum, p87.
11 Senso-ji (Asakusa Kannon Temple), p87.
Restaurants
12 Otafuku, p136.
13 Hatsuogawa, p135.
14 Sometaro, p136.
15 Vin Chou, p136.
Coffee Shops
16 Angelus, p152.
17 ef, p153.
Bars
18 Flamme d'Or, p159.
19 Kamiya Bar, p159.
Shops and Services
20 Nakamise Dori, p173.
21 Meugaya, p183.
Galleries
17 ef, p212.
Gay & Lesbian
22 24 Kaikan Asakusa, p219.
Yado Sadachiyo
KOTOTOI DORI
24 Kaikan Asakusa
Asakusa Ryokan
Hanayashiki
Hanayashiki Amusement Park
Asakusa View Hotel
Kaizen-ji Temple
Tengaku-in Temple
Senso-ji (Asakusa Kannon Temple)
Asakusa Shrine (Asakusa Jinja)
Seisui-ji Temple
KOKUSAI DORI
Five-Storey Pagoda
UMAMICHI DORI
EDO DORI
Shogen-ji Temple
Asakusa Park
Denpouin
Bentendo
Yahata Shrine
SUSHIYA DORI
KAPPABASHI DOGUGAI DORI
DENBOIN DORI
SHIN NAKAMISE DORI
Ryokan Shigetsu
Tobu Asakusa Station
Higashi Hongan-ji Temple
Sometaro
Vin Chou
Drum Museum
ORANGE DORI
CHINYOKO DORI
NAKAMISE DORI
KANNON DORI
Angelus
Kamiya Bar
Sumida River
Tsukaku-ji Temple
KAMINARIMON
Riverboat Pier
Hotel Sunroute Asakusa
Asakusa Station
Hatsuogawa
Tourist Information Centre
AZUMABASHI
ASAKUSA DORI
Tawaramachi Station
ef
Flamme d'Or
Mishima Shrine
Jyohuku-ji Temple
Fudo-in Temple
Toei Asakusa Station
KOMAGATABASHI
Ace World Bags & Luggage Museum

Japanese houses. The *yakata-bune* are also floating restaurants, where passengers can recline on tatami and watch the city's sights slide past while enjoying traditional Japanese cuisine. The boats' speciality is Edomae tempura, using fish caught in Tokyo bay.

By leaving Asakusa station, and standing on the corner of the Umamichi Dori, you are at 1-1-1 Taito-ku – the address of Tokyo's oldest western-style hostelry, Kamiya Bar (*see p159*), renowned as the home of 'Denki-Bran' (Electric Brandy), a dubious alcoholic concoction that produces truly spectacular hangovers. Looking over Azuma Bridge, the Bubble-era **Asahi Building** stands out for its sheer audacity. Designed by Philippe Starck, its bulk is said to remind the onlooker of a glass of dark beer, and is surmounted by a golden 'object' that has been the cause of furtive giggles ever since. The architectural confusion is increased by the addition of a pagoda-style roof for the police box just before the turning on to the bridge.

The little museums of Sumida-ku

On the surface, Sumida-ku looks like any working-class Japanese neighbourhood. Unlike much of Tokyo, however, families have lived here in *shitamachi* (the traditional part of town) for generations. The Little Museums of Sumida-ku, spread between the Sumida and Arakawa rivers, reflect this heritage. Many are functioning shops with displays showing their history and techniques.

Several factors, however, make visits complicated. Museum hours are erratic: appointments are often required, but few of the proprietors speak English. Streets are narrow, and addresses confusing. Luckily, the international section of the Sumida-ku City Cultural Affairs Office can contact the museums and provide detailed maps.

Information is available online at www.city.sumida.tokyo.jp/english/guide/museums.

Sumida-ku Office

Cultural Affairs Department, 1-23-20 Azumabashi (5608 6186). Asakusa station, exit 5. **Open** 8.30am-5.15pm Mon-Fri.

Alloy Casting Museum

2-4-14 Bunka (3612 2773). Tobu Omurai station (Tobu Kameido Line). **Open** 9am-5pm 1st, 2nd & 3rd Fri, Sat of mth.
Moulds and panels on display illustrate the casting process and how the Giant Buddha in Kamakura was made.

Battledore Museum

5-43-25 Mukojima (3623 1305). Tobu Hikifune station (Tobu Isezaki, Kameido lines). **Open** 10am-5pm Thur-Sat. Closed Oct 1-Jan 20.
The history of battledore (the predecessor to badminton) or *hagoita* as it's called in Japan, is explained at this museum. Displays showcase the production process and fine examples of pre-war bats.

Construction Tools & Wooden Frame Museum

1-5-3 Kikukawa (3633 0328). Morishita station (Toei Shinjuku, Oedo lines). **Open** 10am-4pm Sat & 4th Sun of mth.
Wooden houses were traditionally built without nails, here you can see how it was done.

Dry Woodwork Museum

Kanso Mokuzai Kogei Bldg, 2-9-11 Kinshi (3625 2401). Kinshicho station. **Open** 10am-5pm daily. Reservations required.
Exhibits include toys, folk handcrafts, and special furniture made from 'dry wood'.

Edo Textile Designs Museum

Oomatu Dye Factory, 2-26-9 Yahiro (3611 5019/http://e-sumida.gr.jp/daimatsu). Keisei-Hikifune station (Keisei Oshiage Line). **Open** 11am-5pm Mon-Fri (Sat by appointment).
Komon is the word used to describe the intricate patterns seen on kimono and other textiles. Thousands of traditional Edo era fabric patterns can be viewed here.

Folding Screen Museum

1-31-6 Mukojima (3622 4470/www.byoubu.co.jp). Tobu Narihirabashi station (Tobu Isezaki Line). **Open** 9am-5pm Mon-Sat. Closed 2nd and 4th Sat of mth May-Sept.
Screens from the Nara to Edo periods are displayed as well as the tools that were used to make them.

Kobayashi Doll Museum

6-31-2 Yahiro (3612 1644). Keise Yahiro station (Keisei Oshiage Line). **Open** 10.30am-5pm Fri-Sun, by appointment only.
Watch the Kobayashi brothers make handcrafted dolls in their workshop. Upstairs, a small museum displays dolls dating from the Edo period to the present, among them the 'honour dolls' given to *kamikaze* pilots.

Entering **Senso-ji Temple** through the **Kaminarimon** gate, the path to the inner sanctum leads down **Nakamise Dori**, the avenue of tiny stalls selling traditional sweets and toys. Shops of this kind have been here ever since the 1700s, and among the specialities on offer are *kaminari-okoshii* ('thunder' rice crackers), and *ningyo-yaki* (sweet red bean buns moulded into doll-shapes). Just before the main hall stands the *okouro* or incense-burner, with a continual flow of people crowding round to 'bathe' in the smoke, which is said to possess wisdom-giving powers. Behind and to the right of the main hall is **Asakusa Shrine**, the starting point of Tokyo's biggest festival – the Sanja Matsuri, and to the left is a five-storey pagoda, the second highest pagoda in Japan.

Going right through the precincts of Senso-ji Temple will lead you to the Kototoi Dori, and by turning left, you'll walk past the **Goro-Goro Taiken Theatre**, famous for displays of highly stylised swordsmanship. Turning left

Koimari Porcelain Museum

Ace Motors Inc 2F, 5-23-9 Yahiro (3619 3867). Keisei Yahiro station (Keisei Oshiage Line). **Open** 11am-6pm Sat.
Displays of domestic ware from the Edo period.

Noh Mask Museum

5-10-5 Narihira (3623 3055). Narihirabashi station (Tobu Isezaki Line)/Keisei Oshiage station (Keisei Oshiage Line). **Open** 9am-5pm Tue, Sat & 4th Sun of mth.
Learn about the time-consuming process of making a Noh mask and see 50 examples.

Rubber Baseball Museum

2-36-10 Sumida (3614 3501/www.nagase-kenko.com) Tobu Kanegafuchi station (Tobu Isezaki Line). **Open** 10am-4pm Mon-Fri and 1st, 3rd & 5th Sat of mth.
Find out the history and production process of rubber baseballs, bats, gloves.

Safe and Key Museum

3-4-1 Chitose (3633 9151). Morishita station (Toei Shinjuku, Oedo lines) Ryogoku JR station, east exit. **Open** 10am-5pm 1st & 3rd Sat, Sun of mth. Closed Aug.
Unlock the history of safes.

Sumida Housing Centre, Wooden House Museum

1-7-16 Tsutsumi-dori (3612 7724). Higashi Mukojima station (Tobu Isezaki Line). **Open** 10am-4pm Sat & 4th Sun of mth.
How were traditional wooden houses made?

Sumo Photograph Museum

3-13-2 Ryogoku (3631 2150). Ryogoku JR station, east exit or Toei Oedo Line, exit A4). **Open** 10am-5pm Tue; daily during the Jan, May & Sept tournaments.
Sumo history is described through photographs and memorabilia.

Suzuki Carpenter's Museum

6-38-15 Higashi-Mukojima (3616 5008). Tobu Higashi-Mukojima station (Tobu Isezaki Line). **Open** 10am-4pm daily by appointment only.
Here you can see examples of embossing, lathing and other handcrafted woodwork.

Tabi Museum

1-9-3 Midori (3631 0092). Ryogoku JR station, west exit or Toei Oedo Line, exit A1. **Open** 9am-6pm Mon-Sat.
One of only three places still making custom tabi – traditional split toe socks—this has been a family affair for ten generations. Footprints of sumo wrestlers (e.g. Akebono) and other famous tabi-wearers (e.g. the King of Tonga) are exhibited.

Tortoiseshell Museum

2-5-5 Yokoami (3625 5875/www.tukuru.gr.jp/info/info_fl.htm). Ryogoku JR station, west exit orToei Oedo Line, exit A1. **Open** 10am-5.30pm daily.
Tools to carve tortoiseshell hair combs and ornamental hairpins (and the products themselves) are exhibited here.

Traditional Wood Sculpture Museum

4-7-8 Higashi-Komagata (3623 0273). Honjo Azumabashi station (Toei Asakusa Line). **Open** noon-5pm 1st, 2nd & 3rd Fri, Sat of mth.
Learn the history of the wood carvings used to decorate temples and shrines.

Wood Carving Museum

1-13-3 Ishihara (3622 4920/www.tukuru.gr.jp/matsumoku). Ryogoku JR station, west exit or Toei Oedo Line, exit A2. **Open** 10am-4pm Sat.
This museum exhibits carved wood of every type imaginable, from intricate handmade signboards to chopsticks.

again at a small *shotengai* called Hisagao Dori , which terminates at Rokku Broadway, the entrance to **Hanayashiki Amusement Park**. Hanayashiki, opened in 1853, is the home of Japan's oldest steel-track rollercoaster ride, and an exceedingly scary haunted house known as the Obake-yashiki.

Leaving Hanayashiki, you'll find yourself in the small district known as **Rokku**, in pre-war times a thriving downtown area. A revival of interest has led to its recent gentrification, as can be seen by the prominent presence of the Comme Ça Store and Uniqlo – but the *shitamachi* spirit refuses to die. Folk music drifts from the open doorways of Engei Hall, the home of the *rakugoka*, Japan's traditional wits and storytellers. Garish posters of 1960s Yakuza films are pasted outside the Shin-Gekijo, Meiga-za and Toho cinemas. TV screens showing horse-racing – the traditional gambling pursuit of the middle-aged male – can be glimpsed inside the massive Asakusa Winds Building, where racecourse tickets are sold.

Leaving the Asakusa area, the Kokusai Dori will take you to the Kappabashi Dori, with streets lined with stores selling knives, dishes and all forms of kitchen utensils, as well as the plastic models of food that can be seen outside so many Japanese restaurants.

Asakusa is home to festivals both old and new, which means that it still hasn't entirely lost the hedonistic edge acquired during the Edo period. The **Sanja Matsuri** is Tokyo's oldest and biggest festival, a frenzied procession of over a hundred *mikoshi* (portable shrines) held annually in early May. There are many other festivals throughout the year, the most modern of which being the **Tokyo Samba Festival** in late August, when hundreds of Brazilian and Japanese dancers parade through the streets. Japan's biggest annual summertime fireworks display is held annually on the banks of the Sumida river, and broadcast on national TV. For all, *see p194* **Festivals & Events**.

The legend of the founding of Senso-ji Temple tells us that a statue of Kannon was found in the waters on the Sumida, caught in the fishing nets of two brothers. Even though they put it back in the river, it kept returning to them, and they had the temple built to enshrine it. It's a perfect metaphor for Asakusa itself; a place hauled out of time, territory dredged up from the subconscious of the nation itself, that reminds us no matter how fast the city seems to change, some things will never truly be lost.

GETTING THERE

Asakusa is on the Ginza and the Toei Asakusa lines.

Asakusa's **five-storey pagoda**. *See p85.*

Sights

Ace World Bags & Luggage Museum

Ace Bldg 8F, 1-8-10 Komagata, Taito-ku (3847 5515/www.acebag.co.jp/museum). Asakusa station, exit 1. **Open** 10am-4.30pm Mon-Fri. **Admission** free.

This three-room museum takes a look at bags from around the world. Inspired by a leather museum he saw in Germany, Ace Luggage owner Shinkawa Ryusaku opened his own version on the eighth floor of his company's HQ in 1975. From Thailand, there's a 1974 purse made of patchwork frog skin and a 1977 handbag with fanned anteater hide. And check out the Japanese bag made from the skin of an unborn calf, a material now thankfully illegal.

Asakusa Shrine (Asakusa Jinja)

2-3-1 Asakusa, Taito-ku (3844 1575/www.asakusajinja.com/index_2.html). Asakusa station, exits 1, 3, 6, A4. **Open** *Shrine* 6.30am-5pm daily. *Grounds* 24hrs daily.

The Asakusa Shrine was established in 1649 to honour the three fishermen who, 1,000 years before, had found the Kannon statue in their nets, which led to the founding of the Asakusa Kannon Temple. Nicknamed 'Sanja-sama' (the three shrines), the shrine is host to the annual Sanja Matsuri (Sanja festival) in May (*see p198*).

Asakusa's **temple complex** is the biggest tourist attraction in Tokyo.

Drum Museum (Taiko-kan)

Miyamoto Unosuke Shoten, Nishi-Asakusa Bldg 4F, 2-1-1 Nishi-Asakusa, Taito-ku (3842 5622/www.tctv.ne.jp/members/taikokan). Tawaramachi station, exit 3. **Open** 10am-5pm Wed-Sun. **Admission** ¥300; ¥150 concessions.

With a clay drum from Mexico, an *udekki* from Sri Lanka and hundreds of other drums from around the world, this interactive museum is hard to beat. Find your own rhythm by banging on many of them (a blue dot means it's OK, a red one means it's not).
Gift shop.

Hanayashiki

2-28-1 Asakusa, Taito-ku (3842 8780/www.hanayashiki.net/first.html). Asakusa station, exit 3. **Open** 10am-6pm Mon, Wed-Sun. **Admission** ¥900; ¥400 concessions.

Japan's oldest amusement park is close to Asakusa's Senso-ji and has been in business since 1885. It still draws crowds, but while most rides have been upgraded over the years, their scope is limited due to the park's small size. There are around 20 rides, more appealing for nostalgia than for thrills.

Japan Toys Museum

Tsukuda Group Bldg 9F, 1-36-10 Hashiba, Taito-ku (3874 5133/www.toynes.or.jp/e2-1-1.htm). Bus from Asakusa station bound for Minami Senju via Ishihama, then 5min walk from Kiyokawa Itchome bus stop. **Open** 9.30am-5pm Wed-Sun; closed 3rd Wed of mth. **Admission** ¥200; ¥100 concessions.

Serious collectors will appreciate the 8,000 toys, categorised by year, ranging from Meiji-era wooden toys to a remote-controlled Godzilla. Though most toys are stored behind glass, there's a small number available for play.
Gift shop.

Senso-ji (Asakusa Kannon Temple)

2-3-1 Asakusa, Taito-ku (3842 0181). Asakusa station, exits 1, 3, 6, A4. **Open** *Temple* 6am-5pm daily. *Grounds* 24hrs daily.

The origins of Tokyo's oldest temple are said to go back to the year 645, when three fishermen found a statue of Kannon in their nets. The temple is now the centrepiece of Tokyo's biggest tourist attraction.

Tokyo Water Cruise

3841 9178/Hinode Pier 3457 7830/www.suijobus.co.jp/cruise.

Waterbuses cruise the Sumida river along five routes, taking in the old bridges and the newer Rainbow Bridge en route. The lines converge at Hinode Pier, a five-minute walk from Hamamatsucho station. The best point of departure is Asakusa, where the boats leave Azuma Bridge bound for the beautiful Hama-Rikyu Detached Garden (*see p59*). Boats depart every 20-45 minutes and tickets cost ¥620 (there's a separate entry fee for Hama-Rikyu). The last boat for Hama-Rikyu leaves Asakusa at 3pm (the gardens close early), while the last boat leaves Asakusa at 7.55pm.

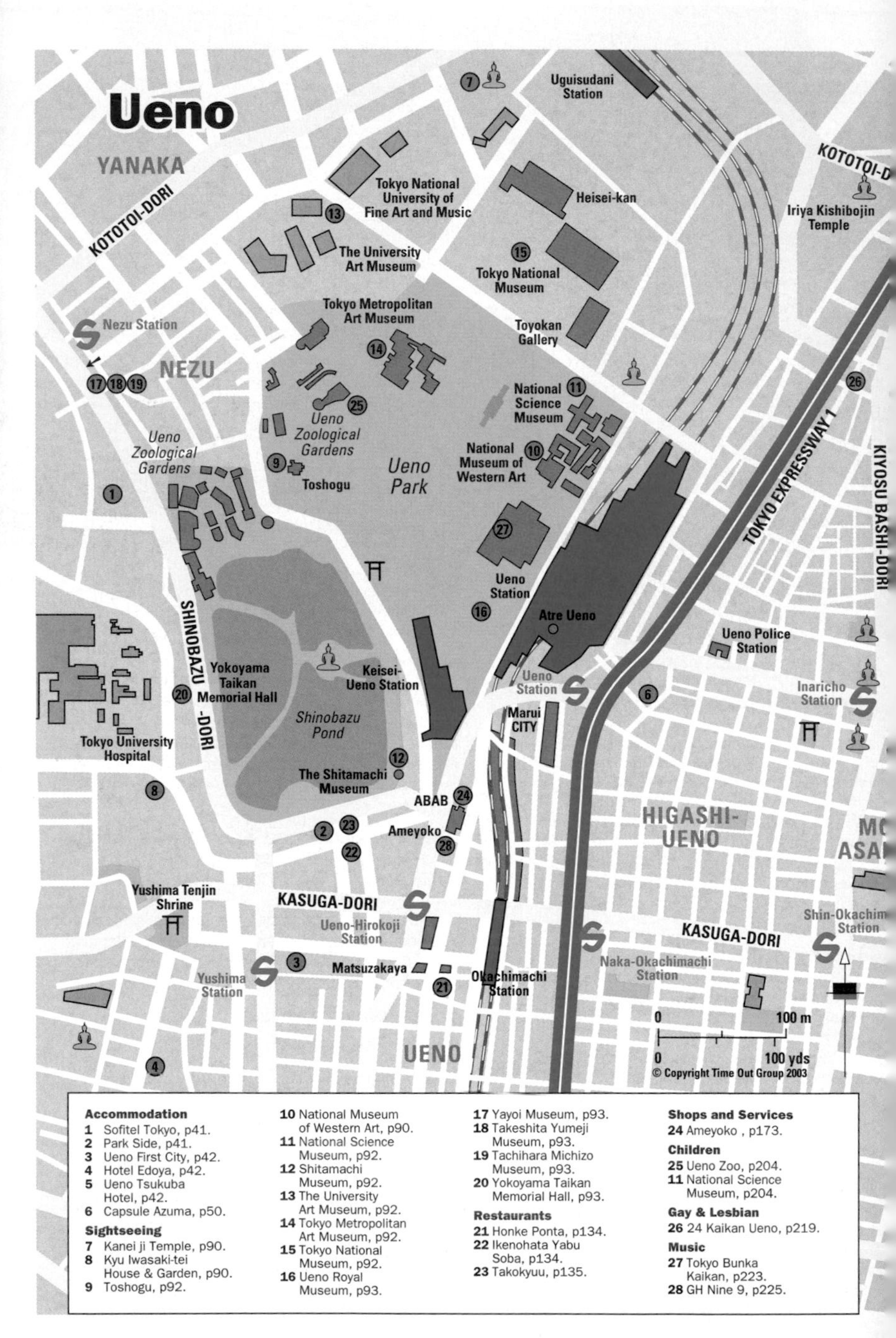
Ueno
YANAKA
KOTOTOI-DORI
Nezu Station
NEZU
Ueno Zoological Gardens
Tokyo National University of Fine Art and Music
The University Art Museum
Tokyo Metropolitan Art Museum
Ueno Zoological Gardens
Toshogu
Ueno Park
Uguisudani Station
Heisei-kan
Tokyo National Museum
Toyokan Gallery
National Science Museum
National Museum of Western Art
KOTOTOI-D
Iriya Kishibojin Temple
TOKYO EXPRESSWAY 1
KIYOSU BASHI-DORI
Ueno Station
Atre Ueno
Ueno Police Station
Ueno Station
Inaricho Station
Marui CITY
SHINOBAZU -DORI
Yokoyama Taikan Memorial Hall
Keisei-Ueno Station
Shinobazu Pond
Tokyo University Hospital
The Shitamachi Museum
ABAB
Ameyoko
HIGASHI-UENO
Yushima Tenjin Shrine
KASUGA-DORI
Ueno-Hirokoji Station
Matsuzakaya
Yushima Station
Okachimachi Station
Naka-Okachimachi Station
KASUGA-DORI
Shin-Okachim Station
UENO
0 100 m
0 100 yds
© Copyright Time Out Group 2003
Accommodation
1 Sofitel Tokyo, p41.
2 Park Side, p41.
3 Ueno First City, p42.
4 Hotel Edoya, p42.
5 Ueno Tsukuba Hotel, p42.
6 Capsule Azuma, p50.
Sightseeing
7 Kanei ji Temple, p90.
8 Kyu Iwasaki-tei House & Garden, p90.
9 Toshogu, p92.
10 National Museum of Western Art, p90.
11 National Science Museum, p92.
12 Shitamachi Museum, p92.
13 The University Art Museum, p92.
14 Tokyo Metropolitan Art Museum, p92.
15 Tokyo National Museum, p92.
16 Ueno Royal Museum, p93.
17 Yayoi Museum, p93.
18 Takeshita Yumeji Museum, p93.
19 Tachihara Michizo Museum, p93.
20 Yokoyama Taikan Memorial Hall, p93.
Restaurants
21 Honke Ponta, p134.
22 Ikenohata Yabu Soba, p134.
23 Takokyuu, p135.
Shops and Services
24 Ameyoko , p173.
Children
25 Ueno Zoo, p204.
11 National Science Museum, p204.
Gay & Lesbian
26 24 Kaikan Ueno, p219.
Music
27 Tokyo Bunka Kaikan, p223.
28 GH Nine 9, p225.

Ueno

Map p88

Ueno Park may have the highest concentration of top-class museums in the world, but there's still an appealing air of lost grandeur about the Ueno area of Tokyo as a whole. Before leaving the station, head to its main (above ground) hall, one of the few station buildings in Tokyo to have largely survived Japan's decades of redevelopment. The height of the ceilings and grandiose architectural style recall a time when this was one of the city's main transport hubs, ferrying people in from the north in the days before the *shinkansen* dragged most of the passengers away to the main terminus at Tokyo station. Those were the days, too, when the east side of Tokyo was king, and Asakusa and Ueno were the city's playgrounds, before the action started to drift westwards, to Shibuya and Shinjuku. The first subway line in Asia opened in 1927 to link Asakusa to Ueno, and is now part of the Ginza Line.

Nowadays, few Japanese make the trip to Ueno, and even fewer foreigners. It's a pity, because this is probably the last major Tokyo centre not to have been entirely colonised by the shopping chain-gang. As a result, it's more low-rise than much of the rest of Tokyo, and although chain coffee shops and stores do exist, they do so in harmony with long-established businesses and the famous, bustling market.

MARKET

To get a full-blast feel of Ueno, head there on a Saturday or Sunday, when the market's in full swing. Head for the Shinobazu exit of the JR station, or exit 5 from the subway, and on the other side of a very wide pedestrian crossing, you'll see **Ameyoko**, the area's bustling shopping centre. The market here grew up in the years following the war. With much of Ueno flattened, this was the place people came to buy provisions, often on the black market. Even today this spirit survives, and in among the myriad fishmongers and fruit and vegetable stalls, there are scores of small shops selling cheap jeans, T-shirts, and goods 'inspired' by exclusive international designers. The market is also one of the few places in Tokyo that is a reliable source of hard-to-find foods and spices.

At the weekend, you'll be shoulder to shoulder with Tokyo's Indian and Thai families stocking up on green chillies, basmati or Thai rice and coriander. And homesick Americans have been known to seek solace here in genuine Milky Way bars or Hershey's chocolate imported from the States, rather than Australia, as is the norm in Japan. At a fork in the road about 90 metres (300 feet) into Ameyoko, there stands a dubious-looking building with an amazing food hall in the basement, selling whole frogs, durian, and other impossible-to-get delicacies from around the world. Meanwhile, under the railway tracks, cheap watches and electronic goods are the order of the day, along with the occasional seller of bootleg CDs.

CULTURE

If down and dirty shopping's not your thing, then Ueno also has much to offer in the way of culture. **Ueno Park** is home to some of Japan's greatest cultural assets, and contains the world's highest concentration of international-class museums. The park is on the opposite side of the station from the market; to get there, take the park exit from inside the station or climb the staircase above Keisei Ueno station, or the hill that runs alongside the JR station. As you enter the park from near the JR station, pause at the information booth to pick up an English map of the various sights on offer, the first of which, the Le Corbusier-designed **National Museum of Western Art**, is right next door. For information on all of Ueno Park's major museums, see individual entries below. For information on the **zoo**, *see p204*.

Culture aside, Ueno's main attractions are historical. Ueno Park was Tokyo's first public park when it opened in 1873. Just five years earlier, it had been the site of a bloody battle between supporters of the new Meiji government and warriors loyal to the Tokugawa shogunate. The government won, but in the process Kanei-ji Temple, where six of Japan's 15 shogun are buried, was destroyed. The main body of the park is littered with memorials and ancient buildings, or at least facsimiles of ancient buildings. If you want to track them all, take a hike down to the southern corner of Shinobazu pond, a shallow boating lake that comes alive with blooming lotus blossoms in summer. Here, the **Shitamachi Museum** provides a charming example of what life was like in 19th-century Edo (Tokyo).

In the centre of the pond itself sits **Benten Hall**. The island and the original temple were built in the early 17th century; the bridge was added later. The hall is dedicated to Bentaizen, first goddess of rivers, eventually goddess of wisdom and pursuit of knowledge and the arts, as well as goddess of money. The current building dates from 1958.

Double back over the bridge and climb two flights of steps, and you'll find yourself on an unremarkable gravel square. To the right at the top of the steps is a statue of Saigo Takamori, a leading figure in the transfer of power from the shogun to the emperor. He resigned from the Imperial forces a few years later and led the

Satsuma rebellion to Tokyo to challenge the government, but killed himself when he failed. The statue depicts him in casual dress – this way his contribution is marked without compromising the Imperial forces' reputation.

Behind to the left is a tomb dedicated to the memory of the Shogitai, the 2,000 or so anti-Imperial rebels who made their last stand at Ueno in 1868, virtually razing the area in the process. In the small enclosure there are prints of the battle and a map of the temple grounds before most buildings were destroyed.

Away to the left is **Kiyomizu Hall**, one of the few buildings to escape destruction in the battle. Originally completed in 1631, the main building has been renovated but the small annexe retains a flavour of old.

Turning left at the top of the steps, then taking the next turn left will take you past an ancient burial mound, **Suribachi**, and down towards **Gojo shrine**, a concentration of small buildings dedicated to the gods of medicine and learning. The small grey *torii* (gate) leads to a tiny manmade cave with a small shrine. The steps under a row of orange *torii* on the right lead back to the main avenue in the park.

Turning left after a few yards will take you to the entrance of **Toshogu shrine**, the finest of the historical monuments in the park. The shrine is dedicated to the first shogun, Tokugawa Ieyasu. The style is similar to the one where he is buried, in Nikko. Toshogu was first built in 1627, then remodeled in 1651. It has withstood earthquakes and numerous fires, as well as the battle of Ueno Hill, and is one of the oldest buildings in Tokyo. The big lantern on the left before the first gate is one of the largest in Japan. The path to the entrance is lined with many smaller stone lanterns. There are also some copper lanterns near the temple, used only for purification and sacred fires in religious ceremonies. They were offerings to the memory of the first shogun by feudal lords. On the right along the path are two separate monuments in memory of the last world war. Karamon, the front gate of the temple, is famous for its dragon carvings. They are said to be so lifelike that they sneak to the pond for a drink at night. The shrine is open every day from 9am-5pm (admission ¥200). The main shrine building is the **Golden Hall** or Konjiki-do, and inside is the armour and sword of the shogun, as well as a few artworks and artefacts. Toshogu shows its age and cannot be described as beautiful, but the atmosphere inside is solemn.

Walking along the path to Toshogu you can see the pagoda, but need to enter the zoo to get a closer look. Following the zoo wall and returning to the main path leads towards the grand fountain, where Kanei-ji temple used to stand. To preserve this memory a small temple was moved from Kawagoe (in Tokyo's north) to the park in 1879 and renamed **Kanei-ji**. This particular building was chosen since it is the work of the same person who supervised the original Kanei-ji. Behind the temple and past the school the road leads along a cemetery to Chokugakumon gate, where six of the Tokugawa shogun are buried. It is not open to the public. The road continues back to the park and at the main road stands **Rinno-ji** temple. The temple itself is relatively recent, but the small structure and lanterns in the grounds are redolent of the days before the battle.

GETTING THERE

Ueno station is on the Ginza and JR Yamanote lines.

Sights

Kanei-ji Temple

1-14-11 Ueno Sakuragi, Taito-ku (3821 1259). Uguisudani station. **Open** 9am-5pm daily.

Built in 1625 to protect the Imperial Palace from spirits from the north-east, Kanei-ji was once the centre of a massive complex of 36 temples, most of which were destroyed in the 1868 battle of Ueno.

Kyu Iwasaki-tei House & Gardens

1-3-45 Ikenohata, Taito-ku (3823 8033/www.tokyo-park.or.jp/english/jpgarden3.html#iwasaki). Yushima station, exit 1. **Open** 9am-5pm daily. Closed Dec 29-3 Jan. **Admission** ¥150; free concessions.

You might expect such an enormous hilltop estate in a wealthy Connecticut enclave, but not here, a stone's skip from Ueno's Shinobazu pond. Built in 1896 for Iwasaki Hisaya, son of the founder of the Mitsubishi conglomerate, this compound reveals the fin-de-siècle sheen beneath Ueno's grimy surface. British architect Josiah Conder designed the recently renovated main residence – a two storey wooden structure with Jacobean and Pennsylvanian country house elements (and the first western-style toilet in Japan) – and the adjacent billiards room in the form of a log cabin. Across the lawn is the Hiroma or Japanese hall. In the large tatami rooms, visitors can sip green tea and admire *fusuma* (sliding doors) painted with seasonal motifs by Hashimoto Gaho. *English pamphlet.*

National Museum of Western Art (Kokuritsu Seiyo Bijutsukan)

7-7 Ueno Koen, Taito-ku (3828 5131/www.nmwa.go.jp). Ueno JR station, Park exit. **Open** 9.30am-5pm Tue-Thur, Sat, Sun; 9.30am-8pm Fri. **Admission** ¥420; free-¥130 concessions; additional charge for special exhibitions. Free admission every 2nd & 4th Sat of mth.

The core collection housed in this 1959 Le Courbusier-designed building, Japan's only national museum devoted to western art, was assembled by

One of Ueno's many cultural delights.

Kawasaki shipping magnate Matsukata Kojiro in the early 1900s. Considering that the collection was begun so recently, it is surprisingly good, ranging from 15th-century icons to Monet to Pollock. Temporary exhibitions often draw Tokyo's biggest crowds, with the 2002 record of over 500,000 visitors set by 'Masterworks from the Prado'.
Cafe. English pamphlet. Gift shop.

National Science Museum (Kokuritsu Kagaku Hakubutsukan)

7-20 Ueno Koen, Taito-ku (3822 0111 Mon-Fri; 3822 0114 Sat, Sun, hols/www.kahaku.go.jp/english/index.html). Ueno JR station, Park exit. **Open** 9am-4.30pm Tue-Thur; 9am-8pm Fri; 9am-6pm Sat, Sun. **Admission** ¥420; ¥70 concessions, free every 2nd Sat of mth.
The main building dates from 1930 and looks it, with dusty displays on evolution and plants and animals. The much livelier new building is packed with kids learning about science by lifting themselves with pulleys, pedalling a cyclecopter, or taking part in hands-on workshops. Impressive tyrannosaurus, stegosaurus and other dinosaur skeletons and fossils will please the little palaeontologist. Newer exhibits have English labels.
Gift shop.

Shitamachi Museum (Shitamachi Fuzoku Shiryokan)

2-1 Ueno Koen, Taito-ku (3823 7451). Ueno JR station, Park exit. **Open** 9.30am-4.30pm Tue-Sun. **Admission** ¥300; ¥100 concessions.
Though *shitamachi* literally means 'downtown', 'old town' is a more accurate translation for the nearly extinct rows of wooden houses and the lively folk who lived in them. Take off your shoes and step into recreations of a merchant's shop, a coppersmith's workshop and a sweet shop. Upstairs, learn how to make Japanese toys or look at the exhibitions focusing on life in *shitamachi*. At weekends, kids will love the live *kamishibai* (paper drama), a traditional form of entertainment in which roaming street performers used painted cards to tell stories (in Japanese).
English pamphlet.

Tokyo Art University (Geidai) Art Museum

12-8 Ueno Koen (5685 7755/www.geidai.ac.jp/museum). Ueno JR station, Park exit. **Open** 10am-5pm Tue-Sun. **Admission** ¥300; ¥100 concessions; additional charge for special exhibitions.
The museum connected to Japan's most prestigious national art and music school has an impressive collection of over 40,000 objects, from Japanese traditional art to western paintings and photos. The large new building, opened in 1999, holds both permanent collections and temporary exhibitions.

Tokyo Metropolitan Art Museum

8-36 Ueno Koen, Taito-ku (3823 6921/www.tobikan.jp). Ueno JR station, Park exit. **Open** *Main gallery* 9am-5pm Tue-Sun. *Library* 9am-5pm daily (closed 1st & 3rd Mon of mth). **Admission** *Library* free. *Galleries* varies. **Credit** (gift shop only, purchases over ¥3,000) JCB, MC, V.
Designed by Maekawa Kunio, this brick-faced museum was largely constructed underground to remain unobtrusive – with limited success. Temporary exhibitions in the main hall feature everything from traditional Japanese art to art nouveau.
Gift shop. Restaurant.

Tokyo National Museum (Tokyo Kokuritsu Hakubutsukan)

13-9 Ueno Koen, Taito-ku (3822 1111/www.tnm.go.jp). Ueno JR station, Park exit. **Open** 9.30am-5pm Tue-Sun (closes 8pm Fri during special exhibitions). **Admission** ¥420; free-¥130 concessions; extra charge for special exhibitions.
If you have just one day to devote to museum-going in Tokyo and are interested in Japanese art and artefacts, this is the place to come. Japan's oldest and largest museum houses a collection of over 89,000 items in several buildings. Past the ornate gateway and guardhouses, taken from the Ikeda Mansion in Marunouchi, there's a wide courtyard and fountain surrounded by three main buildings. Directly in front is the 1937 Honkan, or main gallery, which displays the permanent collection of Japanese arts and antiquities. The 25 rooms regularly rotate their exhibitions of paintings, ceramics, swords, kimono, sculpture and the like. The Toyokan, the faux log cabin-style building to the right, features three floors of artworks from other parts of Asia. The Hyokeikan, the European-style building to the left, opened in 1909, and was the first in Japan to be devoted to modern art after the Meiji period (1912 onwards). It was designed by the imperial architect, Katayama Tokuma, who, greatly influenced by the western architecture he saw while travelling, incorporated an ornate dome, arches and mosaic tiles into the structure. It is currently closed. The modern box behind the Hyokeikan is the Gallery of Horyu-ji Treasures, designed by Taniguchi Yoshio and built in 1999. Inside are some of Japanese Buddhism's most important and ancient artefacts, from the seventh-century Horyu-ji Temple in Nara, the first Buddhist temple in Japan. The highlight is a large open room with dozens of tiny bronze Buddha figurines seated in their own glass vitrines. The Heiseikan, behind the Honkan, is the newest building. It holds month-long temporary blockbusters of Japanese and Asian art.
Café. Lockers. Gift shop.

Toshogu

9-88 Ueno Koen, Taito-ku (3822 3455). Ueno station, exits 7, 8, 9 or Nezu station, exit 2 or Ueno Okachimachi station (Toei Oedo Line), exit 3. **Open** *Main hall* 9am-6pm daily. **Admission** ¥200; ¥100 concessions.
Built in the early 17th century, the shrine is a designated National Treasure, and the dragons on its gates, sculpted by Hidari 'Lefty' Jingoro, are said to be so life-like that they descend to the nearby Shinobazu pond to drink at night.

Ueno Royal Museum (Ueno no Mori Bijutsukan)

1-2 Ueno Koen, Taito-ku (3833 4195/www.ueno-mori.org). Ueno JR station, Park exit. **Open** 10am-5pm daily. **Admission** varies.

This medium-sized *kunsthalle* in the woods of Ueno Park holds the annual VOCA exhibition of emerging Japanese artists and has also recently held exhibitions from New York's MOMA and the Picasso Museum in Barcelona. It has no permanent collection and its temporary shows are sporadic.

Yayoi Museum of Art

2-4-3 Yayoi, Bunkyo-ku (3812 0012). Nezu station, exit 1. **Open** 10am-5pm Tue-Sun. **Admission** ¥800; ¥400-¥700 concessions; ¥1100 for pass also valid for Tachihara Michizo Memorial Museum & Takeshisa Yumeji Museum of Art.

Housed under the same roof as the Takeshisa Yumeji Museum of Art (*see below*). Both museums dedicate themselves to the history of Japanese *manga* (comics) and illustrations.

Takeshisa Yumeji Museum of Art

2-4-2 Yayoi, Bunkyo-ku (5689 0462). Nezu station, exit 1. **Open** 10am-5pm Tue-Sun. **Admission** ¥800; ¥400-¥700 concessions; ¥1,100 for pass also valid for Yayoi Museum of Art & Tachihara Michizo Memorial Museum.

Tachihara Michizo Memorial Museum

2-4-5 Yayoi, Bunkyo-ku (5684 8780/www.orchid.co.jp/~tatihara/tatihara.htm). Nezu station, exit 1. **Open** 10am-5pm Tue-Sun. **Admission** ¥400; ¥200-¥300 concessions; ¥1100 for pass also valid for Yayoi Museum of Art & Takeshisa Yumeji Museum of Art.

The third small museum facing one of Tokyo University's historic gates, along with the Yayoi Museum and the Takeshisa Yumeji Museum (*above*). It is dedicated to Tachihara Michizo, an artist noted for his pastels. Unfortunately, there are no English translations.

Gift shop. Restaurant.

Yokoyama Taikan Memorial Hall

1-4-24 Ikenohata, Taito-ku (3821 1017/www.tctv.ne.jp/members/taikan). Yushima station, exit 1. **Open** 10am-4pm Thur-Sun (closes during bad weather & occasionally in summer). **Admission** ¥500; ¥200 concessions.

Regarded as one of Japan's great modern painters, Yokoyama Taikan was born at the beginning of the Meiji Restoration (1868) and lived through 89 years of change. In his traditional Japanese house (rebuilt after damage from World War II fire bombings) overlooking Shinobazu Pond, Yokoyama practised *nihonga* (traditional Japanese painting), taking Mount Fuji and other images from nature as his inspiration. In 1952, he became Japan's first representative at the Venice Biennale. If his paintings don't impress, his well-planned gardens will.

English pamphlet. Gift shop.

The market at **Ameyoko**. *See p89.*

Yanaka

Map p94

No matter how much you love the frantic pace of Tokyo's bustling main centres, there will come a time when you want to escape the skyscrapers and the crowds. This is when you need to come to the area known as Yanaka, one of the few areas of Tokyo to offer a real glimpse of what life was like in Edo 150 years ago.

Yanaka is a charming area of low-level buildings with the highest concentration of temples in Tokyo, ranging from the grand to the decidedly humble. The temples were moved here from elsewhere in Tokyo by official decree following the 1657 Long Sleeves Fire, which destroyed much of the city. Yanaka has led something of a charmed life ever since. First it became a playground for the wealthy, and then almost a living museum of old Tokyo, escaping destruction in both the 1923 earthquake and the World War II air raids.

The only way to see Yanaka is on foot, and though this route takes in many of the area's most famous sights, if you're prepared to risk getting lost in the area, there's a lot more to be discovered in its steep, winding back streets.

Start by taking the Yamanote Line to Nippori station. Then, from the south exit from the platform, take the west station exit, which will bring you out on a narrow footpath at the foot of a flight of steps.

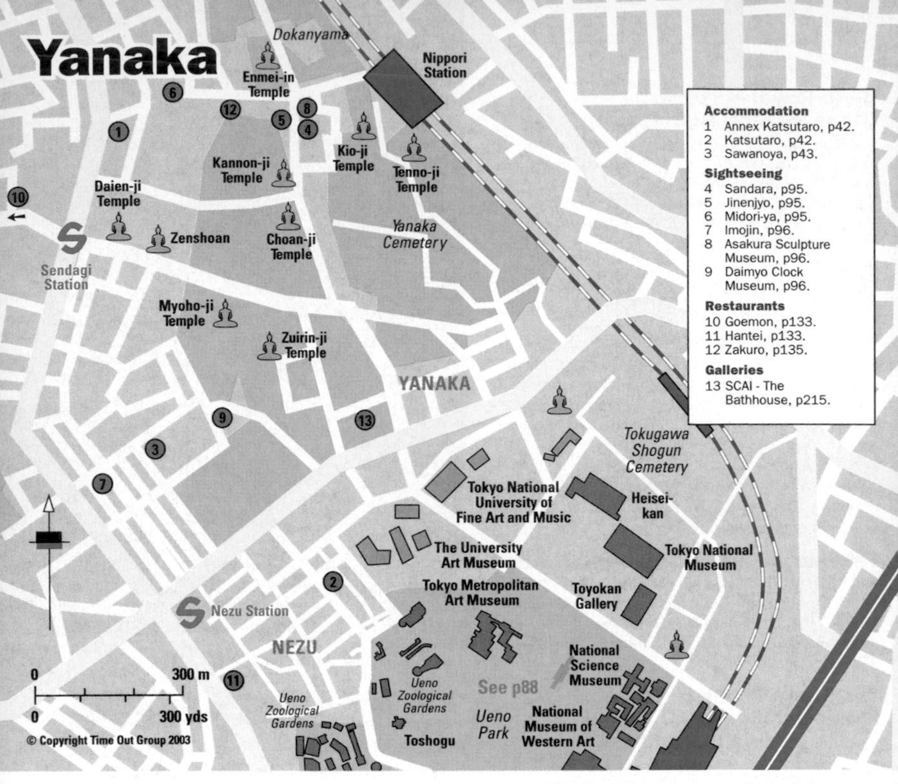

Stretching out in front of you just to the left of the top of the steps is the main road that leads through Yanaka cemetery, one of Tokyo's largest graveyards and, along with Aoyama cemetery, one of its most picturesque. The cemetery, which opened in 1874 on old temple burial grounds, contains the remains of many prominent figures, including Natsume Soseki (1867-1916), author of the novel *I am a Cat*, a whimsical look at human failings through the eyes of a pet. The cemetery is also the resting place of the last Tokugawa shogun, Yoshinobu (1837-1913), who surrendered power to the emperor in 1868, a decision that heralded the Meiji era and paved the way for Japan's transition to a global player. Politics buffs may like to know that the father of Japan's dominant political party, the Liberal Democratic Party, Baba Tatsui (1850-1888), is also buried here, even though his political views got him exiled and he died in Pennsylvania.

Before starting off down the road through the cemetery, take a look in the temple at the beginning of the road. This is **Tennoji Temple**, which was founded over 500 years ago, and whose grounds once covered a far larger area. The prize of the temple is the copper Buddha, which was cast in 1690 but moved here in 1933. The temple gained notoriety in the early 19th century, when it was one of only three temples licensed to hold lotteries. These eventually got so out of hand that they were banned by the Tokugawa shogunate. Also in the grounds is a small bronze *jizo*, supposed to guard the spirits of departed children, which was erected here by a mourning father following the death of his son. Tennoji Temple is also where the god Bishamonten is enshrined, one of the seven lucky Japanese gods. In Edo days, performing a pilgrimage to the shrines of all seven shortly after New Year was thought to guarantee a good year ahead. The pilgrimage can still be made, although it's rather a long walk, starting from Nishi-Nippori station.

Leave the temple grounds and head down the central avenue of the cemetery, a walk made doubly pleasant by the absence of parked cars. Today it's usually quiet, apart from the sightseers, but over 150 years ago, this avenue was a den of iniquity, lined with tea shops that doubled as brothels and illegal gambling dens.

Continue down the path until the *koban* (police box). To the left and slightly behind the *koban* is a small fenced-off area. The rubble inside is all that's left of Yanaka's five-storey pagoda, once the tallest building in Edo. It was built in 1644, but burned down in 1772 and was then rebuilt. It burned down for the last time in 1957, part of a macabre lovers' suicide pact.

Our route here takes us right off the main road, opposite the *koban*, but if you wish to see the tomb of the last Tokugawa shogun, continue straight on until you reach the next set of buildings on the road. Shortly after the grey public toilet, turn left down the road and head straight on to the path. A right turn off the path, followed by a left around 100 metres (350 feet) later will bring you to a walled area of the cemetery. Skirt the wall until you come to a gate. The gate is locked, but inside, in a picturesque miniature garden, lie the remains of Yoshinobu, the last Tokugawa shogun. It's very pretty in April, at cherry blossom time.

Back on the main road near the *koban*, turn right on to the path on the other side of the road, and go straight ahead. On the left you will pass a plaque marking the tomb of Nakamura Masanao (1836-1892), a Meiji-era reformer who was the first person to translate the works of John Stuart Mill into Japanese. In 1877, he revolutionised book printing in Japan with his translation of the contemporary British bestseller *Self Help* by Samuel Smiles. Inspired by the book, he insisted that it be printed properly, in book format, with a cardboard back and set type, no mean feat in a country where most printing was done on woodblocks. The company that printed the book became Dai Nippon Printing, now one of the world's biggest printers and paper concerns.

The path you are on ends in a T-junction just past some modern houses. Facing you at the end of the street is **Choanji Temple**, another of the seven temples to contain a lucky god, in this case Jurojin, a god of long life.

Turn right at the junction, and keep your eyes trained on the left. Soon, down a side street you will catch a glimpse of a particularly impressive, traditional Japanese slate wall, while on your right is an old wooden building that was once a local school and is now a community centre. The wall is part of the complex surrounding **Kannonji**, the next temple on your left. Kannonji is connected with the tale of the 47 ronin (*see p194*), two of whom were students here. Inside the grounds on the right hand side is a small pagoda dedicated to their memory, while deeper inside the temple grounds is a photogenic old stone well.

Turn left out of the temple and continue to walk along the main road. Shortly, on the right, you will pass **Sandara** (7-18-6 Yanaka, Taito-ku, 5814 8618, 10.30am-6pm Tue-Sun), a charming little shop that sells traditional Japanese pottery. A shade further on, on the other side of the road, is **Ryusenji Temple**, a minor temple, but very picturesque with its bending trees and sloping roofs.

If you're feeling in need of a restorative, you may care to stop at **Jinenjiyo** (5-9-25 Yanaka, Taito-ku, 3824 3162, 11.30am-4pm, 5.30-9pm Mon-Fri, 11am-9pm Sat, Sun), a quaint little coffee shop a little further up the road on your left. The speciality here is 'yakuzen curry', which contains traditional Chinese medicines thought to be good for the circulation or the body. The curries come in all the usual flavours – beef, chicken, vegetable – but are guaranteed to put the spring back into your step. You can also stop here for just a coffee, if you can resist the smell of the curry.

Just further down the street from Jinenjiyo, on the other side of the road, is the **Asakura Sculpture Museum**, situated in the black concrete building that was the artist's house. Despite its unprepossessing façade, it's well worth a look.

Turn right out of the museum and continue to the end of the street. On the way, on your right, you will pass a small alleyway lined with small drinking dens, or *nomiya*. This is **Hatsunei Komichi**, one of the last wooden-roofed covered arcades in Tokyo.

At the end of the street, turn left (if you wish to return to Nippori station, turn right) and follow the road to the right, down a flight of steps. On the way, you'll pass eccentric Turkish restaurant **Zakuro** (*see p135*) on your left. Turn right at the bottom of the steps, and 50 metres (160 feet) down the road you'll find **Midori-ya** (3-13-5 Nishi-Nippori, Aragawa-ku, 3828 1746, 10am-6.30pm daily), a traditional maker of Japanese basketware. All items are hand-woven, and past customers include a variety of foreign ambassadors and even the emperor himself. Prices range from ¥500 for trinkets to over ¥30,000 for handbags. Return to the foot of the steps and turn right, into the incongruously named **Yanaka Ginza**, the area's main shopping street. Yanaka Ginza is pedestrianised and uncovered, and a surprising number of traditional businesses still survive, selling such items as *geta* (Japanese wooden shoes), *senbei* (rice crackers) and pottery. It's quaint and seemingly a million miles from the real Ginza.

Turn left at the bottom of Yanaka Ginza, and walk straight, past the Annex Katsutaro Ryokan (*see p42*), until you reach the traffic lights at the end of the street.

Turn left at the lights and walk up the hill to **Daienji Temple**. This is a highly unusual temple building, in that it consists of two totally symmetrical halves. At the time it was built, the

The **Daimyo Clock Museum**. *See p96.*

left half was intended to serve as a shinto shrine, the right as a Buddhist temple, but such plans were kiboshed by a decree from the shogunate, which enforced the separation of the two religions. Inside the grounds, to the right, is a pair of stone monuments, to *ukiyo-e* artist Harunobu and his model Kasamori Osen, a waitress in a Yanaka cemetery tea garden. Kasamori's memorial is the smaller one to the left, and if the caretaker is around he will show you a Harunobu portrait of her in her prime, together with a photograph of one of Kasamori's great granddaughters, who came to visit her ancestor's tomb. The temple is famous for its chrysanthemum festival, which turns the place into a riot of colour in mid October.

Leave the temple, turn left, cross the road at the pedestrian crossing and then turn right by the large white school building with a pagoda. Continue straight down this road, bearing left when it forks, and you will come to the **Daimyo Clock Museum**, a one-room showcase of the strange way Japanese people used to tell the time. The ¥100 English pamphlet is a good investment and makes fascinating reading.

Return to the main street from the museum, turn left and then next left, down a slope with a wonderful Japanese house on the right. Follow the street down past the Sawanoya *ryokan* (*see p43*) and several fine examples of old Japanese shop architecture, standing uneasily next to some not-so-fine recent buildings. On a corner on the left, shortly before the traffic lights, is **Imojin** (2-30-4 Nezu, Bunkyo-ku, 3821 5530, 11am-7pm Tue-Sun), a Japanese sweet shop and ice-cream maker. On a hot day, you'll recognise it by the queue outside.

Cross the main road at the lights and go straight to get to **Nezu Shrine**, a colourful shrine with a giant painted gate and landscaped gardens stretching up a hillside. The shrine dates from 1706, and for most of the year it's amazingly peaceful. In April, however, when the hillside azalea bushes bloom, the whole place swarms with camera-toting visitors.

From here, it's time to return home. Go back to the main road, turn right and you'll hit Nezu station on the Chiyoda Line in five minutes.

GETTING THERE

Yanaka is best reached from Nippori station on the JR Yamanote line.

Yanaka sights

Asakura Sculpture Museum (Asakura Choso Museum)

7-18-10 Yanaka, Taito-ku (3821 4549/www.taitocity.net/taito/asakura/). Nippori JR station, north exit. **Open** 9.30am-4.30pm Tue-Thur, Sat, Sun. **Admission** ¥400; ¥150 concessions.

Asakura Fumio (1883-1964), regarded as the father of modern Japanese sculpture, was crazy about cats. His many sculptures of them can be seen at his former house-studio. The three-level building – designed by the artist in 1936 – melds modernism and traditional Japanese architecture. Asakura worked in the high-ceilinged concrete portion and slept in the tea ceremony-style living quarters behind. The centrepiece of the grounds is a peaceful Japanese water garden, also designed by the artist. *Gift shop.*

Daimyo Clock Museum

2-1-27 Yanaka, Taito-ku (3821 6913). Nezu station exit 1. **Open** 10am-4pm Tue-Sun. Closed July-Sept. **Admission** ¥300; ¥100-¥200 concessions.

Daimyo were feudal lords who controlled vast tracts of land prior to the 19th century Meiji restoration. They were the only people who could afford these clocks, which required adjusting twice a day. Their unique way of keeping time corresponded to sunrise and sunset; the length of an hour changed seasonally, becoming longer in the summer and shorter in winter, and times were named after the signs of the Chinese zodiac. The museum, run by the Japanese Clock Preservation Society, displays dozens of examples from its permanent collection, from alarm clocks to watches that attach to *obi* (kimono belts). *English pamphlet.*

Other sights in east Tokyo

Basho Memorial Museum

1-6-3 Tokiwa, Koto-ku (3631 1448). Morishita station (Toei Shinjuku Line), exit A1. **Open** 9.30am-5pm Tue-Sun. **Admission** ¥100 concessions.

The 17th-century *haiku* poet Basho Matsuo made his home in this corner of timber tycoon (and poetry enthusiast) Sugiyama Sanpu's villa estate on the Sumida river. At one time, plantains (*basho* in Japanese) grew here. Their easily torn leaves reminded Basho of a poet's sensitivity, so he took it as his name. The modest museum holds three floors of Basho's poetry and personal items. Stone trails lead to a shrine marking the location of his cottage. Sadly, there are no English translations.

Edo-Tokyo Museum

1-4-1 Yokoami, Sumida-ku (3626 9974/www.edo-tokyo-museum.or.jp). Ryogoku JR station, west exit. **Open** 9.30am-5.30pm Tue-Sun; 9.30am-8pm Thur, Fri. **Admission** ¥600; free-¥480 concessions; additional fee for special exhibitions.

Inside the museum's spaceship structure, there's a very down-to-earth display of over 400 years of Tokyo's development from the Edo period to today (Edo was renamed Tokyo or 'eastern capital' in 1868). Highlights in this extensive and informative collection of dioramas and displays include an old theatre stage, and reconstructions of historical buildings and the Nihonbashi Bridge. Artefacts outline lifestyles from those of Edo period samurai to World War II families. The museum also shows how disasters both natural and manmade successively altered the city's landscape.

Coffeeshop. English pamphlet. Giftshop. Lockers. Restaurant.

Fukagawa Edo Museum

1-3-28 Shirakawa, Koto-ku (3630 8625). Kiyosumi-Shirakawa station (Toei Oedo Line), exit 3. **Open** 9.30am-5pm daily. Closed 2nd & 4th Mon of mth. **Admission** ¥300; ¥50 concessions.

Tokyo has three museums that recreate Edo period *shitamachi* (downtown areas). This one is better than Ueno Park's cramped Shitamachi Museum (*see p92*), but pales beside the Edo-Tokyo Museum (*see above*). Still, it's worth a visit. Everything about this recreated 1840 town is carefully detailed. You can walk along the street and duck into a vegetable store, rice warehouse, boathouse tavern and tenement There's even rubbish in the bin, next to the outdoor toilets.

English pamphlet.

Japan Stationery Museum

1-1-15 Yanagibashi, Taito-ku (3861 4905). Asakusabashi station, east exit. **Open** 10am-4pm Mon-Fri. Admission free.

Here you can browse the history of writing and calculating implements – from Egyptian papyrus to abacuses to typewriters with interchangeable *kanji* keys. One highlight of this museum is a 14kg (31lb) brush made from the hair of over 50 horses.

Kasai Seaside Park

6-2 Rinkai-cho, Edogawa-ku (3686 6911/www.senyo.co.jp/kasai). Kasai-Rinkai Koen station (Keiyo line). **Open** *Park* 24hrs daily. *Birdwatching centre & visitors' centre* 9.30am-4.30pm daily. *Beach* 9am-5pm daily. *Big wheel* 10am-8pm Mon-Fri; 10am-9pm Sat, Sun. *Tokyo Sea Life Park* 9.30am-5pm Tue-Sun (last admission 4pm). **Admission** free. *Big wheel* ¥700. *Tokyo Sea Life Park* ¥700.

Located by the water at the eastern edge of the city, this park was built to recreate a natural seashore environment. Traces of the city are evident on three sides, but the park still makes a good escape. Inside are the Tokyo Sea Life Park, two small beaches, a Japanese garden and a lotus pond. The birdwatching area includes two ponds and tidal flats.

Museum of Contemporary Art, Tokyo (MoT, or Tokyo-to Gendai Bijutsukan)

4-1-1 Miyoshi, Koto-ku (5245 4111/www.mot-art-museum.jp). Kiba station, exit 3, then 15min walk. **Open** 10am-6pm Tue-Sun. **Admission** ¥500; free-¥400 concessions; additional fee for special exhibitions. **Credit** (shop only) JCB, MC, V.

This huge, city-owned showpiece opened in March 1995 on reclaimed swampland in a far-flung part of Tokyo. Its permanent collection of 3,500 international and Japanese works of art has its moments, but the high-profile temporary exhibitions are the main reason to visit. Visitors can access the large database, extensive video library, and magazine and catalogue collection (all available in English).

Café. Cloakroom. Gift shop. Lockers. Restaurant. English pamphlet.

Tokyo Metropolitan Memorial & Tokyo Reconstruction Museum

2-3-25 Yokoami, Sumida-ku (3623 1200). Ryogoku JR station, west exit. **Open** 9am-4.30pm daily. **Admission** free.

Following the 7.9 Richter scale Great Kanto Earthquake of 1923, approximately 40,000 people who had fled their homes perished on this site when sparks set clothing and bedding alight. The fire continued to rage for nearly a day and a half, destroying three-quarters of the city and killing 140,000 people. Seven years later, a three-storey pagoda-topped memorial building was built. Designed by architect Ito Chuta, it blends Christian pews and a Buddhist incense-filled altar (shinto is represented by the exterior stairs). Following World War II, the memorial's name was changed to include the 100,000 people who died in air raids on Tokyo. The Reconstruction Museum in a nearby building in the park contains wartime mementos. Both buildings are shamefully rundown and receive little attention, most of which is concentrated on the controversial Yasukuni Shrine (*see p12*), which honours the war dead. This place, by contrast, remembers those who died while leading their daily lives. Memorial services are held on 1 September and 10 March.

Gift shop.

West City

Teenage trends, high-end fashion and high-rise buildings dominate the overcrowded streets here.

Harajuku & Omotesando

Map p99

Omotesando and Harajuku are the fashion and youth centres of Tokyo, respectively. That is, if by 'youth centre' one means the collection of trendy hangouts where the latest teen fads are established and followed. And that is, by and large, exactly what youth culture means in Japan in 2003. Fashion and trendiness are the concepts at play in these two hyperactive, fascinating and adjacent Tokyo districts.

Appropriately set slightly uphill from Harajuku, Omotesando is the home of haute couture Tokyo, with every self-respecting fashion house having a store here. The street of Omotesando (Omotesando is both the name of the area and a pleasantly wide, tree-lined boulevard) boasts everything from Hanae Mori to Louis Vuitton, a brand that has become an indispensable accessory for young Japanese women. However, you'll also find upscale toy stores andJapanese goods for tourists, too.

Harajuku is more compact, crammed with clothing stores, eateries and jewellery stores on either side of Tokyo's main artery, Meiji Dori.

The emblematic shopping streets in Omotesando and Harajuku are **Koto Dori** in the former and **Takeshita Dori** in the latter. The first, unsurprisingly, has upscale fashion houses next to effete French restaurants with some posh clubs thrown in. Takeshita Dori, however, is a throng of small clothes stores and crepe stands patronised by the 11-20 set. The street, now a tourist attraction in itself, is a solid mass of humanity at weekends. A shuffle through this awe-inspiring sight is a must.

The main nexus of teeny-bopper Tokyo starts with Takeshita Dori and and extends up towards the **Meiji Shrine**. It is in front of the emperor's holy shrine that Tokyo's teen hipsters (mainly girls) hang out at weekends in outrageous garb. Like Takeshita Dori itself, this expression of youthful exuberance has become a major tourist attraction, and with some justification. The costumes have gone from cool to inventive to bizarre, becoming one of the nation's major articulations of youth creativity. A favourite outfit over the last couple of years has been the 19th-century French maid's kit. Black, white, frilly and naughtily sexy, this get-up can be quite shocking on a 14-year-old Japanese girl. Another eye-catching offering is the nurse's uniform, with a twist. Not content to splatter their smocks with a bit of blood from supposed patients (in vogue a few years ago), the girls now complete the outfit with their own delicately arranged fake blood and bandages. Add to these a variety of sexy, goth, punk,

Sightseeing
1 Anniversaire Gallery, p100.
2 Aoyama Cemetery, p100.
3 GA Gallery, p100.
4 Laforet Museum, p101.
5 Meiji Shrine, p101.
6 Meiji Shrine (Inner garden), p101.
7 Miji Shrine Garden, p101.
8 Ukiyo-e Memorial Museum, p101.
9 Watari-Um Museum, p101.
10 Yoyogi Park, p101.

Restaurants
11 Aux Bacchanales, p144.
12 Crayon House, p145.
13 Daruma-ya, p145.
14 Denpachi, p145.
15 Fujimamas, p146.
16 Fumin, p146.
17 Ghungroo, p146.
18 Giliola, p146.
19 Hokuto, p147.
20 Kyushu Jangara Ramen, p147.
21 La Grotta Celeste, p146.
22 Maisen, p147.
23 Natural Harmony Angoro, p147.
24 Pumpkin Cook Katsura, p148.
25 Roy's, p148.
26 Senba, p149.
27 Soho's, p149.
28 Las Chicas, p145.

Coffee Shops
29 Daibo, p153.

Bars
30 Den Aquaroom, p159.
31 Office, p159.
32 Oh! God, p159.
33 Pink Cow, p159.
34 Radio Bar, p160.
35 Sign, p160.
36 Tokyo Apartment Café, p160.

Shops and Services
37 Glassarea Aoyama, p171.
38 Takeshita Dori, p173.
39 Kikuya, p174.
40 Shu Uemura, p174.
41 Laforet , p176.
42 Little Village, p179.
43 New Funk Inc, p179.
44 UnderCover, p179.
45 Uniqlo, p179.
46 YAB-YUM, p179.
47 Comme des Garçons, p179.
48 Issey Miyake, p181.
49 Yohji Yamamoto, p181.
50 Benetton, p181.
51 Fcuk, p181.
52 Gap, p181.
53 Louis Vuitton, p181.
54 R Newbold, p181.
55 Fuji Torii, p181.
56 Oriental Bazaar, p183.
57 It's Demo, p185.
58 Sputnik Pad, p185.
59 Kinokuniya International, p185.
60 Astro Mike, p187.
61 Pook et Koop, p188.
62 Boudoir, p190.
63 Peekaboo, p191.
64 Sinden, p191.

Children
65 BorneLund, p205.
66 Kiddyland, p205.
12 Crayon House, p206.

Galleries
67 Gallery 360, p213.
68 Design Festa Gallery, p213.
69 Gallery Gan, p213.
70 Nadiff, p213.
28 Las Chicas (Café/D-Zone), p213.
33 Pink Cow, p213.
71 Spiral, p214.
72 TN Probe, p214.

Music
73 Cay, p230.
74 Astro Hall, p229.
75 Mandala Minami-Aoyama, p231.

Nightlife
76 Fai, p237.
77 Maniac Love, p238.
78 Mix, p239.
79 The Orbient, p239.

Performing Arts
80 Punchline Comedy Club, p246.

Sport & Fitness
81 National Yoyogi Stadium 1st Gymnasium, p250.

Harajuku
0
200 m
0
200 yds
© Copyright Time Out Group 2003
Meiji Shrine Inner Garden
Yoyogi Park
SHIBUYA-KU
Harajuku Station
Meiji-Jingumae Station
Togo Shrine
TAKESHITA DORI
MEIJI DORI
INOKASHIRA DORI
National Gymnasium
JIN'NAN
JINGUMAE
RIVER PROMENADE
KYU SHIBUYA
OMOTESANDO
AOYAMA DORI
MINAMI-AOYAMA
Mizuho Bank
Omotesando Station

Yoyogi Park, one of Tokyo's most popular strolling spots. *See p101.*

school and superhero costumes, and Sundays in front of Meiji Shrine become pretty interesting. While you're in the area, be sure to explore the backstreets of Harajuku, in the area sandwiched behind Meiji Dori and Omotesando.

Though perhaps less arresting, people-watching among the designer goods and high-priced cups of coffee in Omotesando any day of the week is good as well. Omotesando itself makes an agreeable walk, and has one feature that may not be here for much longer. Incongruously but wonderfully, there have been *danchi*, or government-subsidised apartment buildings, on a stretch of Omotesando's prime land since the 1920s. These quaint but decidedly untrendy buildings harken back to a different era and offer a great contrast to the boutiques on the other side of the street. Sadly, it seems these monuments may come down soon, so see them while you can. Omotesando also has a lot to offer after sundown. Koto Dori has numerous bars and fun dance clubs. A stroll down this stretch of at night should reveal a mix of well-to-do partiers, hardcore ravers and average folk out for a good time.

While the individual characters of Harajuku and Omotesando are apparent, the two areas are united by an adoration of the fashionable. It's almost as if, with age and money, one graduates from one to the other. No visitor should head home without coming here.

GETTING THERE

Harajuku and Omotesando are best explored from Harajuku station on the Yamanote Line, or Meiji-Jingumae station on the Chiyoda Line.

Sights

Anniversaire Gallery

Anniversaire Bldg B1, 3-5-30 Kita-Aoyama, Minato-ku (5411 4288/www.anniversaire.co.jp). Omotesando station, exit A2. **Open** (exhibitions only) noon-6pm Wed-Sun. **Admission** ¥500.

This chi-chi department store makes use of the small 'museum' in the basement as a lure. Recent exhibitions have featured Chagall prints.

Aoyama Cemetery

2-33 Minami-Aoyama, Minato-ku. Nogizaka station, exit 5. **Open** 24hrs daily.

This giant necropolis occupies some of the most expensive land in Tokyo. Once part of the local *daimyo*'s estate, it has been a cemetery since 1872 after a brief stint as a silk farm. It now contains over 100,000 graves and is a good spot for *hanami* (cherry-blossom viewing, *see p196*) in April.

GA Gallery

3-12-14 Sendagaya, Shibuya-ku (3403 1581/www.ga-ada.co.jp). Yoyogi station, exit A1. **Open** noon-6.30pm Tue-Sun. **Admission** ¥500; free concessions.

Global Architecture's annual 'GA Houses' and 'GA Japan' exhibitions make it one of Tokyo's best places for modern and contemporary Japanese and international architecture. The building also has one of the best architecture bookstores in the city.

Gift shop.

Honda Welcome Plaza

Honda Aoyama Bldg 1F, 2-1-1 Minami-Aoyama, Minato-ku (3423 4118/www.honda.co.jp/welcome-plaza). Aoyama-Itchome station, exits 1, 3. **Open** *Sept-May* 10am-6pm daily. *June-Aug* 10am-7pm daily. **Admission** free.

All of Honda's cars and motorbikes are on display, and most can be touched or petted, though preferably not drooled over. A 20-minute walk or a short subway ride from Omotesando station.

Laforet Museum

Laforet 6F, 1-11-6 Jingumae, Shibuya-ku (3475 0411/www.laforet.ne.jp/harajuku/home). Harajuku station, Omotesando exit or Meiji-Jingumae station, exit 5. **Open** 11am-8pm daily. **Admission** varies with events. **Credit** AmEx, JCB, MC, V.

Tokyo's trendiest fashion nexus has five floors of teeny-bopper shopping heaven with an art museum/event space as the cherry on top.

Meiji Shrine (Meiji Jingu)

1-1 Kamizonocho, Yoyogi, Shibuya-ku (3379 5511/www.meijijingu.or.jp/english/index.htm). Harajuku station, Omotesando exit or Meiji-Jingumae station, exit 2. **Open** *Spring, autumn* 5.40am-5.20pm daily. *Summer* 4am-5pm daily. *Winter* 6am-5pm daily. **Admission** *Shrine* free. *Treasure house* ¥200.

Surrounded by the shady trees of Meiji Shrine Inner Garden (*see below*), this shrine is an impressive example of the austere style and restrained colours typical of Shinto architecture. Originally opened in 1920, it is dedicated to Emperor Meiji, whose long reign (1868-1912) coincided with Japan's modernisation. The current building dates from 1958: a reconstruction after the original was destroyed during World War II. At the entrance on the Harajuku side stands an 11-metre (36ft) *torii* (gate), the largest in the country, built from 1,600-year-old Japanese Cypress trees imported from Taiwan.

Meiji Shrine (Inner Garden)

1-1 Yoyogi-Kamizono-cho, Shibuya-ku. Harajuku station, Omotesando exit, or Meiji-Jingumae station, exit 2. **Open** 5am-5pm daily, but varies with season.

A thickly wooded area with a shrine dedicated to Emperor Meiji and Empress Shoken in the centre. The shrine's atmosphere of serenity encompasses the whole garden, which has many tranquil paths, as well as dense overhanging foliage. The best approach is from the Harajuku end of Omotesando.

Meiji Shrine Garden (Meiji Jingu Gyoen)

Yoyogi-kamizono-cho, Shibuya-ku (3379-5511). Harajuku station, Omotesando exit, or Meiji-Jingumae station, exit 2. **Open** *Nov-Feb* 9am-4pm daily. *Mar-Nov* 9am-5pm daily. **Admission** ¥500.

There are two entrances to this garden, just off the main path to Meiji Shrine, yet few people come here. It's neither large nor especially beautiful, but it is quiet – except in June when the iris field attracts admirers. Vegetation is dense, limiting access to the few trails, which lead to the pond and teahouse.

Nezu Institute of Fine Arts

6-5-1 Minami-Aoyama, Minato-ku (3400 2536/www.nezu-muse.or.jp). Omotesando station, exit A5. **Open** 9.30am-4.30pm Tue-Sun. **Admission** ¥1,000; ¥700 concessions.

Set in tranquil woods, complete with ponds, stone trails and teahouses, the Nezu Institute of Fine Arts is Aoyama's prime art oasis. Tobu Railway founder Nezu Kaichiro had a penchant for Chinese art and collected Shang and Zhou bronzes. Over the years, the museum's collection of over 7,000 objects has grown through donations of Korean ceramics and Japanese ink paintings from private collectors. Some of the most famous works are on permanent display, others rotate in for temporary exhibitions.

Café. English pamphlet. Gift shop.

Okamoto Taro Memorial Museum

6-1-19 Minami-Aoyama, Minato-ku (3406 0801/http://taro-okamoto.or.jp). Omotesando station, exit B1. **Open** 10am-6pm Mon, Wed-Sun. **Admission** ¥600; ¥300 concessions.

For a healthy dose of whimsy, check out this two-storey museum, once the studio of artist Okamoto Taro, who died in 1996. The adjoining café looks into a tropical garden packed with his wacky sculptures.

Cafe. English pamphlet. Gift shop.

Ukiyo-e Ota Memorial Museum of Art (Ota Kinen Bijutsukan)

1-10-10 Jingumae, Shibuya-ku (3403 0880/www.ukiyoe-ota-muse.jp). Harajuku station, Omotesando exit or Meiji-Jingumae station, exit 5. **Open** 10.30am-5.30pm Tue-Sun. Closed from 27 to end of every mth. **Admission** ¥700; ¥200 concessions.

Slip off your shoes and pad through this small, tatami-floored temple to *ukiyo-e* woodblock prints. The late Ota Seizo, chairman of Toho Mutual Life Insurance, began collecting the prints after he saw that Japan was losing its traditional art to museums and collectors in the west. Temporary exhibitions drawn from the 12,000-strong collection often include works by popular masters such as Hiroshige and Hokusai.

English pamphlet. Gift shop.

Watari-Um Museum of Contemporary Art

3-7-6 Jingumae, Shibuya-ku (3402 3001/www.watarium.co.jp). Gaienmae station, exit 3. **Open** 11am-7pm Tue, Thur-Sun; 11am-9pm Wed. **Admission** ¥1,000, ¥800 concessions.

Mario Botta designed this small art museum for the Watari family in 1990. It holds four exhibitions a year, some of which originate at the museum, while others, such as a recent show on folk artist Henry Darger, are brought from abroad. There's a good art bookshop and a pleasant café in the basement.

Cafe. Gift shop.

Yoyogi Park

2-1 Yoyogi-Kamizono-cho, Shibuya-ku (3469 6081). Harajuku station, Omotesando exit or Yoyogi Koen station, exit 4. **Open** 24hrs daily.

A favourite with couples and families, who spend warm afternoons lounging on the grass. Across Inokashira Dori is architect Tange Kenzo's 1964 Yoyogi National Stadium, still one of Tokyo's most famous modern landmarks (*see p23*).

Shibuya
Bunkamura
Tokyu Honten
BUNKAMURA DORI
KOEN DORI
Seibu
109 Building
Hachiko Statue
JR Shibuya Station
Inokashira Line Shibuya Station
Mark City
DOGENZAKA
TAMAGAWA DORI
Tokyu
Toyoko Line Shibuya Station
Tokyu Bunka Kaikan
ROPPONGI DORI
MEIJI DORI
Miyashita Park
Mitake Park
Mitake Shrine
MIYAMASUSAKA
AOYAMA DORI
Children's Castle
United Nations University
Tofuku-ji Temple
Konno Shrine
YAHATAZAKA
0
300 m
0
300 yds

Accommodation
1 Cerulean Tower Tokyu Hotel p43.
2 Arimax, p43.
3 Excel Hotel, p43.
4 Central Land Shibuya, p50.
5 Villa Giulia, p48.
6 P&A, p49.

Sightseeing
7 Bunkamura the Museum, p105.
8 Eyeglass Museum, p105.
9 Gallery TOM, p105.
10 Parco Museum of Art, p106.
11 Shoto Museum of Art, p107.
12 TEPCO , p107.
13 Tobacco & Salt Museum, p107.
14 Toguri Museum, p108.

Restaurants
15 Ankara, p140.
16 Jembatan Merah, p141.
17 Legato, p141.
18 The Lock-Up, p141.
19 Lunchan, p141.
20 Myoko, p141.
21 Raj Mahal, p142.
22 Sonoma, p143.
23 Vingt2, p144.

Coffee Shops
24 Cantina, p153.
25 Coffee 3.4 Sunsea, p153.
26 Lion, p154.
27 Satei Hato, p155.

Bars
28 Bello Visto, p164.
29 The Hub, p164.
30 Insomnia, p164.
31 Soft, p165.
32 Tantra, p165.
33 World Sports Cafe, p166.

Shops and Services
34 Seibu, p169.
35 Tokyu Honten, p170.
36 Mark City, p171.
37 Book First, p173.
38 109, p176.
39 291295, p176
40 Parco, p179.
41 Three Minutes Happiness, p185.
42 Tokyu Hands, p185.
43 COMIX, p187.
44 Hachiko Shop, p188.
45 Nakanukiya, p188.
46 ranKing ranQueen, p188.
47 Cisco, p188.
48 Dance Music Record, p188.
49 HMV, p190.
50 Recofan, p190.
51 Tower Records, p190.
52 Eye Desk, p191.
53 Hatch, p192.
54 Opt Label, p192.
55 Zoff, p192.

Children
56 Children's Castle, p204.
57 Tokyo Metropolitan Children's Hall, p204.

Film
58 Cine Amuse, p207.
59 Cine Quinto, p207.
60 Cinema Rise, p207.
61 Le Cinema, p208.
62 Cine Saison Shibuya, p208.
63 Euro Space, p208.
64 Shibuya Cinema Society, p209.
65 Theatre Image Forum, p209.
66 Uplink Factory, p209.

Galleries
67 Gallerie Le Deco, p214.
68 Saison Art Program Gallery, p214

Music
69 Orchard Hall, p222.
70 JZ Brat, p225.
71 National Yoyogi Stadium, p228.
72 NHK Hall, p228.
73 Shibuya AX, p229.
74 Shibuya Kokaido, p229.
75 Club Asia, p230.
76 Club Eggsite Sibuya, p230.
77 Club Quattro, p230.
78 Crocodile, p231.
79 DeSeo, p231.
80 Gig-antic, p231.
81 La. Mama Shibuya, p231.
82 On Air East, p232.
83 On Air West, p232.
84 Shibuya Nest, p232.

Nightlife
85 Ball, p235.
75 Club Asia, p236.
86 Club Atom, p236.
87 Club Bar Family, p236.
88 Club Chu, p236.
89 Club Hachi, p237.
90 Fura, p237.
91 Ism Shibuya, p238.
92 La Fabriqu, p238.
93 Loop, p238.
94 Lounge Neo, p238.
95 Module, p239.
96 Organ Bar, p240.
97 Rockwest, p240.
98 The Room, p240.
99 Secobar, p241.
100 Simoon, p241.
101 Ruby Room, p240.
102 Vuenos Bar Tokyo, p241.
103 Womb, p241.

Performing Arts
104 Cerulean Tower Noh Theatre, p243.
105 Aoyama Round Theatre, p245.
106 Bunkamura Theatre Cocoon, p245.

Sport & Fitness
107 Esforta, p252.

Shibuya

Map p102

You may not know it, but you've probably already experienced the delights of Shibuya, via your television screen. Think of all the stock images of Tokyo that are presented by TV news companies on the rare occasions they have reason to travel to Japan. The giant TV screens, the incredibly crowded pedestrian crossing, the young people with dyed hair and radioactive fake tans. Welcome to Shibuya.

For the full Shibuya experience, take the Hachiko exit from the station. In the small paved square that greets you on leaving the station you may be lucky enough to see a small bronze statue of a dog, if it's not obscured by people. This is an effigy of the exit's eponymous Hachiko, a faithful dog that accompanied its master to the station every day, and continued to come alone and wait for him until seven years after his death. By the time of Hachiko's own death in 1935, the dog had become a Tokyo legend, and its obituary was carried in newspapers. The statue erected in its honour is the most popular, and crowded, meeting place in Shibuya. People who know the area a little better arrange to meet at another statue, in Easter Island style, that is to be found close to the station's central west exit, on the other side of the railway bridge behind Hachiko.

The Hachiko exit, however, provides the best view of Shibuya, especially at night or on busy weekends. The first things you will notice are the three giant video screens, all of which pump out promotional pop videos and commercials nearly 24 hours a day, with the volume switched on. When all three are showing different things, the cacophony can be unbearable, even in this famously noisy city. Hachiko Square is at the bottom of the valley that gives Shibuya its name (it can be translated as 'valley of good taste'), and all roads lead uphill. While standing here, try to imagine that less than 100 years ago, Shibuya was a tranquil, prestigious Tokyo suburb famous for the quality of its tea.

Now, Shibuya is famous as a rather déclassé playground for the young who have the time, but not the money, to make the most of what the capital city has to offer. Although the area has much in the way of value-for-money diversions – particularly in the field of live music (*see p222*), those looking for a truly outstanding restaurant or bar are, with very few exceptions, recommended to look elsewhere. This is the home of the price-conscious chain gang, where budget coffee shops such as Doutor, Segafredo and Starbucks vie for business with anonymous *izakaya*, cheap restaurants and even cheaper bars.

One area where Shibuya does excel, however, is shopping. Much of Shibuya, including two of the railway lines that terminate in the station, is owned by the giant Tokyu Corporation. Indeed, the station building itself is incorporated into

The giant **Bunkamura** arts centre. *See p105.*

the fabric of the **Tokyu Toyoko** department store (*see p170*). As well as the buildings that bear its name, Tokyu also owns the giant **109** mall (*see p176*), which specialises in clothes for the young and terminably fashionable. 'Tokyu' is one of the possible readings of '10' and '9' in Japanese, although most people refer to the place as 'Ichi Maru Kyu' ('one zero nine'). In recent years, Tokyu has made some attempt to spruce up the image of Shibuya, developing the upmarket **Mark City** shopping complex in 2000 (it's connected to the station), and opening the **Cerulean Tower Hotel** (the tallest building in Shibuya, *see p243*) on the south side of the station in 2002.

Meanwhile, back on street level, the downmarket action goes on. To sample it for yourself, take the hill that runs up the left side of the 109 Building. This is **Dogenzaka**, named in honour of a highwayman called Dogen who haunted its environs in the 13th century. Dogen's modern equivalents are the owners of the *pachinko* (similar to pinball) and massage parlours that now line much of the route. A right turn into one of the side streets off Dogenzaka almost opposite the uphill exit from Mark City will bring you into Shibuya's main love hotel area, with around 100 hotels vying for trade at charges starting from ¥2,000 for a couple of hours. Walking in a straight line will take you past a variety of strange bars, hotels and clubs, past nightclub Club Asia (*see p230*) and live venue On Air West (*see p232*), and you will return to a main road almost opposite **Bunkamura**, Tokyu's giant Shibuya arts complex. Heading back toward the action alongside Bunkamura will eventually bring you to **Centre Gai**, a paved and mostly pedestrianised shopping street packed with young people shopping at the myriad stores that cater for them, or simply hanging around.

The best way to enjoy Shibuya is simply to hang around with them, dip into the area's back streets and take in all the action. Although the tiny streets are winding and disorientating, it's virtually impossible to become seriously lost here, since all the main roads lead back to the station. Just head downhill to get to Hachiko.

If this taste of Shibuya's main section has got you intrigued, you might want to set off in the opposite direction from Hachiko, over the pedestrian footbridges and into the small streets that run parallel to the Yamanote Line. Until recently, this area had remained relatively untouched by commercialism, but rising rents in the main shopping area have pushed many small businesses, mainly catering for young people, back here. These tiny streets of south Shibuya retain an alternative feel that the rest of the area has largely lost. Stick to the railway line for long enough and you'll be in **Ebisu**, another lively area well worth checking out.

GETTING THERE

Shibuya is on the JR Yamanote and Saikyo lines, the Keio Inokashira Line, the Tokyu Toyoko and Denentoshi lines, and the Eidan Ginza and Hanzomon subway lines.

Sights

Beer Museum Yebisu

4-20-1 Ebisu Garden Place, Shibuya-ku (5423 7255/ www.sapporobeer.jp/brewery/ebisu). Ebisu JR station, east exit. **Open** 10am-6pm Tue-Sun. **Admission** free; beer additional ¥200.

Sapporo built this museum on the site of one of its former breweries, obliterated in 1994 by the outdoor mall Ebisu Garden Place. Past the historical photographs, beer labels, old posters and video displays, there's a virtual-reality tour of the brewing process and, at last, a lounge. Alas, the beer's not free.

English pamphlet. Gift shop. Tasting lounge.

Bunkamura The Museum

Bunkamura B1, 2-24-1 Dogenzaka, Shubuya-ku (3477 9111/www.bunkamura.co.jp). Shibuya JR station, Hachiko exit. **Open** 10am-7pm Mon-Thur, Sun; 10am-9pm Fri, Sat. **Admission** varies. **Credit** Amex, MC, V.

Probably the best museum in Tokyo run by a department store chain (it's owned and operated by the Tokyu corporation). It hosts international art blockbusters featuring subjects and artists ranging from Tintin to photographer Sebastiao Salgado. Elsewhere in this major shopping and cultural centre are boutiques, an arthouse cinema, a theatre, restaurants and an art bookstore.

Eyeglass Museum

Iris Optical 6-7F, 2-29-18 Dogenzaka, Shibuya-ku (3496 3315). Shibuya JR station, Hachiko exit. **Open** 11am-5pm Tue-Sun. **Admission** free.

The first spectacles were sighted in Italy in 1280, but the Japanese had to stumble around blindly until the 16th century, when Jesuit priest Francis Xavier brought a pair into the country. The 6,000-piece collection is complemented by a 19th-century eyeglass workshop shipped over from the French Alps.

Gallery TOM

2-11-1 Shoto, Shibuya-ku (3467 8102). 15min walk from Shibuya JR station, Hachiko exit or 6min walk from Shinsen station (Keio Inokashira Line). **Open** 10.30am-5.30pm Tue-Sun. **Admission** ¥600; ¥200 concessions.

Touching the art at this museum is encouraged, not prohibited. It is designed to give blind and visually-impaired visitors an opportunity to discover and explore works by a range of artists.

Japan Folk Crafts Museum (Mingei-kan)

4-3-33 Komaba, Meguro-ku (3467 4527/www.mingeikan.or.jp). Komaba-Todaimae station (Keio Inokashira Line). **Open** 10am-5pm Tue-Sun. **Admission** ¥1,000; ¥200-¥500 concessions.

Kyoto University professor Yanagi Soetsu created this museum in 1936 to spotlight *mingei*, literally 'arts of the people'. The criteria for inclusion in the collection were that objects should be made anonymously, by hand, and in large quantities. Yanagi collected ceramics, metalwork, woodwork, textiles, paintings and other everyday items from Japan, China, Korea, Taiwan and Okinawa at a time when their beauty wasn't always recognised. Handwritten labels (in Japanese) and simple wooden display cases complement the rustic feel.

English pamphlet. Gift shop.

Kume Art Museum

Kume Bldg 8F, 2-25-5 Kami-Osaki, Shinagawa-ku (3491 1510). Meguro JR station, west exit. **Open** 10am-5pm Mon, Tue, Thur-Sun. **Admission** ¥500; ¥200-¥300 concessions.

Kume Kuchiro was one of the first Japanese artists to embrace the Impressionist style. This museum has changing displays of his paintings, with themes taken from his 1871-2 trek across the globe.

Gift shop.

Matsuoka Museum of Art

5-12-6 Shirokanedai, Minato-ku (5449 0251/ www.matsuoka-museum.jp). Shirokanedai station, exit 1. **Open** 10am-5pm Tue-Sun. **Admission** ¥800; ¥500-¥700 concessions.

Over a lifetime that spanned nearly a century, real-estate developer Matsuoka Seiji became a true connoisseur of Japanese paintings, Asian ceramics and ancient sculpture from China, Rome and Egypt. The quality and range of the objects is impressive and the English-language labels excellent.

English pamphlet. Gift shop.

The Hachiko exit of Shibuya JR station leads to this giant pedestrian crossing.

Museum of Contemporary Sculpture

4-12-18 Naka-Meguro, Meguro-ku (3792 5858/ www.museum-of-sculpture.org). Naka-Meguro station, central exit. **Open** 10am-5pm Tue-Sun. **Admission** free.

The Watanabe Collection includes more than 200 pieces by 56 contemporary Japanese artists. Three outdoor areas filled with large, mostly conceptual works complement two storeys of figurative studies inside. The marble tombstones in the adjacent graveyard provide an interesting counterpoint.

Coffee shop.

Nature Study Institute & Park

5-21-5 Shirokanedai, Minato-ku (3441 7176/ www.ins.kahaku.go.jp). Meguro JR station, east exit. **Open** *Sept-Apr* 9am-4.30pm Tue-Sun. *May-Aug* 9am-5pm Tue-Sun. **Admission** ¥210; ¥60 concessions.

A primeval forest in central Tokyo? Yes, it's a remnant of the ancient Musashino Plain. Established as a scientific study area in 1949, it contains about 750 plants, 100 birds and 1,300 types of insect. Admission is limited to a few hundred people at a time so you can enjoy the turtle-filled ponds and forested hills in peace. The one-room museum at the entrance is hardly a destination in itself, but has a couple of interesting points, such as a map showing how the amount of greenery in Tokyo has decreased since 1677, largely as a result of dwindling temple grounds. The park is adjacent to the Tokyo Metropolitan Teien Art Museum (*see p108*).

Gift shop.

Parasite Museum

4-1-1 Shimo-Meguro, Meguro-ku (3716 1264). Meguro JR station, west exit. **Open** 10am-5pm Tue-Sun. **Admission** free.

Medical doctor Kamegai Satoru opened this museum in 1953 after he noticed that his practice increasingly dealt with parasites caused by the unsanitary conditions that were widespread in post-war Japan. The museum now displays some 300 samples of 45,000 parasites he collected, 20 of which were discovered by his foundation. The second floor has a display of an 8.8m (29ft) tapeworm taken from the body of a 40-year-old man, with a ribbon next to it showing you just how long 8.8m really is. The gift shop sells parasites preserved in plastic keyrings and postcards sure to gross out your friends.

Gift shop. English pamphlet.

Parco Museum of Art & Beyond

7F, Parco Dept Store Part 3, 15-1 Udagawacho, Shibuya-ku (3464 5111/www.parco-art.com/ parco_museum). Shibuya JR station, Hachiko exit. **Open** 10am-8.30pm during exhibitions only. **Admission** ¥700; free-¥500 concessions. **Credit** AmEx, DC, JCB, MC, V.

Parco, Seibu department store's hip division, hosts this gallery, inside one of Shibuya's ultimate shoppers' paradises. As only the trendiest photographers and designers from Japan and overseas are invited, this is one of the cooler places to be seen (though not necessarily to see – the shows are variable). Recent exhibitions have featured photographer Kawauchi Rinko and design group Groovisions.

Shinjuku Gyoen is a favourite day out for Tokyo families. *See p112.*

Shoto Museum of Art

2-14-14 Shoto, Shibuya-ku (3465 9421). Shinsen station (Keio Inokashira Line), north exit. **Open** 9am-5pm Tue-Sun. **Admission** ¥300; ¥100 concessions; children free Sat.

The Shoto's rough stone exterior gives way to curved walls encircling a central fountain. It's no Guggenheim, but this odd bit of ageing architecture (owned by Shibuya ward) sometimes hosts inspired shows, such as a recent retrospective of 16th-century Japanese painter Sesson and a survey of south-east Asian textiles. It's also inexpensive and quiet.

Café.

Sugino Costume Museum

4-6-19 Kami-Osaki, Shinagawa-ku (3491 8151/ www.costumemuseum.jp). Meguro JR station, west exit. **Open** 10am-4pm Mon-Sat. Closed 20 July-31 Aug, 23 Dec-7 Jan. **Admission** ¥200; ¥100-¥160 concessions.

Sugino College's four-floor costume museum presents a small collection of old western and Japanese fashions, along with a few 'ethnic' costumes from various parts of the globe. It's a dingy affair, with old linoleum floors, fluorescent lighting, chipped mannequins and dusty display cases, but those interested in historical clothing may appreciate it. A flapper dress from the 1920s greets visitors on the first floor. Upstairs, the selection of Japanese clothing includes Edo period textile swatches, hair accessories, Ainu tribal wear and a reproduction of a woman's Heian period outfit.

Gift shop.

TEPCO Electric Energy Museum (Denryoku-kan)

1-12-10 Jinnan, Shibuya-ku (3477 1191/www5. mediagalaxy.co.jp/Denryokukan). Shibuya JR station, Hachiko guchi exit. **Open** 10am-6pm Mon, Tue, Thur-Sun. *Cinema showings* 10.30am, 1pm, 3.30pm Mon. **Admission** free. *Cinema showings* ¥100.

TEPCO (Tokyo Electric Power Company) juices the city. Seven floors of displays show how electricity's made and where it goes; exhibits range from life-size mock-ups of nuclear power generators to the latest electronic appliances. A more realistic display would include the metal bucket which, when used to mix uranium at a fuel processing plant in Tokaimura in 1999, touched off Japan's worst nuclear accident. Instead there's the benign Energy Monster to host interactive computer games. On Mondays, Hollywood films are screened in the museum's cinema.

Café. Gift shop.

Tobacco & Salt Museum

1-16-8 Jinnan, Shibuya-ku (3476 2041/www.jti.co.jp/ Culture/museum/WelcomeJ.html). Shibuya JR station, Hachiko exit. **Open** 10am-6pm Tue-Sun. **Admission** ¥100; ¥50 concessions.

This quirky four-floor museum provides an introduction to two former Japanese government monopolies. There's a rack holding hundreds of cigarette packets from around the world, historical artefacts and a re-creation of Edo-period tobacco production – and salt harvesting. At the gift shop, smokers can purchase unusual Japanese cigarettes.

Coffee shop. Gift shop.

Toguri Museum of Art

1-11-3 Shoto, Shibuya-ku (3465 0070/www.toguri-museum.or.jp). Shinsen station (Keio Inokashira Line). **Open** 9.30am-5.30pm Tue-Sun. **Admission** ¥1,030; ¥420-¥730 concessions. **Credit** AmEx, DC, JCB, MC, V.

The art of porcelain is the focus of this quiet museum. Its 3,000 antique Chinese and Japanese pieces rotate through four shows a year. All displays are accompanied by captions in Japanese and English.

Gift shop. Lounge.

Tokyo Metropolitan Museum of Modern Japanese Literature

4-3-55 Komaba, Meguro-ku (3466 5150). Komaba-Todaimae station (Keio Inokashira Line), west exit. **Open** 9am-4.30pm Sat, Sun. **Admission** free.

Once owned by the royal Maeda family, the large two-storey brick mansion housing this museum was designed as an example of 'English Tudor' architecture in 1929. Wide stairwells, lofty ceilings and dark-wood accents provide the university-library-like setting for the collection of original manuscripts, first editions, photographs and other memorabilia from modern Japanese writers. Unfortunately, there are no English descriptions. Next door is the Japan Museum of Modern Literature (3468 4181).

Lockers. Lounge.

Tokyo Metropolitan Museum of Photography

Ebisu Garden Place, 1-13-3 Mita, Meguro-ku (3280 0031/www.tokyo-photo-museum.or.jp). Ebisu JR station, east exit. **Open** 10am-6pm Tue, Wed, Sat, Sun; 10am-8pm Thur, Fri. **Admission** varies.

This four-floor museum in one corner of Ebisu Garden Place is Tokyo's premier photography showcase. Regular exhibitions draw from the museum's extensive collection, and temporary shows feature both Japanese and international themes and photographers. In the basement, the small Images and Technology Gallery presents a multimedia history of optics, featuring tricks such as anamorphism, and the occasional temporary media art exhibition.

Café. English pamphlet. Gift shop. Lockers.

Tokyo Metropolitan Teien Art Museum

5-21-9 Shirokanedai, Minato-ku (3443 0201/www.teien-art-museum.ne.jp). Meguro JR station, east exit. **Open** 10am-6pm daily. Closed 2nd, 4th Wed of mth. **Admission** varies with exhibition. *Garden only* ¥200; free-¥160 concessions.

This 1933 art deco mansion, fronted by both a western-style rose garden and a Japanese stroll garden with teahouse, was once the home of Prince Asaka Yasuhiko, the uncle of Emperor Hirohito, and his wife, Princess Nobuko, the eighth daughter of Emperor Meiji. The prince returned from a three-year stint in 1920s Paris enamoured of art deco and decided to build a modern house. Henri Rapin designed most of the interior, while René Lalique added his touch to the crystal chandeliers and the doors. The actual house was completed by architects of the Imperial Household Department, foremost among them Yokichi Gondo. Visits to temporary exhibitions double as house tours, with the artwork spread throughout the rooms.

Gift shop. Lockers. Lounge.

Accommodation
1 Century Hyatt, p43.
2 Keio Plaza, p44.
3 Park Hyatt, p44.
4 Tokyo Hilton, p44.
5 Shinjuku Prince, p44.
6 Washington Hotel, p44.
7 New City Hotel, p44.
8 Shinjuku Palace, p45.
9 Star Hotel, p45.
10 Japan Minshuku Association, p50.
11 Shinjuku Kuyakusho-Mae Capsule, p51.
12 Hotel Listo, p48.
13 Bron Mode, p49.

Sightseeing
14 Bunka Gakuen Costume, p111.
15 Shinjuku Gyoen, p112.
16 Sompo Japan Museum, p112.
17 Tokyo Metropolitan Government Building, p113.
18 Toto Super Space, p113.

Restaurants
19 Angkor Wat, p136.
20 Ban Thai, p136.
21 Le Bistrot d'à Côté, p136.
22 China Grill-Xenlon, p136.
23 Christon Café, p138.
24 Hannibal, p138.
25 Hyakunincho Yataimura, p138.
26 Mysterious Bar, p138.
27 New York Grill, p138.
28 Tokaien, p139.
29 Tsunahachi, p139.
30 Yui-An, p140.

Coffee Shops
31 Bon, p152.
32 Danwashitsu Takizawa, p153.
33 GeraGera, p154.
34 New Dug, p155.
35 Tajimaya, p155.

Bars
36 Angel, p160.
37 Café Hoegaarden, p160.
38 Clubhouse, p161.
39 The Dubliners, p1161.
40 La Jetée, p161.
41 J Fox R&R Bar, p162.
42 Living Bar, p162.
43 Shot Bar Shadow, p162.

Shops and Services
44 Isetan, p167.
45 Keio, p168.
46 Lumine 1&2, p168.
47 My Lord, p169.
48 My City, p168.
49 Odakyu, p169.
50 Kinokuniya, p174.
51 Sakuraya, p176.
52 Yodobashi Camera, p176.
53 Comme Ça Store, p176.
54 Sagemonoya, p183.
55 Franc Franc, p185.
56 Shinanoya, p186.
57 Yamaya, p186.
58 Don Quixote, p188.
59 Disk Union, p190.
60 Like an Edison, p190.
61 Shame Records, p190.
62 Vinyl, p190.
63 Virgin Meagastore, p190.

Children
15 Shinjuku Gyoen, p203.
64 Uniqlo, p206.

Film
65 Cinema Square Tokyu, p207.

Galleries
66 epSITE, p214.
67 Konica Plaza, p215.
68 Nikon Plaza Shinjuku, p215.
69 Shinjuku I-Land, p215.
70 Shinjuku Park Tower, Gallery One, p215.

Gay & Lesbian
71 Ace, p216.
72 Advocates Bar, p216.
73 Advocates Café, p216.
74 Arty Farty, p216.
75 Dragon, p217.
76 Fuji, p217.
77 GB, p217.
78 Hug, p217.
79 Kinsmen, p217.
80 Kinswomyn, p217.
81 Monsoon, p218.
82 New Sazae, p218.
83 Tamago Bar, p218.
84 Word Up, p218.
85 24 Kaikan Shinjuku, p219.
86 Dock, p220.
87 HX, p220.
88 King of College, p220.
89 Slamdunk, p220.
90 Books Rose, p221.
91 Cocolo Café, p221.
92 Hotel Nuts, p221.
93 Karaoke Rafu, p221.
94 Kinkantei, p221.

Music
95 J, p225.
96 Shinjuku Pit Inn, p226.
97 Koseinenkin Kaikan, p228.
98 Antiknock, p229.
99 Liquid Room, p231.
100 Shinjuku Loft, p232.
101 Shinjuku Loft Plus One, p232.
102 Shinjuku Marz, p232.
103 Studio Jam, p232.

Nightlife
104 Club Acid Tokyo, p235.
105 Club Complex Code, p236.
106 Izm, p238.
99 Liquid Room, p238.
107 Oto, p240.

Performing Arts
108 Koma Gekijo, p244.
109 Space Zero, p246.
110 Suehiro-tei, p247.

Sport & Fitness
111 Tipness, p252.

Shinjuku
Ome Kaido
Nomura Building
Sompo Japan Building
Kita Dori
Mitsui Building
Sumitomo Building
Shinjuku Centre Building
Tocho Dori
Chuo Dori
Gijido Dori
Higashi Dori
No.1
Tokyo Metropolitan Govt Twin Towers
No.2
Fureai Dori
NTT
Minami Dori
Koen Dori
Plaza Dori
Keio Shinjuku Station
Odakyu Shinjuku Station
Toei Shinjuku Station
Toei Shinjuku Line
Koshu Kaido
Bunka Women's University
Seibu Shinjuku Station
Marunouchi Line
Studio Alta
JR Shinjuku Station
New South Exit
Takashimaya Times Square
Kuyakusho Dori
Hanazono Shrine
Yasukuni Dori
Shinjuku Sanchome
Meiji Dori
Shinjuku Dori
Gyoen Dori
Seigaku-ji Temple
Seijuin Temple
Taiso-ji Temple
Tenryu-ji Temple
Shinjuku Gyoen
0
200 m
200 yds
© Copyright Time Out Group 2003

Shinjuku

Map p109

Whatever else you do during your time in Tokyo, do not allow yourself to miss out on Shinjuku, the most diverse and interesting area that Tokyo has to offer. Shinjuku is like Tokyo in microcosm. Split neatly into two halves, west and east, by the Chuo and Yamanote railway lines, Shinjuku has a high-rise west side that is the embodiment of Japan's post-war metamorphosis. The highest concentration of skyscrapers in Tokyo is home to a host of top-class hotels, and provides prestigious addresses for several banking and insurance companies' headquarters. Since 1991 it has also been home to the Tokyo Metropolitan Government – its Gotham-like twin towers appropriately overlook the whole area.

On the east side, meanwhile, things get down and dirty. Here is not only the glitz, neon and downright dodgy red light district of **Kabuki-cho** but also the colourful bars of **San-chome** (san cho-may), the gay district of **Ni-chome** (nee cho-may), the tiny watering holes of **Golden Gai**, where the Tokyo of the 1950s is making its last stand (*see p160*), and the grungy music venues that are scattered throughout the area.

Shinjuku is also a transport hub. In fact, Shinjuku is the busiest railway station in the world, with a million punters passing through daily. Those photos you've seen of thrashing commuters being pushed on to crowded trains by uniformed guards in the Tokyo rush hour? Shinjuku station, every morning of the week, from 7.30am onwards. Get up early and take a camera, but don't expect there to be much room to stand on the platform.

One word of warning: like many of Tokyo's railway stations, Shinjuku has tunnels that stretch for miles underground on several basement and sub-basement levels. Before you go anywhere here, make sure you have a good idea of which station exit you need (there are around 50).

It may surprise some that for all Shinjuku's glitz and neon (if you've seen a photo of neon sign after neon sign in Japan chances are it's from Shinjuku), it is also steeped in counterculture. Ni-chome, a self-contained area near Shinjuku San-chome and Shinjuku Gyoenmae stations, is the most active and open gay and lesbian district in the country with gay literature, advertisements and goods openly displayed (something unusual for Japan) on airy sidestreets.

The little alleyways around Kabuki-cho house avant-garde performance houses as well as intellectual hothouses disguised as tiny bars. Indeed, Shinjuku was the explosive epicentre of Japan's (very active) youth movement in the 1960s (something that can be seen in director Nagisa Oshima's 1968 classic *Diary of a Shinjuku Thief*). This feeling has never left some of the smaller, less populated byways of the east side. Going back a bit further, Shinjuku was also the site of one of the most important black markets in Tokyo just after the war: whatever you needed you could find in the area's labyrinth of teeming and seamy sidestreets.

That spirit of consumption (as well as the seaminess) remains, whether it be for good times and/or sex – both of which jump out at you in in-your-face Kabuki-cho – or for department store shopping – myriad stores are located on and around Shinjuku Dori, also on the east side of Shinjuku. For some reason, the city planners (though the notion is a contradiction in terms in Japan) thought there wasn't enough consumption going on in Shinjuku, so in the early 1990s they commissioned **Takashimaya Times Square**, a huge shopping complex built on old train switching grounds, which were clearly dangerously under-consuming. So now Shinjuku's revitalised south exit has joined the east and west as a destination for shoppers and partygoers.

Business, shopping, drinking, partying and the arts all exist side by side in this fascinating, unique section of Tokyo. Take your time here to drink in all the atmosphere you can. No trip to Tokyo is complete without a romp through Shinjuku, steeped in history, consumerism and decadence.

GETTING THERE

Shinjuku is on the JR Chuo, Saikyo, Sobu and Yamanote lines, and on the Marunouchi Line, the Toei Oedo and Shinjuku lines, the Keio Line, the Odakyu Line and the Seibu Shinjuku Line.

Shinjuku sights

Banknote & Postage Stamp Museum

9-5 Ichigaya-Honmuracho, Shinjuku-ku (3268 3271/www.npb.go.jp/ja/museum/index.html). Ichigaya station, exit 6. **Open** 9.30am-4.30pm Tue-Sun. **Admission** free.

The Finance Ministry runs this historical overview of the Printing Bureau, founded in 1871 as the Paper Money Office. Japanese currency is indebted to Edoardo Chiossone, an Italian intaglio plate engraver who helped improve the look of Japan's money in the late 19th century (including making the empress's visage on a banknote look more Japanese). The displays include money and stamps from around the world.

The gateway to **Kabuki-cho**, Shinjuku's very own sin city.

Bunka Gakuen Costume Museum

Endo Memorial Hall 3F, Bunka Gakuen, 3-22-1 Yoyogi, Shibuya-ku (3299 2387/www.bunka.ac.jp/museum/hakubutsu.htm). Shinjuku JR station, south exit. **Open** 10am-4.30pm Mon-Sat. **Admission** ¥500; ¥200-¥300 concessions.

Women's fashion college Bunka Gakuen founded this museum on its 60th anniversary in 1979. The small collection includes examples of historical Japanese clothing, such as an Edo-era fire-fighting coat and a brightly coloured, 12-layer *karaginumo* outfit. Kamakura-period scrolls illustrate the types of dress worn by different classes of people. The displays change four or five times a year.

Gift shop.

Fire Museum

3-10 Yotsuya, Shinjuku-ku (3353 9119/www.tfd.metro.tokyo.jp/ts/museum.htm). Yotsuya-Sanchome station, exit 2. **Open** 9.30am-5pm Tue-Sun. **Admission** free.

This Tokyo Fire Department-owned museum traces the cultural history of fire-fighting, from decorative uniforms to vintage ladder trucks to the elaborate

pompoms used to identify neighbourhood brigades. Between 1603 and 1868, 97 major conflagrations swept through Tokyo. Scale models, sound and lights recreate an Edo-period blaze in miniature. Video monitors show footage of the fires that destroyed the city after the 1923 Great Kanto Earthquake and World War II fire bombing. Elsewhere, cartoon stories (in Japanese) teach children what to do in case fire breaks out at home. Kids also love climbing into the rooftop helicopter.
English pamphlet. Gift shop.

Meiji Memorial Picture Gallery (Seitoku kinen Kaiga-Kan)

Meiji Jingu Outer Garden, 9 Kasumigaoka, Shinjuku-ku (3401 5179/ www.meijijingu.or.jp/gaien/01.htm). Shinanomachi station. **Open** 9am-5pm daily. **Admission** ¥500; ¥200-¥300 concessions.

First built in 1920, this shrine to the Meiji emperor suffered damage during World War II and was rebuilt in 1958. The long, windowless European-style stone block structure with a triple arched entrance and domed roof appears at the end of one of Tokyo's most unusual views, a colonnade of gingko trees that turn bright yellow in autumn. Past the dramatic, high-ceilinged Japanese granite and marble entrance, long galleries of Japanese-style paintings document famous events in the life of the emperor who opened Japan to the world.
English pamphlet.

NTT Inter Communication Centre

Tokyo Opera City Tower 4F, 3-20-2 Nishi-Shinjuku, Shinjuku-ku (0120 144199/www.ntticc.or.jp). Hatsudai station (Keio New Line), central exit. **Open** 10am-6pm Tue-Sun during exhibitions only. Closed 2nd Sun in Feb, 1st Sun in Aug. **Admission** ¥800; ¥400-¥600 concessions. **Credit** (shop only) AmEx, DC, JCB, MC, V.

Opened by telecommunications giant NTT in 1996, this museum is at the leading edge of media design and media arts. The small permanent collection includes a timeline of technology, various art videos and interactive installations, and sound pieces designed for the museum's anechoic chamber.
Gift shop. Internet café. Lockers.

Shinjuku Gyoen

11 Naito-cho, Shinjuku-ku (3350 0151/www.shinjukugyoen.go.jp). Shinjuku Gyoenmae station. **Open** *Park* 9am-4.30pm Tue-Sun. Open daily during cherry blossom (early Apr) and chrysanthemum (early Nov) season. *Greenhouse* 11am-3pm Tue-Sun. **Admission** ¥200; ¥50-free concessions.

Shinjuku Gyoen opened as an imperial garden in 1906, during Japan's push for westernisation, and was the first place in Japan that many non-indigenous species were planted. The fascination with the west is evident in the garden's layout: there are both English- and French-style sections, as well as a traditional Japanese garden. The park is spectacular at *hanami* (cherry blossom viewing, *see p196*), when its 1,500 trees paint the whole place pink.

Sompo Japan Museum (formerly Yasuda Kasai Seiji Togo Memorial Museum)

Sompo Japan Bldg 42F, 1-26-1 Nishi-Shinjuku, Shinjuku-ku (3349 3081/www.sompo-japan.co.jp/museum). Shinjuku JR station, west exit. **Open** 10am-6pm Tue-Sun. **Admission** ¥500; free-¥300 concessions; additional charge for special exhibitions.

The views from this 42nd-floor museum are spectacular. Perhaps to compete, Yasuda, as the insurance company was known at the time, purchased Van Gogh's 1889 *Sunflowers* in October 1987 for the then record-breaking price of over ¥5 billion (£24 million). Though there is now speculation that it's a fake, no one is willing to find out for sure. This symbol of Japan's go-go Bubble years hangs alongside Cézanne's *Pommes et Serviette* (bought in January 1990) in a dim glass box. The museum's core work is by Japanese artists, specifically Togo Seiji (1897-1978), who donated 200 of his own pieces and 250 items from his art collection to the museum. Temporary exhibitions feature early modernists such as Utrillo and often tepid group shows of contemporary Japanese artists.
Gift shop.

Sword Museum

4-25-10 Yoyogi, Shibuya-ku (3379 1386). Sangubashi station (Odakyu Line). **Open** 10am-4.30pm Tue-Sun. **Admission** ¥525; free-¥315 concessions.

The confiscation of swords as offensive weapons during the American occupation threatened the traditional Japanese craft of sword-making. To safeguard it, the Society for the Preservation of Japanese Art Swords was established in 1948. It opened this museum in 1968 to display its collection of centuries-old swords and fittings. Even non-enthusiasts may find themselves mesmerised by their qualities: mysterious, wave-like patterns, sharkskin handles and sculptured guards.
Gift shop.

Takagi Bonsai Museum

Meiko Shokai Bldg, 1-1 Gobancho, Chiyoda-ku (3262 1640/www.bonsaimuseum.org). Ichigaya JR station. **Open** 10am-5pm Tue-Sun. **Admission** ¥800; ¥500 concessions.

Decades ago, Takagi Reiki started a business repairing nylon stockings. He soon expanded his company, Meiko Shokai, into recycling machinery and paper shredders. Now the top two floors of the company headquarters are used for bonsai cultivation and display. The rooftop garden is a serene spot with a 500-year-old pine and surrounding pond. Below it, there's an outdoor nursery and storage area for some of the 300 bonsai in the collection. Inside, the trees on display change seasonally – delicately scented pale apricot in late winter, robust pink cherry in spring, drooping red maple in autumn, and so on. Pots and other craftwork are also on display.
Tearoom. Gift shop. English pamphlet.

The **Tokyo Metropolitan Government Building** towers over the neighbouring park.

Tokyo Metropolitan Government Building Twin Observatories

2-8-1 Nishi-Shinjuku, Shinjuku-ku (5321 1111/ observatory 5320 7890/www.yokoso.metro.tokyo.jp). Tocho-mae station (Toei Oedo Line), exit 4. **Open** *North observatory* 9.30am-10pm Tue-Sun. *South observatory* 9.30am-5.30pm Mon, Wed-Sun. **Admission** free.

Two of the best views over Tokyo have the added bonus of being free. Each of the TMG twin towers has an observatory on the 45th floor, affording a 360° panorama interrupted only by the other tower. Admire the view while sipping a coffee from the cafeteria in the centre of the vast floor. Other buildings in west Shinjuku with free viewing areas include the Shinjuku Centre Building (53F) and the Nomura Building (49F), both of which are open late.

Tokyo Opera City Art Gallery

Tokyo Opera City Tower 3-4F, 3-20-2 Nishi-Shinjuku, Shinjuku-ku (5353 0756/www.operacity.jp/ag). Hatsudai station (Keio New Line), central exit. **Open** noon-8pm Tue-Thur, Sun, noon-9pm Fri, Sat. **Admission** ¥1,000; free concessions.

With money from Odakyu Railways, NTT and other giant corporations, high-ceilinged Opera City has been one of the city's largest and best-funded private contemporary art spaces since it opened in 1999. It brings in travelling shows from around the world and initiates its own exhibitions of Japanese and international artists. Head curator Kataoka Mami's move to the Mori Art Museum at the beginning of 2003 could suggest change – Hori Motoaki, former curator at the Museum of Modern Art, Kamakura, has taken her place. Upstairs from the main galleries is the Terada Collection of Japanese modern art and Project N, a compact space for emerging artists; entry to both is included in the admission price. The museum shares a building with the NTT Inter Communication Centre (*see p112*).

Toto Super Space

L-Tower Bldg 26-27F, 1-6-1 Nishi-Shinjuku (3345 1010). Shinjuku station, exits A17, A18. **Open** 10am-6pm daily. Closed 1st & 3rd Wed of mth. **Admission** free.

It's hard to spend any time at all in Japan without building up an interest in toilet technology. This showroom, operated by the country's leading maker of bathroom hardware, has something to intrigue even the most jaded toilet user. As well as the now standard bidet toilets, Toto also makes baths that fill themselves automatically and can be switched on via the internet. The latest thing is toilets that analyse what's deposited in there. No, really.

Other sites in west Tokyo

See also pp114-120 **Outside the Loop**, for sights further west.

Akasaka Detached Palace (Geihinkan)

2-1-1 Moto-Akasaka, Minato-ku (3478 1111). Yotsuya station, exit 2. Not open to the public.

Tokyo is not famous for the uniformity of its architecture, but even so this building is a surprise. Its construction, in the early years of the 20th century, was intended to prove that Japan could do anything the west could, including build palaces, so they built a hybrid of Buckingham Palace and Versailles. The late Emperor Hirohito lived here when he was crown prince, but the only people allowed in these days are visiting dignitaries. A great pity.

Outside the Loop

There's lots more Tokyo to enjoy outside the bounds of the JR Yamanote Line.

Shimo-Kitazawa

The 1960s, and all of the decade's cultural upheavals, affected Japan in unexpected and sometimes subtle ways. One of the effects was the emergence of a small area south-west of Shinjuku known as Shimo-Kitazawa. If Tokyo is a collection of loose village communities, as some people like to say, then Shimo-Kitazawa is its laid-back bohemian enclave, a mixture of London's Camden and Soho.

The creative impetus behind the area's growth came from the 1960s *sho-gekijou* (small-theatre) movement, a phenomenon born of frustration with theatres dominated by either western realism or tradition-bound *kabuki* and *noh*. The *sho-gekijou* movement gave younger actors and directors the freedom to experiment and express themselves, and as fortune would have it, a large number of these came to be concentrated in Shimo-Kitazawa.

As well as theatre, this area has become famous for its live houses – the dark, dynamic, box-like venues where Tokyo's aspiring bands hone their skills. Every weekend, the live houses – particularly the well-known ones, such as **Shelter**, **Club Que** and **Club 251** (*see p232, p230 and p230*) – are rammed full with a body-pierced, leather-wearing crowd moshing politely in front of a tiny stage.

To get the full Shimo-Kitazawa experience, leave by the north exit and turn right, and the first thing that strikes you is the grotto-like entrance of the **Stone Market** gem and crystal shop (2-25-17 Kitazawa, Setagaya-ku, 5790 2733/www.stone-m.com/shop.html). Coming up to the crossroads with Shiseido on the right corner, the street that stretches away from right to left will take you past shops selling new and second-hand clothes ranging from cute to bizarre, and all points in-between.

The road from the station terminates in a T-junction. Turning right leads back to the train tracks, and straight ahead will take you past **fxg** (*see p191*) – the shop that spearheaded the current wave of cheap, stylish opticians – to Ichibangai Dori.

Over on the other side, the station's south exit crackles with life after dark, as this is where the area's residents and visitors go to eat, drink and mosh themselves into a happy, eardrum-ringing haze.

Directly opposite the exit is the area's main *shotengai* (shopping street), packed full of fast-food shops, *pachinko* parlours and cheap boutiques. Half-way down the street the area's distinctive character starts to come through, with its second-hand book, game and CD shops. A road branching off to the right, with Mr Donuts on the corner, points the way to a quiet, leafy street with one of the best *izakaya* in the area – the stately **Shirube** (*see p149*).

Directly opposite Shirube is the English pub, **Heaven's Door** (*see p166*), a haven for those looking for a decent pint and UK football.

Going back to the *shotengai* and walking right to the bottom, you'll find a knot of streets leading off in five directions. These streets contain hundreds of little bars and restaurants, many of them serving ethnic food and drink.

Back at the south exit, a road off to the left of the Minami-Shotengai leads to where the action is, in terms of theatres and live houses. Halfway down this street is the basement live-house Club Que, while at the end of the street is Chazawa Dori, with Shelter off to the left and Club 251 about ten minutes' walk to the right. The streets between the Minami-Shotengai and the Chazawa Dori are well worth a wander, as they host several 'natural-food' *izakaya* and the **Honda Theatre** (2-10-15 Kitazawa, Setagaya-ku, 3468 0030/www.honda-geki.com).

Arty, lively and occasionally pretentious, Shimo-Kitazawa has the power to restore the faith of those who say Tokyo's losing its soul.

GETTING THERE

Shimo-Kitazawa is on the Keio Inokashira and Odakyu lines.

The Chuo Line

Loved and loathed, the Chuo Line is an essential artery feeding workers from the western suburbs of Tokyo into the city's main business centres. The Japanese love lists, and the orange train is near the top on quite a few. Number one in terms of service-stopping suicides, number two for most crowded trains, the Chuo Line is also notorious for gropers and drunken salarymen, and often both. But it's not the journey, it's where you're going that counts. Towns along the Chuo Line were famous for their writers, musicians and hippies in times past. These people are by and large gone, but

Japan Open-Air Folk House Museum provides a glimpse of old Japan. *See p120.*

many of the charming businesses that served them remain as they were, and with them stays a sense of community. Although the Chuo Line does have its major shopping centres, such as Kichijoji, these tend to be more quirky, with more family-run businesses than in the central areas of Tokyo. The best stations to explore are from Nakano to Kichijoji, although some stations further along the line can yield delights such as the open-air branch of the **Edo-Tokyo Museum**, in Musashi Koganei (*see below*).

Edo-Tokyo Open Air Architectural Museum (Edo-Tokyo Tatemono-en)

3-7-1 Sakura-cho, Koganei Ishi (042 388 3300/ www4.ocn.ne.jp/~tatemono). Musashi Koganei station, north exit, then any bus from No2 or No3 bus stop. Alight at Koganei Koen Nishi-Guchi. **Open** *Apr-Sept* 9.30am-5.30pm Tue-Sun. *Oct-Mar* 9.30am-4.30pm Tue-Sun. **Admission** ¥400; free-¥200 concessions.

Tokyo's façade may be in an never-ending cycle of renewal, but the capital's architectural heritage is well preserved in an unexpectedly rich hoard of buildings at this branch of the Edo-Tokyo Museum. As well as swank private residences and quaint old town shops, there's a host of one-offs, such as an ornate bathhouse and a mausoleum built for a shogun's wife. Even the visitors' centre once served as a ceremonial pavilion in front of the Imperial Palace. Be prepared for lots of slipping in and out of shoes if you want to visit the interiors.

Free umbrella loans in rain. Gift shop. Gift shop.

Nakano

Although best known these days for its cheap shopping, Nakano was once a home for 80,000 dogs. The fifth shogun, Tokugawa Tsunaiyasho, was particularly fond of dogs, and in 1695 he built an *inuyashiki* (dog castle) across the whole of Nakano to keep his tens of thousands of canine mates in comfort. In tribute, a cluster of dogs in green bronze can be found next to the Nakano Council building beside the towering white Nakano Sun Plaza, opposite the north exit of the station.

A must-see for fans of manga, anime (animation) and 'cosplay' (costume play) is the sprawling empire of Mandarake. What was once one shop selling recycled manga comics has spread its tentacles across **Nakano Broadway** (*see p173*), the town's main shopping mall next to the north exit. Now, 14 shops dotted over three floors of the four-floor centre sell comics, figurines, vintage toys, animation cells, CDs, video games, posters, cosplay costumes – in fact anything related to Japan's favourite obsession. Start on the third floor at comic HQ, and lose an afternoon wandering around. Key rings and tiny figurines sell from ¥100, and make cheap and unique souvenirs to take home instead of clichéd chopsticks and fans. Broadway is also home to a host of discount shoe shops and fashion stores, selling at prices far below those charged five minutes' train ride away in Shinjuku.

Inokashira Park, a favourite trysting place for Tokyo's courting couples. *See p118.*

Afterwards, visit the Escher-like, low-wattage confines of Nakano's **Classic** coffee shop (*see p153*) to soak up a ¥400 coffee and a huge sound system playing non-stop classical music. The extensive warren of streets surrounding the Broadway complex has scores of restaurants, bars and *izakaya*, many of them offering food at bargain prices.

Slightly out of Nakano centre are the quirky **Tetsugakudo Park** and the **Toy Museum**.

Tetsugakudo Park

1-34-28 Matsugaoka, Nakano-ku (3954 4881). Nakano station, north exit, then bus bound for Ikebukuro, alighting at Tetsugakudo, or Arai Yakushi-mae station (Seibu Shinjuku Line), then 10min walk. **Open** 9am-5pm daily.

A hillside park founded by philosopher Inoue Enryo, who wanted to enshrine philosophical theory in physical form. The park contains 77 spots that symbolise different doctrines. On the top of the hill are six Meiji-era buildings that are open to the public during *hanami* (cherry blossom viewing, *see p196*), and at weekends and public holidays in October.

Toy Museum

2-12-10 Arai, Nakano-ku (3387 5461/www.toy-art.co.jp/museum.html). Nakano station, north exit. **Open** 10.30am-4pm Mon, Wed, Thur, Sat, Sun. **Admission** ¥500; free uner-2s.

More hands-on than the Japan Toys Museum (*see p87*), the crafts-oriented Toy Museum has no shortage of local kids at play. There's not a video game or TV in sight.

Koenji

The next station after Nakano is the resident wilful teenager of the Chuo Line family. Denim jeans, baggy jumpers and ethnic anoraks all pass the youth test in Koenji, favoured as it is by students, hipsters and a revolving showcase of ignored street musicians. The guitarists are the human hangover from the 'live houses' that dot the backstreets and give Koenji its fame, most of them showcasing headbangers, well-scrubbed punks and hard-rocking bad boy bands. The west side provides the best mix of shops, restaurants and bars. The food and nightlife of Koenji matches its residents, and what it lacks in sophistication it more than makes up for with its honesty and bang for a buck. A good lunch of western dishes, cakes and coffee can be had at the **Yonchome Café** (4-28-10 Koenji Minami, Suginami-ku, 5377 1726, 11am-2am daily), visible from the south exit. In the evening, try **Dachibin** (3-2-13 Koenji-Kita, Suginami-ku, 3377 1532, 5pm-5am daily), an Okinawan oasis. The menu features Okinawan cooking, most of it *chanpuri* (mixed fried things) and many dishes feature the bitter flavours of the local vegetable *goya* – *chanpuri goya* is a good start. If you tire of the pedestrian flavours of Orion, the local draught, then ask for *aomori* – it's the local sake, in two strengths: five-year-old 35 per cent and the older 45 per cent. Drink with respect.

Asagaya

Seeing itself as the prince among the kissed toads of the Chuo Line, Asagaya strives to match the urbanity of inner Tokyo. This self-confidence is based on both slight and solid cultural connections. The area's well-founded reputation for jazz grows every year as its Jazz Street jazz festival, held in October, continues to mutate in size and composition. A number of bars work year round showcasing local jazz players. Although seen and not heard, scribblers of all types laid the foundation for Asagaya's worldview. The Asagaya-kai was a group of prominent Japanese authors that haunted the area from 1910 to the early 1950s. Its leader, Masuji Ibuse, wrote *Black Rain*, the story of a Hiroshima woman's struggle with radiation poisoning. An art renaissance came in the 1970s when the area was a draw for Japan's best manga artists. These days though, its wealthy residents spend rather than create, and a little ambulatory effort will unearth good restaurants and homely, cramped bars.

Worth seeing are the aged trees that line Nakasugi Dori, the main street under the railway tracks, which are at their most gloriously green from May to June. Just off this street can be found **Spicy & Beer Bar** (Watanabe Bldg 1F, 3-31-1 Asagaya-Minami, Suginami-ku, 3220 7752, 11.30am-2am Mon-Thur, 11.30-4am Fri, Sat, 11.30am-midnight Sun), a boozer offering curries and beers from 33 countries. Film buffs note – the square on the south side of the station was a backdrop in the original version of horror movie *The Ring*.

Ogikubo

Key word: *ramen*. One of Tokyo's best known *ramen* shops is in Ogikubo, and people travel from all over Japan to eat there. **Harukiya** (1-4-6 Kami-Ogi, Suginami-ku, 3391 4868, 11am-9pm daily) seats only 16 people, and there's usually a small queue. The *ramen* is great. Ask for *chuka soba* or for extra slices of pork, *chashumen*. Appropriately, Ogikubo's best tourist pull is tied into its past. Harukiya was established in 1952, on the heels of a black market that sprang up after World War II to offset the poverty of those times. What else remains is a good fresh fish, meat and veg market; it sprawls over the basement floor of the Ogikubo Town 7 shopping centre. Sake lovers must partake of the fine flavours on offer at **Saru-no-Kura** (1-8-11 Ogikubo, Suginami-ku, 3391 4366, 5pm-midnight Mon, Tue, Thur-Sun). Fine aesthetics and a menu of sake-enhancing foods all help keep the spotlight on the sake itself, which comes mainly from Niigata prefecture.

Nishi Ogikubo

In the 1960s, peaceful 'Nishi Ogi' rose to heights of civil disobedience as a gathering point for organic veggie-loving hippies. Two cults have arisen as well from these nondescript surroundings – most notorious was Aum Shinrikyo, the religious sect responsible for the subway sarin gas attacks in 1995 that killed 12 people. Now fortunately, Nish Ogi is best known only for antique and bric-à-brac shops – around 65 of them, in fact. Take the north exit from the station and head for the police box. Boldly stride up to the policeman, make no sudden moves, and say 'antique mapu onegaishimasu'. He'll pull one out of the desk, and you'll be on your way to a pleasant day spent strolling the backstreets. Both western and Japanese antiquities are on sale, but don't expect bargains. Overall, the north-west section of the walk has the best furniture, lighting and antique shops. Nishi Ogi is mostly wealthy residential, so as you wander look out for the occasional wicked Japanese garden. Worth browsing are a few eccentric second-hand bookshops. For dinner, try the Mexican food at **El Quixico** (2F, 3-15-14 Nishi-Ogi-Minami, Suginami-ku, 3332 7590, 6pm-2am Tue-Sun), where tasty and fresh Mexican staples go hand in hand with lethal frozen margaritas.

Kichijoji

Resplendent on the edge of Tokyo's 23 wards, Kichijoji serves the local population as a toned-down shopping Mecca when Shinjuku seems too far. Many department stores have branches here, there are cinemas and the supporting cast of bars, restaurants and coffee shops round out the whole. The most popular destination here, though, is **Inokashira Park**. Well-trodden paths surround a carp-filled lake that entices lovers to bond through rowing. In late March and early April, the park fills up with people enjoying *hanami*, cherry blossom-viewing. Any time of the year is good, but summer is best for the **Pepecafe Forest** (4-1-5 Inokashira-Koen, Mitaka-shi, 0422 427081, noon-10pm Mon, Wed-Sun). This groovy park café lies directly across from the central bridge that runs over the lake, and its plastic walls roll up in summer, ideal for evening beers. In between the park and Mitaka, further up the Chuo Line, lies the **Ghibli Museum**, a showcase for the Oscar-winning animation studio of the same name. Elsewhere, ethnic restaurants are something of a speciality. Digging deep among the shopping streets out of the north exit will turn up many more eateries. This plethora of choice makes a Kichijoji an excellent night-time excursion.

The **Ghibli Museum** is the home of *Princess Mononoke* and a host of other anime treats.

Ghibli Museum

1-1-83 Shimorenjaku, Mitaka Shi (0570 055777/ www.ghibli-museum.jp). Kichijoji station, then 15min walk or Mitaka station, south exit, then a community bus. **Open** (tours) 10am, noon, 2pm, 4pm Mon, Wed-Sun. **Admission** ¥1,000; ¥100-¥700 concessions.

Miyazaki Hayao's studio has produced some of the Japan's most popular and complex classics of animation, from *My Neighbour Totoro* to *Princess Mononoke* and *Spirited Away*. Gaining access to this relatively new museum devoted to the studio, however, is tougher than getting into the Kremlin. You need to make reservations and purchase tickets in advance (which can be done from overseas; check the website). Show up on the prescribed day with your ticket and passport or other ID, and you will be escorted into another world. See original prints, play in rooms with painted ceilings and walls, and watch short animations in the cinema. All visitors receive original frames from one of Miyazaki's films as a small souvenir. The gift shop sells original animation cels. *See also p207* **Film**.

Inokashira Park

1-18-31 Gotenyama, Musashino-shi (0422 47 6900). Kichijoji station, park exit, then 10min walk. **Open** *Park* 24hrs daily. *Zoo & boat rentals* 9.30am-4.30pm daily.

Located just 15 minutes from the centre of Tokyo, this park has more than enough to keep you busy for a full afternoon, including a zoo (not the greatest in the world, *see p203*), a pond with amusingly shaped rental boats, a petting zoo and enough playground facilities to keep the little ones happy. At weekends the park comes alive with street traders, musicians and artists.

Daikanyama, the home of upmarket shopping and a giant metal sunflower.

The Tokyu Toyoko Line

The busiest private railway line in Tokyo, the Tokyu Toyoko Line connects Shibuya station in central Tokyo to Yokohama's futuristic mini-city of **Minato-Mirai** (the station is called Sakuragi-cho, *see p256*).

The Shibuya terminus of the railway is a little to the east of the JR Yamanote Line platforms. Because it's a private railway, separate tickets must be purchased. The good news is that it's one of the cheapest lines in Tokyo, with fares starting at ¥110. On its way down to Yokohama, the Toyoko Line cuts through two notable – and exclusive – areas of Tokyo, each with its own character, and each well worth a visit.

Daikanyama

Daikanyama, the first stop out of Shibuya, is a close neighbour of the lively Ebisu area. After the earthquake of 1923, this area was one of few to benefit from a planned reconstruction programme, and the new buildings erected at the time (now mostly gone) set an upmarket tone for the area that survives to this day. Daikanyama remains a resolutely low-rise part of Tokyo, and in recent years has emerged as one of the most fashionable places to shop and stroll, or sip a cappuccino and people-watch at one of the many pavement cafés.

The main reason people come here, though, is the area's plethora of designer fashion outlets. **Jean Paul Gaultier** (28-7 Sarugaku-cho,

Shibuya-ku, 3770 8271, 10.30am-8pm daily) and **Tsumori Chisato** (*see p179*) all have boutiques here, while for younger followers of fashion there are many shops, such as **Love Girls Market** (22-23 Daikanyama-cho, Shibuya-ku, 5459 0150, 11am-8pm daily), selling the latest in outrageous teenage trends.

Of course, in Tokyo, such small outlets are not allowed to thrive alone, and once there's a perceptible profit to be made, older buildings are often cleared away for new designer outlets. Daikanyama's is called **La Fuente** (11-1 Sarugaku-cho, Shibuya-ku, info 3462 8401/ www.lafuente.co.jp, shops 11am-8pm daily, restaurants and bars 11.30am-4am daily), and opened at the end of 2000. This four-storey complex contains about 30 lifestyle stores and fashion outlets, while the basement houses a dozen or so restaurants and bars. Small enough by Tokyo standards to be approachable, as is Daikanyama as a whole.

Jiyugaoka

Step off the train at Jiyugaoka and you might be forgiven for thinking you've arrived in another country. Half of the shop signs and names in this area appear to be written in French, a language that for the Japanese smacks of a certain *exclusivité*. The confusion doesn't stop there, since Jiyugaoka is at the intersection of two railway tracks (the other track being the Tokyu Oimachi Line) and two Tokyo wards, Meguro-ku and Setagaya-ku, with half of the addresses in the area belonging to each *ku*.

The best way to negotiate this confusing area is to leave the station by the central exit, and head straight down the road to the right of the square. By the time you reach the traffic lights, you're within spitting distance of **O'Carolans** (*see p158*), Jiyugaoka's surprisingly spacious Irish bar. It's the other shops in the area, however, that might hold your attention, as Jiyugaoka has probably more lifestyle-related stores than any other area in Tokyo.

These include **Coh House** (2-16-11 Jiyugaoka, Meguro-ku, 3725 6323, 11am-7pm Mon, Tue, Thur-Sun), which imports American furniture from Boston and New England, and **Country Spice** (7-4-12 Okusawa, Setagaya-ku, 3705 8444/www.country-spice.co.jp, 11am-7pm daily), which sells imported antique bric-à-brac such as enamelled bread bins and obscure kitchen equipment, at inflated prices.

People who worry about their food or who have food allergies should check out the Jiyugaoka branch of **Chikyu-Jin Club** (*see p185*), which sells only organically produced produce, from fruit and vegetables to French jams and organic breakfast cereals. Another good alternative bet is **Shala** (*see p185*), which sells Japanese and imported ceramics, as well as its own incense.

A stroll around Jiyugaoka's narrow streets and byways will yield more tiny stores, selling everything from clothing, jewellery and antiques to fresh-baked French pastries. If it all gets too much, head back to the real world at **Rude Boy Café** (5-28-15 Okusawa, Setagaya-ku, 3722 6996, noon-4am daily), where curry and coffee is consumed to a ska soundtrack. In the evening, check out **Café Mardi Gras** (5-29-10 Okusawa, Setagaya-ku, 3277 6892, 8pm-1.30am daily), a bar with a huge selection of vinyl, which hosts live concerts in its basement premises on Monday nights (phone to check). Its food speciality is gumbo, and the master is kind, friendly and tolerant of drunks.

Sights further afield

Art Tower Mito

1-6-8 Gokencho, Mito Shi, Ibaraki Ken (029 227 8111/www.arttowermito.or.jp). Mito station (Joban Line, from Ueno station), north exit or JR highway bus from Tokyo station. **Journey times** Joban Line 1hr; JR highway bus 1hr 40mins. **Open** 9.30am-6pm Tue-Sun. **Admission** ¥800; free concessions.

The Arata Isozaki-designed Art Tower Mito complex (1989) is far, far from Tokyo. But its high-profile exhibitions of contemporary Japanese and international artists may make it worth the day trip. Isozaki's landmark – a twisting tetrahedral spire – rises over the town. From the viewing platform you can see over the Ibaraki plains to the ocean on one side and the mountains on the other.

Cafe. Gift shop.

Japan Open-Air Folk House Museum (Nihon Minka-En)

7-1-1 Masugata, Tama-ku, Kawasaki Shi, Kanagawa Prefecture (044 922 2181/www.city.kawasaki.jp/88/88minka/home/minka.htm). Mukogaoka Yuen station (Odakyu Line), south exit, then a 12-min walk. **Journey time** *30 mins from Shinjuku.* **Open** 9.30am-4.30pm Tue-Sun. **Admission** ¥500; free-¥300 concessions.

The Japanese haven't always lived in concrete shoeboxes. At this wonderful open-air museum in the leafy hills of suburban Kawasaki, you can walk through 23 traditional buildings (*minka*), some up to 300 years old. Authentic structures trucked in from across Japan and reconstructed here include many thatched roof farmhouses, tea huts, a western-style merchant house, a minuscule ferryman's hut, and a working water wheel. In the main museum building at the entrance, videos and displays detail traditional construction techniques. If you feel peckish, one of the farmhouses has a small *soba* shop with a nice view.

Restaurant. English pamphlet.

Mickey and his cartoon compadres come out to play at **Tokyo Disney Resort**. *See p122.*

Jindai Botanical Garden (Jindai Shokubutsuen)

5-31-10 Shindaiji Honcho, Chofu-shi (0424 83 2300). Kichijoji station, park exit, then take Chofu station Kitaguchi-bound bus & alight at Jundai Shokubutsuen stop (20mins). **Journey time** 50mins. **Open** 9.30am-5pm Tue-Sun. **Admission** ¥500.

One of the oldest, and biggest, botanical gardens in Japan. Once you've paid your entrance fee, you're free to wander around, and the place is so spacious that it's almost like a genuine walk in the country. In season, the display afforded by the rose garden in front of the hothouses is truly spectacular. On the other side of the gardens themselves lies an area that has an intriguingly country-like feel, and is complete with a temple, a stream and a couple of soba restauarants. After a walk around the park, it's very relaxing to sit by the stream drinking a locally brewed beer or traditional Japanese soft drink.

John Lennon Museum

Saitama Super Arena 4F-5F, 8 Shin-Toshin, Chuo-ku, Saitama Ken (048 601 0009/www.taisei.co.jp/museum). Kita Yono station (JR Saikyo Line) or Saitama Shin-toshin station (JR Keihin Tohoku Line). **Journey time** 40mins. **Open** 11am-6pm Wed-Mon. **Admission** ¥1,500; ¥500-¥1,000 concessions.

On 9 October 2000, the day that would have marked John Lennon's 60th birthday, the only museum in the world devoted to a single rock musician opened in Saitama. The museum is part of a massive redevelopment that, coincidentally, shares a building with a new arena that hosts rock concerts. With the assistance of Lennon's widow, Yoko Ono, the museum has been able to amass a unique collection of personal belongings. Exhibits are divided into nine zones, each reflecting a stage of Lennon's life, from early childhood to the Beatles to his five-year retire-

ment from music to the 'Imagine' period. Exhibition labels are bilingual, but English speakers may most appreciate reading Lennon's handwriting, from his school scrapbooks to the lyrics for 'Nowhere Man'. The gift shop sells pricey goods under its own label, 'Imagine' (as in 'imagine the profit margin').
Cafe. Gift shop.

Kawasaki City Museum

1-2 Todoroki, Nakahara-ku, Kawasaki Shi, Kanagawa Ken (044 754 4500/http://home.catv.ne.jp/hh/kcm/). Musashi-Kosugi station (Tokyu Toyoko Line), north exit, then bus from No1 stop bound for Nakahara station. **Open** 9.30am-5pm Tue-Sun. **Admission** ¥500; free-¥300 concessions; additional charge for special exhibitions.
This conglomeration of mini-museums hulks in a corner of one of Kawasaki's largest parks. They hold several different types of exhibitions concurrently, usually featuring photography, graphic design, and manga (comics), and also screen art films. A local history section displays various artefacts and rebuilds the area's traditional villages in miniature.
Café. Gift shop.

Sightseeing

Machida City Museum of Graphic Arts

4-28-1 Haramachida, Machida City (0427 260 860/ http://art.by.arena.ne.jp). Machida station (Odakyu Line). **Journey time** 1hr from Shinjuku. **Open** 10am-5pm Tue-Fri; 10am-5.30pm Sat, Sun. **Admission** varies.
Machida is a little out of the way, but it has good shopping, as well as this institution set in airy grounds. Devoted to graphic design, its collection holds 16,000 works on paper from around the world.
Gift shop.

Nikko Edomura

470-2 Karakura, Fujiwara-machi, Shioya-gun, Tochigi-ken (0288 77 1777/www.jidaimura.co.jp/edo/edo02.htm). Kinugawa Onsen station (Tobu Kinugawa Line). **Journey time** 2hrs from Asakusa station. **Open** *mid Mar-Nov* 9am-5pm daily. *Dec-mid Mar* 9am-4pm daily. **Admission** ¥2,800-¥4,500.
While you won't find samurai and geisha strutting the streets of Tokyo, you will find fantastic ninja shows, costumed geisha and other exciting attractions to take you back in time at this sprawling theme park that is a fairly accurate reproduction of old Edo. It's a two-hour ride from Asakusa station.

Sanrio Puroland

1-31 Ochiai, Tama-shi (042 339 1111/www.sanrio.co.jp/english/spl/spl.html). Tama Centre Station (Keio Sagamihara/Odakyu Tama lines). **Open** 10am-5pm Mon-Fri; 10am-8pm Sat, Sun. Closed occasional Wed, Thur. **Admission** 1-day passport ¥4,400; ¥3,300-¥4,000 concessions.
Japanese novelty goods giant Sanrio tries to outdo the American mouse with its own version of a theme park wonderland, whose central character is Hello Kitty. The park features an assortment of rides and mini-adventures squarely aimed at the young children, who are the biggest fans of Kitty-chan. For grown-ups, its biggest attraction may be that it's indoors, and therefore weather-proof, providing somewhere to take the kids when it's pelting down.

Taro Okamoto Museum of Art, Kawasaki

7-1-5 Masugata, Kawasaki City, Kanagawa Prefecture (044 900 9898/www.taromuseum.jp). Mukogaoka-Yuen station, south exit, then a 15-min walk. **Open** 9.30am-5pm Tue-Sun. **Admission** ¥500; free-¥300 concessions; additional fee for special exhibitions.
In the same hillside park as the Japan Open-Air Folk House Museum (*see p120*), this small building is dedicated to the collection, preservation and display of one of Japan's most loved modern artists. It also holds temporary exhibitions of modern and contemporary art, sometimes with unusual angles – Godzilla, for example.
English pamphlet.

Tokyo Disney Resort

1-1 Maihama, Urayasu-shi, Chiba (English-language information 045 683 3333/www.tokyodisneyresort.co.jp/tdr/index_e.html). Maihama station (JR Keiyo or Musashino lines), south exit. **Open** varies. **Admission** 1-day passport ¥5,500; 2-day passport ¥9,800. Starlight passport (after 3pm Sat, Sun, hols) ¥4,500. Admission to either Disneyland or DisneySea, but not both on same day.
Ticket office Tokyo Disney Resort Ticket Centre, Hibiya Mitsui Bldg, 1-1-2 Yurakucho, Chiyoda-ku (3595 1777). Hibiya Station, exit A11. **Open** 10am-7pm daily.
Sitting on a huge tract of land in Tokyo Bay, the Tokyo Disneyland complex was rebranded as the Disney Resort with the opening of an adjacent but separate theme park, DisneySea, in 2001. DisneySea has given the whole enterprise a massive shot in the arm, since room for expansion on land is limited here, and the rest of the park (still known as Disneyland) was starting to show its age in parts. Disneyland's seven main zones boast 43 attractions, while DisneySea has 23 water-based attractions in its seven zones. Whatever you may feel about the Disney machine, it's virtually impossible not to have a great day out here. Go early, and preferably on a week day, to avoid the queues. Tickets may be purchased in advance from the ticket office.

Urawa Art Museum

Urawa Century City 3F, 2-5-1 Naka-cho, Urawa Shi, Saitama Ken (048 827 3215/www.uam.urawa.saitama.jp). Urawa station, west exit. **Open** 10am-8pm Tue-Sun. **Admission** free; additional fee for special exhibitions.
This city art museum, opened in 2000, is noted for its collection of artists' books and a forward-thinking art education programme. Shows focus mainly on modern Japanese artists, especially from the local prefecture of Saitama, but do occasionally feature artists of international standing.
English pamphlet.

Eat, Drink, Shop

Features

Restaurants

What can you sup in the city with more places to eat and drink than anywhere else in the world? Absolutely anything you fancy.

According to the latest official survey, in 2001, there are around 300,000 places that serve food in Tokyo, ranging from the humblest street stall to some of the world's most exclusive, and expensive, restaurants. This means that, if you ate breakfast, lunch and dinner in a different restaurant every day, you would need to live for around 275 years to stand a chance of trying them all out. Naturally, we've tried our best, and the restaurants listed below are all outstanding or unusually long-established.

Another feature of the Tokyo restaurant trade, as with bars and clubs, is that the pace of change is frantic. Businesses may sell up or move as their lease expires or their building demolished, or go out of business altogether, as eating fashions change. All our selections have been checked and double-checked at the time of going to press, but some restaurants may have closed down or moved on by the time you read this. If you have a particular destination in mind, always phone ahead to confirm.

Central

Marunouchi, Kanda, Ochanomizu

Botan

1-15 Kanda Sudacho, Chiyoda-ku (3251 0577). Kanda JR station, north exit. **Open** 11.30am-9pm Mon-Sat. **Average** ¥7,000. **No credit cards**. **Map** p62.

No need to order (except drinks): this place serves only one thing, chicken sukiyaki, and it does it well. Botan, meaning both 'button' and 'peony', was founded more than 100 years ago by a button-maker. A kimono-clad waitress will light the charcoal in the brazier, set a small iron dish on top, then start cooking: chicken, onion, tofu and other vegetables simmering in the house sauce.

Isegen

1-11-1 Kanda Suda-cho, Chiyoda-ku (3251 1229). Kanda JR station, north exit. **Open** 11.30am-2pm, 4pm-10pm Mon-Fri. **Average** ¥6,000. **No credit cards**. **Map** p62.

Isegen has been serving its legendary anko nabe (monkfish casserole) for over 150 years. The present sprawling wooden premises date back to the 1930s. Anko are only in season from September to April, which coincides perfectly with the time you most want to sit down to a steaming nabe. In the off-season it serves river fish.

Izumo Soba Honke

1-31 Kanda-Jinbocho, Chiyoda-ku (3291 3005). Jinbocho station, exit A7. **Open** 11.30am-3.30pm, 5pm-8.30pm Mon-Fri; 11.30am-3.30pm Sat. **Average** ¥2,000. **No credit cards**. **Map** p62.

Here, soba comes in the dark, country style popular in western Japan, served chilled in stacks of five small trays along with a variety of condiments. A good range of hot noodles in broth is also available.

Kandagawa Honten

2-5-11 Soto-Kanda, Chiyoda-ku (3251 5031). Ochanomizu JR station, Hijiribashi exit. **Open** 11.30am-2pm, 5-9.30pm Mon-Sat. Closed 2nd Sat of mth. **Average** ¥4,000. **Credit** DC, MC, V. **Map** p62.

Kimono-clad waitresses serve exquisite unagi (eel) cooked over charcoal and basted with a sweet sauce, The result is succulent and tender, and the ancient Japanese house setting magnificent.

Kanda Yabu Soba

2-10 Kanda-Awajicho, Chiyoda-ku (3251 0287). Awajicho station, exit A3. **Open** 11.30am-8pm daily. **Average** ¥1,500. **No credit cards**. **English menu**. **Map** p62.

Tokyo's most famous soba shop, Yabu is a living museum dedicated to the art of the noodle. The premises are a beautiful old Japanese house with small garden, decorated with shoji screens, tatami and woodblock prints.

Ginza, Shinbashi & Tsukiji

Afternoon Tea Baker & Diner

2-3-6 Ginza, Chiyoda-ku (5159 1635/www.afternoon-tea.net/gshp). Ginza-Itchome station, exit 4. **Open** 11.30am-2.30pm, 5.30-10.30pm Mon-Fri; 11.30am-2.30pm, 5.30pm-9pm Sat, Sun. **Average** ¥7,000. **Credit** AmEx, DC, JCB, MC, V. **English menu**. **Map** p57.

British celebrity chef Jamie Oliver created the menu at this upmarket branch of Tokyu's near-ubiquitous teashop chain. The menu offers a choice of set meals or à la carte, the latter generally thought to be the better option, and fuses local Japanese ingredients with western standards. Highly recommended are raw tuna served on a bed of caramelised onion, and vanilla-flavoured lamb, which comes complete with whole vanilla pods. The solid wine list is reasonably priced, with bottles starting at ¥3,800, the restaurant is light, airy and spacious, and the service will probably be the best you'll encounter in Tokyo: thoughtful and attentive without being intrusive. Pricey, but worth it.

Ajanta

1-8-2 Higashi-Shinbashi, Minato-ku (6215 8860/ www.ajanta.com). Shiodome station, central plaza exit (Toei Oedo or Yurikamome lines). **Open** 11am-11pm daily. **Average** ¥2,000. **Credit** AmEx, DC, JCB, MC, V. **English menu**.

A long-established and popular chain of Indian restaurants. This recently opened branch is very pleasant, nestling inside the newly created mini-city at Shiodome, near Shinbashi. Grab a good seat and watch the action in the shopping square below. At lunchtime, vast set menus are doled out for ¥1,500-¥2,000. The branch in Nibancho is open 24 hours, and the Ebisu branch has great views and a buffet.

Branches: 3-11 Nibancho, Chiyoda-ku (3264 6955); YGP Tower 39F, 4-20-3 Ebisu, Shibuya-ku (5420 7033).

Birdland

Tsukamoto Sozan Bldg B1F, 4-2-15 Ginza, Chuo-ku (5250 1081). Ginza station, exits B8, B10, C6. **Open** 5-10pm Mon-Fri; 5-9pm Sat. **Credit** AmEx, DC, JCB, MC, V. **Average** ¥5,000. **Map** p57.

Birdland was one of the first places to produce gourmet yakitori, served with imported beers and a selection of fine wines. The chefs use top-quality free-range bantam chickens that are so tasty you can enjoy their meat raw as sashimi. It's a small place, and very popular, so some evenings staff impose a time limit (opening hours are divided into two r[illegible] ly equal shifts), to keep a constant flow of orders going. Popular dishes include chicken liver pate, yakitori, and the superb sansai-yaki (breast meat grilled with Japanese pepper).

Daidaiya

8-5 Ginza Nine No.1 Bldg 2F, Ginza-Nishi, Chuo-ku (5537 3566/www.chanto.com/matome/restaurant/ dai.html). Shinbashi JR station, Ginza exit. **Open** 5pm-1am daily. **Average** ¥4,000. **Credit** AmEx, DC, JCB, MC, V. **English menu**. **Map** p57.

With its spectacular lighting and intricate dining arrangements, Daidaya boasts the most remarkable restaurant interior in Tokyo. The food is good too – a confident modern twist on the traditional staples of Japanese cuisine.

Branches: Shinjuku NOWA Bldg 3F, 3-37-2 Shinjuku, Shinjuku-ku (5362 7173); Belle Vie Akasaka 9F, 3-1-6 Akasaka, Minato-ku (3588 5087).

Edogin

4-5-1 Tsukiji, Chuo-ku (3543 4401/www.tsukiji-edogin.co.jp). Tsukiji station, exit 2. **Open** 11am-9.30pm Mon-Sat; 11am-9pm Sun. **Average** ¥3,500. **Credit** AmEx, DC, MC. **English sushi list**. **Map** p57.

The portion sizes at sushi specialist Edogin are legendary, and you're just around the corner from the central fish market, so the ingredients couldn't be

The best Restaurants

For Buddha-like contemplation

Try the pricey Buddhist kaiseki ryori at **Daigo**. *See p128.*

For the full *Bladerunner* experience

Wait for a rainy day, then head for **Yurakucho Under the Tracks**. *See p128.*

For stunning interior design

Daidaya has been open for over three years, but nobody's beaten it yet. *See p125.*

For celebrity name-dropping

Jamie Oliver's **Afternoon Tea Baker & Diner** (pictured) is light and airy, the food's great, and it has cachet. *See p124.*

For the full-on Asian experience

Get shouted at by swarms of menu hawkers at **Hyakunincho Yataimura**. *See p138.*

For reading the weekend paper over scrambled eggs and coffee

Hide from the crowds in the paved square outside **Roti**. *See p134* **The best brunches.**

For dressing up and smoking a hookah pipe

Get an authentic taste of old Turkey in old Tokyo at **Zakuro**. *See p132.*

For top-class American cuisine

The **Zuna Grill** is expensive but inventive, and the food is wonderful. *See p133.*

For dining outdoors

Relax in the leafy glades of the **Terrace Restaurant, Hanezawa Garden**. *See p144.*

fresher. That's why it's always popular, despite the almost production-line service and lack of character. Choose your fish from the tank in the centre of the large dining room and it will be served still quivering.

Kihachi China

2F-4F 3-7-1 Ginza, Chuo-ku (5524 0761/www.kihachi.co.jp). Ginza station, exit C8. **Open** 11.30am-4pm, 5-11pm Mon-Fri; 11.30am-4.30pm, 5-11.30pm Sat, Sun. **Credit** AmEx, DC, JCB, MC, V. **Map** p57.

If it's Chinese with style you're looking for, this understated, tastefully decorated restaurant near the Ginza shopping strip is the place to go. The dim sum lunch set (¥2,500) is a great choice. Booking advisable.

Little Okinawa

8-7-10 Ginza, Chuo-ku (3572 2930/www.little-okinawa.co.jp). Shinbashi JR station, Ginza exit. **Open** 5pm-3am Mon-Fri; 4pm-midnight Sat, Sun. **Average** ¥3,500. **No credit cards**. **Map** p57.

The food of Japan's southernmost islands incorporates many influences from China, especially in the predilection for noodles and pork. The 'national' dish is goya champuru, a stir-fry of tofu and bitter gourd. And the drink of choice is awamori, a rice-based rocket-fuel with a highly distinctive taste. Try it in this cheerful and busy restaurant.

Monja Maruyama

1-4-10 Tsukishima, Chuo-ku (3533 3504). Tsukishima station, exits 5, 8. **Open** 5-10.30pm Tue-Sun. **Average** ¥2,000. **No credit cards**.

Monja, the crêpe-like concoction of batter, vegetables, seafood and meat cooked on a griddle, is not for everyone. But for those who like it, Tsukishima, with its dozens of little monja restaurants, is monja heaven. Mr Maruyama, a Tsukishima native, founded his place ten years ago to experiment with variations on the theme. Thus you'll find rarities such as pitch-black monja with squid's ink, or mochi mochi crêpe, with mochi, the sticky pounded rice used in many Japanese dishes around New Year.

Ohmatsuya

Ail d'Or Bldg 2F, 6-5-8 Ginza, Chuo-ku (3571 7053). Ginza station, exits C2, C3. **Open** 5-10pm Mon-Sat. **Average** ¥9,000. **Credit** AmEx, DC, JCB, MC, V. **English menu**. **Map** p57.

Ascending from the swish streets of Ginza, you emerge in a remarkable faux-rustic inn with wooden beams and folksy decor. Ohmatsuya specialises in the foods of rural Yamagata Prefecture, so that means farmhouse foods, but prepared with style: plenty of mountain herbs and fresh seafood from the Japan Sea coast, not to mention some of the best sake in the country. Every table has a charcoal fireplace on which dishes are grilled in front of your eyes.

Oshima

Ginza Core Bldg 9F, 5-8-20 Ginza, Chuo-ku (3574 8080). Ginza station, exits A3, A4. **Open** 11am-10pm (last order 9pm) daily. **Average** ¥1,800 set lunch; ¥2,800-¥12,000 set dinner. **Credit** AmEx, DC, JCB, MC, V. **Map** p57.

Traditional Japanese food served up in tasteful, modern, comfortable settings. Not all of the courses are great, but the food is always well prepared and beautifully presented.

Branches: Odakyu Halc Annex 8F, 1-5-1 Nishi-Shinjuku, Shinjuku-ku (3348 8080); Hotel Pacific Tokyo 3F, 3-13-3 Takanawa, Minato-ku (3441 8080).

Robata

1-3-8 Yurakucho, Chiyoda-ku (3591 1905). Hibiya station, exit 4. **Open** 5-11pm daily. **Average** ¥5,000. **No credit cards**. **No menu**. **Map** p57.

You can easily walk past this tiny old wooden *izakaya*, but if you do you'll be missing out on one of the most charming dining experiences in central Tokyo. Sit down at one of the old wooden seats and choose from the freshly prepared dishes – salads, pork in cream sauce, tofu dishes or tomato-based vegetable stews – that sit in huge bowls in a semicircle on a giant counter. Then sit back and wait for your dishes to be brought to you, one by one.

Shichirinya

Ginza Corridor 108 Saki, 7 Ginza, Chuo-ku (3289 0020). Ginza station, exit C1 or Shinbashi JR station, Ginza exit. **Open** 5.30pm-4am Mon-Fri; 5.30-11pm Sat, Sun. **Average** ¥4,000. **Credit** AmEx, MC, V. **Map** p57.

The shichirin charcoal brazier used to be synonymous with post-war austerity. Now it's the chic way to prepare food. Smokeless grills, quality ingredients and sophisticated service.

Ten-Ichi

6-6-5 Ginza, Chuo-ku (3571 1949). Ginza station, exits C3, B9. **Open** 11.30am-10pm daily. **Average** ¥5,000 lunch; ¥10,000 dinner. **Credit** AmEx, DC, JCB, MC, V. **English menu**. **Map** p57.

Tokyo's best-known tempura house has a tranquil, pampering atmosphere. You sit at the counter and receive a constant flow of perfectly cooked morsels served straight from the wok. The tempura is light and aromatic, not greasy. Dinner courses start from ¥8,500 and include rice, tea and dessert. The Ginza flagship shop is the most refined, but any of the other branches around the city also guarantee top-quality tempura.

Branches: Imperial Hotel, 1-1-1 Uchisaiwaicho, Chiyoda-ku (3503 1001); Sony Bldg B1F, 5-3-1 Ginza, Chuo-ku (3571 3837); C I Plaza B1F, 2-3-1 Kita-Aoyama, Minato-ku (3497 8465); Mitsui Bldg B1F, 2-1-1 Nishi-Shinjuku, Shinjuku-ku (3344 4706).

Ten-Ichi deux

Nishi Ginza Depato 1F, 4-1 Ginza (3566 4188). Yurakucho JR station, Ginza exit or Ginza station, exits C5, C7. **Open** 11am-10pm daily. **Average** ¥1,300-¥2,800 lunch; ¥2,800-¥4,200 dinner. **Credit** AmEx, DC, JCB, MC, V. **English menu**. **Map** p57.

Casual, lower-priced offshoot of the reputable, and very expensive, Ten-ichi chain. Specialises in light dishes such as ten-don (tempura prawns on a rice bowl) with simple side dishes.

Yurakucho Under the Tracks

2-1 Yurakucho, Chiyoda-ku (no phone). Yurakucho JR station, Hibiya or Ginza exit. **Open** early evening-midnight daily. **Average** ¥2,500. **No credit cards**. **Map** p57.

For a cheap night's entertainment and a quintessential Japanese experience, don't miss the yakitori roadshow that takes place nightly beneath the tracks of the Yamanote Line. Little open-air eateries are wedged into tiny spaces. The master presides behind the counter, dishing out grilled yakitori and other tidbits (*see also pp156-166*).

North

Ikebukuro

Ikebukuro Gyoza Stadium

Namco Namja Town 2F, Sunshine City, 3-1-1 Higashi-Ikebukuro, Toshima-ku (Sunshine 60 Information Centre 3989 3331). Ikebukuro station, exits 35, 41. **Open** 10am-10pm daily. **Admission to Namja Town** ¥300; ¥200 concessions. **Average** ¥300 per portion of gyoza. **No credit cards**. **Map** p69.

Opened in 2002, this complex of restaurants inside the giant Ikebukuro Namja Town complex bills itself as the first theme park in the world to specialise in gyoza, and who are we to disagree? For the uninitiated, gyoza are small fried pasties, originally of Chinese origin but now such an obsession in Japan that many regions have their own special recipes. The centrepiece of all this culinary weirdness is the 'Gyoza Grab Bag Restaurant Mall', which features 22 gyoza restaurants from all over the country.

South

Roppongi & Akasaka

Bangkok

Woo Bldg 2F, 3-8-8 Roppongi, Minato-ku (3408 7353). Roppongi station, exit 1. **Open** 11.30am-2pm, 5-11pm Mon-Sat; 11.30am-9pm Sun. Closed every 3rd Sun of mth. **Average** ¥3,500. **No credit cards**. **English menu**. **Map** p74.

One of the best Thai restaurants in town is also one of the speediest: you'll be back out into Roppongi's bars and clubs in double-quick time. Tom kha kai soup arrives in a clay pot, a beautiful orange colour from a liberal dose of peppers. It goes well with the minced meat larbs, flavoured with lemongrass, cooling mint and tangy onion. Plenty of veggie fare, too.

Bincho

Marina Bldg 2F, 3-10-5 Roppongi, Minato-ku (5474 0755). Roppongi station, exit 5. **Open** 6-11.30pm Mon-Sat; 6-9.30pm Sun. **Average** ¥5,000. **Credit** AmEx, DC, JCB, MC, V. **English menu**. **Map** p74.

Dark, romantic Japanese-style interior complemented by the smoky aroma of charcoal-grilled yakitori and an exhausting array of sake.

Brendan's Pizzakaya

203, 3-1-19 Nishi-Azabu, Minato-ku (3479 8383). Roppongi station, exits 1, 3. **Open** 5.30-10.30pm Tue-Sun. **Average** ¥3,500 for two. **Credit** JCB, MC, V. **English menu**. **Map** p74.

The pizzeria for homesick foreigners *par excellence*, Brendan's has been serving up great American-style pizza for as long as anyone can remember. Not really what you're in Tokyo for, but what the hell?

Chez Pierre

1-23-10 Minami-Aoyama, Minato-ku (3475 1400). Nogizaka station, exit 5. **Open** 11.30am-2.30pm, 6-10pm Tue-Sun. **Average** ¥7,000. **Credit** AmEx, DC, JCB, MC, V. **Menu in French**. **Map** p74.

Charming, unpretentious mom and pop place serving French provincial cuisine. The inside is warm and inviting, while the floor-to-ceiling windows of the café terrace are perfect for lingering over tea and pastries. The seafood is popular. Recommended wines, carefully selected, change regularly.

Coriander

B1F, 1-10-6 Nishi-Azabu, Minato-ku (3475 5720). Roppongi station, exit 2. **Open** 11.30am-2pm, 6-11pm Mon-Sat. **Average** ¥5,000. **Credit** AmEx, DC, JCB, MC, V. **English menu**. **Map** p74.

A cosy basement restaurant that markets itself as 'new Thai', Coriander serves up tasty dishes that are lighter on the chilli-heat factor than its more authentic cousins, and often contain unusual ingredients, as with carrot tom yam soup. Decor is pleasant, heavy on the cushions, greenery and incense, and service is keen if not always very efficient.

Daigo

2-4-2 Atago, Minato-ku (3431 0811). Kamiyacho station, exit 3. **Open** noon-3pm, 5-9pm daily. **Average** lunch from ¥12,000; dinner from ¥14,000. **Credit** AmEx, DC, JCB. **Map** p74.

Daigo started out as a branch of a *ryotei* in Hida-Takayama. It now serves expensive Buddhist temple *kaiseki* meals in private tatami rooms overlooking peaceful gardens. A ten- to 15-course meal revolving around seasonal offerings is lovingly and artfully presented. An elegant slice of Japanese traditional cuisine. Reservations essential.

Densan

Getsusekai Bldg B1F, 3-10-4 Akasaka, Minato-ku (3585 7550). Akasaka-Mitsuke station, Belle Vie exit. **Open** 4.30pm-4am Mon-Sat; 4.30-11pm Sun. **Average** ¥2,000. **Credit** AmEx, DC, JCB, MC, V.

Densan marries two Japanese 'traditions': oden and karaoke. The speciality here is Kyoto-style oden, featuring a soup made with only a hint of soy sauce, allowing the ingredients to shine. The other specialities are yakitori from free-range chickens and sake, with an emphasis on Niigata Prefecture, where the high quality of rice produces some of Japan's best sake. Then, when your vocal cords are well lubricated, Densan saves you the stumble in search of a karaoke box: private rooms are equipped with the latest system.

Botan. *See p124.*

Erawan

Roi Bldg 13F, 5-5-1 Roppongi, Minato-ku (3404 5741). Roppongi station, exit 3. **Open** 5.30-11.30pm Mon-Fri; 5-11.30pm Sat, Sun. **Average** ¥4,000. **Credit** AmEx, DC, JCB, MC, V. **English menu**. **Map** p74.

Regular customers complain that the quality of the Thai food here has declined. Nevertheless, its popularity is ensured by its location in the notoriously 'varied' Roi Building.

Fukuzushi

5-7-8 Roppongi, Minato-ku (3402 4116). Roppongi station, exit 3. **Open** 11.30am-2pm, 5.30-11pm Mon-Sat. **Average** ¥10,000. **Credit** AmEx, DC, JCB, MC, V. **English menu**. **Map** p74.

Reliable sushi is served up here in stylish surroundings. First-time visitors confused by Japanese menus will welcome the English translations, and staff will try to communicate in English if necessary.

Hassan Hinazushi

6-1-20 Roppongi, Minato-ku (3403 8333). Roppongi station, exit 3. **Open** 11.30am-2pm, 5pm-11pm Mon-Fri; noon-10.30pm Sat; noon-10pm Sun. **Average** ¥8,000. **Credit** AmEx, MC, V. **English menu**. **Map** p74.

Serves elaborate all-you-can-eat shabu-shabu meals, featuring beautifully marbled, paper-thin slices of premium Japanese wagyu (domestic beef, usually from Kobe or Matsuzaka). The interior has classic Japanese motifs, including *washi* paper screens and lamps, wooden beams and a miniature bamboo garden.

Jidaiya

Naritaya Bldg 1F, 3-14-3 Akasaka, Minato-ku (3588 0489). Akasaka station, exit 1. **Open** 11.30am-2.30pm, 5pm-4am Mon-Fri; 5-11.30pm Sat. **Average** courses ¥3,000-¥6,000, à la carte ¥2,500. **Credit** AmEx, DC, JCB, MC, V.

Recreates a rustic Japanese farmhouse complete with tatami mats, dried ears of corn, fish-shaped hanging fireplace fixtures and heaps of old-looking wooden furniture. The atmosphere is a bit contrived but fun nevertheless, and large shared tables contribute to the conviviality. The food is all Japanese, with an emphasis on seafood, meat and vegetables cooked at the table.

Branches: Isomura Bldg B1F, 5-1-4 Akasaka, Minato-ku (3224 1505); Uni Roppongi Bldg B1F, 7-15-17 Roppongi, Minato-ku (3403 3563).

Ken's Dining

1-15-4 Nishi-Azabu, Minato-ku (5771 5788/www.chanto.com/main/main.html). Nogizaka station, exit 5. **Open** 6pm-3am Mon-Sat; 6pm-1am Sun. **Average** ¥5,000. **Credit** AmEx, DC, JCB, MC, V. **English menu**. **Map** p74.

Chef Ken Okada has produced an intriguing menu that fuses Japanese with Korean (plenty of kimchee), Chinese and even a touch of Italian. Not only does it work most of the time, it's also quite affordable for this neck of the Nishi-Azabu woods.

Branches: 3-26-6 Shinjuku, Shinjuku-ku (5356 0336).

Kisso

5-17-1 Roppongi, Minato-ku (3582 4191). Roppongi station, exit 3. **Open** 11.30am-2pm, 5.30-10pm (last order 9pm) Mon-Fri; 5.30-8pm Sat. **Average** ¥2,500 lunch; ¥10,000 dinner. **Credit** AmEx, DC, JCB, MC, V. **Map** p74.

Kisso provides Japanese *kaiseki* ryori in a contemporary setting – the main dining area is decked out in stylish black, with deep chairs surrounded by artfully arranged flowers and a subtle jazz soundtrack. The meals are a sequence of small dishes that are ordered as a set; most include sashimi and cooked fish with grated daikon, miso soup with tofu, wakame and mitsuba (Japanese parsley), seasonal and often unusual vegetables, along with a little meat, perhaps chicken or pork, served with pungent hot mustard.

Kusa no Ya

Mita Bldg 3F, 2-14-33 Akasaka, Minato-ku (3589 0779). Akasaka station, exit 2. **Open** 11.30am-midnight Mon-Fri; 5-10pm Sat, Sun. **Average** ¥4,000. **Credit** AmEx, DC, JCB, MC, V.

This popular and famous Korean restaurant started out in the Azabu-Juban area. People come for the yakiniku, thinly sliced marinated beef cooked at the table and devoured family-style with side dishes of pickled kimchee and copious amounts of beer.

Branches: A&K Bldg 8F, 4-6-8 Azabu Juban, Minato-ku (3455 8356); 2-10-1 Shinbashi, Minato-ku (3591 4569).

Monsoon Café

2-10-1 Nishi-Azabu, Minato-ku (5467 5221/ www.global-dining.com/global). Nogizaka station, exit 5. **Open** 11.30am-5am daily. **Average** ¥4,000. **Credit** AmEx, DC, JCB, MC, V. **English menu.**

A reliable chain serving Indonesian/Thai-influenced foods, Monsoon is owned by Tokyo dining giant Global Dining. Food here is always good, and the frozen cocktails really hit the spot in Tokyo's sweltering summers. Start your meal with some of the best Vietnamese spring rolls in town, liberally laced with coriander.

Branches: Campari Bldg 4F, 1-6-8 Jinnan, Shibuya-ku (5489 1611); 15-4 Hachiyama cho, Shibuya-ku (5489 3789); 1-2-3 Ginza, Chuo-ku (5534 3631).

Moti

Hama Bldg 3F, 6-2-35 Roppongi, Minato-ku (3479 1939). Roppongi station, exit 1. **Open** 11.30am-11pm daily. **Average** ¥2,000. **Credit** AmEx, DC, JCB, MC, V. **English menu. Map** p74.

One of the better of the Moti chain of restaurants, with the bonus of being open late and close to disco-central and Roppongi Hills.

Branches: Kinpa Bldg 3F, 2-14-31 Akasaka, Minato-ku (3584 6649); Akasaka Floral Plaza 2F, 3-8-8 Akasaka, Minatoku (3582 3620).

Ninja

Akasaka Tokyu Plaza 1F, 2-14-3 Nagatacho, Chiyoda-ku (5157 3936). Akasaka-Mitsuke station, Sotobori Dori exit. **Open** 5.30pm-4am daily. **Average** ¥4,000. **Credit** AmEx, DC, JCB, MC, V. **English menu.**

Ninja is probably the best-quality themed *izakaya* in town. On arrival you are ushered through a series of winding wooden corridors designed to evoke old village Japan by a waiter dressed as a Ninja warrior. Thereafter, waiters continue to pop out of unlikely places and sneak up with menus and food. There's also an itinerant magician. Food is trad Japanese with a western twist. Grilled wild mushrooms come with a cheese dip, and delicious fresh cold tofu is served with French sea salt. Booking advisable.

Nodaiwa

1-5-4 Higashi-Azabu, Minato-ku (3583 7852). Akabane-Bashi station, Nakano-Hashi exit. **Open** 11am-1.30pm, 5-8pm Mon-Sat. **Average** ¥4,000. **No credit cards. English menu. Map** p74.

Housed in an old *kura* storehouse transported from the mountains, Nodaiwa is arguably the best unagi shop in the city. It only uses eels that have been caught in the wild, and the difference is noticeable in the texture, especially if you try the shirayaki (broiled without any added sauce, and eaten with a dip of shoyu and wasabi). This is true gourmet fare.

Noodles

2-21-7 Azabu-Juban, Minato-ku (3452 3112). Azabu-Juban station, exit 1. **Open** 6pm-4am Mon-Sat; 6am-11pm Sun. **Average** ¥4,500. **Credit** MC, V. **English menu. Map** p74.

You can tell all you need to know from the name, the trendy orange exterior and the eye-catching arrangement of jars of soba, bifun and pasta in the window. Noodles serves its pan-Asian fare with style and verve, with plenty of New World wines, a jazzy sound track and waiters who wear their jeans rolled up to the knee. Things are so relaxed here, the local trendies treat it like a family restaurant.

Olives

West Walk Roppongi Hills 5F, 6-10-1 Roppongi, Minato-ku (5413 9571/www.toddenglish.com/ Restaurants/Olives.html). Roppongi station, exit 1. **Open** 11am-3.30pm, 6-11.30pm daily. **Average** ¥10,000. **Credit** AmEx, DC, JCB, MC, V. **English menu. Map** p74.

American celebrity chef Todd English opened his first restaurant in Tokyo in April 2003, in the spanking new Roppongi Hills complex. The menu is top-quality fusion cuisine, mixing styles and ingredients from Europe, America and Japan. English's wild mushroom risotto is the stuff of legend, although the juicy marinated steaks are also highly recommended.

Phothai Down Under

Five Plaza Bldg 2F, 5-18-21 Roppongi, Minato-ku (3505 1504). Roppongi station, exit 3. **Open** 11.30am-2.30pm, 5-10.30pm Mon-Wed; 11.30am-2.30pm, 6-11pm Thur-Sat. **Average** ¥4,000. **Credit** AmEx, DC, JCB, MC, V. **English menu. Map** p74.

A Thai-Australian restaurant, with a menu of middling-quality Thai food and enormous Aussie steaks. Think of the Thai dishes as starters, choose a cut of meat from the tray brought to your table, and accompany it with Aussie wine or Thai beer.

Shisen Hanten

Zenkoku Ryokan Kaikan 5-6F, 2-5-5 Hirakawa-cho, Chiyoda-ku (3263 9371). Nagata-cho station, exit 5. **Open** 11.30am-2pm, 5-10pm (last order 9pm) daily. **Average** ¥2,000. **Credit** AmEx, DC, MC, V. **English menu.**

Hiyashi chuka, cold Chinese-style noodles and chopped vegetables topped with sesame or vinegar sauce, is a popular summer dish at this Chinese restaurant. Sesame is the speciality here, a rich,

Robata: one of Tokyo's most charming dining experiences. *See p127.*

mildly spicy paste ladled over chilled al dente noodles, topped with sliced chicken and cucmbers. Other Chinese dishes round out the menu.

Shinmasan-ya Namiki

Bldg 1F, 3-12-5 Akasaka, Minato-ku (3583 6120). Akasaka-Mitsuke station, Belle Vie exit. **Open** 11.30am-3am Mon-Sat. **Average** ¥3,500. **Credit** JCB, MC, V.

Shinmasan-ya is a Korean-run place, which serves honest home-style cooking with the emphasis on dishes other than the ubiquitous yakiniku – this place serves Tokyo's best bibimbap, for example. Ask to be seated on the floor; your legs can dangle under the table, while the heated floor warms the parts of you that the food can't reach.

Vietnamese Cyclo

Piramide Bldg 1F, 6-6-9 Roppongi, Minato-ku (3478 4964/www.create-restaurants.co.jp). Roppongi station, exit 1. **Open** 11.30am-3pm, 5-10.30pm daily. **Average** ¥4,500. **Credit** AmEx, DC, JCB, MC, V. **English menu**. **Map** p74.

Heineken
Beer

Serves sleek, upmarket versions of Saigon staples. Not a particularly authentic experience, despite the cyclo trishaw at the entrance: food is toned down for Japanese tastes. Neverthless, it's a stylish space, the goi cuon spring rolls are good and there's 333 beer.

Zakuro
TBS Kaikan Bldg B1F, 5-3-3 Akasaka, Minato-ku (3582 6841). Akasaka station, exit 1. **Open** 11am-11pm daily. **Average** ¥9,000. **Credit** AmEx, DC, JCB, MC, V. **English menu**.
A casual restaurant that captures the best of Japan's traditional haute cuisine: shabu-shabu, sukiyaki, tempura and dishes inspired by fresh seasonal bounties, served in private or common western-style dining rooms, a tempura bar or private tatami rooms.
Branches: Ginza Sanwa Bldg B1F, 4-6-1 Ginza, Chuo-ku (3535 4421); Nihon Jitensha Kaikan B1F, 1-9-15 Akasaka, Minato-ku (3582 2661); Shin Nihonbashi Bldg B1F, 3-8-2 Nihonbashi, Chuo-ku (3271 3791); Shin Yaesu Bldg B1F, 1-7-1 Kyobashi, Chuo-ku (3563 5031).

Zuna Grill
Plaza Mikado Bldg B1F, 2-14-5 Akasaka, Minato-ku (3568 4555). Akasaka station, exit 2. **Open** 11.30am-3pm, 5.30-10pm Mon-Fri; 5.30-10.30pm Sat. **Average** ¥9,000. **Credit** AmEx, DC, JCB, MC, V. **English menu**.
One of the finest western-style restaurants in Tokyo, this upmarket American dining space marks a first foray into the restaurant trade by Hawaiian-born former sumo wrestler Akebono. The interior is moodily lit and pleasantly modern. The menu, while far from extensive, offers a well-thought-out combination of meat and fish dishes. The tuna carpaccio starter and main course of roast chicken, lovingly grilled on a spit in the open kitchen, are highly recommended. The wine list, with all wines from the New World, is expensive, but this is forgiven as soon as you taste the food. If you can, get someone else to pick up the tab.

Further south

Aguri
1-6-7 Kami-Meguro, Meguro-ku (3792 3792). Naka-Meguro station. **Open** 5.30pm-1am daily. **Average** ¥4,000. **Credit** AmEx, MC, V.
Big, friendly, casual and with just enough style to raise it above the average. Platters of prepared foods line the counter tapas style, while cooks stand ready to cook up grilled fish and teppanyaki meat and vegetables. Just point to whatever you like the look of – and that applies to the good choice of sake too.

Jiang's
Kurokawa Bldg 3F, 3-5-7 Tamagawa, Setagaya-ku (3700 2475). Futako-Tamagawa station (Tokyu Denentoshi Line). **Open** 5-10pm Tue-Sun. **Average** ¥3,500. **Credit** AmEx, JCB, MC, V.
Nguyen Thi Giang was born in Hanoi and raised in the south of Vietnam, and the menu in her spotless little restaurant reflects both influences. The hearty cha gio are cooked in northern style, full of tasty pork, while the delicate banh xeo pancakes are as sweet and satisfying as you'd find in Hue. This is the best home-style Vietnamese food in all of Tokyo.

Komahachi
Hashimoto Bldg 1F, Shiba, Minato-ku (3453 2530/ www.komahachi.com). Tamachi station, west exit or Mita station (Toei Mita/Asakusa lines), exits A7, A8. **Open** 5-11pm Mon-Fri; 4-10.30pm Sat. **Average** ¥3,500. **No credit cards**. **English menu**.
Komahachi sums up the experience of the neighbourhood *izakaya*. It's cosy and friendly; there's a variety of interesting dishes and sake; the waiters take care of you; and it's all reasonably priced.
Branches: throughout the city.

Stellato
4-19-17 Shirokanedai, Minato-ku (3442 5588/ www.global-dining.com/global). Shirokanedai station, exit 2. **Open** 5.30pm-2am daily. **Average** ¥7,000. **Credit** AmEx, DC, JCB, MC, V. **English menu**.
Part of the Global Dining chain, Stellato combines a flair for the dramatic (huge chandeliers, a blazing log fire and an immodest faux-Moorish façade) with food that is always interesting, and frequently exceptional. The nicest touch is the rooftop lounge.

T Y Harbor Brewery
2-1-3 Higashi-Shinagawa, Shinagawa-ku (5479 4555/www.tyharborbrewing.co.jp). Tennozu Isle station (Tokyo monorail) or Shinagawa station, east exit. **Open** 11.30am-2pm, 5.30-10.30pm Mon-Fri; 11.30am-3pm, 5.30-10.30pm Sat, Sun. **Average** ¥2,500. **Credit** AmEx, DC, JCB, V. **English menu**.
The food at this bayside microbrew pub-cum-restaurant is mainly casual California-style pasta dishes and sandwiches. But the brews (a selection of porter, pale and amber ales and wheat beer) are drinkable, and the terrace, overlooking a canal, provides something lacking in Tokyo – a place to hang out by the water. *See also p134* **The best brunches**.

East

Ueno & area

Goemon
1-1-26 Hon-Komagome, Bunkyo-ku (3811 2015). Hon-Komagome station. **Open** noon-2pm, 5-10pm Tue-Sat; noon-8pm Sun. Last order 2hrs before closing. **Average** ¥8,000. **No credit cards**. **Map** p94.
With a bamboo-lined entrance and garden with waterfalls and carp ponds, Goemon is almost a substitute for a trip to Kyoto. In winter the speciality is yudofu (hot tofu in broth), in summer chilled hiya yakko.

Hantei
2-12-15 Nezu, Bunkyo-ku (3828 1440). Nezu station, exit 2. **Open** noon-2.30pm, 5-10.30pm Tue-Sun. **Average** ¥6,000. **No credit cards**. **English menu**. **Map** p94.

Kushi-age is not gourmet fare, but Hantei elevates it to new levels, partly due to the care that goes into the ingredients and preparation, but mostly because of the beautiful old wooden building. There's no need to order: staff will bring course after course, stopping after every six to ask if you want to continue.

Honke Ponta

3-23-3 Ueno, Taito-ku (3831 2351). Ueno JR station, south exit. **Open** 11am-2pm, 4.30-8pm Tue-Sun. **Average** ¥4,000. **No credit cards. Map** p88.

Honke Ponta was the first place in Tokyo to serve tonkatsu pork cutlet – deep-fried golden nuggets of succulent pork – but it prefers to think of itself as a western-style restaurant and thus serves steak so tender that knives melt in it. But it's still best to go for the tender katsuretsu (cutlet), ika (squid) or kisu (whiting) fry. Order rice and soup separately and you'll get akadashi soup (red miso, nameko mushrooms and scallions) so dark and viscous it's like eating Brazilian feijoada. There are no prices on the menu.

Ikenohata Yabu Soba

3-44-7 Yushima, Bunkyo-ku (3831 8977). Yushima station, exit 2. **Open** 11.30am-2pm, 4.30-8pm Mon, Tue, Thur-Sat; 11.30am-8pm Sun. **Average** ¥1,500. **No credit cards. English menu. Map** p88.

Kanda Yabu Soba (*see p124*) has spawned numerous shops run by former chefs. This one does predictably excellent soba at reasonable prices in a modern Japanese setting. The soba is some of the best in Tokyo, though the surroundings may disappoint.

The best Brunches

As western influences become ever more pronounced, a growing number of Tokyo restaurants are wising up to the concept of the weekend brunch. That being a slap-up meal to be consumed at a leisurely pace some time between breakfast and lunch time, preferably with friends and while perusing the newspapers. Here's our pick of the best brunch bunch.

Cabana

1F, ATY Bldg, Ebisu 3-28-12, Shibuya-ku (5421 2228/www.cabanacc.com). Ebisu JR station. **Brunch served** 8.30am-4pm Sat, Sun. **Average** ¥2,000. **Credit** AmEx, DC, JCB, MC, V.

Sandwiches, quiche, eggs benedict and mountains of pancakes star on the brunch menu of this highly regarded Californian restaurant. Cabana opens unusually early, which makes it a boon for early risers and those who don't go to sleep at all.

New York Grill

Brunch served 11.30am-2.30pm Sun. **Set brunch** ¥5,800.

The ultimate indulgence: a choice of main dish, plus appetiser and dessert, accompanied by a glass of champagne, can be had at one of the finest hotel restaurants in the world. *See p138.*

Roti

1F Piramide Bldg, 6-6-9 Roppongi, Minato-ku (5785 3671/www.rotico.com). Roppongi station, exits 1, 3. **Brunch served** 11am-5pm Sat, Sun. **All-day breakfast served** 10am-3pm Sun. **Average** ¥2,500. **Credit** AmEx, DC, MC, V.

In addition to the weekend brunch, this superior American restaurant also offers an awesome Sunday all-day breakfast, just the pick-me-up you need after the night before. Choose from one of half a dozen breakfasts, all with endless tea and coffee. At the time of writing, plans are afoot to extend the breakfast deal to Saturday.

Roy's Aoyama

Brunch served 11am-3.30pm Sat, Sun. **Set brunch menu** ¥3,500, ¥5,500.

The weekend brunch here is one of the very best ways to start a weekend – or end it. There's all-you-can-drink wine to accompany home-made muffins, dim sum-style appetisers, devastating entrées and some scrumptious desserts. *See p148.*

TY Harbor Brewery

Brunch served 11.30am-5pm Sat, Sun. **Average** ¥2,000.

The brunch menu at this stylish brew restaurant is unusually exotic, featuring a mixture of Asian-influenced dishes such as sashimi, and western standards such as burgers and pizza. More lunch than breakfast, really, but pleasant all the same. *See p133.*

Tokyo Daihanten

5-17-13 Shinjuku, Shinjuku-ku (3202 0121). Shinjuku station. **Brunch served** 11.30am-3pm daily. **Average** ¥2,000. **Credit** AmEx, DC, JCB, MC. V.

Sadly, this place no longer has trolleys loaded with steaming food plying their trade around the aisles, but the dim sum remains among the finest in Tokyo. Brunch here will be a great weekend treat.

Daigo. *See p128.*

Sasanoyuki

2-15-10 Negishi, Taito-ku (3873 1145). Uguisudani station, north exit. **Open** 11am-9.30pm Tue-Sun. **Average** ¥4,500. **Credit** AmEx, DC, JCB, MC, V. **English menu**.

Tokyo's most famous tofu restaurant since the Edo period has an imperial legacy: it was founded by a tofu-maker lured from Kyoto by Kaneiji temple's imperial abbot. But Sasanoyuki is as down-home as the Nippori neighbourhood it sits in, and also very reasonably priced. Order the top-of-the-line course and you may feel you have had enough tofu to last you for your entire stay in Japan.

Takokyuu

2-11-8 Ueno, Taito-ku (3831 5088). Yushima station, exit 2. **Open** 6pm-midnight Tue-Sun. **Average** ¥100-¥600 per piece. **No credit cards**. **Map** p88.

Four generations have been serving Tokyo-style oden at this Ueno institution for 94 years. Takokyuu is renowned for its heavier, Kanto-type broth, which stews for two days before daikon, onions, oysters and other delicacies are thrown in. The house sake is supposedly available nowhere else in Tokyo.

Zakuro

B1F & 2F, Nippori Konishi Bldg, 3-13-14 Nishi-Nippori, Arakawa-ku (5685 5313). Nippori station, west exit. **Average** ¥3,000. **No credit cards**. **Map** p94.

This Persian/Turkish restaurant thrives in the unlikeliest of surroundings, the olde-world area of Yanaka. The basement premises are lined wall-to-wall with carpets and cushions; take off your shoes on entry and sit cross-legged on the floor. Diners are encouraged to dress up by the ebullient owner, who will then take your photo for his customer scrap book. At lunch, the ¥1,500 set meal includes four dishes (with real Basmati rice, a rarity in Tokyo) and a sheesha pipe. Choose your tobacco flavour and puff away contentedly after the meal. In the evening there's belly dancing and a host of other good-time activities. Booking is essential for dinner, and business is booming so much that the owner will be taking up the lease on the second floor of the same building in late 2003.

Asakusa

Bon

1-2-11 Ryusen, Taito-ku (3872 0375/www.fuchabon.co.jp). Iriya station, exit 3. **Open** noon-2pm, 5-8pm Mon-Fri; 5-8pm Sat, Sun. **Average** ¥7,000. **Credit** AmEx, DC, JCB, MC, V. **English menu**.

Exquisitely prepared fucha ryori, a branch of shojin ryori, in a tranquil setting that is truly Zen. Only one set menu is served, and its individual dishes change with the seasons. Sit back and enjoy the succession of beautiful morsels as a living expression of traditional Japanese culture.

Hatsuogawa

2-8-4 Kaminarimon, Taito-ku (3844 2723). Asakusa station, exits 1, 2, 3, A1, A3, A4. **Open** noon-2pm (last order 1.30pm), 5-8pm (last order 7.30pm) Mon-Sat; 5-8pm (last order 7.30pm) Sun. **Average** ¥3,000. **No credit cards**. **Map** p83.

A tradition-steeped restaurant in historic Asakusa. The tiny entrance is graced with stones, plants, bamboo latticework and a white *noren* emblazoned with the word 'unagi'. Step into this tiny world of wooden beams and traditional Japanese decor and enjoy the taste of succulent broiled eel. The unaju box set is delicious, or try kabayaki: unagi on a stick.

Otafuku

1-6-2 Senzoku, Taito-ku (3871 2521/www.otafuku.ne.jp). Iriya station, exits 1, 3. **Open** *Apr-Sept* 5-11pm Tue-Sat; 5-10pm Sun. *Oct-Mar* 5-11pm Mon-Sat; 4-10pm Sun. **Average** ¥100-¥500 per piece. **Credit** AmEx, DC, JCB, MC, V. **Map** p83.

This place has been serving oden since the Meiji era. It specialises in Kansai-style oden; the broth is much lighter on soy than the Tokyo version. Otafuku also specialises in sake, which goes well with the flavour of vegetables and fish cakes that make up oden.

Sometaro

2-2-2 Nishi-Asakusa, Taito-ku (3844 9502/www.yamani-shoji.co.jp/sometaro/page/sometaro%20official%20top.shtm). Tawaramachi station, exit 3. **Open** noon-10.30pm daily. **Average** ¥3,000. **No credit cards. English menu. Map** p83.

Comfort food in a funky wooden shack, in easy walking distance of the tourist sights of Asakusa. It can get incredibly sweaty in summer, but sitting round the okonomiyaki pan, the intimate atmosphere is wonderfully authentic.

Vin Chou

2-2-13 Nishi-Asakusa, Taito-ku (3845 4430). Tawaramachi station, exit 3. **Open** 5pm-midnight Mon, Tue, Thur-Sat; 4-10pm Sun. **Average** ¥4,000 **No credit cards. Map** p83.

This five-star charcoal-grilled yakitori shop is an offshoot of the nearby French bistro, La Chevre. That explains why it offers Bresse chicken, quail and a range of good wines and cheese. Some of the best food in the neighbourhood.

Further east

Yoshiba

2-14-5 Yokoami, Sumida-ku (3623 4480). Ryogoku JR station, east exit. **Open** 11.30am-1.30pm, 5-10pm Mon-Sat. Also Sun evening during sumo tournaments. **Average** ¥6,000. **No credit cards.**

Chanko nabe is the legendary food of sumo wrestlers, said to help them put on those layers of bulk – when eaten in huge volumes late at night. For the rest of us, it's just a mixed casserole. There's nowhere more authentic to sample it than at Yoshiba, a former vsumo stable, where you sit around the hard-packed mud of the ring where wrestlers used to practise.

West

Shinjuku

Angkor Wat

1-38-13 Yoyogi, Shibuya-ku (3370 3019). Yoyogi station, west or A1 exit. **Open** 11am-2pm, 5-11pm daily. **Average** ¥2,500. **No credit cards. Map** p109.

What this place lacks in ambience it makes up for in food. It may look like a cafeteria, and indeed the food comes with amazing dispatch, but that may only be because they're lining up to get in. Cheerful Cambodian waitresses (daughters of the proprietor) will help you navigate the menu; don't leave out an order of chicken salad and chahan (fried rice).

Ban Thai

Dai-ichi Metro Bldg 3F, 1-23-14 Kabuki-cho, Shinjuku-ku (3207 0068). Shinjuku JR station, east exit. **Open** 11.30am-3pm, 5pm-midnight Mon-Fri; 11.30am-midnight Sat, Sun. **Average** ¥3,000. **Credit** AmEx, DC, JCB, MC, V. **English menu. Map** p109.

Conveniently situated at the opening end of raunchy Kabuki-cho, this is the longest-standing Thai institution in town, and no wonder: while no longer the best, there's nothing on the extensive menu that will disappoint. The curries are especially good.

Le Bistrot d'à Côté

1-6-11 Shinjuku, Shinjuku-ku (3359 3066). Shinjuku Gyoenmae station, exit 1. **Open** noon-2pm, 6-9pm Mon-Sat. **Average** ¥2,000. **No credit cards. French menu. Map** p109.

While Tokyo boasts literally hundreds of so-called authentic French restaurants, most of them fall at the first post by being located in humdrum office blocks. This quaint corner restaurant is altogether different, its tiny premises painstakingly recreating the look and feel of a real French bistro, not an easy feat to pull off in the middle of high-rise Shinjuku. Happily, the food and wine are every bit as painstaking, and the three-course set lunch for ¥1,500 is an absolute bargain. Try the rabbit or the house pâté and your mouth will love you forever. Booking is absolutely essential.

Carmine Edochiano

9-13 Arakicho, Shinjuku-ku (3225 6767). Yotsuya-Sanchome station, exit 4. **Open** noon-2pm, 6-10pm daily. **Average** ¥2,500 lunch; ¥8,000 dinner. **Credit** AmEx, JCB, MC, V. **Italian menu.**

Carmine Cozzolini was one of the pioneers of good, cheap Italian trattoria fare in Tokyo, but this is a daring move upmarket. He has converted a Japanese *ryotei* into a remarkable-looking *ristorante*, fusing traditional architecture with a Tuscan sensibility. The food is adequate, the surroundings great.

China Grill – Xenlon

Odakyu Hotel Century Southern Tower 19F, 2-2-1 Yoyogi, Shibuya-ku (3374 2080). Shinjuku JR station, south exit. **Open** 11.30am-4.30pm, 5-11pm daily. **Average** ¥1,500-¥5,000 lunch; ¥7,000-¥15,000 set dinner, ¥7,000 à la carte. **Credit** AmEx, DC, JCB, MC, V. **English menu. Map** p109.

Impeccable service and impressive views of the neon skyline make this stylish Chinese restaurant well worth the splurge. The Cantonese fare with a nod towards western, rather than Japanese, influences includes dim sum at lunchtime.

Restaurants by cuisine

Japanese

Aguri (general), *p133;* **Bincho** (yakitori), *p128;* **Birdland** (yakitori), *p125*; **Bon** (shojin ryori), *p135*; **Botan** (sukiyaki/shabu-shabu), *p124*; **Chibo** (okonomiyaki), *p140*; **Crayon House Hiroba** (vegetarian), *p145*; **Daidaiya** (general), *p145*; **Daigo** (shojin ryori), *p128*; **Daruma-ya** (noodles), *p145*; **Denpachi** (general), *p145*; **Densan** (oden), *p128*; **Down to Earth** (natural foods), *p140*; **Edogin** (sushi), *p125*; **Fukuzushi** (sushi), *p129*; **Goemon** (tofu ryori), *p133*; **Hantei** (kushi-age), *p133*; **Hassan Hinazushi** (sukiyaki/shabu-shabu), *p129*; **Hatsuogawa** (unagi), *p135*; **Hokuto** (noodles), *p147*; **Honke Ponta** (tonkatsu), *p134*; **Ikenohata Yabu Soba** (noodles), *p134*; **Isegen** (nabe), *p124*; **Izumo Soba Honke** (noodles), *p124*; **Jidaiya** (general), *p129*; **Jigoku Ramen Hyottoko** (noodles), *p141*; **Jinroku** (okonomiyaki), *p141*; **Kandagawa Honten** (unagi), *p124*; **Kanda Yabu Soba** (noodles), *p124*; **Kisso** (kaiseki), *p129*; **Komahachi** (general), *p133*; **Kyushu Jangara Ramen** (noodles), *p147*; **Little Okinawa** (regional cuisine), *p127*; **Maisen** (tonkatsu), *p147*; **Monja Maruyama** (monja), *p127*; **Myoko** (noodles), *p141*; **Mysterious Bar** (general), *p138*; **Natural Harmony Angoro** (natural foods), *p147*; **Ninja** (general), *p130*; **Nodaiwa** (unagi), *p130*; **Ohmatsuya** (regional cuisine), *p127*; **Oshima** (general), *p127*; **Otafuku** (oden), *p136*; **Robata** (general), *p127*; **Sasanoyuki** (tofu ryori), *p135*; **Senba** (noodles), *p149*; **Shichirinya** (aburiyaki), *p127*; **Shirube** (general), *p149*; **Sometaro** (okonomiyaki), *p136*; **Takokyuu** (oden), *p135*; **Ten-Ichi** (tempura), *p127*; **Ten-Ichi deux** (tempura), *p127*; **Torijaya** (noodles), *p139*; **Tsunahachi** (tempura), *p139*; **Vin Chou** (yakitori), *p136*; **Vingt2** (yakitori), *p144*; **Wasabiya** (general), *p144*; **Yoshiba** (nabe), *p136*; **Yurakucho Under the Tracks** (yakitori), *p128*; **Ya-So Poetry Restaurant** (general), *p144*; **Yui-An** (general), *p140*; **Yukun-tei** (general), *p140*; **Zakuro** (general), *p133*.

Asian

Ajanta (Indian), *p125*; **Angkor Wat** (Cambodian), *p136*; **Bangkok** (Thai), *p128*; **Ban Thai** (Thai), *p136*; **China Grill – Xenlon** (Chinese), *p136*; **Coriander** (Thai), *p128*; **Erawan** (Thai), *p129*; **Fumin** (Chinese), *p146*; **Ghungroo** (Indian/Pakistani), *p146*; **Hong Kong Garden** (Chinese), *p141*; **Hyakunincho Yataimura** (Pan-Asian), *p138*; **Ikebukuro Gyoza Stadium** (Chinese), *p128*; **Jap Cho Ok** (Korean), *p147*; **Jembatan Merah** (Indonesian), *p141*; **Jiang's** (Vietnamese), *p133*; **Kaikatei** (Chinese), *p147*; **Kihachi China** (Chinese), *p127*; **Kusa no Ya** (Korean), *p130*; **Monsoon Café** (Pan-Asian), *p130*; **Moti** (Indian/Pakistani), *p130*; **Namaste Kathmandu** (Nepali), *p149*; **Nataraj** (vegetarian Indian/Pakistani), *p149*; **Ninniku-ya** (Pan-Asian), *p142*; **Raj Mahal/ Raj Palace** (Indian/Pakistani), *p142*; **Shinjuku Jojoen** (Korean), *p138*; **Shinmasan-ya** (Korean), *p131*; **Shisen Hanten** (Chinese), *px130*; **Tokaien** (Korean), *p139*; **Vietnamese Cyclo** (Vietnamese), *p131*.

Asian/western fusion

Afternoon Tea Baker and Diner, *p124*; **Las Chicas**, *p145*; **Christon Café**, *p138*; **Dancing Monkey**, *p145*; **Fujimamas**, *p146*; **Ken's Dining**, *p129*; **Kubakan**, *p147*; **Legato**, *p141*; **The Lock-Up**, *p141*; **Nobu Tokyo**, *p147*; **Noodles**, *p130*; **Phothai Down Under**, *p130*; **Pumpkin Cook Katsura**, *p148*; **Rojak**, *p148*; **Sonoma**, *p143*; **Terrace Restaurant, Hanezawa Garden**, *p144*.

French

Aux Bacchanales, *p144*; **Le Bistrot d'à Côté**, *p136*; **Chez Pierre**, *p128*; **La Dinette**, *p138*.

Italian

La Befana, *p149*; **Carmine Edochiano**, *p136*; **Giliola**, *p146*; **La' Grotta Celeste**, *p146*; **Primi Baci**, *px149*; **Soho's**, *p149*.

Mexican & South American

La Casita, *p140*.

Middle Eastern

Ankara, *p140*; **Hannibal**, *p138*; **Zakuro**, *p133*.

North American

Brendan's Pizzakaya, *p128*; **Cardenas Charcoal Grill**, *p140*; **Fummy's Grill**, *p140*; **Good Honest Grub**, *p140*; **Lunchan**, *p141*; **New York Grill**, *p138*; **Olives**, *p130*; **Ricos Kitchen**, *p143*; **Roy's Aoyama**, *p148*; **Stellato**, *p133*; **Tableaux**, *p144*; **T Y Harbor Brewery**, *p133*; **Zuna Grill**, *p133*.

Eat, Drink, Shop

Ramen noodles: Japan's favourite.

Christon Café

Oriental Wave 8-9F, 5-17-13 Shinjuku, Shinjuku-ku (5287 2426/www.ug-gu.co.jp/restaurants/shop/shop-criston.html). Shinjuku JR station, east exit. **Open** 5-11pm Mon; 5pm-5am Tue-Sun. **Average** ¥2,500. **Credit** AmEx, DC, MC, V. **English menu**. **Map** p109.
This Osaka-based chain offers surprisingly good food in a sepulchral setting themed around the decor of a Catholic church. The Asian fusion menu is ambitous and well presented. Dine on pasta, salads or inventive meat dishes in the shadow of the Virgin Mary. *See also p146* **Themed dining**.
Branch: B1F, 2-10-7 Dogenzaka, Shibuya-ku (5728 2225).

La Dinette

2-6-10 Takadanobaba, Shinjuku-ku (3200 6571). Takadanobaba station, Waseda exit. **Open** 11.30am-1.30pm, 6-9pm Mon-Sat. **Average** ¥3,000. **No credit cards**. **French menu**.
Reservations are advised for this authentic bistro in the low-rent student district of Takadanobaba. La Dinette serves simple French cuisine at affordable prices in student-friendly portions.

Hannibal

Urban Bldg B1F, 1-11-1 Hyakunincho, Shinjuku-ku (5389 7313/www.hannibal.cc/). Shin-Okubo station. **Open** 11.30am-2pm, 5.30pm-12.30am Mon-Sat. **Average** ¥3,500. **Credit** AmEx, DC, JCB, MC, V. **English menu**. **Map** p109.
Currently Hannibal is Tokyo's only source of Tunisian food – and it's very good. Chef Mondher Gheribi cooks a confident Mediterranean cuisine with highlights from his home country – including mechoui salad, great roast chicken, home-made khobz bread along with a spicy home-made harissa.

Hyakunincho Yataimura

2-20-25 Hyakunincho, Shinjuku-ku (5386 3320). Shin-Okubo station. **Open** 11am-2.30pm, 5.30pm-4am Mon-Fri; 11pm-4am Sat, Sun. **Average** ¥2,500. **No credit cards**. **English menu (some stands)**. **Map** p109.
Just the spot if you find yourself out all night or just looking for a break from polite Japanese service. It's a low-rent place where the 'waiters' might dish out your rice while puffing on a cigarette in true Asian style. Yataimura ('foodstall village') is a collection of small cooking stands around a central eating area. The proprietors vie aggressively for your custom, so sit down and quickly order some beer and snacks or you will be swamped by people brandishing menus. There are pages of choices from places as diverse as Thailand, Indonesia, Taiwan and Fukien. One of the most fun places in town.

Mysterious Bar

B1F, 1-16-3 Kabuki-cho, Shinjuku-ku (5291 6670/ www.cest-la-vie.co.jp). Shinjuku JR station, east exit. **Open** 5pm-5am Mon-Sat; 5pm-midnight Sun. **Average** ¥2,500. **No credit cards**. **Map** p109.
The greatest mystery here is what's so mysterious. This is a theme restaurant of sorts, as diners are led through a maze into their own cushion-lined private cage. The food's quite acceptable and the waiting staff suitably eccentrically clad in luminous stockings. The same company also runs the Lock-Up. *See also p146* **Themed dining**.

New York Grill

Park Hyatt Tokyo 52F, 3-7-1-2 Nishi-Shinjuku, Shinjuku-ku (5323 3458/www.parkhyatttokyo.com/ Facility/Restaurant/newyorkgrill.html). Shinjuku JR station, west exit. **Open** 11.30am-2.30pm, 5.30-10.30pm daily. **Average** ¥6,000 brunch; ¥5,000 lunch; ¥10,000 dinner. **Credit** AmEx, DC, JCB, MC, V. **English menu**. **Map** p109.
The New York Grill offers a sky-high view and food to match, and it's worth every yen for the fantastic view from this chic pinnacle at the apex of the Park Hyatt Hotel. There's an extensive menu of seafood and meat dishes, highlights of which include baked black mussels, lobster ceviche with ginger, tomato and coriander, and home-grown Maezawa tenderloins and sirloins. Sunday brunch is an ex-pat institution, as are evening cocktails in the adjoining New York Bar. *See also p134* **Brunch**.

Shinjuku Jojoen

Tokyo Opera City Tower 53F, 3-20-2 Nishi-Shinjuku, Shinjuku-ku (5353 0089/www.jojoen.co.jp). Hatsudai station (Keio New Line), central exit. **Open** 11.30am-11.30pm (last order 10.45pm) daily. **Average** ¥5,000. **Credit** AmEx, DC, JCB, MC, V. **English menu**.

The cheap chain gang

As well as a plethora of upmarket restaurants, cafés and bars, Tokyo also has hundreds of chains *izakaya* that cater for people who want to eat (mainly) Japanese food without breaking the bank.

The chains listed below are all reliable, and offer great value for money. While the food on offer is not in the same league as that of some other restaurants listed in this chapter, the bill is much more likely to put a smile on your face.

The following chains have so many branches around the city that wherever you are in the major centres of Tokyo, there's bound to be one close by. Most of the restaurants open from 5pm until 3am during the week, generally staying open until 5am at weekends.

Katsuya

Kanda Sakura Bldg 1F, 1-8-1 Kaji-cho, Chiyoda-ku (5289 0408/www.arcland.co.jp/Service/da01.html). Kanda station, east exit.

A small chain, with just 17 branches in the Tokyo area, Katsuya specialises in tonkatsu, deep-fried breaded pieces of pork cutlet. A katsu-don (pork cutlet on a bed of rice) costs ¥490. This chain is so popular it has its very own fan club. Most branches are in out-of-the-way areas of Tokyo, so the details given above are for the Kanda branch, which is the most easily accessible.

Ootoya

Umeyoshi Bldg 2F, 30-3 Udagawa-cho, Shibuya-ku (3476 1128/www.ootoya.com/op.html). Shibuya station, Hachiko exit.

A full-on Japanese curry here will set you back ¥680. the menu also features salads, in addition to other Japanese staples. This chain has around 100 branches in central Tokyo, most of which close at midnight, but the branch listed here is open 24 hours.

Shirokiya/Uotani

Information 0120 80 5088/www.monteroza.co.jp.

Two chain *izakaya* among a dozen operated by the Monteroza group. Shirokiya and Uotani between them have over 200 branches in central Tokyo. Shirokiya is a general *izakaya* offering complete set meals of eight dishes from ¥1,850, while Uotani specialises in fish.

Tengu

Information 0120 109 549/www.teng.co.jp.

Look for the sign of the eponymous red-nosed goblin to spot a branch of this chain, which has over 200 restaurants in central Tokyo and serves a range of dishes from ¥400.

Watami

Information 5737 2780/www.watami.co.jp.

Has over 150 branches in central Tokyo, serving salads from ¥380, yakitori from ¥250 and sushi rolls from ¥380. Draught beer and shochu cocktails cost ¥420.

This is not honest, down-home Korean cooking; it's yakiniku with a view. And what a view! From this 53rd-floor eyrie, the Shinjuku skyline at night is breathtaking. If there are only two of you, make a reservation (Mon-Sat only) for the 'pair seats' – ten pairs of comfortable chairs facing the window.

Tokaien

1-6-3 Kabuki-cho, Shinjuku-ku (3200 2934). Shinjuku JR station, east exit. **Open** 11am-4am daily. **Average** ¥2,250 all-you-can eat/90mins; à la carte varies. **Credit** AmEx, DC, JCB, MC, V. **Map** p109.

If yakiniku is a religion, then Tokaien is its temple: nine floors of this building in Kabuki-cho are turned over to yakiniku and home-style Korean cooking. The sixth floor features all-you-can-eat ('tabe-hodai' in Japanese) yakiniku.

Torijaya

4-2 Kagurazaka, Shinjuku-ku (3260 6661). Kagurazaka station, Kagurazaka exit or Ushigome Kagurazaka station (Toei Oedo Line), exit A3. **Open** 11.30am-2.30pm, 5-10.30pm Mon-Sat; 11.30am-3pm, 4-10pm Sun. **Average** ¥2,500-¥4,000 set lunch; ¥6,500 dinner. **Credit** AmEx, JCB, MC, V.

This traditional restaurant in Kagurazaka specialises in Kyoto-style udon cuisine. It calls itself udon *kaiseki*, but things never get too formal. The centrepiece of any meal here is udon-suki, and hearty nabe of chicken, vegetables and thick-cut wheat noodles. Courses start from ¥5,500.

Tsunahachi

3-31-8 Shinjuku, Shinjuku-ku (3352 1012/www.tunahachi.co.jp). Shinjuku JR station, east exit. Shinjuku-Sanchome station, exits A1-5. **Open** 11am-10pm daily. **Average** ¥5,000. **Credit** AmEx, DC, JCB, MC, V. **English menu**. **Map** p109.

Surviving amid the gleaming modern buildings of Shinjuku, Tsunahachi's battered wooden premises are a throwback to the early post-war era. So are the prices: this is the best bargain for tempura in town. The food is quite good enough for everyday fare. So what if the whole place is filled with the whiff of oil?

Yui-An

Shinjuku Sumitomo Bldg, 52F, 2-6-1 Nishi-Shinjuku, Shinjuku-ku (3342 5671/www.sanwa-kosan.co.jp/yuian/yuian.html). Shinjuku JR station, west exit. **Open** 5-11.30pm Mon-Sat; 4-10.30pm Sun. **Average** ¥4,000. **Credit** AmEx, JCB, MC, V. **Map** p109.

The waiters act like automata and the modern *izakaya* food is average. But the view over the night sky of Shinjuku is nothing short of spectacular, so call ahead and ask for one of the tables by the 52nd floor window. Prices are reasonable, which has made Yui-an very popular with dating couples and groups of young people.

Yukun-tei

3-26 Arakicho, Shinjuku-ku (3356 3351/www.akasakayukun.com). Yotsuya-Sanchome station, exit A4. **Open** 11.30am-2pm, 5-10.30pm Mon-Sat. **Average** ¥1,000 lunch; ¥8,000 dinner. **Credit** AmEx, DC, JCB, MC, V.

A friendly Kyushu *izakaya* with cheerful Kyushu waitresses and delightful Kyushu cuisine. Many of the names on the *washi* menu sound foreign even to Japanese ears and indeed there's something undeniably exotic – and southern – about the food. The lunch sets are absolutely fantastic: onigiri teishoku has two enormous onigiri (rice balls), while the inaka udon teishoku will net you a very generous bowlful of udon with rice and mysterious little side dishes. In the evening take your pick from the extensive selection of sashimi, plus grilled and simmered goodies. The smooth house sake, which is also called Yukun Sakagura, is available nowhere else.

Branches: Seio Bldg B1F, 2-2-18 Ginza Chuo-ku (3561 6672); Tokyo Tatemono Dai 5 Yaesu Bldg B1F, 1-4-14 Yaesu, Chuo-ku (3271 8231); Toranomon Jitsugyo Kaikan Bldg B2F, 1-1-21 Toranomon, Minato-ku (3508 9298); Akasaka Tokyu Plaza 3F, 2-14-3 Nagatacho, Chiyoda-ku (3592 0393).

Shibuya, Daikanyma, Ebisu & Hiroo

Ankara

Social Dogenzaka B1F, 1-14-9 Dogenzaka, Shibuya-ku (3780 1366/ankara.theshoppe.com). Shibuya JR station, Hachiko exit. **Open** 5-11.30pm daily. **Average** ¥2,500. **Credit** MC, V. **English menu**. **Map** p102.

Tucked away in the backstreets of Shibuya, this snug little Turkish restaurant serves up an array of delicious and healthy meze and a range of other Turkish delights.

Chibo

Yebisu Garden Place Tower 38F, 4-20-3 Ebisu, Shibuya-ku (5424 1011). Ebisu JR station, east exit. **Open** 11.30am-3pm, 5-11pm (last order 10pm) Mon-Fri; 11.30am-10pm Sat, Sun. **Average** ¥2,500. **Credit** AmEx, DC, JCB, MC, V. **English menu**.

This branch of an Osaka okonomiyaki restaurant uses the original Osaka-style recipe. In addition to the usual meats and seafood, stuffings include asparagus, mochi or cheese, and of course mayonnaise. Friendly staff, reasonable prices and a large menu, plus a gorgeous view, make this a popular place for okonomiyaki.

Cardenas Charcoal Grill

1-12-14 Ebisu-Nishi, Shibuya-ku (5428 0779/www.cardenas.co.jp/chacoal/chacoal1.html) Ebisu JR station, west exit. **Open** 11.30am-2pm Mon-Fri; 5.30-2am daily. **Average** ¥5,000 dinner. **Credit** AmEx, JCB, MC, V. **English menu**.

The latest, most stylish and satisfying of the three Californian restaurants that now share the Cardenas name and distinctive take on Pacific Rim fusion food. The centrepiece here is the eponymous grill from which issue chicken, steaks, fish and seafood. There is a strong selection of US West Coast wines.

Branches: (not all Pacific Rim), throughout the city.

La Casita

Selsa Daikanyama 2F, 13-4 Daikanyama-cho, Shibuya-ku (3496 1850/www.lacasita.co.jp). Daikanyama station (Tokyu Toyoko Line). **Open** 5pm-11pm Mon; noon-11pm Tue-Sun. **Average** courses from ¥2,500; la carte ¥3,500. **No credit cards. English menu**.

Like most of Tokyo's south-of-the-border restaurants, La Casita isn't authentically Mexican. But the heady aroma of corn tortillas grabs you upon entering this airy 'little house' and won't let go until you've sampled the near-perfect camarones al mojo de ajo (grilled shrimp with garlic Acapulco style) or the enchiladas rojos bathed in spicy tomato sauce.

Down to Earth

2-5 Sarugaku-cho, Shibuya-ku (3461 5872). Daikanyama station (Tokyu Toyoko line). **Open** noon-3pm, 6-10.30pm Mon-Fri; noon-10.30pm Sat. **Average** ¥1,500. **Credit** AmEx, DC, JCB, MC, V. **English menu**.

Down to Earth attracts a mostly young clientele (and even the occasional celebrity) with its casual atmosphere and wholesome food. While not completely vegetarian, hefty garden burgers and a mixed bag of ethnic offerings will satisfy even the vegans.

Fummy's Grill

2-1-5 Ebisu, Shibuya-ku (3473 9629/www.cardenas.co.jp/chacoal/chacoal1.html). Ebisu JR station, east exit. **Open** 11.30am-2am daily. **Average** ¥4,500 dinner. **Credit** AmEx, JCB, V. **English menu**.

Fumihiro Nakamura opened his original Californian casual bistro back in 1996, and in many people's books it's still the best. That's because it's casual, friendly and cheap, and the food still has a creative spark. BYO wine, or explore his mostly New World offerings in the company of a heterodox crowd of arty types and business suits, locals and expats.

Good Honest Grub

1-11-11 Ebisu-Minami, Shibuya-ku (3710 0400). Ebisu JR station, west exit. **Open** 11.30am-11.30pm Mon-Fri; 9am-11.30pm Sat, Sun. **Average** ¥1,500 lunch; ¥3,500 dinner. **Credit** AmEx, JCB, MC, V. **English menu**.

No-nonsense North American food in sidewalk cafe setting. Portions are generous, and there's plenty for vegetarians too. Awesome shakes.

Hong Kong Garden

4-5-2 Nishi-Azabu, Minato-ku (3486 8611/www.hongkong-garden.co.jp/). Hiroo station, exit 3. **Open** *Dim sum* 11.30am-3pm Mon-Fri; 11.30am-4.30pm Sat, Sun. *Dinner* 5.30-10.30pm daily. **Average** ¥6,000 (dinner). **Credit** AmEx, JCB, MC, V. **English menu**.

Huge gastrodome (seating 800-plus) devoted to the pleasures of Hong Kong-style cooking. The main dishes are Cantonese-lite, but very pleasant, especially the stir-fried organic beef with subtle hints of star anise. The trolley-borne dim sum are not totally authentic, but as good as you can expect in Tokyo.

Jembatan Merah

109 Bldg 8F, 2-29-1 Dogenzaka, Shibuya-ku (3476 6424/www.alpha-net.ne.jp/users2/jembatan/index1.html). Shibuya JR station, Hachiko exit. **Open** 11am-11pm Mon-Sat; 11am-10pm Sun. **Average** ¥2,500. **Credit** (bills over ¥5,000) AmEx, DC, JCB, MC, V. **English menu**. **Map** p102.

The Indonesian fare at JM is not quite up to the standard of Tokyo's best, but with branches dotted conveniently around the Yamanote Line, it's pretty convenient, with the added attraction of good vegetarian offerings. There are seven dishes starring tempeh (a fermented soybean patty with a nutty flavour), middling gado gado salad, and an extravagant 12-course 'special menu' for those who can't be troubled to navigate the many pages of the menu.

Branches: I-Land Tower B1F, 6-5-1 Nishi-Shinjuku, Shinjuku-ku (5323 4214); 3-20-6 Akasaka, Minato-ku (3588 0794); Sunshine City Alpa B1F, 3-1 Higashi-Ikebukuro, Toshima-ku (3987 2290).

Jigoku Ramen Hyottoko

1-8-4 Ebisu-Minami, Shibuya-ku (3791 7376). Ebisu JR station, west exit. **Open** 2-10pm Mon-Fri; 2-7pm Sat. **Average** ¥1,000. **No credit cards**.

Jigoku means 'hell', and the house speciality here is ramen in a bright red soup in varying degrees of spiciness, with various colourful names: aka-oni (red ogre, shoyu broth); ao-oni (green ogre, salt broth); enma (king of hell, spicy miso); jigoku (hell, spicy miso); and jigoku ramen special (spicy miso). A sign on the wall warns that if you order the special and can't finish it, you have to wash dishes.

Jinroku

6-23-2 Shirokane, Minato-ku (3441 1436). Hiroo station, exits 1, 2. **Open** 6pm-3am (last food order 1.30am) Tue-Sat; 6-11pm Sun. **Average** ¥4,500. **Credit** AmEx, MC, V. **English menu**.

Okonomiyaki raised to a new level, in gleaming, modern, upmarket surroundings. Besides the standard pancakes, the chefs at Jinroku also serve up excellent gyoza dumplings, teppanyaki seafood, tofu steak and fried yaki-soba. Be sure to try the negi-yaki – which substitutes chopped green leek in place of the more usual Chinese cabbage. Wash it all down with Chilean wine.

Legato

E Space Tower 15F, 3-6 Maruyama-cho, Shibuya-ku (5784 2121/www.global-dining.com/global/). Shibuya JR station, Hachiko exit. **Open** 5pm-2am daily. **Average** ¥5,000. **Credit** AmEx, DC, JCB, MC, V. **English menu**. **Map** p102.

The latest restaurant to be opened in Tokyo by the Global Dining Group, which also owns Monsoon and Stellato (*see p130* and *p133*), among others, Legato opened in 2002 in a new tower building on Dogenzaka. The theme is theatrical: food as an experience to be savoured amid lavish decor (Shibuya unfolds 15 floors below). The menu mixes Asian and western influences, in accordance with Tokyo's current vogue, and so features Vietnamese spring rolls or Chinese noodles alongside lamb chops and pizza.

The Lock-Up

B1F, 33-1 Udagawacho, Shibuya-ku (5728 7731/www.cest-la-vie.co.jp). Shibuya JR station, Hachiko exit. **Open** 5pm-1am Mon-Thur; 5pm-5am Fri, Sat; 5pm-midnight Sun. **Average** ¥2,000. **No credit cards**. **Map** p102.

On arrival at this prison-themed *izakaya*, you'll be asked if it's your first visit. Just say, 'Hai.' After this, you will be handcuffed by the waitress and led to your cell to await a selection of run-of-the-mill *izakaya* fare. Every hour, the monsters escape from jail to terrorise diners, until they are brought under control by police girls clad in unfeasibly short skirts. Don't say we didn't warn you. *See also p146* **Themed dining**.

Branches: 5F, 1-29-1 Higashi-Ikebukuro, Toshima-ku (5960 6755); Oriental Wave 5F, 5-17-13 Shinjuku, Shinjuku-ku (5272 7055).

Lunchan

1-2-5 Shibuya, Shibuya-ku (5466 1398). Shibuya JR station, Miyamasusaka (east) exit. **Open** 11.30am-11pm Mon-Sat; 11am-10pm Sun. **Average** ¥2,500. **Credit** AmEx, DC, JCB, MC, V. **English menu**. **Map** p102.

No one can figure out the name. Is it a misspelling? Or is it diminutive of someone named Lun? Why is the interior so ugly? Ah well, no matter. Aside from the reasonably priced Sunday brunch of ample proportions with complimentary champagne, Lunchan does a credible array of California-meets-Asia curries, pizza and pasta, complemented by a friendly little wine list.

Myoko

Shinto Bldg 1F, 1-17-2 Shibuya, Shibuya-ku (3499 3450). Shibuya JR station, Miyamasusaka (east) exit. **Open** 11.30am-2pm, 5-9pm Mon-Fri; 11.30am-2pm Sat. **Average** ¥1,200. **Credit** AmEx, DC, JCB, MC, V. **Map** p102.

The speciality here is houtou, a hearty mountain-style stew made with flat wide udon noodles. Other ingredients include oysters, kimchee, mushroom, pork, or sansai, cooked in a miso-based broth with lots of vegetables and served bubbling hot in an iron kettle. There are also many cold dishes, such as 'salad udon' (chilled noodles and vegetables),

Japanese cuisine

Kaiseki ryori

Kaiseki ryori is Japan's formal haute cuisine. A kaiseki meal is a sequence of small dishes, apparently simple but always immaculately prepared and presented to reflect the seasons. Courses follow one after the other, but slowly; a one-hour parade would be considered hurried. The formal order of the meal will be a starter, then sashimi, a clear soup, then a series of dishes that are grilled, steamed, served with a dressing, deep-fried, and with a vinegar dressing. The main ingredients are fish and vegetables, plus small amounts of meat, either beef or chicken. Rice is served at the end of the meal. Be warned, Kaiseki is very pricey. Courses rarely start at under ¥10,000.

Shojin ryori

Shojin ryori follows the same lines as mainstream kaiseki, except that no fish is used, and stocks are prepared with shiitake mushrooms and kombu seaweed. Tofu and yuba feature prominently in shojin meals.

Tofu ryori

Beancurd is celebrated for its protein content and its versatility, and features strongly in Japanese cooking. Because tofu restaurants tend to use small amounts of fish or chicken (often in the soup stocks), they are classified separately from the strict shojin tradition.

Sushi

The classic style of arranging raw fish and other delicacies on patties of vinegared rice dates back to the 18th century, when it became a popular street food in Edo (present-day Tokyo). Since it used seafood from the Bay, it became known as Edo-mae sushi. Top sushi shops can be daunting, as they don't post their prices, and customers are expected to know their uni from their ikura. The best (and cheapest) way to learn your way around the etiquette and vocabulary is to explore the many *kaiten* (conveyor belt) sushi shops, where prices are fixed and you can take what you want without having to order.

Sukiyaki & shabu-shabu

Sukiyaki is a dish of tender, thinly sliced meat (usually beef, but sometimes pork, horse or chicken), plus vegetables, tofu and other ingredients, such as shirataki (devil's tongue noodles), cooked in a soy sauce broth that has been slightly sweetened with sugar and mirin (sweet cooking sake). As they are cooking, you fish them out and dip them into beaten raw egg. Shabu-shabu refers to the sound made as paper-thin beef is swished back and forth in a bubbling broth, cooked at the table, usually in a special copper pot.

Tempura

The Portuguese are credited with introducing the technique of deep-frying fish, seafood and vegetables – and also the name itself. But in Japan the dish has been elevated to a fine art. Good tempura has a batter covering that is thin and crisp, and never too oily.

Nabemono & one-pot cooking

One-pot stews cooked at the table, in a casserole (nabe) of iron or heavy earthenware, over a gas flame. Everyone is served from the one pot: pluck out seasonal titbits with long chopsticks, drop them into the bowl provided or dip in sauce. Favourite nabe styles include chicken, oyster and chanko nabe, the sumo wrestlers' stew of meat, fish and vegetables.

plus several good-value set lunches. A large picture menu makes ordering a simple business despite the lack of an English menu.

Ninniku-ya

1-26-12 Ebisu, Shibuya-ku (3446 5887). Ebisu JR station, west exit. **Open** 6-10pm Tue-Thur, Sun; 6-11pm Fri, Sat. **Average** ¥5,000. **No credit cards. English menu.**

Ninniku is the Japanese word for garlic, and everything on the menu, with the possible exception of the drinks, is laced with it. The odours of towering garlic bread, vicious Thai curries, mouthwatering pasta and rice dishes with Chinese, Thai, Indian and other ethnic twists waft out on the streets.

Raj Mahal/Raj Palace

Jow Bldg 5F, 30-5 Udagawa-cho, Shibuya-ku (3770 7677). Shibuya JR station, Hachiko exit. **Open** 11.30am-11pm daily. **Average** ¥3,500. **Credit** AmEx, DC, JCB, MC, V. **English menu.** **Map** p102.

Despite their chain status, the Raj Mahal/Palace restaurants are known for their good service and above average Moghul-style food. The restaurant menus are extensive.

Branches: Urban Bldg 4F, 7-13-2 Roppongi, Minato-ku (5411 2525); Peace Bldg 5F, 3-34-11 Shinjuku, Shinjuku-ku (5379 2525); Hakuba Bldg 4F, 26-11 Udagawa-cho, Shibuya-ku (3780 6531); Taiyo Bldg 4F, 8-8-5 Ginza, Chuo-ku (5568 8080).

Yakitori & kushiyaki

Yakitori are skewered pieces of chicken cooked over a charcoal grill, served with salt or a slightly sweet soy-based glaze. Yakitori means 'grilled chicken', but most yakitori-ya also do wonderful things with vegetables.

Unagi

Unagi, or eel, is another of Japan's great delicacies. Eels are filleted, basted and very slowly broiled (often over charcoal). Unagi is thought to be a restorative, and is consumed with a fanaticism that is almost religious during the hot months of July and August for stamina, to improve eyesight and even virility.

Teppanyaki, okonomiyaki & monja

Beef is a luxury item in Japan, but Japanese beef (especially Kobe beef) is very good. Grilled on the teppan ('metal surface'), this is a wonderful way to experience Japanese-style steak. Thin slices of beef, seafood and vegetables will be grilled in front of you.

Okonomiyaki ('grilled whatever you like') is often described as a Japanese pancake, though you can also think of it as a well-stuffed omelette. Many okonomiyaki restaurants also do yaki-soba (fried Chinese-styles noodles). Originally from western Japan (Hiromshima and Osaka both lay claim to it) okonomiyaki is cheap, robust and satisfying. The Tokyo version is known as monja.

Oden

Oden is a simple seasonal dish of fish cakes, tofu, vegetables and konyaku (devil's tongue), simmered in a light, kelp-based broth, served with a dash of karashi (hot mustard) for flavouring. It is usually accompanied by sake and often served at outdoor *yatai* (covered street stalls). Although the cheap oden of outdoor stands and convenience stores has a smell that can be chokingly pungent, the subtle flavours of oden in fine restaurants can be a revelation.

Kushi-age

Pieces of meat, seafood and vegetables are skewered and deep fried to a golden brown in a coating of fine breadcrumbs. Usually eaten with a sweetened soy-based sauce, salt or even a dab of curry powder. Perfect when washed down with beer, and rounded off with rice and miso soup.

Tonkatsu

The 'katsu' in 'tonkatsu' means cutlet, a very popular dish first introduced during the Meiji period when eating meat began to catch on. The katsu is now almost always pork, usually lean cuts of sirloin, dredged in flour, dipped in egg, rolled in breadcrumbs and deep-fried.

Noodles

Noodles are hugely popular, especially at lunchtime. There are two main indigenous varieties: soba (thin grey-coloured noodles made form buckwheat and wheat); and udon (chunkier wheat noodles, usually white). These can be eaten either chilled, served on a bamboo 'plate' with a soy-based dipping sauce; or hot, usually in soy-flavored broth topped with chopped spring onions, tempura or other ingredients. Even more popular than these are the crinkly, yellowish Chinese-style noodles known as ramen, which are served in a rich, meat-based stock, flavoured with miso, soy sauce or salt, and topped with vegetables or cha-shu, sliced barbecued pork.

Ricos Kitchen

4-23-7 Ebisu, Shibuya-ku (5791 4649) Ebisu JR station, east exit. **Open** 11.30am-3pm, 5.30-11pm daily. **Average** ¥6,000 dinner. Credit AmEx, MC, V. **English menu**.

Chef Haruki Natsume produces a suave and never less than satisfying cucina nueva americana, served in a chic and airy space. Perhaps this is why Ricos has been full virtually every day since it opened.

Sonoma

2-25-17 Dogenzaka, Shibuya-ku (3462 7766). Shibuya JR station, Hachiko exit. **Open** 11.30am-midnight Sun-Thur; 11.30-4am Fri, Sat. **Average** ¥4,000. **Credit** AmEx, DC, JCB, MC, V. **English menu**. **Map** p102.

Sonoma is run by the same people who gave Tokyo one of its legendary, and now deceased, clubs, Sugar High. Their past is reflected in the clientele which seems to consist of just about every foreign DJ or VJ currently living in Tokyo. Decor is simple and pleasant, and the food is of the fusion variety that seems to be on every Tokyo restaurant's menu these days. Dishes can be variable: on a recent visit chicken tortilla in a blue cheese sauce was a success, but lamb chops with red currants was not. A reasonable selection of mainly New World wines starts at around ¥3,600. Eating here gets you free admission to the Ruby Room club upstairs (*see p241*), the spiritual successor of Sugar .

Tableaux

11-6 Sarugakucho, Shibuya-ku (5489 2201/ www.global-dining.com/global/). Daikanyama station (Tokyu Toyoko Line). **Open** 5.30pm-1am daily. **Average** ¥7,500. **Credit** AmEx, MC, V. **English menu**.

There is more than a touch of kitsch to the decor here, but the eclectic Pac-Rim fusion food is entirely serious. Tableaux has become a favourite port of call with the well-heeled Daikanyama set, many of whom drop by just for a Havana and cognac in the adjoining cigar bar.

Terrace Restaurant, Hanezawa Garden

3-12-15 Hiroo, Shibuya-ku (3400 2013). Hiroo station, then a 15min walk. **Open** *Summer* 11am-1.30pm (BBQ only), 6-11pm daily. **Average** ¥2,000. **Credit** AmEx, MC, V.

The march of time leaves none of us untrampled and in recent years this venerable garden dating from the Meiji era, which once served as a scenic yakitori house, has been spruced up and westernised, with a meat and pasta menu, to cater for current trends. Sadly, the eating area has also been extended, leaving the garden itself all but invisible under wooden planking. Still, eating al fresco under the trees is such a rare experience in Tokyo that it's worth the trip. An adjacent cocktail lounge is open year-round.

Vingt2

ICI Bldg 1F, 1-6-7 Shibuya, Shibuya-ku (3407 9494). Shibuya JR station, Miyamasusaka (east) exit. **Open** 11.30am-3pm, 5-11pm Mon-Sat. **Average** ¥900 lunch; ¥3,500 dinner. **Credit** AmEx, DC, JCB, V. **Map** p102.

An extensive selection of charcoal-grilled fish, meat and vegetable kushi-yaki (skewered foods) near Children's Castle (*see p204*) and Aoyama Dori.

Wasabiya

ITO Bldg. B1F, 2-17-8 Ebisu-Nishi, Shibuya-ku (3770 2604). Ebisu JR station, east exit. **Open** 6pm-midnight Mon-Fri; 6-11.30pm Sat. **Average** ¥4,500. **Credit** AmEx, MC, V. **English menu**.

This is where the stylish people of Daikanyama like to graze these days. The owner sports a pony tail. The decor is in the best modern-Japanese vein. Sit at the counter or install yourself at low tables on the floor. There's a good variety of dishes from sashimi through grills to tempura – much of it served wth a dab of the trademark pungent wasabi.

Ya-So Poetry Restaurant

4-10-3 Nishi Azabu, Minato-ku (3499 0233). Hiroo station, exit 3. **Open** 6pm-6am Mon-Sat. **Average** ¥3,000. **Credit** AmEx, DC, JCB, MC, V.

With walls and room dividers festooned with snippets of poetry, this upscale *izakaya* is a romantic departure from the farmhouse feel most such places strive for. Lighting is by candle and corner lights wrapped in *washi*. The food is as distinctive as the interior: classic Japanese with an unusual approach. Ume no tataki is a creative dish of piquant ume paste served like sushi, with nori, slivered onion and ginger. Finish with a delicious twist on a traditional meal-ender: udon chazuke, in which chewy noodles in tea broth take the place of rice.

Harajuku & Omotesando

Aux Bacchanales

Palais France 1F, 1-6-1 Jingumae, Shibuya-ku (5474 0076/www.auxbacchanales.com). Harajuku station, Takeshita exit or Meiji-Jingumae station, exit 5. **Open** *Brasserie/café* 10am-midnight daily. *Restaurant* 5.30pm-midnight daily. **Average** ¥2,000. **Credit** (restaurant only) AmEx, DC, JCB, MC, V. **French menu**. **Map** p99.

One of the rare places in Tokyo where the action spills out on to the streets and people go to watch and be watched – and drink themselves silly on relatively inexpensive red wine. Features French cooking in a casual bistro setting, with 'authentic' French café

Street food

Japan is not really an eat-on-the-street country. In fact, it is generally considered rude to eat or drink in public, but there are exceptions. During festivals, or late at night around certain busy transport hubs, you may find vendors serving some of the foods below from *yatai*, small portable carts with their own cooking equipment and, sometimes, minimal counter space.

Taiyaki are a pancake-like batter stuffed with sweet red bean jam and cooked in fish-shaped moulds ('tai' means sea bream). They are extremely popular with children, and making a comeback with nostalgia-minded adults.

Takoyaki are found at special stalls denoted by a banner featuring a cheerful-looking red octopus. They're something of an acquired taste, consisting of diced octopus cooked in egg batter and moulded into balls, often with pickled ginger and a sweet glaze sauce.

The **yakisoba** found at yatai is a far cry from the yakisoba, or lo mein, served in Chinese restaurants. These noodles, grill-fried with cabbage, bean sprouts or carrot are doused in sweet sauce and sprinkled with red pickled ginger and nori (seaweed).

Yaki-imo are charcoal-cooked sweet potatoes, roasted until the skin is flaky and the inside soft and very hot. Some people take them home, add a little butter and wolf them down, although most eat them just as they are.

Fujimamas: a confident fusion of east and west. *See p146.*

furniture. All things considered, the food's pretty good. The less atmospheric branch is in an office block in the business district; opening hours differ.
Branch: Ark Mori Bldg 2F, 1-12-32 Akasaka, Minato-ku (3582 2225).

Las Chicas

5-47-6 Jingumae, Shibuya-ku (3407 6865/www.vision.co.jp/index2.html). Omotesando station, exit B2. **Open** 11am-11pm daily. **Average** ¥1,000 lunch; ¥4,000 dinner. **Credit** AmEx, DC, JCB, MC, V. **English menu. Map** p99.
One of the most creative and foreigner-friendly spaces in town, Las Chicas is part of a gorgeous complex encompassing several restaurants and bars (Las Chicas, Tokyo Salon, Nude and Crome) that host revolving exhibitions of local talent. The bilingual staff (mostly Australian) are friendly and helpful, and so on the cutting edge of fashion as to almost constitute an exhibition in themselves. Dishes such as potato wedges with sour cream and Thai chilli sauce, cheesy polenta chips or homemade bread with real butter are all meals in themselves, and make perfect mates for the earthy, sensuous Australian wines.

Crayon House Hiroba

3-8-15 Kita-Aoyama, Minato-ku (3406 6409/www.crayonhouse.co.jp). Omotesando station, exit B2. **Open** 11am-2pm, 2.30-5pm (for tea), 5-10pm daily. **Average** ¥1,500. **Credit** AmEx, DC, JCB, MC, V. **Map** p99.
Set up alongside a natural foods store, Crayon House is not exclusively vegetarian, but offers a good selection of well-prepared wholesome dishes, many with organic ingredients. Consists of two mini restaurants: Hiroba, offering Japanese food, and Home, offering western stuff.

Dancing Monkey

Minami-Aoyama Homes B1F, 6-2-2 Minami-Aoyama, Minato-ku (6418 4242/www.global-dining.com/global). Omotesando station, exit B1. **Open** 11.30-5am daily. **Average** ¥2,000. **Credit** AmEx, DC, JCB, MC, V. **English menu.**
Another Global Dining restaurant, the curiously named Dancing Monkey offers a reasonably priced sample of what's on the menu at other restaurants in the Global Dining empire. Thus choose everything from Zest-style beef jamabalaya to Monsoon-style Vietnamese spring rolls. Lunch sets at ¥1,000 yen or less, including the salad bar, are a bargain.

Daruma-ya

5-9-5 Minami-Aoyama, Minato-ku (3499 6295). Omotesando station, exit B1. **Open** 11am-10pm daily. **Average** ¥1,500. **No credit cards. English menu. Map** p99.
Daruma-ya takes its name from daruma, roly-poly legless caricatures of the fifth-century Indian priest Bodhidarma that are a Japanese good luck charm. Famous for its hand-made Chinese noodles (ramen) executed with a Japanese twist; the most popular is takana soba – ramen noodles topped with a leafy domestic vegetable that defies translation.

Denpachi

5-9-9 Minami-Aoyama, Minato-ku (3406 8240). Omotesando station, exit B1. **Open** 5pm-midnight daily. **Average** ¥2,000. **No credit cards. Map** p99.
An *izakaya* known among regulars as 'the sardine place', Denpachi also serves up a mean array of beef tongue dishes. But mostly it does wicked things to the humble sardine (iwashi). Small strips of very tender fish appear as iwashi sashimi, while iwashi tataki is a tender rendering of sardines into small, carpaccio-like pieces. Don't miss the iwashi wonton

Themed dining

'The monsters have escaped! The monsters have escaped!' screams a high-pitched voice above the screech of an emergency siren. Suddenly your space is invaded by a blood-drenched mummy; the creature is about to swat you aside with its ghastly hand when a mini-skirted policewoman intervenes and carts it off to jail. This scene is recreated nightly for diners at **The Lock-Up** (*see p141*), one of a growing band of theme restaurants springing up all over Tokyo. Monsters aside, the Lock-Up has a prison theme – diners are handcuffed and led in chains to their tables, which are situated in individual prison cells.

If you fear such excitement may be too much for you, then the **Christon Café** (*see p138*) offers the more contemplative surroundings of a Christian church, complete with statues of the Virgin Mary and a bleeding Christ on the cross. Diners at the Shinjuku branch can book themselves a table in the confessional booths by the altar.

Over in Akasaka, meanwhile, **Ninja** (*see p130*) returns to Japan's roots with a basement recreation of a medieval Japanese village, populated by black-clad staff who appear out of wall panels clutching the parchment scrolls that act as menus. The most upmarket of the theme chains, Ninja serves high-quality Japanese food with a western twist.

At the bottom of the heap, quality wise, is the **Mysterious Bar** (*see p138*), where diners eat in cushion-lined cages that are suspended in mid-air. The biggest mystery here seems to be why people bother coming to the restaurant, since the food is mediocre and there's no special show.

All of these places are phenomenally popular, particularly with groups of young Japanese on a boisterous night out (though Ninja's clientele is slightly more mature). Queues can get very lengthy, particularly at weekends. Reservations advised.

soup, a delicately flavoured broth in which swim two wonton stuffed with ground sardine.
Branches: 4-8-7 Ginza, Chuo-ku (3562 3957); 1-15-8 Kabuki-cho, Shinjuku-ku (3200 8003).

Fujimamas

6-3-2 Jingumae, Shibuya-ku (5485 2262). Harajuku, Omotesando exit or Meiji-Jingumae station, exit 4. **Open** 11am-11pm daily. **Average** ¥3,000. **Credit** AmEx, DC, JCB, MC, V. **English menu**. **Map** p99.
Confident east-west fusion cuisine in a casual setting. Servings are large and prices reasonable, given the swanky address and sunny decor.

Fumin

Aoyama Ohara Bldg B1F, 5-7-17 Minami-Aoyama, Minato-ku (3498 4466). Omotesando station, exit B1. **Open** 1-2.30pm, 5.30pm-9.30pm Mon-Fri; 1-2.30pm, 5pm-9pm Sat; 1-2.30pm Sun. **Average** ¥4,000. **No credit cards**. **Map** p99.
Most people in Tokyo haven't actually gone to Fumin; they've tried to go and given up because of a wait made torturous by the heady smells of garlic and Chinese seasonings. But thc extensive menu of funky home-style Chinese food characterised by large servings, liberally seasoned, makes all that waiting worthwhile. Don't miss the (scallion) wonton.

Ghungroo

Seinan Bldg 2F, 5-6-19 Minami Aoyama, Minato ku (3406 0464/www.ghungroo-jp.com). Omotesando station, exit B1. **Open** 11.30am-10.30pm Mon-Thur; 11.30am-11pm Fri; noon-11pm Sat; noon-9.30pm Sun. **Average** ¥1,500 lunch; ¥3,000 dinner. **Credit** AmEx, DC, JCB, MC, V. **English menu**. **Map** p99.
This restaurant perhaps offers the closest experience in Tokyo to a British-style Indian curry. The place is divided into two rooms, the furthest from the door being the more inviting. The menu contains few surprises, but the chicken dishes and bindi (okra) curry are especially good. Like most Indian places in Tokyo, it lets itself down by only serving Japanese rice. It's better to stick with a naan, fresh from the tandoor, instead.

Giliola

Aoyama Ohara Kaikan B1F, 5-7-17 Minami-Aoyama, Minato-ku (5485 3516). Omotesando station, exit B1. **Open** 11.30am-2.30pm, 5.30-11pm, Mon-Sat. **Average** ¥5,000. **Credit** (dinner only) AmEx, DC, JCB, MC, V. **Italian menu**. **Map** p99.
This tiny underground trattoria serves up a delightful selection of home-style Italian cooking. There's a small list of Italian wines, and a larger selection of grappa to round off the meal. Dishes such as penne with gorgonzola and linguine al pesto genovese, and main courses of salmon on mushroom risotto and lamb chops are all fantastically executed.

La' Grotta Celeste

Aoyama Centre Bldg 1F, 3-8-40 Minami-Aoyama, Minato-ku (3401 1261/www.unimat-offisco.co.jp). Omotesando station, exit A4. **Open** 11.30am-3pm, 5.30-11pm daily. **Average** ¥1,000-¥1,800 lunch; ¥5,000 dinner. **Credit** AmEx, DC, JCB, MC, V. **Italian menu**. **Map** p99.
A place for a special-occasion splurge, with excellent service and exquisite Italian food serve in a delightful pink-hued setting. It's hard to decide

which is better: the grotto room with its brick lattice walls and Italianate ceiling fresco or the centre room complete with a view of the open kitchen and its wood-burning stove.

Hokuto

Haruki Bldg B1F, 3-5-17 Kita-Aoyama, Minato-ku (3403 0078). Omotesando station, exit A3. **Open** 11am-midnight Mon-Fri; 11am-10pm Sat, Sun. **Average** ¥1,500. **No credit cards. Map** p99.

Hokuto is really a Chinese restaurant, but its ramen are so good that it deserves to be in a class all by itself. The atmosphere, too, is a step above what you find in the average ramen joint, while the goma ramen (sesame noodles) have been known to send people into raptures.

Branches: 1-17-1 Jingumae, Shibuya-ku (3405 9015); 7-8-8 Ginza, Chuo-ku (3289 8683).

Jap Cho Ok

4-1-15 Minami-Aoyama, Minato-ku (5410 3408). Gaienmae station, exit 1A. **Open** 11.30am-2pm, 5.30pm-3am Mon-Sat; 11.30am-2pm, 5.30-11pm Sun. **Average** ¥5,000. **Credit** AmEx, MC, V. **English menu**.

Demonstrating that there's much more to Korean food than yakiniku and kimchee, Jap Cho Ok is a cross between a Buddhist temple refectory and an oriental apothecary. Medicinal herbs hang from the walls, while the paper screens and lamps evoke the spare grandeur of a Korean mountain monastery. The menu includes a raft of vegetarian options, as well as meat and fish. A stylish crowd gathers here, as much for the ambience as the cuisine.

Kaikatei

7-8-1 Minami-Aoyama, Minato-ku (3499 5872). Omotesando station, exit B1. **Open** 11am-2pm, 6-11pm Mon-Sat. **Average** ¥3,500. **No credit cards**.

Like taking a step back in time to 1930s Shanghai: old beer posters, wooden clocks, dated LPs and odd murals of barbarian foreigners lend an air of wartime mystery to this atmospheric Chinese restaurant. Shrimp in crab sauce is delicately flavoured, with ginger, spring onion and shrimp predominating. It's a good match for mildly spicy Peking-style chicken with cashew nuts and rich black bean sauce. Avoid the gyoza and flat Heartland beer.

Kubakan

Raika Annex Bldg B1F, 6-4-6 Minami-Aoyama, Minato-ku (5467 7135/www.kubakan.com). Omotesando station, exits A5, B1. **Open** 6pm-1am Tue-Sat; 11.30am-3pm (brunch), 5.30-11pm Sun. **Average** ¥5,000. **Credit** AmEx, DC, JCB, MC, V. **English menu**.

Chef Mark Vann of Fujimamas fame created this new upmarket restaurant, taking his love of fusion cuisine and pushing it up a notch. All the ingedients used here are organic, but if you can't decide between the duck enchilada with Mexican red chilli sauce or soy-basted lamb chops, then there's also a tasting menu featuring selected dishes with a glass of recommended wine from the excellent list. Finish off the evening in grand style, at Kubakan's annexe, Republica, which is Tokyo's only dedicated champagne bar.

Kyushu Jangara Ramen

Shanzeru Harajuku Ni-go-kan 1-2F, 1-13-21 Jingumae, Shibuya-ku (3404 5572/www.kyusyujangara.co.jp). Harajuku station, Omotesando exit or Meiji-Jingumae station, exit 3. **Open** 10.45am-2am Mon-Thur; 10.45am-3.30am Fri; 10am-3.30am Sat; 10am-2am Sun. **Average** ¥1,000. **No credit cards. Map** p99.

This whimsically decorated ramen restaurant always has queues snaking down the stairs. Don't worry: with 73 seats, an opening will quickly appear. Kyushu ramen from Fukuoka City is the speciality here, but it comes with a little twist: the customer selects whether they want the broth light or heavier, the noodles thin, thick or somewhere in between, and finally the quantity – big or small.

Branches: 3-11-6 Soto Kanda, Chiyoda-ku (3512 4059); 7-11-10 Ginza, Chuo-ku (3289 2307); 2-12-8 Nagata cho, Chiyoda-ku (3595 2130); 1-1-7 Nihonbashi, Chuo-ku (3281 0701).

Maisen

4-8-5 Jingumae, Shibuya-ku (3470 0071). Omotesando station, exit A2. **Open** 11am-10pm daily. **Average** ¥2,000. **Credit** DC, JCB, MC, V. **English menu. Map** p99.

This branch of this chain tonkatsu shop is a converted bath-house. If you're able to get a seat in the huge and airy dining room in the back, you'll notice several tell-tale signs: very high ceilings and a small garden pond. You can't miss with any of the teishoku (set meals); standard rosu katsu or lean hire katsu are both good choices, each coming with rice, soup and pickled daikon.

Branch: 1-1-5 Yurakucho, Chiyoda-ku (3503 1886).

Natural Harmony Angoro

3-38-12 Jingumae, Shibuya-ku (3405 8393/www.naturalharmony.co.jp). Gaienmae station, exits 2, 3. **Open** 11.30am-2pm, 6-10pm Tue-Sun. **Average** ¥1,500 lunch; ¥3,500 dinner. **No credit cards. English menu. Map** p99.

Currently Tokyo's best natural food restaurant, this place boasts a simple wood-clad interior that's no-smoking and additive-free. The food is very tasty, and although some fish is served, the ethos is strongly supportive of vegetarians. The baked eggplant is great; the wholewheat pizzas less so. There's a good range of organic beer, sake and wine.

Nobu Tokyo

6-10-17 Minami-Aoyama, Minato-ku (5467 0022/www.soho-s.co.jp). Omotesando station, exit B1, then a 10-min walk. **Open** *Restaurant* 11.30am-3.30pm (last order 2.30pm) Mon-Fri; 6-11.30pm (doors close at 10pm) daily. *Bar* 6pm-4am (last order 3.30am) Mon-Sat; 6-11pm (last order 10.30pm) Sun. **Average** ¥5,000 lunch; ¥8,000 dinner. **Credit** AmEx, DC, JCB, MC, V. **English menu**.

Soho's. *See p149.*

Nobu Matsuhisa started his career as a sushi chef in Tokyo before striking out for Peru, Argentina and the US. His restaurant, Nobu, electrified jaded New York palates and set the standard for nouvelle Japanese cuisine throughout the world. Nobu comes home to Japan in an elegant, sophisticated setting serving world-class fusion cuisine – and the celebrated sushi rolls.

Pumpkin Cook Katsura

4-28-28 Jingumae, Shibuya-ku (3403 7675). Harajuku station, Omotesando exit or Meiji-Jingumae station, exit 5. **Open** noon-2.30pm, 4-10.30pm Mon, Wed-Sun. **Average** ¥2,000. **No credit cards**. **English menu**. **Map** p99.

This is a decidedly odd little restaurant, where everything on the menu contains pumpkin, a theme that carries all the way through to the squash-laden decor. You might fancy trying pumpkin-tinged lasagne or salad, and round the meal off with a pumpkin-flavoured dessert.

Rojak

B1F, 6-3-14 Minami-Aoyama, Minato-ku (3409 6764). Omotesando station, exit A5, B1. **Open** noon-4pm, 6pm-midnight daily. **Average** ¥1,200 lunch; ¥3,000 dinner. **Credit** AmEx, DC, JCB, MC, V. **English menu**.

Western-influenced Asian food in a lovely basement with candlelit nooks and crannies, high ceilings and jungle-motif wall coverings. Next to the dining room is a comfy bar area with soft sofas and a cigar humidor. Fantastic salads are served in large, dark wood bowls that match the tables. Noodles, curries and seafood, especially sashimi, get reinvented at Rojak in sublime ways. There's a fair selection of wines (mostly Australian), as well as beers.

Roy's Aoyama

Riviera Minami-Aoyama Bldg 1F, 3-3-3 Minami-Aoyama, Minato-ku (5474 8181/www.soho-s.co.jp). Gaienmae station, exits 1A, 1B. **Open** 11.30am-3.30pm, 5.45-11pm daily. **Average** ¥5,000. **Credit** AmEx, DC, JCB, MC, V. **English menu**. **Map** p99.

A fabulous selection of simple but exciting Euro-Asian-Pacific cuisine that's combined with intimate service. At Roy's you'll find traditional Japanese flavours – shoyu, ginger and miso – featuring in exquisitely arranged masterpieces such as seared shrimp with a spicy miso butter sauce or Mediterranean-style seafood fritata accompanied by pickled ginger and spicy sprouts. The weekend brunch is one of the very best ways to start a weekend – or to end it. *See p134* **Brunch**.
Branch: **Roy's Café Atago** MORI Tower 2F, 2-5-1 Atago, Minato-ku (5733 3400).

Senba

4-4-7 Jingumae, Shibuya-ku (5474 5977). Omotesando station, exit A2. **Open** 11am-10.30pm Mon-Fri; 11am-9.30pm Sat, Sun. **Average** ¥1,500. **Credit** DC, MC, V. **Map** p99.
Senba specialises in soba, udon and kishimen noodles. The star of the line-up is kurumi soba, a choice of noodles served with a creamy dipping sauce. A nice way to sample a number of dips is the makunouchi: three to five pretty little bowls served in a (fake) wooden box. You can try oroshi (grated daikon with mushrooms), tororo (grated mountain yam), tempura, walnut and sansai (wild mountain vegetables).
Branches: 4-1-13 Nihonbashi-Honcho, Chuo-ku (3270 7100); 11-1 Kanda Matsunagacho, Chiyoda-ku (3251 8645); Sanshin Bldg B1F, 1-4 Yurakucho, Chiyoda-ku (3591 7384); 2-9-7 Kanda-Kajicho, Chiyoda-ku (3251 8007).

Soho's

V28 Bldg 4F, 6-31-17 Jingumae (5468 0411/www.soho-s.co.jp). Harajuku station, Omotesando exit or Meiji-Jingumae station, exit 4. **Open** 11.30am-4am Mon-Sat; 11.30am-11.30pm Sun. **Average** ¥3,000. **Credit** AmEx, DC, JCB, MC, V. **English menu**. **Map** p99.
A recently opened designer restaurant that serves up enjoyable Italian food in a decidedly space-age setting. A selection of pasta and pizza dishes costs around ¥1,500 each, and the pumpkin and prosciutto risotto is highly recommended. The bar area is equally impressive. You are free to drink here without eating (though there's a snack menu), and gaze down through the curved windows on to the shopping mecca of Omotesando four floors below.
Branches: **Soho's West** 5-25-9 Nakamachi, Setagaya-ku (5707 8833); **Soho's Vino Rosso** 35-4 Udagawacho, Shibuya-ku (3462 5646).

Further west

La Befana

5-31-3 Daita, Setagaya-ku (3411-9500). Shimo-Kitazawa station, north exit. **Open** 11.30am-3pm, 5.30-11pm daily. **Average** ¥4,000. **Credit** AmEx, MC, V. **Italian menu**.
Angelo Cozzolini, brother of Carmine, has created one of Tokyo's best pizzerias, with a real wood-fired oven and plenty of style. He also serves solid, dependable oven-roasted fish and tasty side dishes.

Namaste Kathmandu

Yokose Bldg B1F, 2-11-7 Kichijoji-Honcho, Musashino-shi (0422 21 0057). Kichijoji station, north exit. **Open** 11am-4pm, 5-10.30pm Tue-Sun. **Average** ¥3,000. **No credit cards**. **English menu**.
One of the sincerest places in Tokyo, this cosy little den makes you feel as if you've walked into someone's home; the proprietors treat customers like family, passing around snapshots from Nepal and urging you to visit. There's only one chef, six tiny tables and a counter. You may find that the alu tama – a dish purportedly much loved in Nepal – is an aquired taste; you'll be fine with anything else.

Nataraj

B1F, 5-30-6 Ogikubo, Suginami-ku (3398 5108/www.nataraj.co.jp). Ogikubo station, south exit. **Open** 11.30am-11pm daily (lunch menu only 11.30am-2.30pm Mon-Fri). **Average** ¥2,000. **Credit** AmEx, DC, JCB, MC, V. **English menu**.
Vegetarian fare is hard to come by in Tokyo, especially food that isn't holier-than-thou. At Nataraj (God of Dance) the food is sure to satisfy. Servings are moderate, so choose an assortment from the extensive curry menu or select from one of five special sets with rice, naan, salad, chutney, popadom, dalwara and a choice of curries.

Primi Baci

Inokashira Parkside Bldg 2F, 1-21-1 Kichijoji Minami-cho, Musashino-shi (0422 72 8202). Kichijoji station, Inokashira Koen exit. **Open** 11.30am-2.30pm, 5pm-11pm daily. **Average** ¥4,000. **Credit** AmEx, DC, JCB, MC, V. **English menu**.
In a splendid setting overlooking Inokashira Park, Primi Baci (which translates as 'First Kisses') has both exquisite service and well-executed Tuscany cuisine. An open and airy interior boasts well-spaced tables set with fresh flowers and charming, unpretentious waiters who are eager to test their English. For starters try the tartara di tonno, a column of tender tuna tartare garnished with marche salad and slivered fried leeks, or the torretta di melanzane, an aubergine, mozzarella and tomato tower bathed in swirls of basil sauce.

Shirube

Pine Crest Kitazawa Bldg 1F, 2-18-2 Kitazawa, Setagaya-ku (3413 3785). Shimo-Kitazawa station (Inokashira or Odakyu lines), south exit. **Open** 5.30-11.30pm daily. **Average** ¥3,000. **No credit cards**.
Anyone who goes to Shirube immediately adopts it as one of their favourite restaurants. A riotous cacophony of mostly young people can be observed having the time of their lives here, ordering dish after dish of *izakaya* food cooked with flair. Don't let the lack of an English-language menu discourage you from eating here; the offerings change so often that it would be hard to keep it up to date. Just ask for a seat at the counter and point at whatever takes your fancy.

Menu Reader

MAIN TYPES OF RESTAURANT

寿司屋 ***sushi-ya***
sushi restaurants

イクラ *ikura* salmon roe

タコ *tako* octopus

マグロ *maguro* tuna

こはだ *kohada* punctatus

トロ *toro* belly of tuna

ホタテ *hotate* scallop

ウニ *uni* sea urchin roe

エビ *ebi* prawn

ヒラメ *hirame* flounder

アナゴ *anago* ark shell

イカ *ika* squid

玉子焼き *tamago-yaki* sweet egg omelette

かっぱ巻き *kappa maki* rolled cucumber

鉄火巻き *tekka maki* rolled tuna

お新香巻き *oshinko maki* rolled pickles

蕎麦屋（そば屋） ***soba-ya***
Japanese noodle restaurants

天ぷらそば うどん *tempura soba, udon*
noodles topped with shrimp tempura

ざるそば うどん *zaru soba, udon*
noodles served on a bamboo rack in a lacquer box

きつねそば うどん *kitsune soba, udon*
noodles in hot broth topped with spring onion and fried tofu

たぬきそば うどん *tanuki soba, udon*
noodles in hot broth with fried tempura batter

月見そば うどん *tsukimi soba, udon*
raw egg broken over noodles in their hot broth

あんかけうどん *ankake udon*
wheat noodles in a thick fish bouillon/soy sauce soup with fishcake slices and vegetables

鍋焼きうどん *nabeyaki udon*
noodles boiled in an earthenware pot with other ingredients and stock. Mainly eaten in winter.

居酒屋 ***izakaya***
Japanese-style bars

日本酒 *nihon-shu* Japanese sake

冷酒 *rei-shu* cold sake

焼酎 *shoochuu* grain wine

チュウハイ *chuuhai*
grain wine with soda pop

生ビール *nama-biiru* draft beer

黒ビール *kuro-biiru* dark beer

梅酒 *ume-shu* plum wine

ひれ酒 *hirezake*
sake with toasted blowfish fins

焼き魚 *yaki zakana* grilled fish

煮魚 *ni zakana*
fish cooked in various sauces

刺し身 *sashimi*
raw fish in bite-sized pieces, served with soy sauce and horseradish

揚げ出し豆腐 *agedasi doofu*
lightly fried plain tofu

枝豆 *edamame*
boiled young soybeans in the pod

おにぎり *onigiri*
rice parcel with savoury filling

焼きおにぎり *yaki onigiri*
grilled rice balls

フグ刺し *fugusashi*
thinly sliced sashimi, usually spectacularly arranged and served with ponzu sauce

フグちり *fuguchiri*
chunks of fugu in a vegetable stew

雑炊 *zosui*
cooked rice and egg added to the above

焼き鳥屋 *yakitori-ya*
yakitori restaurants

焼き鳥 *yakitori*
barbecued chicken pieces marinated in sweet soy sauce

つくね *tsukune* minced chicken balls

タン *tan* tongue

ハツ *hatsu* heart

シロ *shiro* tripe

レバー *reba* liver

ガツ *gatsu* intestines

鳥皮 *tori-kawa* skin

ネギ間 *negima* chicken with spring onions

おでん屋 *oden-ya*
oden restaurants or street stalls

さつま揚げ *satsuma-age* fish cake

昆布 *konbu* kelp rolls

大根 *daikon* radish

厚揚げ *atsu-age* fried tofu

OTHER TYPES OF RESTAURANT

料亭 *ryotei*
high-class, traditional restaurants

ラーメン屋 *ramen-ya*
Japanese-style ramen or Chinese noodle restaurants

天ぷら屋 *tempura-ya* tempura restaurants

すき焼き屋 *sukiyaki-ya*
sukiyaki restaurants

トンカツ屋 *tonkatsu-ya*
tonkatsu restaurants

お好み焼き屋 *okonomi yaki-ya*
okonomiyaki restaurants

ESSENTIAL VOCABULARY

A table for..., please ***...onegai shimasu***

one/two/three/four
hitori/futari/san-nin/yo-nin

Is this seat free? ***kono seki aite masu ka***

Could we sit...? ***...ni suware masu ka***

over there ***soko***

outside ***soto***

in a non-smoking area ***kin-en-seki***

by the window ***madogiwa***

Excuse me
sumimasen/onegai shimasu

May I see the menu, please
menyuu o onegai shimasu

Do you have a set menu?
setto menyuu/teishoku wa arimasu ka

I'd like... ***...o kudasai***

I'll have... ***...ni shimasu***

a bottle/glass...
...o ippon/ippai kudasai

I can't eat food containing...
...ga haitte iru mono wa taberare masen

Do you have vegetarian meals?
bejitarian no shokuji wa arimasu ka

Do you have a children's menu?
kodomo-yoo no menyuu wa arimasu ka

The bill, please
o-kanjyoo onegai shimasu

That was delicious, thank you
gochisou sama deshita

We'd like to pay separately
betsubetsu ni onegai shimasu

It's all together, please
issho ni onegai shimasu

Is service included?
saabisu-ryoo komi desu ka

Can I pay with a credit card?
kurejitto caado o tsukae masu ka

Could I have a receipt, please?
reshiito onegai shimasu

Coffee Shops

Tokyo's café society caters for connoisseurs of the mighty bean.

The mushrooming number of Starbucks outlets in the metropolis may mean a Seattle-style caffeine fix is now never far away, but Tokyo has a lot more to offer devotees of the mighty bean than branches of the all-conquering franchise. Long before the arrival of the overseas invader in 1996, the Japanese capital already boasted coffee shops (*kissaten*) in profusion, with wood-panelled traditionalists and cosy family-run operations jostling for attention alongside grand cafés and an eclectic mix of strange specialists.

Since 1981, the number of coffee shops nationwide has fallen from a peak of around 155,000 to fewer than 90,000 today. In 2002, even Starbucks Japan reported red ink and scaled back its ambitious expansion plans. For owners of individual establishments in Tokyo, fierce competition from well-heeled chain operators and the effects of the endless recession mean a continuing struggle just to survive. But while some long-time favourites like Shinjuku's The Scala have been forced to shut up shop, many more continue to hold out against all odds.

Café society has followed the winds of change in Tokyo since the city's first coffee shop opened in Ueno back in 1888. Meiji modernisation gave way to the elegant Ginza café of the jazz age, post-war havens for music fans and courting couples, and smoky Shinjuku student dives of the 1960s. During the halcyon days of the Bubble era, it is claimed that ultra-swanky establishments even put flecks of gold leaf into the coffee. More recently, the economic downturn of the last decade helped give rise to a new breed of cheaper chains espousing an unfamiliar gulp-and-run ethos.

Expense is always a consideration in Tokyo. The price of a cup of coffee in a non-franchise *kissaten* may be around ¥500-¥600, but that doesn't mean that the virtues of this more traditional style of coffee shop should be missed. Each place has its own unique character and style. Here, once you've ordered a single cup, you're free to sit all day in some of the world's most expensive real estate. With the city rushing by outside, the pleasant surroundings, constantly topped-up iced water and unlimited sitting time make the price of that single cup a bargain.

Coffee shops don't accept credit cards.

Angelus

1-17-6 Asakusa, Taito-ku (3841 2208). Asakusa station, exits 1, 3. **Open** 10am-9.30pm Tue-Sun. **Map** p83.

Out front is a smart counter selling a fancy selection of western-style cakes; further inside, the coffee shop section is a more Spartan affair of plain walls and dark-wood trimmings. Perhaps, at some point in the dim and distant past, this was the way in which local operations got to grips with handling new-fangled foreign delicacies.

Ben's Café

1-29-21 Takadanobaba, Shinjuku-ku (3202 2445/ www.benscafe.com). Takadanobaba station, east exit. **Open** 11.30am-midnight daily.

A New York-style café, famed locally for its cakes, bagels and easygoing ambience. Also hosts occasional art shows, comedy evenings and weekend poetry readings. The friendly staff speak English and serve great coffee.

Bon

B1F, 3-23-1 Shinjuku, Shinjuku-ku (3341 0179). Shinjuku station, east exit. **Open** 12.30-11.50pm daily. **Map** p109.

The search for true coffee excellence is pursued with surprising vigour at this pricey but very popular Shinjuku basement. The cheapest choice from the menu sets you back a cool ¥1,000, but cups are selected from an enormous bone china collection. Special coffee-tasting events are held periodically for caffeine connoisseurs.

Café Canaan

2-7-5 Kitazawa, Setagaya-ku (3467 9052). Shimo-Kitazawa station, south exit. **Open** 10am-10pm Mon-Wed, Fri-Sun.

With just one table and a counter, this is something of a hideaway from the madding crowds of Shimo-Kitazawa. The lack of space is compensated for by an unfussy interior, quality coffee and softly piped classical music.

Le Café Doutor Espresso

1F San'ai Bldg, Ginza 5-7-2, Chuo ku (5537 8959). Ginza station, exits A1, A2. **Open** 7am-11pm Mon-Sat; 8am-10pm Sun. **Map** p57.

A one-off upmarket branch of the cheap and cheerful chain that proliferated across the city during the recession-hit '90s. Located on a prime piece of real estate at Ginza 4-chome crossing, it has drinks and sandwiches beyond the standard Doutor fare. Outside tables provide places for watching the bustling crowds and checking out the famous Wako clock tower across the street.

Café Fontana

Abe Building B1F, 5-5-9 Ginza, Chuo-ku (3572 7320). Ginza station, exits B3, B5. **Open** noon-midnight Mon-Fri; 2-11pm Sat; 2-7pm Sun. **Map** p57.
A typically genteel Ginza basement establishment, but one where the individually served apple pies come in distinctly non-dainty proportions. Each steaming specimen contains a whole fruit, thinly covered in pastry, then doused thoroughly in cream.

Cantina

Shibuya Homes B1F, 2-1 Udagawacho, Shibuya-ku (5489 2433/www.cantina.co.jp). Shibuya station, Hachiko exit. **Open** 11am-11pm Tue-Sun. **Map** p102.
Toys and movies provide the twin themes for Cantina's airy new premises, but there's more than a hint of *Star Wars* obsession about the place. A large-as-life C3-PO still greets visitors at the entrance, R2D2 is perched noisily on the bar and a Harrison Ford lookalike sits moodily on a nearby stool. Fashionably chic, but good for kids of all ages. May the force be with you.

Classic

5-66-8 Nakano, Nakano-ku (3387 0571). Nakano station, north exit. **Open** noon-9.30pm Tue-Sun.
This ramshackle relic of eccentricity is a creaky one-off that's survived the winds of change since 1930. Classical music drifts eerily over the sound system as the ill-lit Gothic gloom gradually reveals strangely sloping floors, ancient leather chairs, long-deceased and undusted clocks. The paintings that adorn the walls are all by the shop's original, now dead, owner. Tickets for coffee, tea or juice are ¥400 and purchased at the entrance.

Coffee 3.4 Sunsea

Takano Bldg 1F, 10-2 Udagawacho, Shibuya-ku (3496 2295). Shibuya station, Hachiko exit.
Open 1-11pm daily. **Map** p102.
Kathmandu hippy chic and postmodern Shibuya cool meet in this laidback retreat, with classical Indian sitar and tabla on soundtrack. Cushion-strewn sofas, ethnic wooden carvings and a large tank of hypnotic tropical fish all add to the dreamy effect. Self-indulgent sensory overload is guaranteed from the sensational coffee float. It's somehow in keeping with the mood of the place that the owners don't have fixed days off; they close whenever they feel like it, so call ahead to confirm.

Daibo

2F, 3-13-20 Minami-Aoyama, Minato-ku (3403 7155). Omotesando station, exits A3, A4. **Open** 9am-10pm Mon-Sat; noon-8pm Sun. **Map** p99.
The biggest treat at this cosy wood-bedecked outpost is the excellent milk coffee, which comes lovingly hand-dripped into large pottery bowls. Even the regular blend coffee reveals a true craftsman's pride, and comes in four separate varieties. There's just one long wooden counter plus a couple of tables, but the restrained decoration and low-volume jazz on the stereo combine to soothing and restful effect.

Danwashitsu Takizawa

B1F, 3-36-12 Shinjuku, Shinjuku-ku (3356 5661). Shinjuku station, east exit. **Open** 9am-9.50pm Mon-Sat; 9am-9.30pm Sun. **Map** p109.
If you ever want to experience the perverse pleasure of blowing ¥1,000 on a single cup of coffee, this is the place to do it. Artfully simple yet completely comfortable, it's the kind of spot where you could stay all day: water trickles over rocks for a vaguely Zen-like sense of tranquillity and staff bow with quite extraordinary politeness. Discount tickets for future visits after you pay the bill.
Branches throughout the city.

ef

2-19-18 Kaminarimon, Taito-ku (3841 0114/gallery 3841 0442/www.tctv.ne.jp/get2-ef/). Asakusa station, exit 2. **Open** *Café & gallery* 11am-7pm Mon, Wed-Sun. *Bar* 6pm-midnight Mon, Wed, Thur, Sat; 6pm-2am Fri; 6-10pm Sun. **Map** p83.
This retrofitted hangout is a welcome attempt to inject a little Harajuku-style cool into musty Asakusa. Among its own more surprising attractions is a small art gallery converted from an old

Ben's Café. *See p152.*

Jazz Coffee Masako.

warehouse. Duck through the entrance at the back and suddenly you're out of 1950s Americana and into tatami territory, admittance to the main exhibits being up a steep set of traditional wooden steps.

Football Café

Plaza (courtyard), Tokyo International Forum, 3-5-1 Marunouchi, Chiyoda-ku (5223 6861). Yurakucho station, Tokyo International Forum exit or Ginza station, exit C9. **Open** 11.30am-11pm daily. **Map** p57.

Banks of TV screens showing the latest Italian and English league matches mean you're never far from the action in this smartly upmarket operation. Table football on the balcony.

GeraGera

B1F, B2F 3-17-4 Shinjuku, Shinjuku-ku (3350 5692/ shop.geragera.co.jp/sjk_hon/index.html). Shinjuku station, east exit. **Open** 24hrs daily. **Map** p109.

Manga coffee shops spread like wildfire after emerging in the mid 1990s with a winning combination of coffee and Japanese comic books. More recently, computer games and online access have also been added as regular features. This branch of one of the main chains has 250 seats, with internet use at ¥380 for the first hour and ¥50 per 10 minutes after that. Self-service hot and cold drinks are ¥180.

Jazz Coffee Masako

2-20-2 Kitazawa, Setagaya-ku (3410 7994). Shimo-Kitazawa station, south exit (Odakyu/Inokashira lines). **Open** 11.30am-11pm daily.

A real homely feel, as well as all the jazz coffee shop essentials present and correct: excellent sound system, enormous stack of records and CDs behind the counter, walls and low ceiling painted black and all plastered in posters and pictures. The noticeboard at the flower-filled entrance proudly announces newly obtained recordings; inside, there are bookcases and sofas among the well-lived-in furnishings.

Ki No Hana

4-13-1 Ginza, Chuo-ku (3543 5280). Higashi-Ginza station, exit 5. **Open** 10.30am-8.30pm Mon-Fri. **Map** p57.

The pair of signed John Lennon cartoons on the walls is the legacy of a chance visit by the former Beatle one afternoon in 1978. With its peaceful atmosphere, tasteful floral decorations, herbal teas and lunchtime vegetarian curries, it isn't too difficult to understand Lennon's appreciation of the place. Apparently, the overawed son of the former owner also preserved the great man's full ashtray, including butts. Alas, he kept this as a personal memento, so it isn't on display.

Kissa Hibiya

1-2-5 Yurakucho, Chiyoda-ku (3580 0203). Hibiya station, exit A5. **Open** 9.30am-10.30pm Mon-Sat; 9.30am-8.40pm Sun. **Map** p57.

A classic old-school operation, inviting you to shut out the rest of the world and snuggle down for a long stay. It's comfortable and spacious, with three floors to spread out on, but it's the top one that offers the best place to admire the distinctively retro use of coloured glass for interior lighting. Blend coffee is only ¥450 till 2pm, the price rising to ¥500 from 2pm until 5pm and ¥600 after 5pm.

Lion

2-19-13 Dogenzaka, Shibuya-ku (3461 6858). Shibuya station, Hachiko exit. **Open** 11am-10.30pm daily. **Map** p102.

A church-like air of reverence pervades this sleepy shrine to classical music. A pamphlet listing the stereophonic offerings is helpfully laid out before the customer, seating is arranged in pew-style rows facing an enormous pair of speakers, and conversations are discouraged. If you must talk, whisper. The imposing grey building is an unexpected period piece set amid the gaudy love hotels of Dogenzaka.

Marunouchi Café

1F Fuji Bldg, 3-2-3 Marunouchi, Chiyoda-ku (3212 5025/www.marunouchicafe.com). Yurakucho station, Tokyo International Forum exit. **Open** 8am-8pm Mon-Fri; 10am-6pm Sat, Sun. **Map** p57.

If the Japanese coffee shop is essentially a place to hang out, this popular innovator could be a glimpse of a new low-cost future. Connoisseurs may not care for canned coffee dispensed from vending machines, but it's hard to argue with the price. Surroundings are comfortably spacious and Asian generic, with internet access and magazines available.

Mignon

2F, 4-31-3 Ogikubo, Suginami-ku (3398 1758/ http://members.jcom.home.ne.jp/stmera/mignon). Ogikubo station, south exit. **Open** 11am-10pm Mon-Tue, Thur-Sat; 11am-7pm Sun.

Classical music is the name of the game here, with an awesome collection of vinyl lining the shelves behind the counter. There's just the single room, plus a small side gallery of pottery items, but it's comfortable and doesn't feel cramped. That's despite the large pair of speakers standing alongside one wall.

Miro

2-4-6 Kanda-Surugadai, Chiyoda-ku (3291 3088). Ochanomizu station, Ochanomizubashi exit. **Open** 8.30am-11pm Mon-Sat.

Named after Catalan surrealist Joan Miró (1893-1983), several of whose works adorn the walls. Ambience and decor appear untouched by the passing decades. The location is pretty well hidden, down a tiny alley opposite Ochanomizu station.

Mironga

1-3 Kanda-Jinbocho, Chiyoda-ku (3295 1716). Jinbocho station, exit A7. **Open** 10.30am-11pm Mon-Fri; 11.30am-7pm Sat, Sun.

Probably the only place in the metropolis where non-stop tango provides seductive old-style dance music accompaniment to the liquid refreshments. Argentina's finest exponents feature in the impressive array of fading monochromes up on the walls, and there's also a useful selection of printed works on related subjects lining the bookshelves. Of the two rooms, the larger and darker gets the nod for atmosphere. A good selection of imported beers and reasonable food, as well as a wide range of coffees.

New Dug

B1F, 3-15-12 Shinjuku, Shinjuku-ku (3341 9339/ www.dug.co.jp). Shinjuku station, east exit. **Open** noon-2am Mon-Fri; noon-11.30pm Sat, Sun (bar from 6.30pm). **Map** p109.

Way back in the 1960s and early 1970s, Shinjuku was sprinkled with jazz coffee shops. Celebrated names of that bygone era include Dug, an establishment whose present-day incarnation is a cramped brick-lined basement on Yasukuni Dori. Everything about the place speaks serious jazz credentials, with carefully crafted authenticity and assorted memorabilia. A basement bar annexe below the nearby KFC is used for live performances.

Pow Wow

2-7 Kagurazaka, Shinjuku-ku (3267 8324). Iidabashi station, west exit. **Open** 10.30am-10.30pm Mon-Sat; 12.30-7pm Sun.

Heavy on the old-fashioned virtues of dark wood and tastefully chosen pottery, this spacious traditionalist establishment features an extraordinary coffee-brewing performance in its narrow counter section, where large glass flasks bubble merrily away over tiny glass candles in the manner of some mysterious chemistry experiment. There's also an upstairs gallery space.

Rihaku

2-24 Kanda-Jinbocho, Chiyoda-ku (3264 6292). Jinbocho station, exits A3, A4. **Open** 11am-8pm Mon-Sat.

Named after Sung dynasty Chinese poet Li Po (701-62), whose works include the celebrated lament 'Drinking Alone', this is a place more attuned to eastern tradition than most. The high ceiling and wooden layout of the interior are reminiscent of some old Japanese farmhouse, but resist the temptation to slip off the shoes as you enter.

Sabouru

1-11 Kanda-Jinbocho, Chiyoda-ku (3291 8404). Jinbocho station, exit A7. **Open** 9am-11pm Mon-Sat.

Wooden masks on the walls, tree pillars rising to the ceiling, and a menu that features banana juice all lend a strangely South Sea island air to this cosy triple-level establishment squeezed into a brick building reverting to jungle on a Jinbocho back street. It's cheap, too, with blend coffee a snip at ¥400. Next door is the less extravagantly furnished sequel, Sabouru 2 (3291 8405).

Satei Hato

1-15-19 Shibuya, Shibuya-ku (3400 9088). Shibuya station, Miyamasusaka (east) exit. **Open** 11am-11.30pm daily. **Map** p102.

Step through the marble-tiled entrance and into top-grade kissaten territory of a traditionalist inclination. A huge collection of china cups stands behind the counter, while sweeping arrangements of seasonal blooms add colour to a dark wood interior that recalls an earlier age. Most expensive item on the menu is Blue Mountain at ¥1,000.

Tajimaya

1-2-6 Nishi-Shinjuku, Shinjuku-ku (3342 0881). Shinjuku station, west exit. **Open** 10am-11pm daily. **Map** p109.

Caught between the early post-war grunge of its immediate neighbours and the skyscraper bustle of the rest of west Shinjuku, Tajimaya responds with abundant bone china, coffees from all over the world, non-fetishist use of classical music, and milk in the best copperware. Scones on the menu and the unusual selection of ornaments provide further evidence of advanced sensibilities, but the deeply yellowed walls and battered wood suggest a struggle to keep up appearances.

Bars

Dress up as a frog, drink in a library, office or padded cell, avoid anywhere that says 'snack', and take advantage of some laudably lax licensing laws.

Drinking is a major activity in Tokyo, and a serious social lubricant. Most deals are sealed over a glass or ten of beer or sake, and many friendships have been forged or, indeed, destroyed by the demon drink.

Drinking here is almost always accompanied by eating. Even in western-style bars, a plate of snacks will often appear unbidden if you do not order food with your drink. This can make the dividing line between bars and restaurants difficult to draw. Most serious drinking is still done in *izakaya*, a word often misleadingly translated as 'Japanese pub'. These places offer reasonably priced menus of Japanese food, and because people rarely entertain at home, this is where most socialising goes on. Some have special 'all you can drink' deals – look for signs.

Most other bars have some food to keep customers happy, and many demand a table charge (usually ¥500, but sometimes more) to cover the cost of snacks. Most bars listed here make no charge unless otherwise indicated. Normally, a no-charge bar will say so clearly outside. As a rule, if you can't see a price list, don't go in.

If out drinking with Japanese business partners or friends over a meal, you will not normally be expected to refill your own glass. Someone else at the table will keep a close eye on the level and top it up when appropriate. 'No' is generally not accepted as an answer, so drinking slowly is the surest way to control your consumption. Be sure to return the favour by refilling your companions' glasses.

Luckily, public drunkenness is treated with tolerance. No one will frown at you for staggering around trying to find that last train home, and public vomiting is an all too frequent occurrence, especially on the Chuo Line.

'PUB', 'BAR' AND 'SNACK'

If you see a small Japanese bar with the welcoming word 'pub', 'bar' or 'snack' outside, it's best not to venture in unless you know what you're doing. The words usually mean a bar with an owner whose job includes keeping the patrons entertained (usually with karaoke or conversation) and expects a cover charge in return. Cover charges are often not fixed, and are likely to be less painful for regulars than for those who wander in off the street, so beware.

Central

Ginza & Shinbashi

Hibiki

Caretta Shiodome 46F, 1-8-1 Higashi-Shinbashi, Minato-ku (6215 8051/www.dynac.co.jp). Shiodome station (Yurikamome or Toei Oedo lines). **Open** 11am-4pm, 5-11.30pm daily. **Credit** AmEx, DC, JCB, MC, V.

A pleasantly upmarket *izakaya* with great Japanese food and even better views, near the top of one of the towers in the recently opened Shiodome district near Shinbashi. Prices are reasonable, with beer costing around ¥700, and each dish around the same, but book early to be sure of the best views. *See p163* **Booze with a view**.

Kagaya

B1F, 2-15-12 Shinbashi, Minato-ku (3591 2347/ www1.ocn.ne.jp/~kagayayy). Shinbashi JR station, Karasumori exit. **Open** 5.30pm-midnight (or until empty) Mon-Sat. Booking only Sun. **No credit cards**.

A warm, eccentric welcome is guaranteed to all readers of this book by Mark, the Japanese crackpot host of this Shinbashi institution. When you arrive, choose a country-themed drink from a list, and Mark will disappear into his magic cupboard to re-emerge in a costume that reflects your choice. Drinks come in glasses that move, shake or make noises, and serve as the prelude to games such as table football or Jenga. You can, if you wish, also dress as a frog or giant teddy bear. The place is as unique as its billing system, which always seems to come to ¥2,500 a head, no matter how much you eat or drink. Delicious food is prepared by Mark's very tolerant mother, who wishes it to be known that much of her food is vegetarian.

Lion Beer Hall

7-9-20 Ginza, Chuo-ku (3571 2590/ www.ginzalion.jp). Ginza station, exit A4. **Open** 11.30am-11pm Mon-Sat; 11.30am-10.30pm Sun. **Credit** AmEx, MC, V. **Map** p57.

This 1930s beer hall, part of the Sapporo Lion chain, is a tourist attraction in itself. The tiled, wood-panelled interior looks as if it's been transplanted from Bavaria, and a menu laden with sausage choices adds to the effect. To complete the illusion, Friday night sessions have been known to descend into mass karaoke demonstrations. For those who want to eat more than drink, there is a restaurant upstairs.

Pop Inn 2

7-2-20 Ginza, Chuo-ku (3289 8557). Ginza station, exit C2. **Open** 5pm-midnight Mon-Thur; 5pm-2am Fri. **No credit cards. Map** p57.
A complete antidote to the swanky restaurants and bars of the Ginza area, this tiny bar is really a Japanese-style bar that serves Guinness, rather than the Irish bar it claims to be. It's certainly a no-frills affair, with a cobbled stone floor and wooden seats that can inflict severe damage to the coccyx. Nevertheless, it's popular with local workers and one of the few such bars in Tokyo that doesn't depend on expats for its custom.

Centre elsewhere

Ieyasu Hon-jin

1-30 Kanda Jinbocho, Chiyoda-ku (3291 6228). Jinbocho station, exit A7. **Open** 5-10pm Mon-Fri. **No credit cards. Map** p62.
Genial host Taisho bangs the drum behind the bar to greet each new customer to this cosy, top-class *yakitori* bar named after the first of the Tokugawa shoguns. There are only a dozen seats, so everyone crowds around the counter, where a wide choice of foodstuffs (including mushrooms and beef as well as the usual chicken) lies in glass cases, already on sticks, ready to be popped on the coals and grilled. All the food is excellent, as is the beer and sake, which Taisho dispenses with natural flair, pouring into small cups from a great height. Not cheap (expect around ¥4,000-¥7,000 for a couple of hours' eating and drinking), but still good value. Try to avoid the 6-8pm after-work rush and don't go in a group of more than two or three.

North

Ikebukuro and area

Artist's Café

Tokyo Dome Hotel 43F, 1-3-61 Koraku, Bunkyo-ku (5805 2243/www.tokyodome-hotels.co.jp). Suidobashi station, east exit. **Open** 11.30am-11pm daily. **Credit** AmEx, DC, JCB, MC, V.
Surprisingly pleasant jazz-themed bar and restaurant with great views on the top floor of a swanky hotel. *See p163* **Booze with a view**.

Bobby's Bar

Milano Bldg 3F, 1-18-10 Nishi-Ikebukuro, Toshima-ku (3980 8875/http://plaza.rakuten.co.jp/bobbysbar). Ikebukuro JR station, west exit. **Open** 6pm-empty Mon-Thur, Sun; 6pm-5am Fri, Sat. **No credit cards. Map** p69.
Small foreigner-friendly bar on the west side of Ikebukuro station offering a fine selection of imported beers with live music most nights. It shares a building with the New Delhi Indian restaurant, which offers good food at reasonable prices, and a conveniently placed bolthole after a few lagers.

Asakusa stalwart **Kamiya Bar**. *See p159.*

South

Roppongi

Bauhaus

Reine Roppongi Bldg 2F, 5-3-4 Roppongi (3403 0092/www.e-bauhaus.jp). Roppongi station, exit 3. **Open** 7pm-1am Mon-Sat. **Credit** AmEx, DC, JCB, MC, V. **Map** p74.
One of those 'only in Japan' experiences, this is a live music venue that has featured the same band for over 20 years. Nowhere else in the world can you jam to flawless covers of the Rolling Stones, Pink Floyd or Madonna, by men and women who can't speak three words of English, and then have them serve you food and drink in between sets. It's on the pricey side, though, with a ¥2,800 music charge. Sets every hour.

Bernd's Bar

Pure 2F, 5-18-1 Roppongi, Minato-ku (5563 9232). Roppongi station, exit 3. **Open** 5-11pm Mon-Sat (or until empty). **Credit** AmEx, MC. **Map** p74.
A small second-floor corner of Germany, with fresh pretzels on the tables, and Bitburger and Erdinger on tap for washing down your Wiener schnitzel. Try to get a table by the window for the view over the

nightlife area of Roppongi. If you happen to meet owner Bernd Haag, you'll find he can chat with you in English, German, Spanish, as well as Japanese.

Cavern Club

Saito Bldg 1F, 5-3-2 Roppongi (3405 5207/ www.kentos-group.co.jp/cavern). Roppongi station, exit 3. **Open** 6pm-2.30am daily. **Credit** AmEx, DC, JCB, MC, V. **Map** p74.

Tokyo's finest Beatles imitators play here nightly, and some say they sound better live than the originals. In low light, if you're very drunk and wearing dark enough glasses, you might convince yourself you're back in Liverpool. Music fee is ¥1,500.

Gas Panic

3-15-24 Roppongi, Minato-ku (3405 0633/ www.gaspanic.co.jp). Roppongi station, exits 3, 5. **Open** 6pm-5am daily. **No credit cards**. **Map** p74.

A Roppongi institution of depravity, where young people go to meet other young people, grope them and (often) vomit on them. To give an idea of what it's like, note that you must have an alcoholic drink in your hand at all times, and that drinking water is not allowed. Unsurprisingly, bargain drink night on Thursday is the busiest night, with everything priced at ¥400. There are several Gas Panic installations: one in Shibuya's Centre Gai (3462 9049), three in the Gas Panic Building and one closer to Roppongi Dori, Gas Panic Club (3402 7054). The club is allegedly more classy, but that's not saying much.

George's Bar

9-7-55 Akasaka, Minato-ku (3405 9049). Roppongi station, exit 7. **Open** 8pm-5am daily. **No credit cards**. **Map** p74.

If the Tokyo government gave out blue plaques for historic monuments, then this tiny place would definitely get one. George's has been going since the early 1960s, and the real jukebox contains many songs from the period to prove it. Can get very raucous indeed at weekends, with frequent impromptu demonstrations of karaoke. Be warned: opening times vary at the whim of the master.

Paddy Foley's Irish Pub

B1F, 5-5-1 Roppongi, Minato-ku (3423 2250). Roppongi station, exit 3. **Open** 5pm-1am daily. **Credit** AmEx, MC, V. **Map** p74.

One of Tokyo's first Irish pubs, this place still offers a good craic, despite increasing competition. Guinness, naturally, is the house speciality and the food is good. Can get as crowded as a London pub at weekends, something the locals (who always sit down to drink) regard with mild bemusement.

Shanghai Bar

6-2-31 Roppongi, Minato-ku (5772 7655/www.kiwa-group.co.jp/shanghaibar). Roppongi station, exit 1. **Open** 11am-4am Mon-Sat; 11am-11pm Sun. **Credit** AmEx, DC, JCB, MC, V. **Map** p74.

Forget all images of Chinese pagodas and lion statues. The city to which this bar pays tribute with its sleek, polished decor is the Shanghai of the 21st century. House specialities are cocktails and champagne, costing around ¥1,000 per glass, and there's a good menu of Japanese- and Chinese-influenced dishes. Non-drinkers will be heartened by some inventive alcohol-free cocktails.

Shunju

Sanno Park Tower 27F, 2-11-1 Nagatacho, Chiyoda-ku (3592 5288/www.shunju.com/top.html). Tameike-Sanno station, exit 7 or Kokkaigijidomae station, exit 5. **Open** 11.30am-2.30pm, 5-11pm Mon-Sat. **No credit cards**.

From this upmarket whisky and cigar bar high in the Sanno Park Tower you get a good view of the jumbled cityscape towards Shibuya. The illuminated glass wine cellar and shelf after shelf of scotch (from ¥1,000 to ¥10,000 a glass) stand out amid the bar's dark elegance, and you feel a world away from the buzzing chaos 27 floors below. The seasonal cocktails are recommended and they serve a mean martini. The bar menu dishes from the adjoining restaurant are minuscule, but tasty and beautifully presented. A welcome feature is the separate, glass-walled cigar room with extractor fans.

These

2F, 2-13-19 Nishi-Azabu, Minato-ku (5466 7331/ www.these-jp.com). Roppongi station, exit 1. **Open** noon-4am Mon-Sat. **Credit** MC, V. **Map** p74.

As much library as bar – and pronounced 'tay-zay' – this strange place exudes the feel of a British gentlemen's club, but with superior service. The bar has shelves and shelves of magazines and books for browsing, both foreign and Japanese, and a large central room where you are free to chat while indulging in one of the long list of whiskies. If you're lucky, you may be offered a cocktail made with the fresh fruit of your choice. Harry Potter fans watch out for the secret room.

Tokyo Sports Café

7-15-31 Roppongi, Minato-ku (3404 3675/www. tokyo-sportscafe.com). Roppongi station, exits 2, 4. **Open** 6pm-6am Mon-Sat (closing time depends on matches). **Credit** DC, JCB, MC, V. **Map** p74.

One of the longest established and largest sports bars in Tokyo, this place screens all major sporting events from around the world, with space to show two things at once. Has an extensive range of beers and cocktails, and a generous happy hour, until 9pm.

South elsewhere

Meguro Tavern

Sunwood Meguro 2F, 1-3-28 Shimo-Meguro, Meguro-ku (3779 0280/www.themegurotavern.com). Meguro station, west exit. **Open** 6pm-1am Mon-Fri; 5pm-1am Sat; noon-11pm Sun. **No credit cards**.

Above-average English pub with menu designed to reassure expats. The roast beef and Yorkshire pud Sunday lunch is a local institution. One of the best places, too, for traditional Christmas dinner, if you happen to be in town at the time.

O'Carolan's
3F, 2-15-22 Jiyugaoka, Meguro-ku (3723 5533/www.o-carolan.co.jp). Jiyugaoka station (Tokyu Toyoko Line), central exit. **Open** 11am-midnight daily. **No credit cards.**
Unusually spacious Irish bar with a pleasant greenhouse area where you can sip your drinks on wicker sofas as the sunshine comes through the ceiling.

Omocha
3-16-13 Kamimeguro, Meguro-ku (5725 8766). Naka-Meguro station. **Open** noon-2am Mon-Thur; noon-4am Fri, Sat; noon-midnight Sun. **Credit** AmEx, DC, JCB, MC, V.
An unbelievably fashionable DJ bar in unbelievably unfashionable Naka-Meguro. Most people come here to eat as well as drink, and individual dishes cost around ¥500. The decor, all peach, is unsettling at first, but not so much that the feeling can't be fixed by a couple of drinks from the extensive menu.

East

Asakusa

Flamme d'Or
Asahi Super Dry Hall 1F, 2F, 1-23-36 Azumabashi, Taito-ku (5608 5381/www.asahibeer.co.jp/rest/azuma/flam_fme.html). Asakusa station, exits 4, 5, A5. **Open** *June-Aug* 11.30am-11pm daily. *Sept-Mar* 11.30am-10pm daily. **Credit** AmEx, MC, V. **Map** p83.
One of Tokyo's quirkier landmarks, the enormous golden object atop Philippe Starck's ultra-modern building across the river from the temples of Asakusa is most often compared with an unknown root vegetable. Or a golden turd. The dark tetrahedral Super Dry Hall itself is said to be modelled on the shape of a cut-off beer glass, and was named after a brand of beer. The beer hall inside is also distinctive: oddly shaped pillars, tiny porthole windows high overhead and sweeping curved walls covered in soft grey cushioning. English menus are available, as is a choice of German-style bar snacks and Asahi draught beers. On the 22nd floor of the building next door is another bar, the Asahi Sky Room, serving beer and soft drinks from 10am to 9pm.

Kamiya Bar
1-1-1 Asakusa, Taito-ku (3841 5400/www.kamiya-bar.com). Asakusa station, exits 3, A5. **Open** 11.30am-10pm daily. **No credit cards.** **Map** p83.
Established in the late 1800s, Kamiya is the oldest Western-style bar in Tokyo and is quintessential Asakusa. The crowds aren't there for décor or even drink: the interior is Formica-table coffee shop and too-bright lighting. But the atmosphere – loud, smoky, occasionally raucous – is typical of this working-class area. Try the house Denki Bran (Electric Brandy) – not so much for the taste, but for the experience. It imparts amazing hangovers and also makes a dubious gift to take home.

West

Harajuku & Omotesando

Bar Ho
Backborn House B1F, 6-2-10 Minami-Aoyama, Minato-ku (5774 4390/homepage.mac.com/bar_ho/index.html). Omotesando station, exit B1. **Open** 6pm-2am Mon-Thur; 6pm-5am Fri, Sat; 3pm-midnight Sun. **Credit** AmEx, DC, JCB, MC, V.
A pleasant little bar that specialises in single-malt scotch whiskies, of which it has over 60 on the menu, with many more exotic and expensive ones off it. The atmosphere is olde worlde calm, with soft jazz and soft furnishings making it the perfect place to unwind after a hard day. Head upstairs, flop down on a sofa with a double Macallan and let your worries drift away.

Den Aquaroom
FIK Bldg B1F, 5-13-3 Minami-Aoyama, Minato-ku (5778 2090). Omotesando station, exit B1. **Open** 6pm-2am Mon-Thur, Sat; 6pm-4am Fri; 6-11pm Sun. **Credit** AmEx, DC, JCB, MC, V. **Map** p99.
Fish tanks, and lots of them, are the defining feature of this fashionable yet comfortable bar. Before you sink into one of the red armchairs or perch at the crowded bar, be aware of the ¥1,000 cover charge. To soften the blow, there's a wide selection of cocktails and an intriguing menu (in English) of reasonably priced Asian-influenced food.

Office
Yamazaki Bldg 5F, 2-7-18 Kita-Aoyama, Minato-ku (5786 1052). Gaienmae station, exit 2. **Open** 5pm-3am daily. **No credit cards.** **Map** p99.
What's the perfect place for someone who can't tear themselves away from the office to come and relax? That's right, another office! Surely the only bar in Tokyo with a photocopier as part of the decor, along with the necessary green lamps, desks and power points for customers to plug in their laptop computers. Somehow, the turntables feel out of place. Drinks are around ¥600, making it a pleasant, if odd, venue for a spot of overtime.

Oh God!
B1F, 6-7-18 Jingumae, Shibuya-ku (3406 3206). Harajuku station, Omotesando exit or Meiji-Jingumae station, exit 4. **Open** 6pm-6am daily. **Credit** AmEx, DC, JCB, MC, V. **Map** p99.
Films are shown nightly on a giant screen to an audience more interested in knocking back the ¥700 beer. Also has pool and pinball tables. A schedule for the week's films is posted outside.

Pink Cow
1-10-1 Jingumae, Shibuya-ku (5411 6777/www.thepinkcow.com). Harajuku station, Omotesando exit or Meiji-Jingumae station, exit 3. **Open** 5pm-empty Tue-Sun. **No credit cards.** **Map** p99.
One of the cosiest bars in Tokyo, started by American artist Traci Consoli, the Cow has become

the de facto gathering place for Tokyo's foreign artistic community. The premises are a former house, with a warren of rooms to explore, and on Fridays and Saturdays there's a home-cooked all-you-can-eat buffet for ¥2,500. Also plays host to writers' workshops and the Pink Cow Conspiracy, a forum for foreigners who want to do business in Japan without dealing with Japanese banks.

Radio Bar

2-31-7 Jingumae, Shibuya-ku (3405 5490). Harajuku station or Meiji-Jingumae station. **Open** 7pm-2am Mon-Sat. **No credit cards**. **Map** p99.

Dazzlingly designed in a 19th-meets-21st-century style, and dazzlingly expensive, this is a wonderful place to enjoy superior cocktails or sample a wide range of Scotch whiskies. For around ¥1,500 per cocktail plus ¥1,500 cover charge, you get attentive service by tuxedo-clad barmen. There are nine tall bar stools at the wooden counter, and in a corner, in dim light, sits the star of the show – an antique short-wave radio. The cover charge includes a beautiful arrangement of fruits, vegetables and cheese.

Sign

2-7-18 Kita-Aoyama, Minato-ku (5474 5040). Gaienmae station, exit 3. Open 10am-midnight Mon-Fri; 11am-midnight Sat, Sun. **No credit cards**. **Map** p99.

An unashamedly artistic and artsy bar-cum-restaurant-cum-gallery a stone's throw from the station, Sign manages the difficult trick of being all things to all punters. While nearby office workers drop in and treat it as their local, artistic or creative types flock to the basement gallery, and clubbers come here to listen to the occasional live shows by local DJs. The pristine interior reflects the venue's many purposes perfectly, being both starkly simple (in a designerly way) and colourful and fun.

Tokyo Apartment Café

Green Fantasia 1F, 1-11-11 Jingumae, Shibuya-ku (3401 4101/www.harajuku-ac.com). Harajuku station, Omotesando exit or Meiji-Jingumae station, exit 3. **Open** 11-4am daily. **No credit cards**. **Map** p99.

Fairly new and extremely stylish bar that offers a good selection of beers and whiskies at reasonable prices. Changes character after dark, once the area empties of shoppers.

Shinjuku, Takadanobaba

Angel Irish Pub

Tohokaikan Bldg B1F, 1-19-2 Kabuki-cho, Shinjuku-ku (5273 8642/www.angel-tokyo.com/index.htm). Shinjuku JR station, east exit. **Open** 5pm-1am Mon-Thur; 5pm-4am Fri, Sat; 3pm-midnight Sun. **No credit cards**. **Map** p109.

The most recent addition to the Irish pub scene in Shinjuku, the Angel opened in early 2002. Decor is identikit Oirish, although the pub's small size makes the atmosphere more friendly than most, and its location in the heart of Kabuki-cho makes it a great early evening meeting place for clubbers off to sample the delights of the area. The other two Angel bars (one of which is just around the corner) are standard Japanese drinking joints, with the usual range of beers and snacks.

Branches: 1-29-1 Kabuki-cho, Shinjuku-ku (5272 8642); 1-34-6 Numabukuro, Nakano-ku (5343 8642).

Café Hoegaarden

2-20-16 Yoyogi, Shibuya-ku (5388 5523/ www.brussels.co.jp/index.html). Shinjuku JR station, south exit. **Open** 5.30pm-2am Mon-Fri; 5.30-11pm Sat. **Credit** AmEx, DC, JCB, MC, V. **Map** p109.

An upmarket cousin of the local Brussels chain, this light and airy bar, done out in pine, is popular with local office ladies so you may have to wait for a table during the week. On draught, as well as the eponymous wheat beer, is Kriek cherry beer and a guest beer that changes weekly. The bottled beer menu contains over 50 highly priced but popular Belgian brews. Food is standard pub stuff, with a Belgian twist in the form of sausages and potato-based dishes. Great frites and mayonnaise.

Branches: (Brussels chain) 3-16-1 Kanda Ogawacho, Chiyoda-ku (3233 4247); 75-1 Yaraicho, Shinjuku-ku (3235 1890); 1-10-23 Jingumae, Shibuya-ku (3403 3972); 3-21-14 Nishi-Azabu, Minato-ku (5413 5333).

Golden Gai

While the building boom goes on around it, this tiny section of east Shinjuku remains resolutely stuck in the 1950s. The four streets that constitute this fascinating little area play host to some 200 tiny *nomiya*, or drinking dens, most of which cannot accommodate more than eight customers at a time. The area is phenomenally popular with Japanese salarymen in their forties and fifties; many bars cater to them exclusively, and do not welcome foreign customers. The bars we have selected (*see below*) are all foreigner-friendly.

At the time of writing, there are signs that the winds of change are starting to blow here. Many of the leases on the bars came up for renewal in late 2002 and early 2003, and some have been taken over by a younger breed of master, who are introducing rock music and DJing to their bars, much to the chagrin of older regulars. There's life in Golden Gai yet. Grab it while you can in bars like **J Fox R&R Bar** (*see p162*), **La Jetée** (*see p161*) and **Shot Bar Shadow** (*see p162*).

Focusing can be a problem after a few at the **Angel**. *See p160.*

Clubhouse Tokyo

Marunaka Bldg 3F, 3-7-3 Shinjuku, Shinjuku-ku (3359 7785/www.clubhouse-tokyo.com). Shinjuku-Sanchome station, exits C3, C4. **Open** 5pm-midnight daily (later for special sporting events). **No credit cards**. **Map** p109.

Run by a Japanese rugby fanatic who may have spent too long in Wales, Clubhouse is the only specialist sports bar in Shinjuku and can be phenomenally crowded on big game nights. Premiership football is also screened here, and the owner has a big library of classic sporting events on tape that he's happy to play to request if there's nothing else on. Monday night is prize darts night. British and Irish beers on tap.

The Dubliners

Shinjuku Lion Hall 2F, 3-28-9 Shinjuku, Shinjuku-ku (3352 6606). Shinjuku JR station, east exit. **Open** noon-1am Mon-Sat; noon-11pm Sun. **Credit** AmEx, MC, V. **Map** p109.

The oldest and scruffiest of the growing chain of Irish pubs owned by Sapporo, one of Japan's largest brewers, which is the sole importer of Guinness in Japan. Draught Guinness has recently been joined on the drinks list by cider (little known in Japan), while the menu has expanded to feature pizzas, in addition to the ever-popular, and very crunchy, fish and chips. The Shibuya branch is the cosiest, the Ikebukuro branch the most raucous, and the Sanno Park Tower branch the quietest.

Branches: Sun Grow Bldg B1F, 1-10-8 Nishi-Ikebukuro, Toshima-ku (5951 3614); Sanno Park Tower B1F, 2-11-1, Nagata-cho, Chiyoda-ku (3539 3615); 2-29-8 Dogenzaka, Shibuya-ku (5459 1736); 1-1-18 Toranomon, Minato-ku (5501 1536).

The Fiddler

B1F, 2-1-2 Takadanobaba, Shinjuku-ku (3204 2698/www.thefiddler.com). Takadanobaba station, Waseda exit. **Open** 6pm-3am Mon-Thur, Sun; 6pm-5am Fri, Sat. **No credit cards.**

Run by UK expats, this place smells like pubs back home, only it's open until the wee hours. There's free live music or comedy on many nights. Most acts are local foreign groups, but the odd Japanese band plays here too. The menu features ploughman's lunch, and the kitchen stays open until midnight.

La Jetée

1-1-8 Kabuki-cho, Shinjuku-ku (3208 9645). Shinjuku JR station, east exit. **Open** 7pm-empty Mon-Sat. **No credit cards**. **Map** p109.

One of the friendliest Golden Gai bars that welcomes foreigners, this tiny bar is run by film fanatic Kawai Tomoyo, who speaks fluent French but no English. Popular with French expats and creative types. *See p160* **Golden Gai**.

At Golden Gai's **J Fox**, drinking is a serious business. *See below.*

J Fox R&R Bar

1-1-9 Kabuki-cho, Shinjuku-ku (090 1502 5547). Shinjuku JR station, east exit. **Open** 7pm-late daily. **No credit cards**. **Map** p109.

We can only hope that this newish bar in Shinjuku's Golden Gai is the first of many like it. Master Higuchi Hirotaka is one of the youngest bar owners in the area, which has made his tiny venue popular with less wrinkly Golden Gai habitués. Possibly the friendliest bar in Golden Gai, although to get the most out of it, you should be prepared to speak a bit of Japanese. *See p160* **Golden Gai**.

Living Bar

Shinjuku Nomura Bldg 49F, 1-26-2 Nishi-Shinjuku, Shinjuku-ku (3343 8101/www.j-group.jp). Shinjuku JR station, west exit. **Open** 11.30am-2pm, 5-11pm Mon-Fri; 5-11pm Sat; 5-10pm Sun. **Credit** AmEx, DC, JCB, MC, V. **Map** p109.

An unremarkable chain of Japanese-style *izakaya*, but the cheap food and great views at the Shinjuku branch make it noteworthy.

Branches: 2-1-20 Hamamatsucho, Minato-ku (5472 3808); 5-2-1 Roppongi, Minato-ku (3423 3808).

Saci Perere

B1F, 9 Honshio-cho, Shinjuku-ku (3226 5888/ www.saciperere.co.jp). Yotsuya JR station, Yotsuya exit. **Open** 6pm-midnight Mon-Sat. **No credit cards**.

More of a restaurant and club than a straightforward bar, Saci Perere hosts live Brazilian music every night. The ¥1,500 table charge is for the music, but if you eat the ¥3,500 set menu, the music charge is thrown in. The friendly master speaks English and even writes the odd poem, and lone travellers are made welcome at the impressive semi-circular bar. Food is tasty and filling, particularly the black bean stew, and on Fridays and Saturdays the joint really starts jumping. Only real complaint is the early closing time.

Shot Bar Shadow

1-1-8 Kabuki-cho, Shinjuku-ku (3209 9530). Shinjuku JR station, east exit. **Open** 5pm-midnight Mon-Fri; 6pm-midnight Sat (members only after midnight). **No credit cards**. **Map** p109.

The master of this tiny Golden Gai bar speaks Arabic, German, Russian and French, thanks to his time in the Foreign Legion. For you to become a member, and be allowed in after midnight, he must be able to remember your name, which is not as easy a feat as it might sound. A friendly place where six is a crowd, typical in Golden Gai, but stay clear of the food. *See p160* **Golden Gai.**

Shibuya, Ebisu, Daikanyama

Bar

1-9-11 Ebisu-Minami, Shibuya-ku (5704 0186). Ebisu JR station, west exit. **Open** 7pm-1am Mon, Sun; 7pm-5am Tue-Sat. **Credit** AmEx, DC, JCB, MC, V.

Perhaps the owners couldn't think of a better name for this ethereal drinking den, or perhaps they used up all their imagination on the interior, where glass beads on the pillars twinkle like distant stars in the orange glow of Japanese paper lanterns, all to a backdrop of space-like sounds. The speciality is scotch whisky, with 200 single malts on offer at around ¥1,000.

Bar Kitsune

Chatolet Shibuya B1F, 2-20-13 Higashi, Shibuya-ku (5766 5911/www.usen.com/tenpo/kitsune/shibuya.html). Ebisu JR station, west exit. **Open** 6pm-3am Mon-Thur; 6pm-5am Fri, Sat; 6pm-midnight Sun. **No credit cards.**

Situated on Meiji Dori between Ebisu and Shibuya, this bar pushes back the boundaries between restaurant, DJ bar and club but stops short of providing a dancefloor. That doesn't stop the ever-changing DJs from getting the punters grooving in the aisles, or the acrobatic waiters from serving food late into the night. It's rare to see a foreign face here, as Kitsune hasn't been colonised by bar and club hoppers, who vilify the lack of dancing space. The most striking aspect of the slick interior is the phenomenal, ever-changing light radiating from all four walls. There's an entry charge (¥2,000 with two drinks) at weekends, but once you're inside drinks at the bar are ¥500 a throw, so you get your money's worth, provided you stay long enough.

Booze with a view

In a city that rises as high as Tokyo does in parts, it seems a shame to restrict your drinking to ground level. As the sun sets, raise a glass in one of Tokyo's towering bars. Be warned, though. The higher the lift goes, the higher the prices. Most of Tokyo's upmarket high-rise hotels have bars on their upper floors, but the four venues we've chosen here are especially worth the trip, and the money. Each is in a different area of Tokyo, to offer a variety of views.

From the tallest building in Shibuya, the Cerulean Tower Hotel, take a pew in the well-named **Bello Visto** bar (*see p164*) on the 40th floor. Enormous glass windows open up the city before you, with the surprisingly low-rise skyline of Shibuya by night particularly impressive. The bar's focus is on wine, with a frankly terrifying list of expensive wines from all over the world. Prices start at ¥900 a glass, and a 10 per cent service charge will be added to your bill. To ensure a seat by the window, booking is advisable.

Meanwhile, up in mainly low-rise Suidobashi sits the Tokyo Dome Hotel, a 43-storey monster that towers above the neighbouring Tokyo Dome baseball ground. Ride the glass elevator up to the 43rd floor and you'll find yourself in the **Artist's Café** (*see p157*), a pleasant jazz-themed bar and restaurant. If you only want to drink, take a seat at a stool in a window and take in the view. CD players under the counter give you a chance to listen to some of the artists who have appeared here, while live music starts nightly at around 6.30pm. The nice thing here is that the two main windows to the left and right of the lift offer totally different views. To the right, you tower over houses and small local businesses, while to the left the monoliths of Shinjuku heave into view.

To get an even closer view of Shinjuku, for a surprisingly reasonable price, head to the Nomura Building on the west side of the station. Here, on the 49th floor, is a branch of the small and otherwise unremarkable Japanese *izakaya* chain **Living Bar** (*see p162*), which serves a mix of Japanese and western food, with dishes starting at ¥500, and beer for the same price. The dining room is surrounded by huge windows offering a vista over neighbouring skyscrapers towards the neon lights of east Shinjuku. There are also four private rooms, all with their own windows, that can be booked for parties of six to 25 people.

A more upmarket *izakaya* experience is provided by **Hibiki** (*see p156*), on the 46th floor of a newly opened tower in the Shiodome area near Shinbashi. Food here is freshly prepared Japanese grill fare, at around ¥800 a dish, while drinks cost around ¥700. The view over the river towards Odaiba is spectacular, taking in both Rainbow Bridge and the Odaiba big wheel, but window tables should be reserved in advance.

Tokyo tipples

The best-selling form of alcohol in Japan is **beer** (almost invariably lager), which overtook sake as the nation's drink of choice in the early 20th century. Japan's major brewers Kirin, Asahi, Suntory and Sapporo are recognised the world over, but since a 1994 liberalisation of relevant laws, there has been an explosion in local microbrews, known in Japanese as *ji-biru*. Many better bars will carry some of these; brands to watch out for include Akagi Jibeer, Akasaka Beer, Tama no Megumi and Tokyo Ale. TY Harbor Brewery (*see pp124-149*) sells only its own brewed-on-the-premises concoctions.

A Japan-only phenomenon is ***happoshu***, an alcoholic drink designed to look and taste like beer but containing very low levels of malt in order to escape Japan's beer tax. *Happoshu* is typically ¥30 per can cheaper than the real thing. Despite what the adverts would have you believe, it does not taste nice.

Japanese ***sake***, more commonly referred to as *nihonshu* since 'sake' also means 'booze', is rice wine, and connoisseurs exist here in much the same way as they do for wine in the west. Everybody has their own favourite region, and there are good years and bad years. *Nihonshu* is delicious hot or cold, typically 10-20 per cent alcohol by volume, and drinking cheap stuff to excess produces phenomenal hangovers.

Japan's very own distilled spirit is called ***shochu***. It's made from grain, and typically contains 25 to 40 per cent alcohol by volume. *Shochu* is rarely drunk straight, but mixed with fruit juices and soda water, or with Oolong tea to form an Oolong *hai*. If you want to try a *shochu* drink, first ask if it's possible to have a *nama* fruit *hai*, meaning (usually) that the customer gets to squeeze his own juice out of the fruit. Cheaper *izakaya* do not offer this option, and the juice is likely to come from a box. Fruit *hai* do not taste alcoholic, but have the curious effect of getting one drunk from the ankles up, so be careful when getting to your feet.

Bello Visto

Cerulean Tower 40F, 26-1 Sakuragaoka-cho, Shibuya-ku (3476 3000/www.ceruleantower-hotel.com). Shibuya JR station, south exit. **Open** 4pm-midnight Mon-Fri; 3pm-midnight Sat, Sun. **Credit** AmEx, DC, JCB, MC, V. **Map** p102.

Very pricey high-rise bar with great views. *See p163* **Booze with a view**.

Crangi Café Martini

COM BOX Bldg 2F, 1-32-16 Ebisu-Nishi, Shibuya-ku (5728 2099). Daikanyama station (Tokyu Toyoko Line) or Ebisu JR station, west exit. **Open** 11.45am-3am Mon-Thur; 11.45am-5am Fri, Sat. **Credit** AmEx, DC, JCB, MC, V.

A martini specialist in upmarket Daikanyama, with an interior festooned with work by New York silversmith Philip Crangi. As well as over 30 different martinis (around ¥1,200), the bar offers all manner of champagne tipples.

The Footnik

Asahi Bldg 1F, 1-11-2 Ebisu, Shibuya-ku (5795 0144/www.footnik.net). Ebisu JR station, east or west exit. **Open** 11.30am-1am Mon-Thur; 11.30am-4.30am Fri; 3pm-4.30am Sat; 3pm-1am Sun. **No credit cards**.

The first pub to offer live English Premiership matches in Tokyo abandoned its down-at-heel premises in Takadanobaba to move to these spacious surroundings in late 2001. Live football remains the *raison d'être*. Good range of imported draught beers, including Guinness.

The Hub

Poan Shibuya Bldg B1F, 3-10 Udagawa-cho, Shibuya-ku (3496 0765/www.pub-hub.com/english/shop.html). Shibuya JR station, Hachiko exit. **Open** noon-midnight Mon-Thur, Sun; noon-2am Fri, Sat. **No credit cards**. **Map** p102.

One of a chain of Japanese-run British-style pubs. This branch has the added attraction of a real table football table. See website for others.

Insomnia Lounge

Ikuma Building B1F, 26-5 Utagawacho, Shibuya-ku (3476 2735). Shibuya JR station, Hachiko exit. **Open** 6pm-5am daily. **Credit** AmEx, DC, JCB, MC, V. **Map** p102.

Welcome back to the womb. This spacious basement bar, tucked away opposite one side of the 109 Building, is covered from floor to ceiling in soft red fabrics, the cushioned walls reminiscent of a padded cell. For the ultimate queasy experience, try sitting at the bar and gazing into the mirrored lights above it. And don't miss a trip to the toilet. There's an extensive food and cocktail menu, but beware the cover charge of ¥500 per person. Take your shoes off when you enter.

Kissa Ginza

1-3-9 Ebisu-Minami, Shibuya-ku (3710 7320). Ebisu JR station, west exit. **Open** 6pm-late Mon-Sat. **No credit cards**.

Here's a recipe for post-modern kitsch, Tokyo style. Take a 40-year-old coffee shop that hasn't seen a decorator in 30 years, install a glitter ball and two turntables and… absolutely nothing else. Result: this place has changed from a deserted coffee shop to one of Ebisu's hippest hang-outs. The turntables spin on Fridays and Saturdays, and the music is deep, deep lounge. The neon sign outside, incidentally, just reads Ginza.

Soft

B1F, 3-1-9 Shibuya, Shibuya-ku (5467 5817). Shibuya JR station, east exit. **Open** 7pm-4am Mon-Fri; 9pm-4am Sat. **No credit cards**. **Map** p102.

Bizarre *Alice in Wonderland* kind of space with one of the city's most impressive selections of imported bottled beers. Lights flicker on automatically as you descend the curved stairs into the surprisingly small bar, which is decked out in orange and white with funky chairs, foam matting and some little tables suspended from the ceiling. Don't forgo a visit to the bathroom, entered through a tiny waist-high door, where the toilet paper hangs from high above your head and the taps in the basin are like nothing else. Soft is also on the underground DJ circuit most weekends. Depending on the DJ, there may be a cover charge of between ¥1,000-¥2,500, including one or two drinks.

Space Punch

Sato Bldg 1F, 1-13-5 Ebisu-Nishi, Shibuya-ku (3496 2484). Ebisu JR station, west exit. **Open** 8pm-3am daily. **No credit cards**.

This small watering hole on Ebisu's west side resembles a bar in a big nuclear cooling tube. The warm glow of the illuminated orange bar bounces off rounded metal walls punctuated with mini TVs to create a futuristic vibe. There's also a selection of cool pop-up toys and games to keep you amused, and the red toilet is a must-use. It's too clean to be *Blade Runner*, but it's certainly a taste of the futuristic Tokyo for which many come hunting.

Tantra

Ichimainoe Bldg B1F, 3-5-5 Shibuya, Shibuya-ku (5485 8414). Shibuya JR station, Miyamasusaka (east), new south exits. **Open** 8pm-5am daily. **No credit cards**. **Map** p102.

Blink and you'll miss the entrance, the only sign of which is a small, dimly lit 'T' above a nondescript stairwell on the corner of a nondescript office building on the south side of Roppongi Dori near Shibuya. Heave open the imposing metal door and you'll find yourself in what resembles a secret, subterranean

A spontaneous outbreak of Spanish dancing at **Las Meninas**. *See p166.*

drinking club, with stone pillars, veiled alcoves, flickering candles and statues depicting scenes from the *Kama Sutra*. On your first visit you'll feel like you've gatecrashed a very private party, but have courage and don't be put off by the ice-cool staff. The ¥1,000 cover charge is a warning not to enter without a substantial wad in your wallet.

What the Dickens

Roob 6 Bldg 4F, 1-13-3 Ebisu-nishi, Shibuya-ku (3780 2099/www.ookawara-kikaku.com/dickens). Ebisu JR station, west exit. **Open** 5pm-1am Tue, Wed; 5pm-2am Thur-Sat; 3pm-midnight Sun. **No credit cards.**

At the top of the building that houses nightclub Milk is this popular British-style pub. The walls are decorated with Dickens manuscripts, which have been liberally re-captioned in the gents' toilets. Unfortunately, food is of genuine British pub standard. Local bands play live nightly.

World Sports Café

World Sports Plaza East Bldg B1F, 1-16-9 Shibuya, Shibuya-ku (3407 7337/www.worldsportscafe.co.jp). Shibuya JR station, Miyamasusaka (east) exit. **Open** 5.30pm-4.30am Tue-Fri; 11.30-4.30am Sat, Sun. **Credit** AmEx, DC, JCB, MC, V. **Map** p102.

An *izakaya* that shows every sport imaginable on over 60 TV screens. The staff' uniforms are modelled on sports kits, with numbers on the back. On arrival, you will be asked which sport you are interested in, and then be shown to a seat closest to a screen showing your choice. Not great for atmosphere, but a comfortable and casual place to chat while taking in a game.

Further west

A-Sign Bar

3F, 5-32-7 Daizawa, Setagaya-ku (3413 6489). Shimo-Kitazawa station, south exit. **Open** 5pm-1.30am Tue-Sun. **No credit cards.**

The name of this Okinawa-style bar refers to the 'Approved for US Military' signs that appeared outside select drinking holes on the southern Japanese island during its American occupation. An interesting interior includes old pictures, a fantastic old jukebox and an antique pinball machine. An even more interesting drinks policy means that the per-glass price for spirits gets cheaper if you bulk order. As well as the island's own Orion beer, on offer are 47 types of Okinawan sake, or *awamori*, notorious for its strength. Food from the Okinawan restaurant below can be ordered at the bar.

Heaven's Door

Takimoto Bldg 2F, 2-17-10 Kitazawa, Setagaya-ku (3411 6774). Shimo-Kitazawa station (Odakyu/Keio Inokashira lines), south exit. **Open** 6pm-late daily. **No credit cards.**

An extremely comfortable bar run by charismatic Brit expat Paul Davies. Soft furnishings, a Joe Orton-style approach to interior design, a crowd of friendly regulars and a complete absence of food mark this place out. One of the best places in town to watch live football. Call ahead to confirm that it's on.

Las Meninas

Plaza Koenji 2F, 3-22-7 Koenji-Kita, Suginami-ku (3338 0266). Koenji station, north exit. **Open** 6pm-late Tue-Sun. **No credit cards.**

This tiny, pristine place stands out among the myriad late-night dives of Koenji, out in west Tokyo. Run by exiled Brit Johnny and his Japanese wife, it's the best place in the area for tapas and Spanish wine. The food, prepared with the day's freshest ingredients, complements an extensive wine list and impressive choice of reasonably priced beers. Can be difficult to get a table at weekends. Great bread.

Mother

5-36-14 Daizawa, Setagaya-ku (3421 9519). Shimo-Kitazawa station (Odakyu/Keio Inokashira lines), south exit. **Open** 6pm-2am Mon-Thur; 5pm-2am Fri-Sun. **No credit cards.**

The extreme kitsch of this only-in-Japan bar, which resembles a mix of gingerbread house, treehouse and sub-aquatic pub, betrays what is in fact a classy establishment. The no-hard-edges interior is hard to describe: a combination of ceramic mosaic walls dotted with glowing blue 'stone' lights and faux wood seating. The drinks are generous and there is a wide range of bottled beers, as well as a high-quality menu of freshly made Okinawan and Thai dishes. You can bring your own CDs and staff will play them, although Mother's own playlist, mostly legends such as Sly and the Family Stone, the Rolling Stones, Bob Dylan and the like, is pretty flawless.

Pierrôt

2-1-8 Kitazawa, Setagaya-ku (090 8042 7014/ http://members.tripod.co.jp/shimokitapierrot/top.htm). Shimo-Kitazawa station (Odakyu/Keio Inokashira lines), south exit. **Open** 8.30pm-late daily. **No credit cards.**

By day a used clothes shop, at 8pm the racks are wheeled away and this shack at the bottom of the main shopping street turns into an open-air bar. The Tokyo climate is not well suited to such bars, and while in summer the city needs far more al fresco watering holes like this, in winter Pierrôt is left out in the cold, so to speak. Nevertheless, it's worth stopping by any time of the year for the almost always excellent free live music. In winter there is a variety of warm cocktails on offer as well as the usual range of beers and mixers. The coffee is best avoided. Note that the bar has no toilet, but offers customers free use of the 'Toilet Express' bike, on which they can speed themselves to the nearest convenience.

The Shamrock

Sunny City Kichijoji Bldg B1F, 1-18-3 Kichijoji Honcho (0422 23 4669/www.shamrock-no1.co.jp/timee.html). Kichijoji station, central exit. **Open** 11am-5am daily. **No credit cards.**

Small, friendly Irish pub, with the best Guinness in this increasingly fashionable area.

Shops & Services

In Tokyo, shopping is about more than just buying things, it's a way of life.

Tokyo is shopping city. There may be a recession on, but someone seems to have forgotten to mention it to the thousands of wide-eyed shoppers in a permanent frenzy of consumerism in the main shopping centres of Shinjuku, Ikebukuro, Shibuya and Ginza.

In this city, if you look hard enough you can buy almost anything, and outside the major centres, which all tend to have branches of the same stores, Tokyo is a warren of small, fascinating shopping streets, many of them with long-established characterful businesses selling everything from secondhand comics to rice crackers.

The Japanese and local governments have long been fiercely protective of local shopkeepers and reluctant to let the local shopping experience boil down to a choice of giant supermarkets, as has happened in many western countries. The result is that walking down an out-of-centre Japanese shopping street, or *shotengai*, can be like taking a trip back in time, with traditional greengrocers and rice shops nestling up to newcomers such as fast-food shops.

As with everywhere in Tokyo, our recommendations are just a starting point for the serious shopper. Don't be frightened to wander where your fancy takes you. Who knows what bargains await around the next corner?

One-stop shopping

Department stores

All Japanese *depato* share certain basic similarities. Food halls are always in the basement, along with some restaurants and cafés. The first two floors are women's clothing and accessories, with menswear beginning on the third or maybe the fourth. The higher levels include restaurants that stay open at night after the main store has closed, and the rooftops are used as beer gardens in the summer. Almost all stores offer tax-exemption services for purchases (mainly clothing) over ¥10,000, if you take your passport with your purchase to the customer service counter. Most have sections where you can buy Japanese craft products as souvenirs, and some have delivery services to anywhere in the world. Store guides in English are often available at the information desk. *Depato* are closed approximately one day every two months, so it's worth calling before you go if you're looking for something specific. Also, remember that closing times may differ from branch to branch of the same store.

Daimaru

1-9-1, Marunouchi, Chiyoda-ku (3212 8011/www.daimaru.co.jp/english/tokyo.html). Tokyo JR station, Yaesu central exit. **Open** 10am-9pm Mon-Fri; 10am-8pm Sat, Sun. *Restaurant floor* 11am-10pm daily. **Credit** AmEx, DC, JCB, MC, V. **Map** p62.

This store is conveniently located inside Tokyo railway station. The first six floors are devoted to fashion and accessories, restaurants are on the eighth floor, Japanese souvenirs are on the seventh and tenth and the Daimaru Museum is on the 12th. The money exchange and tax exemption counters are on the seventh floor; a shipping service is also available.

H2 Sukiyabashi Hankyu

5-2-1 Ginza, Chuo-ku (3575 2231/www.hankyu-dept.co.jp). Ginza station, exit C2, C3. **Open** 10.30am-9pm daily. **Credit** AmEx, DC, JCB, MC, V. **Map** p57.

This store is one of a pair, along with the neighbouring Yurakucho Hankyu. H2 stocks numerous household goods and accessories, houses the giants HMV and Gap, and has a customer service counter on the third floor. Yurakucho Hankyu sells mainly clothes and cosmetics.

Isetan

3-14-1 Shinjuku, Shinjuku-ku (3352 1111/www.isetan.co.jp). Shinjuku-Sanchome station, exit B3, B4, B5. **Open** 10am-8pm daily. **Credit** AmEx, DC, JCB, MC, V. **Map** p109.

Isetan runs the I-Club, a special free service for foreign customers that provides English-speaking shopping assistants and other assistance. Membership enquiries can be made at the customer services desk on the eighth floor of the store's Annex Building. The club's monthly newsletter contains comprehensive news of forthcoming sales, discounts and special promotions, plus details of clothing ranges available in sizes larger than the usual Japanese ones. Isetan is split into seven buildings very close to each other. The overseas shipping service is in the basement of the Main Building and the tax exemption counter is on the eighth floor of the Annex Building. BPQC – an eclectic selection of Japanese and foreign concession stores selling cosmetics, perfumes, CDs and household goods – is on the basement second floor of the Main Building.
Branch: 1-11-5 Kichijoji Honcho, Musashino-shi (0422 211 111).

Out and about in Ginza, one of Tokyo's main shopping centres.

Keio

1-1-4 Nishi-Shinjuku, Shinjuku-ku (3342 2111/www.keionet.com). Shinjuku JR station, west exit. **Open** 10am-8pm daily. *Restaurant floor* 11am-10pm daily. **Credit** AmEx, DC, JCB, MC, V. **Map** p109.

Situated between Odakyu, My Lord and Lumine, with entrances leading directly from Shinjuku station, Keio has ladieswear and accessories on the first four floors, menswear on the fifth, kimono, jewellery and furniture on the sixth, children's clothes and sporting goods on the seventh, and office supplies on the eighth. The Lilac range of clothing is available in westerner-friendly larger sizes. The tax exemption and currency exchange counters are situated on the sixth floor.

Branch: Keio Seiseki-Sakuragaoka, 1-10-1 Sekido, Tama-shi (042 337 2111).

Lumine 1 & 2

Lumine 1: 1-1-5 Nishi-Shinjuku, Shinjuku-ku; Lumine 2: 3-38-2 Shinjuku, Shinjuku-ku (3348 5211/www.lumine.co.jp). Shinjuku JR station, south exit. **Open** 11am-10pm daily. **Credit** AmEx, DC, JCB, MC, V. **Map** p109.

This very confusingly laid-out store takes up two sides of Shinjuku station, near the south exit. Lumine 1 contains clothes and jewellery for women, with the food hall on the basement second floor. Lumine 2 sells menswear, accessories and sporting goods. There was no duty-free service available at the time of writing.

Matsuya

3-6-1 Ginza, Chuo-ku (3567 1211/www.matsuya.com). Ginza station, exits A12, A13. **Open** 10am- 8pm daily. **Credit** AmEx, DC, JCB, MC, V. **Map** p57.

Clothing at Matsuya includes menswear and womenswear by Issey Miyake on the third floor. Traditional Japanese souvenirs are on the seventh, with shopping services for foreigners – tax exemption and overseas shipping – on the third floor. The money exchange counter is on the first.

Matsuzakaya

6-10-1 Ginza, Chuo-ku (3572 1111/www.matsuzakaya.co.jp/ginza/index.shtml). Ginza station, exits A1, A2, A3, A4. **Open** 10.30am-7.30pm Mon-Thur; 10.30am-8pm Fri, Sat; 10.30am-7pm Sun & national holidays. **Credit** AmEx, DC, JCB, MC, V. **Map** p57.

The main branch of Matsuzakaya is actually in Ueno, but visitors from abroad are usually more familiar with this branch in Ginza. Here, the tax exemption and money exchange counters are on the basement second floor, and there's a kimono shop on the sixth. The annexe contains a beauty salon, an art gallery and even a ladies' deportment school.

Branch: 3-29-5 Ueno, Taito-ku (3832 1111).

Mitsukoshi

1-4-1 Muromachi, Nihonbashi, Chuo-ku (3241 3311/www.mitsukoshi.co.jp). Mitsukoshimae station, exit A3, A5. **Open** 10am-7.30pm daily. **Credit** AmEx, DC, JCB, MC, V. **Map** p62.

The oldest surviving department store in Japan, Mitsukoshi owns the Japanese franchise to the jewellery giant Tiffany's. The Ginza store has a tax exemption counter on the basement third floor, plus a Japanese souvenir store called Japanesque.

Branches: 4-6-16 Ginza, Chuo-ku (3562 1111); 3-29-1 Shinjuku, Shinjuku-ku (3354 1111); 1-5-7 Higashi-Ikebukuro, Toshima-ku (3987 1111).

My City

3-38-1 Shinjuku, Shinjuku-ku (5269 1111/www.e-mycity.co.jp/). Shinjuku JR station, east exit. **Open** 10am-9pm daily. *Restaurant floors* 11am-11.30 pm daily. **Credit** AmEx, DC, JCB, MC, V. **Map** p109.

Department stores vs malls

It all seemed so simple back in the Bubble days. Japan's department stores could do no wrong; their venerable names ensured a steady stream of reverent shoppers, and their embarrassingly polite staff were the stuff of legend. Today, the national recession is a tarpit sucking the economy down inch by inch, and the *depato* mammoths are being pulled under by their own weight. Over the last five years, *depato* sales have consistently declined, and restructuring measures once believed unthinkable – closing loss-making outlets and cutting workforces – are a grim reality.

Now, the *depato* are trying every trick in the book to attract customers. They offer incentives such as free shipping, discounts for membership card holders, and free gifts (such as 'character goods').

They've also successfully diversified into non-traditional areas, known as *depa-res* and *depa-chika*. The *depa-res* are high-quality gourmet restaurants, usually on the top floors of the stores; the *depa-chika* are basement food halls featuring branches of internationally famous delis, patisseries and confectioners. In fact, in recent years the only clear profits the *depato* have made are in these food halls.

The recession's not the only thing the *depato* have to worry about, however. They also have increasingly severe competition in the form of a new generation of shopping malls. These malls are built into the design of brand-new urban developments that are changing the face of the city. The last two years have seen the opening of mammoth projects such as the **Marunouchi Building**, the **Shiodome** site near Shinbashi and **Roppongi Hills** (for all, *see p171*). Soon, these will be joined by the Aoyama complex, a centre which is due to replace the much-loved Dojunkai low-rent apartments in the otherwise upmarket Omotesando area.

'Malls' seems too simple a word for these new areas; they are more like theme parks dedicated to consumption. Their exteriors, such as that of the Caretta Shiodome, designed by American architect Jon Jerde, are breathtaking; their interiors hold so many retail outlets they have been called 'cities within cities'; and even more damning, they beat the *depato* in the *depa-chika* game too. Their basement floors have a sophistication and elegance that welcome the foreign visitor. In comparison, the chaotic *depato* food halls with their confusing layout and constantly shouting *happi*-coated vendors can simply bewilder.

There is a Japanese saying, '*okyaku-sama wa kami-sama desu*' – the customer is God. In an increasingly competitive future, Japan's consumers really will have the power of life or death over the *depato*.

Situated above the east exit of Shinjuku station, My City is chiefly notable for the Shunkan gourmet restaurant area on the seventh and eighth floors. Created by celebrated designer Takashi Sugimoto and opened in late 2002, it's been a smash hit.

My Lord

1-1-3 Nishi-Shinjuku, Shinjuku-ku (3349 5611/www.shinjuku-mylord.com). Shinjuku JR station, south exit. **Open** *Fashion floors* 11am-9pm daily. *Mosaic Street* 10am-9pm daily. *Restaurant floor* 11am-10.30pm daily. **Credit** AmEx, DC, JCB, MC, V. **Map** p109.

My Lord (pronounced mih-lord-oh) has a number of boutiques, but perhaps its greatest attraction is Mosaic Street, a closed alleyway running between the Keio and Odakyu department stores. Here are many shops-within-shops devoted to kitsch, retro, and cute cartoon characters from around the world, such as Pingu, Powerpuff Girls and the Sony Post Pets.

Odakyu

1-1-3 Nishi-Shinjuku, Shinjuku-ku (3342 1111/www.odakyu-dept.co.jp). Shinjuku JR station, west exit. **Open** 10am-8pm daily. *Restaurant floor (12F)* 11am-10pm daily. *Restaurant floors (13F, 14F)* 11am-10.30pm daily. **Credit** AmEx, DC, JCB, MC, V. **Map** p109.

The store is split into two buildings, the Main Building and the Annex (Halc) Building, which are connected by an elevated walkway and underground passageways. The Main Building has kimono on the sixth floor and furniture on the eighth, while the Odakyu Halc has menswear, sportswear, three floors of the electronics retailer Bic Camera and a Troisgros delicatessen in the basement food hall. The top three floors of the Main Building contain restaurants. The tax exemption counter is on the fifth floor of the Main Building.

Seibu

21-1 Udagawa-cho, Shibuya-ku (3462 0111/www.seibu.co.jp). Shibuya JR station, Hachiko exit. **Open** 10am-8pm Mon-Wed, Sun; 10am-9pm Thur-Sat. *Restaurant floor annex A (8F)* 11am-9pm daily. *Restaurant floor annex A (B2F)* 11am-11pm daily. **Credit** AmEx, DC, JCB, MC, V. **Map** p102.

The Shibuya main store is split into two buildings, Annexes A and B, which face each other across the street. Annex A sells mainly ladieswear, and Annex B menswear, children's clothes and accessories. The tax exemption counter is on the M2 (mezzanine) floor of Annex A. Seibu also runs the stores Loft and Movida, both of which are within easy walking distance of the Shibuya store. Loft is designed for the 18-to-35 age range, selling goods for household and beauty care. Movida has a number of designer boutiques on each floor.
Branches: 1-28-1 Minami-Ikebukuro, Toshima-ku (3981 0111); 2-5-1 Yurakucho, Chiyoda-ku (3286 0111).

Takashimaya

2-4-1 Nihonbashi, Chuo-ku (3211 4111/www.takashimaya.co.jp). Nihonbashi station, exit B2. **Open** 10am-7.30pm daily. Credit AmEx, DC, JCB, MC, V. **Map** p62.
This store shares much of the outward opulence and grandeur of its neighbour Mitsukoshi, having based a lot of its interior style on Harrods of London. Menswear is on the first and second floors, ladieswear is on the third and fourth, childrenswear on the fifth, furniture on the sixth and kimonos on the seventh. The tax exemption counter is on the first floor and the overseas shipping service is on the basement first floor. The massive Shinjuku branch (Takashimaya Times Square) contains a large number of boutiques, a branch of the hardware store Tokyu Hands, the Kinokuniya International Bookshop in the Annex building and the Times Square theatre on the 12th floor.
Branch: Takashimaya Times Square, 5-24-2 Sendagaya, Shibuya-ku (5361 1122).

Tobu

1-1-25 Nishi-Ikebukuro, Toshima-ku (3981 2211/www.tobu.co.jp). Ikebukuro JR station, west exit. **Open** 10am-8pm daily. **Credit** AmEx, DC, JCB, MC, V. **Map** p69.
The Main Building houses clothing for all occasions on the lower floor (including kimono on the ninth), with an enormous selection of restaurants from the 11th to 17th floors. The Central Building sells clothing in larger sizes, plus a good range of interior goods and office supplies. The Plaza Building contains the designer collection. The currency exchange and tax exemption counters are on the basement first floor of the Central Building. The website is in Japanese only.

Tokyu Honten

2-24-1 Dogenzaka, Shibuya-ku (3477 3111/www.tokyu-dept.co.jp/honten). Shibuya JR station, Hachiko exit. **Open** 11am-7pm daily. *Tokyu Food Show (B1F)* 11am-8pm daily. *Restaurant floor (8F)* 11am-10.30pm daily. **Credit** AmEx, DC, JCB, MC, V. **Map** p102.
Tokyu Honsten sells designer fashions for men and women and interior goods for the home. The Tokyu Toyoko store is situated directly above Shibuya JR

Go mobile

You've probably heard about the Japanese obsession with their *keitai denwa* (as mobile phones are called in Japan), and the good news is that it's not difficult to find one with a bilingual service and instruction manual. The main telecommunications companies are NTT DoCoMo, KDDI, J-Phone (owned by Vodaphone), and Tuka. These companies have offices in every high street; alternatively, it's possible to buy a mobile phone from one of the major electronics retailers.

Japan's 3G technology, after a shaky start, is now widely used, and most new phones include digital cameras and are capable of internet access. Each company has a wide range of billing plans and discount services, depending on the customer's needs, and the cost of the actual handset itself can vary considerably. When buying, you'll need to present a passport, driving licence or alien registration card as ID.

If you're only in Japan for a short time, a prepaid phone with a prepaid account card may prove the best option. To buy a prepaid phone you'll need the above ID, and the cost consists of the application charge (around ¥1,000), the price of the prepaid card (from ¥3,000 to ¥10,000) and the price of the handset.

In Japan, part of the charm of having a *keitai* is the amazing range of accessories that go with it. Don't forget to check out the straps, pouches and antenna rings that have turned an everyday functional object into a fetish.

Contact information is listed below (these are toll-free numbers):

NTT DoCoMo
0120-005-250.

KDDI
0077-7-111.

J-Phone
0088-21-2000.

Tu-Ka Cellular Tokai Customer Centre
0077-788-151.

station; the gourmet food hall in the basement, the Tokyu Food Show, holds branches of the extremely popular delicatessens Seijo Ishii and Kinokuniya (not to be confused with the bookstore below). The Tokyu Plaza store, behind Shibuya station, sells ladies' fashion, cosmetics and accessories, and has a CD shop and a branch of the Kinokuniya bookshop (however, it does not sell books in English). All the stores are linked together and in close proximity.

Shopping malls

Caretta Shiodome

1-8-2 Higashi-Shinbashi, Minato-ku (6218 2100/ www.caretta.jp). Shiodome station (Toei Oedo Line), exit 5, 6. **Open** varies. **Credit** varies.

This mall opened in late 2002 and got bigger in April 2003 with the opening of another mall, the Shibuya City Center, over the way. Part of the giant, brand-new Shiodome complex, what it lacks in quantity it makes up for in quality. The two basement floors hold an eclectic mix of shops, cafés and restaurants, including an Andersen bakery and a Buitoni pasta bar, and there are more restaurants on the first three floors of the Canyon Terrace building. The complex also houses the main offices of advertising giant Dentsu, the ADMT Advertising Museum (*see p59*) and the Dentsu Shiki Theatre (*see p245*).

Decks

1-6-1 Daiba, Minato-ku (3599 6500/www.odaiba-decks.com). Odaiba Kaihin Koen station (Yurikamome Line). **Open** 11am-9pm daily. **Restaurants** 11am-11pm daily. **Credit** varies. **Map** p78.

A seaside shopping arcade that opened on Odaiba in 2000, Decks is notable for its two themed shopping and restaurant areas: one a mini-Chinatown, the other a nostalgic recreation of a 1950s shopping street. The centre also contains a giant Sega arcade. The eponymous decks at the front of the building offer a pleasant view over Tokyo bay.

Glassarea Aoyama

5-4-41 Minami-Aoyama, Minato-ku (5485 3466). Omotesando station, exit B1. **Open** varies. **Credit** varies. **Map** p99.

This intriguing plaza, designed by the Tokyu Corporation, is an example of the new 'micro-malls' that have opened up in recent years in places such as Aoyama and Daikanyama. Instead of inspiring awe through their sheer size, they give the visitor a homelier, cosier impression. Glassarea Aoyama is host to boutiques, household goods stores, and an *izakaya* offering eastern Fukui Prefecture cuisine.

Mark City

1-12-1 Dogenzaka, Shibuya-ku (3780 6503/ www.s-markcity.co.jp). Directly connected to Shibuya station. **Open** varies. **Credit** varies. **Map** p102.

A major addition to the Shibuya shopping scene, presenting a number of boutiques and 'lifestyle' stores in one building, opposite Shibuya station. Restaurants and cafés are on the fourth and third floors, ladieswear is on the second, accessories and cosmetics are on the first.

Marunouchi Building

2-4-1 Marunouchi, Chiyoda-ku (5218 5100/www.marubiru.jp/index2.html). Tokyo JR station, Shin Marubiru exit. **Open** *Shops* 11am-9pm Mon-Sat; 11am-8pm Sun. *Restaurants* 11am-11pm Mon-Sat; 11am-10pm Sun. **Credit** AmEx, DC, JCB, MC, V. **Map** p62.

Extensively renovated and reopened in late 2002, the new and elegant 'Marubiru' devotes its first four floors to the Shopping Zone, while the fifth, sixth, 35th and 36th floors belong to the Restaurant Zone. The basement food hall has an emphasis on big-name gourmet products, and there are branches of American Pharmacy and Meidi-ya. The two-floor Terence Conran shop is the UK designer's biggest outlet in Tokyo, but don't expect any bargains.

Roppongi Hills

6-10 Roppongi, Minato-ku (www.roppongihills.com). Roppongi station, exits 1, 3. **Open** varies. **Credit** varies. **Map** p74.

The brainchild of Tokyo property magnate Mori Minoru, this giant shopping and entertainment development opened to a great fanfare at the end of April 2003. Most similar developments in Tokyo are restricted in scale, due the cost of land and the difficulty of acquiring it, but Mori spent some 20 years making all of this 40-acre site his own. The result is impressive: a series of wide pedestrian squares and walkways meander over three levels between the tower at the centre of the complex, its apartment blocks and its three separate shopping centres, which contain around 200 premium shops and restaurants, a nine-screen cinema and a public amphitheatre. An art gallery, the first in the world to be linked with New York's Museum of Modern Art, is due to open in October 2003. On its opening weekend, one million people flocked to Roppongi Hills; 100,000 are expected to visit daily.

Sunshine City

3-1 Higashi-Ikebukuro, Toshima-ku (3989 3331/ www.sunshinecity.co.jp). Ikebukuro station, east exit, exits 35, 41. **Open** *Shops* 10am-8pm daily. *Restaurants* 11am-10pm daily. **Credit** AmEx, DC, JCB, MC, V. **Map** p69.

The prototype for the huge malls that are beginning to dominate Tokyo, Sunshine City has most of its stores and restaurants in the Alpa Shopping Centre. There is also the indescribable indoor theme park Namja Town, home to 25 attractions, and the Gyoza Stadium (a collection of restaurants devoted to *gyoza*, the Chinese dumplings that the Japanese adore).

Venus Fort

Palette Town, 1 Aomi, Koto-ku (3599 0700/ www.venusfort.co.jp/conbine.html). Aomi station (Yurikamome Line). **Open** *Shops* 11am-9pm Mon-Fri, Sun; 11am-10pm Sat. *Restaurants* 11am-11pm daily. **Credit** varies. **Map** p78.

Widely touted as the 'first theme park exclusively for women', this unusual mall is decorated in a faux-classic Greco-Roman style designed to evoke feelings of strolling through Florence or Milan (it even has an artificial sky that changes colour with the time of day outside). Venus Fort contains mainly European-style boutiques and patisseries, and even a half-decent crêperie, and is part of the giant Odaiba bayfront complex.

Yebisu Garden Place

4-20 Ebisu, Shibuya-ku & 13-1/4-1 Mita, Meguro-ku (5423 7111/www.gardenplace.co.jp/english). Ebisu JR station, east exit. **Open** varies. **Credit** varies.
Within the spacious precincts of Yebisu Garden Place can be found the Westin Hotel, the Tokyo Metropolitan Museum of Photography, the Yebisu Beer Museum and a large number of boutiques. In late 2002 the complex was completed by the addition of Glass Square, a stylish self-enclosed new shopping centre.

Shopping streets

Ameyoko Plaza Food & Clothes Market

6-10-7 Ueno, Taito-ku (no phone/www.ameyoko.net). Ueno JR station, Shinobazu exit, or Okachimachi station, north exit. **Open** 9am-7pm daily. **No credit cards**. **Map** p88.
This maze of streets is two markets, Ueno Centre Mall (3831 0069/www.ameyoko-centerbldg.com) and Ameyoko itself. The Centre Mall sells souvenirs and clothes; the other market specialises in fresh food, especially fish. Vendors knock down their prices towards the end of the day.

Nakamise Dori

Asakusa, Taito-ku (no phone). Asakusa station, exits 1, 3, A4. **Open** 8am-8pm daily. **No credit cards**. **Map** p83.
This maze of stalls and tiny shops leading up to the entrance to Sensoji Temple in Asakusa sells Japanese souvenirs, some dating back to the Edo era. It also sells the kind of food that is traditionally associated with festivals, and traditional snacks such as *kaminari-okoshii* (toasted rice crackers), and *ningyo-yaki* (red bean-filled buns moulded into humorous shapes).

Nakano Broadway

Opposite north exit of Nakano station (office 3387 1610/3388 7004/www.nakano-broadway.jp). **Open** varies. **Credit** varies.
Walk down this cathedral-like shopping street and you will come to the covered Broadway section. On the second and third floors can be found several branches of Mandarake, a store selling a selection of new and secondhand *manga*; branches of Fujiya Avic, a secondhand CD/DVD/anime store where rarities and bootlegs can invariably be found; and a large number of stores selling a vast range of collectable action figures.

Nishi-Ogikubo

Nishi-Ogikubo station, Suginami-ku (sugishoren.com/street/400.htm). **Open** varies. **Credit** varies; cash preferred.
The area of the four main roads that cross at the Zenpukuji river is the home of around 75 antique, secondhand and 'recycle' shops. They sell everything from Japanese ceramics to 1950s American memorabilia. Go out of the station's north exit, stop at the *koban* (police box) and ask for a copy of the 'an-tik-ku map-pu'.

Takeshita Dori

Opposite Takeshita exit of Harajuku station (www.harajuku.jp/takeshita/index.html). **Open** varies. **Credit** varies. **Map** p99.
Takeshita Dori, in Harajuku, is the centre of teenage culture in Tokyo. Down this packed street can be found secondhand clothes and CD stores with bizarre Jap-lish names like Junk Jewel, Lip Hip and Gal Fit, stores that specialise in teen *idoru* (from the Japanese rendition of 'idol') memorabilia, and the flamboyant costumes of the 'Visual Kei' tribe. There's also a large branch of the bargain cosmetics store Daiba, popular with the teen crowd. Many more offbeat shops await in the tiny alleys that branch off the main street.

Books

The shops listed below are the best stores for books in English and other languages, on any subject. If you're looking for curiosities and bargains and have a day to spare, head for the **Kanda-Jinbocho** area (Jinbocho station) and browse among the secondhand bookstores that line Yasukuni Dori.

Book First

33-5 Udagawa-cho, Shibuya-ku (3770 1023/www.book1st.net Japanese only). Shibuya JR station, Hachiko exit. **Open** 10am-10pm daily. **Credit** AmEx, DC, JCB, MC, V. **Map** p102.
The most centrally located bookstore in Shibuya. Has a large number of English, French and German books on the third floor, including textbooks for studying Japanese and teaching English.
Branches: 2-6-1 Kaji-cho, Chiyoda-ku (5295 3131); 4F Aqua-City, 1-7-1 Daiba, Minato-ku (5531 5400); 4-3-1 Toranomon, Minato-ku (5776 6787).

Caravan Books

2-21-5 Ikebukuro, Toshima-ku (5951 6406/www.booksat caravan.com). Ikebukuro station, exit C1. **Open** 11am-8pm Mon-Thur; 11am-9pm Fri, Sat; noon-6pm Sun. **No credit cards**. **Map** p69.
At last Good Day Books (*below*) has some competition, in the form of this pleasant secondhand English-only bookshop in the nether reaches of Ikebukuro. Come here and browse, drink coffee and chew the fat with owner Nick Ward, who'll also buy your old books. A book search service is also available, and the website is excellent.

Fiona Bookstore

5-41-5 Okusawa, Setagaya-ku (3721 8186/www.fiona.co.jp). Jiyugaoka station (Tokyu Toyoko Line), central exit. **Open** 11am-8pm daily. **Credit** AmEx, DC, JCB, MC, V.

Stocks mainly books for children in both English and Japanese. There are also educational toys, games, videos and dolls.

Good Day Books

3F 1-11-2 Ebisu, Shibuya-ku (5421 0957/www.gooddaybooks.com). Ebisu JR station, east exit. **Open** 11am-8pm Mon, Wed-Sat; 11am-6pm Sun. **No credit cards**.

Stocks over 30,000 used books and 7,000 new ones, most of them in English. There's also an extensive selection of secondhand books on Japan and Japanese-language texts. This shop is a must-visit for anyone looking for a bargain, and also gives credit against customers' old paperbacks.

Kinokuniya Bookstore

3-17-7 Shinjuku, Shinjuku-ku (3354 0131/www.kinokuniya.co.jp). Shinjuku JR station, east exit. **Open** 10am-8pm daily. **Credit** AmEx, DC, JCB, MC, V. **Map** p109.

Kinokuniya has perhaps the largest selection of new books in Tokyo, but this does come at a price. A recent paperback costs about ¥1,500, around twice as much as on the Japanese site of Amazon. It claims to have around a million books in English and other languages in stock, on the sixth floor. Although the main store is near Studio Alta, the branch behind nearby Takashimaya (Shinjuku station south side) is much larger.

Branches: throughout the city.

Maruzen

2-3-10 Nihonbashi, Chuo-ku (3273 3313/www.maruzen.co.jp). Nihonbashi station, exit B3. **Open** 10am-8pm Mon-Sat; 10am-7pm Sun. **Credit** AmEx, DC, JCB, MC, V. **Map** p62.

Stocks a wide range of bestsellers and other fiction, and non-fiction and textbooks. Convenient for people working in central Tokyo.

Branches: throughout the city.

Nellie's English Books

Sunbridge Bldg 1F/2F, 1-26-6 Yanagibashi, Taito-ku (3865 6210/0120 071329/www.nellies.jp). Asakusabashi JR station, east exit, Asakusabashi station (Toei Asakusa Line), exit A3. **Open** 10am-7pm Mon, Tue, Thur, Fri; 10am-6pm Wed, Sat. **Credit** AmEx, DC, JCB, MC, V.

Stocks a wide selection of materials useful for English teachers working in Japan. The range includes books, readers, videos, songbooks and software.

Confectionery

The Japanese have a sweet tooth, but the notion of what consititutes sweet is markedly different from that in the west. The taste of traditional Japanese confectionery is based on *anko* – a red paste made from azuki beans. A slightly more refined choice is *wagashi*, a colourful candy made from sugar and sometimes used in tea ceremonies. Products vary according to the season, and most are meant to be eaten quickly, so be sure to enquire as to how long they'll keep.

Akebono

5-7-19 Ginza, Chuo-ku (3571 0483/www.ginza-akebono.co.jp/top.html). Ginza station, exit A1. **Open** 9am-9pm Mon-Sat; 9am-8pm Sun. **Credit** AmEx, DC, JCB, MC, V. **Map** p57.

This small but lively store's variety of traditional Japanese sweets is also available in the basement food halls of Tokyo's major department stores.

Branches: throughout the city.

Iidabashi Mannendou

1F Toku Bldg, 2-19 Ageba-cho, Shinjuku-ku (3266 0544/www.omedeto.co.jp/index2.htm). Iidabashi JR station, east exit; Iidabashi subway station, exits B1, C1. **Open** 10am-7pm Mon-Fri; 10am-5pm Sat. **No credit cards**.

Japanese sweets prepared according to traditional recipes dating back to 17th-century Kyoto.

Kikuya

5-13-2 Minami-Aoyama, Minato-ku (3400 3856). Omotesando station, exit B1. **Open** 9.30am-5pm Mon-Fri; 9.30am-3pm Sat. **Credit** AmEx, DC, JCB, MC, V. **Map** p99.

A small takeaway-only spot that sells a varied range of handcrafted and mouth-watering sweets.

Kimuraya

4-5-7 Ginza, Chuo-ku (3561 0368/www.kimuraya-sohonten.co.jp). Ginza station, exits A9, B1. **Open** 10am-9.30pm daily. **No credit cards**. **Map** p57.

This venerable shop is historically and culturally significant for being the first in Tokyo to sell *anpan* – bread rolls filled with *anko*.

Toraya

4-9-22 Akasaka, Minato-ku (3408 4121/www.toraya-group.co.jp). Akasaka-Mitsuke station, exit A. **Open** 8.30am-8pm Mon-Fri; 8:30am-6pm Sat, Sun. **Credit** AmEx, DC, JCB, MC, V.

This highly distinguished shop sells *wagashi* to the imperial family. Also has branches in New York and Paris.

Branches: throughout the city.

Cosmetics

Japan's two biggest cosmetics companies are Kanebo and Shiseido, whose products adorn the shelves of all department stores, and even some 24-hour convenience stores.

Shu Uemura

5-1-3 Jingumae, Shibuya-ku (3486 0048/www.shu-uemura.com/www.shu-uemura.co.jp). Omotesando station, exit 1. **Open** 10am-8pm daily. **Credit** AmEx, DC, JCB, MC, V. **Map** p99.

Antiquarian, or just plain old, books and maps are on sale by the ton in Kanda-Jinbocho.

Perhaps the closest Japanese equivalent to the British Boots chain of chemists. Stylish cosmetics at reasonable prices, and a presence on almost every high street.
Branches: throughout the city.

Electronics

For the visitor, the place of interest for buying electronics is **Akihabara**, the only area in Tokyo where bartering is common. Of course, there are other stores almost matching Akihabara prices in other parts of the city. The most notable of these are **Bic Camera**, **Yodobashi Camera** and **Sakuraya**, but note that these are geared to domestic consumption. If you are interested in photography, take a stroll around the back streets of **Shinjuku** near Studio Alta, where there's a host of secondhand camera shops.

Akky

1-12-1 Soto-Kanda, Chiyoda-ku (5207 5027/email: akky@akky-jp.com). Akihabara JR station, Electric Town exit. **Open** 10am-8pm daily. **Credit** AmEx, DC, JCB, MC, V.
A well-presented store with efficient and friendly bilingual staff, selling all kinds of electrical appliances. All products are sold duty-free, and all are export models. Of particular interest are the plasma televisions on the second floor. Goods are sold with an international warranty and English instructions.

AsoBitCity

4-3-3 Soto-Kanda, Chiyoda-ku (3251 3100/www.laox.co.jp). Akihabara JR station, Electric Town exit. **Open** 10am-9pm daily. **Credit** AmEx, DC, JCB, MC, V.
This extraordinary store doesn't mess about in getting your attention; outside the main entrance, an arcade showcases the latest games while girls dressed in *anime* costumes accost pedestrians with flyers. That's just the prelude to what's inside – seven floors of high-tech mayhem, with games, software, PCs, peripherals and 'character goods' (based on cartoon characters). There's a shooting gallery and a large model train set on the fifth floor, while the seventh floor is exclusively devoted to adult DVDs and CD-ROMs.

Bic Camera

1-41-5 Higashi-Ikebukuro, Toshima-ku (5396 1111/www.biccamera.co.jp). Ikebukuro JR station, east exit. **Open** 10am-8pm daily. **Credit** AmEx, DC, JCB, MC, V. **Map** p69.
As is the case with other large electronics retailers Sakuraya and Yodobashi Camera, Bic Camera's range of stock is so huge that different branches specialise in different kinds of goods. The company sells every kind of modern electronic appliance, as well as a limited amount of household furniture. However, all branches stock easy moneyspinners like mobile phones and Walkmen. Some knowledge of Japanese is necessary for making enquiries.
Branches: throughout the city.

Duty Free Akihabara

1-15-3 Soto-Kanda, Chiyoda-ku (3255 5301/www.laox.co.jp). Akihabara JR station, Electric Town exit. **Open** 10am-8pm Mon-Sat; 10am-7.30pm Sun.
Laox's main duty-free branch sells anything and everything electrical you could ever want, and more besides. Visitors should remember to check voltages or buy a cheap transformer.

Laox

1-2-9 Soto-Kanda, Chiyoda-ku (3253 7111/ www.laox.co.jp). Akihabara JR station, Electric Town exit. **Open** 10am-8pm Mon-Sat; 10am-7.30pm Sun. **Credit** AmEx, DC, JCB, MC, V.

In the main store, the duty-free section is located on the fourth to seventh floors. A worldwide delivery service is available, and most of the staff speak good English. There are English-language catalogues and instruction manuals for most products.

Branches throughout the city (not duty-free goods).

Sakuraya

1-1-1 Nishi-Shinjuku, Shinjuku-ku (5324 3636/www. sakuraya.co.jp). Shinjuku JR station, west exit. **Open** 10am-9pm daily. **Credit** AmEx, DC, JCB, MC, V. **Map** p109.

Sakuraya's flagship store is located next to Shinjuku's Odakyu department store and sells every kind of modern electric appliance. Some knowledge of Japanese is necessary for making enquiries.

Branches: throughout the city.

Takarada

1-14-7 Soto-Kanda, Chiyoda-ku (3253 0101/www. takarada-musen.com/). Akihabara JR station, Electric Town exit. **Open** 11am-8.30pm daily. **Credit** AmEx, DC, JCB, MC, V.

This small but very busy shop is close to the station, and has a number of bilingual staff to help you find what you want. The top floor also stocks a range of Japanese souvenirs, ceramics and so on.

Tsukumo Robocon Magazine Kan

Yamaguchi Bldg 1F, 3-2-13 Soto-Kanda, Chiyoda-ku (3251 0987/www.rakuten.co.jp/tsukumo/). Akihabara JR station, Electric Town exit. **Open** 10.45am-7.30pm Mon-Sat; 10.15am-7pm Sun. **Credit** AmEx, DC, JCB, MC, V.

This fascinating store specialises in robots – not only the cute, semi-intelligent kind that the Japanese have been working on in recent years, but also DIY AI projects for serious hobbyists. Mechanical cats, dogs, turtles and insects – the store's robots come in all shapes and sizes, and some simply defy description. Unfortunately the only robot kit that comes with English explanations is the imported Lego Mindstorms, but the lower-price-range robots are fairly easy to understand and operate. There are many Tsukumo branches scattered around Akihabara; ask in one and they'll give you a map showing where this shop is.

Branches: throughout the city.

User's Side 2

4F, K&S Ebisu Bldg 2, 1-16-2 Hiroo, Shibuya-ku (5447 7011/www.users-side.co.jp/2/index.php). Ebisu JR station, west exit. **Open** 11am-7pm daily. Closed 1st, 3rd Wed of mth. **Credit** AmEx, DC, JCB, MC, V.

This shop is a godsend to the expatriate. It sells export models of Japanese technology, with English software. It also has an affordable repair and troubleshooting service, with English-language technical support available and bilingual shop staff. There are branches of User's Side 2 in the USA as well, so products and parts can be ordered quickly and conveniently.

Yodobashi Camera

1-11-1 Nishi-Shinjuku, Shinjuku-ku (3346 1010/ www.yodobashi.co.jp). Shinjuku JR station, west exit. **Open** 9.30am-9pm daily. **Credit** AmEx, DC, JCB, MC, V. **Map** p109.

Like its rivals Bic and Sakuraya, this store's main presence consists of half a dozen branches scattered around Shinjuku. Sells every kind of electrical appliance. Some knowledge of Japanese is necessary for making enquiries.

Branches: **Multi Media Kinshicho** 3-14-5 Koutou-bashi, Sumida-ku (3632 1010); 4-9-8 Ueno, Taito-ku (3837 1010).

Fashion

109

2-29-1 Dogenzaka, Shibuya-ku (3477 5111/www. shibuya109.jp). Shibuya JR station, Hachiko exit. **Open** 10am-9pm daily. *Restaurants* 10am-10.30pm daily. **Credit** varies. **Map** p102.

This mall is the mecca of the 'Joshikosei' – the fashion-obsessed teenage girls who swarm around central Tokyo. It's worth a visit to see the flashy, sometimes bizarre trends that appear and disappear with lightning speed. Warning: you may leave feeling very old. Nearby 109-2 caters to pre-teens.

Branch: **109-2** 1-23-10 Dogenzaka, Shibuya-ku (3477 8111).

291295 = Homme

6-19-1 Jingumae, Shibuya-ku (3407 2912/www. 291295.com). Shibuya JR station, Miyamasusaka (east) exit or Harajuku station, Omotesando exit or Meiji-Jingumae station, exit 4. **Open** 11am-8pm daily. **Credit** AmEx, DC, JCB, MC, V. **Map** p102.

The numbers in the shop's name signify the date it was founded. It sells its own casual urban streetwear for young males, made of weathered fabrics with a slight hip hop influence, at reasonable prices.

Comme Ça Store

3-26-6 Shinjuku, Shinjuku-ku (5367 5551). Shinjuku JR station, east exit. **Open** 11am-9pm Mon-Sat; 11am-8pm Sun. **Credit** AmEx, DC, JCB, MC, V. **Map** p109.

The company's name is 'FIVE FOXes' (sic), its brand's name is 'Mono Comme Ça' – and it is no relation to Comme des Garçons (*see p179*). As well as affordable fashions in warm colours and fabrics, the company also produces toys, stationery and household goods.

Branches: throughout the city.

Laforet Harajuku/Foret Harajuku

1-11-6 Jingumae, Shibuya-ku (3475 0411/ www.laforet.ne.jp/harajuku). Harajuku station, Omotesando exit or Meiji-Jingumae station, exit 5. **Open** *B Laforet Harajuku* 11am-8pm daily. *5F Books Laforet and B1F HMV* 11am-9pm daily. *Foret Harajuku* 11am-9pm daily. **Credit** varies. **Map** p99.

Fads and fashions

When it comes to fashion, it's easy to think of Japan as One Nation under a Brand, and the name of that brand is Louis Vuitton. It's a puzzle as to why this particular name has such a hold over the Japanese female, but the result is that Japanese purchases account for over one-third of Louis Vuitton's global sales. What some observers find unsettling is the degree of unquestioning acceptance of the label's desirability, as if ownership of a Vuitton bag was a vital part of the survival instinct. 'Japan's an advanced country technologically, but it's still developing mentally,' says 22-year-old fashion student Yumi Uehara. 'If people lack self-confidence, owning Louis Vuitton goods can be comforting.'

A good section of the younger generation is, however, asserting its individuality, with fashion statements coming up direct from the streets. Twenty-first-century trends for girls so far have been *sukapan* – jeans worn under lacy skirts – and *oyapan* – baggy slacks with tucks and clear creases. Also, to reflect these troubled times, military chic has been big; camouflage pants, PLO scarves, bandannas and knee-high boots have caught on with both sexes, and the trend shows no sign of fading away.

And what of Japanese fashion's heavy hitters? In the early 1980s, the creations of Issey Miyake, Rei Kawakubo and Yohji Yamamoto put Japan on the map; and over 20 years later, they still dominate the scene. Younger, up-and-coming Japanese designers are conspicuous by their absence from the European fashion houses. Popular Japanese labels have responded by either trying to retain their underground feel, or by cultivating a 'bad boy' image, as with Takahashi's Jun's UnderCover (*see p179*).

Whatever the future holds for the Japanese, one thing is certain: on the day of reckoning they'll be perfectly dressed.

Boasting an interior created by the UK's Tomato (the design wing of the Underworld techno team), Laforet contains about a hundred small boutiques whose clothes are aimed at young wearers of garish, eccentric fashion. Various exhibitions and multimedia events are also held here.

Little Village

3-21-18 Jingumae, Shibuya-ku (3470 1936/ bb.bidders.co.jp/a-little-village/). Harajuku station, Takeshita exit or Meiji-Jingumae station, exit 5. **Open** 11am-8pm daily. **Credit** AmEx, DC, JCB, MC, V. **Map** p99.

Clubbers, take note. This shop sells original lines of cyber-freak and retro-cool clubwear, and is affiliated to Camden's legendary Cyberdog store (the Tokyo branch of which is just further down the same street).

New Funk inc

6-16-7-202 Jingumae, Shibuya-ku (5485 3033). Harajuku station, Omotesando exit or Meiji-Jingumae station, exit 4. **Open** 11am-8pm Mon-Fri; noon-8pm Sat, Sun. **Credit** AmEx, DC, JCB, MC, V. **Map** p99.

Set up by an enterprising New Zealander, New Funk inc sells dancewear and all kinds of club-related merchandise. It also releases its own 'True Trance' DJ- mix CD series.

non-sens

28-3 Sarugaku-cho, Shibuya-ku (3462 5430). Daikanyama station (Tokyu Toyoko line). **Open** 11am-8pm daily. **Credit** AmEx, DC, JCB, MC, V.

An elegant ladieswear store that stocks both domestic and imported designs.

Branch: 1-3-1 Jinnan Shibuya-ku (3462 6116).

Parco

15-1 Udagawa-cho, Shibuya-ku (3464 5111/ www.parco.co.jp). Shibuya JR station, Hachiko exit. **Open** 10am-8.30pm daily. **Credit** AmEx, DC, JCB, MC, V. **Map** p102.

The main branch of this mid-range clothing store is split into three buildings. Part 1 also houses a theatre on the top floor and an art bookshop. Part 3 contains an exhibition hall hosting innovative young artists. Another branch in Shibuya is the home of the concert hall Club Quattro (*see p230*).

Branches: 1-28-2 Minami-Ikebukuro, Toshima-ku (5391 8000); 1-5-1 Kichijoji-Honcho, Musashino-shi (0422 21 8111).

POV Beams

1F-2F 19-7 Sarugaku-cho, Shibuya-ku (5428 5253/ www.beams.co.jp). Daikanyama station (Tokyu Toyoko line). **Open** 11am-8pm daily. Closed third Wed of mth. **Credit** AmEx, DC, JCB, MC, V.

The stores in this cosy mini-mall have all been opened by the stylish fashion chain Beams. They stock the label's own streetwear, along with a range of affordable jewellery and the famous Yoshida Kaban brand of accessories.

Branches: throughout the city.

Screaming Mimi's

18-4 Daikanyama-cho, Shibuya-ku (3780 4415). Daikanyama station (Tokyu Toyoko line). **Open** noon-8pm daily. **Credit** AmEx, DC, JCB, MC, V.

A small store packed with original, secondhand and imported clothes and accessories for both sexes, ranging from the cute to the psychedelic. Also has a branch in New York.

Tsumori Chisato

11-1 Sarugaku-cho, Shibuya-ku (5728 3225). Daikanyama station (Tokyu Toyoko line). **Open** 11am-8pm daily. **Credit** AmEx, DC, JCB, MC, V.

Designer Tsumori Chisato once said, 'I never want to grow up.' This attitude is reflected in her bright, youthful designs and choice of fabrics, which have struck a chord with shoppers of all ages.

Branches: 3-7-3 Ebisu-Minami, Shibuya-ku (5720 7335); also outlets in many department stores.

UnderCover

5-3-18 Minami-Aoyama, Minato-Ku (3407 1232). Omotesando station, exit A5. **Open** 11am-8pm daily. **Credit** AmEx, DC, JCB, MC, V. **Map** p99.

Designer Takashi Jun has walked the thin line between the anarchy of punk and the security of the mainstream for over ten years; visit his stores to judge whether he's still the angry young man of Japanese fashion.

Branches: outlets in many department stores.

Uniqlo

6-10-8 Jingumae, Shibuya-ku (5468 7313/ www.uniqlo.co.jp). Harajuku station, Omotesando exit or Meiji-Jingumae station, exit 4. **Open** 11am-9pm daily. **Credit** AmEx, DC, JCB, MC, V. **Map** p99.

Residents of the UK will already be familiar with the name. This is the store that revolutionised retail and distribution practices in Japan with its cut-price but reasonably high-quality apparel. However, sales are currently nosediving as rivals catch on to the formula.

Branches: throughout the city.

YAB-YUM

3-6-24 Jingumae, Shibuya-ku (5775 2257/www.yab-yum.com). Harajuku station, Takeshita exit or Meiji-Jingumae station, exit 5. **Open** noon-8pm daily. **Credit** AmEx, DC, JCB, MC, V. **Map** p99.

The name means 'ying' and 'yang' in Nepalese, and it's the interplay between light and shade, hard and yielding, male and female that drives the label's creations. YAB-YUM was set up by Yoshida Mami and Brit Patrick Ryan.

Branches: outlets in many department stores.

Designer

Comme des Garçons

5-2-1 Minami-Aoyama, Minato-ku (3406 39519). Omotesando station, exit A5. **Open** 11am-8pm daily. **Credit** AmEx, DC, JCB, MC, V. **Map** p99.

LOUIS VUITTON

Comme des Garçons' Rei Kawakubo is one of the pioneers who put Japanese designers on the fashion map. The extraordinary exterior of the main store beckons the shopper into a maze of psychedelic prints, classically themed suits and smart formal wear. Tax exemption service available.
Branches: outlets at many department stores.

Issey Miyake
3-18-11 Minami-Aoyama, Minato-ku (3423 1407/ 1408/www.isseymiyake.com). Omotesando station, exit A4. **Open** 11am-8pm daily. **Credit** AmEx, DC, JCB, MC, V. **Map** p99.
The recent 'Matsuri' line shows that Issey Miyake and his design protégé Naoki Takizawa are still at the forefront of modern Japanese fashion. Tax exemption service available.
Branches: outlets at many department stores.

Yohji Yamamoto
5-3-6 Minami-Aoyama, Minato-ku, (3409 6006/ www.yohjiyamamoto.co.jp). Omotesando station, exit A5. **Open** 11am-8pm daily. **Credit** AmEx, DC, JCB, MC, V. **Map** p99.
It was largely due to Yamamoto Yohji's innovative fashion shows in the 1980s that the colour black became the cool, timeless choice of clothing that it is today. His Aoyama store reflects that in its muted, reflective ambience. The clothes, however, shine with originality. Tax exemption service available.
Branches: throughout the city; many outlets in department stores.

International fashion

Benetton
4-3-10 Jingumae, Shibuya-ku (5474 7155/www. benetton.co.jp). Harajuku station, Omotesando exit or Omotesando station, exit A2. **Open** 11am-8pm Mon-Thur, Sun; 11am-8.30pm Fri, Sat. **Credit** AmEx, DC, JCB, MC, V. **Map** p99.
Flagship store on this extremely fashionable Omotesando shopping street.
Branches: throughout the city.

fcuk
4-3-3 Jingumae, Shibuya-ku (5786 0556/www.french connection.com). Harajuku station, Omotesando exit or Omotesando station, exit A2. **Open** 11am-8pm daily. **Credit** AmEx, DC, JCB, MC, V. **Map** p99.
A chain that has become tremendously popular with Japanese clubbers.
Branches: 14-23 Daikanyama-cho, Shibuya-ku (5728 0555); **Printemps** Ginza 3-2-1 Ginza, Chuo-ku (3566 0555); **Venus Fort**, Palette Town 1 Aomi, Koto-ku (3570 0555).

Gap
4-30-3 Jingumae, Shibuya-ku (5414 2441/www. gap.co.jp). Harajuku station, Omotesando exit or Meiji-Jingumae station, exit 5. **Open** 10am-9pm daily. **Credit** AmEx, DC, JCB, MC, V. **Map** p99.
Gap has been a tremendous success in Japan, providing the template for Uniqlo (*see p179*).
Branches: throughout the city.

Louis Vuitton
5-7-5 Jingumae, Shibuya-ku (0120 07 1854/ www.vuitton.com). Omotesando station, exit A1. **Open** 10am-8pm daily. **Credit** AmEx, DC, JCB, MC, V. **Map** p99.
Come and see what all the fuss is about in this shrine to consumerism, Louis Vuitton's ultra-stylish flagship store in Omotesando.
Branches: throughout the city.

R Newbold
6-15-9 Jingumae, Shibuya-ku (5485 0560/www.r-newbold.com). Harajuku station, Omotesando exit or Meiji-Jingumae station, exit 4. **Open** 11am-8pm daily. **Credit** AmEx, DC, JCB, MC, V. **Map** p99.
This store is licensed to the UK's Paul Smith brand, but commissions quality menswear from local Japanese designers.
Branches: throughout the city.

Gift & craft shops

Aoi Art
4-22-11 Yoyogi, Shibuya-ku (3375 5553/www.aoi-art.ab.psiweb.com). Sangubashi station (Odakyu Line). **Open** 11am-7pm Tue-Sun. **Credit** AmEx, DC, JCB, MC, V.
The sword is an enduring image of Japan and its samurai warriors. Aoi Art is one of Tokyo's oldest buyers and sellers of swords and armour, with some pieces dating back to the Kamakura era. A certificate of authenticity is presented with each purchase, with the signature of the swordsmith. Don't try to carry it home as hand luggage.

Fuji Torii
6-1-10 Jingumae, Shibuya-ku (3400 2777). Harajuku station, Omotesando exit or Meiji-Jingumae station, exit 4. **Open** 11am 6pm Mon, Wed-Sun. Closed 3rd Mon of mth. **Credit** AmEx, DC, JCB, MC, V. **Map** p99.
Fuji Torii's wares cover almost all aspects of Japanese crafts. Pieces include screens, hanging scrolls, furniture, and bronze ornaments. All are handmade originals.

Hara Shobo
2-3 Kanda-Jinbocho, Chiyoda-ku (5212 7801/ www.harashobo.com). Jinbocho station, exit A6. **Open** 10am-6pm Tue-Sat. **Credit** AmEx, DC, JCB, MC, V. **Map** 62.
Hara Shobo sells all kinds of woodblock prints – both old and new. The company issues a catalogue, *Edo Geijitsu* (Edo Art), twice a year. The staff speak good English.

Hasebe-ya
1-7-7 Azabu-Juban, Minato-ku (3401 9998). Azabu-Juban station, exit 5. **Open** 10am-7pm daily. **Credit** AmEx, DC, JCB, MC, V.
Specialises in pottery (*yakimono*) and furniture (*kagu*) from both Japan and Korea. The furniture is not all antique, and there are occasional bargains to be found here.

Tea sets at the **Oriental Bazaar**, one of Tokyo's best-known gift shops. *See p183.*

Hasegawa Ginza
1-7-6 Ginza, Chuo-ku (5524 7576/0120 58 7676 (free)/www.kuyou.com). Ginza-Itchome station, exit 7 or Ginza station, exit 9. **Open** 11am-7pm daily. **Credit** AmEx, DC, JCB, MC, V. **Map** p57.
This fascinating store specialises in ceremonial Buddhist objects, such as incense, rosaries and the fantastically ornate altars. Prices may be steep, but it's an excellent place to browse, and the Hasegawa Museum on the sixth floor contains some extraordinary arts and crafts

Hayashi Kimono
International Arcade 2-1-1 Yurakucho, Chiyoda-ku (3501 4012). Yurakucho station, exit A1. **Open** 10am-7pm Mon-Sat; 10am-6pm Sun. **Credit** AmEx, DC, JCB, MC, V. **Map** p57.
Hayashi Kimono has the largest stock of secondhand kimono in Tokyo, and offers tax-free shopping and a mail order service. The shop is located inside the International Arcade opposite the Imperial Hotel; the arcade's entrance is under the train tracks that stretch between Yurakucho and Shinbashi. The arcade also contains a number of other stores that sell a wide range of high-quality Japanese souvenirs.

Ito-ya
2-7-15 Ginza, Chuo-ku (3561 8311/www.ito-ya.co.jp). Ginza station, exit A13. **Open** 10am-7pm Mon-Sat; 10.30am-7pm Sun. **Credit** AmEx, DC, JCB, MC, V. **Map** p57.
This narrow, very busy store specialises in Japanese paper. The main store (Ito-ya 1 Bldg) sells conventional stationery and calligraphic tools. The Annex (Ito-ya 3 Bldg), directly behind it and accessible by walking through the main store, has origami paper, traditional letter paper and ink, and many other paper-related crafts.
Branches: throughout the city.

Japan Sword
3-8-1 Toranomon, Minato-ku (3434 4321). Kamiyacho station, exit 3. **Open** 9.30am-6pm Mon-Fri; 9.30am-5pm Sat. **Credit** AmEx, DC, JCB, MC, V. **Map** p74.
The oldest and possibly most famous purveyor of samurai swords in Tokyo.

Japan Traditional Craft Centre
Metropolitan Plaza 1F-2F, 1-11-1 Nishi-Ikebukuro, Toshima-ku (5954 6066/www.kougei.or.jp). Ikebukuro JR station, Metropolitan exit or via Tobu department store. **Open** 11am-7pm daily. **Credit** AmEx, DC, JCB, MC, V. **Map** p69.
This organisation was founded with the aim of promoting awareness of Japan's traditional crafts. It frequently runs special exhibitions, kimono dressing lessons and 'craft clinics'. Wares on display and for sale include wood, metal and bamboo craftwork, textiles, stonework, household Buddhist altars and more. It closes at irregular times, so call ahead.

Kimono Arts Sunaga
2-1-8 Azabu-Juban, Minato-Ku (3457 0323). Azabu-Juban station, exit 4. **Open** 11am-8pm Mon, Wed-Sun. **Credit** AmEx, DC, JCB, MC, V.
Sells new and secondhand kimono, also crafts and ornaments made from recycled kimono material.

Lynn Matsuoka Studio
Aries Court 101, 2-9-10 Moto-Azabu, Minato-ku (3443 1443/www.traditions.jp/). Hiroo station, exits 1, 2. **Open** by appointment. **Credit** MC,V.
This studio houses the drawings, paintings and prints of American artist Lynn Matsuoka, who has been living and working in the esoteric worlds of sumo and *kabuki* for 28 years. In addition, the studio offers posters, postcards and portrait commissions. It also represents the work of furniture designer Keith Barker.

Akihabara

Step out of the station and you are surrounded by a neon frenzy of Chinese ideograms, crawling their way up and down the walls of the buildings. Young men and women with Chinese characters painted on their tunics chant incomprehensible slogans through megaphones. And in the back streets off the main drag, sullen-looking dealers slouch behind their folding tables, used laptops stacked upright in plastic baskets, cases of software spread on the table's black cloth. Welcome to Akihabara – Tokyo's Electric Town.

This messy scrum of over 550 electronics retailers huddled together has a long history. In the late 1920s, Akihabara became known as a district of radio shops, supplying parts for enthusiasts inspired by the new technology and eager to listen to the NHK, Japan's equivalent of the BBC. As the country rebuilt itself after World War II, the range of products increased, led by the government's single-minded drive to ensure that consumer spending became the engine of economic recovery. It was then that the area became known as Electric Town, and even today retailers regard it as the ultimate testing ground for new technologies before they enter national and world markets.

For foreign visitors, the main reason for coming to Electric Town is to buy tax-exempt goods for export. The duty free shops are clearly signposted outside, and the staff within generally speak good English. For some of the best of these shops, *see p175.* To qualify for tax-exempt goods you must be visiting Japan for less than six months and must buy something for over ¥10,000. Bring a copy of your passport with you.

Along with other retailers, those in Akihabara have been affected by Japan's interminable recession. The retail trade has coped by developing new markets in old goods. Ten years ago, for example, no one bought secondhand computers, but today a new breed of small vendors are doing a brisk trade.

Meanwhile pornography has thrust itself brazenly into the mainstream, with stores hoping to tempt Akihabara's overwhelmingly male browsers with adult DVDs and CD-ROMs. Another growth area has been surveillance. Tiny spy cameras, concealed microphones, infra-red scopes – they're all up for grabs in Electric Town.

For many visitors, Akihabara is the perfect bridge between Tokyo's hectic past and chaotic, data-fuelled future. There is even a shrine nearby, which does a brisk trade in 'IT charms', tiny embroidered pouches to be fastened to your screen. Welcome to 21st-century Akihabara, where the invisible guardian spirits of new technology watch over us users.

Meugaya

2-27-12 Asakusa, Taito-ku (3841 6440). Asakusa station, exits 1, 6. **Open** 10am-7pm Mon, Tue, Thur-Sun. **No credit cards. Map** p83.

This small store has been in business for over 200 years. It sells clothing and goods related to Japanese *matsuri*, such as *happi*-coats (short, colourful tunics), *tabi*, kimono, *hakuma* and much more.

Ohya Shobo

1-1 Kanda-Jinbocho, Chiyoda-ku (3291 0062/ www.ukiyoe.or.jp/ohya). Jinbocho station, exits A5, A7. **Open** 10am-6pm Mon-Sat. **No credit cards. Map** p62.

Boasts the world's largest stock of old illustrated books (some dating back 300 years), *ukiyo-e* and other prints, old maps, early *manga*, and any kind of Japanese graphic art.

Oriental Bazaar

5-9-13 Jingumae, Shibuya-ku (3400 3933). Harajuku station, Omotesando exit or Meiji-Jingumae station, exit 4. **Open** 10am-7pm Mon-Wed, Fri-Sun. **Credit** AmEx, DC, JCB, MC, V for purchases of ¥2,000 or more. **Map** p99.

Probably the best-known gift shop in Tokyo. Kimono, *yukata* and chinaware are in the basement, stationery and furniture are on the first floor, and antiques, screens, lamps and books on Japan are on the third. The staff speak fluent English.

Branch: Narita airport, No.1 Terminal Building 4F (0476 32 9333).

Sagemonoya

Yabane KK, 4-28-20-703 Yotsuya, Shinjuku-ku (3352 6286/www.netsuke.com). Shinjuku-Gyoenmae station, exit 2. **Open** 1.30-6pm Tue-Sat or by appointment. **Credit** AmEx, DC, JCB, MC, V. **Map** p109.

Sagemonoya specialises in *netsuke* and *sagemono* – the tiny, ornate accessories designed to hang from the belt of a kimono and to hold tobacco, medicines and other small objects. This shop holds hundreds of collectibles, and the staff can answer enquiries in English, French or German.

Tanogokoro

1-8-15 Ginza, Chuo-ku (3538 6555/www. tanagokoro.com). Ginza-Itchome station, exits 7, 9. **Open** 11am-8pm Mon-Fri; 11am-7pm Sat, Sun. **Credit** AmEx, DC, JCB, MC, V. **Map** p57.

Sells products, clothes, jewellery and ornaments made of *binchotan* – Japanese charcoal. Shoppers can indulge in the curative powers of *binchotan*'s delicate fragrance in a basement healing room.

Home & garden

Cherry Terrace

29-9 Sarugaku-cho, Shibuya-ku (3770 8728/www. cherryterrace.co.jp). Daikanyama station (Tokyu Toyoko Line). **Open** 11am-7pm Tue-Sun. **Credit** AmEx, DC, JCB, MC, V.

Part of Daikanyama's characteristically upmarket shopping complex Hillside Terrace, Cherry Terrace sells high-quality kitchenware and utensils, along with labour-saving devices such as coffee-makers. It hosts frequent cookery workshops in both Japanese and western cuisine.

Flying Saucer

2-15-10 Numabukuro, Nakano-ku (3387 5474/ www.flyingsaucer.co.jp). Numabukuro station (Seibu Shinjuku Line). **Open** 11am-7pm Mon, Tue, Thu-Sun. **Credit** AmEx, DC, JCB, MC, V purchases of ¥3,000 or more.

This curiously named shop describes itself as a 'home chef workshop', and sells everything you might need for your kitchen, and lots more you might not. It holds themed kitchen workshops twice a month for those so inclined.

Japanese gifts and souvenirs

In Japanese society, the concept of the *omiyage* is crucial. It means that whenever you travel, you return with some kind of gift for your family and friends, something representative of the area you have visited. So when it comes to your own souvenirs of Japan, something for the people back home (or indeed to keep for yourself), what should you choose?

There are three elements to consider: affordability, portability and originality. If money and transport headaches are of no consequence, then a stone lantern might be just right for your garden. But if you're looking for something smaller, lighter and cheaper, there's still a bewildering variety of gifts to choose from – and bear in mind that not all shops have staff who can explain what they are in English.

One vastly popular category of gifts is clothing, and the obvious choice will be the kimono, although prices can be steep. A more reasonable and easier-to-wear option is the *yukata,* a gown that can be worn by both sexes. The designs used on kimono and *yukata* are highly detailed and use seasonal motifs such as cherry blossom, plum blossom, maple and pine. For men, the *happi* coat is a short tunic used in festivals, and for both sexes there is the *tabi* (uniquely shaped socks) and the *tenugui* (towel worn around the head at festivals, often decorated with some form of heraldic symbol). Accessories include the *netsuke* – a small, carved pouch that is hung from the kimono.

If you are looking for something for the home, prints of *ukiyo-e* paintings by Hiroshige or Hokusai are very popular. Ceramics, *urushi-nuri* lacquerware and chopsticks also make good gifts: all vary according to their region of origin. Many kinds of ornamental goods that are suitable as souvenirs, such as lanterns and fans, are made utilising the unique properties of Japanese *washi* paper and its close cousin, origami paper.

Japanese dolls are another choice: there is a surprising variety of faces, figures and hairstyles available, from the stylised wooden *kokeshi* to the delicate Imperial Doll Family displayed in every Japanese house on Girls' Day (3 March).

If you're looking for something a little more unusual, however, *fuurin* (windchimes) make a charming addition to any home, and will remind you of the cooling, melodic sound heard in the heat of the Japanese summer. Japanese *hagoita* (battledores) are sold in November as good-luck charms for the New Year, and are painted with decorative scenes from *kabuki* plays.

Also, for the culturally minded, there are the numerous implements used in the tea ceremony, and the card games Hyakkunin-isshu Karuta and Hanafuda (each has a long and fascinating history).

Finally, food. One imperishable gift that is sure to arouse interest is *shichimi-togarashi,* the seven-flavoured seasoning that can be used to spice up so many dishes. And if you have a browse among the stores of Kappabashi Dori, you can even buy some tasty-looking sushi that will stay fresh forever – because it's finely crafted out of plastic.

Franc Franc

Shinjuku Southern Terrace, 2-2-1 Yoyogi, Shibuya-ku (5333 7701/www.francfranc.com Japanese only). Shinjuku JR station, south exit. **Open** 11am-10pm daily. **Credit** AmEx, DC, JCB, MC, V. **Map** p109.

A popular and reasonably priced interior goods shop, with a wide range of candles, incense, bathroom goods, lamps, and furniture. It also has its own brand of compilation CDs, catering to the massive market for bossa nova music.

Branches: throughout the city.

It's Demo

1-9-18 Jingumae, Shibuya-ku (5414 0738). Harajuku station, Omotesando exit or Meiji-Jingumae station, exit 5. **Open** 11am-10pm daily. **Credit** AmEx, DC, JCB, MC, V. **Map** p99.

The name is the English-style pronunciation of the Japanese *itsudemo*, meaning 'whenever'. In addition to household goods, it sells cards, cosmetics, a small selection of ladieswear and 'loungecore' CDs.

Branches: throughout the city.

Mujirushi Ryohin

3-8-3 Marunouchi, Chiyoda-ku (5208 8241/www.muji.co.jp). Yurakucho JR station, Kyobashi exit or Yurakucho subway station, exit A9. **Open** 10am-9pm daily. **Credit** AmEx, DC, JCB, MC, V. **Map** p57.

The shop better known as Muji – the original no-brand designer brand. This is the biggest Tokyo outlet of the all-purpose one-stop store that went on to conquer London and Paris.

Branches: throughout the city.

Shala

Miyazawa Bldg 1, 2F, 2-10-19 Jiyugaoka, Meguro-ku (5726 2326/www.shala-japan.com). Jiyugaoka station (Tokyu Toyoko Line), central exit. **Open** 11am-8pm. **Credit** AmEx, DC, JCB, MC, V.

Shala has a nice line in Japanese and imported ceramics, as well as glassware, lamps and candles. It also sells its own incense in fragrances such as lotus, bamboo and *yuzu*.

Sputnik Pad

1F-3F, 5-46-14 Jingumae, Shibuya-ku (6418 1330/www.gosputnik.com). Omotesando station, exit B2. **Open** 11am-7pm daily. **Credit** AmEx, DC, JCB, MC, V. **Map** p99.

Sputnik Pad is the brainchild of Teruo Kurosaki, who has been called the 'Terence Conran of Japan'. Its furniture boasts designers from Scandinavia and Italy as well as Japan, and its innovative, postmodern housewares are well worth a look.

Three Minutes Happiness

3-5 Udagawa-cho, Shibuya-ku (5459 1851). Shibuya JR station, Hachiko exit. **Open** 11am-9pm daily. **Credit** AmEx, DC, JCB, MC, V. **Map** p102.

Think of this as a high-class 100-yen shop, selling an eclectic mix of original household goods, most costing less than ¥1,000. This lively store is owned by the Comme Ça fashion chain, and there is even a Comme Ça Deli selling snacks in the shop's front.

Toko-Toko

20-23 Daikanyama, Shibuya-ku (5489 0105). Daikanyama station (Tokyu Toyoko Line). **Open** 11am-7pm daily. Closed first, third Mon of mth. **Credit** AmEx, DC, JCB, MC, V.

A small, welcoming store offering furniture made in Japan and a variety of Pacific countries.

Tokyu Hands

12-18 Udagawa-cho, Shibuya-ku (5489 5111/www.tokyu-hands.co.jp). Shibuya JR station, Hachiko exit. **Open** 10am-8pm daily. **Credit** AmEx, DC, JCB, MC, V. **Map** p102.

This is the largest hardware store in Tokyo. Here you'll find all those things you never realised you needed. The basement is particularly worth noting: moving away from the hardware theme, it sells novelty goods, fancy dress costumes and games, and is a perfect introduction to the Japanese sense of humour. Be warned, however, that the layout of the Shibuya main store can be very confusing.

Branches: Takashimaya Times Square, 5-24-2 Sendagaya, Shibuya-ku (5361 3111); 1-28-10 Higashi-Ikebukuro, Toshima-ku (3980 6111).

Imported food & other goods

If you're staying in Japan for more than a few weeks, you may start to miss the tastes and comforts of home. The stores below cater to expatriates, and to Japanese people looking for something a bit different.

Chikyu-Jin Club

1-5-29 Azabu-Juban, Minato-ku (5771 6145) Azabu-Juban station, exit 4, 7. **Open** 10am-8pm daily. **Credit** AmEx, DC, JCB, MC, V.

This warm, homely store imports organic foods, cosmetics and health-related products. Discount service for card members.

Branch: 2-15-8 Jiyugaoka, Meguro-ku (3725 2710).

Kinokuniya International

3-11-7 Kita-Aoyama, Minato-ku (3409 1231/www.e-kinokuniya.com). Omotesando station, exit B2. **Open** 9.30am-8pm daily. **Credit** AmEx, DC, JCB, MC, V. **Map** p99.

A wide range of international foods is on offer at Kinokuniya, at vastly inflated prices, as well as English-language newspapers and magazines. This is the best known, and most prestigious, of Tokyo's foreign food specialists.

Branches: throughout the city.

Meidi-ya

2-6-7 Ginza, Chuo-ku, Tokyo (3563 0221/www.meidi-ya.co.jp). Ginza-Itchome station, exit 8. **Open** 10am-9pm Mon-Sat, 10am-8pm Sun. **Credit** AmEx, DC, JCB, MC, V. **Map** p57.

Meidi-ya has an attractive array of imported foods, and an impressive wine cellar. It also has regular themed fairs at discount prices.

Branches: 5-6-6 Hiroo, Shibuya-ku (3444 6221); 7-15-14 Roppongi, Minato-ku (3401 8511).

Plastic food is a popular novelty gift.

National Azabu

4-5-2 Minami-Azabu, Minato-ku (3442 3181). Hiroo station, exit 1. **Open** 9.30am-8pm daily. **Credit** AmEx, DC, JCB, MC, V.

National Azabu has a long history of serving the international community, and is one of very few places in Tokyo that sells English-style sausages, making it worth the trip in its own right. Like Kinokuniya, it's far from cheap. There's also a book store and stationery shop on the second floor.

Sanmi Discount Store

4-8-12 Ginza, Chuo-ku (3561 9891). Ginza station, exit A14. **Open** 9am-8pm Mon-Fri; 10am-7pm Sat, Sun. **No credit cards. Map** p57.

Small, but extremely well-stocked, and close to the heart of the Ginza shopping district.

Shinanoya

1-12-9 Kabuki-cho, Shinjuku-ku (3204 2365/www.shinanoya.co.jp/home/main.html). Shinjuku JR station, east exit. **Open** 11-4am Mon-Sat; 11am-9pm Sun. **Credit** MC, V. **Map** p109.

This is a scotch whisky lover's paradise. Hundreds of single malts line the walls, at prices cheaper than in the UK. Snap up a Glen Grant single malt unavailable in the UK for just ¥1,500, and some Highland Spring mineral water to go with it. There's also a small selection of foreign foods and snacks, and some imported beers.

Branches: Daida Wine House 1-42-1 Daida, Setagaya-ku (3412 2418); 8-6-22 Ginza, Chuo-ku (3571 3315).

Yamaya

3-2-7 Nishi-Shinjuku, Shinjuku-ku (3342 0601/www.yamaya.co.jp/). Shinjuku JR station, south exit. **Open** 10am-10pm daily. **Credit** AmEx, DC, JCB, MC, V. **Map** p109.

A medium-sized foreign food and booze specialist with one unique feature for Tokyo: it's cheap. Yamaya has a vast selection of imported wines priced from a budget-beating ¥280 to a wallet-stretching ¥10,000 per bottle, along with cheap cheeses and snack foods. Delivery of large orders can be arranged for an extra ¥500 within the 23 wards of central Tokyo.

Branches: 1-43-6 Higashi-Ikebukuro, Toshima-ku (3980 2977); 1-6-8 Shibuya, Shibuya-ku (3409 3258); 2-14-33 Akasaka, Minato-ku (3583 5657).

Jewellery

4 degrees C

2-6-4 Ginza, Chuo-ku (3538 2124/www.fdcp.co.jp). Ginza-Itchome station, exit 8. **Open** 10am-8pm daily. **Credit** AmEx, DC, JCB, MC, V. **Map** p57.

The name of this upmarket store is pronounced 'yon-do-shi'. It has a stylish, modern range of gold, silver and platinum jewellery made by Japanese designers, as well as its own brand of watches, perfume, apparel and accessories.

Branches: throughout the city; many outlets in department stores.

Ginza Diamond Shiraishi

2-6-3 Ginza, Chuo-ku (3567 5751/www.bridal diamond.co.jp). Ginza station, exit A13. **Open** 11.30am-8pm Mon, Wed-Sun. **Credit** AmEx, DC, JCB, MC, V. **Map** p57.

A striking shopfront houses an impressive selection of rings and necklaces produced by Japanese designers. Its most popular sellers are the elegant Myuthos and Arpia brand of rings.

Mikimoto

4-5-5, Ginza, Chuo-ku (3535 4611/www.mikimoto.com). Ginza station, exit A9. **Open** 11am-7pm daily. **Credit** AmEx, DC, JCB, MC, V. **Map** p57.

The story of how the first cultured pearls in the world were developed in Japan is the story of Kokichi Mikimoto, the founder of this world-famous store. This flagship branch has a magnificent range of pearl jewellery on display, and there's a museum upstairs.

Branches: Imperial Hotel Arcade, 1-1-1 Uchisaiwaicho, Chiyoda-ku (3591 5001).

Tasaki Shinju

5-7-5 Ginza, Chuo-ku (3289 1111/www.tasaki.co.jp). Ginza station, exit A2. **Open** 10.30am-7.30pm daily. **Credit** AmEx, DC, JCB, MC, V. **Map** p57.

The flagship Ginza store is known (with good reason) as the Jewellery Tower. Each floor of this huge building is devoted to a particular jewellery theme; the museum on the fifth floor is particularly worth a look.

Branches: throughout the city.

Wako

4-5-11 Ginza, Chuo-ku (3562 2111/www.wako.co.jp). Ginza station, exit A9, A10, B1. **Open** 10.30am-6pm Mon-Sat. **Credit** AmEx, DC, JCB, MC, V. **Map** p57.

The building's grand exterior is matched only by the hushed ambience of the interior. As well as fine jewellery, it also sells designer apparel and accessories.

Novelties & toys

Astro Mike

5-25-2 Jingumae, Shibuya-ku (3499 2588/www.mike-toys.com/index.html). Harajuku station, Omotesando exit or Meiji-Jingumae station, exit 4. **Open** 11am-8pm daily. **Credit** AmEx, DC, JCB, MC, V. **Map** p99.

Japanese and western toys and action figures dating from the 1960s to the present are displayed on the overflowing shelves.

COMIX by Manga no Mori

12-10 Udagawa-cho, Shibuya-ku (5489 0257/www.thecomix.com). Shibuya JR station, Hachiko exit. **Open** noon-9pm Mon-Fri; 11am-9pm Sat, Sun. **No credit cards. Map** p102.

Most branches of Manga no Mori specialise in Japanese comics, or *manga*, but this recently renovated store's stock in trade is American comic books, carrying the latest, imported titles from Marvel, DC and others.

Branches (Manga no Mori): 6-16-16 Ueno, Taito-ku (3833 3411); 3-10-12 Takada, Toshima-ku (5292 7748); 1-28-1 Higashi-Ikebukuro, Toshima-ku (5396 1245).

Opening times

Tokyo may not be the city that never sleeps, but it's certainly on its way to raging insomnia. With people working longer shifts and going home later, stores are staying open longer to catch those bleary-eyed commuters and thereby survive the recession. In fact, some stores are not closing at all; Japan's 24-hour convenience stores are legendary for the variety of goods and services they offer, but they're not alone anymore. Boutiques, beauty salons, novelty stores, bowling alleys and golf driving ranges are going 24/7 in some places.

The regular opening hours of shops in general and department stores in particular are becoming more and more flexible. Opening at 10am or sometimes 11am, most retail outlets stay open until 8pm, with some exceptions; popular boutiques close at 9pm, and centrally located stores close at 10pm.

Sunday is a normal shopping day in Japan, as it has no religious significance. That means that large stores are usually very crowded, becoming almost unbearable during the summer sales and the New Year holiday. While department stores are open seven days a week, they do have the occasional closed day; look for large notices inside the shops announcing whether they are closed on one day of that month.

There is plenty of festive tack on display during the Christmas season. However, Christmas is not a holiday in Japan; 25 December is a normal working day with ordinary office hours. What's more, the Christmas decorations come down on the stroke of midnight, to make space for the more traditional New Year celebrations – a practice that can be bewildering and disconcerting for foreign visitors.

As far as the national holidays (*see p278* **Directory**) are concerned, most stores (except the traditional, craft-orientated shops) will be open, but if you have a specific place in mind, it's worth calling before you go, to make sure.

Don Quixote

1-16-5 Kabuki-cho, Shinjuku-ku (5291 9211/www.donki.com). Shinjuku JR station, east exit. **Open** 24hrs daily. **No credit cards. Map** p109.

Roughly the same concept as Japan's 100-yen stores (*see p189* **Bargain hunting**), but the interior and some of the products could have been designed by Salvador Dalí with a hangover. Snacks, liquor, toys, 'character goods', kitchen utensils and designer brands, all at bargain prices.

Branches: throughout the city.

Full Dog

2F Daikanyama Roob-1 Bldg, 28-13 Sarugaku-cho, Shibuya-ku (3770 8081/www.fulldog.jp). Daikanyama station (Tokyu Toyoko Line). **Open** 11.30am-8.30pm daily. **Credit** AmEx, DC, JCB, MC, V.

How many dog-related novelty items can you cram into one shop? The answer is here, in the swanky Daikanyama district.

Hachiko Shop

1F South Bldg, Tokyu Department Toyoko branch, 2-24-1 Shibuya, Shibuya-ku (3477 3111). Connected to Shibuya station. **Open** 10am-9pm daily. **Credit** AmEx, DC, JCB, MC, V. **Map** p102.

This shop is inside Tokyu department store, within Shibuya station, and sells products dedicated to the faithful dog Hachiko, which gave the nearby famous meeting area its name.

Nakanukiya (aka Two Tops)

1-11-3 Jinnan, Shibuya-ku (5459 2173/www.nakanukiya.com). Shibuya JR station, Hachiko exit. **Open** 10am-11pm daily. **Credit** AmEx, DC, JCB, MC, V. **Map** p102.

This store opposite Tower Records has to be seen to be believed. Cut-rate designer brands are sold on the first two floors, but the ambience gets weirder and stranger the further up you go, until you are facing replica guns, action figures, sex toys and ethnic ornaments all crammed into the same few square metres.

Pokemon Centre

3-2-5 Nihonbashi, Chuo-ku (5200 0707/www.pokemoncenter-online.com). Nihonbashi station, exit B3. **Open** 10am-7pm daily. **Credit** AmEx, DC, JCB, V. **Map** p62.

Pocket Monster may have lost ground to Yugi-Oh and a variety of other games, but Pikachu's furry yellow paw still has an iron grip on Japanese pop culture. Come and see the monster-masters in their central Tokyo stronghold.

Pook et Koop

6-15-9 Jingumae, Shibuya-ku (5466 8504/www.pook.co.jp). Harajuku station, Omotesando exit or Meiji-Jingumae station, exit 4. **Open** 11.30am-8pm daily. **No credit cards. Map** p99.

A tiny shop crammed with all kinds of cult comic, TV and film paraphernalia, from Japan, the US, the UK and all points between.

ranKing ranQueen

2F West Bldg, Tokyu Department Toyoko branch, 2-24-1 Shibuya, Shibuya-ku (3770 5480/www.ranking-ranqueen.net). Inside Shibuya JR station. **Open** 10am-11.30pm daily. **Credit** AmEx, DC, JCB, MC, V. **Map** p102.

In recent years, the Japanese have become obsessed with making lists and charts of what's popular, which they call 'rankings' (hence the puns in this shop's name, which, in case you were wondering, is pronounced 'ranking ranking'). Inside this shop, you'll find the top ten products for CDs, cosmetics, dieting aids, magazines and so on. It's an intriguing way of gaining an insight into the mind of the Japanese consumer.

Branches: Shinjuku station, east exit (5919 1263); Jiyuugaoka station (Tokyu Toyoko Line), central exit (3718 8890).

Tora no Ana

B1-4F, 4-3-1 Soto-Kanda, Chiyoda-ku (5294 0123/www.toranoana.co.jp/). Akihabara JR station, Electric Town exit. **Open** 11am-9pm Mon-Thur; 10am-9pm Fri-Sun. **Credit** AmEx, DC, JCB, MC, V.

This flagship store of the Tora no Ana *manga* chain, in Akihabara, has a Godzilla-size cartoon character painted on the outside wall. As well as the nation's best-selling new comics, the shop also sells a selection of *dojinsha*, fanzines created by devoted *manga* amateurs.

Branches: 1-18-1 Nishi-Shinjuku, Shinjuku-ku (5908 1681); 1-13-4 Higashi-Ikebukuro, Toshima-ku (5957 7138); Akihabara Part 2, Kimura Bldg 2-4F, 1-9-8 Soto-Kanda, Chiyoda-ku (5256 2055); Akihabara Part 3, Kyoeki Soto Kanda Bldg 4-6F, 4-4-2 Soto-Kanda, Chiyoda-ku (3526 7211).

Records & CDs

Cisco

11-1 Udagawa-cho, Shibuya-ku (3462 0366/www.cisco-records.co.jp). Shibuya JR station, Hachiko exit. **Open** 11am-9pm daily. **Credit** AmEx, DC, JCB, MC, V. **Map** p102.

Cisco is at the cutting edge of dance music. Its Shibuya branch is actually five buildings close to each other, divided according to sub-genre of techno. This is the place to see well-known DJs holding earnest discussions with the shop owners across the turntables.

Branches: Studio Alta 6F, 3-24-3 Shinjuku, Shinjuku-ku (3341 7495).

Dance Music Record

36-2 Udagawa-cho, Shibuya-ku (3477 1556/www.dmr.co.jp). Shibuya JR station, Hachiko exit. **Open** noon-10pm daily. **Credit** AmEx, DC, JCB, MC, V. **Map** p102.

'Dance Music Record' is the name of the shop and, indeed, dance music records is what it sells. The first floor is a wide, open space with a comprehensive collection of the latest domestic and international vinyl releases. All genres of house, as well as jazz and loungecore, are catered for.

Bargain hunting

They don't call it the 'golden recession' for nothing. Japan has been the first G7 nation to suffer from major deflation, and this has meant a lowering of prices across the board. This is by no means a good thing in the long term, but it has meant stores and companies resorting to desperate means to attract consumers. In Tokyo, it has meant that it's easier than ever before to find what you want at bargain prices.

In the high streets, new specialist stores have sprung up offering items such as suits, shoes and eyeglasses with 10, 20 or 30 per cent slashed off normal retail prices. Department store food halls hold off-season sales of certain food items. Tokyo's trendiest areas are full of tiny stores stocked with secondhand CDs, bootlegs and rarities. Just a good browse around Shinjuku, Shibuya, Shimo-Kitazawa or Ochanomizu should be quite educational.

It's even possible to find discounted, authentic brand-name goods, thanks to legal loopholes and the appearance of new 'designer pawn shops'. Stores such as Two Tops (*see p188*), opposite Tower Records in Shibuya, are packed everyday with Japanese shoppers snapping up whatever designer goods they can afford, while it lasts.

Hundred yen shops exist on most local shopping streets, with goods such as toys, stationery and household goods being sold at the aforementioned price. Eighty-eight yen shops have recently sprung up, based in certain supermarkets.

Secondhand shops have mushroomed – just look for the word 'recycle' (which means secondhand in Japanese). There are also the *kinken* shops, which sell discounted tickets for *shinkansen* (bullet train), cinemas and so on. Be prepared for the fact that signs on their shop fronts and interiors are entirely in Japanese script, which can make them intimidating places. Two well-known *kinken* shops are **Ticket Showa** (Shinbashi station, 3580 7175) and **Go Go Ticket** (near Tokyu Hands, Shibuya, 3463 3000).

Department stores have sales at set times of year. The New Year sales start on 3 January, and continue for about a week. The summer sales start in either July or August, and there are sometimes special one-off sales, for example if a baseball team sponsored by the store wins the Japan series. One gimmick that's caught on with all the department stores is the *fukubukuro* or lucky bag. They sell at various prices, and contain a lucky dip of designer accessories worth more than the price of the bag.

For cheap reads, browse among the secondhand bookshops of **Yasukuni-Dori** near Jinbocho station. An area of sports discount stores is just up the road, too, towards Ochanomizu station.

For low-priced traditional Japanese memorabilia, wander down one of the streets lined with antique shops, such as **Nishi-Ogikubo**, **Koto-Dori** in Aoyama, or **Nakamise-Dori** in Asakusa. There's a lot of junk, but you may find some surprises if you're prepared to search carefully.

Homesick foreigners appreciate the **Foreign Buyers Club** (www.fbcusa.com), which imports food and many other goods at discount prices. The expatriate community in Tokyo is in a constant state of flux, which means there are plenty of opportunities to acquire bargains. People advertise things they want to leave behind through '*sayonara* sales' – classified ads – in magazines such as *Tokyo Notice Board* and *Metropolis*.

Disk Union

3-31-4 Shinjuku, Shinjuku-ku (3352 2691/www.diskunion.co.jp/top.html). Shinjuku JR station, east or central exit. **Open** 11am-9pm Mon-Sat; 11am-8pm Sun. **Credit** AmEx, DC, JCB, MC, V. **Map** p109.

Disk Union deals mainly in used CDs and vinyl, and has thousands of items for sale in its racks. The Shinjuku main store is a tall, narrow building where each floor is devoted to a different genre, including world music, soundtracks and electronica. There are separate branches nearby that specialise in dance music, jazz, and that much-maligned genre, progressive rock.

Branches: throughout the city.

High Line Records

Kitazawa Bldg B1F, 2-14-16 Kitazawa, Setagaya-ku (5432 7411/www.e-highline.net). Shimo-Kitazawa station (Odakyu/Keio Inokashira lines), south exit. **Open** 11.30am-8pm daily. **Credit** AmEx, DC, JCB, MC, V.

This is a great little store specialising in Japanese independent and small labels in rock (pop, hard rock, punk and so on) along with some dance. Over a dozen listening stations are stocked with the latest releases. Also sells vinyl, cassettes, videos and T-shirts.

HMV

24-1 Udagawa-cho, Shibuya-ku (5458 3411/www.hmv.co.jp). Shibuya JR station, Hachiko exit. **Open** 10am-midnight daily. **Credit** AmEx, DC, JCB, MC, V. **Map** p102.

A crowded, hectic branch of one of the world's most celebrated record stores. It holds regular special events, with nationally and internationally renowned musicians appearing in-store.

Branches: throughout the city.

Like an Edison

7-15-14 Nishi-Shinjuku, Shinjuku-ku (3369 3119). Shinjuku JR station, west exit. **Open** 11am-8pm daily. **Credit** AmEx, DC, JCB, MC, V. **Map** p109.

This obscure little shop is a stronghold of 'Visual-Kei' bands, the sound that inspired the gothic Lolitas that haunt Harajuku and Yoyogi Park. An intriguing look into the heart of one of the most puzzling developments in Japanese youth culture.

Recofan

Shibuya BEAM 4F, 31-2 Udagawa-cho, Shibuyaku (3463 0090/www.recofan.co.jp). Shibuya JR station, Hachiko exit. **Open** 11.30am-9pm daily. **Credit** AmEx, DC, JCB, MC, V. **Map** p102.

Recofan has a policy of selling new releases at bargain rates – in some cases, half the retail price. Each branch also has a large selection of used CDs of all genres. Regular shoppers receive a loyalty card that gives even bigger discounts.

Branches: throughout the city.

Shame Records

7-16-15 Nishi-Shinjuku, Shinjuku-ku (5330 3970). Shinjuku JR station, west exit. **Open** 2-10pm daily. **No credit cards**. **Map** p109.

Crates upon crates of funk, jazz, Latin and rare groove vinyl from the 1960s and 1970s, all just waiting to be sampled.

Tower Records

1-22-14 Jinnan, Shibuya-ku (3496 3661/www.towerrecords.co.jp). Shibuya JR station, Hachiko exit. **Open** 10am-11pm daily. **Credit** AmEx, DC, JCB, MC, V. **Map** p102.

Perhaps the expatriate's favourite Tokyo music store. Under the leadership of CEO Keith Cahoon, Tower has excelled in its policy of promoting Japanese independent bands and labels as well as new releases from around the world. In addition, the seventh floor holds one of Tokyo's best bookshops, stocking magazines and newspapers that are unavailable elsewhere.

Branches: Flags Bldg 7-10F, 3-37-1 Shinjuku, Shinjuku-ku (5360 7811); Ikebukuro P'Parco 5-6F, 1-50-35 Higashi-Ikebukuro, Toshima-ku (3983 2010).

Vinyl

7-4-7 Nishi-Shinjuku, Shinjuku-ku (3365 0910/www.vinyljapan.com). Shinjuku JR station, west exit. **Open** noon-9pm daily. **Credit** AmEx, DC, JCB, MC, V for purchases over ¥5,000. **Map** p109.

The sheer range of this shop's stock beggars the imagination. Rare 1960s and 1970s sounds, progressive rock, punk, mod, hip hop, Japanese indies: it's all here on CD and, of course, vinyl.

Branches: **Shop Two** 7-5-5 Nishi-Shinjuku, Shinjuku-ku (5330 9141); **Shop Three** 7-5-14 Nishi-Shinjuku, Shinjuku-ku (3371 5961).

Virgin Megastore

3-1-13 Shinjuku, Shinjuku-ku (3353 0056/www.virginmegastore.co.jp). Shinjuku-Sanchome station, exit C1. **Open** 10am-11pm daily. **Credit** AmEx, DC, JCB, MC, V. **Map** p109.

As you would expect, Virgin has a comprehensive selection of CDs. The Shinjuku main store also sells English-language magazines and has an internet café, where access is free with a drink.

Branch: B1F, Marui City Ikebukuro, 3-28-13 Nishi-Ikebukuro, Toshima-ku (5952 5600).

Services

Beauty salons

For cosmetics shops, *see p174.*

Boudoir

Mansion Kawai 101, 2-25-3 Jingumae, Shibuya-ku (3478 5898/www.boudoirtokyo.com). Harajuku station, Takeshita exit or Meiji-Jingumae station, exit 5. **Open** 10am-9pm Mon-Fri; 10am-8pm Sat; 10am-6pm Sun. **Credit** AmEx, DC, JCB, MC, V. **Map** p99.

Mostly non-Japanese beauticians offer a full range of beauty and body treatments in this salon located in one of the most stylish areas of the city. Services available include facials, waxing, massage and relaxation therapy.

Don Quixote: anything and everything at knock-down prices, round the clock. *See p188.*

C'bon Biyu Body Salon

7-18-12 Roppongi, Minato-ku (3404 7535/www.cbon.co.jp/home/home.html). Roppongi station, exit 2. **Open** 11am-8.30pm Mon-Fri; 11am-6.30pm Sat, Sun. **Credit** AmEx, DC, JCB, MC, V. **Map** p74.

Offers a range of skincare services including oil massages, body packs and anti-ageing treatments, along with saunas and jacuzzis.

Nail Bee

Minochi Bldg 4F, 3-11-8 Roppongi Minato-ku (3470 9665/www.nailbee.com). Roppongi station, exit 5. **Open** 12.30pm-8pm daily. **Credit** AmEx, DC, JCB, MC, V. **Map** p74.

The Nail Bee salon offers sculptured nails, French manicures and waxing.

Hairdressers

Peekaboo EXT

4-3-15 Jingumae, Shibuya-ku (5411 0848/www.peek-a-boo.co.jp/). Omotesando station, exit A2. **Open** 10am-10pm (book by 8pm) Tue-Fri; 10am-9pm (book by 7pm) Sat; 10am-7.30pm (book by 5.30pm) Sun. **Credit** AmEx, DC, JCB, MC, V. **Map** p99.

Famous throughout Japan, this stylish chain of unisex salons features internationally trained stylists, many of whom speak English. All forms of hair treatment available.

Branches: throughout the city.

Sinden

3-42-12 Jingumae, Shibuya-ku (3405 4409/www.sinden.com). Gaienmae station, exit 3. **Open** 10am-7.30pm daily. **Credit** AmEx, DC, JCB, MC, V. **Map** p99.

Sinden has mostly non-Japanese staff with a wide range of expertise. Colouring, perming and styling are offered for men and women.

Who-Ga

1F Akasaka Kyo Bldg, 2-16-13 Akasaka, Minato-ku (5570 1773/www.who-ga-newyork.com). Akasaka station, exits 5A, 5B. **Open** 11am-9pm Mon, Wed-Fri; 10am-7pm Sat, Sun. **Credit** AmEx, DC, JCB, MC, V.

The bilingual staff here trained in Who-Ga's New York salon. Discounts of up to 25% are available to female customers.

Opticians

Recent years have seen an explosion of shops specialising in stylish eyewear at discount prices in Japan. This development is partly due to the deflationary economy, and partly to a self-conscious nation always hungry for a new trend. Below is a selection of the best of these new-wave opticians. Although the styles of the frames vary considerably, the similarity of their prices reflects the competitive nature of the specs business. All these opticians employ the latest technology for their speedy, convenient, and often free, eye tests.

Eye Desk

2-19-15 Shibuya, Shibuya-ku (5468 9667). Shibuya station, Miyamasuzaka (east) exit, exit 12. **Open** 11am-9pm Mon-Sat; 11am-7pm Sun. **Credit** AmEx, DC, JCB, MC, V. **Map** p102.

Fxg (Face By Glasses)

2-35-14 Kitazawa, Setagaya-ku (5790 8027/www.fxg.co.jp). Shimo-Kitazawa station (Odakyu/Keio Inokashira lines), north exit. **Open** *Jan-June, Aug-Nov* 11am-8pm Mon, Tue, Thur-Sun. *July, Dec* 11am-8pm daily. **Credit** AmEx, DC, JCB, MC,

Vending machines

One thing guaranteed to bewilder the visitor upon arrival in Japan is the sheer number of vending machines (known in Japanese as *jidohanbaiki*). On every street corner, down every small alleyway, they encrust the buildings at ground level like a host of white metallic barnacles.

In the constantly harassed world of the Japanese commuter, nothing tops the vending machine for speed and convenience; even in the local convenience store, you can't get away from the lines of people waiting at the till, and that time-consuming courteous exchange with the person who serves you. With the *jidohanbaiki*, however, instant gratification is just a couple of coins away.

The first wave of *jidohanbaiki* hit the city during the Tokyo Olympics in 1964, when huge numbers of people descended on an already crowded and understaffed city. Over the years since then, the variety of goods sold has increased dramatically, as has the number of vending machines, which is currently well over six million.

Although there is a vast and frequently bizarre range of goods sold through *jidohanbaiki*, over half of them sell drinks, both soft and alcoholic. These include the 'stamina drinks' targeted at Japan's fatigued workforce and containing ingredients such as vitamins, minerals, ginseng, viper tincture, and – of course – caffeine.

Due to concern over underage drinking and smoking, beer (and cigarette) machines shut down automatically at 11pm each day. And some machines have been introduced that require the insertion of an ID such as a driver's licence before alcoholic drink can be dispensed. But as these machines are near 24-hour convenience stores, where staff generally ask no questions about age, the ID-checking machines are regarded as a bit of a joke.

All machines take coins and ¥1,000 notes, but some do not accept 500 yen coins, thanks to a run of fake coin scams across the country. One other gripe – and a major one at that – is that in the summer, for some incomprehensible reason, the majority of these machines stop selling hot coffee. Coffee in a can is certainly a novelty, but cold coffee in a can is not to be recommended.

Hatch

2-5-8 Dogenzaka, Shibuya-ku (5784 3888/www.e-hatch.jp). Shibuya JR station, Hachiko exit. **Open** 11am-8pm daily. **Credit** AmEx, DC, JCB, MC, V. **Map** p102.

Hatch is so named because it sounds like *hachi*, which means 'eight' in Japanese – and the figure-of-eight symbol looks like a pair of glasses.

Branches: 1-20-16 Jinnan, Shibuya-ku (5784 4788); 1-16-2 Jingumae, Shibuya-ku (5772 8788).

Opt Label

1-21-1 Jinnan, Shibuya-ku (5458 9081/www.opt-label.com). Shibuya JR station, Hachiko exit. **Open** 11am-8pm daily. **Credit** AmEx, DC, JCB, MC, V. **Map** p102.

Zoff

4F Mark City, 1-12-1 Dogenzaka, Shibuya-ku (5428 3961). Connected directly to Shibuya station. **Open** 10am-9pm daily. **Credit** AmEx, DC, JCB, MC, V. **Map** p102.

Branches: 6-35-3 Jingumae, Shibuya-ku (5766 3501); 2-23-13 Kitazawa, Setagaya-ku (3466 1225); Metropolitan 5F, 1-11-1 Nishi-Ikebukuro, Toshima-ku (5911 4677).

Pharmacies

The following pharmacies all have English-speaking staff (except Roppongi Pharmacy, which does, however, have a late-night service, until 2am daily). Under Japanese law, western medicines are not generally available, but pharmacy staff will be prepared to try to find the best Japanese remedy for any complaint. For emergency medical information, *see p278* **Directory**.

American Pharmacy

Marunouchi Bldg B1F, 2-4-1 Marunouchi, Chiyoda-ku (5220 7716/www.tomods.jp/). Tokyo JR station, Shin Marubiru exit or south exit. **Open** 8am-9pm Mon-Fri; 10am-9pm Sat; 10am-8pm Sun. **Credit** AmEx, DC, JCB, MC, V. **Map** p62.

American Pharmacy

Hibiya Park Bldg 1F, 1-8-1 Yurakucho, Chiyoda-ku (3271 4034). Hibiya station, exits A6, A7. **Open** 9.30am-8pm Mon-Sat; 10am-6pm Sun & bank holidays. **Map** p57.

Koyasu Drug Store Hotel Okura

Hotel Okura Main Bldg B1F, 2-10-4 Toranomon, Minato-ku (3583 7958). Roppongi-Itchome station, exit 2. **Open** 8.30am-9pm Mon-Sat; 10am-9pm Sun. **Credit** AmEx, DC, MC, V. **Map** p74.

Roppongi Pharmacy

6-8-8 Roppongi, Minato-ku (3403 8879). Roppongi station, exit 3. **Open** 10.30-1am daily. Closed 2nd Sun of mth. **No credit cards**. **Map** p74.

Arts & Entertainment

Features

Festivals & Events

From blossom viewing to bean hurling, Tokyo is a city for all seasons.

Winter

Toyota Cup

National Stadium, Kasumigaoka-machi, Shinjuku-ku. Sendagaya station (JR Sobu Line). **Information** www.toyotacup.com. **Tickets** Pia Sports 0570 02 997/http://t.pia.co.jp. **Date** late Nov.

This annual one-off match on neutral Tokyo turf between the holders of Europe's and South America's premier club titles has long been recognised as the unofficial world club championship.

47 Ronin Memorial Service (Ako Gishi-sai)

Sengakuji Temple, 2-11-1 Takanawa, Minato-ku. Sengakuji station (Toei Asakusa Line), exit A2. **Information** 3441 5560/info@sengakuji.or.jp. **Date** 14 Dec (also 1-7 Apr).

The famous vendetta attack celebrated here (*see p8*) took place in the early hours of 31 January 1703, or 15 December by the old Japanese calendar. Two days of events, including dances, a parade in period costume and a Buddhist memorial ceremony, take place at the temple where the warriors are buried alongside their former master. There's also a parade in Ginza, with participants in samurai outfits.

Battledore Market (Hagoita Ichi)

Asakusa Kannon Temple (Sensoji), 2-3-1 Asakusa, Taito-ku. Asakusa station, exit 1, 3, 6, A4. **Information** 3842 0181. **Map** p83. **Date** 17-19 Dec.

Hagoita are paddle-shaped bats used to hit the shuttlecock in *hanetsuki,* the traditional New Year game. Ornamental versions come festooned with colourful pictures and many temples hold markets selling them in December. The one at Sensoji is Tokyo's largest.

Emperor's Birthday (Tenno Tanjobi)

Date 23 Dec.

The only day apart from 2 January when the public is allowed to enter the inner palace grounds.

Christmas Eve/Day

Date 24-25 Dec.

The most romantic day of the year is Christmas Eve: couples celebrate with extravagant dates, involving fancy restaurants and love hotels. Not many locals do anything special to mark the following day, despite the battery of fairy lights, decorated trees and piped carols deployed by department stores.

Year End

Date 28-31 Dec.

The year's last official day of work is 28 December; after work people begin a frantic round of last-minute house cleaning, decoration-hanging and food preparation ready for the night's celebrations. Many stay at home to catch NHK's eternally popular *Red and White Singing Contest,* although huge crowds also go out to shrines and temples for the hour of midnight, when bells are rung 108 times to welcome in the New Year.

New Year's Day (Ganjitsu)

Many locations, inc Meiji Shrine & Asakusa Kannon Temple (Sensoji). **Information** 3201 3331. **Date** 1 Jan.

The most important annual holiday of the year sees large crowds fill temples and shrines to bursting point for that all-important first visit of the year. Otherwise, New Year's Day tends to be a quiet family affair, except for postmen staggering under enormous sacks of New Year cards, which all Japanese people send to friends and colleagues. Only the first day of the year is an official holiday, but people stay away from work for longer, with most shops and businesses closing until 4 January.

Emperor's Cup Final

National Stadium, Kasumigaoka-machi, Shinjuku-ku. Sendagaya station (JR Sobu Line). **Tickets** Pia Sports 0570 02 997/http://t.pia.co.jp. **Date** 1 Jan.

The showpiece event of Japan's domestic soccer season is the climax of the main cup competition. It kicks off at 1.30pm.

New Year Congratulatory Visit (Ippan Sanga)

Chiyoda, Chiyoda-ku. Tokyo station. **Map** p62. **Date** 2 Jan.

The public is allowed into the inner grounds of the Imperial Palace on two days a year; this is one of them (the emperor's birthday in December is the other, *see above*). Seven times during the day, between 9.30am and 3pm, the symbol of the state appears on the palace balcony with other members of the royal family to wave to the crowds from behind bullet-proof glass.

Tokyo Metropolitan Fire Brigade Parade (Dezome-shiki)

Plaza in front of Tokyo Big Sight, 3-21-2 Ariake, Koto-ku. Kokusai-tenjijo Seimon station (Yurikamome Line). **Information** 3201 3331. **Map** p78. **Date** 6 Jan. **Time** morning.

The highlight of this day, which celebrates the work of the city's fire fighters, is a display by members of the Preservation Association of the old Edo Fire Brigade, who dress in traditional *hikeshi* firefighters' garb and perform acrobatic stunts at the top of long ladders. Items of modern equipment are also featured.

New Year Grand Sumo Tournament (Ozumo Hatsu Basho)

Kokugikan, 1-3-28 Yokoami, Sumida-ku. Ryogoku station, west exit. **Information** 3623 5111. **Date** mid Jan. **Time** 10am-6pm.
The first of the year's three full 15-day sumo tournaments held in Tokyo. The tournaments take place from the second to the fourth Sunday of January, May and September.

Coming of Age Day (Seijin no Hi)

Meiji Shrine & others. **Information** 3201 3331. **Date** 2nd Mon of Jan.
Those reaching the age of 20 in the 12 months to April make their way to shrines in their best kimono and suits for blessings and photos. The traditional date of 15 January generally coincides with New Year's Day under the old lunar calendar.

Chinese New Year

Yokohama Chinatown, East Gate. Ishikawacho station (JR Keihin Tohoku/Negishi Line), Chinatown exit. **Information** 045 641 4759/Yokohama Chinatown Development Association 045 662 1252/www.chinatown.or.jp/1index.html. **Date** Jan/Feb.
Cymbals crash and dragon dancers weave their way along the restaurant-lined streets of Yokohama Chinatown as the local community celebrates its big party of the year.

Setsubun

Various locations, including Sensoji Temple & Zojoji Temple. **Information** 3201 3331. **Date** 3 Feb.
Much hurling of soybeans to cries of '*oni wa soto, fuki wa uchi*' ('demons out, good luck in') as the last day of winter by the lunar calendar is celebrated in homes, shrines and temples. The tradition is to eat one bean for every year of one's age. Sumo wrestlers and other celebrities are among those doing the casting out in ceremonies at well-known Tokyo shrines.

Chocs away, it's Valentine's Day.

National Foundation Day (Kenkoku Kinen no Hi)

Date 11 Feb.
A public holiday commemorating the supposed beginnings of Japan's imperial line in 660 BC, the date when mythical first emperor Jimmu, a descendent of sun goddess Amaterasu Omikami, is said to have ascended to the throne. After World War II, the public holiday on 11 February was abolished; this one was inaugurated, amid controversy, in 1966.

Valentine's Day

Date 14 Feb.
Introduced into Japan by confectionery companies as the day when women give chocolates to men: there's a heart-shaped treat for that special someone, plus *giri choko* (obligation chocolates) for a wider circle of male associates.

Plum Blossoms

Yushima Tenjin Shrine, 3-30-1 Yushima, Bunkyo-ku. Yushima station, exit 3. **Information** 3836 0753. **Map** p88. **Date** mid Feb-mid Mar.
The delicate white blooms arrive a little earlier than the better-known cherry blossoms, and are generally celebrated in a more restrained fashion. Yushima Tenjin Shrine, a prime viewing spot, also holds a month-long festival featuring traditional arts such as *ikebana* (flower-arranging) and tea ceremony.

Dolls Festival (Hina Matsuri)

Date 3 Mar.
A special festival for girls. Kimono-clad dolls representing traditional court figures are displayed on a multi-tiered red stand, and the arrangement takes pride of place in the home on the big day.

Daruma Fair

Jindaiji Temple, 5-15-1 Jindaiji Motomachi, Chofu-shi. Bus from Chofu station (Keio Line) north exit to terminus at Jindaiji Temple. **Information** 0424 86 5511. **Date** 3-4 Mar.
After meditating in a cave for nine years, Bodhidharma, a Zen monk from ancient India, is reputed to have lost the use of all four limbs. The cuddly red figure of the Daruma doll, which is modelled after him, also lacks eyes; the first gets painted in for good luck when a difficult task is undertaken, the second on its successful completion. Jindaiji's Daruma fair is one of the biggest.

Spring

Fire-Walking Ceremony(Hi-watari)

Kotsu Anzen Kitosho, near Takaosan-guchi station (Keio Line). **Information** 0426 61 1115/www.takaosan.com/index2.htm). **Date** 2nd Sun in Mar.
At the foot of Mount Takao, hardy *yamabushi* mountain monks from Yakuoin Temple walk barefoot across burning coals while chanting incantations.

You don't have to be Irish to celebrate **St Patrick's Day**.

Brave members of the public are then invited to test their own hardiness of soul and sole by following in their footsteps (literally).

White Day

Date 14 Mar.

Male recipients of Valentine's Day chocs return the compliment with white chocolate for the ladies.

St Patrick's Day Parade

Omotesando Dori. Harajuku station, Omotesando exit. **Information** www.inj.or.jp. **Map** p99. **Date** 17 Mar or nearest Sun, from 11am.

Enthusiastic local devotees of Gaelic culture demonstrate their baton-twirling, drumming, pipe-playing and dancing skills at this popular parade led by Ireland's ambassador. Revelries continue through the day at the city's many Irish hostelries.

Vernal Equinox Day (Shumbun no Hi)

Date around 21 Mar.

Many people visit family graves on this day, since it falls in the middle of *higan*, a week-long, twice yearly Buddhist memorial service.

Geisai

Various venues. **Information** www.geisai.net. **Date** Mar/Sept.

Started by artist Murakami Takashi, Geisai, like older brother Design Festa, is a chance for individuals and groups to rent booths and get discovered (or at least sell something). Geisai has a slight professional edge because it includes a few major galleries and also holds a competition where winners are given a chance to break into the commercial art market. *See p211.*

Cherry Blossom Viewing (Hanami)

Various locations including Ueno Park, Sumida Park, Yasukuni Shrine, Shinjuku-Gyoen, Aoyama Cemetery. **Information** 3201 3331. **Date** late Mar-early Apr.

The great outdoor event of the year sees popular viewing spots invaded by hordes of nature-loving locals. Some prefer quiet contemplation of the explosion of pink petals up in the trees, while others use the occasion for some serious partying. Cases of alcohol poisoning are not unknown and ambulance crews remain on alert.

New Fiscal Year

Date 1 Apr.

April Fool's Day marks the start of Japan's financial and academic calendars. Big companies hold speech-filled ceremonies to welcome the year's graduate intake to the rigours of corporate life.

47 Ronin Memorial Week

Sengakuji Temple, 2-11-1 Takanawa, Minato-ku. Sengakuji station (Toei Asakusa Line), exit A2. **Information** 3441 5560/info@sengakuji.or.jp). **Date** 1-7 Apr.

Sengakuji's most famous inmates (*see p8*) get a whole week of services to honour them.

Tokyo Motorcycle Show

Tokyo Big Sight, 3-21-2 Ariake, Koto-ku. Kokusai-Tenjijo Seimon station (Yurikamome Line). **Information** 5457 2106/www.motorcycleshow.org. **Admission** ¥1,500. **Map** p78. **Date** early Apr.

Everything to warm any biker's heart, with models from Japan and the rest of the world. Event celebrated its 30th anniversary in 2003.

Nippon International Contemporary Art Fair

Tokyo International Forum, 3-5-1 Marunouchi, Chiyoda-ku. Yurakucho JR station, exit 6.
Information 5212 1925/www.nicaf.com. **Admission** ¥1,000; ¥500 students. **Map** p57. **Date** early Apr.
The largest art fair in Asia is held every two years or so, featuring galleries from across Japan and Asia.

Start of Baseball Season

Tokyo Dome or Jingu Baseball Stadium.
Information 5800 9999 Tokyo Dome; 3404 8999 Jingu Baseball Stadium. **Tickets** Pia Sports 0570 02 997/http://t.pia.co.jp/. **Date** early Apr.
The long and winding road to the October play-offs usually gets under way with a three-game Central League series featuring the Giants, the city's perennial favourite. There's extra spice if the opposition is the Swallows, the capital's other big team, or the Giants' oldest and deadliest rivals, the Hanshin Tigers. For stadium details, *see p248*.

Horseback Archery (Yabusame)

Sumida Park. Asakusa station. **Information** 5246 1111. **Date** mid Apr.
Mounted riders in medieval warrior gear shoot arrows at stationary targets while galloping along at full tilt. There's also a big *yabusame* festival at Tsurugaoka Hachiman Shrine in Kamakura (*see p266*) in mid September; the practice can also be seen during the autumn festival at Meiji Shrine on 3 November (*see p200*).

Design Festa

Tokyo Big Sight, 3-21-2 Ariake, Koto-ku. Kokusai-tenjijo Seimon station (Yurikamome Line).
Information 3479 1433/www.designfesta.com.
Admission ¥1,000; free under-12s. **Map** p78.
Date Apr, Nov.
Showcases young designers, artists, musicians and performers. Hundreds of them rent small booths, turning the convention centre into a big art fair.

Meiji Jingu Shrine Spring Festival (Haru no Taisai)

Meiji Jingu Shrine, 1-1 Kamizonocho, Yoyogi, Shibuya-ku. Harajuku station, Omotesando exit or Meiji-Jingumae station, exit 2. **Information** 3379 5511. **Admission** free. **Map** p99.
Date 29 Apr-early May.
Daily free performances of traditional entertainment, including *gagaku* and *bugaku* imperial court music and dance, plus *noh* and *kyogen* drama.

Golden Week

Date 29 Apr-5 May.
Put three public holidays (Greenery Day, Constitution Day and Children's Day) in close proximity and there's the vacation opportunity known as Golden Week. Planes, trains and automobiles hit gridlock as people flee the city en masse, then all head home again at the same time. Tokyo remains relatively quiet, with many smaller shops and restaurants closed for the duration.

Greenery Day (Midori no Hi)

Date 29 Apr.
A nature appreciation day to begin Golden Week (*above*). Previously celebrated as the birthday of Emperor Showa (Hirohito).

International Labour Day

Date 1 May.
Despite falling in the middle of Golden Week, the day when workers of the world unite in celebration is not an official holiday in Japan. Many vacationing trade unionists meet for a rally in Yoyogi Park.

Constitution Day (Kempo Kinenbi)

Date 3 May.
Commemorates the day in 1947 when the US-imposed pacifist constitution came into operation.

Children's Day (Kodomo no Hi)

Date 5 May.
A traditional festival for boys; the corresponding one for girls is the Dolls Festival on 3-4 March (which isn't a public holiday). Celebrations include the hanging of paper streamers in the shape of carp.

Kanda Festival

Organised from Kanda Myojin Shrine. **Information** 3254 0753. **Date** mid May.
One of the city's traditional 'Big Three' festivals, this is held in odd-numbered years, alternating with the Sanno festival. In Edo days, it was a particular favourite of the local townspeople, due to Kanda Myojin's links with the popular tenth-century rebel Taira no Masakado. Events include *shinkosai* rites with participants parading in Heian costume, plus a gala procession that crisscrosses the Kanda area and features a number of festival floats and *mikoshi* portable shrines.

Sanja Festival

Organised from Asakusa Shrine. **Information** 3844 1575/www.asakusajinja.com/index_2.html.
Date mid May.
The biggest of the city's annual festivals, Sanja attracts enormous crowds to Asakusa and honours the three seventh-century founders of Sensoji Temple. It climaxes after several days of events with three huge *mikoshi* portable shrines (*sanja*) that carry the spirits of the three men being paraded around local streets. Each shrine needs dozens of people to carry it.

Summer

Sanno Festival

Organised from Hie Shrine. **Information** 3581 2471.
Date mid June.
Another of the 'Big Three' festivals, Sanno alternates with the Kanda festival and is held in its full splendour on even-numbered years. Hie Shrine, which had close links with the Tokugawa shoguns, is near today's central government district. The main procession goes round the edge of the Imperial

Palace, with participants in Heian-period costumes and priests riding on horses, plus all the usual festival floats and *mikoshi*.

Iris Viewing

Various locations, including Meiji Shrine Inner Garden, Horikiri Iris Garden & Mizumoto Park. **Information** 3201 3331. **Date** mid June.

The annual blooming of the purple and white flowers falls during the grey humid days of the rainy season, but is no less popular for that.

Mount Fuji

Climbing season 1 July-31 Aug.

It's claimed that everyone should climb Mount Fuji once in their life, though more than that is said to be excessive. The perfectly formed cone of Japan's favourite dormant volcano is all but lost in the summer haze from most Tokyo vantage points, but many enthusiastic walkers head out for that one-off push to the summit, often at night in order to catch the dawn sunrise. *See also p270.*

Ground-Cherry Market (Hozuchi-ichi)

Asakusa Kannon (Sensoji) Temple, 2-3-1 Asakusa, Taito-ku. Asakusa station, exit 1, 3, 6, A4. **Information** 3842 0181. **Map** p83. **Date** 9-10 July.

On these two days in July, prayers at Sensoji are said to be the spiritual equivalent of 46,000 days' worth at other times. Big crowds are attracted by this spiritual bargain. A ground-cherry market takes place at the temple over the same period.

International Lesbian & Gay Film Festival

Spiral Bldg, 5-6-23 Minami-Aoyama, Minato-ku. Omotesando station, exit B1. **Information** 5380 5760/http://l-gff.gender.ne.jp. **Map** p99. **Date** mid July.

Held for the 12th time in 2003, the annual LGFF lasts around five days and offers a rare chance for locals to catch up on the best of gay cinema.

Marine Day (Umi no Hi)

Date 20 July.

Introduced in 1996, this is a public holiday celebrating the benefits and bounty of the sea.

Sumida River Firework

Asakusa station area. **Information** 5246 1111. **Map** p83. **Date** last Sat in July, 7pm.

First held in 1733, this is the daddy of Tokyo's many summer firework events: the oldest, biggest and most crowded. Up to 20,000 *hanabi* ('flower-fires') light up the night skies, and as many as a million people pack streets, bridges and rooftops, eyes trained upward. Waterfront locations also tend to be favoured for other big displays.

Fuji Rock Festival

Naeba Ski Resort, Niigata. **Information** 3444 6751/http://smash-jpn.com. **Date** late July/early Aug.

This annual outdoor music mega-festival pulls together major rock and dance acts from Japan and overseas. Its 2003 line-up featured Audio Active, Bjork, Elvis Costello, Iggy Pop and Underworld, among others. Despite the name, the festival has not been held near Mount Fuji since the inaugural event back in 1997 was hit by a typhoon.

Summersonic

Chiba Marine Stadium, Makuhari Messe Makuhari-Hongo station (JR Sobu Line) or Kaihin Makuhari station (Keiyo Line), south exit. **Information** 0180 993 0300/www.summersonic.com. **Date** early Aug.

Multi-band, multi-venue weekend rock event that provides an urban-based summer alternative to the big outdoor festivals out in the countryside. Line-up for 2003 included Radiohead and Blur.

Reggae Japansplash

Yomiuri Land Open Air Theatre East. Yomiuri Land Mae station (Odakyu Line). **Information** 3498 9999/www.tfm.jp/jps. **Date** late July-early Aug.

The long-standing high point of the summer for local reggae fans made a welcome return in 2002 after a one-year break.

Obon

Date 13-15 Aug.

The souls of the departed are supposed to return to the world of the living during this Buddhist festival honouring the spirits of ancestors. Observances include welcoming fires, Bon dances and night-time floating of lanterns on open water. Although there's no public holiday, many companies give workers time off to visit the folks back home, leaving the capital unusually quiet for a few days.

War-End Anniversary

Yasukuni Shrine, 3-1-1 Kudankita, Chiyoda-ku. Kudanshita station, exit 1. **Map** p62. **Date** 15 Aug.

The annual anniversary of Japan's surrender to the allied forces is still a source of diplomatic friction with neighbouring countries, as many leading politicians mark the day by visiting Yasukuni Shrine, where the souls of Japan's war-dead, including those executed as war criminals, are honoured. *See also p12* **War and peace**.

Tokyo Jazz

Ajinomoto stadium, 376-3 Nishi-cho, Chofu Shi. Tobitakyu station (Keio Line). **Information** www.tokyo-jazz.com. **Date** late Aug.

Stadium-based jazz weekend event.

Asakusa Samba Carnival

Asakusa station area. **Information** 3842 5566. **Map** p83. **Date** late Aug.

Thousands of gorgeously costumed samba dancers, some Brazilian but most Japanese, shake their stuff out in the streets in the heart of old downtown Tokyo. It's a startling and colourful spectacle, with a competition among teams for the cash prize that goes to the parade's top troupe.

Awa Odori

Koenji station area. **Information** 3312 2728. **Date** late Aug.

Street carnival Japanese-style. This annual shindig features a form of traditional Tokushima folk dance known as the Fool's Dance. As the raucous refrain of its light-hearted song puts it, 'You're a fool whether you dance or not, so you may as well dance'.

Autumn

Tokyo Earthquake Anniversary

Date 1 Sept.

The city authorities test emergency relief preparations and hold practice drills in locations across the city on the anniversary of the 1923 disaster.

Tokyo Lesbian & Gay Parade

Yoyogi Park. Harajuku station. **Information** 3380 0363/www.tlgp.org/index.html. **Date** early Sept.

Supposedly an annual event, but the 2003 parade was cancelled due to a lack of volunteers. Organisers hope it will resume in 2004. *See also p220* **Tokyo's gay & lesbian calendar**.

Yokohama Triennale

Pan Pacific Yokohama, 2-3-7 Minato-Mirai, Nishi-ku & other venues. Yokohama station. **Information** 045 441 7300/www.jpf.go.jp. **Date** Sept-Nov.

The inaugural exhibition in 2001 placed Yokohama, Japan's second largest city, on the contemporary art world map, with 110 international artists featured. Next scheduled for 2004.

International Super Track & Field

Yokohama International Stadium. Shin-Yokohama station. **Information** 045 477 5000. **Tickets** Pia Sports 0570 02 997/http://t.pia.co.jp. **Date** mid Sept.

Usually the last big outdoor meeting of the international athletics calendar, so there tends to be a relaxed end-of-term atmosphere among the assembled galaxy of record-setters, medal-winners and other track stars.

Respect for the Aged Day (Keiro no Hi)

Date 15 Sept.

Held on the anniversary of the 1966 enactment of the Law on Welfare for the Aged. Japan has an ageing population and the world's highest life expectancy.

Autumnal Equinox Day (Shubun no Hi)

Date around 23 Sept.

Like the spring equinox, the autumn equinox coincides with the mid-point of *higan*, the seven-day Buddhist memorial service.

Tokyo Game Show

Makuhari Messe Convention Centre. Makuhari-Hongo station (JR Sobu Line) or Kaihin Makuhari station (JR Keiyo Line). **Information** 3591 1421/ www.cesa.or.jp/english/index.html. **Admission** ¥1,200. **Date** late Sept.

Yabusame, horseback archery. *See p197*.

The biggest computer and video game show on the planet is now held on just one weekend a year, with 2002 setting a new record for visitor numbers.

Moon Viewing (Tsukimi)

Date late Sept.

Parties to view the harvest moon have been held in the city since the Edo era, but the search for clear night skies means that somewhat less urban venues are favoured nowadays. Non-traditionalists may find solace in the annual Tsukimi Burger promotion, recognising a distinctly lunar quality to the fried egg that comes as an added seasonal ingredient.

Art-Link Ueno-Yanaka

Various locations. Ueno and Nippori stations. **Information** 5685 7685. **Date** late Sept-mid Oct.

Annual art event that includes exhibitions and events in galleries, shops and temples around the old cultural centre of Ueno and the artists' district of Yanaka. Keep an eye out for flyers or announcements in the media.

Takigi Noh

Various venues. **Date** Sept-Oct.

Atmospheric outdoor performances of medieval *noh* drama are staged at a number of shrines, temples and parks, illuminated by flickering flames from bonfires and torches.

CEATEC Japan

Makuhari Messe Convention Centre. Makuhari-Hongo station (JR Sobu Line) or Kaihin Makuhari station, south exit (Keiyo Line). **Information** 5402 7603/www.ceatec.com/index.html. **Admission** ¥1,000; students ¥500. **Date** early Oct.

Not only the place to check out all the latest gadgets before they hit the shops, but also an opportunity to see cutting-edge Japanese communications and information technology in action.

Tokyo Designer's Block/Designer's Week/Swedish Style

Various venues. **Information** www.tokyodesignersblock.com/www.tdwa.com/www.swedishstyle.net. **Date** early Oct.

These three big annual design events usually happen around the same time at various venues. Though not directly related, each draws product, fashion and other designers from around the world. The Swedish event also usually includes artists and musicians.

Japan Tennis Open

Metropolitan Ariake Tennis Woods Park, 2-2-22 Ariake, Koto-ku. Ariake station (Yurikamome Line). **Information** 3481 2321. **Tickets** Pia Sports 0570 02 997/http://t.pia.co.jp. **Map** p78. **Date** early Oct.

The international tennis circus hits town for the nation's premier event. Local interest tends to focus on the women's tournament.

Sports Day (Taiiku no Hi)

Date 2nd Mon in Oct.

The traditional date of 10 October commemorates the opening day of the 1964 Tokyo Olympics.

Tokyo Motor Show

Makuhari Messe Convention Centre. Makuhari-Hongo station or Kaihin Makuhari station, south exit (Keiyo Line). **Information** 3211 8829/www.tokyo-motorshow.com. **Admission** ¥1,200. **Date** late Oct-early Nov.

An important showcase for the gleaming new products of car manufacturers both domestic and foreign. Passenger cars and motorbikes are featured in odd-numbered years; commercial vehicles in even ones.

Chrysanthemum Festival

Meiji Shrine Inner Garden, Yoyogi-kamizono-cho, Shibuya-ku. Harajuku station, Omotesando exit. **Information** 3379 5511. **Map** p99.
Date late Oct-late Nov.

The start of autumn was traditionally marked by the Chrysanthemum Festival on the ninth day of the ninth month of the old lunar calendar. The delicate pale blooms are also represented on the crest of Japan's Imperial family.

Culture Day (Bunka no Hi)

Date 3 Nov.

Leading Japanese artists and writers, plus other luminaries, pick up Order of Culture government awards on a day set aside for cultural activities to celebrate the peaceful democratic ideals of the post-war constitution, promulgated on this day in 1946.

Meiji Jingu Shrine Grand Autumn Festival (Reisai)

Meiji Jingu Shrine, 1-1 Kamizonocho, Yoyogi, Shibuya-ka. Harajuku station, Omotesando exit. **Information** 3379 5511. **Map** p99. **Date** 3 Nov.

In former times, Culture Day celebrated the birthday of the Meiji Emperor, and the biggest annual festival of the Meiji Shrine still takes place on the same date. There are performances of traditional music and theatre, and *yabusame* horseback archery.

Tokyo International Fantastic Film Festival

Cinemas in Shibuya. **Information** 5777 8600/http://forum.nifty.com/fanta/tokyo. **Map** p102.
Date late Oct-early Nov.

A feast of horror and science fiction from around the world, cheekily timed to coincide with the main International Film Festival (*see below*). Specialises in previewing new films and reviving old classics.

Tokyo International Film Festival

Le Cinema, Bunkamura (see p208) & other venues in Shibuya. **Information** 3563 6305/www.tiff-jp.net.
Map p102. **Date** early Nov.

The largest film festival in Japan attracts a glittering influx of international movie talent, gathered for the serious business of the competitions and special promotional screenings of upcoming Hollywood blockbusters. There are also showings of Japanese cinema classics and an Asian film award, as well as the International Fantastic Film Festival *(see above)*, Women's Film Week and other related events.

Seven-Five-Three Festival (Shichi-go-san)

Various locations, including Meiji Jingu Shrine. **Information** 3201 3331. **Date** 15 Nov.

Tradition has it that children of certain ages (three, five and seven) are strangely susceptible to misfortune. One way to avoid this problem is to get any family member with the wrong number of birthday cake candles on their cake down to a Shinto shrine on 15 November to pray for divine blessings and protection. Important shrines are besieged by hordes of kids in their best kimono on this day.

Autumn Leaves (Koyo)

Various locations including Shinjuku Gyoen, Ueno Park & Meiji Jingu Gaien Park. **Information** 3201 3331. **Date** 2nd half of Nov.

The spectacular autumnal colours of maple and gingko trees transform many of Tokyo's parks and gardens into a blaze of reds and yellows.

Labour Thanksgiving Day (Kinro Kansha no Hi)

Date 23 Nov.

This is the public holiday when the people of Japan are supposed to thank one another for all their hard work through the year.

Japan Cup

Tokyo Racetrack, 1-1 Hiyoshi-cho Fuchu City. Seimonmae station (Keio Line). **Information** 042 363 3141. **Tickets** Pia Sports 0570 02 997/http://t.pia.co.jp. **Date** late Nov.

Top horses and jockeys from round the world race over 2,400m.

Children

Little monsters, big city, big choice.

For children, Tokyo is stimulus city, offering an enviable range of suitable pastimes, events and venues. The falling birth rate in Japan means that the Tokyo child is pampered like never before. As parents have fewer children, so they lavish more money on the ones they've got. To meet this new demand, scores of specialist shops catering exclusively to young consumers have opened in recent years.

Tokyo's also great for more traditional entertainment. Zoos, aquariums, shops, museums, nature spots and mountains are all close by, and while nature here may not be as grand as in Australia, say, and some amusement parks may look like scaled-down versions of American originals, such shortcomings are offset by the sheer accessibility and variety of children's facilities.

Children's facilities in Tokyo can get very crowded at weekends and during school holidays; this is particularly true of indoor facilities on wet and cold days. At museums and aquariums, the problem is compounded by the inadequate provision of English displays, preventing foreign visitors from making the best of them. You may prefer to avoid them at weekends, particularly during school holidays (usually 21 March-7 April, 20 July-31 August, and 23 December-7 January). Almost all the facilities listed here can be accessed by public transport, and are often within an hour's train ride of major stations such as Shinjuku.

Amusement parks

Going to amusement parks is a pricey business, so it's worth noting that tickets are often available cheaply at '*kinken* shop' discount ticket stores, sometimes at a fraction of the regular prices (*see p189* **Bargain hunting**). See also **Tokyo Disney Resort**, *p122*.

Tamatech

5-22-1 Hodokubo, Hino-shi (042 591 0820/www.tamatech.com). Bus from Tama Dobutsu Koen station (Keio Line). **Open** 9.30am-5.30pm daily. **Admission** *All rides* ¥3,900; ¥3,100 3-12s. *Three rides* ¥2,300; ¥1,500 3-12s. *Entry only* ¥1,600; ¥800 3-12s; each ride then costs ¥200-¥800.

Despite a wide variety of other attractions, including a rollercoaster and a free-fall ride, it's the go-karts that are most popular here – ideal for children who want to drive themselves, rather than sit in a machine-driven ride. There are several racing circuits for small riders to test their driving skills. Tamatech is run by the Honda motor company.

Tokyo Sesame Place

600 Kamiyotsugi, Akiruno-shi (042 558 6511/www.sesameplace.co.jp). Bus bound for Keio Hachioji from Akigawa station (Itsukaichi Line); get off at Tokyo Summerland for free shuttle bus to Sesame Place. **Open** *July-Sept* daily. *Oct, Nov, Mar-June* Mon-Wed, Fri-Sun. Dec-Feb Fri, Sat & hols. Times vary. **Admission** ¥2,000; ¥1,000 2-12s. *Summer* ¥2,200; ¥1,200 2-12s.

This theme park based on the *Sesame Street* TV show has reproduced some of the most exciting attractions of the original park in Pennsylvania, including big ball pools, a gigantic air mattress, cargo nets, tunnels and climbs. Various interactive shows, including English play-along and musical revues, are certain to keep your children busy and excited. There is a small section for water activities, including a paddling pool and a water maze, which open in summer. Poor access is one of the few shortcomings of this otherwise excellent park.

Aquariums

Itabashi Ward Aquarium

3-50-1 Itabashi, Itabashi-ku (aquarium 3962 8419/zoo 3963 8003). Itabashi Kuyakusho-Mae station (Toei Mita Line), exit A1. **Open** *Mar-Nov* 10am-4.30pm Tue-Sun. *Dec-Feb* 10am-4pm Tue-Sun. **Admission** free.

This freshwater aquarium is inside Itabashi Higashi Park, which also contains the Itabashi Ward Children's Zoo. The zoo and aquarium, although small, are among the least explored such facilities in Tokyo, and offer a real opportunity to mingle with animals. Most of the creatures in the aquarium, including turtles and shrimps, are kept in open tanks, so you can see and smell them close up. The zoo offers free pony rides twice a day at 10.30am and 1.30pm – riding tickets are handed out 30 minutes ahead of each ride. The zoo has two petting sections, one for guinea pigs and another for sheep and goats. Zoo staff keep the petting sections clean and tidy, and washing facilities are provided to make sure your kids go home the same way.

Shinagawa Aquarium

3-2-1 Katsushima, Shinagawa-ku (3762 3431/www.aquarium.gr.jp Japanese only). Omori Kaigan station (Keihin Kyuko Line), east exit. **Open** 10am-5pm Mon, Wed-Sun. **Admission** ¥1,100; ¥600 primary & middle school children; ¥300 4-6s.

Meeting the animals at **Inokashira Park Zoo**. *See p203.*

The best aquarium in Tokyo is located somewhat inconveniently on the western coast of the Tokyo Bay. Its highlight is a water tank tunnel, in which visitors walk under swimming green turtles, stingrays and scores of other fish. From another tank, huge sand tiger sharks peer out with cold, steely eyes. The aquarium also runs Tokyo's only dolphin shows. They take place at the outdoor stadium four or five times a day and always attract huge crowds, so it's best to check the show schedules on arrival. The aquarium is in a public park with its own facilities, including a long cycling course. Bikes are available for free rental.

Tokyo Sea Life Park

6-2-3 Rinkai-cho, Edogawa-ku (3869 5152). Kasai Rinkai Koen station. **Open** 9.30am-5pm Tue-Sun (last admission 4pm). **Admission** ¥700; ¥250 middle school children living or studying outside Tokyo.

Located across Tokyo Bay from Shinagawa Aquarium is this new facility built on the 77 hectares of reclaimed land that constitute Kasai Seaside Park. Its main attraction is a large doughnut-shaped water tank, home to 200 enormous tuna fish. Because of its novelty, proximity to Tokyo Disneyland and better transport access, this aquarium is always more crowded than its Shinagawa sibling. The aquarium itself, however, seems rather small for its setting. A walk on the sandy beach outside provides a welcome break from the crowds.

Playgrounds

Koganei Park

1-13-1 Sekino-machi, Koganei-shi (042 385 5611). Musashi-Koganei station, north exit, then any bus from bus stop 2 or 3 and alight at Koganei Koen Nishi-Guchi.

A cycle track lets you explore the central part of this 77-hectare park in western Tokyo. About 120 bikes are available for pre-schoolers and their parents. If your child tires of pedalling, they can try sledging down an artificial turf-covered slope, built into one of the park's grassy knolls. The 17-degree slope is wide enough for at least a dozen sledges to race down at the same time. Many visitors to the park bring their own sledges, but you can buy one at a nearby concession stand or borrow one of the park's by queueing at the bottom of the slope. With plenty of grass to sit on, Koganei Park is one of Tokyo's most pleasant, for both parents and children. It also houses the outdoor branch of the Edo-Tokyo Museum, a fascinating collection of buildings saved from the bulldozer.

Mount Takao

For parents looking for something more than a city park for their energetic kids, this western Tokyo mountain may be the place to go. At 600m (2,000ft), the mountain is challenging, but not too difficult for small kids. There are six trails to get to the top. The No.6 trail takes you alongside a small stream and requires some rock-hopping towards the peak. If the children don't fancy climbing, a cable-car ride (with a gradient of 31.18 degrees, the steepest in Japan) can take you half way up the mountain. The mountain is very accessible by train, a 47-minute ride from Shinjuku on an express train on the Keio Line, a trip that costs just ¥350.

National Showa Memorial Park

3173 Midori-machi, Tachikawa-shi (042 528 1751/ www.ktr.mlit.go.jp/showa). Nishi-Tachikawa station (Ohme Line). **Open** *Mar-Oct* 9.30am-5pm daily. *Nov-Feb* 9.30am-4.30pm daily. **Admission** ¥400; ¥80 6-14s. *Rainbow Pool* (including park admission) ¥2,250; ¥1,220 6-14s; ¥310 4-5s.

A paradise for athletic children, this 180-hectare park has a large play area called Children's Forest, with giant trampoline nets, bouncy domes, and 'foggy woods' that get covered by clouds of artificial fog from time to time. The Forest House in the centre of the forest sells children's favourite snacks and drinks and provides a resting space. If it's too hot to walk to the Children's Forest from the main gate in summer, you can pop into the Rainbow Pool for a paddle. There are three paddling pools containing waterfalls and squirt fish. For bigger children, there is a running-water pool, a wave pool and water slides. The park also has long cycling courses. Renting a bike costs ¥250 for three hours for children under 15 and ¥410 for adults.

Nogawa Park

6-4-1 Osawa, Mitaka-shi (0422 31 6457). Shin-Koganei station (Seibu Tamagawa Line), then 15mins walk (follow railway tracks south till you arrive at Nogawa River). **Open** 24hrs daily. *Nature centre* 9.30am-4.30pm Tue-Sun.

A natural spring on the northern side of the Nogawa river bisects this picturesque park. The area around the spring is a popular paddling spot in summer. There is a small nature centre upstream, which has samples of various insects and allows visitors to listen to recorded sounds of birds in Tokyo woodland. Various climbing structures and other wooden play equipment also dot the extensive grassy areas.

Shinjuku Gyoen

11 Naito-cho, Shinjuku-ku (3350 0151/www. shinjukugyoen.go.jp). Shinjuku Gyoen-Mae station. **Open** *Park* 9am-4.30pm Tue-Sun. *Greenhouse* 11am-3pm Tue-Sun. Open daily during cherry (early Apr) and chrysanthemum (early Nov) flowering. **Admission** ¥200; free-¥50 concessions. **Map** p109.

The lawn in this park is not just huge, but very clean, thanks apparently to its ¥200 entrance fee. Parents can safely let their toddlers crawl around without worrying about canine presents. The use of balls and other play equipment is forbidden here, but the wide-open field is enough to satisfy any energetic child. There are also small ponds in a section near the Shinjuku Gate, called the Mother and Child's Forest, where catching American crayfish is a very popular pastime in summer. You can always take shelter in a large greenhouse when it gets chilly.

Trim Sports Center (Jingu Gaien 'Jido Yuen')

1-7-5 Kita-Aoyama, Minato-ku (3478 0550/www. meijijingu.or.jp/gaien). Shinanomachi station. **Open** *Mar-Oct* 9.30am-5pm daily. *Nov-Feb* 9.30am-4.30pm daily. **Admission** ¥200; ¥50 2-12s.

Despite its compact size and central location, this popular playground within the Outer Garden of the Meiji Jingu Shrine possibly has more play equipment than any other park in Tokyo. Children can try swings, slides and climbs of various sizes and shapes, and picnic at beautiful log houses equipped with large tables and chairs. The park has three areas, each for a different age group, but children are allowed to wander anywhere under parental supervision. Snacks and light food are available at the stand in the park or from a line of vending machines installed just outside the entrance gate.

Zoos

The three zoos listed here are all run by the Tokyo metropolitan government. They arrange special programmes from time to time, such as a one-day zoo-keeper session and an evening barbecue. Call for details.

Inokashira Park Zoo

1-17-6 Gotenyama, Musashino-shi (0422 46 1100). Kichijoji station, park (south) exit. **Open** 9.30am-5pm Tue-Sun. **Admission** ¥400; ¥150 middle school children living or studying outside Tokyo.

This small zoo's best attraction is its setting. A five-minute walk from Kichijoji station, a major commercial hub in Tokyo's western suburb, it is set in Inokashira Park, with a pond, woods, a playground and an outdoor swimming pool all close by. The zoo, officially called Inokashira Nature and Culture Park, has two sections, one near the pond housing an aviary and a freshwater aquarium, the other lying near the wood and containing an animal zoo, a petting zoo, a greenhouse and a small amusement park. The entrance fee will buy you tickets for both sections, which can be used separately. If you are tired of watching animals and riding a mini train at the amusement park, you can return to the pond for a boat ride, take a rest at one of the cafés lining the street leading to the park from the station, or go shopping in the malls on the other side of the station.

Tama Zoo

7-1-1 Hodokubo, Hino-shi (042 591 1611). Tama Dobutsu Koen station (Keio Line). **Open** 9.30am-5pm Mon, Tue, Thur-Sun. **Admission** ¥600; ¥200 7-12s; ¥300 over-65s; free 5 May, 29 Apr, 1 Oct.

Animals are displayed in more natural settings here. Built over several low hills, the zoo allows visitors to enjoy hiking and animal-watching at the same time. Main attractions include koalas, lions in a 'safari' setting, and above all, a huge insectarium with butterflies, hoppers and beetles. Enjoy the sensation of friendly butterflies coming to rest their weary wings on your hand.

Ueno Zoo

9-83 Ueno-Koen, Taito-ku (3828 5171). Ueno station, park exit. **Open** 9.30am-5pm Tue-Sun. **Admission** ¥600; ¥200 middle school children living or studying outside Tokyo. **Map** p88.

Japan's oldest zoo, established in 1882, is also the most popular, thanks mainly to a giant panda. But there's a lot more to Ueno Zoo. Its eastern section houses mammals, including giraffes, elephants, polar bears and sea lions. Don't be discouraged by the crowd in the eastern section; the western section across the bridge is less crowded and offers more opportunities to interact with animals. Children can touch goats, sheep, horses and ducks in the petting zoo, while the reptile and amphibian house is home to a large number of toads and a huge alligator in a water tank. Being centrally located, the zoo is limited in size, but its elaborate presentations work well.

Barbecuing

Akigawa River

www.akirunokanko.com/bbq.html.

Most of the popular barbecuing spots in Tokyo are found along the Akigawa river in the Oku-Tama region. One is located just a five-minute walk from Musashi-Itsukaichi station, the last stop on the Itsukaichi Line. There is plenty of space for barbecuing on the wide riverbank, but cooking equipment must be rented at a cost of ¥500-¥1,500, depending on size. Charcoal is sold for ¥400. Sinks and clean toilets are provided. There is parking space for 400 cars, costing ¥1,000. The river is shallow and fit for paddling a little upsteam near the next bridge.

Indoor facilities

National Children's Castle

5-53-1 Jingumae, Shibuya-ku (3797 5666/ www.kodomono-shiro.or.jp). Shibuya station, Miyamasuzaka (east) exit, or Omotesando station, exits B2, B4. **Open** 12.30-5.30pm Tue-Fri; 10am-5.30pm Sat, Sun. **Admission** ¥500; ¥400 3-17s. **Map** p102.

A fabulous play hall with facilities including indoor climbing equipment and a playhouse on the third floor, and a music lobby on the fourth floor where children can indulge their love of noise. The playport in the roof garden on the fifth floor is the Castle's biggest attraction, combining a jungle gym with large ball pools. Access to the playport is restricted to children over the age of three, and it closes on rainy days. A swimming pool on the second basement floor reopened in April 2001, but requires an additional fee of ¥100-¥300.

Tokyo Metropolitan Children's Hall

1-18-24 Shibuya, Shibuya-ku (3409 6361/www. jidokaikan.metro.tokyo.jp). Shibuya station, Miyamasuzaka (east) exit. **Open** *Sept-June* 9am-5pm daily. *July, Aug* 9am-6pm daily. Closed 2nd, 4th Mon of mth, 29 Dec-3 Jan. **Admission** free. **Map** p102.

Located conveniently near Shibuya, this public facility – the largest of 600 public children's halls in Japan – is a gem, its six-storey building packed with recreational and educational facilities. The second floor is reserved for pre-schoolers, with large wooden climbing frames and wooden toys. The third floor features a handicraft section, the 'human body maze' and a ball pool, the most popular play area. Books can be borrowed from a library on the fifth floor, while on the roof, kids can try their hand at roller-skating and unicycling. Each floor has plenty of lockers to stash belongings. On the way home, be sure to pick up a copy of the monthly event schedule at the information centre. For information about other children's halls, contact the Tokyo Metropolitan Government Foreign Residents' Advisory Centre, *see chapter* **Resources A-Z: telephone helplines**.

Museums

Japan Science Foundation Science Museum

2-1 Kitanomaru Koen, Chiyoda-ku (3212 8544/ www.jsf.or.jp). Kudanshita station, exit 2. **Open** 9.30am-4.50pm daily. **Admission** ¥600; ¥250-¥400 concessions. **Map** p62.

Compared with the National Science Museum (*below*), this place is more like a school, dedicated to raising interest in science and technology through interactive programmes and exhibits. Check the whiteboard at the entrance for programme schedules, then head to the fifth floor, where most of the interactive programmes and classes take place. In one programme children learn about the principle of flight by making a boomerang. In another, they learn about the mechanics of pulleys by manoeuvring a crane to lift a ball. The interactive exhibits are as much fun as they are educational.

National Science Museum

7-20 Ueno Koen, Taito-ku (3822 0111/www. kahaku.go.jp/english/index.html). Ueno station. **Open** 9am-4.30pm Tue-Thur; 9am-8pm Fri; 9am-6pm Sat, Sun. **Admission** ¥420; ¥70 concessions. Free every 2nd Sat of mth. **Map** p88.

The museum has a good collection of dinosaur fossils, including an Arosaurus that greets you at the entrance of the main building and a Tyranosaurus, Triceratops and giant Apatosaurus in the basement of the new building. Kids may get a kick out of the interactive displays in the Discovery Forest on the third floor of the new building.

Transportation Museum

1-25 Kanda-Sudacho, Chiyoda-ku (3251 8481/www. kouhaku.or.jp). Akihabara station, Electric Town exit, or Kanda station, north exit. **Open** 9.30am-5pm Tue-Sun. **Admission** ¥310; ¥150 4-15s.

Young train fans congregate here to clamber over a variety of steam engines, train carriages and drivers' cabs. A simulator offers the chance to drive a train for yourself.

Weird and wonderful faces at the **National Children's Castle**. *See p204.*

Shopping

Toys

For more toys and novelties, *see p187.*

BorneLund

Hara Bldg 1F, 6-10-9 Jingumae, Shibuya-ku (5485 3430/www.bornelund.co.jp). Harajuku station, Omotesando exit or Meiji-Jingumae station, exit 4. **Open** 11am-7.30pm daily. **Credit** AmEx, DC, JCB, MC, V. **Map** p99.

This small shop near Omotesando has a great selection of wooden toys, mostly imports from Europe and North America. Unless you are looking specifically for Japanese toys, you are more likely to find better Christmas presents here than in other local rivals, such as Kiddyland (*below*).

Kiddyland

6-1-9 Jingumae, Shibuya-ku (3409 3431/ www.kiddyland.co.jp). Harajuku station, Omotesando exit or Meiji-Jingumae station, exit 4.
Open 10am-8pm. Closed third Tue of mth. **Credit** AmEx, DC, JCB, MC, V. **Map** p99.

Kiddyland excels in 'character goods', some of them imported, such as Snoopy, and some of them home-grown, such as Sanrio's omnipresent Kitty-chan.

Toys'R'Us

Aqua City Odaiba 1F, 1-7-1 Daiba, Minato-ku (5564 5011/www.toysrus.co.jp). Daiba or Odaiba Kaihin Koen station (Yurikamome Line). **Open** 11am-9pm daily. **Credit** AmEx, DC, JCB, MC, V. **Map** p78.

This US toy chain sells the same range of toys as department stores but at more competitive prices. There is another central Tokyo outlet in the Sunshine City complex, Ikebukuro (*see p171*).

Clothes

Children Museum

1-25-17 Jiyugaoka, Meguro-ku (3718 8855/www. children-museum.com). Jiyugaoka station. **Open** 10.30am-7pm daily. **Credit** varies.

This small tile-covered building houses 21 shops for children's clothes, shoes, accessories and toys. A purchase of more than ¥1,000 entitles you to a ride on a mini Thomas train.

Dear Kids Park

Palette Town 1F, 1 Aomi, Koto-ku (3599 1749/ www.palette-town.com). Aomi station (Yurikamome Line) or Tokyo Teleport station (Rinkai Line). **Open** 11am-8pm daily. **Credit** varies. **Map** p78.

Part of the Sun Walk mall in Palette Town, this shopping area contains 13 shops, all devoted to children. There's also a small space with play equipment.

Mujirushi Ryohin

3-8-3 Marunouchi, Chiyoda-ku (5208 8241/www. mujiyurakucho.com). Yurakucho JR station, Kyobashi exit or Yurakucho subway station, exit A9. **Open** 10am-9pm daily. **Credit** AmEx, DC, JCB, MC, V. **Map** p57.

This no-brand store chain deals in almost everything you need for babies and children. The flagship shop in Ginza has a feeding room and a play area. **Branches**: throughout the city.

Uniqlo

3-13-3 Shinjuku, Shinjuku-ku (5369 0731/www.uniqlo.com). Shinjuku San-Chome station, exit B2. **Open** 11am-9pm daily. **Credit** AmEx, DC, JCB, MC, V. **Map** p109.

The choice of babies' and children's clothes at this casual-wear chain is very limited, but clothes are priced competitively and are great value for money.

Hairdressing

Choki Choki

Aqua City Odaiba 6F, 1-7-1 Minato-ku (3528 4005/www.choki-choki.com). Daiba station (Yurikamome Line). **Open** 11am-9pm daily (last appointment 7.30pm). **Credit** AmEx, DC, JCB, MC, V. **Map** p78.

Opened in November 2002, this is Japan's largest hair salon for children. Junior customers are covered in a plastic cape printed with cartoon pictures, and sit on a chair that's actually a pedal car. While they are 'steering' and watching a video shown in a side mirror, the hairdressers go about their business.

Zusso-f

Isetan department store 4F, 1-11-5 Kichijoji-Honcho, Musashino-shi (0422 20 4790/www.zusso.com/zusso-f). Kichijoji station, north exit. **Open** 10am-7.30pm daily. **Credit** AmEx, DC, JCB, MC, V.

Tokyo's first hair salon for children. Small customers can watch a video while getting a haircut. Games are provided in a waiting room, too.

Restaurants

Eating out with small children can be a problem in any city. Luckily Tokyo has the institution of the 'family restaurant'. Such restaurants are usually spacious, have child seats and serve special meals for children at reasonable prices. Restaurants in the Skylark chain serve a Kid's Plate for ¥380, and similar meals at Jonathan's and Denny's cost ¥480.

Crayon House Hiroba

3-8-15 Kita-Aoyama, Minato-ku (3406 6409/www.crayonhouse.co.jp). Omotesando station, exit B2. **Open** 11am-10pm daily. **No credit cards. Map** p99.

This organic restaurant, in the basement of the Crayon House children's bookstore, runs an eat-as-much-as-you-like buffet for ¥1,200. The bookstore on the first floor stocks 50,000 books, while the toy shop on the second handles imported wooden toys.

Sylvanian Families

i-Bldg 3F, 2-13-11 Kichijoji-Honcho, Musashino-shi (0422 23 2030). Kichijoji station, north exit. **Open** 11am-10pm daily. **Credit** DC, JCB, V.

This small restaurant in Kichijoji, run by the Japanese licensee of the Sylvanian Families characters, is filled with Sylvanian dolls and dolls' houses. For ¥650, kids can have lunch with bears, rabbits and other residents of Sylvanian Village. The restaurant also has a small play area.

Babysitting

The following babysitter services come highly recommended by Tokyo parents. If you're staying at a reputable hotel, staff may be able to arrange babysitting, but the following agencies all have qualified, well-trained and caring staff.

Rates vary but expect to pay between ¥1,500 and ¥2,200 per hour. Some agencies demand a minimum of three hours at a set rate before they agree to send out a sitter, then you pay for each additional hour, with different rates for late-night and early-morning services.

As a rule, do not expect sitters from agencies to speak a wide variety of languages, though from time to time some do have babysitters who speak a little English or French.

Japan Baby-Sitter Service

7-19-16 Oizumi-Gakuen-cho, Nerima-ku (3423 1251/www.jbs-mom.co.jp). **Open** 5am-noon daily. **No credit cards.**

One of the oldest services in Tokyo, specialising in grandmotherly types. Reserve 24 hours in advance.

Little Mate

3-6-23 Ooka, Minami-ku, Yokohama-shi (045 712 3253/www.tokyolm.co.jp). Nursery at Keio Plaza Hotel (3345 1439) & Okura Hotel (3586 0360). **Open** 7am-midnight daily. **No credit cards.**

Little Mate is a day nursery where you can drop your children off for an hour or more, or even overnight at the two hotels listed. Reservations are required by 7pm the previous day (4pm at the Okura Hotel). For hotel addresses, *see pp34-52*.

Poppins Service

Tekku Hiroo Bldg 8F, 1-10-5 Hiroo, Shibuya-ku (3447 2100/www.poppins.co.jp). **Open** 7am-9pm Mon-Sat. Membership only. **No credit cards.**

Expect either a young lady trained in early childhood education or a retired veteran teacher when you request a sitter from Poppins. At the Toys'R'Us nursery in Odaiba, a glass exterior lets parents check how their little ones are looked after. Bookings must be made two days in advance.

Branch: *in front of Toys'R'Us, Aqua City Odaiba 1F, 1-7-1 Daiba, Minato-ku (3599 4510).*

Royal Baby Salon

Ginza Kosumion Bldg 7F, 1-5-14 Ginza, Chuo-ku (3538 3238/www.royalbaby.co.jp). Ginza-Itchome station, exit 6. **Open** 10am-6 pm daily. **Credit** (with extra charge) AmEx, DC, JCB, MC, V. **Map** 57.

This nursery comes in handy when you want to leave your children in safe hands while you go shopping in the Ginza area. Children under two years of age receive individual, one-on-one attention from a highly experienced sitter. When making a reservation, ID, such as a passport, must be produced, and bookings must be made by 5pm the day before. Sitting periods can be extended later into the evening by prior arrangement.

Film

Going to the cinema can be a daunting experience if you don't know the ropes.

A visit to the cinema in Tokyo can be one of the most frustrating, dispiriting experiences known to mankind. For a start, it's expensive, with major cinemas charging an average of ¥1,800 for on-the-day admission. If you want to save money, advance tickets can be bought at convenience stores and ticket agencies for around ¥300 less. The problem with this system is that the tickets are sold for the film, not the cinema, so in theory any number of people can descend on a given cinema to catch the latest blockbuster. And they do. To be sure of a good seat, people regularly arrive one hour in advance, and then charge in to take the best places as soon as the doors open. Seats can be booked through agencies such as Pia (*see p225*), but this adds an extra ¥200-¥1,000 to the price.

The cluster of Japanese cinemas in areas such as Shinjuku, Ginza and Shibuya all operate this ridiculous system. However, hope comes in the form of the new breed of multiplexes, which offer reserved seating at the point of sale without a premium.

Despite the inconvenience, cinema-going is a popular pastime here, and most Hollywood or other foreign films are screened in their original version with Japanese subtitles. Major Japanese cinemas in Tokyo's busiest centres are not listed, simply because we can't recommend the experience. None of the cinemas listed here accept credit cards.

Cinemas

Athénée Français Cultural Centre

4F, 2-11 Kanda Surugadai, Chiyoda-ku (3291 4339/ www.athenee.net/culturalcenter/). Suidobashi JR station, exit A1. **Tickets** vary. **Seats** 80.

Screens classics and discovers new filmmakers.

Ciné Amuse

ÇSF, 2-23-12 Dogenzaka,Shibuya-ku (3496 2888/ www.cineamuse.co.jp/). Shibuya JR station, Hachiko exit. **Tickets** ¥1,800; ¥1,000-¥1,500 concessions; ¥1,000 on 1st of mth except Jan. **Seats** 132 in East Screen, 129 in West Screen. **Map** p102.

Programming ranges from Japanese classics such as *Ai no Corrida* to new international films.

Ciné La Sept

2-8-6 Yurakucho, Chiyoda-ku (3212 3761/www. cqn.co.jp/). Yurakucho JR station, Chuo exit. **Tickets** ¥1,800; ¥1,000-¥1,500 concessions; ¥1,000 on 1st of mth. **Seats** 159. **Map** p57.

A mixture of home-grown films and less well-known international charmers are shown in this authentic-looking art-house cinema. The programme also includes morning and late-night screenings.

Ciné Pathos

4-8-7 Ginza, Chuo-ku (3561 4660). Ginza station, exit A6. **Tickets** ¥1,800; ¥1,000-¥1,500 concessions; ¥1,000 for all on 1st of mth. **Seats** 200 in screen 1, 144 in screen 2, 81 in screen 3. **Map** p57.

A three-screen cinema that mixes new films and classic revivals.

Ciné Quinto

Parco Part3 8F, 14-5 Udagawa-cho, Shibuya-ku (3477 5905/www.parco-city.co.jp/cine_quinto/). Shibuya JR station, Hachiko exit. **Tickets** ¥1,800; ¥1,000-¥1,500 concessions; ¥1,000 1st of Mar, June, Sept & Dec. Keep ticket stub for ¥800 discount next time. **Seats** 227. **Map** p102.

Good sound equipment and comfortable seats are a welcome feature of this cinema, which often screens new British films. It also offers bizarre film-based discounts. For example, when Hong Kong film *The Eye* was on, anyone carrying a photo of a ghost got an ¥800 discount. Different rules are stipulated for each film.

Cinema Rise

13-17 Udagawa-cho, Shibuya-ku (3464 0051/ www.cinemarise.com./). Shibuya JR station, Hachiko exit. **Tickets** ¥1,800; ¥1,000-¥1,500 concessions; ¥1,000 for last show Sun; ¥1,000 on 1st of mth (not Jan). **Seats** 220 in screen 1, 303 in screen 2. **Map** p102.

A champion of independent cinema, this is the place where *Trainspotting* and *Buena Vista Social Club* first hit Tokyo. Overseas students pay only ¥1,000, but must show valid ID.

Cinema Shimo-Kitazawa

1-45-15 Kitazawa, Setagaya-ku (5452 1400/ www.cinekita.co.jp/). Shimo-Kitazawa station (Keio Inokashira or Odakyu Line), south exit. **Tickets** ¥1,500, ¥1,000-¥1,300 concessions. **Seats** 50.

A shed built by film studio staff. Shows independent films from around the world.

Cinema Square Tokyu

Tokyu Milano Bldg 3F, 1-29-1 Kabukicho, Shinjuku-ku (3202 1189/www.tokyu-rec. co.jp/table.html). Shinjuku JR station, east exit. **Tickets** ¥1,800; ¥1,000-¥1,500 concessions; ¥1,000 for all on 1st of mth. **Seats** 224. **Map** p109.

The pioneer of art house cinemas in Tokyo, showing mainly recent independent films.

Ebisu Garden Cinema.

Le Cinema

Bunkamura 6F, 2-24-1 Dogenzaka, Shibuya-ku (3477 9264/www.b-lecinema.com/). Shibuya JR station, Hachiko exit. **Tickets** ¥1,800; ¥1,000-¥1,500 concessions; ¥1,000 on 1st of mth. **Seats** 150 in screen 1, 126 in screen 2. **Map** p102.

Two screens in the giant Bunkamura arts complex offer a diet of mainly French fare. Also the main venue for the Tokyo International Film Festival.

Ciné Saison Shibuya

The Prime 6F, 2-29-5 Dogenzaka, Shibuya-ku (3770 1721/www.webs.to/sibuya/). Shibuya JR station, Hachiko exit. **Tickets** ¥1,800, ¥1,000-¥1,500 concessions, ¥1,000 on 1st of mth & Wed. **Seats** 221. **Map** p102.

Revivals, mini festivals and independent productions are the lifeblood of this comfortable cinema.

Ciné Switch Ginza

Ginza-Hata Bldg B1F, 4-4-5 Ginza, Chuo-ku (3561 0707/www.cineswitch.com/). Ginza station, exit A10. **Tickets** ¥1,800; ¥1,000-¥1,500 concessions; ¥1,000 on 1st of mth. **Seats** 273 in screen 1, 182 in screen 2. **Map** p57.

Recent European and American films.

Ebisu Garden Cinema

4-20-2 Ebisu Garden Place, Ebisu, Shibuya-ku (5420 6161/www.cineplex.co.jp/). Ebisu JR station, east exit. **Tickets** ¥1,800; ¥1,000-¥1,500 concessions; ¥1,000 on 1st of mth. **Seats** 232 in screen 1, 116 in screen 2.

Two comfortable screens show a mix of blockbusters and limited-release foreign films. Film-goers are summoned in numbered batches, according to when they bought their tickets, so there's never any stampede for seats.

Euro Space

Tobu-Fuji Bldg 2F, 24-4 Sakuragaoka-cho, Shibuya-ku (3461 0211/www.eurospace.co.jp/). Shibuya JR station, south exit. **Tickets** ¥1,700; ¥1,000-¥1,400 concessions; ¥1,000 on 1st of mth (not Jan). **Seats** 75 in screen 1, 106 in screen 2. **Map** p102.

This cinema specialises in independent films from Europe and Asia. Retrospectives have included an Eric Rohmer revival.

Ginza Théâtre Cinema

Ginza-Théâtre Bldg 5F, 1-11-2 Ginza, Chuo-ku (3535 6000/http://webs.to/ginza/). Kyobashi station, exit 2. **Tickets** ¥1,800; ¥1,000-¥1,500 concessions; ¥1,000 on 1st of mth. **Seats** 150. **Map** p57.

Late-night shows with interesting programmes.

Haiyu-za

4-9-2 Roppongi, Minato-ku (3470 2880/www.haiyuzagekijou.co.jp/jindex.html). Roppongi station, exit 6 from Toei Oedo Line, exit 4A from Hibiya Line. **Tickets** vary. **Seats** 300. **Map** p74.

Roppongi's venerable old fleapit only opens irregularly these days, but when it does its speciality is weird and avant-garde films from all continents.

Hibiya Chanté Ciné

Chanté Bldg 2F, 1-2-2 Yurakucho, Chiyoda-ku (3591 1511/www.toho.co.jp/). Hibiya station, exit A5. **Tickets** ¥1,800; ¥1,000-¥1,500 concessions; ¥1,000 on 1st of mth. **Seats** 226 in screens 1 & 2, 192 in screen 3. **Map** p57.

Shows mainly recent European and American films.

Iidabashi Ginrei Hall

2-19 Kagurazaka, Shinjuku-ku (3269 3852/www.cam.hi-ho.ne.jp/ginrei/). Iidabashi JR station, west exit or Iidabashi subway station, exit B4A, B4B. **Tickets** ¥1,500; ¥1,000-¥1,200 concessions; ¥1,000 on 1st of mth. **Seats** 206.

Special double-feature screenings offer interesting combinations of second-run films. If you pay ¥10,000 to join the Cinema Club, you can go as often as you like for a year without paying another yen,.

Iwanami Hall

Iwanami Jinbocho Bldg 10F, 2-1 Kanda Jinbocho, Chiyoda-ku (3262 5252/www.iwanami-hall.com/). Jinbocho station, exit A6. **Tickets** ¥1,800; ¥1,400-¥1,500 concessions; ¥1,400 on 1st of mth. **Seats** 400. **Map** p62.

This high-brow cinema has been screening international works of social realism since the 1970s.

Kichijoji Baus Theatre

1-11-23 Kichijoji-Honmachi, Musashino-shi (0422 22 3555/www.baustheater.com/). Kichijoji station, north (Chuo) exit. **Tickets** ¥1,800; ¥1,000-¥1,500 concessions; ¥1,000 on 1st of mth. **Seats** 220 in screen 1, 50 in screen 2, 106 in screen 3.

Three screens showing everything from Hollywood blockbusters to Japanese independent films.

Kineca Omori

Seiyu Omori 5F, 6-27-25 Minami Oi, Shinagawa-ku (3762 6000/kineca.m78.com/). Omori station, east exit. **Tickets** ¥1,800; ¥1,000-¥1,500 concessions; ¥1,000 on Wed. **Seats** 168 in screen 1, 82 in screen 2, 52 in screen 3.

Three screens, with one showing only Asian films. Late-night shows often have interesting programmes, such as the films of John Cassavetes.

Laputa Asagaya

Laputa Bldg 2F, 2-12-21 Asagaya-Kita, Suginami-ku (3336 5440/www.laputa-jp.com/). Asagaya station, north exit. **Tickets** ¥1,200; ¥1,000 concessions; ¥1,000 on Wed. **Seats** 50.

Tiny cinema that shows everything from Mikio Naruse to Ken Loach. A meal in the top-floor restaurant is a nice way to finish off a night at the pictures.

National Museum of Modern Art Film Centre

3-7-6 Kyobashi, Chuo-ku (5777 8600/www.momat.go.jp). Kyobashi station, exit 1 or Takara-cho station (Toei Asakusa Line), exit A4. **Tickets** ¥500. **Seats** 310 in screen 1, 151 in screen 2. **Map** p57.

This museum hosts two cinemas, an exhibition gallery, library and café. The museum has a 19,000-strong collection of rare films, and often revives Japanese classics. Programme information and schedules are posted on the bilingual website.

Sanbyakunin Gekijo

2-29-10 Honkomagome, Bunkyo-ku (3944 5451/www.bekkoame.ne.jp/~darts). Sengoku station (Toei Mita Line), exit A1. **Tickets** ¥1,800; ¥1,000-¥1,500 concessions; ¥1,000 on 1st of mth. **Seats** 302.

Art house cinema specialising in classic features. It recently held a Fritz Lang retrospective.

Sangenjaya Chuo Gekijo

2-14-5 Sangenjaya, Setagaya-ku (3421 4610). Sangenjaya station (Tokyu Denentoshi Line) Setagaya dori exit. **Tickets** ¥1,300, ¥800-¥1,100 concessions; ¥1,000 1st of mth; ¥1,100 Fri. **Seats** 262.

Good old second-run cinema with interesting double features.

Shibuya Cinema Society

Fuji-Bldg37 B1F, 1-18 Dogenzaka, Shibuya-ku (3496 3203). Shibuya JR station, west exit. **Tickets** ¥1,800, ¥1,000-¥1,500 concessions; ¥1,000 on 1st of mth. **Seats** 104. **Map** p102.

Shows range from recent European and American films to revivals of work from world cinema. On Mondays, couples – gay or straight – pay ¥2,800.

Shimo-takaido Cinema

3-27-26 Matsubara, Setagaya-ku (3328 1008). Shimo-Takaido station (Keio or Tokyu Setagaya lines). **Tickets** ¥1,600; ¥1,000-¥1,300 concessions; ¥1,000 on 1st of mth. **Seats** 126.

Repertory cinema with an interesting programme, from revivals to recent major films.

Shin-Bungeiza

Maruhan-Ikebukuro Bldg 3F, 1-43-5 Higashi-Ikebukuro, Toshima-ku (3971 9422/www.shin-bungeiza.com). Ikebukuro JR station, east exit. **Tickets** ¥1,300; ¥900-¥1,200 concessions. **Seats** 266. **Map** p69.

Legendary repertory cinema that reopened after rebuilding in 2000. Shows a wide range of films, from Japanese classics to Hollywood no-brainers.

Theatre Image Forum

2-10-2 Shibuya, Shibuya-ku (5766 0114/www.imageforum.co.jp/). Shibuya JR station, east exit. **Tickets** ¥1,800; ¥1,000-¥1,500 concessions. **Seats** 64 in screen 1, 108 in screen 2. **Map** p102.

Two screens show cutting-edge contemporary films, classics and avant-garde features.

Tollywood

2F, 5-32-5 Daisawa, Setagaya-ku (3414 0433/homepage1.nifty.com/tollywood/) Shimo-Kitazawa station (Odakyu/Keio Inokashira lines), south exit. **Tickets** ¥600-¥1,500. **Seats** 46.

Art house cinema specialising in short films, famous directors' early works and new independent films.

Uplink Factory

Yokoyama Bldg 5F, 1-8-17 Jinnan, Shibuya-ku (5489 0750/www.uplink.co.jp/). Shibuya JR station, Hachiko exit. **Tickets** vary. **Seats** 50. **Map** p102.

Fascinating programme that runs from features such as Roman Polanski's early works to Eurotrash. Also holds film workshops and live performances.

Multiplexes

Cinema Mediage

Mediage, Aqua City Odaiba 1/2F, 1-7-1 Daiba, Minato-ku (5531 7878/www.cinema-mediage.com). Odaiba Kaihin Koen station (Yurikamome Line). **Tickets** ¥1,800; ¥1,000-¥1,500 concessions; ¥6,000 super premium for two; ¥2,000-¥2,200 premium; ¥1,000 for all on 1st of mth. **Seats** 114-612 (varies over 13 screens). **Map** p78.

The home of the super premium love seat, designed for canoodling couples, Warners-owned Mediage provides a superior film-going experience, with all seats reserved at no extra charge.

Shinagawa Prince Cinema

Shinagawa Prince Hotel Executive Tower 3F, 4-10-30 Takanawa, Minato-ku (5421 1113/www.princehotels.co.jp/info1/shinagawa-executive/cinema_imax/site/cinema/index.html). Shinagawa station, Takanawa exit. **Tickets** ¥1,800; ¥1,000-¥1,500 concessions; ¥1,000 on 1st of mth; ¥2,500 premier screens. **Seats** 96-219 (varies over 10 screens).

All the latest hits appear at this ten-screen giant. Premium screens have wide, high-backed seats, and parents can leave kids in the hotel's day nursery (call ahead to confirm a place).

Virgin Cinemas Roppongi

Roppongi Hills (www.virgincinemas.co.jp/roppongi/index.html). Roppongi station, exit 1. **Tickets** ¥1,800; ¥1,000-¥1,500 concessions; ¥3,000 premier screen; ¥1,800 premier art screen; ¥1,000 on 1st of mth (not premier screen). **Seats** 81-652 (varies over 9 screens). **Map** p74.

This giant of a cinema in the Roppongi Hills has all-night screenings on Thursdays, Fridays and Saturdays. The so-called premium screens offer art-house movies.

Galleries

A brief tour through Tokyo's increasingly lively contemporary art scene.

Tokyo purportedly has more than 1,000 art galleries. Volume alone, however, doesn't create focus or momentum. To understand the limitations of the local scene, tour the tiny storefront galleries in the art centre of Ginza. Most are halfway homes for resold ceramics or Cezannes, basements for rent to the unrepresented, temples to the traditional, on-again off-agains, or corporate trophies. That doesn't mean there's nothing good. There are a handful of consistent, internationally minded contemporary art galleries scattered around, and the rental and corporate spaces often bear surprises. But at times it can feel like a treasure hunt with the odds of a lottery.

Recently this situation has begun to improve dramatically. A number of progressive young galleries throughout the city have begun to band together loosely, raising the standard and increasing transparency.

One result is *Favorite!*, a free, bilingual, bi-monthly map and exhibition schedule to what's on at the best contemporary galleries (and two private museums) in Tokyo (pick it up at any of the spaces marked 'F' in the listings).

Another is the consolidation of several premier galleries into two must-see complexes. The atmospheric Shokuryo Building in Sagacho accomplished this for a number of years, but fell to redevelopers' bulldozers at the end of 2002. Most of the Shokuryo galleries moved to a former paper warehouse in nearby Shinkawa (Kayabacho station) at the beginning of 2003. Following renovations, the new home of **Taka Ishii**, **Shugo Arts**, **Tomio Koyama** and **Viewing Room Koyanagi** has given Tokyo a novel, Chelsea-type destination. And, like the Shokuryo, it's spitting distance from the Sumida river and the Museum of Contemporary Art (MoT, *see p97*). About 20 minutes away from Shinkawa on the Hibiya subway line, **Ota Fine Arts**, **Roentgen** and **Taro Nasu Gallery** joined forces in a complex in Roppongi, opened in April 2003, near the new Mori Art Museum (MAM, *see p75*).

There are two additional high-density, centrally located art spots worth stopping by. The **Okuno Building** in Ginza has five floors of closet-sized rental galleries inside one of the area's oldest tenements. Just a few blocks away, a large number of galleries cluster in the **Kyobashi** district. Across town in Omotesando, the super white **Galeria Building** houses **Skydoor Gallery**, **Promo-Arte** and **Gallery Gan**. Further down the same street you'll find **Yasu** and other small galleries.

Despite these agglomerations, Tokyo galleries and museums still tend to be fairly spread out so planning is essential. Check the latest listings in the free weekly magazine, *Metropolis* (available at various shops on Fridays and online at www.metropolis.co.jp), the weekly art sections of newspapers – the *Japan Times* on Wednesday, the *Daily Yomiuri* on Thursday and the *International Herald Tribune* on Friday – and the quarterly *Tokyo Journal*.

Other useful media sources are **Japan Art Scene Monitor**, a website supported by the Australian Embassy which summarises recent cultural developments (www.jasm.australia.or.jp), and **Real Tokyo**, a website and e-newsletter that keeps readers updated on upcoming cultural activities around the capital (www.realtokyo.co.jp/english).

In addition to young galleries, energetic new organisations have brought fresh viewpoints to Tokyo's ossified art structures. The most exciting is **Arts Initiative Tokyo**, a group of young independent curators who run classes on how to think about, talk about and curate contemporary art (skills rarely taught at Japanese art schools). Though most of their classes are in Japanese, they also host bilingual guest lectures as well as temporary exhibitions and parties (www.a-I-t.net). Elsewhere, alternative groups such as **Video Art Collective** (5380 8755) carry on, but unfortunately the groups command N (www.commandn.net) and eyesaw (www.eyesaw.org) have been put on hold.

Big organisations are stirring things up at the grassroots level, too. Major corporations including Kirin and Philip Morris sponsor regular competitions for young artists. In 2002, the Mori Art Museum produced a CD of young art musicians and also held a video art competition and subsequent seven-month-long screening series at their space, Think Zone. In April 2004, they will sponsor their first biennial show of 50 contemporary artists living in Japan. The 2001 **Yokohama Triennale**, initiated by the Japan Foundation, introduced 110 artists from Japan and overseas and gave the Tokyo area a much needed high-profile international art event. Look for the second instalment in 2004 (www.jpf.go.jp).

To see art from young people who don't win competitions, who have no access to commercial galleries, but still want to show and sell their work, visit one of the semi-annual art festivals put on by **Design Festa** or **Geisai** (*see p196,* started by Takashi Murakami). At these events fashionistas, performers, designers, illustrators and artists all pay a small amount to do their thing in booths measuring little more than three feet square.

Note that many of the galleries below open only when they have an exhibition on. Call ahead to confirm, or check the relevant website.

Akasaka-Roppongi

Canadian Embassy Gallery

B2, 7-3-38 Akasaka, Minato-ku (5412 6200/www.canadanet.or.jp/). Aoyama-Itchome station, exit 4. **Open** 9am-5.30pm Mon-Fri; 1-5pm Sat.

Canada's best appears in the spacious, high-ceilinged granite basement of Moriyama and Teshima Architects' award-winning building.

Gallery MA

TOTO Nogizaka Bldg #3, 3F, 1-24-3 Minami-Aoyama, Minato-ku (3402 1010/www.toto.co.jp/GALLERMA/index.htm). Nogizaka station, exits 3, 4. **Open** 11am-7pm Tue-Sat. **Map** p74.

Sponsored by toilet giant Toto, this gallery holds some of the city's best modern and contemporary architecture shows. It usually publishes catalogues to accompany exhibitions, which are sold in the small bookstore. Recent shows have featured the work of Konstantin Melnikov and Yamamoto Riken.

Gallery Min Min

Complex 3F, 6-8-14 Roppongi, Minato-ku (5414 2360). Roppongi station, exits 1, 3. **Open** 2-7pm Tue-Sat. **Map** p74.

A relatively new gallery showing international artists, especially photo-based painting.

Gallery Side 2

Mitsuba Bldg 1F, 2-18-3 Akasaka, Minato-ku (6229 3669). Tameike-Sanno station, exit 12. **Open** 11am-7pm Tue-Sat. **Map** p74.

This daring space shows emerging Japanese (Shinoda Taro, Fujita Jun) and hot international artists (Andrea Zittel). F.

Hiromi Yoshii + Gallery Koyanagi Viewing Room

Complex 1F, 6-8-14 Roppongi, Minato-ku (5786 3566). Roppongi station, exits 1, 3. **Open** 11am 7pm Tue-Sat. **Map** p74.

This young gallerist specialises in prints by well-known contemporary Japanese artists.

Hiromi Yoshii.

Ota Fine Arts

Complex 1F, 6-8-14 Roppongi, Minato-ku (5786 2344/www.jade.dti.ne.jp/~aft/home.html). Roppongi station, exits 1, 3. **Open** 11am-7pm Tue-Sat. **Map** p74.

Some of Japan's best-known contemporary artists such as Kusama Yayoi, Ozawa Tsuyoshi and others dealing with the politics of identity show at this well-established gallery. F.

roentgenwerke

Complex 3F, 6-8-14 Roppongi, Minato-ku (3475 0166). Roppongi station, exits 1, 3. **Open** 11am-7pm Tue-Sat. **Map** p74.

Roentgen (German for x-ray) was first the largest and then the smallest gallery in Tokyo. Now it's a happy medium-small, and features conceptual work mostly by European and Japanese artists.

Taro Nasu Gallery

Complex 2F, 6-8-14 Roppongi, Minato-ku (5411 7510). Roppongi station, exits 1, 3. **Open** 11am-7pm Tue-Sat. **Map** p74.

Young and emerging Japanese and international artists such as Matsue Taiji show under Nasu's unusually thin fluorescent strip lighting.

Asakusa

Contemporary Art Factory

1-15-3 Sumida, Sumida-ku (5630 3216/www.ask.ne.jp/~factory/infomation/infomation.html). Higashi Mukojima station (Tobu Isezaki Line from Asakusa). **Open** noon-7pm Wed-Fri; noon-6pm Sat-Sun.

Forward-looking if irregular exhibitions, performances and other events are held in a 40-year-old *shitamachi* warehouse.

Gallery ef

2-19-18 Kaminarimon, Taito-ku (3841 0442/www.tctv.ne.jp/get2-ef). Asakusa station, exit 2. **Open** 11am-7pm Mon, Wed-Sun. **Map** p83.

The beamed ceilings and lacquer floors of this extremely rare example of a 19th-century earthen-walled warehouse are tough competition for the contemporary international art that is shown here. *See also p153.*

Ginza

Base Gallery

Kindai Bldg, 1F, 3-7-4 Kyobashi, Chuo-ku (3567 8543/www.gaden.com/base.html). Kyobashi station, exits 1, 2. **Open** 11am-7pm Mon-Sat. **Map** p57.

This well-established space on the edge of Ginza shows blue-chip contemporary Japanese artists such as painter Ohtake Shinro and younger names including photographer Yokozawa Tsukasa.

Creation Gallery-G8

Recruit Ginza 8 Bldg 1F, 8-4-17 Ginza, Chuo-ku (3575 6918/www.recruit.co.jp/GG/). Shinbashi JR station, Ginza exit. **Open** 11am-7pm Mon-Fri. **Map** p57.

Massive Japanese publishing house Recruit shows contemporary Japanese graphic design in one of its office buildings.

Dai-Ichi Seimei Minami Gallery

DN Tower 21, Dai-ichi Honkan Bldg 1F, 1-13-1 Yurakucho, Chiyoda-ku (5221 3242/www.dai-ichi-life.co.jp/company/activity/index.html). Hibiya station, exit B2. **Open** 11am-6pm Mon-Fri. **Map** p57.

A major life insurance company sponsors this showcase for young, emerging Japanese artists.

Forum Art Shop

B Block, Tokyo International Forum, 3-5-1 Marunouchi, Chiyoda-ku (3286 6716/http://paper.cup.com/forum). Yurakucho JR station, Tokyo International Forum exit. **Open** 10am-8pm daily. **Map** p57.

Inside architect Rafael Vinoly's stunning landmark convention and performance centre, this space shows contemporary Japanese arts and crafts.

Galleria Grafica

Ginza S2 Bldg 1, 2F, 6-13-4 Ginza, Chuo-ku (5550 1335/www2.big.or.jp/~adel/grafica.html). Higashi Ginza station, exit A1 or Ginza station, exit A3. **Open** 11am-7pm Mon-Sat. **Map** p57.

There's a busy rental space on the ground floor of the building that houses Galleria Grafica, and a commercial gallery upstairs.

Gallery Koyanagi

1-7-5 Ginza, Chuo-ku (3561 1896). Ginza station, exit A13 or Ginza-Itchome station, exit 7. **Open** 11am-7pm Mon-Sat. **Map** p57.

This major Tokyo white cube features international and Japanese artists with an emphasis on photography (Thomas Ruff, Sugimoto Hiroshi). F.

Gallery Yamaguchi

Kyoei Bldg, B1, 1F 3-5-3 Kyobashi, Chuo-ku (3564 6167/www.jade.dti.ne.jp/~g-yama/www.gaden.com/yamaguchi.html). Kyobashi station, exit 2. **Open** 11am-7pm Mon-Sat. **Map** p57.

This pair of galleries (rental and commercial) mostly shows young Japanese artists.

Ginza Graphic Gallery

DNP Ginza Bldg 1F, 7-7-2 Ginza, Chuo-ku (3571 5206/www.dnp.co.jp/gallery). Ginza station, exit A2. **Open** 11am-7pm Mon-Fri; 11am-6pm Sat. **Map** p57.

One of Japan's largest printing companies presents contemporary design and graphics.

Guardian Garden

Recruit Ginza 7 Bldg B1F, 7-3-5 Ginza, Chuo-ku (5568 8818/www.recruit.co.jp/GG/). Shinbashi JR station, Ginza exit. **Open** 11am-7pm Mon-Fri. **Map** p57.

This Recruit-sponsored gallery often features group shows of young photographers.

INAX Gallery

Inax Plaza 2F, 3-6-18 Kyobashi, Chuo-ku (5250 6530/www.inax.co.jp/Culture/gallery/1_tokyo.html). Kyobashi station, exit 2. **Open** 10am-6pm Mon-Sat. **Map** p57.

Major ceramics maker INAX runs an architecture bookstore on the ground floor and two galleries upstairs at this premises. One gallery caters for emerging artists with a craft edge, while the other deals with exhibitions of traditional craft techniques from around the world.

Kobayashi Gallery

Yamato Bldg B1, 3-8-12 Ginza, Chuo-ku (3561 0515). Ginza station, exit A12. **Open** 11.30am-7pm Mon-Sat. **Map** p57.

Young Japanese artists rent this well-established space to show their stuff.

Kodak Photo Salon

Tokaido Ginza Bldg 3F, 6-4-1 Ginza, Chuo-ku (3572 4411/www.kodak.co.jp). Ginza station, exit C3. **Open** 10am-6pm daily. **Map** p57.

Contemporary photography.

Leica Gallery Tokyo

Matsushima Gankyo Bldg 3F, 3-5-6 Ginza (3567 6706). Ginza station, exit A13. **Open** 10.30am-5.30pm Tue-Sat. **Map** p57.

Contemporary photography.

Maison Hermès

Maison Hermès 8F Forum, 5-4-1 Ginza, Chuo-ku (3569 3611). Ginza Station, exit B7. **Open** 11am-7pm Mon, Tue, Thur-Sun. **Map** p57.

The curved glass block walls of this beautiful, Renzo Piano-designed space both filter daylight and magnify neon at night. The gallery holds shows of Japanese and international contemporary art and crafts, organised according to annual themes such as 'the hand'.

Moris Gallery

Dai 5 Taiyo Bldg, 7-10-8 Ginza, Chuo-ku (3573 5328). Ginza station, exit A3. **Open** 11.30am-7pm Mon-Sat. **Map** p57.

This tiny gallery space provides a starting point for young artists.

Nishimura Gallery

Nishi Ginza Bldg B1F, 4-3-13 Ginza, Chuo-ku (3567 3906/http://members.aol.com/nishig1). Ginza station, exit B4. **Open** 10.30am-6.30pm Tue-Sat. **Map** p57.

Yokoo Tadanori, Oshie Chieko, David Hockney and other Japanese and international artists appear here.

Okuno Building

1-9-8 Ginza, Chuo-ku. Ginza station, exit A13 or Ginza-Itchome station, exit 10. **Open** 11am-7pm Mon-Sat (hours vary). **Map** p57.

One of Ginza's oldest buildings (c1932), this tenement has plants hanging off verandas and five floors of tiny rental galleries including Gallery Kobo (3567 8727/www.spinn-aker.co.jp) and Ono Gallery II (3535 1185).

Shiseido Gallery

Tokyo Ginza Shiseido Bldg B1, 8-8-3 Ginza, Chuo-ku (3572 3901/www.shiseido.co.jp/gallery/html). Shinbashi JR station, Ginza exit. **Open** 11am-7pm Tue-Sat; 11am-6pm Sun. **Map** p57.

Like Maison Hermès (*see above*), this is more of a *kunsthalle* than a commercial gallery, with important group and solo shows by contemporary Japanese and international artists such as Roman Signer and Nakamura Masato. The cosmetics giant runs it in the basement of its Ricardo Bofill-designed headquarters.

Tokyo Gallery

8-6-18 Ginza, Chuo-ku (3571 1808/www.tokyo-gallery.com/). Shinbashi JR station, Ginza exit. **Open** 11am-7pm Mon-Fri; 11am-5pm Sat. **Map** p57.

Tokyo Gallery shows modern and contemporary Japanese, Chinese and Korean artists. It opened a Beijing branch in 2003.

Wacoal Ginza Art Space

Miyuki No.1 Bldg B1, 5-1-15 Ginza, Chuo-ku (3573 3798/www.wacoal.co.jp/company/artspace/). Ginza station, exit C2. **Open** 11am-7pm Mon-Fri; 11am-5pm Sat. **Map** p57.

Underwear manufacturer Wacoal sponsors this space for exhibitions of contemporary art in fabric and other media.

Zeit-Foto Salon

Matsumoto Bldg 4F, 1-10-5 Kyobashi, Chuo-ku (3535 7188/www.zeit-foto.com/). Tokyo JR station, Yaesu exit. **Open** 10.30am-6.30pm Tue-Fri; 10.30am-5.30pm Sat. **Map** p62.

Reliable and wide-ranging photo exhibitions by Japanese and international photographers.

Harajuku

Las Chicas Café/D-Zone

5-47-6 Jingumae, Shibuya-ku (3407 6865/www.vision.co.jp/index2.html). Omotesando station, exit B2. **Open** 11am-11pm daily. **Map** p99.

Fashion-conscious restaurant, bar and shop complex with frequent photo and painting shows (especially by ex-pats) in a splendid al fresco environment off the main drag. English-friendly.

Design Festa Gallery

3-20-18 Jingumae, Shibuya-ku (3479 1442/www.designfesta.com). Harajuku station, Takeshita exit. **Open** 11am-8pm daily. **Map** p99.

There's a rabbit warren of rental galleries inside this super-funky apartment house with a colourful café in the backyard. It sponsors the semi-annual Design Festa, a huge fair for young artists.

Gallery Gan

Galeria 1F, 5-51-3 Jingumae, Shibuya-ku (5468 6311). Omotesando station, exit B2. **Open** 11am-7pm Mon-Sat. **Map** p99.

Contemporary Japanese and international artists, such as Vik Muniz.

Gallery 360°

2F, 5-1-27 Minami-Aoyama, Minato-ku (3406 5823/www.360.co.jp). Omotesando station, exits B4, A5. **Open** noon-8pm Tue-Sun. **Map** p99.

This well-located space emphasises works on paper and multiples by Lawrence Wiener, Homma Takashi and other contemporary artists. F.

Nadiff

Casa Real B1F, 4-9-8 Jingumae, Shibuya-ku (3403 8814/www.nadiff.com). Omotesando station, exit A2. **Open** 11am-8pm daily. **Map** p99.

The city's best art and art-music bookstore (the main store in a chain) has a small gallery showing hot young Japanese artists.

Pink Cow

1-10-1 Jingumae, Shibuya-ku (5411 6777/www.thepinkcow.com). Harajuku station, Omotesando exit or Meiji-Jingumae station, exit 3. **Open** varies with exhibitions. **Map** p99.

Bar that sometimes shows work by local artists. *See p159.*

Promo-Arte

Galeria Bldg 2F, 5-51-3 Jingumae, Shibuya-ku (3400 1995/www.promo-arte.com). Omotesando station, exit B2. **Open** 11am-7pm Tue-Sun (but can vary with exhibition). **Map** p99.

Tokyo's main Latin American art space.

Saison Art Program Gallery

Cosmos Aoyama 1F, 5-53-67 Jingumae, Shibuya-ku (5464 0197/www.smma-sap.or.jp). Omotesando station, exit B2. **Open** 11am-6pm Tue-Sat. **Map** p102.

Sponsored by the Saison group of companies, the SAP Gallery holds exhibitions by the winners of its grant programme for young artists.

Sign

Yamazaki Bldg B1, 2-7-18 Kita-Aoyama (5474 5040). Gaienmae station, exit 2. **Open** 10am-2am daily.

This hip little café fills its awkwardly shaped basement gallery with photography and illustrations.

Spiral

Spiral Bldg 1F, 5-6-23 Minami-Aoyama, Minato-ku (3498 1171/www.spiral.co.jp). Omotesando station, exit B1. **Open** 11am-8pm daily. **Map** p99.

A ramp spirals around the circular open space at one end of the Maki Fumihiko-designed building, hence the name. A wide range of hip fashion, art, and design shows appear here. There's also a café, bar and CD shop.

TN Probe

Hanae Mori Bldg 5F, 3-6-1 Kita-Aoyama, Minato-ku (3498 2171/www.tnprobe.com). Omotesando station, exit A1. **Open** varies with exhibitions. **Map** p99.

Construction firm Obayashi Corporation opened TN Probe in 1995. It holds two major architecturally themed exhibitions a year, with smaller shows, lectures and other programmes in between.

Viewing Room, Yoyogi/Garage

21-5 Moto-Yoyogicho, Shibuya-ku (5465 6064/ www.ycassociates.co.jp). Yoyogi-Hachiman station (Odakyu Line) or Yoyogi Koen station, exit 1. **Open** 11am-7pm Tue-Sat.

Yes, it's in a cute but hard-to-find room at the back of a garage. Shows contemporary Japanese artists.

Kayabacho-Shinkawa

ShugoArts

2F, 1-31-6 Shinkawa, Chuo-ku (5542 3468/www. shugoarts.com). Kayabacho station (Hibiya, Tozai lines), exit 3. **Open** 11am-7pm Tue-Sat.

One of three major galleries in the new, must-see Shinkawa Gallery Complex, ShugoArts' first dedicated space shows an eclectic range of contemporary Japanese and international artists such as Shimabuku and Candice Breitz. F.

Taguchi Fine Art

4F, 2-17-13 Kayabacho, Chuo-ku (5652 3660/www. taguchifineart.com). Kayabacho station (Hibiya, Tozai lines), exit 3. **Open** 1-7pm Tue-Sat (10am-1pm by appointment only).

Contemporary Japanese and international art. F.

Taka Ishii Gallery

1F, 1-31-6 Shinkawa, Chuo-ku (5542 3615/www. takaishiigallery.com). Kayabacho station (Hibiya, Tozai lines), exit 3. **Open** 11am-7pm Tue-Sat.

Taka Ishii has moved from Otsuka, his base for eight years, to the Shinkawa Complex. His gallery emphasises photography by major international and Japanese artists (Araki Nobuyuki, Hatakeyama Naoya, Thomas Demand). F.

Tomio Koyama Gallery

1F, 1-31-6 Shinkawa, Chuo-ku (6222 1006/www. c-channel.com/c00808). Kayabacho station (Hibiya, Tozai lines), exit 3. **Open** 11am-7pm Tue-Sat.

One of Japan's most powerful contemporary galleries represents Murakami Takashi and Nara Yoshitomo as well as international artists like Dennis Hollingsworth. The third Shinkawa Complex resident. F.

Shibuya, Ebisu & Daikanyama

Gallerie Le Deco

Le Deco Bldg, 3-16-3 Shibuya, Shibuya-ku (5485 5188/http://home.att.ne.jp/gamma/ledeco). Shibuya JR station, Miyamasusaka (east) exit. **Open** 11am-7pm Tue-Sun. **Map** p102.

Regular exhibitions are spread over the six floors of this rental space. There's a café and lounge on the ground floor.

Gallery Speak For

Speak For Bldg B2, 28-2 Sarugakucho, Shibuya-ku (5459 6385/www.abahouse.co.jp/). Daikanyama station (Tokyu Toyoko Line). **Open** 11am-8pm Tue-Sun.

Uber-hip young designers and fashion photographers from Japan and abroad show here.

Mizuma Art Gallery

Fujiya Bldg 2F, 1-3-9 Kamimeguro, Meguro-ku (3793 7931/www.mizuma-art.co.jp). Nakameguro station (Hibiya, Tokyu Toyoko lines). **Open** 11am-7pm Tue-Sat.

Features some of Japan's hottest contemporary artists, such as Aida Makoto and Ujino Muneteru. F.

Shinjuku

epSITE

Shinjuku Mitsui Bldg 1F, 2-1-1 Nishi-Shinjuku, Shinjuku-ku (3345 9881/http://epsite.epson.co.jp). Shinjuku JR station, west exit. **Open** 10.30am-6pm daily. **Map** p109.

Epson uses its latest digital technology to create the enormous, impressively detailed photo prints displayed its showcase gallery.

Kenji Taki Gallery

3-18-2 Nishi-Shinjuku, Shinjuku-ku (3378 6051/ www2.odn.ne.jp/kenjitaki). Hatsudai station (Keio New Line), east exit. **Open** noon-7pm Tue-Sat.

Kenji Taki and Wako Works (*see p215*) are neighbours here in the shadow of Tokyo Opera City. Taki shows contemporary Japanese and international artists such as Watanabe Eiji and Wolfgang Laib. F.

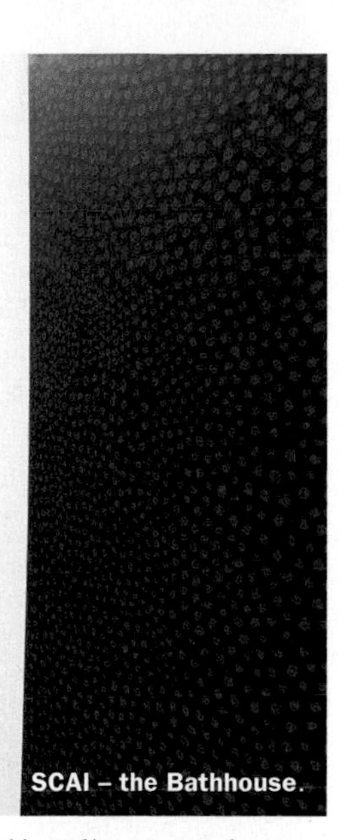

SCAI – the Bathhouse.

Konica Plaza

Shinjuku Takano Bldg 4F, 3-26-11 Shinjuku, Shinjuku-ku (3225 5001/www.konica.co.jp/corporate/culture/plaza/). Shinjuku JR station, east exit. **Open** 10.30am-7pm daily. **Map** p109.
Contemporary photography.

Nikon Plaza Shinjuku

Shinjuku L Tower 28F, 1-6-1 Nishi Shinjuku, Shinjuku-ku (3344 0565/www.nikon-image.com/jpn/service/salon/index.htm). Shinjuku JR station, west exit. **Open** 10am-7pm daily. Closed 11, 12 Feb, 3rd Sun and following Mon in Aug. **Map** p109.
In addition to the photos, Nikon's Plaza Shinjuku gallery has a good view.

Shinjuku I-Land

6-5-1 Nishi-Shinjuku, Shinjuku-ku. Shinjuku JR station, west exit. **Open** 24hrs daily. **Map** p109.
Public art by Daniel Buren, Luciano Fabro, Roy Lichtenstein and others is installed around the bases of Nishi-Shinjuku skyscrapers.

Shinjuku Park Tower, Gallery One

3-7-1 Nishi-Shinjuku, Shinjuku-ku (5322 6633/www.shinjukuparktower.com). Tochomae station (Toei Oedo Line), exit A4/free bus from in front of UFJ Bank at Shinjuku L Tower, Shinjuku JR station, west exit. **Open** varies with exhibition. **Map** p109.
Contemporary and modern art and crafts.

Wako Works of Art

3-18-2-101 Nishi-Shinjuku, Shinjuku-ku (3373 2860). Hatsudai station (Keio New Line), east exit. **Open** 11am-7pm Tue-Sat.
Wako shows blue-chip and/or conceptual contemporary Japanese and international artists such as Gerhard Richter. F.

Ueno

SCAI – the Bathhouse

Kashiwayu-Ato, 6-1-23 Yanaka, Taito-ku (3821 1144/www.scaithebathhouse.com). Nippori station, west exit. **Open** noon-7pm Tue-Sat. **Map** p94.
Formerly a bathhouse (the building is 200 years old), this high-ceilinged space in a charming neighbourhood near Ueno Park features contemporary Japanese artists such as Miyajima Tatsuo and international artists like Li Bul and Julian Opie. F.

Other areas

Kojimachi Gallery

3-4-2 Kojimachi, Chiyoda-ku (3511 2348). Kojimachi station, exit 3. **Open** varies with exhibition.
Strong emerging artists pop into this tiny space.

MDS/G

36-18 Ohyamacho, Shibuya-ku (3481 6711). Yoyogi-Uehara station. **Open** 1-7pm Tue-Sat.
Miyake Design Studio holds irregular contemporary art shows in this Shigeru Ban-designed building.

Soh Gallery

2-14-35 Midori-cho, Koganei City (042 382 5338/www.soh-gallery.com). Higashi-Koganei station, north exit. **Open** 1-7pm Fri-Sun; by appointment Wed, Thur.
Contemporary Japanese and international art.

Gay & Lesbian

Come out and play; Tokyo's closet is full.

Tokyo's modern-day gay and lesbian scene is centred on Shinjuku Ni-chome, a district about halfway between Shinjuku-Sanchome and Gyoenmae subway stations. But this area's brash vitality provides no clue to the long and venerable history of Japanese homosexuality.

In the 16th century Tokugawa period, love between men (or often between a man and a boy) was considered purer than heterosexual love and was celebrated in the art and writing of the time. The import of Christian values from the west during the period of Japan's industrialisation soon put an end to that. Nevertheless, Japan remains a relatively irreligious country and homosexuality is not morally condemned as it still is in many places. Instead, Japanese gays and lesbians suffer a social stigma of embarrassing non-conformity that visiting foreigners will find hard to appreciate. The concepts of public and private are handled differently in Japan. Having something to hide is not considered a 'bad' thing. And when obligations are at stake, it makes the closet seem a very comfortable place to stay: it's private, so you can do what you like there.

Ni-chome today is a hidden warren of tiny bars, restaurants and host clubs – a thriving centre of sexual diversity. There are similar bars, bathhouses, fetish clubs and saunas across the city, if you know where to look; the realm of sexual fantasy is one outlet repressed Japanese males – gay or straight – use to escape from the heavy social obligations of their daily lives. Unfortunately for some, this is a world most foreign visitors or even long-term residents never get to see: of more than 300 establishments in Ni-chome, only a handful welcome foreigners. Of these, not all are open to women and even fewer cater specifically to lesbians.

Even if you can't read Japanese it's probably worth picking up a copy of the brick-sized *Badi* magazine just get an idea of the true scope of the scene – the pictures, ads and comic strips will be a good enough indication. (*Badi* is sold in any of the sex/book shops along Naka Dori.)

With Japanese people's relatively weak command of English and inherent shyness, it's fair to say that meeting locals in Tokyo is not always easy. Any unfriendliness you encounter is more likely to be a lack of confidence than outright hostility. And it's worth making the effort because, at the very least, the friends you make will never forget you.

None of the places listed below accept payment by credit card.

Bars & clubs

Ace

Daini Hayakawa Bldg B1F, 2-14-6 Shinjuku, Shinjuku-ku (3352 6297/www.akiplan.com/ace/). Shinjuku-Sanchome station, exits C7, C8. **Open** 8pm-5am (depends on event) Thur-Sun. **Admission** varies. **Map** p109.

This venue for many of Tokyo's smaller gay dance parties has events most weekends. Particularly noteworthy are Cyclon, Pink House and any number of hip hop events.

Advocates Bar

7th Tenka Bldg B1F, 2-18-1 Shinjuku, Shinjuku-ku (3358 8638/www.f-impression.com/). Shinjuku-Sanchome station, exits C7, C8. **Open** 8pm-4am daily. **Map** p109.

Sister to Advocates Café (*see below*) this basement bar around the corner is the latest reincarnation of the short-lived Blue Oyster Lounge, briefly the most fabulous joint in Ni-chome. Gone is the big round bar, in favour of a decent dancefloor. Weekend DJ nights are hit and miss; follow the crowds from Advocates Café. There may be a cover charge depending on the event.

Advocates Café

7th Tenka Bldg 1F, 2-18-1 Shinjuku, Shinjuku-ku (3358 3988/www.f-impression.com). Shinjuku-Sanchome station, exits C7, C8. **Open** 6pm-5am daily. **Map** p109.

Punters spill out on to the street in front of this tiny café/bar in summer. (It's one of the only places in the whole of Tokyo where the police tolerate this; there are people who pull strings in Ni-chome.) In winter, wrap up warm because there's almost no space inside. Happy hour is 6-9pm Monday to Friday, and there's also a 'beer blast' on Sunday from 6pm to 9pm (drink all the beer you can for a set price). Open to all sexes and sexualities. A good place to find out where the crowds are heading.

Arty Farty

Dai 33 Kyutei Bldg 2F, 2-11-6 Shinjuku, Shinjuku-ku (3356 5388/www.arty-farty.net/). Shinjuku-Sanchome station, exit C8. **Open** 7pm-midnight Mon; 7pm-5am Tue-Sat; 6pm-5am Sun. Gay men only on Sat. **Admission** ¥800 Mon-Thur; ¥900-¥1,000 Fri-Sun. **Map** p109.

This 'Wild West' bar is now in a new location across the street from the side entrance of Dragon (*see below*). The move has seen the creation of a dancefloor and a noticeable improvement in the music policy, with DJs on weekends. The decor is also better, but the staff are as humourless as ever. The Sunday afternoon 'beer blast' (all the beer you can drink 4-8pm for ¥1,000) remains popular. Women are allowed 'with their gay friends' on Fridays and Sundays.

Dragon

Accord Bldg B1F, 2-12-4 Shinjuku, Shinjuku-ku (3341 0606/www.bekkoame.ne.jp/ha/id25304/dragon.html). Shinjuku-Sanchome station, exits C7, C8. **Open** 6pm-5am Mon-Thur; 8pm-5am Fri, Sat; 5pm-5am Sun. **Admission** ¥1,000 men, ¥2,000 women Fri, Sat; free Mon-Thur, Sun. **Map** p109.

Shameless handbag music policy, video entertainment and nearly naked staff make Dragon the club of last resort at weekends. Be warned that it can get very crowded and sweaty if there is no other gay event on in the city on a Friday or Saturday night. The dancefloor gets turned into a dark room on Sunday afternoon and on some weekday evenings. Dragon is opposite GB (*see below*).

Fuji

B1F, 2-16-2 Shinjuku, Shinjuku-ku (3354 2707/www.14you.jp/fuji). Shinjuku-Sanchome station, exits C7, C8. **Open** 8pm-2am Mon-Thur; 8pm-5am weekends. **Map** p109.

A basement karaoke bar that's been around for years and caters mostly to an older crowd. Don't be put off by the dingy decor; this is a fun place open to both men and women, with plenty of English songs for karaoke singing. And if the staff are rude, then just sing louder.

GB

Business Hotel T Bldg B1F, 2-12-3 Shinjuku, Shinjuku-ku (3352 8972/www.techtrans-japan.com/GB/index.htm). Shinjuku-Sanchome station, exits C7, C8. **Open** 8pm-2am Mon-Thur, Sun; 8pm-3am Fri, Sat. **Map** p109.

The most infamous bar in Tokyo for east-meets-west interaction, handily attached to a 'business hotel'. The bar caters to an older clientele than Arty and Advocates (for both, *see p216*) and admits men only, except for one day in the year (Halloween – and we're not kidding).

Hug

2-15-8 Shinjuku, Shinjuku-ku (5379 5085). Shinjuku-Sanchome station, exits C7, C8. **Open** 9pm-6am Mon-Sat. **Map** p109.

Hug is a women-only karaoke bar that attracts an over-30 clientele.

Kinsmen

2F, 2-18-5 Shinjuku, Shinjuku-ku (3354 4949/www.11.ocn.ne.jp/~kinsmen/). Shinjuku-Sanchome station, exits C7, C8. **Open** 9pm-3am Mon, Wed-Fri, Sun; 9am-5pmSat. **Map** p109.

Once one of the most popular foreigner-friendly bars in Ni-chome, these days Kinsmen is the place to go to get away from everyone else. Famous for its *ikebana* flower arrangements.

Kinswomyn

Daiichi Tenka Bldg 3F, 2-15-10 Shinjuku, Shinjuku-ku (3354 8720). Shinjuku-Sanchome station, exits C7, C8. **Open** 8pm-3am Wed-Sun. **Map** p109.

Kinswomyn (a sibling of the men's bar above) is Tokyo's most popular women-only bar. Old guard butch-femme types occasionally drop by, but for the most part it's a cosy, relaxed crowd.

Crisis of ignorance

It's vital to proactively practise safe sex in Japan. Overall infection rates remain low compared to other countries, but it's young Japanese – both straight and gay – who are most at risk. In 2002, people in their teens and twenties accounted for nearly 40 per cent of all Japanese newly infected with AIDS. The Health Ministry blames it on lax use of condoms, a casual attitude towards sex, and misconceptions about the risks.

Studies have shown that young, free-loving Japanese of all orientations do not practise safe sex as a rule, even the 40 per cent that have several sex friends at one time. Condom sales fell by 25 per cent over the 1990s, as many refuse to believe that HIV/AIDS is anything more than a foreign disease.

Several valiant volunteer groups are making brave efforts to increase awareness in the face of shameful popular indifference and inadequate government action. Gay men seem to have more access to information about the risks than other groups, but it seems they are even worse at protecting themselves than promiscuous young straight kids. In 2002, twice as many people were infected with HIV in Japan through homosexual sex as through the heterosexual variety.

Practise safe sex and you'll be no more at risk in Japan than anywhere else. But make an extra effort to do so – in the saunas and sex clubs, and in private – because many of your hosts may not.

Monsoon

Shimazaki Bldg 6F, 2-14-9 Shinjuku, Shinjuku-ku (3354 0470/www.geocities.co.jp/Foodpia-Celery/3441/home.html). Shinjuku-Sanchome station, exits C7, C8. **Open** 3pm-6am daily. **Map** p109.

A small, friendly, men-only bar with conveniently long opening hours, catering to a young crowd. The place was recently renovated with an eye to stealing some of the customers from Advocates (*see p216*). The drinks got cheaper too.

New Sazae

Ishikawa Bldg 2F, 2-18-5 Shinjuku, Shinjuku-ku (3354 1745/new_sazae.tripod.co.jp/open.htm). Shinjuku-Sanchome station, exits C7, C8. **Open** 9pm-6am Mon-Sat; 10pm-6am Sun. **Map** p109.

New Sazae's ancestor (Old Sazae) was rumoured to have been the favourite haunt of famed, crazed gay novelist Mishima Yukio. The New Sazae, in the same location, is still going strong, although it looks as if it hasn't been redecorated since Mishima's day. The place gets going late and has good music and an attitude-free, anything-goes atmosphere that's rare among the foreigner-friendly bars in Ni-chome. Fabulous old seen-it-all drag queens can sometimes be found propping up the bar.

Tamago Bar

Nakae Bldg 1F, 2-15-13 Shinjuku, Shinjuku-ku (3351 4838). Shinjuku-Sanchome station, exits C7, C8. **Open** 9pm-5am daily. **Map** p109.

A pricey women-only bar. One of its draws is that customers are served by *onabe* hosts (women dressed as men).

Word Up

Tom Bldg 2F, 2-10-7 Shinjuku, Shinjuku-ku (3353 2466). Shinjuku-Sanchome station, exits C7, C8. **Open** 7pm-5am Tue-Sun. **Map** p109.

Big B-Boy-style bar that until recently attracted the best-looking patrons around. In April 2003, however, the managers put up a sign suggesting foreigners go elsewhere. It was quickly replaced with a sign describing the place as a bar for Japanese/Asians to meet other Japanese/Asians, and requiring customers to order their drinks in Japanese. Although staff don't actually appear to be refusing to serve anyone, the intention is clear. That the young Japanese owner and his staff can even contemplate such a policy is an unfortunate commentary on the ignorance and prejudice that is still too prevalent in Japan. Many customers – both Japanese and foreigners – have since boycotted the place.

Saunas

Not surprisingly in a country where people like nothing better than stripping off with strangers for a piping hot bath, the sauna scene is big and popular. Dump your shoes in a locker, buy a ticket at the vending machine, and hand it in at

Leopardskin and foliage decorate the bar area at **Advocates Bar**, *see p217*.

the counter, where you'll be given a pack of essentials in return. (Bring your own condoms anyway, and practise safe sex, because not all your fellow clients do.) Don't be surprised to find many patrons sleeping soundly. After all, it's cheaper than a taxi home, and a lot more fun.

Jinya

2-30-19 Ikebukuro, Toshima-ku (5951 0995). Ikebukuro JR station, west exit. **Open** 24hrs daily. **Admission** ¥2,200. **Map** p69.

Respectable-looking establishment at ease with foreigners. Facilities include a refreshment/TV room, private rooms and a porn viewing area.

24 Kaikan Asakusa

2-29-16 Asakusa, Taito-ku (5827 2424). Asakusa station, exits 1, 3, 6. **Open** 24hrs daily. **Admission** ¥2,300-¥2,800. **Map** p83.

The original of the three 24 ('Ni-Yon') Kaikans caters to an older, rougher clientele (true to its *shitamachi* roots in the old side of the city). Most cruising for non-Japanese goes on in the bath/shower area.

24 Kaikan Ueno

1-8-7 Kita-Ueno, Taito-ku (3847 2424). Ueno JR station, Iriya exit. **Open** 24hrs daily. **Admission** ¥2,400. **Map** p88.

An enormous six-floor sauna that boasts a rooftop sun deck, plus gym, restaurant and karaoke bar, as well as various other spots to enjoy yourself in public and private.

24 Kaikan Shinjuku

2-13-1 Shinjuku, Shinjuku-ku (3354 2424). Shinjuku-Sanchome station, exits C7, C8. **Open** 24hrs daily. **Admission** ¥2,600. **Map** p109.

The newest branch of the 24 Kaikan chain opened in the heart of Ni-chome in January 2003, and not surprisingly it tends to attract younger patrons than its sister saunas. Because of its central location, it gets packed at weekends. It may have 24-hour opening times, but don't go too late: by 3am most of the exhausted young customers are sleeping soundly. It's handily located on the street along the side of the cruising park near Ace.

Club events

Most of Tokyo's major gay or gay-mixed club events happen outside Ni-chome. Nights bounce in and out of favour with the club set regularly, so it's best to check where's hot and where's not with the pre-club crowds at Advocates in Ni-chome. The music at these events is mostly techno, although some have secondary dance floors with alternative sounds.

At the time of writing, **Red** at Luners in Azabu-Juban (*see p238*) is probably the most popular gay-mix party. It takes place on the second Saturday of the month and is renowned for its cute customers and strictly techno music policy. A new entry that's proving popular is **Funk** – a reincarnation of the old Passion party – on the third Friday at Code in Kabuki-cho (*see p236*). The music is more housey, poppy and, yes, funky, than at most parties, and the so-called VIP dance floor is usually packed with the best-dressed party people vying for strutting space. **Boys Life** at Shinjuku Kabukicho's Liquid Room (*see p238*) on the first Saturday of the month is for men only. The cavernous main dance floor and smaller hip hop lounge are always jam-packed. Tokyo's longest-running gay-mix party, **The Ring**, takes place on the last Saturday of the month, and is also at Luners.

Although it's not a gay event per se, **Department H** (for *echi*, a Japanese word for sex) is Tokyo's biggest fetish gathering, at **On Air West** near Club Asia in Shibuya (*see p236*) on the first Saturday in the month. The main attractions for most will be the fetish shows and unusually dressed (or undressed) patrons. You don't have to be in costume, so fetish tourists can go as well.

Back in Ni-chome, **Pink House** and **Cyclon** at Ace (*see p216*) are worth looking out for. Pink House is an always-popular mixed party, while hard techno and muscle boys rule the roost at Cylon. Check the flyers at Advocates to see when they are happening.

The number of women-only parties has fallen in recent years with the (hopefully temporary) passing of Diamond Cutter and Duralmin Bitch. The main monthly women-only event, **Goldfinger**, happens on the last Friday of the month at various venues. Worth a special mention is the after-hours party on Sunday mornings at **Maniac Love** in Aoyama (*see p238*), where every big night out ends with a bang, often until late the following evening if you're up for it.

There are usually another couple of large events most months advertised in the CIA club guide booklet, or in flyers at Advocates or at dance music shops such as Cisco in Shibuya (*see p188*). This being Tokyo, things change rapidly, parties come and go, venues change, new clubs open and old ones close all the time. For the latest information check *CIA* or *Metropolis*.

Tokyo's gay & lesbian calendar

Tokyo's **Lesbian and Gay Parade** usually takes place in late August or early September. While having nothing on the wild Pride events of London, Sydney and San Francisco, it's remarkable to many that it happens at all. Three thousand marchers in 2002 was a significant achievement, given that being 'out' is not an option for most Japanese homosexuals, especially outside Shinjuku Ni-Chome's gay ghetto. Marchers and supporters congregate at the outdoor event space between NHK and Yoyogi Park before the parade leaves for a tour through the trendy Shibuya and Harajuku districts. The genuine support of many onlookers for previous parades may be evidence of a real change in attitudes towards gays and lesbians in this country. Sadly, the event was cancelled in 2003, although organisers promise to bring it back in 2004.

The evening of the parade is the Shinjuku Ni-chome Matsuri, when the area's Naka Dori thoroughfare becomes a sweaty summer street party. It's much like any other summer festival in Japan, with food stalls, plenty of beer, fan dancing and parades of traditional portable shrines. (You will spot the differences though, such as the fact that the fan dancers are all male and wearing leather and chains.)

There are also gay festivals in Sapporo, Nagoya, Fukuoka and Osaka in August, although Sapporo's is the only one worth making a special effort to go to.

Promoters for other events like to call July 'gay pride month'. It's when the **Tokyo Lesbian and Gay Film Festival** takes place at Spiral Hall in Aoyama (*see p214*), and also the month of **Lesbian and Gay Day** at Tokyo Disney Resort (*see p122*). The film festival lasts several days at the end of July, showcasing films from both home and abroad, and usually squeezes in at least one big party to celebrate.

Organisers of Gay Day say as many as 3,000 participants have converged on Chiba Prefecture's own Magic Kingdom for the event in each of the last three years. It's not official, and there's no discount. In 2002, the event took place at the then newly opened Disney Sea Park next door. Following in the traditions of Gay Days at Disney parks in the US, visitors are encouraged to show their pride by wearing red. Check the press for details of events.

Sex clubs

There are literally hundreds of *hattenba* (sex clubs) in Tokyo, as listed in the back pages of *Badi* magazine. They're generally small apartments or offices turned into cruising spaces with flimsy partition walls, dim lighting and dodgy music. Some have themes (naked, swimwear, jock straps and so on) on different nights of the week – but the general theme is always the same. The ones listed below accept foreign customers. Condoms may be provided, but it's best to bring your own. When you arrive, a voice behind the counter may ask if you speak Japanese. Just say *hai*.

Dock

B1F, 2-18-5 Shinjuku, Shinjuku-ku (3226 4006/ www.bar-dock.com/index_pc.html). Shinjuku-Sanchome station, exits C7, C8. **Open** 9pm-4pm daily. **Admission** ¥1,200 including one drink. Dress code nude (but don't take off your shoes!) Tue-Sat. **Map** p109.

Minuscule cruising bar two doors down from Arty Farty. Friday is naked night; jock straps are allowed on Saturday. There's also a 'dark room' cruising area (read: three square metres curtained off in the corner).

HX

UI Bldg 1F, 5-9-6 Shinjuku, Shinjuku-ku (3226 4448/www.ruftuf-jp.com/hx). Shinjuku-Sanchome station, exits C7, C8. **Open** 24hrs daily. Closed 10am-3pm on 2nd & 4th Thur of mth. **Admission** ¥1,500; ¥1,000 4-11am. **Map** p109.

Small sex club for mostly young, fit guys that's also open to foreigners. It's the other side of Yasukuni Dori from Ni-chome, down the alley next to MosBurger on the right. Ask for condoms at the door.

King of College

2-14-5 Shinjuku, Shinjuku-ku (3352 3930). Shinjuku-Sanchome station, exits C7, C8. **Open** 6pm-4am daily. **Map** p109.

Friendly, English speaking staff (a novelty in this industry in Tokyo) make this place ideal. You can rent 'hosts' by the hour in a private room at the club or at your home or hotel room.

Slamdunk

2-4-12 Shinjuku, Shinjuku-ku (3355 7178/www.ask.ne.jp/~doberman/works/slamdunk.html). Shinjuku-Gyoenmae station, exit 1. **Open** 24hrs. **Admission** ¥1500; ¥1000 4am-11am. **Map** p109.

Small club open to foreigners. Go down the alley next to am/pm on the other side of Shinjuku Dori from Ni-chome; it's behind the small brown door at the end.

New Sazae: foreigner-friendly and attitude-free. *See p221*.

Treffpunkt

Fukutomi Bldg 4F, 2-13-14 Akasaka, Minato-ku (5563 0523/www1.odn.ne.jp/treffpunkt). Akasaka station, exits 2, 5. **Open** noon-11pm daily. **Admission** ¥1,700; ¥1,000 noon-3pm Mon-Fri.

This is a small club close to the business areas of the city that – unlike some others of its ilk – welcomes foreign customers. Underwear forbidden at weekends. Closes early.

Other places

Books Rose

2-14-11 Shinjuku, Shinjuku-ku (3352 7023/www.books-rose.com). Shinjuku-Sanchome station, exits C7, C8. **Open** 11am-1am Mon-Thur, Sun; 11am-2am Fri, Sat. **Map** p109.

You can get a window on the Japanese gay scene by browsing in any of the bookshops that stretch along Naka Dori. Books Rose, at the bottom of the street, is the best – a veritable treasure trove of magazines and videos, sex toys and stimulants, and all sorts of other paraphernalia.

Cocolo Café

Daiichi Hayakawaya Bldg 1F, 2-14-6 Shinjuku, Shinjuku-ku (5366 9899). Shinjuku-Sanchome station, exits C7, C8. **Open** 11am-5am Mon-Fri; 3pm-7am Sat; 5pm-5am Sun. **Map** p109.

Cocolo Café is an atmospheric all-night restaurant and bar that serves pretty decent food. A good place to go when you've had your fill of overcrowded, smoke-filled bars.

Hotel Nuts

1-16-5 Shinjuku, Shinjuku-ku (5379 1044). Shinjuku-Sanchome station, exits C7, C8. **Open** 24hrs daily. **Admission** ¥5,800-¥7,400 for 2hrs. **Map** p109.

One of Tokyo's few gay love hotels. The basic rooms are decorated in pink and have decent bathrooms with big baths, but will disappoint lovers expecting the ultimate über-kitsch experience. The management has been known to refuse entry if neither customer is Japanese. Rooms come with one free condom and a novelty souvenir lighter.

Karaoke Rafu

B1F, 2-16-8 Shinjuku, Shinjuku-ku (3353 0290). Shinjuku-Sanchome station, exits C7, C8. **Open** 5pm-5am Mon-Fri; noon-5am Sat, Sun. **Admission** ¥300 for 1hr with 1 drink before 5pm; ¥650 for 1hr with limited free drinks after 5pm. **Map** p109.

Cheap, grungey basement karaoke box venue in serious need of a makeover. Thin walls make listening to other Whitney wannabes an inevitable, if not always pleasurable, experience. Prices go up by ¥100 on Friday, Saturday and Sunday.

Kinkantei

2-17-1 Shinjuku, Shinjuku-ku (3356 6556). Shinjuku-Sanchome station, exits C7, C8. **Open** 7pm-4am Mon-Sat. **Map** p109.

When in Ni-chome don't miss the chance to visit one of the best *soba* restaurants in Tokyo. It's a small, fading old place with unassuming staff and delicious food, a bit like stepping into a time warp. The *tenzaru* cold *soba* and tempura are a delight in the summer.

Music

Every night is a live music night in Tokyo.

As you would expect from the largest city in the world and the second biggest market for recorded music, Tokyo has a thriving live scene in all the major musical genres – so much so that there's often too much to choose from on any given night. Most international acts and orchestras drop by on their world tours while local artists increasingly provide originality to match their talent. With more Japanese musicians gaining recognition and success abroad, more kids than ever before are picking up instruments, decks, computers – whatever it takes.

Venues in all genres run the gamut from charming but tatty fleapit to state-of-the-art hall, with facilities usually reflected in ticket prices.

Classical music

Classical music has been hugely popular in Japan ever since the country opened itself up to the outside world in the 19th century. In recent years, Japan has produced its own classical music stars – from conductor Seiji Ozawa and composer Takashi Yoshimatsu to pianist Mitsuko Uchida and young violinist Midori – and the country now counts hundreds of professional and amateur orchestras, many of them based in Tokyo.

In fact, there are more classical music events in Tokyo than in any other city in the world, with a host of high-quality venues catering for the needs of every classical music buff. Many of these halls are run by private companies, such as Suntory, in a typically Japanese partnership between industry and the arts. Tickets are best purchased well in advance, especially for a performance by one of the many foreign orchestras that stop by.

Casals Hall

1-6 Kanda-Surugadai, Chiyoda-ku (3294 1229). Ochanomizu JR station, Hijiribashi exit. **Capacity** 511.

This beautiful hall was designed exclusively for chamber music and small ensembles. Opened in 1987 in the heart of Tokyo's university and bookstores district, it's recognised for its great acoustics.

Hakuju Hall

1-37-5 Tomigaya, Shibuya-ku (5478 8867 /www.hakujuhall.co.jp). Yoyogi-Koen station or Yoyogi-Hachiman station (Odakyu Line). **Capacity** *Normal seats* 300. *Reclining seats* 162.

Scheduled to open in October 2003, this small hall aims to provide an unrivalled musical experience. Every seat can be reclined (a world first!) and, with the state-of-the-art acoustics, the intention is to bring the 'spirit of comfort' to all music fans.

Kan'i Hoken Hall

8-4-13 Nishi-Gotanda, Shinagawa-ku (3490 5111/ www.u-port.kfj.go.jp). Gotanda JR station, west exit. **Capacity** 1,826.

A mainstay for over 20 years, this venue is appreciated mainly for its acoustics. Classical music and ballet are the usual fare here, but musicals, rock and jazz concerts, plus crooners both local and international, also make the bill.

Orchard Hall

2-24-1 Dogenzaka, Shibuya-ku (3477 9111/ www.bunkamura.co.jp). Shibuya JR station, Hachiko exit. **Capacity** 2,150. **Map** p102.

The largest shoe-box hall in Japan with high walls and ceilings, designed to produce the best possible acoustics, to which end the stage can be moved. The second- and third-level seating seems far away from the stage but distance only improves the sound. Classical, opera and ballet are the norm, although this hall is occasionally used for other genres.

Sogetsu Hall

7-2-21 Akasaka, Minato-ku (3408 1129 9113). Aoyama-Itchome station, exit A4. **Capacity** 530.

This relatively small venue, which belongs to the sogetsu-ryu school of ikebana (flower arranging), is used for classical music but also hosts Japanese music recitals, poetry readings and even film previews. The venue's funnel shape may frustrate those concert-goers who have sharp ears, but it's much more intimate than other halls.

Sumida Triphony

1-2-3 Kinshi, Sumida-ku (5608 1212/www.njp.or.jp/sumida). Kinshicho station, north exit. **Capacity** *Large hall* 1,800. *Small hall* 250.

Just across the Sumida river, this relatively new hall has a beautiful old-style lobby and a warm atmosphere. Sumida Triphony is the home of the New Japan Philharmonic Orchestra, which makes regular appearances, but various international artists play here, too, including jazz greats and world music events such as gamelan orchestras.

Suntory Hall

1-13-1 Akasaka, Minato-ku (3505 1001/ www.suntory.co.jp/suntoryhall/english). Roppongi-Itchome station, exit 3. **Capacity** *Large hall* 2,006. *Small hall* 430. **Map** p74.

This hall's most striking visual feature is the massive organ, giving it an almost church-like appearance. The acoustics are superb, though, with even legendary conductor Herbert von Karajan moved to describe the place as 'truly a jewel box of sound'. Operated by local brewer Suntory mainly for recitals and classical music, it's also used by others such as contemporary jazz guitarist Bill Frisell.

Tokyo Bunka Kaikan

5-45 Ueno Koen, Taito-ku (3828 2111/www.t-bunka.jp). Ueno JR station, park exit. **Capacity** *Large hall* 2,303. *Small hall* 649. **Map** p88.

These halls near the park exit of Ueno station, both over 40 years old, were recently refurbished to make up for ground lost to newer venues. They're now back with a vengeance, presenting full schedules every month. The main hall is the largest in Tokyo and high enough to have four balconies. On the fourth floor of the building is Tokyo's main music library (open to the public), holding over 100,000 CDs, records, scores, music books and more.

Tokyo Metropolitan Art Space

1-8-1 Nishi-Ikebukuro, Toshima-ku (5391 2111/ www.geigeki.jp). Ikebukuro station, west exit, exits 2a, 2b. **Capacity** *Large hall* 1,999. *Middle hall* 841. *Small hall* 1 300. *Small hall 2* 220-300. **Map** p69.

The first thing that strikes you about this building is the long escalator, travelling from the ground floor up to the fifth floor. Not to be outdone, the halls also have some unusual features – the middle hall's UFO-like shape is especially peculiar. Unlike the large hall, the middle hall is used for musicals and plays as well as classical music.

Tokyo Opera City

3-20-2 Nishi-Shinjuku, Shinjuku-ku (5353 0770/ www.operacity.jp/en/concert.html). Hatsudai station (New Keio Line), central exit. **Capacity** *Main hall* 1,632. *Recital hall* 286.

The lobby's fusion of architectural styles is just a sign of what's to come in the main hall. The base is in the prevalent shoe box shape but it ends as a pyramid with a glass window at the top. Opened in 1997, the hall was built for the most advanced sound technology, with an oak interior and a 3,826-pipe organ as centrepiece. There's a hall for solo performances, too, also built to give the best acoustic experience.

Jazz

The jazz scene in Tokyo is thriving. The 30 larger jazz clubs, plus 20 or so smaller clubs (with more in nearby Yokohama), are crowded every night of the week. On any given night, Latin, bop, free, big band, swing, experimental, fusion, jazz-funk and blues can be heard in clubs all over the city. In summer, over 50 festivals offer jazz in relaxing, outdoor settings. Though it may seem unusual to hear an

Tokyo Opera City.

originally American art form in Japan during a short stay, the atmosphere at Tokyo's many small clubs is unique. Jazz fans are almost always friendly, speak a little English, and are loquacious about their obsessive love of jazz.

Unlike rock or classical venues, many jazz venues have a fixed door price, which we've given where available. Not that the times given are performance times. Doors usually open at least 30 minutes, usually one hour, beforehand. Many places offer two live sessions per night, which can mean paying twice (although the second set usually comes with a discount). Most major clubs accept credit cards, while the smaller ones do not.

Akai Karasu

Shirakaba Bldg 4F, 1-13-2 Kichijoji Honcho, Musashino-shi (0422 21 7594/www.akaikarasu.co.jp). Kichijoji station, north exit. **Admission** ¥1,500-¥2,500.

This mom and pop club, whose name means 'Red Crow', is a real delight. This is a place to unwind, with solid, straight groups. A variety of jazz nightly from 7.30pm, specialising in vocals.

Aketa no Mise

Yoshino Bldg B101, 3-21-13 Nishi Ogi Kita, Suginami-ku (3395 9507/www.aketa.org/mise.html). Nishi-Ogikubo station, north exit. **Admission** ¥2,500.

Feels more like a dorm room than a club, with handwritten signs, milk carton stands, cast-off furniture and music that's challenging and eclectic. Cutting-edge jazz from free to piano trio to Latin and back again, nightly from 7.30pm.

Alfie

Hama Roppongi Bldg 5F, 6-2-35 Roppongi, Minato-ku (3479 2037/homepage1.nifty.com/live/alfie/index.html). Roppongi station, exit 1. **Admission** ¥3,500. **Map** p74.

Alfie has a sleek interior and upscale audience. It's always comfortable and there's always room. Owner Hino-san picks the groups with a good ear. Jazz nightly from 8pm; jam sessions start after midnight.

B Flat

Akasaka Sakae Bldg B1F, 6-6-4 Akasaka, Minato-ku (5563 2563/www.bflat.jp). Akasaka station, exits 5A, 5B. **Admission** ¥2,500-¥7,000. **Map** p74.

A large venue serving decent food as well as drinks. The jazz groups are often the best in the city and the club also brings in groups from the US and Europe a couple times a month. Jazz nightly from 7.30pm.

Blue Note Tokyo

6-3-16 Minami Aoyama, Minato-ku, (5485 0088/www.bluenote.co.jp). Omotesando station, exits B1, B3. **Admission** ¥6,000-¥10,000.

The fanciest, largest club in the city, with prices to match, is part of the international Blue Note chain and well supported by the industry. Only top international performers are allowed on this stage. World music also from time to time. The one-set policy is aggravating, but the club is impressive and the musicians top class. Music nightly, with separate sets at 7pm and 9.30pm (6.30pm and 9pm on Sun).

Blues Alley

Hotel Wing International Meguro B1F, 1-3-14 Meguro, Meguro-ku, (5496 4381/www.bluesalley.co.jp). Meguro JR station, west exit. **Admission** ¥3,000-¥5,000.

Akai Karasu.

Showcases everything from jazz, big band, Latin, Brazilian, fusion and soul to pop and, yes, blues. The service is impeccable, the sound system crisp and the food tasty. Music nightly from 7.30pm.

Body & Soul

Anise Minami Aoyama B1, 6-13-9 Minami Aoyama, Minato-ku (5466 3348/www.bodyandsoul.co.jp). Omotesando station, exit B1. **Admission** ¥3,500.

This sophisticated, well-run club is comfortable and dedicated to jazz and jazz only, nightly from 8.30pm. The best players in the city love to play to the savvy crowd here. Good food and wine as well.

Buddy

Futaba Hall B2F, Asahigaoka 1-77-8, Nerima-ku, (3953 1152/www.buddy-tokyo.com). Ekoda station (Seibu Ikebukuro Line), south exit. **Admission** ¥1,500-¥2,800.

This rather large club is a little out of the way, a few stops from Ikebukuro, but worth the trip. The main focus is jazz, but tango or prog-rock groups are almost as common. Music nightly from 7.30pm.

GH Nine 9

UNO Bldg 9F, 4-4-6 Ueno, Taito-ku (3837 2525/ http://homepage1.nifty.com/ghnine). Okachimachi station, north exit or Ueno Hirokoji station, exit 3. **Admission** ¥3,000. **Map** p89.

This futuristic space at the top of a post-mod building is always a little eerie, but the music is consistently high quality. Jazz nightly from 8pm.

Hot House

Liberal Takadanobaba B1F, 3-23-5 Takadanobaba, Shinjuku-ku (3367 1233/ www2.vc-net.ne.jp/~winning/menu/hothouse/ hothouse.html). Takadanobaba station, Waseda exit. **Admission** ¥3,500.

Hot House is the world's smallest jazz club. An evening here might remind you of listening to live jazz in your living room, only with 15 or so other jazz lovers on the same sofa bench. Don't come late – it's so small you can't get in when the pianist is seated. Duos and trios and no amps. Warm and friendly atmosphere. Jazz nightly from 8.30pm.

J

Royal Mansion B1, 5-1-1 Shinjuku, Shinjuku-ku (3354 0335/www.jazzspot-j.com). Shinjuku JR station, east exit or Shinjuku-Sanchome station, exit C7. **Admission** ¥1,500-¥2,000. **Map** p109.

This jazz maniacs' place showcases up-and-coming talent, particularly singers, nightly from 7.15pm.

Jirokichi

Koenji Bldg B1, 2-3-4 Koenji-kita, Suginami-ku (3339 2727/www.jirokichi.net). Koenji station, north exit. **Admission** ¥2,500-¥4,000.

As eclectic as any spot in town, with everything from klezmer to didgeridoo to jive blues to jazz piano trios. The place has a young, hip vibe. There's hardly room to dance, but people do anyway. Well-run and fun. Music nightly from 7.30pm.

JZ Brat

Cerulean Tower Tokyu Hotel 2F, 26-1 Sakuragaokacho, Shibuya-ku (5728 0168/ www.jzbrat.com). Shibuya JR station, south exit. **Admission** from ¥5,000. **Map** p102.

The newest, most upscale club in the city, housed inside a huge hotel. The large interior has room to move and chat while the music plays. Consistently good booking of groups with occasional overseas players. Jazz nightly from 7.30pm.

Naru

Jujiya Bldg B1, 2-1 Kanda Surugadai, Chiyoda-ku (3291 2321/www.jazz-naru.com/index.html). Ochanomizu JR station, Ochanomizubashi exit. **Admission** ¥2,500.

Naru has a black lacquer interior and comfortable seats, and a bar top that winds around the piano, where you can also sit. Music consists of mostly young, hot players, and there are straight-ahead, satisfying old favourites, too. There's also good food and wine. Jazz nightly from 7.30pm.

Rooster

Inoue Bldg B1, 5-16-15 Ogikubo, Suginami-ku (5347 7369/www.rooster.jp). Ogikubo station, west exit. **Admission** ¥1,500-¥2,500.

Getting tickets

Tickets for almost any gig are available at the door but that's only if there are any left. Many concerts sell out quickly – even lesser-known acts, local or foreign, tend to fill venues. Advance tickets are a safe option and usually a bit cheaper too. There's a better chance of finding last-minute tickets at live houses; in fact, some venues only sell at the door, but, in these cases, it's wise to go and queue up ahead of opening time. Or trust the touts, always around at bigger venues.

Tokyo's main ticket agency is **Pia**, and it has numerous ticket outlets throughout the city, and also in Tokyu department store (*p170*). Pia publishes a weekly magazine listing thousands of events, each with its own six-digit code. Staff can also handle enquiries in English (05 7002 9999 probleme!/http://t.pia.co.jp).

The easiest ticket agency to find is probably the *konbini* chain **Lawson** (3569 9900 probleme!/www2.lawsonticket.com), but be prepared that using the vending machine requires the knowledge of a fair bit of Japanese. A third agency is **CN Playguide** but its outlets are more limited. There's also a new online option at http://eee.eplus.co.jp.

Music nightly from 8pm at the best blues club in the city. Small and intimate, it features the best blues (and bluesy jazz) from all over Tokyo, including acoustic, electric, New Orleans, East Side Chicago, slide and all points in between.

Roppongi Pit Inn

3-17-7 Roppongi, Minato-ku (3585 1063/www.pit-inn.com). Roppongi station, exits 3, 5. **Admission** from ¥3,000. **Map** p74.

This is a large space with excellent sound system close to the action of Roppongi. The Pit Inn features electric music and fusion, but also many other kinds of jazz nightly from 7.30pm.

Shinjuku Pit Inn

Accord Shinjuku B1F, 2-12-4 Shinjuku, Shinjuku-ku (3354 2024/www.pit-inn.com). Shinjuku-Sanchome station, exits C7, C8. **Admission** ¥3,500-¥5,000. **Map** p109.

Shinjuku Pit Inn is one of Tokyo's best clubs. All chairs face the stage in reverence for the most respected jazz groups in town, who offer their latest to the adoring in attendance. Irregular afternoon slot at 2.30pm gives the stage to newly emerging bands. Otherwise jazz nightly from 7.30pm.

Someday

1-20-9 Nishi Shinbashi, Minato-ku (3506 1777). Shinbashi JR station, Karasumori exit. **Admission** ¥2,500-¥3,700. **Map** p62.

Moved to the business area of Shinbashi towards the end of May 2003, where owner Mori-san continues to indulge his love of big bands. Jazz features every night from 7.45pm.

Sometime

1-11-31 Kichijoji Honcho, Musashino-shi (0422 21 6336/www.sometime.co.jp/sometime). Kichijoji station, north exit. **Admission** from ¥1,500.

One of the most popular clubs in the city. The stage sits in the centre of the club so you can see and hear up close. Don't come late and get stuck in the half-downstairs, though. Almost every top-notch player comes through sometime. The club has kept its music charge reasonable for years. Great, friendly service. Jazz nightly from 7.30pm.

Sonoka

2-15-19 Kami Osaki, Shinagawa-ku (3446 8680/ www7.plala.or.jp/mic_t/). Meguro JR station, east exit. **Admission** ¥2,800.

Vying with Hot House for the honour of smallest jazz club in the world, you have to pass drinks down the line of tables to those farthest from the bar. No need for mikes and amps. Excellent selection of established and soon-to-be groups, nightly from 8pm.

Tokyo TUC

Tokyo Uniform Center Honsha Biru B1F, 2-16-5 Iwamotocho, Chiyoda-ku (3866 8393/www.tokyouniform.com/tokyotuc/). Kanda station, north exit or Akihabara JR station, Showa Dori exit. **Admission** ¥3,000-¥11,000.

This great club is unfortunately out of the way, and doesn't have jazz playing every night. But when it does have shows, and if you can find a place to sit or stand, it has only the best Japanese and international musicians as part of its schedule. Tokyo TUC is so popular, it was voted one of the world's best jazz clubs in *Downbeat* magazine.

Rock/electronica/ world music

The rock scene here is incredibly active – venues abound and run the whole gamut: from relaxed wine-and-dine seating to trashy underground pits, from tiny crammed spaces to enormous stadiums, with just about every shape, size and ambience in between.

The bigger places will host any style as the size is more important than what's on. Live houses often tend to stick within limited genres to build a following – making it possible to take a gamble on a gig by the venue alone. Medium-sized venues pick at everything in between and often offer the most interesting options.

Gigs often start at 7pm, even at weekends. At a few live houses, events kick off at 11pm or midnight, but more likely you'll be back on the streets by about 9.30pm. Expect to pay ¥2,000-¥4,000 for a local gig, a bit more money for established medium-sized bands, while big overseas acts cost twice as much, if not more. Events in smaller venues often have three to four bands every night.

Stadiums & large venues

Club Citta Kawasaki

1-26 Ogawacho, Kawasaki-ku, Kawasaki-shi, Kanagawa-ken (044 246 8888/http://clubcitta.co.jp). Kawasaki station, east exit. **Capacity** *Standing* 1,300. *Seated* 600.

Halfway to Yokohama, Club Citta Kawasaki is a great hive of activity, with a large hall for live gigs. The lighting gear and stage-side speaker stacks are put to good use by loud and proud rock acts, but there are also other styles here, even dance stuff. Club Citta is an aggressive promoter, too, some foreign bands playing only here. Sometimes it turns into a cinema with all-night festivals.

Hibiya Kokaido

1-3 Hibiya Koen, Chiyoda-ku (3591 6388). Kasumigaseki station, exits B2, B3a, C4; Hibiya station, exit A10, A14. **Capacity** 2,075. **Map** p57.

Built in 1929, Hibiya Kokaido is one of the oldest concert halls in Tokyo. It's a versatile venue too, used for all sorts of events from political rallies to magic shows; it can even lay claim to being the scene of the mid-speech assassination of the chairman of the Socialist Party in 1960.

Nippon Budokan. *See p229.*

Hibiya Outdoor Theatre (Hibiya Yagai Ongakudo)

1-3 Hibiya Koen, Chiyoda-ku (3591 6388). Kasumigaseki station, exits B2, B3A, C4, or Hibiya station, exits A10, A14 or Uchisaiwaicho station, exits A6, A7. **Capacity** 3,114. **Map** p57.

Used since 1923, this outdoor venue puts enjoyment at the mercy of the weather. Umbrellas are not allowed, but turn up on a nice day and enjoy one of Tokyo's few open-air venues. Unfortunately, it is an ode to concrete, including the seats, even though it was rebuilt 20 years ago.

Koseinenkin Kaikan

5-3-1 Shinjuku, Shinjuku-ku (3356 1111/www.kjp.or.jp/hp_20/). Shinjuku-Sanchome station, exit C7. **Capacity** 2,062. **Map** p109.

An early 1960s construction that went through major refurbishment a decade ago, this classical music-style hall is an enduring venue known for its great acoustics. The place where Bowie, Led Zep and many other '70s legends once played, it's still the venue of choice for many.

Makuhari Messe

2-1 Nakase, Mihama-ku, Chiba-shi, Chiba-ken (043 296 0001/www.m-messe.co.jp). Makuhari Hongo station (JR Sobu Line) or Kaihin Makuhari station (JR Keiyo Line). **Capacity** 9,000.

The Event Hall in this huge convention complex on the outskirts of Tokyo is the place for all-night concert and DJ parties. It doesn't matter that after all that dancing there's a long trek back to town in the wee hours; it also doesn't matter that it is actually nothing more than an arena, as this is where the likes of Kraftwerk, Underworld and Foo Fighters, plus a bunch of big-name DJs entertain full houses.

Nakano Sun Plaza Hall

4-1-1 Nakano, Nakano-ku (3388 1151/ www.sunplaza.or.jp/hall). Nakano station, south exit. **Capacity** 2,222.

Unassuming venue a few stops from Shinjuku, this hall has hosted top bands including the Clash and PiL, as well as many bluesmen and world music artists. The list of prohibitions recited before any concert is far more suited to a classical music hall. At the time of writing, the local council, the venue's owner, is considering putting it up for sale.

National Yoyogi Stadium

2-1-1 Jinnan, Shibuya-ku (3468 1171/www.ntgk.go.jp/yoyogi). Harajuku station, Omotesando exit or Meiji-Jingumae station, exit 1. **Capacity** *Gymnasium 1* 13,665. *Gymnasium 2* 3,202. **Map** p102.

Another 1964 Olympics structure, this one used rarely and mainly for big-selling J-pop stars. More interestingly, the adjacent public space near NHK has a live stage with irregular free gigs.

NHK Hall

2-2-1 Jinnan, Shibuya-ku (3465 1751/www.nhk-sc.or.jp/nhk_hall). Harajuku station, Omotesando exit or Meiji-Jingumae station, exit 1 or Shibuya JR station, Hachiko exit. **Capacity** 3,700. **Map** p102.

The second main hall in this area is operated by state TV and radio broadcaster NHK. Concerts featured on the programmes are recorded here.

Get rocking at **La.mama Shibuya**, a good place to see new bands. *See p231.*

Recognised for good acoustics, it hosts various types of music, from classical to rock and jazz. The grander the performance, the higher the ticket price.

Nippon Budokan

2-3 Kitanomaru-Koen, Chiyoda-ku (3216 5100/ www.nipponbudokan.or.jp). Kudanshita station, exit 2. **Capacity** 14,950. **Map** p62.

Built for martial arts competition in the 1964 Olympics and an unlikely venue for rock concerts. When the Beatles played here in the mid '60s it sparked protests but now music happily shares with sports events. It's the main venue of this size and attracts many bigger overseas artists. Not only can't you buy alcohol on the premises, but the sound is below average.

Shibuya AX

2-1-1 Jinnan, Shibuya-ku (5738 2020/www.shibuya-ax.com). Harajuku station, Omotesando exit, or Meiji-Jingumae station, exit 1, or Shibuya station, Hachiko exit. **Capacity** *Standing* 1,500. *Seated* 700. **Map** p102.

Opened at the end of 2000, this medium-sized hall is proving quite popular and deservedly so. The odd cup-like shape (with the band at the bottom) and speaker positioning is a successful experiment in acoustics. Mainly hosts middling and up-and-coming local rock acts. A word of warning: the left luggage lockers are outside and you're not allowed to go out the door and back again once you're in.

Shibuya Kokaido

1-1 Udagawacho, Shibuya-ku (3463 3022). Shibuya station, Hachiko exit. **Capacity** 2,318. **Map** p102.

Yet another 1964 Olympics structure, this one for weightlifting competition, that survived the transition with the best reputation thanks to its acoustics. Seems to attract overseas mainstream rock groups and electric guitar players, but the many Japanese artists who play here add a bit of variety.

Tokyo Bay NK Hall

1-8 Maihama, Urayasu-shi, Chiba (047 355 7007/ www.nkhall.co.jp). Maihama station (JR Keiyo Line). **Capacity** 7,000.

A strange capitol-like structure with old-world columns, Tokyo Bay NK Hall looks more like the venue for a gala dinner than a concert. Built more recently than similar-sized venues, it has had a good run of acts including Beck, Massive Attack and the 2003 Free Tibet in Tokyo event. It may be out of the way, but since all the concerts here finish early there's no problem with getting back.

Tokyo Dome

1-3-61 Koraku, Bunkyo-ku (5800 9999/www.tokyo-dome.co.jp/). Suidobashi station, west exit or Korakuen station, exit 2. **Capacity** 55,000.

Also known as 'Big Egg', this is the mega-band venue where you need a giant screen to see the details on stage and the sound is one or two seconds behind the action. Unfortunately some bands need to play here and you'll have to pay a lot to see them, from the price of your ticket to your drinks as well. In the height of summer the roof might keep the rain away but the humidity seeps through and the plastic chairs don't feel too comfortable.

Tokyo International Forum

3-5-1 Marunouchi, Chiyoda-ku (5221 9000/ www.tif.or.jp). Yurakucho station, Tokyo International Forum exit or Ginza station, exit C9. **Capacity** *Hall A* 5,012. *Hall C* 1,502. **Map** p57.

The smaller three-level Hall C at the Tokyo International Forum was built in 1996 to provide the ideal in acoustics for music with its special 'concert hall shaper' device. With walls the colour of Chinese quince to match the colour of violins, this venue seems a bit too stylish for most gigs – but the sound quality can be a boon. Hall A is an enormous conference space, but best-selling groups that have a large following occasionally play.

Zepp Tokyo

Palette Town 1F, 1 Aomi, Koto-ku (3599 0710/www.zepp.co.jp/tokyo). Aomi station (Yurikamome Line) or Tokyo Teleport station (Rinkai Line). **Capacity** 2,700. **Map** p78.

Part of a chain with locations in four other cities, Zepp Tokyo is now sparingly used, although a number of good gigs and all-night events took place when it opened. Odaiba is not really the place to spend an evening, even though this space has been designed for good sightlines and acoustics.

Clubs & live houses

Antiknock

Ray Flat Shinjuku B1F, 4-3-15 Shinjuku, Shinjuku-ku (3350 6670/www.music.ne.jp/~antiknock). Shinjuku JR station, new south exit. **Capacity** 300. **Map** p109.

Antiknock is a small venue near Takashimaya Times Square where Tokyo's colourful hardcore punks gather. Its aim is to present 'original' music, but, most importantly, the music has to rock. If you need to vent your frustration with the crowds at Shinjuku station, just pop down here and get rocking with a different type of crowd.

Astro Hall

New Wave Harajuku Bldg B1F, 4-32-12 Jingumae, Shibuya-ku (3401 5352/www.astro-hall.com). Harajuku station, Takeshita exit or Meiji Jingumae station, exit 5. **Capacity** 400. **Map** p99.

When it opened in 2000 this was the venue of choice for many local indie bands but it's been up and down since. Some foreign acts also play here, but nearby Shibuya AX is better suited to live bands and it's dragging people away.

Bullet's

Kasumi Bldg B1F, 1-7-11 Nishi-Azabu, Minato-ku (3401 4844/www.bul-lets.com). Roppongi station, exit 2. **Capacity** 120. **Map** p74.

Finding information in English

Pia magazine has the major disadvantage of printing the names of foreign bands in katakana. It's annoying since many local acts use the Roman alphabet for their names.

One way around this is to check out the flyers at record stores – a lot use the alphabet for the artists and venues as well. Many stores stick to genres and finding the right shop means access to good info. Bigger stores have corners within sections or floors with flyers and fanzines – Disk Union and Tower Records in Shinjuku are good bets. More and more venues have their own websites, usually with the schedule, some with English versions.

Another option is to check out the websites of the promoters. Main ones are Smash (http://smash-jpn.com), Creativeman (www.creativeman.co.jp), Disk Garage (www.diskgarage.com), Hot Stuff (www.red-hot.ne.jp), Sogo (www.sogopr.co.jp), Flip Side (www.flipside.co.jp) and UDO (www.udo.co.jp).

A dark, cosy bar with sofas and cushions that's sometimes used for world music-influenced or ambient artists such as Terre Thaemlitz or Makyo. A better alternative to a live house for mellow events.

Cave-be

Kitazawa Plaza B1F, 2-14-16 Kitazawa, Setagaya-ku (3412 7373/www.cave-be.com). Shimo-Kitazawa station (Keio Inokashira/Odakyu lines), south exit. **Capacity** 150.

Opened in early 2003 next to the Japanese indie music shop High Line Records, this venue presents small local bands in all sorts of rock styles. It's already quite busy with bands on most nights.

Cay

Aoyama Spiral Bldg B1F, Aoyama 5-6-23, Minato-ku (3498 5790/www.spiral.co.jp/event). Omotesando station, exit B1. **Capacity** 400. **Map** p99.

This is a restaurant, regularly turned into a live or all-night events venue. The whole building is a centre for contemporary arts and design and the music selection matches that with new electronica, various world music-influenced and 'fusion' acts such as Karsh Kale or Holger Czukay. The view from the back is far from the best on all standing nights.

Club Asia

1-8 Maruyama-cho, Shibuya-ku (5458 1996/ www.clubasia.co.jp/asia). Shibuya JR station, Hachiko exit. **Capacity** 800. **Map** p102.

Club Asia is a big name on the scene. A bit more of a club than a live venue, it's currently hosting many hip hop events and acts, after doing a lot of techno and other dance music.

Club 251

Mikami Bldg B1F, 5-29-15 Daizawa, Setagaya-ku (5481 4141/www.club251.co.jp). Shimo-Kitazawa station (Keio Inokashira/Odakyu lines), south exit. **Capacity** 400.

One of the main venues in Shimo-Kitazawa and a reliable place to drop in to. There are no restrictions on musical styles, but it tends to be rock oriented, with a twist. This black, bare place shows its age but that's a sign of popularity rather than neglect.

Club Eggsite Shibuya

1-6-8 Jinnan, Shibuya-ku (3496 1561/www.egg-man.co.jp/eggsite). Shibuya JR station, Hachiko exit. **Capacity** 350. **Map** p102.

Club Eggsite Shibuya is close to the bigger Shibuya venues and is a bit of an institution, too. Most nights you'll see local bands playing here, those with an eye on a deal with a record company. A good venue for assorted rock-oriented music styles, this is also a good place to catch upcoming talent.

Club Goodman

AS Bldg B1F, 55 Kanda-Sakumagashi, Chiyoda-ku (3862 9010/www.clubgoodman.com). Akihabara JR station, Showa Dori exit. **Capacity** *Standing* 280. *Seated* 100.

This venue may be isolated in Akihabara, but it's worth a mention for its varied choice of acts. Club Goodman is not the cosiest place to spend a night but there's some unusual stuff on at times.

Club Quattro

Quattro by Parco 4, 5F, 32-13 Udagawa-cho, Shibuya-ku (3477 8750/www.net-flyer.com). Shibuya JR station, Hachiko exit. **Capacity** 750. **Map** p102.

Club Quattro is a superior venue that hosts quality acts most of the time, situated on the top floor of the Parco department store. It's not limited by genre, with varied overseas acts plus some of the best local bands, even ones that would normally prefer to play at bigger venues. Despite some architectural features that restrict views, this is one of the most appealing music venues in town.

Club Que

Big Ben Bldg B2F, 2-5-2 Kitazawa, Setagaya-ku (3412 9979/www.ukproject.com/que). Shimo-Kitazawa station (Keio Inokashira/Odakyu lines), south exit. **Capacity** 250.

In eight years, this place has built a strong reputation and, despite its small size, some not-so-small local indie bands sometimes appear. Club Que is keen on variety, not only genre-wise, as it also becomes a late-night DJ club on weekends. Irregular early afternoon gigs on weekends or holidays.

Crocodile

New Sekiguchi Bldg B1F, 6-18-8 Jingumae, Shibuya-ku (3499 5205/www.music.co.jp/~croco). Shibuya JR station, Miyamasusaka (east) exit or Harajuku station, Omotesando exit or Meiji-Jingumae station, exit 4. **Capacity** *Standing* 250. *Seated* 120. **Map** p102.

Although this venue bills itself as a modern music restaurant, it's best to skip the food and stick to the music. Crocodile presents anything from salsa to country, rock and jazzy stuff, at times mixed in any combination. Be prepared that there are not such good seats for the last ones arriving on a busy night.

DeSeO

Dai 2 Okazaki Bldg 1F, 3-3 Sakuragaoka-cho, Shibuya-ku (5457 0303/www.deseo.co.jp). Shibuya JR station, south exit. **Capacity** *Standing* 300. *Seated* 120. **Map** p102.

This small live house along the JR tracks is another spot for bands warming up for bigger things. At times some more established acts perform, too.

440

Mikumi Bldg 1F, 5-29-15 Daizawa, Setagaya-ku (3422 9440/www.club251.co.jp/440). Shimo-Kitazawa station (Keio Inokashira/Odakyu lines), south exit. **Capacity** *Standing* 180. *Seated* 100.

A recent addition to the scene, 440 takes a softer approach to live music, and is one of very few café-style live houses outside the jazz circuit. Being part of the same group as Club 251 (only two minutes down the road) means it's already booked for weeks ahead. Open for food and drinks the rest of the time.

Gear

Tokyo Bldg B1F, 4-25-4 Koenji-Minami, Suginami-ku (3318 6948). Koenji station, south exit. **Capacity** 180.

The place for bands that might not be allowed to play anywhere else. All sorts of 'core' stuff with event names like 'Fangs Anal Satan'. Gear is a small venue that has a big following.

Gig-antic

Sound Forum Bldg 2F, 3-20-15 Shibuya, Shibuya-ku (5466 9339/www.gig-antic.co.jp). Shibuya JR station, Miyamasusaka (east) exit. **Capacity** 150. **Map** p102.

Gig-antic is a small live house, situated by the JR tracks, that presents bands from around the country while on tour in Tokyo. Mix of hardcore and punk, some events sold out in advance.

Heaven's Door

Keio Hallo Bldg B1F, 1-33-19 Sangenjaya, Setagaya-ku (3410 9581/www.geocities.jp/xxxheavensdoorxxx). Sangenjaya station (Tokyu Denentoshi Line), south exit. **Capacity** 300.

Heaven's Door is another institution, in a rites-of-passage sense, for many loud Tokyo bands. Only a few established acts play here, yet everybody knows about it. There's not much decoration but there are huge speakers for true music lovers.

La.mama Shibuya

Premier Dogenzaka B1F, 1-15-3 Dogenzaka, Shibuya-ku (3464 0801/http://la.mama.gr.jp). Shibuya JR station, south exit. **Capacity** *Standing* 300. *Seated* 120. **Map** p102.

La.mama has been presenting bands at the start of (hopefully) successful careers for over 20 years. Tends to host more J-pop and commercial rock than other venues in the area.

Liquid Room

7F Humax Pavilion, 1-20-1 Kabuki-cho, Shinjuku-ku (3200 6831/www.liquidroom.net). Shinjuku JR station, east exit. **Capacity** 1,000. **Map** p109.

Venues are not usually seven floors up but Liquid Room stands out for much better reasons. Simply a big black square room, it's been at the forefront of the music scene for ten years now. And busy, too – on weekends shows start early so that all-night dance parties can kick off by 11pm; and those are usually headed by a world famous DJ. No limitations on style and always likely to be a good event. There's special flooring that moves when the whole crowd's in motion and it can feel like an earthquake. On that subject, there's only one set of stairs out.

Live Inn Rosa

Rosa Kaikan B2F, 1-37-12 Nishi-Ikebukuro, Toshima-ku (5956 3463/www.live-inn-rosa.com). Ikebukuro JR station, west exit. **Capacity** *Standing* 350. *Seated* 100. **Map** p69.

Proudly J-pops, this Ikebukuro venue also presents other types of music, including events combining live bands and DJs, and many artistes on their first few appearances.

Live Spot 20,000V

Dai 8 Tokyo Bldg B2F, 4-25-4 Koenji-Minami, Suginami-ku (3316 6969/homepage2.nifty.com/20000volt/index.html). Koenji station, south exit. **Capacity** 180.

Another institution, 'Niman Volt', as it's known, is the place for hard listening, with more than a nod to the experimental and noise set. Current local stars have played here, as do big names in lesser known incarnations, such as Diskaholics Anonymous Trio who played here in late 2002.

Mandala Minami-Aoyama

MR Bldg B1F, 3-2-2 Minami-Aoyama, Minato-ku (5474 0411/www.mandala.gr.jp/aoyama.html). Gaienmae station, 1A exit. **Capacity** 120. **Map** p99.

This is a live-house-cum-restaurant that presents nightly shows of the milder variety, such as ballads and soft jazz, but also sometimes ventures into more esoteric styles and formats.

Mandala2 Kichijoji

2-8-6 Kichijoji Minami-cho, Musashino-shi (0422 42 1579/www.mandala.gr.jp/man2.html). Kichijoji station, south exit. **Capacity** 80.

More of a live house than its Minami-Aoyama sister, this branch of Mandala specialises in more experimental music. A hotbed of activity (one of the live CDs on John Zorn's Tzadik label was recorded here) where local stars sometimes show up unannounced for one-off gigs with friends.

Milk

Roob 6 B1F-B2F, 1-13-3 Ebisu-Nishi, Shibuya-ku (5458 2826/www.milk-tokyo.com). Ebisu JR station, west exit. **Capacity** *Live music floor* 300.

The website says Milk is 'the world's greatest enjoy space'. Not quite, perhaps, but it's definitely an inviting venue, and one that has a sub-basement bar and lounge area. The live area may be an odd shape, but that doesn't seem to bother the lesser-known but respected local talents who regularly perform here.

On Air East

2-14-9 Dogenzaka, Shibuya-ku (no phone/www.onair-web.co.jp/hall). Shibuya JR station, Hachiko exit. **Capacity** 1,300. **Map** p102.

The biggest space in the On Air family, this was a very popular venue that had a good schedule with local and international acts. Unfortunately, On Air East was then demolished, though it is due to reopen in the autumn of 2003. Watch this space.

On Air West

2-3 Maruyama-cho, Shibuya-ku (5458 4646/ www.onair-web.co.jp/hall/). Shibuya JR station, Hachiko exit. **Capacity** 500. **Map** p102.

Situated in the centre of the love hotels zone, On Air West mainly hosts Japanese bands of medium standing. Music tends to be rock oriented, but you can expect a bit of J-pop, neo-goth and other bands to get thrown in to the mix.

Shelter Shimo-Kitazawa

Senda Bldg B1F, 2-6-10 Kitazawa, Setagaya-ku (3466 7430/www.loft-prj.co.jp). Shimo-Kitazawa station (Keio Inokashira/Odakyu lines), north exit. **Capacity** 250.

Part of the Loft group (*see below*), this venue is constantly booked with upcoming or even established local bands that you might normally see at bigger venues. Overseas touring bands play here on occasion. The venue has been around for over ten years and is very popular, so arrive early.

Shibuya Nest

On Air West 5F-6F, 2-3 Maruyama-cho, Shibuya-ku (3462 4420/www.onir-web.co.jp/hall/). Shibuya JR station, Hachiko exit. **Capacity** *Standing* 250. *Seated* 100. **Map** p102.

Also part of the On Air family and on top of On Air West, this smaller venue presents artistes with little regard to genre. It's a cosy space on two floors used by locals and touring groups alike.

Shinjuku Loft

Tatehana Bldg B2F, 1-12-9 Kabuki-cho, Shinjuku-ku (5272 0382/www.loft-prj.co.jp). Shinjuku JR station, east exit. **Capacity** *Live stage* 550. *Sub-stage* 100. **Map** p109.

Loft has been around for more than 25 years and is a dedicated promoter. It reopened in a new space in 1999 without a dent to its reputation. Inside are two areas, one for live shows and the other a bar with a small stage. They like loud music in any genre here. At times a bit more than a live house, with all-night events that include DJs.

Shinjuku Loft Plus One

Hayashi Bldg B2F, 1-14-7 Kabuki-cho, Shinjuku-ku (3205 6864/www.loft-prj.co.jp). Shinjuku JR station, east exit. **Capacity** 100-200. **Map** p109.

An unusual live house billing itself as a 'talk show live performance' space. No music, just people of all ages and walks of life talking about their passions.

Shinjuku Marz

Daiichi Tokiwa B1F, 2-45-1 Kabuki-cho, Shinjuku-ku (3202 8248/www.marz.jp). Shinjuku JR station, east exit. **Capacity** 300. **Map** p109.

Funk, rock and J-pop – what the bands have in common here is the ambition to set off on a musical career. Opened in 2001, Shinjuku Marz is doing well despite stiff local competition.

Star Pine's Café

1-20-16 Kichijoji-Honcho, Musashino-shi (0422 23 2251/www.mandala.gr.jp/spc.html). Kichijoji station, central exit. **Capacity** 350.

The biggest of the three Mandala venues, this one's a bit more bar style. The artists are mostly experimental, and genres range from progressive or jazzy to avant-garde and dancey; most of the music is a high quality. Star Pine's Café is the venue of choice for various obscure-ish overseas acts. All-night events follow gigs at weekends.

STB139

6-7-11 Roppongi, Minato-ku (5474 1395/ http://stb139.co.jp). Roppongi station, exit 3. **Capacity** *Standing* 500. *Seated* 315. **Map** p74.

You can watch some world-class talent while wining and dining at this venue. The only competition to Blue Note Tokyo, STB 139 does some things better. The layout is much friendlier and the atmosphere a bit more relaxed. There's more variety in the music, too, which veers towards soul, Latin, R&B and classics rather than just plain jazz.

Studio Jam

Central Bldg 1F-B1F, 2-3-23 Kabuki-cho, Shinjuku-ku (3232 8169/www.h4.dion.ne.jp/~studio/jam). Shinjuku JR station, east exit. **Capacity** 200. **Map** p109.

Open since 1980, Studio Jam specialises in 1960s-1970s music with a bit of guitar pop thrown in.

Y2K

Aban Bldg B1F, 7-13-2 Roppongi, Minato-ku (5775 3676/www.explosionworks.net). Roppongi station, exits 4a, 7. **Capacity** 450. **Map** p74.

Opened in 1999 in the heart of Roppongi with a mission to bring live music to clubbers, this venue concentrates on smaller local rock-minded bands.

Tokyo International Forum. *See p229*.

Nightlife

The Tokyo club scene is as wild, varied and full of surprises as the city itself.

Japan might still be feeling the pinch, but you'd never know it from the country's dance venues. Significant investment in improved sound-systems, interior aesthetics and – most importantly – the music, have helped to keep Japan's clubs full.

The latest clubs to emerge are trying to provide a complete night out, including great food at restaurants attached to clubs. These places include **Air** (Italian/Japanese), **Alife** (Italian/Japanese), **La Fabrique** (French) and **The Orbient** (Chinese).

The last five years have also seen a steady influx of foreign DJs, but this doesn't mean there's no local talent. Japanese names to look out for include Yamataka Eye (inspirational experimental techno), Emma (house), Takyu Ishino (techno), Krash (hip hop), and Ken Ishii (techno electronica).

Newcomers to Japan should also take the opportunity to observe the subtle cultural differences between clubbing in the east and west. You will notice a lack of security at the door, the issuing of tickets for drinks after payment at the door, the far-out (or acutely spot-on) fashion, the static feel on – and the relaxed attitude off – the dance floor.

Another difference is the kind of friendly atmosphere that's been missing in, say, the UK since the illegal raves of the late 1980s. And as far as the locals are concerned, the novelty of aggressive drinking and excessive hitting on women has long worn off.

There has also been a change in the prevailing clubbing philosophy. Although considered taboo by practically all Japanese, the use of dance-enhancing drugs is on the rise and moving from the underground to some respected dance venues. It is still a delicate matter, however, and most clubbers as well as clubs do not want to draw attention to it. If this is part of your scene, a cautious approach is advisable. Japanese clubs are generally safe environments, but – despite what others may tell you – the police have been known to actually do their jobs and arrest people.

Clubs come in all shapes and sizes – with prices to match. The smaller ones are usually dimly lit but cosy, costing around ¥2,000 with one or two drinks tickets. Thanks to their intimacy, the smaller clubs are good places to make lasting friendships.

If your stay is short, it might be better to hit one of the larger clubs. Although more expensive – around ¥3,500 with one drink ticket – you will definitely know where your money has gone.

Not sure where to go, or who's playing? Head for any CD or record shop, particularly in the Shibuya area, and pick up a selection of the flyers that litter the counters. Some will save you ¥500 on the entry charge.

Also worthy of investigation is the 'After Dark' section of the weekly *Metropolis* free magazine, also to be found at most main CD shops, including Shibuya HMV and Tower. But if your Japanese is up to scratch, get yourself a copy of *Floor*.

Don't be too dismayed by the apparent early-to-bed nature of the club scene as revealed in the listings below. For an explanation of club opening hours, *see p237* **The witching hour**.

328 (San Ni Hachi)

B1F, 3-24-20 Nishi-Azabu, Minato-ku (3401 4968/ www.02.246.ne.jp/~azabu328/). Roppongi station, exit 1. **Open** 8pm-midnight daily. **Admission** ¥2,000 Mon-Thur, Sun (incl 2 drinks); ¥2,500 Fri, Sat (incl 2 drinks). **Dress code** none. **Map** p74.

You'll spot 328's large neon sign from the Nishi-Azabu crossing. First opened in 1979, it underwent total refurbishment in 1998. Music is a mixture of genres, ranging from soul to dance classics, attracting an older crowd. On Saturdays, this small venue plays more rare groove tunes and gets packed, so make sure to come early.

Air

Hikawa Bldg B1F/B2F, 2-11 Sarugaku-cho, Shibuya-ku (5784 3386/www.air-tokyo.com/). Daikanyama station (Tokyu Toyoko Line). **Open** only for special events. **Admission** varies with event (incl 1 drink). **Dress code** casual.

Air is situated in a quieter part of Shibuya, a bit of a trek from the station. Deep inside this rabbit's burrow you'll find a comfortable DJ lounge. Go still further and there's a cheap bar and spacious dance floor. The array of international talent on offer here is impressive, as is the sound system.

Alife

1-7-2 Nishi-Azabu, Minato-ku (5785 2531/www.e-alife.net). Roppongi station, exit 2. **Open** *Club* 9pm-midnight Thur-Sat. *Lounge & restaurant* 11pm-5am Mon-Sat. **Admission** (club only) ¥3,500 men (incl 2 drinks); ¥2,500 women (incl 2 drinks). **Dress code** not too casual. **Map** p74.

This huge new club has it all, with a spacious party lounge on the second floor, a stylish café (which wouldn't be out of place in a designer furniture shop) on the ground floor, and a large dance area in the basement. The main music on offer is a mixture of dance, which creates a vibrant party atmosphere during the night, but the place is a haven for hard-core clubbers, with guest DJs playing trance or house on Sunday mornings.

Ball

Kuretake Bldg 4F, 4-9 Udagawa-cho, Shibuya-ku (3476 6533/www.club-ball.com). Shibuya JR station, Hachiko exit. **Open** 10pm-5am Mon-Sat; varies with events Sun. **Admission** ¥2,000 Mon, Thur, Fri (incl 2 drinks); ¥2,000 Sat, Sun (incl 1 drink); ¥1,000 Tue, Wed (incl 1 drink). **Dress code** none. **Map** p102.

There's a great night view of Shibuya to be had from this small venue, but sadly that's its best feature, despite the reasonably priced bar (drinks from ¥600). The PA here simply isn't up to scratch – and given that the choice of music is house, this is a very serious shortcoming indeed. What's more, the dance floor is tiny.

Bar Drop

2F, 1-29-6 Kichijoji-Honcho, Musashino-shi (0422 20 0737/www.drop.co.jp). Kichijoji station, central exit. **Open** 9.30pm-midnight Mon-Thur; 11pm-midnight Fri, Sat; varies Sun. **Admission** ¥1,500 Mon-Thur (incl 1 drink); ¥2,000 Fri-Sun (incl 1 drink). Can vary with events. **Dress code** none.

Bar Drop features a variety of '90s US and UK pop music on its two dance floors (2F and B1F), with the downstairs floor offering a slightly more eclectic choice of sounds. Unusually for Tokyo, there's a large lounge space, with tables and chairs to cool off at when you've danced until you dropped.

Bed

Fukuri Bldg B1F, 3-29-9 Nishi-Ikebukuro, Toshima-ku (3981 5300/www.ikebukurobed.com). Ikebukuro JR station, west exit. **Open** 10pm-5am daily. **Admission** ¥2,000 Mon-Thur, Sun (incl 2 drinks); ¥2,500 Fri, Sat (incl 2 drinks). **Dress code** none. **Map** p69.

As you descend to Bed, you will be greeted by photo montages of previous, presumably satisfied, customers. Clientele here is generally young, and the music consists of mainly hip hop, but there's also the occasional techno and warp house.

Bullet's

Kasumi Bldg B1F, 1-7-11 Nishi-Azabu, Minato-ku (3401 4844/www.bul-lets.com). Roppongi station, exit 2. **Open** 10pm-5am Wed-Sat. **Admission** varies with events. **Dress code** none. **Map** p74.

If you want an altogether different experience, this is your place. As soon as you enter Bullet's, you have to leave your shoes at the door, then you can either chill out on the carpeted floor or dance barefoot at the back. Music varies from trance to ambient depending on events. Attracts an arty crowd.

Club Acid Tokyo

Kowa Bldg B1F, 2-3-12 Shinjuku, Shinjuku-ku (3352 3338/www.acid.jp). Shinjuku-Gyoenmae station, Shinjuku Gate exit. **Open** 8pm-midnight, but can vary with event. **Admission** ¥2,000 (incl 2 drinks), but can vary. **Dress code** none. **Map** p109.

Finding the entrance to Club Acid is a challenge in itself. Only a small sign on Shinjuku Dori gives any hint of its existence. The best way of finding it is to pay attention to the stairways of neighbouring buildings and follow your ears: on different nights you can hear anything booming out of here, from ska to rock, hip hop to Latin, R&B to techno to drum 'n' bass. Check the schedule to see what's on when.

Alife. *See p234.*

Take off your shoes and shake your body at **Bullet's**. *See p235.*

Club Asia

1-8 Maruyama-cho, Shibuya-ku (5458 1996/www.clubasia.co.jp). Shibuya JR station, Hachiko exit. **Open** varies. **Admission** from ¥2,000. **Dress code** no beach sandals. **Map** p102.

Club Asia is a favourite space with private-party organisers, so for individual events you should be sure to check out the schedule by the entrance. There is a bar and cloakroom on the first floor, a small dance floor and bar on the second, and by the stairway that leads from the second floor there's a moderately roomy dance floor and bar. The stairway to the main hall is an unusual feature, but it can get very crowded, particularly on Friday nights. The main hall's high ceiling looks great but can make the sound appear a bit uneven.

Club Atom

Dr Jeekahn's 4F/5F/6F, 2-4 Maruyama-cho, Shibuya-ku (5428 5195). Shibuya JR station, Hachiko exit. **Open** 9pm-5am Thur-Sat. **Admission** ¥3,000 (incl 2 drinks). **Dress code** not too casual, no sandals. **Map** p102.

This large venue has two reasonably open dance floors. The dance floor on the fifth floor devotes itself to mainstream trance or house while the one on the fourth floor, with its cave-like interior, plays more R&B and hip hop.

Club Bar Family

Shimizu Bldg B1F, 1-10-2 Shibuya, Shibuya-ku (3400 9182). Shibuya JR station, Miyamasusaka (east) exit. **Open** 10pm-4am daily. **Admission** varies with events. **Dress code** none. **Map** p102.

A small venue with a bar and dance floor where you can dance the night away to soul and dance classics, R&B and hip hop. The interior is not especially memorable, and the clientele is relatively young, including herds of young girls with fake tans. Drinks are around ¥600.

Club Chu

Oba B-Bldg B1F, 28-4 Maruyama-cho, Shibuya-ku (3770 3780/www.fbi-tyo.com). Shibuya JR station, Hachiko exit. **Open** 10pm-5am daily, but phone to check. **Admission** ¥2,000 (incl 2 drinks). **Dress code** none. **Map** p102.

In Japanese, the word '*chu*' means sky or space, and the decor at this club is designed to give you the feeling that you are floating in space. The cool ambience is intended to attract a more adult clientele than many other clubs – people seeking a lounge space with good music and drink, rather than serious dance nuts or date-hunters.

Club Complex Code

Shinjuku Toho Kaikan 4F, 1-19-2 Kabuki-cho, Shinjuku-ku (3209 0702/www.clubcomplexcode.com/index-pc.html). Shinjuku JR station, east exit. **Open** 8pm-midnight daily. **Admission** ¥3,000 (incl 2 drinks) Mon-Thur, Sun; ¥3,500 (incl 2 drinks) Fri, Sat. **Dress code** not too casual, no sandals. **Map** p109.

With three dance floors (two small, one gigantic), Club Complex Code is a monster nightclub that can host a variety of different events and special nights (sometimes at the same time). Its location, on the fourth floor of a Kabuki-cho building, means that from the outside you get no impression of its size:

The witching hour

A quick look through the listings in this section will reveal a surprising number of clubs that close at midnight. How can this be in a city where bars close at 5am, and many restaurants are open round the clock?

The simple answer is that it isn't like this at all. There is a ridiculous law that prohibits dancing after midnight in local neighbourhoods in order to ensure that it is quiet late at night. This rule is universally ignored but, when asked, many clubs still pretend to toe the line by claiming that they close at midnight. In fact, most clubs stay open till 4am or 5am.

with a capacity of 2,000 people, Code is one of the biggest clubs in Japan. The biggest of the three dance floors is called En-Code, and is sometimes used as a live stage. En-Code itself has a capacity of 1,000 people and four gigantic screens where you can watch the VJs doing their stuff. Sub-floor De-Code holds 120. There is also a main bar room and lounge, Ba-Code, and a snack bar beside the main floor, where a ¥500 token buys you anything from a bottle of mineral water to a small buffet.

Club Hachi

Aoyama Bldg 1-4F, 4-5-9 Shibuya, Shibuya-ku (5766 4887). Shibuya JR station, Miyamasusaka (east) exit. **Open** 10pm-5am daily. **Admission** ¥2,000 (incl 1 drink). Can vary with events. **Dress code** none. **Map** p102.

Club Hachi is a dingy but funky venue that occupies the whole of a run-down four-storey building situated on Roppongi Dori. Although far from roomy, each floor has its own individual character. The first floor is a western-style *yakitori* bar, the second floor has a DJ bar, the third is the main dance area, and the fourth is the lounge bar. The venue was once the home of globally fêted DJs Ken Ishii and Kensei, who used to play here regularly. The monthly schedule has a wide selection, from drum 'n' bass to R&B, house, techno, hip hop and jazz.

Club Jamaica

Nishi-Azabu Ishibashi Bldg B1F, 4-16-14 Nishi-Azabu, Minato-ku (3407 8844/www.club-jamaica.com). Roppongi station, exit 1. **Open** 10pm-5am Thur-Sat. **Admission** ¥1,000 Thur (incl 1 drink); ¥2,500 Fri, Sat (incl 2 drinks). **Dress code** none. **Map** p74.

Opened by a reggae fanatic in 1989, with a back wall piled up with speakers, Club Jamaica blasts out roots reggae on Thursday nights, attracting a younger crowd at the weekend with faster sounds. It's a small venue with an entrance that can be difficult to find, but the atmosphere is friendly and the sound system has some serious bass.

Club Que Shimo-Kitazawa

Big Ben Bldg B2F, 2-5-2 Kitazawa, Setagaya-ku (3412 9979/www.ukproject.com/que). Shimo-Kitazawa station (Inokashira/Odakyu lines), south exit. **Open** 6.30pm-4am daily. **Admission** around ¥2,500, but varies with events. **Dress code** none.

Club Que's main raison d'être is as a live house for rock bands, but once the weekend gigs are over it transforms itself into a club. Music tends to be rock-oriented, with healthy doses of alternative rock, guitar pop and vintage rock thrown in. Worth a trip.

Core

TSK CCC Bldg B1- B2F, 7-15-30 Minato-ku (3470 5944/www.clubcore.net). Roppongi station, exit 4b. **Open** 10pm-midnight daily. **Admission** ¥2,500 (incl 1 drink), but varies with events. **Dress code** none. **Map** p74.

Discretion is taken to new heights at Core, whose owner claims he didn't put a sign outside because he didn't want everyone to know it was there. The dance floor is quite roomy given its sub-basement location. For a club, the bar snacks are impressive. Drinks start at ¥600. Core features mostly house and techno, and it has proved popular with TV and sports personalities on their nights off. Every second Friday, it hosts a house and R&B event, 'Scene', where DJs Funakoshi and Yo-Gin spin the tracks.

Discotheque Byblos

Jule A Bldg B1F, 1-10-10 Azabu-Juban, Minato-ku (3568 2380/www.byblos-group.com). Azabu-Juban station, exits 4, 7. **Open** 6pm-1am Mon-Thur; 6pm-midnight Fri, Sat. **Admission** *Men* ¥3,000 Mon-Thur (incl 2 drinks); ¥3,500 Fri, Sat (incl 2 drinks). *Women* ¥2,500 (incl 2 drinks). **Dress code** smart.

This club recently dissolved its association with Salem cigarettes to concentrate on the 'mature' end of the club-going market, people between the ages of 30 and 50. Expect besuited salarymen a-go-go.

Fai

5-10-1 Minami-Aoyama, Minato-ku (3486 4910/ www.fai-aoyama.com/). Omotesando station, exit B1. **Open** 10pm-(midnight)-5am daily. **Admission** ¥2,000 Mon-Thur (incl 2 drinks), varies with events; ¥2,500 Fri-Sun (incl 3 drinks). **Dress code** not too casual, no beach sandals at weekends. **Map** p99.

Only punk and techno are left off the musical menu at Fai, whose speciality is music from the '70s and '80s. Fine drinks start at ¥700.

Fura

3-26-25 Shibuya, Shibuya-ku (5485 4011/ www.fura.co.jp). Shibuya JR station, Miyamasusaka (east) or south exit. **Open** 9pm-5am Thur-Sun.

Admission around ¥3,000 (incl 1 or 2 drinks). **Dress code** not too casual, no beach sandals. **Map** p102.
Fura used to be a four-storey complex with an Italian restaurant on the first floor. It now consists of two levels. On the second floor is a relatively roomy dance area playing commercial music; on the floor above is a bar-cum-lounge space playing trance. The club attracts a younger, over-suntanned crowd, with Saturday its busiest night.

Ism Shibuya

Social Dogenzaka Bldg 2F, 1-14-9 Dogenzaka, Shibuya-ku (3780 6320/http://club-ism.com). Shibuya JR station, Hachiko exit. **Open** 10pm-midnight daily. **Admission** varies with events. **Dress code** none. **Map** p102.
Sister venue of Rockwest (*see p240*), located in the area between the Mark City complex and 246 Street. Rockwest has now abandoned its original small-club purpose to attract the crowds by hosting a variety of events. Ism takes the old Rockwest ethos and hosts a number of small techno, house, trance and happy hardcore parties.

Izm

J2 Bldg B1F/B2F, 1-7-1 Kabuki-cho, Shinjuku-ku (3200 9914). Shinjuku JR station, east exit. **Open** 10pm-5am daily. **Admission** ¥2,000 Mon-Thur, Sun (incl 1 drink); ¥2,500 Fri, Sat (incl 1 drink). **Dress code** none. **Map** p109.
Hidden in the seediest part of Kabuki-cho, this small venue attracts a teenage clientele. The music is mainly hip hop, with a touch of R&B and reggae.

La Fabrique

Zero Gate B1F, 16-9 Udagawa-cho, Shibuya-ku (5428 5100). Shibuya JR station, Hachiko exit. **Open** 6pm-2am Mon-Thur; 6pm-5am Fri; 11am-5am Sat; 11am-11pm Sun. **Admission** free Mon-Thur, Sun; ¥2,500-¥4,000 Fri, Sat (varies with event). **Dress code** casual. **Map** p102.
Primarily a French restaurant, serving nouvelle cuisine and lighter vegetable dishes, this place is transformed into a spacious dance venue at night time. Although the resident DJs start playing from 6pm, guest DJs do not begin their sets before 11pm. Downtempo sounds are usually played during the week and the music is speeded up by the weekend to include a mix of house and disco. La Fabrique is a popular venue, with decent house wine, but does get crowded around the bar area.

Liquid Room

Humax Pavilion 7F, 1-20-1 Kabuki-cho, Shinjuku-ku (3200 6831/www.liquidroom.net). Shinjuku JR station, east exit. **Open** varies with events. **Admission** varies with events. **Dress code** none. **Map** p109.
Liquid Room is a large club and live house located in the middle of frantic Kabuki-cho. Although it does host its own events two or three times a month, most of the time the space is rented out, so you never know what might be happening: it could be a live house one night and a hip hop club the next. Liquid Room has two bars and plenty of toilets. You can pick up its free monthly schedule from big music stores such as Tower or HMV (for both *see p190*).

Loop

B1F, 2-1-13 Shibuya, Shibuya-ku (3797 9933/www.baseplanning.co.jp). Shibuya JR station, Miyamasusaka (east) exit, or Omotesando station, exit B1. **Open** 10pm-5am daily. **Admission** ¥2,000 Mon-Thur (incl 1 drink); ¥2,500 Fri-Sun (incl 1 drink), ¥2,000 with flyer (incl 1 drink). **Dress code** none. **Map** p102.
Loop is located between Shibuya and Omotesando stations. A warmly lit lounge space with stylish bare concrete interiors serves as an ideal hide-out for die-hard techno buffs seeking to keep their distance from wannabe club-goers. The dance floor has a friendly vibe, moody lighting and an excellent sound system. DJ Mochizuki hosts the Saturday event 'In the Mix', featuring techno, broken beats and future jazz; on Saturdays you might also catch the occasional invited foreign, mainly British, performers.

Lounge Neo

TLC Building 5F, 2-21-7 Dogenzaka, Shibuya-ku (5459 7230/www.clubasia.co.jp). Shibuya JR station, Hachiko exit. **Open** varies. **Admission** varies. **Dress code** smart. **Map** p102.
Although more a deluxe lounge bar than a club, Lounge Neo does offer some good chill-out sounds in the late hours for those who have clubbed too hard. It's opposite Club Asia (*see p236*), and owned and operated by the same company.

Luners

Fukao Bldg B1F, 1-4-5 Azabu-Juban, Minato-ku (3586 1231/www.luners.co.jp). Azabu-Juban station, exits 4, 7. **Open** varies with events. **Admission** varies. **Dress code** none.
Luners is a relatively large venue and has a huge mirror ball hanging above the main floor. You can admire the whole clubbing crowd from the lounge in the loft. If the main stage and its giant screen leave you cold, make your own stage out of the terrace between the down and upstairs. A first-floor restaurant offers internet access and a quiet environment for a tête-à-tête.

Maniac Love

B1F, 5-10-6 Minami-Aoyama, Minato-ku (3406 1166/www.maniaclove.com). Omotesando station, exit B1. **Open** 10pm-midnight Mon-Sat (plus after-hours party Sun am, *see p237* **The witching hour**). **Admission** ¥2,000 Mon-Thur (incl 1 drink); ¥2,500 Fri, Sat (incl 1 drink); ¥1,000 Sun from 5am (incl free coffee). **Dress code** none. **Map** p99.
With its immense sound system and cool lighting effects, Maniac Love was designed to be a mecca for dance music in Tokyo. The venue, like many others in the city, is a little tricky to find, located in the basement of a plain-looking building. It attracts serious dance music lovers, so don't come here looking for

a date. Drinks start at ¥700. The after-hours party on Sunday mornings has built up a loyal following, and it's not unusual to see the place full to bursting at 7am. It's worth checking out the techno/break beats event, 'Machine Gun', with DJ Captain Funk, the first Friday of every month.

Milk

Roob 6 Bldg B1F/B2F, 1-13-3 Ebisu-Nishi, Shibuya-ku (5458 2826/www.milk-tokyo.com). Ebisu JR station, west exit. **Open** varies with events. **Admission** around ¥2,500, but varies with events. **Dress code** none.

Milk's mission when it opened in 1995 was to bring the best of rock, punk and hardcore to Tokyo. These days, however, even Milk has succumbed to the techno and house sound that has swept Tokyo clubland, although it does go back to its roots and occasionally hosts live rock acts (check website for monthly schedule). The venue itself is maze-like, occupying three sub-surface floors of the same building as the What The Dickens pub (*see p166*). At the bottom of the club is a lounge area with a mysteriously lit morgue-like kitchen, where you can have a quiet conversation while up above the dancing continues on the cramped dance floor.

Mix

B1F, 3-6-19 Kita-Aoyama, Minato-ku (3797 1313/www.at-mix.com). Omotesando station, exits A1, B4. **Open** varies with events. **Admission** ¥2,000 Mon-Thur, Sun (incl 2 drinks); ¥2,500 Fri, Sat (incl 2 drinks). **Dress code** none. **Map** p99.

This tiny, narrow club makes full use of its limited space. Somehow, it manages to fit a seating area between the dance floor and bar. Packed at the weekends, it's a squeeze to get past people in order to get a drink but there is a good selection of dance music with a mixed friendly crowd.

Module

M&I Bldg B1F/B2F, 34-6 Udagawa-cho, Shibuya-ku (3464 8432/www.clubmodule.com). Shibuya JR station, Hachiko exit. **Open** 10pm-midnight Mon-Sat, but can vary. **Admission** ¥2,000 Mon-Thur (incl 1 drink); ¥2,500 Fri, Sat (incl 1 drink). **Dress code** none. **Map** p102.

There is a relaxing split-level bar on the first floor of the basement, with drinks from ¥600. When you get down to the second level you'll find a marked contrast: a loud sound system causes the foundations to shudder below the pitch-black small dance floor, which has only a glitter ball for light.

The Orbient

Crystal Bldg B1F/B2F, 3-5-12 Kita-Aoyama, Minato-ku (5775 2555/www.orbient.jp). Omotesando station, exits A2, A3. **Open** *Restaurant* 6pm-midnight Mon-Thur, Sun; 6pm-5am Fri, Sat. *Club* 7pm-1am Wed-Sun. **Admission** *Men* ¥3,000 Wed-Sun (incl 2 drinks). *Women* free Wed, Thur; ¥2,500 Fri-Sun (incl 2 drinks). Free admission before 8.30pm. **Dress code** not too casual. **Map** p99.

Club Que Shimo-Kitazawa. *See p237.*

La Fabrique. See p238.

Looking smart is advisable if you want to fit in at this upmarket, golden-walled club. There are three bars and a reasonably sized dance floor. The sound system is adequate and the music varies each night – it gets busy on Fridays with dance classics and disco. Its reasonably priced Chinese restaurant is justifiably popular. Advance reservation is necessary and at the weekend there is a table charge of ¥1,000. Once you've finished dining, however, you can get into the club for free.

Organ Bar

Kuretake Bldg 3F, 4-9 Udagawa-cho, Shibuya-ku (5489 5460/www.organ-b.net). Shibuya JR station, Hachiko exit. **Open** 9pm-5am daily. **Admission** ¥2,000 (incl 1 drink) or ¥1,000 (no drink) Mon-Thur, Sun; ¥2,000 Fri, Sat. **Dress code** none. **Map** p102.
Another small joint in the same building as Ball (*see p235*). It features soul, jazz and bossanova, all of which attract a slightly older crowd. What the tiny dance floor lacks in space it makes up for in atmosphere. Drinks are all ¥700.

Oto

2F, 1-17-5 Kabuki-cho, Shinjuku-ku (5273 8264/ www.club-oto.com). Shinjuku JR station, east exit. **Open** 10pm-midnight daily. **Admission** ¥2,000 Mon-Thur, Sun (incl 1 drink); ¥2,500 Fri, Sat (incl 1 or 2 drinks). **Dress code** none. **Map** p109.
Oto (meaning 'sound' in Japanese) lives up to its name, with a sound system that would do a much larger place credit. Music runs from hip hop to techno, and drinks are all ¥700.

Rockwest

Tosen Udagawa-cho Bldg 7F, 4-7 Udagawa-cho, Shibuya-ku (5459 7988/www.rockwest.to/). Shibuya JR station, Hachiko exit. **Open** varies with events. **Admission** varies with events. **Dress code** none. **Map** p102.
Rockwest was once one of the best places in town for a happy hardcore night. It still is a good night out – if you want to listen to a mixture of hip hop and soul. Plus points are that there's a good sound system, air-conditioning and a relatively roomy dance floor. Re-entry to the club is allowed.

The Room

Daihachi Tohto Bldg B1F, 15-19 Sakuragaoka, Shibuya-ku (3461 7167/www.theroom.jp). Shibuya JR station, south exit. **Open** 10pm-5am Mon-Sat. **Admission** ¥1,000-¥2,000 Mon-Thur (incl 1 drink); ¥2,500 Fri, Sat (incl 2 drinks). **Dress code** none. **Map** p102.
The Room is well hidden, so look for a red street light poking out from the basement. This small venue is split in two with one half a concrete-walled bar and the other half a pitch-black dance floor. Music varies, but usually the flavour is house, jazz, crossover or breakbeats. The Room sometimes plays host to top DJs who come here to practise new routines on their nights off.

Ruby Room

Kasumi Bldg 4F, 2-25-17 Dogenzaka, Shibuya-ku (3780 3022). Shibuya JR station, Hachiko exit. **Open** 7pm-5am daily. **Admission** free Mon-Thur, Sun; ¥1,000 (incl 1 drink) Fri, Sat. **Dress code** none. **Map** p102.
From Shibuya station, head left at the intersection of 109, climb up the Dogenzaka slope for about 200m (650ft), take the first right and head down, and you'll see the Sonoma sign on your left. Sonoma is the restaurant run by the people who run Ruby Room, and who formerly ran Shibuya's now-defunct legendary Sugar High club. Ruby Room caters for a twentysomething clubbing crowd, and hosts a lot of foreign DJs. Eat at Sonoma and get free admission to the club.

Secobar

3-23-1 Shibuya, Shibuya-ku (5778 4571/www.community-s.co.jp). Shibuya JR station, Miyamasusaka (east) exit. **Open** *Café* 11am-5am Mon-Sat; 11.30am-1am Sun. *Club* 7pm-5am daily. **Admission** varies with event (incl 1 drink). **Dress code** none. **Map** p102.

Neatly situated under the railway tracks, this lounge café doubles up as a dance venue in the evenings. Full capacity is around 200 people and at weekends it gets packed with a trendy crowd. Music ranges from bossanova to house. Check out Friday's 'electronic pub' night, where techno electronica is played until early in the morning.

Simoon

3-26-16 Shibuya, Shibuya-ku (5774 1669/www.simoon.net). Shibuya JR station, new south exit. **Open** varies with events. **Admission** varies with events. **Dress code** no shorts, sandals. **Map** p102.

Simoon is a cosy, decent-sized dance space that opened in December 2000. The entrance may look like a bicycle parking lot, but once you're inside, a warmly lit lounge space with comfortable couches awaits. The basement dance floor boasts a good-quality sound system for its size. Selected hard house and techno tunes are Simoon's main lines.

Space Lab Yellow

Cesaurus Nishi-Azabu Bldg B1F, B2F, 1-10-11 Nishi-Azabu, Minato-ku (3479 0690/www.club-yellow.com). Roppongi station, exit 2. **Open** varies with events. **Admission** varies with events. **Dress code** none. **Map** p74.

Better known as Yellow, this relatively large space is a popular venue for events and parties. The dance floor gets packed at weekends and is big enough to accommodate the occasional live act. There's also a snack bar and roomy lounge. On Saturdays, guest appearances by visiting foreign DJs fill the place.

Sugar Hill

Azabudai Mansion B1F, 3-4-14 Azabudai, Minato-ku (3583 6223). Azabu-Juban station, exit 6. **Open** 8pm-4am daily. **Admission** ¥700. **Dress code** none.

A lounge-style hideout in Roppongi. One apartment room is stuffed with thousands of classic records from the late '70s and early '80s. As well as finding your favourite dance track at Sugar Hill, you can also indulge in your favourite Japanese food: *tempura* and *udon* are brought in from neighbouring restaurants and sold at reasonable prices.

Twin Star

2-11-3 Kagurazaka, Shinjuku-ku (3269 0005/www.twinstar.co.jp). Iidabashi JR station, west exit. **Open** 6.30pm-midnight Tue, Thur, Fri; 8pm-midnight Wed. **Admission** *Men* ¥4,000 (incl 5 drinks) Tue; ¥3,000 (incl 5 drinks) Wed; ¥3,000 (incl 3 drinks) Thur; ¥2,000 (incl 5 drinks) Fri. *Women* ¥3,000 (incl 5 drinks) Tue, Wed; ¥2,000 (incl 3 drinks) Thur; ¥1,000 (incl 3 drinks) Fri. **Dress code** not too casual.

This giant disco, opened in late 1991, has a garish interior and a spacious dance floor, reviving memories of Japan's Bubble economy. But this sanctuary for *parapara*, a once-fashionable dance craze that involves little leg movement, is now slowly trying to evolve in a new direction, as evidenced by Friday's 3-D event. Tuesday's *parapara* party is worth checking out, for novelty value alone.

Velfarre

Velfarre Bldg, 7-14-22 Roppongi, Minato-ku (3402 8000/http://velfarre.avex.co.jp). Roppongi station, exit 4. **Open** 7pm-1am Mon-Thur, Sun. **Admission** usually ¥3,000 (incl 2 drinks) but varies with events. **Dress code** not too casual. **Map** p74.

The largest disco in Asia, this gigantic club and live house space, with a capacity of over 2,000, is a real throwback to the heady days of the '80s, with marble staircases and other extravagances. It has a vast dance floor with an automated movable stage and giant mirrorball, and more bars, restrooms and snack bars than you can count. If you're feeling brave, try and blag your way into one of the VIP lounges, from where you can watch the action without actually having to dance.

Vuenos Bar Tokyo

1F/B1F, 2-21-7 Dogenzaka, Shibuya-ku (5458 5963/www.clubasia.co.jp). Shibuya JR station, Hachiko exit. **Open** varies. **Admission** varies. **Dress code** no beach sandals. **Map** p102.

Across from and owned by Club Asia (*see p236*), Vuenos opened in October 1998 with a mission to spread the word about Latin, soul and dance music. At weekends, however, the line-up tends to be hip hop, R&B, and reggae. It attracts a younger crowd.

Web

B1F, 3-30-10 Ikejiri, Setagaya-ku (3422 1405/www.m-web.tv). Ikejiri-Ohashi station (Tokyu Shin-Tamagawa, Denentoshi lines). **Open** 10pm-4.30am Mon-Fri; 10pm-5am Sat, Sun. **Admission** varies with event. **Dress code** none.

A small joint that squeezes in nearly 100 people. Web proudly serves a variety of cocktails, and the menu changes monthly. DJs spin music of all genres.

Womb

2-16 Maruyama-cho, Shibuya-ku (5459 0039/www.womb.co.jp). Shibuya JR station, Hachiko exit. **Open** varies with events, Fri, Sat. **Admission** varies with events. **Dress code** no sandals. **Map** p102.

In the middle of one of the biggest love hotel districts of Tokyo, this gymnasium-like disco sits in a bare concrete building. The main floor, whose ceiling is almost nine metres high, is enormous and its huge mirrorball, almost two metres in diameter, is amazing when lit up. The venue also boasts upstairs lounge areas and a super-bass sound system shipped all the way from New York. Although each night varies, there is always an impressive line-up of international DJs.

Performing Arts

Forget realism and bathe in the spectacle of Japanese drama.

The **Kabuki-za** in Ginza, home of *kabuki*. *See p243.*

Japanese theatre is a feast of colour and texture: the exquisite costumes, the make-up, the colourful backdrops, even the embroidered fire curtains. To the colour and texture add sound and smell – the exotic tones of various instruments that accompany the actors' intriguing speech patterns and impassioned exchanges, and in some plays the perfume or incense wafting over the audience. Japanese theatre is to be felt, too – in the tingling of your scalp, the stirred emotions, the held breath and the collective tension of the audience.

In common with the performing arts throughout Asia, Japanese traditional theatre genres integrate dance, music and lyrical narrative. The emphasis is on aesthetic beauty, symbolism and imagery as opposed to western theatre's preoccupation with realism and logic. Another important element distinguishing Japanese theatre from the theatrical traditions of the west is *ma*, perhaps best translated as a 'pregnant pause'. It is considered to be more than just silence; rather it is the space that interrupts musical notes or words and is used to heighten the intensity of the dramatic moment.

The various genres of Japanese drama tend to share certain popular themes, the most common of which are clan squabbles; family, group or servant-master loyalty; commitment to or longing for one's home town or homeland; conflicts between duty and feelings; revenge; corruption and justice; and the supernatural.

NOH AND *KYOGEN*

Noh plays are ritualistic and formulaic.They are grouped into categories, which can be likened to five courses of a formal meal, each with a different flavour. Invigorating celebratory dances about gods are followed by battle plays of warrior-ghosts; next are lyrical pieces about women, then themes of insanity, and finally demons. Presentation is mostly sombre, slow and deliberate. Plays explore the transience of this world, the sin of killing and the spiritual comfort to be found in Buddhism.

There are no group rehearsals: there is a pre-performance meeting, but the actors and musicians do not play together until the performance. This spontaneity is one of the appeals of this kind of theatre.

Kyogen are short, humorous interludes that show the foolishness of human nature through understated portrayal. They are interspersed for comic relief with *noh* pieces, but are intended to produce refined laughter, not boisterous humour.

BUNRAKU

The puppets used in *bunraku* are a half to two-thirds human size and require great skill and strength to operate. Each puppet is operated by two assistants and one chief puppeteer. Becoming a master puppeteer is a lengthy process, beginning with ten years' operating the legs, followed by another ten on the left arm before being permitted to manipulate the right arm, head and eyebrows. Four main elements comprise a *bunraku* performance: the puppets themselves; the movements they make; the vocal delivery of the *tayu*, who chants the narrative and speaks the lines for every character, changing his voice to suit the role; and the solo accompaniment by the three-stringed *shamisen*.

KABUKI

Of all the traditional performing arts in Japan, probably the most exciting is *kabuki*. The actor is the most important element in *kabuki*, and everything that happens on stage is a vehicle for displaying his prowess.

Because the actor is central, the props are used only as long as they show him to his best advantage. *Koken*, stage hands dressed in black, symbolising their supposed invisibility, hand the actor props, make running adjustments to his heavy costume and wig, and bring him a stool to perch on during long speeches or periods of inactivity.

The *onnagata* female role specialists portray a stylised feminine beauty. There is no pretence at realism, so the actor's real age is irrelevant, and there is no incongruity in a 75-year-old man portraying an 18-year-old maiden.

Most *kabuki* programmes feature one *shosagoto* dance piece, one *jidaimono*, and one *sewamono*. *Jidaimono* are dramas set in pre-Edo Japan. They feature gorgeous costumes and colourful make-up called *kumadori*, which is painted along the lines of the actor's face. The actor uses melodramatic elocution, but because *jidaimono* originated in the puppet theatre, the plays also feature accompaniment from a chanter who relates the storyline and emotions of the character while the actor expresses them in movement, facial expressions or poses. *Sewamono* are stories of everyday life during the Edo period (1603-1867) and are closer in style to western drama.

Every *kabuki* theatre features a *hanamichi*, an elevated pathway for the performers that runs through the audience from the back of the theatre to the main stage. This is used for entrances and exits and contains a traplift through which supernatural characters emerge.

SAMURAI AND HISTORICAL DRAMAS

Samurai dramas set in the Edo period, called *jidai geki*, are the most frequently portrayed type of historical drama on stage. Unlike in *kabuki*, female roles are played by women.

No matter how tragic, *jidai geki* must end with a satisfactory resolution, whether it is the successful revenge of a murder or the ascent into heaven of the dead heroine aloft a podium. However, influenced by western drama, plays with happy endings are on the increase.

MODERN DRAMAS AND MUSICALS

The major source for other domestic modern theatre productions are famous western plays and musicals translated into Japanese. In particular, the **New National Theatre** (*see p246*) in the Opera City complex provides a forum for the most respected Japanese directors, who take a contemporary approach to western classics and other productions.

Musicals are popular and are often staged annually. Favourites include *Fiddler on the Roof* and *The Wizard of Oz*. There is also a thriving underground avant-garde theatre subculture in the suburb of Shimo-Kitazawa (*see p114*), with dozens of small venues. For a city as cosmopolitan as Tokyo, it may come as a surprise to learn that only a handful of productions in English are available each year, and some of these are possible only because of touring troupes from Britain or America.

Traditional Japanese theatre

Cerulean Tower Noh Theatre

26-1 Sakuragaoka-Cho, Shibuya-ku (3477 6412/ www.ceruleantower.com/english). Shibuya JR station, south exit. **Box office** tickets sold at Cerulean Tower Tokyu Hotel (3476 3000). No telephone reservations. **Tickets** prices vary. **Credit** AmEx, DC, JCB, MC, V. **Map** p102.

The Cerulean Tower, Tokyo's newest Japanese theatre, opened to the public in May 2001. It hosts professional and amateur *noh* and *kyogen* performances, without English translation.

Kabuki-za

4-12-15 Ginza, Chuo-ku (info 3541 3131/box office 5565 6000/www.shochiku.co.jp/play/kabukiza/ theater). Higashi-Ginza station, exits A2, 3. **Box office** 10am-6pm daily. **Tickets** ¥2,520-¥16,800. **Credit** AmEx, DC, JCB, MC, V. **Map** p57.

The **Cerulean Tower Noh Theatre** stages trad theatre in mod surroundings. *See p243.*

A splendid place to see *kabuki*. An English-language programme (¥1,000) and earphone guide (¥650 plus a refundable deposit of ¥1,000) are invaluable. Performances last up to five hours, including intervals. Tickets to watch just one act from the fourth floor can be bought from one hour beforehand; unfortunately the English earphone guide can't be used on the fourth floor.

Koma Gekijo

1-19-1 Kabuki-cho, Shinjuku-ku (3200 2213/www.koma-sta.co.jp/). Shinjuku JR station, east exit. **Box office** 9.30am-7pm daily. **Tickets** ¥3,000-¥8,500. **Credit** MC, JCB, V. **Map** p109.

A famous theatre with a revolving stage, and some great posters outside. Most performers are famous singers who appear in a period drama, then give a concert. No English.

Meiji-za

2-31-1 Nihonbashi-Hamacho, Chuo-ku (3660 3900/www.meijiza.co.jp). Hamacho station (Toei Shinjuku line), exit A2. **Box office** 10am-5pm daily. **Tickets** ¥5,000-¥12,000. **Credit** DC, V.

Usually stages samurai dramas, often starring actors who play similar roles on TV. No English.

National Theatre Large Hall

4-1 Hayabusa-cho, Chiyoda-ku (3230 3000/www.ntj.jac.go.jp/english/index.html). Hanzomon station, exits 1, 2. **Box office** 10am-5pm daily. **Tickets** ¥1,500-¥9,200. **No credit cards. Map** p62.

Kabuki is staged approximately nine months a year in the Large Hall. The programme (¥800) includes the story in English; an earphone guide is available.

National Noh Theatre

4-18-1 Sendagaya, Shibuya-ku (3230 3000/www.ntj.jac.go.jp/english/index.html). Sendagaya station. **Box office** 10am-6pm daily. **Tickets** ¥2,300-¥6,000; ¥1,700 concessions. **No credit cards.**

Noh performances four or five times a month. A one-page explanation of the story in English is available.

National Theatre Small Hall

4-1 Hayabusa-cho, Chiyoda-ku (3230 3000/www.ntj.jac.go.jp/english/index.html). Hanzomon station, exits 1, 2. **Box office** 10am-5pm daily. **Tickets** ¥3,500-¥5,800. **No credit cards. Map** p62.

Bunraku is performed here for about four months a year. Programmes with the story in English are available, and there is also an earphone guide. Tickets can be reserved by phone up to the day before a performance.

Shinbashi Embujo

6-18-2 Ginza, Chuo-ku (3541 2600/www.shochiku.co.jp/play/index.html). Higashi-Ginza station, exit A6. **Box office** 10am-6pm daily. **Tickets** ¥2,100-¥15,750. **Credit** AmEx, DC, JCB, MC, V. **Map** p57.

The programme features English explanation of the story when Ichikawa Ennosuke stages his 'Super-Kabuki' (April-May), a jazzed-up, modernised version of the real thing. Samurai dramas other months.

Tokyo Takarazuka Gekijo

1-1-3 Yurakucho, Chiyoda-ku (5251 2001/kageki.hankyu.co.jp/english/index.html). Yurakucho JR station, Hibiya exit. **Box office** 10am-6pm Mon, Tue, Thur-Sun. **Tickets** ¥3,500-¥10,000. **Credit** JCB, MC, V. **Map** p57.

One of those 'only in Japan' phenomena, *takarazuka* bridges the gap between traditional and modern theatre in ways that can seem bizarre, and unbelievably camp. All performers are women, even in male roles, as are 90 per cent of the adoring audiences, yet there are no sexual overtones to this at all. Adaptations of western musicals or plays are a particular favourite – anything, in fact, that allows for spangly jackets and big swirly skirts.

Western theatres

Dentsu Shiki Theatre Umi (SEA)

1-8-2 Higashi-Shinbashi, Minato-ku (information 0120 489444/www.shiki.gr.jp/siteinfo/english/theatres.html). Shiodome station (Toei Oedo/Yurikamome lines), Showa Dori exit. **Box office** 10am-8pm daily. **Credit** AmEx, DC, JCB, MC, V.

The newest western-style theatre in Tokyo opened in December 2002 in advertising giant Dentsu's new headquarters in the new Shiodome area of Tokyo. The theatre's remit is to provide western musicals, sung in Japanese. It opened with the hit ABBA-inspired show *Mamma Mia!*.

Tokyo International Players

*Performances held at the Tokyo American Club, 2-1-2 Azabudai, Minato-ku (*TIP information *090 6009 4171/www.tokyoplayers.org/*American Club *3224 3670/www.tokyoamericanclub.org). Kamiyacho station, exit 2.* **Tickets** ¥4,000; ¥2,500 concessions. **No credit cards. Map** p74.

The Tokyo International Players is a group of keen amateurs; their season runs from late September until late May. Productions are in English and usually take place at the Tokyo American Club. The 2003 season included such ambitious productions as *Dial M for Murder* and *Amadeus*.

Dance

Aoyama Round Theatre

5-53-1 Jingumae, Shibuya-ku (3797 5678/box office 3797 1400/www.aoyama.org). Omotesando station, exit B2. **Box office** 10am-6pm daily. **Tickets** prices vary. **No credit cards. Map** p102.

As its name suggests, this is a theatre that can be used in the round, one of very few in Tokyo, and it attracts leading contemporary performers keen to make the most of the space.

Art Sphere

2-3-16 Higashi-Shinagawa, Shinagawa-ku (5460 9999/www.tennoz.co.jp/sphere/). Tennozu Isle station (Tokyo Monorail). **Box office** 10am-6pm daily. **Tickets** prices vary. **No credit cards.**

This theatre caters to the whims of well-off young fans of contemporary modern dance and is sure to book things that are considered 'in', but not too avant-garde or risqué. The larger of Art Sphere's two theatres seats 746, while Sphere Mex seats from 100 to 300. The venue's location, on Tennozu Isle, makes it one of the more interesting, and less accessible, of Tokyo's theatrical venues.

Bunkamura Theatre Cocoon

2-24-1 Dogenzaka, Shibuya-ku (3477 9999/www.bunkamura.co.jp). Shibuya JR station, Hachiko exit. **Box office** 10am-7pm daily. *Phone bookings* 10am-5.30pm daily. **Tickets** prices vary. **Credit** AmEx, DC, JCB, MC, V. **Map** p102.

The giant arts centre's medium-sized venue, with 750 seats, is used mainly for musicals, but stages the occasional dance performance.

Theatre-going with a difference

The theatre-going experience in Japan is markedly different from in the west. Cast aside all notions of hushed reverence and fur coats: a trip to the theatre here is a social outing, and many people come for an afternoon at, say, Ginza's Kabuki-za, armed with flasks of hot drinks, packed meals and bags full of goodies, which are noisily chomped throughout the performance. Nor is it unusual for people to comment on the action they're seeing while it is still going on, rather than waiting until after a show. A particularly fine tableau may well elicit a burst of spontaneous applause.

Of course, a trip to the theatre here is hardly a spontaneous affair. Tickets go on sale a month or more in advance, and it's a good idea to reserve seats as soon as you can, if you don't fancy being stuck at the back of the house. Tickets to touring western shows, particularly those starring well known actors, sell out especially quickly.

If you don't want to bring your own packed meal, most traditional Japanese theatres have a stall or cafeteria that will sell one to you, but be prepared to pay through the nose for the privilege. Theatres here generally do not have bars, but sake and beer can often be purchased in cans. Indulge too much, though, and you may find yourself facing a trip to a Japanese-style squat toilet, which are still prevalent in older buildings.

Intrigue Theatre

It's been a long time coming, but Tokyo now has its first semi-professional English-language theatre company, Intrigue Theatre, which burst on to the scene in 2002 with a thoroughly enjoyable staging of Molière's *The Miser*. The group, which produced two further shows in early 2003, is the brainchild of artistic director Mozaffar Shafeie, a Kurdish-born actor who was a member of the Royal National Theatre in England before taking the plunge and coming to Tokyo. By persuading a few foreign sponsors, including the *Financial Times*, the European Commission and the British Council, to stump up some cash, Shafeie has managed to bring professional British actors over to Tokyo to play the leads in each of Intrigue's productions, with able backing provided by a talented local amateurs. Future plans include a proper theatre workshop – it's hoped that this will lead to more regular productions. The company's present theatre in Akasaka is tiny, but if Intrigue's first year is anything to go by, Shafeie will be looking for bigger premises very soon.

Intrigue Theatre

Performances held at Studio Akasaka Playbox, 8-12-12 Akasaka, Minato-ku (090 9955 0200/www.intriguetheatre.com). Nogizaka station, exit 1. **Tickets** ¥4,000. **No credit cards.**

Hibiya Outdoor Theatre (Hibiya Yagai Ongaku-do)

1-3 Hibiya Koen, Chuo-ku (3591 6388). Kasumigaseki station, exits B2, B3A, C4 or Hibiya station, exits A10, A14 or Uchisaiwaicho station, exits A6, A7. **Map** p57.

This large open-air arena, used mainly for music concerts and open only during the summer months, plays host to Yoko Komatsubara and her flamenco group for one night every summer.

National Engei Hall

4-1 Hayabusa-cho, Chiyoda-ku (3230 3000/www.ntj.jac.go.jp/english/index.html). Hanzomon station, exits 1, 2. **Box office** 10am-5pm daily. **Tickets** ¥1,500-¥9,500. **No credit cards. Map** p62.

It's old, it's established, but it's still the best place to see traditional and contemporary Japanese dance. The National has three stages, of which one is devoted to puppet theatre. What you see here will usually be of a high standard.

New National Theatre

1-1-1 Honmachi, Shibuya-ku (5352 9999/www.nntt.jac.go.jp/). Hatsudai station (Keio New line), central exit. **Box office** 10am-7pm daily. **Tickets** prices vary. **Credit** AmEx, MC, V.

The National Theatre was and is for traditional dance and theatre, but the New National Theatre caters to the modern generation. It calls its spaces the Opera House, the Playhouse and the Pit, the last two catering for dance, mostly modern, although the Opera House does sometimes stage classical ballet. The Pit, holding over 500 people, is a leading venue on the dance circuit. The complex that houses the spaces is worth a visit in its own right.

Session House

158 Yaraicho, Shinjuku-ku (3266 0461/www.interq.or.jp/tokyo/session/webRoom/). Kagurazaka station, Kagurazaka exit. **Box office** 10am-7pm daily. **Tickets** ¥2,000-¥2,500. **No credit cards.**

Naoko Itoh, a modern dancer with her own company, started Session House in order to give solo dancers the opportunity to experiment. She presents not only local contemporary dancers, but also performers from Europe and America. The aim is to showcase pure dance without extensive use of theatrical props and high-tech lighting.

Setagaya Public Theatre

4-1-1 Taishido, Setagaya-ku (5432 1526/www.setagaya-ac.or.jp/sept/). Sangenjaya station (Tokyu Denentoshi line). **Box office** 10am-7pm daily. **Tickets** prices vary. **No credit cards.**

Like the New National Theatre, this venue is a favourite with fans and performers. Although modelled on a Greek open-air theatre, the space can be changed to proscenium-style. The theatre contains two auditoria, the smaller of which, Theatre Tram, is a popular venue for dance. The adopted home of the Sankai Juku Butoh troupe, when they're in town.

Space Zero

2-12-10 Yoyogi, Shibuya-ku (3209 0222). Shinjuku JR station, south exit. **Box office** 10am-6pm Mon-Fri. **Tickets** prices vary. **No credit cards. Map** p109

A medium-sized venue (capacity around 550) that stages mainly modern jazz dance.

Comedy

Although Japan has a tradition of humorous story-telling, called *rakugoh*, nowhere in Tokyo offers translations of such events for the English speaker. Occasional performances are held at the **Edo-Tokyo Museum** (*see p97*).

Punchline Comedy Club

Performances at Pizza Express, 3F, 4-30-3 Jingumae, Shibuya-ku (5775 3894/www.punchlinecomedy.com/tokyo). Harajuku station, Omotesando exit, or Meiji-Jingumae station, exit 5. **Tickets** ¥10,000 incl dinner & 2 drinks. **Credit** AmEx, DC, JCB, MC, V. **Map** p99.

A poster advertises the latest attraction at **Koma Gekijo**. *See p244.*

John Moorhead started the Tokyo branch of this pan-Asian comedy club in Tokyo in 2001. Its mission is to bring top comedians from around the world, many of them from the UK, to perform before an expat crowd. The whole venture is sponsored by Virgin Atlantic. Simon Bligh and the cast of *Whose Line is it Anyway?* have appeared recently.

Suehiro-tei

3-6-12 Shinjuku, Shinjuku-ku (3351 2974/http://suehirotei.com). Shinjuku-Sanchome station, exits B2, C4. **Box office** noon-8.15pm daily. **Tickets** ¥2,200-¥2,700. **No credit cards**. **Map** p109.

A charming old theatre that looks alarmingly like a bathhouse. It seats 325 and hosts regular performances of *rakugoh*. No English translation.

Tokyo Comedy Store

Bar Isn't It, MT Bldg 3F, 3-8-18 Roppongi, Minato-ku (3746 1598/www.tokyocomedy.com). Roppongi station, exit 5. **Performances** 1st & 3rd Thur of mth. **Tickets** ¥2,000 (incl 1 drink). **No credit cards**. **Map** p74.

Tokyo's best-organised English-language comedy group may have the same name as the celebrated London venue, but there the similarity ends. Performers are keen amateurs ranging from the hilarious to the dire. New material is always sought, from both Japanese and foreign performers or those keen to have a go. Performance times can change, so check the website for details before heading out. Also holds improv classes and workshops in Japanese and English.

Tokyo Cynics

The Fiddler, Tajima Bldg B1F, 2-1-2 Takadanobaba, Shinjuku-ku (3204 2698/www.thefiddler.com). Takadanobaba station, Waseda exit. **Performances** 2nd Tue of mth. **Admission** free.

A ramshackle bunch of English-speaking amateur comics and outright eccentrics who regularly enliven evenings at one of Tokyo's longest-established and most popular British-style pubs. From May 2003, they also began to perform in the Footnik bar in Ebisu (*see p164*). Shows are free, and provide the occasional laugh.

Sport & Fitness

From sumo to skiing and soccer, Tokyo's got something for every sports fan.

Sport may not be the first thing visitors associate with Japan's crowded capital, but Tokyo can boast a unique range of top-level attractions across the whole of the sporting spectrum. For starters, the metropolis hosts three professional baseball teams, two top-flight football J.League sides, and three full sumo tournaments a year. In terms of infrastructure, the 1964 Olympics left Tokyo with a string of custom-built venues in the Yoyogi area, including the **National Stadium** in Sendagaya, as well as the **Nippon Budokan** in Kudanshita. More recently, the 2002 World Cup bequeathed the 64,000-seat **Saitama Stadium** on the edge of the capital.

Tokyo also offers a full range of facilities to those interested in taking part in sport themselves, although the types of sports that require more space can sometimes be a problem. Finding a *dojo* (gym) for instruction in martial arts usually poses few difficulties. There is also no shortage of fitness clubs or local authority sports facilities. For team sports, fellow enthusiasts can usually be unearthed via the weekly listings of *Metropolis* magazine (*see chapter* **Directory: Media**).

Spectator sports

American football

The climax of the domestic season is the brilliantly named Rice Bowl at the **Tokyo Dome** in early January, when the college champions take on the winners of the company-based X-League. The same venue also hosts regular NFL pre-season tour matches in August under the American Bowl banner.

Athletics

The IAAF Japan Grand Prix is held every spring in Osaka, which will also host the 2007 World Championships. The long-running International Super Track and Field event, the Tokyo area's main annual taste of top-class competition, was scheduled for Yokohama International Stadium in 2003. Japan's real athletics favourite, though, has long been the marathon. Tokyo's two big events have strict entrance requirements and attract some of the world's top runners.

Tokyo International Marathon

Usually held in mid February, the Tokyo International Marathon starts and finishes at the National Stadium.

Tokyo International Women's Marathon

Follows the same route as the International Marathon, but this one's in November. It was also the world's first women's marathon.

Baseball

Introduced to Japan by Horace Wilson in 1873, baseball has long held a firm grip on local hearts and minds. The first pro side, the Yomiuri Giants, was founded in 1934, and by 1950 a professional competition had been set up, comprising 12 teams in two leagues. Each side plays 140 games a season (April to October), with the winners of the Central and Pacific leagues meeting in the Japan Series to decide the championship. Tokyo has three teams: the **Yomiuri Giants**, the **Nippon Ham Fighters** and the **Yakult Swallows**.

Interest is high at amateur level, too. The national high school baseball tournament is televised live and brings much of the country to a virtual standstill.

More worrying for the future of the professional game in Japan is the recent drain of local superstars to the US major leagues and the growing audiences for live satellite broadcasts from across the Pacific.

Jingu Baseball Stadium

13 Kasumigaoka, Shinjuku-ku (3404 8999). Sendagaya station. **Capacity** 46,000. **Tickets** ¥1,500-¥4,500.

Jingu Baseball Stadium is part of the complex that includes the National Stadium and was built for the 1964 Olympics. It is now home to the Yakult Swallows (Central League).

Tokyo Dome

1-3-61 Koraku, Bunkyo-ku (5800 9999/www.tokyo-dome.co.jp/dome). Suidobashi JR station, west exit or Korakuen station, exit 2. **Capacity** 55,000. **Tickets** ¥1,000-¥5,900.

The Tokyo Dome, known as the Dome, or Big Egg, is home to the Yomiuri Giants (Central League) and the Nippon Ham Fighters (Pacific League). Tickets for games can be very difficult to acquire, particularly for Giants games.

Football

The 2002 World Cup saw the eyes of planet football focused firmly on Japan and co-hosts South Korea, but the closest Tokyo came in terms of venues was suburban Saitama and nearby Yokohama, which hosted the final. Tokyo was also left on the sidelines when the J.League was founded in 1993, but the capital now has two top-flight teams, **FC Tokyo** and **Tokyo Verdy 1969**, which share a ground out in the west of the city. **Urawa Reds** in Saitama and the **Yokohama Marinos** are the other major local clubs. The J.League official website (www.j-league.or.jp) features English-language information on clubs, players and fixtures. The two-stage season runs from March to October with a summer break, followed by the Emperor's Cup in December.

Ajinomoto Stadium

376-3 Nishimachi, Chofu (0424 40 0555/www.ajinomotostadium.com). Tobitakyu station (Keio Line). **Capacity** 50,000. **Tickets** *J.League matches* ¥1,200-¥6,000.
The impressive home of FC Tokyo and Tokyo Verdy 1969 opened in 2001.

National Stadium

Kasumigaoka-machi, Shinjuku-ku (3403 4150). Sendagaya station. **Capacity** 60,057.
The 1964 Olympic stadium still hosts Japanese international football matches, the Emperor's Cup final and the Toyota Cup (*see p194*).

Saitama Stadium 2002

500 Nakanodu, Saitama (048 812 2002/www.stadium2002.com). Urawa Misono station (Nanboku Line, Saitama Railway) or Urawa station, west exit, then bus. **Capacity** 63,700. **Tickets** *J.League matches* ¥2,000-¥4,500.
Saitama Stadium is the home of Urawa Reds and the country's largest soccer-only stadium. It also hosted a 2002 World Cup semi-final.

Horse racing

Horse racing in Japan is run under the auspices of the Japan Racing Association (JRA), which manages the ten national tracks, and the National Association of Racing (NAR), which oversees local courses. Race tracks are one of the few places in the country where gambling is legal. For schedules and details in English, check the Japan Association for International Horse Racing's website (www.jair.jrao.ne.jp).

Ooi Racecourse

2-1-2 Katsushima, Shinagawa-ku (3763 2151). Ooi Keibajomae station (Tokyo monorail).
Ooi Racecourse is run under the auspices of the NAR, with around 120 days' racing every year. Twinkle Races, which are evening events that Ooi pioneered in the 1990s, have proved very popular with office workers. Other NAR courses in the Tokyo region include Funabashi in Chiba.

Former sumo *yokozuna* Akebono. *See p251.*

Tokyo Racecourse

1-1 Hiyoshi-cho, Fuchu City (042 363 3141/www.jra.go.jp/turf/tokyo/index.html). Fuchu-Honmachi station (JR Musashino Line) or Fuchu Keiba Seimonmae station (Keio Line).
One of the ten national tracks run by the JRA. There are 40 days' racing a year, all at weekends. Many of the country's most famous races are held here, including the Japan Cup in November. The latter is an international invitational race that attracts top riders and horses from around the world.

Hydroplane racing (*kyotei*)

Next to horse racing, this is the most popular focus of betting in Japan (bets start at just ¥100). The race itself is between six motor-driven boats in what is essentially a very large swimming pool; boats go round the 600-metre (1,970-foot) course three times, regularly reaching speeds of over 80 kilometres per hour (50 miles per hour). **Edogawa Kyotei** is the Tokyo favourite. The schedule is published in sports newspapers and at: www.edogawa-kyotei.co.jp.

Edogawa Kyotei

3-1-1 Higashi-Komatsugawa, Edogawa-ku (3656 0641). Funahori station (Toei Shinjuku Line), south exit or Shin-koiwa station, then 21 bus.
Admission ¥50.

Ice hockey

The economic recession has hit the Japan Ice Hockey League hard in recent years. The number of teams is down from six to five and there is talk of joining forces with the South Korean league. Amid the uncertainty, **Kokudo** and **Seibu Tetsudo**, the only two teams based near Tokyo, were set to merge in 2003.

For schedules, team details and results, log on to the official website: www.jihf.or.jp/jihl/index-e.htm. The season runs from October to March.

Higashi-Fushimi Ice Arena

3-1-25 Higashi-Fushimi, Hoya-shi (0424 67 7171). Higashi-Fushimi station (Seibu Shinjuku Line).
Home of Seibu Tetsudo.

Shin-Yokohama Prince Hotel Skate Centre

2-11 Shin-Yokohama, Kohoku-ku, Yokohama, Kanagawa (045 474 1112). Shin-Yokohama station, north exit.
Home of Kokudo.

National Yoyogi Stadium 1st Gymnasium

2-1-1, Jinnan, Shibuya-ku (3468 1171). Harajuku station, Omotesando exit. **Map** p99.
Occasional internationals and exhibition games.

Martial arts

For more about Japan's national sport, *see p251* **Sumo**. For information on how to contact individual *dojo* (gyms), *see p252*. For details of federations for other martial arts, *see p253.*

Nippon Budokan

2-3 Kitanomaru Koen, Chiyoda-ku (3216 5100/ www.nipponbudokan.or.jp/). Kudanshita station, exit 2. **Map** p62.
The Budokan stages the All-Japan championships or equivalent-level demonstration events in all the martial arts except sumo. Advance tickets are not required, and in most cases admission is free. Dates vary slightly from year to year, but the schedule for 2004 is as follows: 15 February, kobudo (demonstration); 20 April, jukendo; 29 April, judo; 24 May, aikido (demonstration); 21-22 June, kyudo (student championships); 3 November, kendo; 7 December, naginata; 14 December, karate. In the same complex, martial arts classes may be viewed at the Budokan Gakuen school; phone for details (3216 5143).

Motor sports

Motor sports have a devoted following in Japan. The **Suzuka** circuit, in Mie prefecture towards Nagoya (0593 78 1111/www.suzukacircuit.co.jp/index.html), is the venue of the annual Formula 1 Japan Grand Prix (it is possible to make the return trip in a day). Closer to the capital, **Twin Ring Motegi** boasts two types of circuit, including an oval course that's suitable for US-style motor sports. The permanent circuit hosts local Formula 3 and Formula Nippon races.

Mixed martial arts

Wildly popular in Japan, the professional combat world of MMA crashes through the barriers that separate old-style fighting disciplines. Combining a hard competitive edge with a knowing dose of showbiz hype, huge one-off extravaganzas bring together ex-amateur judo and karate stars, East European hard men, Brazilian jiu-jitsu specialists, former pro wrestlers and awesome man-mountain behemoths to fight it out with few holds barred.

Among the welter of different styles to emerge over the last decade, PRIDE and K-1 stand out. The former imposes few restrictions on competitors. Winners are decided by submission, knockout, TKO or judges' decision, and bouts often end in mat-based confrontations. K-1, which helped spark the initial MMA boom of the mid 90s, is based on a mixture of karate, kick-boxing and tae kwon-do, with gloved fighters and no submissions. Cross-promotional shows will lay down the rules to be followed in individual contests. Top fighters are accorded the sort of adulation normallly reserved for film stars.

There are frequent MMA events in Tokyo throughout the year. PRIDE concentrates on one-off specials, while K-1 features a regular championship calendar that culminates in an annual eight-man World Grand Prix final at Tokyo Dome in early December. The same venue also hosts a year-end MMA television spectacular that started in 2001 and features all the top names.

For information and event schedules, see the PRIDE official homepage at www.pridefc.com or its K-1 equivalent at www.k-1gp.net.

Get your fitness fix at a gym: **Tipness** has 19 branches around the capital. *See p252.*

Twin Ring Motegi
120-1 Hiyama, Motegi-machi, Haga-gun, Tochigi-ken (0285 64 0001/www.twinring.jp/english/index.html). Motegi station (Mooka Line).

Rugby

Japanese rugby is divided between corporate- and university-level teams. The National Stadium in Sendagaya stages the annual Waseda-Meiji match, which is the big university fixture that has traditionally been the season's most popular game. Corporate sides often feature a majority of imported talent, some of whom now appear in the Japanese national side.

The Japan championship, which is held from January to February, features the top four sides from the corporate and university worlds, with results in recent years showing that the standard of university rugby is now far below that of the corporate game.

Ticket information is available at the official site of the Japan Rugby Football Union (www.rugby-japan.or.jp).

Prince Chichibu Memorial Stadium
2-8-35 Kita Aoyama, Minato-ku (3401 3881). Gaienmae station, exits 2, 3 or Sendagaya station or Kokuritsu Kyogijomae station (Oedo Line).
Prince Chichibu Memorial Stadium can be found right next door to the Jingu baseball stadium (*see p248*). This is where you come to see internationals and other big rugby matches that are not held at the National Stadium.

Sumo

With a history dating back 2,000 years, Japan's national sport uniquely blends tradition, athleticism and religion. Its rules are simple: each combatant must try to force the other out of the ring (*dohyo*) or make him touch the floor with a part of his anatomy other than his feet. Tournaments take place over 15 days, with wrestlers fighting once a day. Those who achieve regular majorities (winning more than they lose) progress up through the rankings, the top of which is *yokozuna* (grand champion). Wrestlers failing to achieve a majority are demoted. *Yokozuna* must achieve a majority in every tournament or are expected to retire. Tournaments take place in Tokyo three times a year, in January, May and September, at the **Kokugikan**. This venue also hosts one-day tournaments and retirement ceremonies. For ticket information, results and interviews, see the websites of the Sumo Association (www.sumo.or.jp/index_e.html) and *Sumo World* magazine (www.sumoworld.com).

To learn more about sumo, and to witness the rigorous training wrestlers undergo, it is also possible to visit a sumo stable, or *heya*. Most allow visitors, on condition that they remain quiet. Call ahead to ask permission, in Japanese if possible. It's a good idea to take along a small gift, such as a bottle of sake, for the stablemaster, to show your appreciation. Be warned: the day starts early. Junior wrestlers are up and about at 4am, and gruelling practice sessions start at around 5am. The higher ranked wrestlers start to appear at around 8am.

There are over 40 stables in Tokyo, most situated close to the Kokugikan. There's also an up-to-date list of addresses online at www.accesscom.com/~abe/03haruheya.html.

Ryogoku Kokugikan

1-3-28 Yokoami, Sumidaku (3623 5111/ to book balcony seats 5237 9310). Ryogoku station, west exit. **Tickets** *Balcony* ¥2,100-¥8,200.
Advance tickets are on sale at the box office and regular ticket outlets (*see p225*) about a month before the start of each tournament. They're not difficult to get hold of, but weekends generally sell out and the most expensive box seats are nearly impossible to obtain without corporate connections at any time. A number of unreserved back-row balcony seats are always held back for sale from 8am on the day of the tournament at ¥2,100 (one per person). Many spectators watch bouts between younger fighters from downstairs box seats until the ticket-holders arrive in the mid afternoon.

Tennis

In professional tennis, it's the women's game that gets the most attention in Japan. The biggest event is the annual **Japan Open** (*see p200*) every October at **Ariake Colliseum.** The indoor **Pan Pacific Open** in January and February is held at Tokyo Gymnasium in Sendagaya (*see below*).

Municipal courts exist for those who want a game themselves, but applications are often by lottery. Log on to www.tokyotennis.com for online information.

Metropolitan Ariake Tennis Woods Park

2-2-22 Ariake, Koto-ku (3529 3301/www.tptc.or.jp/park/ariake.htm). Ariake station (Yurikamome Line). **Open** 9am-9pm daily. **Admission** ¥3,000 2 hrs Mon-Fri; ¥3,600 2 hrs Sat, Sun. **Map** p78.
The home of the annual Japan Open tournament has 48 tennis courts.

Volleyball

Doffing its cap to soccer's J.League, in name at least, volleyball's V.League has been rather less successful, with financial problems leading to a number of team closures in recent years. There are two leagues of eight teams; one for women, one for men.

Tokyo Gymnasium

1-17-1 Sendagaya, Shibuya-ku (5474 2111/www.tef.or.jp/tmg/). Sendagaya station.
The only place within Tokyo that regularly hosts V.League volleyball matches.

Active sports & fitness

Golf

With time and expense posing big obstacles to the capital's legion of would-be golfers, driving ranges dot the city. The cost of membership at private golf clubs can easily run to millions of yen, but only three of Tokyo's 19 courses are public facilities. Hotel chains such as Prince Hotels (www.princehotels.co.jp/english/) have reasonably priced golf packages, though prices can shoot up during the summer. Those who want access to the many courses within range of the capital should consult the *Tokyo Golf Course Guide*, www.JapanGolfCourses.com.

Tokyo Metropolitan Golf Course

1-15-1 Shinden, Adachi-ku (3919 0111). Oji-kamiya station (Nanboku Line). **Open** dawn to dusk daily. **Admission** ¥5,000-¥6,000 Mon-Fri; from ¥8,000 Sat, Sun.
The cheapest of Tokyo's public courses. Eighteen holes at par 63. Booking essential at weekends.

Gyms

Membership of private gyms can be very expensive. Large hotels may have swimming pools or gyms, but if you are in need of some muscle-pumping action, head for one of the following. A cheaper alternative is to visit one of Tokyo's public sports centres (*see p254*).

Esforta

Shibuya Infos Tower B1F, 20-1 Sakuragaoka-cho, Shibuya-ku (3780 5551/www.esforta.com). Shibuya JR station, south exit. **Open** 7am-10pm daily. Closed 1st Sun of mth. **Joining fee** ¥50,000 membership, then ¥17,000 per mth. **Map** p102.
Facilities typically include aerobics, sauna, weight machines and sunbeds. The Akasaka and Suidobashi branches have swimming pools.
Branches: throughout the city.

Konami Sports Club

Bunka Kaikan 5F, Sunshine City, 3-1-4 Higashi-Ikebukuro, Toshima-ku (5956 7744/www.konamisports.com). Ikebukuro JR station, east exit. **Open** 10am-1am Mon, Wed-Fri; 10am-11pm Sat; 10am-7pm Sun. **Joining fee** ¥3,000 membership, then ¥11,000 per mth. **Map** p69.
Most branches have a pool, sauna and weight gyms.
Branches: throughout the city.

Tipness

Kaleido Bldg 5F-7F, 7-1 Nishi-Shinjuku, Shinjuku-ku (3368 3531/0120 208 025 free dial/www.tipness.co.jp). Shinjuku station, east or west exit. **Open** 7am-11.15pm Mon-Fri; 9.30am-10pm Sat; 9.30am-8pm Sun. Closed 15th of mth. **Joining fee** ¥3,150 membership, then ¥11,000 per mth.
Map p109.

Serena Williams on court in Tokyo: attention here is focused on the women's game.

There are 19 Tipness branches in Tokyo. Most of the branches have a swimming pool, aerobics classes and weight gyms.
Branches: throughout the city.

Horse riding

Tokyo Horse Riding Club

4-8 Yoyogi Kamizono-cho, Shibuya-ku (3370 0984/ www.tokyo-rc.or.jp/). Sangubashi station (Odakyu Line). **Open** *Mar-Nov* 9am-5.45pm Tue-Sun. *Dec-Feb* 9am-4.45pm. **Admission** ¥6,500 Tue-Fri; ¥7,500 Sat, Sun.
The oldest riding club in Japan boasts 45 horses and seven instructors. Luckily, visitors don't have to pay the annual membership fee of ¥96,000 (after a joining fee of ¥2 million; you also need to be recommended by two members). Booking is necessary.

Ice skating

Championship events are held at the National Yoyogi Gymnasium (*see p250)*. Other ice hockey venues are also open to those who want to skate themselves, as are the following centrally located rinks.

Meiji Jingu Ice Skating Rink

Gobanchi, Kasumigaoka, Shinjuku (3403 3458/ www.meijijingu.or.jp/gaien/05.htm). Kokuritsu Kyogijo station (Toei Oedo Line), exit A2. **Open** noon-6pm Mon-Fri; 10am-6pm Sat, Sun. No entry after 5pm. **Admission** ¥1,300 adults (¥1,000 after 3pm); ¥900 children (¥500 after 3pm). *Skate rental* ¥500. *Locker* ¥100.
Discount coupons allow adults to get 12 entries to the rink for the price of ten.

Takadanobaba Citizen Ice Skating Rink

4-29-27 Takadanobaba, Shinjuku-ku (3371 0910/ www.h2.dion.ne.jp/~c.i.s/). Takadanobaba station, east exit. **Open** noon-7.45pm Mon-Sat; 10am-7.45pm Sun. **Admission** ¥1,300 adults (¥1,000 after 5pm); ¥800 children (¥500 after 5pm). *Skate rental* ¥500. *Locker* ¥100.

Martial arts

There are nine recognised modern martial arts – aikido, judo, jukendo, karate, kendo, kyudo, naginata, shorinji kempo and sumo – and a series of more traditional forms, known collectively as *kobudo*. Almost five million people practice in Japan today. The national associations of each discipline may have training facilities where spectators can view sessions. They may also know of *dojo* (gyms) that welcome visitors or potential students.

Aikido

Aikikai Federation, 17-18 Wakamatsu-cho, Shinjuku-ku (3203 9236/www.aikikai.or.jp).

Judo

All-Japan Judo Federation, 1-16-30 Kasuga, Bunkyo-ku (3818 4199/www.judo.or.jp).

Jukendo

All-Japan Jukendo Federation, 2-3 Kitanomaru Koen, Chiyoda-ku (3201 1020/www.jukendo.or.jp).

Karate

Japan Karatedo Federation, 6F Nihon Zaidan Dai 2 Bldg, 1-11-2 Toranomon, Minato-ku (3503 6637/ www.karatedo.co.jp).

Kendo
All-Japan Kendo Federation, Yasukuni Kudan Minami Bldg 2F, 2-3-14 Kudan Minami, Chiyoda-ku (3234 6271/www.kendo.or.jp).

Kobudo
Nippon Kobudo Association, 2-3 Kitanomaru Koen, Chiyoda-ku (3216 5114).

Kyudo
All-Japan Kyudo Federation, Kishi Kinen Taiikukaikan, 1-1-1 Jinnan, Shibuya-ku (3481 2387/www.kyudo.jp).

Naginata
All-Japan Naginata Federation (Tokyo Office), Kishi Kinen Taiikukaikan, 1-1-1 Jinnan, Shibuya-ku (3481 2411/www.konishi.co.jp/naginata).

Shorinji Kempo
Shorinji Kempo Federation (Tokyo Office), 1-3-5 Uehara, Shibuya-ku (3481 5191/www.shorinjikempo.or.jp).

Sumo (Amateur)
Japan Sumo Federation, 1-15-20 Hyakunin-cho, Shinjyuku-ku (3368 2211).

Running

The big events for hobby runners, held close to the date of the Tokyo Marathon, are the ten-kilometre and 30-kilometre road races out in Ome in north-west Tokyo Prefecture (information 0428 24 6311). Those looking for a little gentle jogging might want to check out the five-kilometre route marked out at 100-metre intervals around the Imperial Palace.

Skiing & snowboarding

Just 90 minutes by train from Shinjuku there's a wide range of slopes that are snowy in winter. And between December and March, JR ticket windows in the metropolis have all-in-one deals covering ski-pass and day-return transport for the destination of your choice, with weekday prices starting from under ¥10,000. Closer at hand, there are year-round indoor slopes where you can ski when it's 30°C outside.

Snova Mizonokuchi-R246
1358-1 Shimo-sakunobe, Takatsu-ku, Kawasaki City, Kanagazawa (044 844 1181/www.snova246.com). Tsudayama station. **Open** 10am-11pm Mon-Fri; 9am-11.30pm Sat; 9am-11pm Sun. **Admission** ¥2,300 90mins, ¥3,500 4hrs Mon-Fri; ¥2,800 Sat, Sun. ¥1,000 membership payable on first visit.

Serves both skiers and snow-boarders, although there are lessons for snow-boarders only. Clothing, boots and board rental available, either as separate items or in a set at ¥3,000. Snova also has another facility, in Shin-Yokohama (045 570 4141).

Sports centres

Each of the 23 wards of Tokyo has sports facilities, with bargain prices for residents and commuters. Except for those in Shibuya-ku, sports centres are also open to non residents and those that don't commute, but only at higher prices.

Chiyoda Kuritsu Sogo Taiikukan Pool
2-1-8 Uchi-Kanda, Chiyoda-ku (3256 8444). Kanda JR station, west exit or Otemachi station, exit A2. **Open** *Pool* noon-9pm Mon, Tue, Thur, Sat; 5.30-9pm Wed, Fri; 9am-5pm Sun. *Gym* 9am-noon, 1-5pm, 6-9pm daily. Closed every 3rd Mon. **Admission** *Pool* ¥600 2hrs. *Gym* ¥350. **Map** p62.

Swimming pool and gym within a weight's throw of Tokyo's business district.

Chuo-ku Sogo Sports Centre
Hama-cho Koen Nai, 2-59-1 Nihonbashi-Hama-cho, Chuo-ku (3666 1501/www.city.chuo.tokyo.jp/index/000456/008169.html). Hama-cho station (Toei Shinjuku Line), exit A2. **Open** *Pool* 9am-9.10pm daily. *Gym* 9am-8.30pm daily. Closed every 3rd Mon. **Admission** *Pool* ¥500. *Gym* ¥400.

Minato-ku Sports Centre
3-1-19 Shibaura, Minato-ku (3452 4151/www.anox.net/minato/sports/sp01.html). Tamachi station, Shibaura exit. **Open** 9am-9pm daily. Closed 1st & 3rd Mon of mth. **Admission** ¥700.

Minato-ku has a swimming pool, sauna, studio, weight gym, and aerobics classes.

Shinagawa Sogo Taiikukan Pool
5-6-11 Kita-Shinagawa, Shinagawa-ku (3449 4400/www1.cts.ne.jp/~ssa/index.html). Osaki JR station, east exit. **Open** varies. **Admission** *Pool* ¥350 2hrs.

No-frills swimming pool. Other sports available include tennis and badminton.

Shinjuku-ku Sports Centre
3-5-1 Okubo, Shinjuku-ku (3232 0171). Takadanobaba station, east exit. **Open** 9am-9pm daily. Closed every 4th Mon. **Admission** *Pool* ¥400 2hrs. *Gym* ¥400 3hrs.

Tokyo Metropolitan Gymnasium Pool
1-17-1 Sendagaya, Shibuya-ku (5474 2111/www.tef.or.jp/tmg/index.html). Kokuritsu Kyogijo station (Toei Oedo Line), exit A4 or Sendagaya station. **Open** 9am-8pm daily. Closed every 3rd Mon, plus occasional other days. **Admission** *Pool* ¥450.

Run by the Tokyo Metropolitan Government, this centre has both 25m and 50m swimming pools, a weight gym (¥350 extra for 2hrs), arena and athletics field. The 25m pool is not open to the public every day and rarely before 1.30pm, phone to check.

Trips Out of town

Yokohama

Japan's second city is a spectacular metropolis, just 40 minutes from Tokyo.

Yokohama is Japan's second city, with a population of 3.25 million. Around 40 minutes by train from Tokyo's Shibuya station, it has a very different feel and atmosphere to Tokyo, largely thanks to its recently redeveloped bay area, known as Minato Mirai, where cool breezes off the sea and a wide expanse of water create a feeling of spaciousness and ease that Tokyo lacks. The city also has many notable historic sites, gardens, museums and spectacular views.

YOKOHAMA IN A DAY

Compared with Tokyo, the key areas of Yokohama are close together and accessible. It's perfectly possible to leave Tokyo in the morning, see most areas of interest here and return – exhausted – in the evening.

The best way to begin exploring the city is from Sakuragi-cho station, *see p261* **Getting there**. From the station, take the exit for Minato Mirai, and head for the tourist booth just outside the exit, which provides detailed maps of Yokohama in English.

In front of you is the well-named **Landmark Tower**, at 296 metres (987 feet) the tallest building in Japan and home to the world's fastest lift, which travels to the top at 45 kilometres (28 miles) per hour. A moving walkway from just behind the station can whisk you into the connected complex, which houses the usual assortment of restaurants and designer boutiques. This whole area is built on the port's old dry docks, one of which has been preserved for use as a public amphitheatre, adjacent to the Queen's Square shopping centre, reached through the Landmark complex.

If the Landmark Tower doesn't tickle your fancy, cross the road almost straight from the tourist information centre and head for Kisha-Michi Promenade, which spans the water towards the giant Ferris wheel of amusement park **Yokohama Cosmoworld** on an old goods railway track. It leads to **Yokohama World Porters**, another giant shopping centre housed in a former dockside warehouse.

Skirt the edge of World Porters and follow the signs for the **Red Brick Warehouse** (*Aka Renga Sogo*), which is in fact two warehouse buildings. A Yokohama landmark, they lay empty from 1989 until reopening as a shopping centre and municipal arts centre in 2002. Brick warehouse number two contains shops and restaurants, including a pleasant glass-covered terrace, and cutting-edge jazz club, **Motion Blue**, supported by Tokyo's Blue Note. The smaller warehouse number one is home to an arts centre and exhibition space, and several crafts shops. The paved plaza between the two leads down to the water's edge, and is a pleasant place for an aimless stroll.

From a road bridge just behind warehouse number one is one of the legacies of the World Cup clean-up, a pedestrian walkway on an old elevated railway line that leads to Yamashita Park. You may see a red metal tower in the distance. This is **Marine Tower**, once the highest structure in Yokohama and still the world's tallest inland lighthouse, but now a tawdry amusement arcade and collection of snack and souvenir shops. Shortly before the walkway deposits you close to Yamashita Park, you will see **Osanbashi Pier** on your left, jutting out into the sea. This is the terminal for international cruise ships, and was extensively remodelled in 2002. The passenger terminal at the end of the pier has a viewing platform that provides panoramic views of the harbour.

Yamashita Park itself is a pleasant seaside area of greenery that contains a famous statue of the Little Girl in Red Shoes, based on a Japanese song about the real-life case of Iwasaki Kimi, a young girl born in 1902 and adopted by American missionaries, who was thought to be living a life of ease in the United States. In fact Kimi never left Japan, but was abandoned by her foster parents to die alone, aged nine, of tuberculosis. The park is also home to the *Hikawa Maru*, a 1930s cruise ship that once ferried Charlie Chaplin to Yokohama. His cabin has been preserved. Note that access to some areas of the park may be restricted until 2005 because of work on a new subway line.

From the far end of the park the walkway continues past the **Yokahama Doll Museum** in the direction of **Harbour View Park** (*Minato no Mieru Oka Koen*), which lies at the top of a hill called France Yama. It's quite a steep climb, but the view of Yokohama Bay and its bridge make it worth it. This park represents the boundary of one of the most historic areas of Yokohama, and the building that housed the first British legation to Japan – which is now called **British House Yokohama** – still stands near the rose garden

Take in the sights of **Minato Mirai**. *See p256.*

beside one of the park's gates. The park also contains a museum dedicated to local novelist Osaragi Jiro (1897-1973).

Leave the park by the gates near the British House, cross the road at the traffic lights to the right and continue straight on until you arrive at the **Foreign Cemetery**, which was originally established to bury sailors who had accompanied Commodore Perry (*see p9*). The cemetery has a small museum, but its grounds are not open to the public.

Looking down the road from the cemetery, you will notice something strikingly different about this area of Yokohama. In fact, it's unlike anywhere in Japan, and resembles an English village, complete with a picture-postcard church, Christ Church of the Bluff. The area is known as Yamate Bluff, a clifftop that once overlooked the port (where Landmark Tower now stands) and provided the city's most prestigious addresses for its new foreign residents. An intriguing overview of the history of the area is provided at the **Yamate Museum**, shortly before the church, housed in the last remaining period wooden building to stand in its original location. Dotted around the Bluff area are the houses of many of the first foreign settlers in Japan, although in many cases the houses have been moved here from elsewhere. A map is available from the museum, and most of the houses are open to visitors. Facing the museum is Motomachi Park, at the top of which stands the Ehrismann residence, built in 1925 by Antonin Rayond, a Czech assistant of American architect Frank Lloyd Wright. It was moved here in 1990 when its original site was turned into condominiums.

Once you've seen enough of this charming area, skirt the park and head downhill. The road will eventually lead to the Motomachi shopping street, the most upmarket street of shops and restaurants in Yokohama. Head down towards the canal and make for the bridge on your left.

On the other side of the bridge over the canal stands the Sazaku-mon entrance gate to Yokohama's **Chinatown**, the biggest such community in Japan, and home to hundreds of restaurants and Chinese shops, some selling spectacular souvenirs. Leave Chinatown by the Choyo-mon gate near the Holiday Inn, and head straight to return to Yamashita Park. From here, take the Sea Bass ferry service across the harbour to Yokohama station (or Sakuragi-cho) and return to Tokyo.

Diplomat's House

16 Yamate-cho, Naka-ku (045 662 8819/www.city.yokohama.jp/me/green/ygf/youkan.html). Ishikawa-cho station, Motomachi (south) exit. **Open** *Sept-June* 9.30am-5pm daily. *July, Aug* 9.30am-6pm daily. Closed 4th Wed of mth. **Admission** free.

Part of the Italian garden, a collection of period dwellings, this house was once the family dwelling of Japanese diplomat Uchida Sadatsuchi. It's one of the finest houses open to the public in the area.

Foreign Cemetery

96 Yamate-cho, Naka-ku (045 622 1311/www.city.yokohama.jp/me/naka/contents/boti.html). Ishikawa-cho station, Motomachi (south) exit, then a 15-min walk. **Open** *Museum* 10am-5pm Tue-Sun. **Admission** free.

Disappointingly not open to the public, this cemetery is the final resting place for some 4,500 non-Japanese who died here. The cemetery first opened in 1854, to bury the dead from Commodore Perry's mission to open up Japan to foreign trade. It stands at the top of Yamate Bluff.

Harbour View Park

114 Yamate-cho, Naka-ku (045 622 8244/www.city.yokohama.jp/me/green/keikaku/kouen007.html/ British House 045 623 7812/Osaragi Jiro Memorial Museum 045 622 5002). Ishikawa-cho station, Motomachi (south) exit, then 20-min walk. **Open** *British House* 9.30am-5pm daily. Closed 4th Wed of mth. *Osaragi Jiro Memorial Museum* 10am-5.30pm daily. Closed 4th Mon of mth. **Admission** *Park & British House* free. *Osaragi Jiro Memorial Museum* ¥200; ¥100 concessions.

One of the city's first attempts at redevelopment, this park opened in 1962, and boasts spectacular views over Japan's busiest port. It contains the British House, home of the first British legation to Japan, and a museum dedicated to writer Osaragi Jiro.

Kirin Yokohama Beer Village

1-17-1 Namamugi, Tsurumi-ku (045 503 8250/ www.kirin.co.jp/about/brewery/factory/yoko/index.html). Namamugi station (Keihin Kyuko Line), then a ten-min walk. **Open** *Oct-May* 10am-5pm Tue-Sun. *June-Sept* 10am-5pm daily. **Admission** free.

Take a guided tour of the Kirin brewery here, and then pause to sip a sample or two. If you can't tear yourself away, there's a pleasant restaurant offering run-of-the-mill *izakaya* fare and Kirin beer.

Landmark Tower & Sky Garden

2-2-1-1 Minato-Mirai, Nishi-ku (Sky Garden 045 222 5030/www.landmark.ne.jp). Sakuragicho station. **Open** *Sky Garden* Sept-mid July 10am-9pm Mon-Fri, Sun. Mid July-Aug 10am-9pm Mon-Fri, Sun; 10am-10pm Sat. **Admission** *Sky Garden* ¥1,000; ¥200-¥800 concessions.

Take the world's fastest elevator to the top of Japan's tallest building to take in the spectacular views. On a clear day, you can make out Mount Fuji in the distance. The rest of the building is devoted to offices and a hotel, the world's highest, naturally.

Marine Tower

15 Yamashita-cho, Naka-ku (045 641 7838/www.hmk.co.jp/). Ishikawa-cho station, north or south exit, then a 15-min walk. **Open** *Mar-Dec* 10am-9pm daily. *Jan, Feb* 10am-7pm daily. **Admission** ¥700; ¥350 concessions.

This inland lighthouse once towered above the whole of Yokohama, but now it's been left in the shade the view from the top is no longer anything to write home about. The rest of the building contains a rather sad amusement arcade, the Motion Display Museum, devoted to old American toys and some tatty coffee and souvenir shops.

Negishi Memorial Racetrack & Equine Museum

1-3 Negishi-dai, Naka-ku (045 662 7581/www.bajibunka.jrao.ne.jp). Negishi or Sakuragi-cho stations, then 21 bus to Takinoue. **Open** *Park* 9.30am-5pm daily. *Equine Museum* 10am-4.30pm Tue-Sun. **Tickets** *Park* free. *Museum* ¥100; ¥30 concessions.

A wonderful park built on the site of Japan's first western-style racetrack. A derelict grandstand survives from its 19th-century glory days, but it's now inside an American naval base. The museum concerns itself with the history of gee-gees and man's relationship with them.

Osanbashi Pier

045 211 2304/www.city.yokohama.jp/me/port/general/gaiyou/osanbasi.html. Kannai station, then a 15-min walk. **Open** 9am-9pm daily. **Admission** free.

Yokohama's passenger terminal for ocean liners has recently been refurbished. A viewing platform in the older terminal provides interesting views of the bay.

Free trade – or else

Yokohama was little more than a small fishing village when American Commodore Perry arrived in his 'black ships' in 1853 and demanded that Japan end 300 years of self-imposed national isolation and open itself to international trade. Under threat of force, the Japanese government signed the US-Japan Treaty of Amity in 1858, opening the port of Yokohama the following year.

A tax office was set up to deal with trade and to serve as a boundary dividing the village into two areas: the southern, foreign, quarter for traders and their families (now the Motomachi and Yamate areas); and the northern one, for Japanese. A period of mutual distrust followed until, in 1868, the Edo shogunate was overthrown and replaced by the Meiji government, which believed that in order to compete with foreigners the Japanese would have to learn and employ their secrets instead of trying to ignore them.

Yokohama then underwent a rapid wave of modernisation, developing into a major trading port linked to the capital by Japan's first railway. It became a city in 1889, when its population passed 120,000, and is now a port into which more foreign vessels enter and out of which more domestic exports leave than any other in the country. The pace of development was stepped up in 2002, when the city played host to the football World Cup final, the key waterfront area being one of the most obvious beneficiaries, with the creation of new pedestrian walkways and shopping areas.

Sankeien Garden

58-1 Honmoku-Sannotani, Naka-ku (045 621 0635/www.sankeien.or.jp). Yokohama station east exit, then 8 or 125 bus from bus stop 2 to Honmoku Sankeien-mae. **Open** *Outer garden* 9am-5pm daily. *Inner garden* 9am-4.30pm daily. **Admission** *Outer garden* ¥300; ¥60 concessions. *Inner garden* ¥300; ¥120 concessions.

A beautiful, traditional Japanese garden that was constructed by a silk merchant in 1906. The enormous grounds include a number of designated Japanese historic monuments saved from the bulldozer elsewhere in Japan and moved here, including a three-storey pagoda.

Shin-Yokohama Ramen Museum

2-14-21 Shin-Yokohama, Kohoku-ku (045 471 0503/ www.raumen.co.jp/top). JR Shin-Yokohama station, then a 5-min walk. **Open** 11am-11pm Mon-Fri; 10.30am-11pm Sat, Sun. **Admission** ¥300; ¥100 concessions.

A couple of floors are devoted to the history of the variety of noodle that has become a national obsession in Japan, but the main attraction here is the eight ramen shops selected from around the country to offer their wares in the basement. Each shop sells a different style of ramen, ranging from Sapporo ramen from the north (miso-based soup), to Hakata from the south (pork and chicken-based soup). Highly recommended is the miso ramen at Sumire – the shop with the longest queue.

Tin Toy Museum

239 Yamate-cho, Naka-ku (621 8710/www.toyspress.co.jp/toysclub/tc_shop.html). Ishikawa-cho station, Motomachi (south) exit, then a 15-min walk.
Open 10am-7pm daily. **Admission** ¥200; ¥100 concessions.

A collection of 3,000 tin toys dating from the 1890s to the 1960s is on display in this small museum close to the Yamate Museum.

World Cup Stadium Tours

International Stadium Yokohama, 3300 Kozukue-cho, Kohoku-ku (045 477 5006/www.hamaspo.com/ stadium). Shin-Yokohama station, then a 15-min walk. **Admission** ¥500; ¥250 concessions. **Tours** 10.30am, noon, 1.30pm, 3pm daily (except for when stadium is in use).

The venue that hosted the 2002 World Cup final has started to offer tours taking in the dressing rooms, practice area and pitch of the stadium that was the focus of world attention on 30 June, 2002. See the Brazil tactical whiteboard, take a shot at a silhouette of Oliver Kahn and gaze in awe at the rubbish left behind in their dressing room by the teams. There's also a chance to run out (almost) on to the pitch with the World Cup anthem blazing.

Yamashita Park

Yamashita Koen, Yamashita-cho, Naka-ku (Hikawa Maru 045 641 4362). Kannai station, then 20-min walk. **Open** *Park* 24hrs daily. *Hikawa Maru* Jan, Apr 9.30am-9pm daily. Feb, Mar 9.30am-6.30pm daily. May, June 9.30am-8pm daily. July, Sept 9.30am-9pm daily. Aug 9.30am-9.30pm daily. Nov, Dec 9.30am-7.30pm daily. **Admission** free.

Yamashita Park is a pleasant patch of seaside greenery popular with courting couples too poor to rent a room. Moored beside the park is the 1930s ocean liner *Hikawa Maru*, which has been preserved in its original state. A walk around it provides a fascinating glimpse of shipboard life. The ship's most famous passenger in its heyday was Charlie Chaplin, whose luxury cabin has been preserved.

Yamate Museum

247 Yamate-cho, Naka-ku (045 622 1188/www.city.yokohama.jp/me/sisetu/naka/yamatesiryo.htm). Ishikawa-cho station, Motomachi (south) exit.
Open 11am-4pm daily. **Admission** ¥200; ¥150 concessions.

Housed in the last remaining western-style wooden building still in its original place, this museum provides a fascinating insight into the early days of Yokohama's development, and the thriving foreign community that soon grew here.

Yokohama Archives of History

3 Nihon Odori, Naka-ku (045 201 2100/www.kaikou.city.yokohama.jp). Kannai station. **Open** 9.30am-5pm Tue-Sun. **Admission** ¥200; ¥100 concessions. **No credit cards**.

In a building that served as the British Consulate until 1972, the archives host a permanent exhibition devoted to the development of the city, and four special exhibitions per year.

Yokohama Cosmoworld

2-8-1 Shinkou, Naka-ku (045 641 6591/www.senyo.co.jp/cosmo/). Sakuragi-cho station, then a 10-min walk. **Open** *mid Mar-Nov* 11am-9pm Mon-Fri; 11am-10pm Sat, Sun. *Dec-mid Mar* 11am-8pm Mon-Fri; 11am-9pm Sat, Sun. **Admission** free.

The Ferris wheel at the centre of this small amusement park, with its giant digital clock, is a true Yokohama landmark. It can hold 480 passengers, making it one of the largest in the world. The park has 27 rides in all, including a water rollercoaster.

Yokohama Curry Museum

1-2-3 Isezaki-cho, Naka-ku (045 250 0833/www.currymuseum.com). Kannai station, north exit.
Open 11am-9.30pm daily. **Admission** free.

A small museum tracing the history of curry in Japan since its arrival in the 19th century. The main reason to come here is the seven curry restaurants.

Yokohama Doll Museum

18 Yamashita-cho, Naka-ku (045 671 9361/ www.welcome.city.yokohama.jp/eng/doll/index.html). Ishikawa-cho station, Motomachi (south) exit, then 15-min walk. **Open** 10am-6pm daily. Closed 3rd Mon of mth. **Admission** ¥300; ¥150 concessions.

Home to nearly 10,000 dolls from 150 countries, this museum appeals to children and serious collectors alike. It also holds occasional puppet shows and exhibitions of the dollmaker's art.

Japan's largest **Chinatown**. *See p257.*

Yokohama Museum of Art

3-4-1 Minato Mirai, Nishi-ku, Yokohama City, Kanagawa Prefecture (045 221 0300/ www.art-museum.city.yokohama.jp). Sakuragi-cho station (Tokyu Toyoko/JR lines). **Open** 10am-6pm Mon-Wed, Fri-Sun. **Admission** ¥500; ¥100-¥300 concessions; additional fee for special exhibitions.

One of the region's major art museums and a Yokohama landmark, this Tange Kenzo-designed building occupies a prime, tree-lined plaza in Minato Mirai ('Port Future'). Abundant natural light pours in through a huge skylight above the open court in the centre of the entrance hall. Up to the right, temporary exhibitions range from Leonardo da Vinci to contemporary artist Nara Yoshitomo. On the left, exhibitions drawn from the permanent collection of European, American, and Japanese modern art and photography change regularly.

Yokohama by boat

Marine Rouge

Information 045 671 7719/www.yokohama-cruising.com. Boats leave from Yamashita Pier. **Daily departures** *Lunch cruise* 11am (90mins). *Afternoon cruise* 1.30pm (90mins). *Sunset cruise* 4pm (90mins). *Dinner cruise* 7pm (2hrs). **Admission** from ¥2,500; ¥1,250 concessions.

Marine Shuttle

Information 045 671 7719/www.yokohama-cruising.com. Boats leave from Yamashita Pier. **Departures** *Mon-Fri* 10.20am (1hr), 12.20pm (1hr), 2.10pm (1hr), 3.40pm (40mins), 4.50 pm (1hr), 6.30pm (90mins). *Sat, Sun* 10.20am (1hr), 11.40am (1hr), 1pm (1hr), 2.20pm (1hr), 3.40pm (40mins), 4.40pm (40mins), 5.30pm (40mins), 6.30pm (90mins). **Admission** *1-hr cruises* ¥2,800; ¥1,400 concessions. *90-min cruises* ¥4,000; ¥2,000 concessions. *40-min cruises* ¥900.

Royal Wing

Information 045 662 6125/www.royalwing.co.jp. Boats leave from Yamashita Pier. **Departures** *Lunch cruise* noon (105mins) daily. *Tea-time cruise* 2.45pm, 5.15pm (90mins) daily. *Dinner cruise* 7.30pm (2hrs) daily. **Admission** *Lunch cruise* ¥2,000-¥20,000. *Tea-time cruise* ¥1,000-¥2,000. *Dinner cruise* ¥2,000-¥25,000.

Sea Bass

Information 045 671 7719/www.yokohama-cruising.com. Boats travel between Yokohama station east exit & Yamashita Pier via Minato Mirai. **Departures** every 20-30mins from 6am until 8.25pm daily. **Admission** *Full trip* ¥600; ¥300 concessions. *From Minato Mirai to either of other destinations* ¥350; ¥180 concessions.

Sea Bass is the Japanese transliteration of 'bus', rather than a giant fish.

Where to eat

Chinatown

www.chinatown.or.jp/1index.html

Dohatsu Honkan

148 Yamashita-cho, Naka-ku (045 681 7273/www.douhatsu.co.jp). Kannai station, exit 1 or south exit or Ishikawa-cho station, China Town (north) exit. **Open** 11.30am-9.30pm Mon, Wed-Sun. **Credit** DC, V. **Average** ¥5,000.

This restaurant is popular for its Hong Kong-style seafood dishes. So popular, in fact, that lunchtime is a spectacle, with customers jostling for position while the strict *mama-san* tries to keep everyone in check. While waiting, take a look at the window display of mouth-watering meats, whole chickens, sausages and other less recognisable animal parts.

Manchinro Honten

153 Yamashita-cho, Naka-ku (045 681 4004/www.manchinro.co.jp/index2.htm). Kannai station, exit 1 or south exit, or Ishikawa-cho station, China Town (north) exit, then 7-min walk. **Open** 11am-10pm daily. **Average** ¥1,500 lunch. ¥3,000 dinner. **Credit** AmEx, DC, MC, V.

This Cantonese restaurant opened in 1892, making it prehistoric by Japanese standards.

Peking Hanten

79-5 Yamashita-cho, Naka-ku (045 681 3535/ www.chinatown.or.jp/shop0002/store/0265.html). Kannai station, exit 1 or south exit, or Ishikawa-cho station, China Town (north) exit. **Open** 11.30am-2am daily. **Average** ¥1,500 lunch; ¥3,000 dinner. **Credit** AmEx, DC, V.

This charming restaurant claims to be the first in Japan to serve Peking duck. An English dinner menu with pictures might be a tad naff, but takes the pain out of choosing.

Motomachi

Aussie

1-12 Ishikawa-cho, Naka-ku (045 681 3671/ www.juno.dti.ne.jp/~aussie/). Ishikawa-cho station, Motomachi (south) exit, then 3-min walk. **Open** 5pm-1am Mon, Wed-Sun. **Average** ¥3,500. **Credit** AmEx, JCB, MC, V.

As the name suggests, this place serves up anything Australian, the most popular dishes on the menu being barbecued kangaroo and crocodile. Get there early for half-price wine (5-7pm).

Mutekiro

2-96 Motomachi, Naka-ku (045 681 2926/www. mutekiro.com). Ishikawa-cho station, Motomachi (south) exit, then 10-min walk. **Open** noon-3pm, 5-10pm daily. **Average** ¥4,000 lunch; ¥15,000 dinner. **Credit** AmEx, DC, MC, V.

Motomachi's most celebrated and upmarket French restaurant has the motto '*Mode française, coeur japonais*', meaning that the dishes often contain typical Japanese ingredients, with a particular emphasis on seafood, but are prepared in a French way. Reservations are essential.

Pas a Pas

1-50 Motomachi, Naka-ku (045 651 5070). Ishikawa-cho station, Motomachi (south) exit, then 15-min walk. **Open** 11am-9pm Tue-Sun. **Average** ¥1,000. **No credit cards**.

Appropriately situated near the France Yama end of the Motomachi shopping area, this French-style café serves up adventurous lunchtime sarnies from noon to 2pm. The rest of the time it's cakes and coffee.

Shopping

Motomachi Shopping Street

www.motomachi.or.jp. Ishikawa-cho station, Motomachi (south) exit, then 2-min walk. **Open** varies.

Yokohama's most prestigious shopping street is a pleasant pedestrianised thoroughfare containing more than 200 shops, from global brands such as Gap to local designers such as Kitamura.

Queen's Square

2-3 Minato-Mirai, Nishi-ku (information 045 682 1000/www.qsy.co.jp/english/index.htm). **Open** *Shops* 11am-8pm daily. *Restaurants* 11am-10pm daily.

A giant shopping and dining complex consisting of several separate but linked tower blocks, Queen's Tower A and B, At! and East, and a hotel by the name of the Pan-Pacific Yokohama. The complex houses over 50 restaurants and cafés, hundreds of shops and a concert hall.

Red Brick Warehouse

1-1-1 & 1-1-2 Shinkou, Naka-ku (Building One 045 211 1515/Building Two 045 227 2002/www. yokohama-akarenga.jp). Sakuragi-cho station, then 15-min walk. **Open** varies.

A pair of renovated customs houses first built 100 years ago is Yokohama's newest tourist attraction. The first warehouse is home to an art space that houses occasional exhibitions and performances, while the warehouse two comprises three floors of shops and restaurants, along with Motion Blue, a top-notch jazz club.

Yokohama World Porters

2-2-1 Shinkou, Naka-ku (045 222 2000/www. yim.co.jp). Kannai station, north exit or Sakuragi-cho station, then 10-min walk. **Open** *Shops* 10.30am-9pm daily. *Restaurants* 10.30am-11pm daily. *Cinema* 10am-midnight daily.

Another giant shopping complex, this time loosely themed around the concept of international trade. It's a good place, therefore, to pick up foreign foods in the basement food hall. Yokohama World Porters also has a branch of the HMV music store and an eight-screen cinema.

Tourist information

The Yokohama Convention & Visitors Bureau also has an excellent English-language website, at www.welcome.city.yokohama.jp/ eng/tourism/.

YCVB Yokohama station *2-16-1, Takashima, Nishi-ku (045 441 7300). Yokohama station, on the east-west walkway.* **Open** 9am-7pm daily.
YCVB Shin-Yokohama station *2937 Shinohara-cho, Kohoku-ku (045 473 2895). Shin-Yokohama station.* **Open** 10am-1pm, 2-6pm daily.
YCVB Sakuragi-cho station *1-1-62 Sakuragi-cho, Naka-ku (045 211 0111). Sakuragi-cho station, Minato-Mirai exit, exit 1.* **Open** 9am-7pm daily.
YCVB Sangyo Boeki Centre 2 *Yamashita-cho, Naka-ku (045 641 4759). Opposite Yamashita Park, Kannai station, then a 15-min walk.* **Open** 9am-5pm Mon-Fri.

Getting there

By train

Take a 40-minute express or 35-minute super-express Tokyu Toyoko Line train from Shibuya station, to its terminus at Sakuragi-cho, ignoring Yokohama station en route. This is the cheapest option, although those with a JR travel pass may prefer to take the JR Keihin Tohoku Line to Sakuragi-cho from Tokyo station.

Hakone

Bubbling hot springs, dramatic scenery and a selection of world-class museums make this Tokyo's playground in the mountains.

Hakone is where Tokyo comes to relax and get a taste of the countryside. Around one-and-a-half hours from Shinjuku station by Odakyu line train, this mountainous area offers convenient transportation, beautiful scenery, a host of attractions and, best of all, a natural hot spring bath, or *onsen*, around virtually every bend of the roads that twist through the mountains.

The best way to see Hakone is to buy the Hakone Free Pass (*see p265*), available at all Odakyu railway stations. The pass covers all public transport in Hakone – and what public transport it is. As well as a picturesque railway and a bus service, the Hakone area also has a funicular railway, a cable car and a boat that crosses Lake Ashinoko at its centre. All of these means of transport are interlinked, making it possible to 'do' the whole of the Hakone area in a day from Tokyo.

THE HAKONE CIRCUIT

Those in a hurry can make the most of their time by trying the 'Hakone circuit'. Get off the train at either Odawara or Hakone Yumoto. From there, transfer to the Tozan mountain railway for the 50-minute ride to its terminus at Gora. At Gora, transfer on to the funicular railway up to the end of the line at Sounzan. Here, transfer to the cable car, which takes you down to the banks of Lake Ashinoko at Togendai station. To get across the lake, board one of the pleasure boats and stay on until Hakone-Machi or Moto-Hakone, from where you can take a bus back to where you started, at Hakone-Yumoto or Odawara. The round-trip should take about three hours, although in the busy summer months it may take longer.

THE FULL HAKONE

While the circuit will give you your fill of glorious scenery, you'll be missing out on a lot of what Hakone has to offer. If you decide to start your journey at Odawara, it's worth making a detour out of the east exit of the station to take the ten-minute walk to **Odawara Castle**, perched on a hill overlooking the town. First built in 1416, and rebuilt in 1960, this picturesque castle was for centuries an important strategic stronghold.

Back on the train, the next major stop, or the starting point for some, is Hakone-Yumoto station. 'Yumoto' means 'source of hot water', which should give you some clue as to what this small town is about. First mentioned in eighth-century poetry as a place to bathe,

Pola Museum of Art.
See p264.

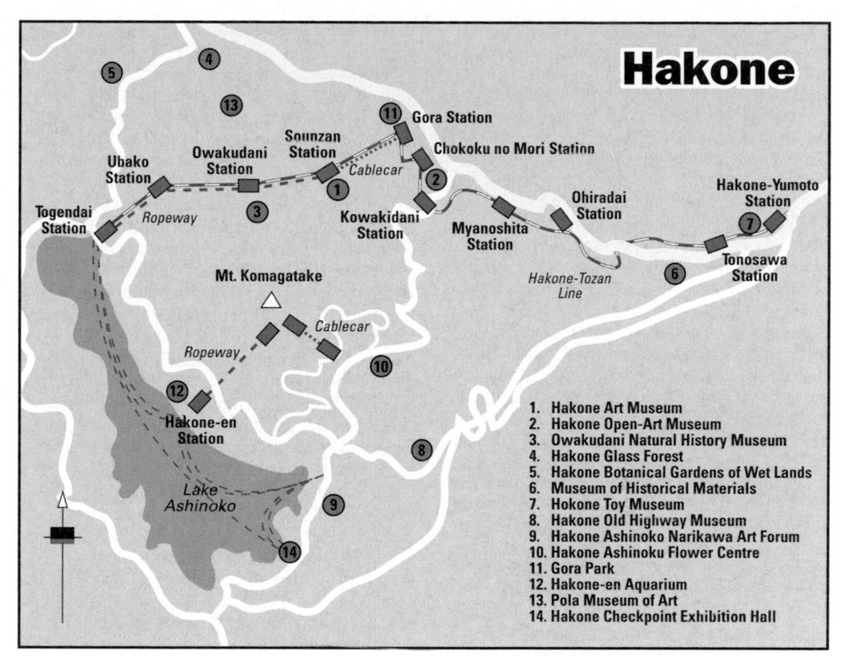

Hakone became a great favourite in the time of the Tokugawa shogunate (1600-1854), with bathers travelling two or three days on foot from Tokyo (then Edo) along the Tokaido Way, portions of which can still be seen over the other side of the river from the modern railway station. The station houses a small tourist office, but the main office is up the hill on the left-hand side. Here, you will find English-speaking assistants, who are happy to hand out maps and pamphlets.

For dedicated modern bathers, the day may end in Hakone-Yumoto. Although the modern town is unremarkable, it is dotted with hot spring baths: just about every building of any size is a hotel or *ryokan*, and many allow non-guests to use their facilities. One of the locals' favourites is located on the hillside on the other side of the tracks from the station. **Kappa Tengoku** has segregated open-air baths surrounded by dense woodland, and a steady army of bathers can be seen trooping up the steep steps to the baths well into the night. Bring your own towel and wash cloth if you want to save money.

Up the hill from the bath is the intriguing **Hakone Toy Museum**. The souvenir shop sells charmingly retro goods imported from China and elsewhere.

Back on the train from Hakone-Yumoto, take some time to enjoy the train itself. This is the world's steepest train line and so sharp are the bends that at three points the train enters a switchback, going forward and then reversing out of a siding in order to continue its ascent. As you climb the mountain you will see water pouring out of the hillside and cascading under the tracks, some of it still hot.

The next station of any note is Miyanoshita. This is home to one of the highest concentrations of *onsen* baths in the area, and is where the first foreigners in Japan came to bathe in the 19th century. To cater for them, the **Fujiya Hotel** (*see p265*) was built in 1878. Miraculously, it's still standing today, a wooden mix of Japanese and western styles. Non-residents are free to stop here for a coffee, a bite to eat or something stronger in the bar.

Two stops up the line, at Chokoku no Mori station, is one of the great glories of Hakone. The **Hakone Open-Air Museum** must be one of the most spectacular in the world. Set on a mountainside overlooking a series of valleys leading to the sea, the museum is dedicated to modern sculpture from all over the globe. Exposed to the elements are works by Moore, Rodin, Antony Gormley and Taro Okamoto.

There's also a world-beating collection of ceramics by Picasso in a separate pavilion.

From here, it's a ten-minute walk to the next station, Gora, the terminus of the Tozan railway and the start of the funicular railway that climbs the steep mountainside. If you're changing from the train, there will be a carriage waiting for you. The first stop on the funicular, Koen Shita, provides a pleasant diversion in the shape of **Gora Park**, a landscaped hillside garden that makes great use of the natural hot water in its hot houses. A walk uphill through the park will bring you to the next stop on the funicular.

This is a good point to visit the **Pola Museum of Art**, deep in the surrounding forest. The museum houses 9,500 works by the likes of Renoir, Picasso and Monet. To avoid damaging the beauty of the countryside, the building is constructed three floors underground, and is only eight metres (27 feet) tall on the surface. To reach the museum, take a bus from Gora station bound for Shisseikaen.

The funicular terminates at Sounzan station, and it's here that many people's favourite part of the Hakone experience begins: the cable car, or Hakone Ropeway, as it's known. Riding over the peaks and valleys of Hakone, this 4.3-kilometre (2.7-mile) ride is Japan's longest cable car route. Around halfway along its length is Owakudani ('big boiling valley'), one of the most breathtaking sights in Hakone. The car passes over, at a height of around 60 metres (200 feet), a smoking hillside streaked with traces of sulphur from the volcanic activity below. The air simply reeks of rotten eggs. On top of a mountain peak sits Owakudani station, the centre of a large tourist complex comprising restaurants, gift shops and the **Owakudani Natural History Museum**. On a clear day you can see the peak of Mount Fuji looming over the mountain range in the distance. There's also a walk to the source of some of the steam that rises out of the mountain, the ancient crater of Mount Kamiyama, the pathway passing over hot streams of water bubbling up. The air is thick with hydrogen sulphide, and signs warn of the dangers of standing in one place for too long for fear of being overcome by fumes. If you feel like a snack, the best bet is a hard-boiled egg. Sold by the half-dozen for ¥500, these eggs have been cooked in the hot spring water, the sulphur turning their shells black.

From Owakudani, the Hakone Ropeway passes over several more valleys before descending to terminate at Togendai on the banks of Lake Ashinoko. The lake is believed to be in the crater of a volcano that blew its top 400,000 years ago. The volcanic activity that goes on beneath the waters to this day ensures that it never freezes over. From here, a pair of incredibly tacky pleasure boats, one done out as a Mississippi steamer, one as a Spanish galleon, cross the lake to Hakone-Machi and Moto-Hakone. Only 500 metres or so separate the two destinations, but for ease of walking, get off at Hakone-Machi and turn left with the lake behind you, to head for Moto-Hakone.

On the way is the site of the **Old Hakone Checkpoint**, where travellers to and from Tokyo (then Edo) were stopped and often interrogated by border guards. Ruins of the original checkpoint still stand, while other buildings have been reconstructed and opened to the public as a museum. Set back a little from the modern road is what's left of a cedar avenue, planted along the Tokaido Way in the early 17th century. Paved sections of the Tokaido Way are still extant, and keen walkers can take a short hike from here along one such section, away from the lake towards Hatajuku.

On a promontory into the lake between the two boat stops is the **Hakone Detached Palace Garden**. The garden of an 1887 villa that once belonged to the imperial family but was destroyed in an earthquake, it has been open to the public since 1946. Further along, past Moto-Hakone and down the side of the lake, is **Hakone Shrine**, its history going back 1,200 years. The site is clearly marked by a red gate, or *torii*, that stands in the lake.

Once you've walked your fill of the area, head back to Moto-Hakone and take a bus back to Odawara. All buses to Odawara stop in Hakone-Yumoto, too.

Gora Park

1300 Gora, Hakone-Machi, Shimogun (0460 22825/ www.hakone-tozan.co.jp). **Open** 9am-5pm daily. **Admission** ¥900; ¥400 concessions.

Hakone Detached Palace Garden

171 Moto-Hakone, Hakone-Machi, Ashigara-Shimogun (0460 37484). **Open** *July, Aug* 9am-5pm daily. *Sept-June* 9am-5pm Mon, Wed-Sun. **Admission** free.

Hakone Open-Air Museum

Ninotaira, Hakone-Machi (0460 21161/www. hakone-oam.or.jp). **Open** *Mar-Nov* 9am-5pm daily. *Dec-Feb* 9am-4.30pm daily. **Admission** ¥1,600; ¥800 concessions.

Hakone Toy Museum

740 Yumoto, Hakone-Machi, Ashigara-Shimogun (0460 64700/www.hakonetoys.com). **Open** 9am-5pm daily. **Admission** ¥800; ¥400 concessions.

Kappa Tengoku

777 Yumoto, Hakone-Machi, Ashigara-Shimogun (0460 56121). **Open** 10am-10pm daily. **Admission** ¥700 (10% discount with Hakone Free Pass). *Towel* (to buy) ¥900.

Odawara Castle

0465 231373. **Open** 10am-4pm Tue-Sun. **Admission** *Park* free. *Castle* ¥400; ¥150 concessions.

Old Hakone Checkpoint

Hakone-Machi (0460 36635). **Open** 9am-4pm daily. **Admission** ¥300; ¥150 concessions.

Owakudani Natural History Museum

1251 Sengokuhara, Hakone (0460 49149). **Open** 9am-4.30pm daily. **Admission** ¥400; ¥250 concessions.

Pola Museum of Art

1285 Kozukayama, Sengokubara, Hakone-Machi, Ashigara-Shimogun (0460 42111/www.polamuseum.or.jp). **Open** 9am-5pm daily. **Admission** ¥1,800; ¥700 concessions.

Fujiya Hotel.

Where to eat & drink

Given the fact that most of the area's activity centres around the hotels, it's hardly surprising that there are remarkably few independent restaurants worth seeking out. For the truly hungry, there are snack bars serving curry, noodles and the like at Owakudani and Togendai stations, and on the lake at Hakone-Machi. The **Bella Foresta** restaurant in the Open-Air Museum (*see p264*) serves a decent buffet lunch for around ¥1,500, while all of the large hotels have at least four restaurants that are open to non-residents. The **Pola Museum** (*above*) has both a café serving snacks and drinks (10am-4.30pm daily) and an upmarket French-style restaurant (11am-4pm daily), with lunch sets starting at ¥1,600.

Where to stay

There are hundreds of places to stay in Hakone, ranging from cheap *ryokan* to top-class hotels. All have their own hot springs. Many have separate rates for weekdays and weekends, the former being cheaper. Expect top prices at peak periods such as New Year and Golden Week in May. If you intend to use Hakone-Yumoto as a base, cheap options include **Kappa Tengoku** (777 Yumoto, Hakone-Machi, Ashigara-Shimogun, 0460 56121), where a double room costs ¥6,200 per night on weekdays (¥7,200 or more at weekends), although its proximity to the railway tracks might mean an earlier awakening than you'd bargained for. A plusher option is the **Kajikasou** (777 Yumoto, Hakone-Machi, Ashigara-Shimogun, 0460 55561/www.kajikaso.co.jp), which has a plethora of different baths, including private ones. Rates start at ¥22,000 on weekdays (¥25,000 weekends).

Up in the mountains, the **Fujiya Hotel** (359 Miyanoshita, Ashigara-Shimogun, 0460 22211/www.fujiyahotel.co.jp) is peerless, with double rooms starting at ¥16,000 on weekdays (¥21,000 weekends). Overlooking Lake Ashinoko is the **Palace Hotel** (1245 Sengokuhara, Hakone-Machi, Ashigara-Shimogun, 0460 48501/hakone.palacehotel.co.jp), where doubles start at ¥15,000 during the low season. This luxury hotel often advertises special-stay plans in the Tokyo press, which can bring the price down further.

Tourist information

Hakone-Yumoto Tourist Information *Kankou Bussankan, 698 Yumoto, Hakone-Machi, Ashigara-Shimogun (0460 58911).* **Open** 9am-5pm daily.
Odakyu Railway Information *Odakyu Shinjuku station (5321 7877).* **Open** 9am-5pm daily.
Odawara Tourist Information *East exit, Odawara station (0465 331521).* **Open** 9am-5pm daily.

Getting there

By train

There are two types of Hakone Free Pass, available at all Odakyu stations and many travel agents. The weekday pass gives you unlimited journeys for two days and costs ¥4,700 from Shinjuku station. The weekend pass gives three days' unlimited transport and costs ¥5,500 from Shinjuku station. The ticket price also covers the basic fare on an Odakyu train from Shinjuku to Hakone. If you want to travel in comfort on the super express Romance Car, you will need to pay an express supplement of ¥870. If you hold a JR Pass (*see p278* **Getting Around**), the most cost-effective way of reaching the area is to take a JR Tokaido *shinkansen* to Odawara station, then buy your Hakone Free Pass there. As this pass does not include transport to Tokyo, it costs ¥3,410 (weekdays) or ¥4,130 (weekends). The Free Pass also gives discounts at many local attractions. Look out for the Hakone Free Pass sticker.

Kamakura

The ghosts of feudal Japan live less than an hour from Tokyo.

For almost 150 years Kamakura was the military and administrative centre of Japan, and the factors that made it a strategic location for the first military government – it has hills on three sides and Sagami Bay on the other – has also kept it separate from the creeping city. Kamakura is one of Tokyo's greenest suburbs and the feeling is still that of the country, yet it's less than one hour from the city.

TEMPLE TOWN

Kamakura was the base of the Minamoto family, which attacked and beat the Taira clan in the 12th century to establish the first military government of a united Japan – the start of 700 years of shogun rule. The Minamoto made Kamakura their seat of power. They encouraged Zen Buddhism, which appealed for its strict self-discipline, and temples of various sects were established in the area. While traces of the government and military rule quickly faded after the Minamoto defeat 150 years later, the religious influence endures to this day.

There are still more than 70 temples and shrines around Kamakura, from the large and eminent to the small and secluded, and many are within walking distance of Kamakura or Kita-Kamakura stations. They are still active today and represent different buddhist sects, among them Rinzai, Pure Land and Nichiren. Over the years the grounds of most temples have been lost through fires and earthquakes, or, in the case of Engaku-ji in Kita-Kamakura, to make way for the railway line. Few buildings remain intact from the Kamakura period (1185-1333), but many temples and shrines appear unspoilt, giving visitors a rare opportunity to view authentic remnants of old Japan.

Kamakura is now a major tourist destination, and the temples and grounds are well looked after. Most temples require a small entry fee (¥100-¥300) – a contribution towards upkeep rather than an admission charge. The directions and distances to temples in each vicinity are marked in English at regular intervals all around town. For a detailed map ask the Tourist Information Service just to the right of the station gates at the east exit. Most temples are open daily, usually from 9am until 4pm, but museums, treasure houses and some shops usually close on Mondays. The town and the main attractions are surprisingly busy at weekends and holidays.

Festival days are also crowded. The main ones are the Grand Festival (14-16 September) and the Kamakura Festival (from the second to the third Sunday in April). Both take place at **Tsurugaoka Hachiman**. In addition to these main events, each temple and shrine holds its own festival, and the beach fireworks on the second Tuesday of August attract big crowds.

Kamakura's main attractions are scattered around and take a day to see in themselves; you may do better to pick an area and check out the temples and sights there.

Walking to temples in any area will take you through small streets in quiet residential areas, with well-tended gardens, old wooden houses, coffee shops and teahouses. There are also some hiking courses on ridges that link different parts of town and various temples. After the initial ascent they are generally fairly easy walks, some leading to picnic areas and parks. The starting points are indicated on the road, as are destinations and estimated durations.

You can also rent bicycles to move faster between areas. The rental office is behind the police box on the right at the east exit of Kamakura station (0467 24 2319). It's open daily from 8.30am to 6pm (¥500 first hour, ¥250 extra hour, full day ¥1,500 weekdays and ¥1,600 weekends; bring ID).

What follows is a list of highlights of the Kamakura area. For information on more sights or special events, check with the Tourist Information Service.

Tsurugaoka Hachiman

The main and most popular shrine in Kamakura, Tsurugaoka Hachiman is 15 minutes' walk from Kamakura station. Hachiman is seen today as the god of war, but in the past was regarded as the guardian of the Japanese nation. The guardian shrine of the Minamoto family, the warring clan that took control of the area in the 12th century, it's one of the most popular destinations in the area.

To get to the shrine, follow Komachi Dori, through the *torii* (gate) on the left on the station's east exit. It's a pedestrianised road, full of souvenirs and craft shops, boutiques, food stalls and shops, as well as restaurants. At the end, turn right. The wide road (Wakamiya Dori) at the main gate is the true entrance to the

The 750-year-old **Great Buddha**. *See p268.*

shrine and leads directly to the sea, where a port flourished in the heyday of the city.

The shrine and grounds of Tsurugaoka (Hill of Cranes) were built to subtle and strict specifications, the most striking example of which is found near the entrance. On the right (the east, the rising sun) is a large pond with three islands (a propitious number), symbolising the Minamoto family. On the left (the west, the setting sun) is a smaller pond with four islands (an unlucky number) symbolising the Taira clan, whom the Minamoto defeated to take control of the area. Going straight on, you'll come to a dancing stage, then to the steps to the main hall. The two guardian figures in the gate are Yadaijin and Sadaijin, but the gingko tree on the left of the steps dwarfs them in majesty. It's purported to be at least as old as the shrine, which was here even before the arrival of the Minamoto. The tree is also famous for having concealed the murderer of the third Minamoto shogun, taken by surprise and beheaded on the spot.

The main hall is at the top. The steps descending on the right lead to other buildings and the treasure house, where historic religious artworks from the area are on display.

Kita-Kamakura

This area is home to many Rinzai sect temples, among them the famous **Engaku-ji**, the largest Zen establishment in Kamakura, only a few metres from Kita-Kamakura station. The temple was founded in 1282, but the main gate, housing statues of Kannon and Rakan, was reconstructed in 1780. Engaku-ji is also famous for having the largest bell in Kamakura.

On the road along the tracks is the **Kamakura Old Pottery Museum** (10am-5pm Tue-Sun, ¥500) and across the tracks is **Tokei-ji**, for a long time a nunnery offering asylum to women wanting a divorce. It's worth a visit for its beautiful garden and grounds as well as the treasure house, which keeps old sutras and scrolls.

Nearby is **Jochi-ji**, noted for the small ancient bridge and steps at the entrance, its bell tower, the burial caves at the back and a tunnel between cemeteries. A mountain path towards Kamakura's west side starts from the left of the entrance. On the other side of the road is **Meigetsuin**, approached by a pleasant street. This temple has the biggest *yagura* (burial cave) in the area, a small stone garden and statues carved out of the rock in the caves.

The main road towards Kamakura leads to **Kencho-ji**, the oldest Zen temple in Japan. It's an imposing place with large buildings and grounds, though only ten of the original 49 sub-temples survive. Its arrangement hasn't changed for over 700 years, however. On the second floor of the main gate are the statues of 500 *rakan* (Buddha's disciples). Behind the last building there's a garden, and, further along, the path leads to steps climbing to Hanso-bo, the shrine protecting the temple. Up the stairs near the tunnel on the road is **Eno-ji**, a very small temple housing statues representing the judges of hell.

West of Tsurugaoka Hachiman

Eisho-ji, the only active buddhist nunnery in the area, is closed to the public. At nearby **Jufuku-ji**, some of the temple grounds are closed too, but you can wander in the old cemetery behind by following the path to the left of the gate. It's a quiet place with many burial caves, some reputed to date from the Kamakura period. From the mountain trail, or back on the road, it's a short walk to **Kaizoji**, a quaint temple known mostly for its wells.

About 30 minutes away on foot is **Zeniarai Benten** ('Money-washing Shrine'), an unforgettable place. Go through a tunnel through the mountain and enter another world, with small shrines carved in the cliffs, a stream, ponds and eerie music in the air. The main cave has bamboo baskets to put your money in, notes and all, and dip in the water. The more you wash the more you'll get back.

Back towards the town at a nearby crossing a lane leads to **Sasuke Inari Shrine**, up steps through more than 100 *torii*. There's not much to see up here, but it is marvellously peaceful at the end of the valley.

Another 30 minutes' walk leads to **Kotokuin** temple, home of the Daibutsu or Great Buddha (entry ¥200). The temple dates from AD 741 and the statue of Buddha from 1252. Nobody really knows how it was cast and put together but it's marvelled at for the skills involved and the fact that the proportions are perfect from the ground. It was once in a hall that suffered fires and earthquakes and was finally demolished by a tidal wave in 1495. The Daibutsu was unscathed and has been in the open ever since. For ¥20 you can wander around inside the statue.

Hase Kannon or **Hase Dera** temple is just down the road. The main feature is a nine-metre (30-foot), 11-faced statue of Kannon (goddess of mercy and compassion), reputedly the tallest in Japan. It was carved in AD 721 out of a single camphor tree. The temple is especially known for its thousands of small *jizo* figures offered in memory of deceased children and babies.

There's also a revolving sutra library containing Buddhist scriptures – worshippers causing the library to rotate receive merit equivalent to reading the entire Buddhist canon – and a small network of caves with statues carved out of the rock. The treasure house (open 9am-4pm daily) contains objects and artefacts excavated from the temple during rebuilding. From Hase Kannon there's also a panoramic view of the town, the beach and Sagami Bay. The ¥300 entry fee is well worth it.

East of Tsurugaoka Hachiman

This least grandiose of the sightseeing areas is quieter, with many smaller temples. The first shrine as you come from Tsurugaoka Hachiman is **Egara Tenjin**, founded in 1104. Tenjin is the patron deity of scholarship and literature, so every 25 January marks a ritualistic burning of writing brushes. Nearby is **Kamakura Shrine**, founded by the Meiji Emperor in 1869.

Turn left up the lane to **Kakuon-ji**. This small temple offers 40-minute tours by a priest (on the hour from 10am to 3pm daily, though not on rainy days). The tour through the grounds is in Japanese only, but the thatched buildings and old wooden statues speak for themselves.

A 15-minute walk from Kamakura Shrine is **Zuisen-ji**, famous for its trees and flowers, especially the plum blossoms in February. It's a small temple, with an old Zen garden created in

The gate to **Tsurugaoka Hachiman**. *See p266.*

A guardian at the gate of **Kencho-ji**. *See p267.*

the 14th century by the celebrated priest and landscape gardener Muso-Kokushi.

From the intersection near Kamakura Shrine you can reach **Sugimotodera**, the oldest temple in Kamakura. The gate and temple both have thatched roofs and were originally built in AD 734. Further up across the road is **Hokoku-ji**, known as the bamboo temple. From here it's a short walk to Shakado Tunnel. It is closed to traffic, but pedestrians still use it.

Down the road (towards the station) is **Hongaku-ji**, a small temple with a very old gate and guardian statues. Shortly after is **Myohon-ji**, founded in 1260. Nestled within mountainsides, it's surprisingly quiet, given its proximity to the town. Between this temple and the beach are many Nichiren sect temples; this is the oldest and largest.

Another 15 minutes or so away is **Myoho-ji**, also known as the Moss Temple. The priest Nichiren is said to have resided here and the summit was one of his favourite spots.

Towards the beach along the main road you'll come to **Choso-ji**, a recently renovated structure (though there's been a temple here since 1345). A statue of Nichiren stands between the statues of four celestial kings that protect the place against evil. Close to the beach is **Komyo-ji**, a large temple established in 1243. There is a path on the right between the temple and the playground leading back up to the road above. On a clear day you can see Mount Fuji towering behind the beach and Enoshima island.

Down at the beach towards the east are the remains of **Wakaejima**, the first artificial port in Japan, built in 1232. It went into terminal decline when Kyoto was restored to being the Japanese capital.

Where to eat & stay

Kamakura is less than an hour from Tokyo by train, so it's easy to do the trip in a day. You can try a Japanese *kaiseki* meal at **Kaiko-tei** (3-7 Sakanoshita, Kamakura-shi, Kanagawa-ken, 0467 25 4494, ¥5,500 lunch, ¥7,000-¥13,000 dinner), an atmospheric restaurant that serves *soba* and *udon* at lunchtime.

On the pedestrianised shopping street near the east exit of Kamakura station, the friendly **T-Side** (Kotobuki Bldg 2F, 1-6-12 Komachi, Kamakura-shi, 0467 24 9572, lunch sets from ¥850) offers great Indian food.

Just outside the west exit of Kita-Kamakura station, the small *soba* shop **Yamamoto** (10.30am-4.30pm, closed Tue, 0467 22 3310, ¥600-¥900) serves tasty noodle dishes.

Facing the ocean in Inamuragasaki on the Enoden line, the **Taverna Rondino** (2-6-11 Inamuragasaki, Kamakura-shi, 0467 25 4355, set meals ¥2,500-¥6,500 plus à la carte in the evenings) serves Italian food. The bright yellow building also has a small outside terrace.

Tourist information

Kamakura City Tourist Information Service
1-1-1 Komachi, Kamakura Eki Konai, Kanagawa-ken (0467 22 3350). **Open** 9am-5pm daily. **English guides** ¥200.

Getting there

By train

It's possible to start sightseeing from either Kita-Kamakura or Kamakura stations. Both are on the JR Yokosuka line from Tokyo station. Fares are ¥780 and ¥890 respectively.

Mountains

Find the spiritual side of Japan, on a mountain peak within easy reach of Tokyo.

Mount Fuji

Once a pilgrimage, the climb to the summit of Mount Fuji is now an experience for all. Japan's highest mountain is renowned for its beauty and spiritual significance. Pilgrimages used to start at Hongu Fuji Sengen, a shrine established in AD 788 and dedicated to Konohanasakuya-hime, patron of Fuji and goddess of the volcano. Mount Fuji is now dormant and only a wisp of smoke wafts from the crater. The last eruption in 1707 covered Edo (now Tokyo), 100 kilometres (62 miles) away, with ash.

The pilgrimage was opened to women only a few years after the Meiji Restoration (*see p10*). The shrines on the way up doubled as inns; pilgrims would pray and rest at each stage before reaching the summit in time for *goraiko*, the sunrise. People still go up to see the sunrise, but most use transport to the fifth stage, where the road stops. Since Fuji is covered in snow most of the year, the climbing season is limited to July and August, although transport to the fifth stage is available from April until November (out of season the trails are open but facilities are closed). The best time is the middle four weeks of the official climbing season. The climb is worthwhile but not easy: a saying goes that there are two kinds of fools, those who never climb Fuji and those who climb it twice.

The climb typically starts from the fifth stage in the afternoon, and includes a sleep in the huts along the way before an early rise to reach the summit in time for *goraiko*. Try to get a weather forecast from the tourist information office before you set out, as the view from the peak may be obscured by cloud.

The temperature at the summit can be 20°C lower than at the base. The average in July is 4.9°C and in August 2.7°C. It's often below zero before sunrise. Essential items to take along include rainwear, torch, water and food (available at huts, but not cheap). Don't forget toilet paper and some bags for your rubbish.

However you decide to approach Fuji, the only way up from the fifth stage is to walk. On the Kawaguchiko side the 7.5-kilometre (4.7-mile) climb takes five hours, the descent about three. From Gotemba (south side) it's six and a half hours up and three down. From the western fifth stage it's a five-hour ascent and three and a half hours to come down.

Some start the climb later in the evening from the fifth stages to avoid staying in the huts. These can cost over ¥7,000 for the few hours, are basic, and busy with people coming and going. Don't expect a good night's sleep. Camping is prohibited – and there's no grassy or soft area for a kip under the stars.

It's still possible to do the climb from the base through the nine stages. You start at **Hongu Fuji Sengen Shrine** and follow the old pilgrim route, the Yoshidaguchi Trail. The shrine is in Fujiyoshida (20 minutes' walk from the station, two stops from Kawaguchiko, *see below* **Getting there**) and it takes up to five hours to the fifth stage. The trail is quiet, passing historical buildings and monuments.

There's not much to do on the summit but enjoy the views and walk around the 220-metre-deep (722 feet) crater, contemplating your own insignificance in the galactic scheme of things.

Tourist information

Kawaguchiko Tourist Information *In front of Kawaguchiko station, 3631-5 Funatsu, Kawaguchiko-Machi (0555 72 6700).* **Open** 8.30am-6pm daily.

Yamanashi Prefectural Fuji Visitors' Centre *6663-1 Kenmarubi, Funatsu, Kawaguchiko-Machi (0555 72 0259).* **Open** *Mar-Jun, Oct-Nov* 9am-5pm Tue-Sun. *July-Sept* 9am-6pm Tue-Sun. *Dec-Feb* 9am-4pm Tue-Sun.

Getting there

By bus

Fastest and cheapest way to Kawaguchiko, main starting point for a Fuji trip, is by bus from Nishi Shinjuku's Keio Shinjuku Expressway Bus Terminal. Fare is ¥1,700 each way; journey time 1hr 45mins. Buses leave regularly from opposite the main Yodobashi Camera store. From the Keio bus terminal at Kawaguchiko station to the fifth stage the fare is ¥1,700 one way or ¥2,000 return. There are five buses a day Apr-Nov (no buses Dec-Mar). There are also six daily buses direct to the fifth stage from Shinjuku (fare ¥2,600 one way). For info call Keio Teito Dentetsu reservation centre (5376 2222).

By train

JR Kaisoku rapid trains (¥2,390) leave Shinjuku in the early evening (with an extra morning service at weekends) and take 2.5-3hrs. Change at Otsuki to the Fuji Kyuko line – timetables can be checked with JR in Otsuki (0554 22 0125) or Fuji Kyuko in

Mount Fuji: don't climb it twice.

Kawaguchiko (0555 72 2911). From Kawaguchiko station to the fifth stage by bus takes another hour.

You can also climb Fuji from the south side, starting at one of two new fifth stages, one near Gotemba, another further west. There are four direct trains daily on the Odakyu line (express Asagiri) from Shinjuku to Gotemba, taking 2hrs and costing ¥2,720. From Gotemba there are three to four buses to the new fifth stage (July, Aug only); taking 1hr and costing ¥1,500 one way or ¥2,000 return.

Mount Takao

Most of Tokyo lies in the Kanto Plain and is surrounded by mountains. Most of these mountainous areas, with the exception of the main valleys, have remained in their natural state; Mount Takao, an hour west of Shinjuku, is a favourite getaway. Like Fuji, a sacred mountain, it has managed to retain some tranquillity despite many visitors. The main route to the 600-metre (1,969-foot) summit is often busy and has tourist attractions along the way, but other paths leading to the top and circling the mountain are more peaceful. On a clear day you can see the sprawl of the city on one side and on the other a mountain range with Fuji towering in the background.

From the station a brick-lined path lined with restaurants and shops leads to the base of the mountain. This is also the boarding area for the cable car and chairlifts to the observatory (¥470). The start of the main path (hiking course No.1) to the observatory is steep, so you may appreciate the option.

The principal attraction along the main path, **Yakuoin Temple**, was founded in 744 and has large grounds. It's one of few temples around Tokyo dedicated to Tengu, the long-nosed goblin. The other path leading to the top (hiking course No.6) starts to the left of the cable car and is a slow steady climb, except for the last stretch. It's a popular but quiet path where passers-by will say '*konnichiwa*' (hello). It runs alongside a stream, and there are religious artefacts in the woods along the way, plus a temple by a waterfall. Information boards describe the local flora and fauna. The course can be done in about an hour.

Mount Takao is probably most crowded during the fire-walking festival, usually the second Sunday of March.

Where to eat

The approach to the mountain is dotted with *soba* shops and run-of-the-mill cafés, but for a special Japanese dining experience, **Ukai Toriyama** (3426 Minami Asakawa-cho, Hachioji-shi, 0426 61 0739, 11am-8pm daily) is the place to go. Nestled in a steep valley a few minutes from town, it consists of several traditional-style buildings, seating two to 25 people, in a large manicured garden with ponds. Free buses run from the station. It serves seasonal food from the area for around ¥7,000 a head. Menus are in English and reservations are highly recommended.

Tourist information

Hachioji City Office *Moto-Hongo 3-24-1, Hachioji-shi (0426 26 3111/fax 0426 26 2381).*
Open 8.30am-7pm Mon-Fri.

Getting there

By train

Catch the Keio line from Shinjuku station to the end of the line at Takao-san Guchi. It takes less than an hour and costs only ¥370. Another option is to take the JR Chuo line to the terminal at Mount Takao: a special rapid from Tokyo will take a little over an hour and cost ¥890. You then transfer to the Keio line for Takao-san Guchi (a further ¥120).

Beaches

Surf and sand are just an hour out of town.

Like just about everything else in Japan, beaches have their official season, falling in July and August. Outside this period, beaches are usually quiet, though surfers and other sporty types congregate even in winter. Come summer, swarms of cafés and restaurants open up, along with plenty of shops where you can buy and hire equipment for sports and activities. The infrastructure and facilities are well organised and dependable, especially at Tokyo's nearest beaches, just over an hour out of town. As a rule, the more distant the beach the more attractive it will be, though it won't necessarily be any less crowded.

Kamakura & Enoshima

Closest to Tokyo, Kamakura's beaches are also some of the busiest. In summer it's hard to find a spot to lie in, and, in part due to their popularity, the beaches are not the cleanest – but that doesn't deter anyone, especially the young and beautiful. The east exit of the station leads to Wakamiya-dori, Kamakura's main street, from which a right turn and a 15-minute walk brings you to the shore. On the left is the Nameri river and then **Zaimokuza beach**, on the right lies **Yuigahama beach**. It stretches to Inamuragasaki Point, and on the other side is another long sandy expanse to Koyurugi Point, just before **Enoshima**, a picturesque island connected to the mainland by a bridge.

The beach facing Enoshima island is nicknamed the Oriental Miami Beach. With many tourist attractions and facilities, it's a magnet for families. It's also as busy as Kamakura, with similar sands, so arriving early is a good idea. Popular activities are yachting, surfing, fishing and, at the western end, cycling.

The five-kilometre (three-mile) beach has been popular since the Meiji era. The town itself is quiet and one of the few attraction is **Ryuko-ji** (Dragon's Mouth Temple), where the priest Nichiren is said to have escaped execution as lightning broke the sword that was about to behead him. The temple was founded in 1337 and its many old wooden buildings include a five-storey pagoda.

The island of Enoshima is also a popular religious site with a history going back 1,000 years. The main approach across the bridge turns into a shopping street that climbs over the mountainous island to reach the western side. The island has three shrines: Hetsunomiya; Nakatsunomiya, founded in AD 853 and rebuilt in 1689; and Okutsunomiya. The main path up and across the island leads through the three shrines and a botanical garden at the island's peak. There are escalators to help the climb, each costing ¥100 to ¥200, but they only go a short distance.

As the path descends towards the shore on the other side, the restaurants on the left offer views of Mount Fuji and a respite from walking. From the rocks by the sea another path leads to caves hollowed out by waves. They can be visited in about 20 minutes; entry is ¥500.

Ryuko-ji

3-13-37 Katase, Fujisawa-shi, Kanagawa-ken (0466 25 7357). **Open** 10am-4pm daily. **Admission** free.

Getting there

By train

Kamakura: trains go directly to Kamakura from Tokyo station (¥890; Yokosuka line); journey time 55mins.

Katase Enoshima: the Odakyu line goes directly from Shinjuku to Katase Enoshima. The local train takes around 85mins and costs ¥610. Express trains run regularly, cost ¥1,210 and take about 70mins.

The historic Enoden railway line also connects Kamakura and Enoshima (23mins; five times an hour; ¥250). The JR Kamakura-Enoshima Free Kippu ticket, valid for two days, gives unlimited access to JR trains, the Enoden railway and Shonan monorail between Ofuna, Fujisawa, Enoshima and Kamakura. It costs ¥1,970 and allows one return trip to Tokyo.

Izu Peninsula & islands

This popular resort area is one of the most seismically active regions in Japan, though most of the quakes that occur are too small to be felt. As a result of this activity the region is dotted with *onsen* (natural hot spring baths), the most accessible in towns along the east coast, which the train line follows. The terminus is at **Shimoda**, where special US envoy Commodore Perry arrived with his Black Ships in 1853 (*see p9*). There's plenty to do in Shimoda, and attractions include a small castle, a floating aquarium and a cable car up Mount Nesugata, from where the peninsula and the Izu Islands are visible.

Trips Out of Town

Enoshima: a shrine for surfers. *See p272.*

The main beach around Shimoda is **Shirahama**, three kilometres (two miles) north-east of the town and a short bus ride from the station. It stretches over 700 metres (2,330 feet,) divided in the middle by a rocky outcrop topped by a *torii* (Japanese gate). The side nearest Shimoda has restaurants and shops along the road and is the closest thing to a 'beach town' near Tokyo. It's packed with swimmers and surfers, even out of season. There are other beaches around Shimoda – a few without any concrete in sight – all accessible by bus or taxi.

There's also a bus from Shimoda that cuts across the peninsula to **Matsuzaki** in about 45 minutes. The part of town near the port has some historic buildings and old neighbourhoods. More buses lead to beaches and smaller towns along the west coast. The waters are even clearer on this side and there are famous diving spots around – notably Mikomoto Island, Kumomi, Ita/Ose.

Between the peninsula and Tokyo lie the Seven Izu Islands, although there are more. Geologically part of the Izu Peninsula, they're administered by the Tokyo Metropolitan Government. The main island is **Oshima**, famous for its volcano (an eruption forced the island's evacuation in 1986), beaches, camping and *onsen* (hot spring baths). The main surfing beaches are **Kobohama**, **Sanohama** and **Fudeshima**. Nearby lie the smaller islands of **Niijima** and **Shikinejima**, the former with many beautiful clean beaches with good waves for surfing and the latter with small beaches for swimming. These three islands are easier to access than ones further south.

Getting there

Shimoda: take the Odoriko train from Tokyo or Shinagawa stations. It takes about two and a half hours and costs ¥5,480 to ¥6,460 each way.

Izu Islands: a ferry leaves Takeshiba Pier near Hamamatsucho station around 10pm daily in summer (Fri-Sun in winter), arriving in Oshima very early (¥3,810-¥11,430), then stopping at Niijima and Shikinejima (both an extra ¥1,130). The return boat leaves in the early afternoon and arrives in Tokyo about 10pm. Contact Tokai Chisen for info (5472 9009) or reservations (5472 9999) between 9.30am-8pm daily. There are also direct 35-min flights from Haneda airport to Oshima.

Boso Peninsula

East of Tokyo across the bay lies the Boso Peninsula, a favourite destination of daytrippers because of its mountains and beaches. The beaches are concentrated near the towns of Tateyama, Chikura, Katsura and Onjuku, but the most famous – especially for surfing – is **Kujukurihama** on the east coast.

Kujukurihama stretches 60 kilometres (38 miles) between Cape Taito and Cape Gyobu and can get rough since it's open on to the Pacific Ocean. To the south on the Sotobo line are **Katsura** and **Onjuku**, both of which have a number of beaches. Every morning except Wednesday, Katsura has a fair dating back 400 years. South on the Uchibo line, there is surfing around **Chikura**, **Setohama** and **Maebara**. On the other side of the peninsula, **Tateyama** has various bathing beaches, **Kagamigaura** being the busiest. Between Tateyama and Chikura at the tip of the peninsula are beaches accessible only by road.

Getting there

It's possible to do a circular trip of the peninsula on the JR Uchibo and Sotobo lines, as they meet at Awa-Kamogawa on the east coast. Both lines leave from Tokyo station; the Uchibo goes along Tokyo Bay (¥2,940 but no direct trains) while the Sotobo (¥4,020 direct Express train or ¥2,210 local) cuts across to follow the Pacific shore south of Kujukurihama.

Nikko

One of Japan's greatest treasures, and home to the three wise monkeys.

Nikko has been famous for its natural beauty since it became a centre of mountain worship more than 1,200 years ago. Eight centuries later, the first shogun, Tokugawa Ieyasu, was so impressed by the place that he chose to be enshrined and buried here. Today, Toshogu Shrine and Shinkyo Bridge, the sacred river crossing, are among Japan's biggest attractions, with over seven million visitors a year.

Nikko means 'sunlight', and the name derives from nearby Futarasan, now called Mount Nantai, home of the goddess Kannon. The priest Shodo Shonin established a centre for Buddhist asceticism on the mountain, and temples flourished, drawing many religious, military and government figures to the area.

Other sights not to be missed around Nikko include Taiyuin Shrine, Lake Chuzenji and Kegon Falls. Also around town are Rinno-ji and Futarasan temples, Ganmangafuchi Abyss, several museums and the botanical gardens. Further out is a vast national park, a popular place for sightseeing, *onsen* (natural hot springs), hiking, camping, boating, skiing and skating.

Nikko is two hours from Tokyo, right at the edge of the Kanto Plain, where the mountains start to rise. From either of the two stations it's a 25-minute walk or five-minute bus ride (¥190; from either platform at Tobu station) to Shinkyo. Antiques shops and restaurants line the main road, many with signs in English. The local delicacy, *yuba* (soy milk skin), features prominently on menus and in souvenir shops.

The road to the left at Shinkyo leads to Lake Chuzenji via the newer part of Nikko, which is filled with souvenir shops. Toshogu and the other temples and shrines are in the national park across the road, ten minutes' walk away.

Shinkyo Bridge

According to legend, the first bridge across the Daiyagawa river was made by two snakes to allow priest Shodo Shonin through on his pilgrimage to Futarasan. In reality, the bridge was built at the same time as Toshogu and is its main approach.

Destroyed by floods in 1902 and rebuilt five years later, Shinkyo Bridge is such a draw with tourists that it's being rebuilt again and is due to reopen some time in 2005.

Rinno-ji, Toshogu, Futarasan & Taiyuin

The cluster of religious buildings on the far side of the bridge includes Rinno-ji, Toshogu, Futarasan and Taiyuin. Entrance fees are ¥900, ¥1,300, ¥200 and ¥550 respectively, but combined tickets for ¥1,000 are available in front of Rinno-ji. The ticket also allows entry to Yakushido (inside Toshogu Shrine), though not to the Sleeping Cat, Tokugawa Ieyasu's mausoleum, or Shin'en in the grounds of Futarasan.

Rinno-ji's main hall is called Sanbutsudo (Three Buddhas). Founded in AD 766, it's the largest temple in the area. Inside are a few artefacts and statues, including the large golden-wood statues of the Three Buddhas. They stand over five metres (16 feet) high, depicting Amida Buddha, the Thousand-armed Kannon and the Horse-headed Kannon. The exit leads to Sorinto, a tall pillar to repel evil, built in 1643, as well as another hall.

Located in front of Sanbutsudo is Rinno-ji Treasure House (8am-4pm daily), where more artefacts from the temple are displayed. Next door is the Edo-style Shoyo-en Garden (¥300), with a 200-year-old cherry tree so revered it has been declared a national monument. On the left of Sanbutsudo stands a black gate, Kuremon, and the path that leads to Toshogu.

Toshogu (summer 8am-5pm daily, winter 8am-4pm daily; last entry 30 minutes before closing time) is the main attraction, and should not be missed even though its flamboyance gets mixed reactions. The buildings include both Shinto and Buddhist elements, and some are more Chinese than Japanese in design. Nearly all are brightly painted with extremely ornate and intricate carvings. The grounds are usually packed from morning, but quieten down towards the end of the afternoon.

Toshogu was built during the reign of the third shogun, Iemitsu, according to instructions left by Tokugawa Ieyasu himself, who died in 1616. It's not clear when work began, but Toshogu was completed in 1636. The finest craftspeople were brought in and it's said that as many as 15,000 people took part in the construction.

Hey hey, we're the three wise monkeys.

After the first *torii* (gate) is a five-storey pagoda built in 1818. Up the stairs is Otemon, also known as the Deva gate after its statues, said to scare away evil spirits. The building on the left after the gate is Shinkyusha (Sacred Stable), where the sacred horse lives. It's the only unpainted building in the grounds, famous for its set of eight carvings of the Sanzaru (three monkeys) representing the ideal way of life ('hear no evil, see no evil, speak no evil'). The three buildings from the right of Otemon are repositories for costumes and other items used in festivals.

To the left at the top of the stairs is Yakushido, famous for the dragon painted on the ceiling and for the roaring echo, which the priest regularly demonstrates. There are also a dozen old statues inside.

The next gate is Yomeimon, meaning 'twilight gate'. Its 400 carvings reputedly make it the most elaborate in Japan. Following is Karamon, leading to the oratory and the main hall. These two gates are decorated in the Chinese style with a dragon, phoenix and other imaginary creatures. The oratory's entrance has more dragon carvings, and inside are another 100 more.

To the right of Karamon is the entrance to the shoguns' mausoleum (an extra ¥500 if you hold the combined ticket). At the top of the first door is the carving of the Nemurineko (Sleeping Cat), famed for depicting the Buddhist question and answer: 'What about a sleeping kitten under peonies in bloom? I would have nothing to do with it.' The stairs lead up the mountain to a quiet and secluded area with two small buildings simply painted in blue and gold, and behind is the mausoleum.

Toshogu's festivals take place on 17 and 18 May and 17 October. On 17 May there's horseback archery in hunting attire of the Middle Ages, held in front of the shrine, while on 18 May the Sennin Gyoretsu procession recreates the transfer of the remains of Ieyasu. The 1,000 people taking part are dressed as samurai, priests and others in the style of the days of the shogun. The 17 October festival combines both, but on a smaller scale.

The path leading to the left before the entrance *torii* goes to the **Toshogu Treasure Museum** (Apr-Nov 8am-5pm daily, Dec-Mar 8am-4pm daily; last entry 30 minutes before closing; admission ¥800), where a small selection of the treasures is exhibited on a rotational basis.

The second path to the left (between the pagoda and Otemon) leads to **Futarasan Temple**, one building from a group of four, the others located on the summit of Mount Nantai, the shore of Lake Chuzenji and the bank of the Daiyagawa river. Exhibits and access inside this temple are quite limited.

Further on is **Taiyuin Shrine** (Apr-Nov 8am-5pm daily; Dec-Mar 8am-4pm daily), where the third shogun, Iemitsu, is buried. It was built in 1652, in the Buddhist style only, and while similar in tone to Toshogu, it's not as extravagant and extensive. The first gate has Nio (heavenly kings) guardian figures; soon after comes Nitenmon Gate, with statues of Komokuten and Jikokuten, two Buddhist deities. The next gate is Yashamon, with four statues of Yashan, and the last is Karamon, before the hall of worship. A few artefacts and old treasures are displayed inside. A walk around the main hall leads to Kokamon Gate and towards the mausoleum, though this is locked at all times.

Back near Shinkyo at the Daiyagawa river, there's a trail that leads upstream to the **Ganmangafuchi Abyss**, famous for a series of old mossy statues along a stretch of the river filled with large volcanic rocks.

Lake Chuzenji & Kegon Falls

Lake Chuzenji is the most popular example of Nikko's famed natural beauty. The lake attracts tourists for swimming, fishing and boating, with many campsites and hiking trails nearby. At **Kegon Falls**, the lake's waters plunge 100 metres (328 feet) into the Daiyagawa river. The falls, which include 12 minor cascades, are reputedly among Japan's finest – especially so in winter when they freeze over. Nearby is the **Chanokidaira ropeway**, and from the top are views of the lake, Kegon Falls and Mount Nantai. There's also a botanical garden with alpine plants.

North of the lake, **Mount Nantai** rises to almost 2,400 metres (7,877 feet). There is a crater at the top, but most climbers making the five-hour ascent (between May and October only) do so for religious reasons, to visit Okumiya Shrine. The side of the mountain gets crowded with worshippers during its festival (31 July-8 August).

There are buses from both train stations to Chuzenji Spa. The Tobu buses cost ¥1,100 each way and depart from either platform.

Where to stay & eat

Although it's possible to take a day trip to Nikko, there are the following atmospheric hotels if you want to stay longer. One of the oldest hotels in Japan, the **Nikko Kanaya Hotel** (1300 Kamihachiisi-machi, Nikko-shi, Tochigi-ken, 0288 54 0001/www.kanayahotel.co.jp, rates ¥8,000-¥35,000) opened for business in 1873. It's a five-minute ride from either station on a Tobu bus (¥190) heading for Nishisando, Kiyotaki, Okuhosoo, Chuzenji or Yumoto onsen. Get off at the Shinkyo stop.

Another option is the **Nikko Tamozawa Hotel** (2010 Hanaishi-machi, Nikko-shi, Tochigi-ken, 0288 54 1152, rates ¥8,000-¥15,000), a 12-minute ride on the same buses. Alight at Rengeseki Tamozawa.

There's also the **Turtle Inn Nikko**, a small inn by the river near Shinkyo (2-16 Takumi-cho, Nikko-shi, Tochigi-ken, 0288 53 3168/www.sunfield.ne.jp/~turtle/index.htm, rates ¥4,200-¥5,000). It has an annex (8-28 Takumi-cho, Nikko-shi, Tochigi-ken, 0288-53-3663/same URL, rates ¥5,800) a few minutes away. Get off at the Sogo Kaikanmae bus stop for either. Staff speak English.

It would be a shame to leave Nikko without trying *yuba*, the local skin of soya milk speciality. **Gyoushin-Tei** (2339-1 Yamauchi, Nikko, Tochigi-ken, 0288 53 3751, 11am-7pm, closed Thur) is set in a 12th-century garden, where it serves *yuba* in *shojin ryori* (¥3,500) or *kaiseki ryori* (¥5,000) courses. **Enya** (443 Ishiya-Machi, Nikko, 0288 53 5605, 11am-2pm, 5-11pm, closed Mon) offers a selection of Japanese and western meat dishes with over 80 different beers from around the world.

Tourist information

Tobu Nikko Station Information Centre *Tobu Nikko station, 4-3 Matsubara-cho, Nikko, Tochigi-ken (0288 53 4511).* **Open** 8.30am-5pm daily.
Nikko Information Centre *591 Goko-Machi, Nikko, Tochigi-ken (0288 53 3795).* **Open** 9am-5pm daily.

Getting there

By train

Two rail lines, Tobu and Japan Railways (JR) go to Nikko and terminate at separate but near-neighbouring stations in the centre of town. Tobu trains are faster and cheaper, and their bus service to the sights is more regular. The Tobu terminal in Tokyo is at Asakusa. Limited express trains go directly to Tobu Nikko station, leaving about every hour from 7.30am.

They cost ¥2,740 each way and take around 1hr 50mins. Other express trains stop at Shimo-Imaichi, requiring a local train ride to Tobu Nikko (a few minutes away). Local trains from Asakusa are the cheapest, at ¥1,320, and take 30mins longer, stopping at most stations and requiring a change at Shimo-Imaichi. Tickets for local trains are always available before departure, but Limited Express trains can be full, so you should book, especially on weekends and holidays. Check with Tobu in Tokyo (03 3623 1171), 9.30am-6.30pm weekdays; to 5.30pm on weekends and holidays. JR trains leave from Tokyo or Ueno stations and require a transfer at Utsunomiya; tickets are ¥2,520. From there it's 45mins on a local train. Each Nikko station has a bus terminal with services to Lake Chuzenji and beyond.

Directory

Features

Directory

Getting Around

Arriving & leaving

To & from the airport

Tokyo International Airport at Narita is nearly 70km (45 miles) from Tokyo and well served by rail and bus links to the city.

JR's Narita Express (3423 0111/www.jreast.co.jp/e/index.html) rail service is the fastest way to get to Tokyo from Narita, but it's also the most expensive. Seats must be reserved and there's no standing room, so during particularly busy times you may have to wait around. All trains go to Tokyo station (¥2,940), with some also serving Shinjuku (¥3,110), Ikebukuro (¥3,110), Omiya (¥3,740) and Yokohama (¥4,180). Trains depart every 30-40 minutes.

The **Keisei Skyliner** (0476 32 8505 Narita/3831 0131 Ueno/www.keisei.co.jp/keisei/tetudou/accessj/index.htm), operated by a private rail company, is a cheaper option. Trains on this line will take you into Ueno station (¥1,920) in around an hour. Cheaper still is a Keisei limited express (Tokkyu), a regular train that makes a few stops on its 75-minute route to Ueno station (¥1,000).

Limousine buses (3665 7220/www.limousinebus.co.jp) also run regularly; fares are ¥3,000.

Taxis from the airport are recommended only for those with bottomless wallets: it costs from ¥30,000 yen and is often slower than the train.

It's more unlikely that you'll arrive at **Haneda International Airport**, which handles mainly internal flights. But if you do, Haneda is served by monorail (www.tokyo-monorail.co.jp) (¥470), which leaves every 5-10 minutes from 5.10am to 11.50pm, linking up to Hamamatsu-cho station on the JR Yamanote Line in a little over 20 minutes. The Keikyu line (045 441 0999/www.keikyu.co.jp) can take you to Shinagawa in central Tokyo in 19 minutes (¥400). Here you can link up with major JR lines.

Limousine buses from Haneda to Tokyo cost in the region of ¥1,000, depending on which part of the city you want to go to. A taxi will cost a minimum of ¥6,000.

Tokyo International Airport at Narita
Flight information & English-language enquiries 0476 34 5000/www.narita-airport.or.jp/airport/.

Haneda International Airport
Flight information 5757 8111/www.tokyo-airport-bldg.co.jp/index2.html.

Leaving town

By train

One of the fastest but most expensive ways to travel Japan's elongated countryside is by *shinkansen* bullet train. Tickets can be purchased at JR reservation 'Green Window' areas or travel agents, or online (Japanese only) at www.eki-net.com. Trains depart from different stations depending on destination; most leave from Tokyo or Ueno. Slower, cheaper trains go to many destinations. Marks on the train platforms show where the numbered carriages will stop. Most carriages have reserved seats only (reservations cost extra), but some carriages are set aside for unreserved seating on each train. Arrive early if you want to sit down.

By coach

Long-distance buses are one of the cheapest ways to travel, though anyone over five feet, six inches tall may find the seats small. Most long-distance buses leave at midnight and arrive early the next morning. All are air-conditioned and have ample space for luggage. Seats can be reserved through a travel agent. Long-distance buses are run by the railway companies. For information, see JR trains and private lines, below.

Tokyo Bus Association
5360 7111/www.tokyobus.or.jp/index.html.
The website and phone line provide information on all bus routes within and leaving Tokyo, in Japanese.

Public transport

Trains & subway

Tokyo has one of the world's most efficient train systems: in the rare event of delays in the morning rush, staff give out apology slips to office workers to show their bosses. Trains and subways are fast, clean, safe and reliable. Most stations have signs in English as well as Japanese, and signs telling you which exit to take. Subways and train lines are colour-coded.

Subways and trains operate from 5am to around midnight (JR lines slightly later). Rush hours are 7.30-9.30am and 5-7pm. The last train can be a nightmare.

Tokyo's rail network is run by several different companies, and changing trains between competing systems can mean paying for two tickets. Transfer tickets are usually available to take you from one line to another, but cost the same as buying two separate tickets. When travelling in Tokyo, try to stay on one network.

Tickets & passes

Japan Rail Pass

This provides for virtually unlimited travel on the national JR network, including *shinkansen* (bullet trains) and all JR lines in Tokyo. The pass cannot be used on the new 'Nozomi' super-express *shinkansen*. It's available only to visitors from abroad travelling under the entry status of 'temporary visitor', and must be purchased before coming to Japan. You must show your passport when changing the Exchange Order to a ticket. It costs from ¥28,300 for a week, about the same price as a middle-distance *shinkansen* return ticket. JR East, which runs trains in and around Tokyo, has its own version of the pass, which costs from ¥20,000 for five days. The same conditions apply.

Exchange Orders for the pass can be purchased at overseas offices of the Japan Travel Bureau International, Nippon Travel Agency, Kinki Nippon Tourist, Tokyu Tourist Corporation and other associated local travel agents, or at an overseas Japan Airlines office if you're travelling by Japan Airlines.

Suica

Suica is a prepaid travel pass issued by JR that contains an integrated circuit. Ticket gates detect the pass if it's swiped over the right point. The minimum fare is automatically deducted you're your balance on entry to the station, with the balance being picked up on exit at your destination. Suica cards can be purchased at JR 'Green Window' areas or at ticket machines. A card costs ¥2,000, including a ¥500 returnable deposit. Credit on the card can be topped up at ticket machines (up to ¥10,000).

Passnet

This advance purchase ticket covers all of Tokyo's railway lines, except for JR. Available in denominations from ¥1,000, it allows you to transfer from one operator's line to another without buying new tickets. The fare is automatically deducted from your remaining credit at the computerised ticket barriers. The ticket saves you only a small amount of cash, but does save fiddling for change.

Frequent-travel tickets

There's a huge number of frequent-travel tickets available, from pre-paid cards to 11-for-the-price-of-ten trip tickets. There are also combination tickets and one-day passes for one, two or three networks, though these are unlikely to be worth buying. For more details, call the JR East Infoline (3423 0111).

Regular tickets

Regular tickets for travelling in Tokyo can be purchased from vending machines at the station. Many vending machines will have a symbol on them to say which notes they accept. At many stations, the touch-screen vending machines can display information in English, but should you be unsure of your destination (or unable to read it from the Japanese map), buy a ticket for the minimum fare and settle up in a fare adjustment machine at the other end. All stations have them. Tokyo does not have punitive fines for travellers with incorrect tickets. Children under six travel free, under 12 pay half price.

Transferring from one line to another, provided it is run by the same operator (see below), will be covered in the price of your ticket. If your journey involves transferring from one network to another, you will have to buy a transfer ticket, if available. Or buy another ticket when you arrive at your transfer point.

Subways

Most subways are run by the Teito Rapid Transit Authority, which is often referred to as Eidan (www.tokyometro.go.jp/index.htm). Its eight lines are: Chiyoda (dark green), Ginza (orange), Hanzomon (purple), Hibiya (grey), Marunouchi (red), Namboku (light green), Tozai (turquoise) and Yurakucho (yellow).

Four subway lines are run by the metropolitan government. These 'Toei' (5322 0400/www.kotsu.metro.tokyo.jp/) lines are slightly more expensive. They are: Toei Asakusa Line (pale pink), Toei Mita Line (blue), Toei Oedo Line (bright pink) and Toei Shinjuku Line (green). If transferring from Eidan to Toei trains, buying a transfer ticket is ¥70 cheaper than buying separate tickets. For subway map, *see p312*.

JR trains

Overland trains in Tokyo are operated by Japan Railways East (JR). It's impossible to stay in Tokyo for more than a few hours without using JR's Yamanote Line, the loop that defines the city centre. All Tokyo's subway and rail lines connect at some point with the Yamanote Line (*see p309*).

JR's major lines in Tokyo are: Yamanote (green), Chuo (orange), Sobu (yellow) and Keihin Tohoku (blue).

JR also operates the long-distance trains and *shinkansen*, which run from Tokyo or Ueno stations.

Private lines

Tokyo's private lines mainly ferry commuters to the outlying districts of the city. Because most were founded by companies that also run department stores, they usually terminate inside, or next to, one of their branches.

The major private lines are run by Keio (3325 2121/ www.keio.co.jp), Odakyu (www.odakyu-group.co.jp), Seibu (www.seibu-group.co.jp/ railways), Tobu (3621 5061/ www.tobuland.com), Tokyu (5481 6866/www.tokyu.co.jp/ index_flash.html), Keisei and Keikyu (for both *see above* **Arriving & leaving**). You can pick up a full map showing all lines and subways from the Airport Information counter on arrival. The Keio lines are the only ones to offer women-only carriages on services after 11pm during the week.

Buses

Like the trains, buses here are run by several companies. Travelling by bus can be confusing if you're new to Japan, as signs are rarely in English. Toei and Keio bus fares cost ¥200, other buses are ¥210, no matter what the distance (half price for kids). Get on the bus at the front, and off at the back. Drop the exact fare into the slot in front of the driver. If you don't have it, use the change machine, normally to the right, which will deduct your fare from the change. Fare machines accept ¥50, ¥100 and ¥500 coins, and ¥1,000 notes. Stops are usually announced by a pre-recorded voice. A Toei bus route guide in English is available at Toei subway stations and hotels.

Cycling

The bicycle remains the most common form of local transport in Tokyo, and theft is rare, although unattended bikes should always be locked. Areas in and around stations are usually no-parking zones for bikes, a rule that locals gleefully ignore, but which can result in your bike being impounded.

Eight Rent

Sumitomo-seimei Bldg 1F, 31-16 Sakuragaoka-cho, Shibuya-ku (3462 2383). Shibuya station, south exit. **Open** 9am-6pm Mon-Fri. **Rates** ¥1,920 a day. Call to make an appointment. Bring your passport.

Jingu-Gaien Cycling Centre

10 Kasumigaoka-machi, Shinjuku-ku (3405 8753). Shinanomachi station. **Open** 10am-3.30pm Sun & public holidays.
Free of charge, but restricted to Jingu-Gaien.

Driving

Rental costs for garages are equivalent to those for small apartments in Tokyo, so if you rent a car you will have to pay astronomical parking fees (usually around ¥100 for 30 minutes, more in the centre). If you do decide to hire a car you'll need an international driving licence backed up by at least six months' driving experience. English-speaking rental assistance is available at many of the large hotels as well as at the airport.

Japan Automobile Federation (www.jaf.or.jp) publishes a 'Rules of the Road' guide in English. Call or visit one of the following branch offices to request one: 3-11-6 Otsuka, Bunkyo-ku (5976 9716); 2-4-5 Azabudai, Minato-ku (3578 1471).

A Metropolitan Expressway map, in English, is available from the Metropolitan Expressway Public Corporation, Isomura Bldg 5F, 1-1-3 Toranomon, Minato-ku (3580 1881).

If you want to drive outside Tokyo (much safer), JR offers rail and car rental packages. Call the JR East Infoline (3423 0111) for details.

Toyota Rent-a-lease

Narita International Airport Terminals 1 & 2 (0476 32 1020/fax 0476 32 1088/ http://rent.toyota.co.jp/top.asp). **Open** 7am-10pm daily. **Branches** throughout the city.

Walking

Tokyo is great for walking. There are no no-go areas, and the whole place is 99.9 per cent safe 24 hours a day. Walking is the best way to discover the hidden nooks and crannies that exist in nearly every neighbourhood. The TIC offers information on free walking tours of parts of Tokyo.

The worst thing about walking in Tokyo is the crowds. Because it's so safe here, Japanese people have no sense of personal space, and are often unaware of what's going on behind them. This results in colossal 'people jams'. People here also tend to walk at speeds associated with village fêtes, rather than capital cities, so be prepared to experience some frustration.

When crossing the road, always do so at marked crossings and always wait for the green man. If you cross on red, you may be responsible for the death of those behind you, who will blindly follow you into the traffic.

Taxis

Taxi fares begin at ¥660 for the first two kilometres and then keep climbing. Prices rise at weekends and between 11pm and 5am. Taxi stands are located near stations, most hotels, department stores and major intersections. The rear doors open automatically, so look out.

Hinomaru Limousine

Ark Hills Mori Bldg, 1-12-32 Akasaka, Minato-ku (3505 1717/ fax 3589 2445).
Stretch limos and the like, with English-speaking chauffeurs.

Guided tours

Bus tours

Hato Bus Tokyo Sightseeing Tour Company

World Trade Centre Bldg, 2-4-1 Hamamatsucho, Minato-ku (3435 6081/fax 3433 1972/www.hatobus.co.jp/english/index.html). Hamamatsucho station, south exit. **Bookings** 9am-7pm daily. **Credit** AmEx, DC, MC, V.
Offers a variety of tours, including half-day, full-day and night tours with English-speaking guides. Only the Edo Tokyo tour requires advance booking, with seats subject to availability on other tours. Prices for tours start at around ¥4,000; the Amazing Night Tour is the most expensive, at ¥14,000. Tour buses usually depart from Tokyo station.

Japan Gray Line Company

3-3-3 Nishi-Shinbashi, Minato-ku (3433 5745/fax 3433 8388/ www.jgl.co.jp/inbound/index.htm). Shinbashi station. **Bookings** 7am-5.45pm daily. **Credit** AmEx, DC, MC, V.
A selection of morning, afternoon and evening tours of the biggest sights the city has to offer, in English. Prices range from ¥4,000-¥15,000. Buses pick up at many hotels.

Sunrise Tours

JTB Bldg 14F, 2-3-11 Higashi-Shinagawa, Shinagawa-ku (5796 5454/www.jtb.co.jp/sunrisetour/index.html). Shinagawa station, Konan (east) exit. **Bookings** 9am-6pm Mon-Fri. **Credit** AmEx, DC, MC, V.
Run by leading travel agent Japan Travel Bureau, Sunrise provides the widest range of English-language tours in Tokyo, and also offers trips out of town to Mount Fuji (*see p270*), Tokyo Disney Resort (*see p122*) and the hot springs of Hakone (*see p262*), plus full-day, half-day or night-time tours of the city. Telephone enquiries for Tokyo tours can be made at any time of day or night.

By taxi

Tokyo Jumbo Hire

4-26-3 Aoto, Katsushika-ku (5629 8188/www.jet-harmony.com). **Bookings** 9am-6pm Mon-Fri. **No credit cards.**
If you feel like seeing the city in style, splash out on a taxi tour. Prices are based on four people travelling together. Four-hour courses start at ¥28,000; an eight-hour ride will set you back ¥49,000. Because of a shortage of English-speaking drivers, it is best to book in advance.

On foot

Mr Oka's Walking Tours of Tokyo

(0422 51 7673/www5d.biglobe.ne.jp/ ~mroka). **Telephone** 7-10pm only. **No credit cards.**
Reitred historian Oka-san offers a variety of informative introductory walking tours of Tokyo in English, ranging in price from ¥2,000 to ¥4,000. Private tours can be arranged for parties of up to ten people. The fee does not include any necessary transportation costs. No matter how much you think you know, you're bound to pick up some informative snippet, as Mr Oka's passion for Tokyo is matched only by his detailed knowledge.

Taxis

Taxi drivers in Tokyo wear blue uniforms with a peaked cap, and sparkling white gloves. Virtually all of them drive Toyota Crowns, a Japan-only model that is powered by liquid petroleum gas for reasons of economy and because they have lower emissions.

Generally speaking, Tokyo taxi drivers are courteous to their customers and hell on wheels for any other road users. Nervous passengers may care to close their eyes or wear dark glasses.

As is the case with London's black-cab drivers, Tokyo taxi drivers are supposedly obliged to accept fares for short journeys. In practice, a non-Japanese customer standing in the pouring rain in Shinjuku at 2am is likely to be completely ignored by taxis in favour of the hordes of Japanese clients in the area. Since the drivers control the back doors, a backseat hijack, London-style, is out of the question. In fairness, Tokyo drivers' reluctance may be down to nervousness about communication, since not many of them know the city intimately, and they often require directions to reach a destination. Things have improved recently on this front, since nearly all taxis are now fitted with programmable global positioning satellite equipment, which can tell the driver where to make a turn.

If you do speak Japanese, taxi drivers can turn out to be garrulous companions. This may be more than you've bargained for on the way home after a hard night on the tiles.

Smoking is the norm in all Japanese cabs, and though drivers are required by law to keep their cabs clean, many wait until the ashtrays overflow before putting the rubber gloves on.

If you have a dispute with a taxi driver, he or she will take you to the nearest *koban*, or police box, where you can resolve it together. The driver usually wins.

Resources A-Z

Age restrictions

There is no age of consent in Japan, and the legal age for smoking and drinking is 20, although the ubiquity of vending machines makes the law virtually impossible to enforce. The minimum voting age is also 20.

Attitude & etiquette

Japanese people are generally forgiving of visitors' clumsy attempts at correct behaviour, but there are certain rules that must be followed to avoid offending your hosts.

Shoes: when entering a house, temple or Japanese-style hotel, remove your shoes. Wear shoes that are easy to pull off and on, and make sure your socks are in good condition.

Blowing your nose: while it's common to hear old men hawking up great gobs of phlegm, for some reason it's considered rude to blow one's nose in public. If you really must do it, go to the toilet.

For bathing etiquette, *see below*. For business etiquette, *see p283*.

Bathing

Bathing is one of the great delights of Japanese life, and every area has a *sento* (public bath) identified by a sign that looks like flames coming out of a handleless frying pan.

Bathing can be enjoyed without heading out of town to the *onsen* of Hakone (*see p262*). *Sento* are perhaps the last urban bastions of 'Japanese-ness'. Though rapidly disappearing from the city centre, nostalgia and necessity have kept bathhouse culture alive in residential Tokyo, and there is a singular pleasure to be had from an hour of simply scrubbing and dipping on a cold, hungover afternoon.

Few overseas visitors to Tokyo ever get as far as the *sento*. This may be due mostly to unfamiliarity – but certainly, inhibitions about public nudity and the strictly adhered-to rules of the *sento* can also dampen enthusiasm. There's little to add to the topic of communal nakedness, but *sento* rules are relatively straightforward.

Upon entering, pay at the *bandai* (usually an aged mama-san sits there) before going through to your changing room, where you fully undress. No towels or any items of clothing are allowed in the bath area. Stow away all belongings in a locker and enter the bathing area. Close the door firmly behind you. Pick up a stool and bucket from a stack near the door and select a 'scrubbing station'.

Here, wash yourself thoroughly (using this opportunity to become acclimatised to the scalding water), before entering one of an array of tubs, some of which can, for the uninitiated, be extremely hot.

Make sure that no soap, either on your body or in your hand, follows you into the bath. It is for soaking in, not washing in. Never put your head under water or immerse your washcloth.

At the time of going to press, admission to all *sento* is pegged at ¥400. If you have a tattoo or have had too much to drink, you will be refused entry.

Aqua

4-9-22, Higashi-Nakano, Nakano-ku (5330 1126). Higashi-Nakano station west exit, exit A1. **Open** 3pm-midnight Tue-Sun.

A modern *sento* with a variety of baths, including a *rotemburo* (outside bath) and sauna. Stocks cold beers.

Daikoku-yu

32-6 Senju Kotobuki-cho, Adachi-ku (3881 3001). Kita-Senju station, west exit, then 15min walk. **Open** 3pm-midnight Tue-Sun.

A beautifully structured bathhouse of classic Japanese design. It is serenely spacious, and houses its own *rotemburo*. Also has cold beer in stock.

Hakusan-yu

2-28-11 Narita-Higashi, Suginami-ku (3311 2396). Shin-Koenji station, exit 1 then 15min walk. **Open** 4-11.30pm Mon-Wed, Fri-Sun.

Retains the essential charm of a neighbourhood bathhouse. There's no beer here, but it does have a *denkiburo* (electric bath).

Travel advice

For up-to-date information on travel to a specific country – including the latest news on safety and security, health issues, local laws and customs – contact your home country government's department of foreign affairs. Most have websites packed with useful advice for would-be travellers.

Australia
www.dfat.gov.au/travel

Canada
www.voyage.gc.ca

New Zealand
www.mft.govt.nz/travel

Republic of Ireland
www.irlgov.ie/iveagh

UK
www.fco.gov.uk/travel

USA
http://travel.state.gov/travel

Shimizu-yu
3-12-3, Minami-Aoyama, Minato-ku (3401 4404). Omotesando station. **Open** 4pm-midnight Tue-Sun. Located in the heart of Omotesando.

Tamano-yu
1-13-7, Asuguyu Kilu, Suginami-ku (3338 7860). Asagaya station, north exit. **Open** 3.30pm-1am Tue-Sun. Tamano-yu is a recently renovated, traditional *sento* with a number of novelty tubs, including a *denkiburo*.

Business

Etiquette

Doing business in Japan is a very different proposition to doing it in the west. Japanese place great emphasis on personal relationships between business partners, and socialising before and after the deal is done is de rigueur.

- Carry plenty of business cards. You will be spraying them around like confetti.
- When out eating with a group, wait for your comrades to indicate your seat.
- Do not write on another person's business card. During a meeting, keep the cards that you have just received face up on the table.
- If you need an interpreter, hire one of your own and ask them to interpret body language for you.
- Never offer to split a restaurant bill. Just say thank you if someone else is paying.
- If you receive a gift from your host, do not open it in front of them. If you give a gift, make sure it is professionally wrapped.
- Be prepared to give details of your personal life in a way that would be inappropriate elsewhere.

Chambers of commerce

American Chamber of Commerce *3433 5381/fax 3433 8454/ www.accj.or.jp.*

Australian & New Zealand Chamber of Commerce *5214 0710/fax 5214 0712/www2.gol.com/ users/anzccj/.*

British Chamber of Commerce *3267 1901/fax 3267 1903/ www.bccjapan.com.*

Canadian Chamber of Commerce *3556 9566/fax 3556 9567/ www.cccj.or.jp.*

Delivery services

Federal Express *0120 003200/www.fedex.com.*

Hubnet Ltd *0120 881084/www.hub-net.co.jp.*

UPS Yamato Express *0120 271040/www.ups.com.*

General information

JETRO (Japan External Trade Organisation) *3582 5511/ www.jetro.go.jp/top-j/index.html.*

Graphic design

Kinko's *0120 001 966 toll-free/ www.kinkos.co.jp.*
A complete range of print services.

Office space

Servcorp *5288 5100/www.servcorp.net/offices@servcorp.net.*
Has several locations in Tokyo with executive service starting from ¥250,000 yen per month plus deposit.

Public relations

IRI *Hatchobori Building 7F, 2-19-8, Hatchobori, Chuo-ku (5543 1221/ www.iri-japan.co.jp/fax 5543 1250/ info@iri-japan.co.jp). Hatchobori station, exit A5.*

Kyodo PR *7-2-22 Ginza, Chuo-ku (3571 5171/www.kyodo-pr.co.jp/fax 3571 8171/info@kyodo-pr.co.jp). Ginza station, exit C3.*

Secretarial service

Telephone Secretary Centre *5413 7320/gh6m-situ@asahi-net.or.jp.*
An answering service (¥10,000 a month). Service includes bilingual secretaries, word processing and typing. Free Japanese lessons for new customers are thrown in.

Telephone answering service

Bell24 System *3590 4646/ freephone 0120 600 024/www. tas.bell24.co.jp.*
Services start from ¥15,000, but bilingual service is provided at a slightly higher cost.

Translation

Simul International *Tranomon 34 MT Bldg 1F, 1-25-5 Toranomon, Minato-ku (3539 3900/www.simul. co.jp). Toranomon station, exits 1, 4.*

Transpacific Enterprises
Orizuru Bldg 201, 3-11-12 Shibasaki, Tachikawa-shi (042 528 8282/fax 042 529 3350/www. transpacific.jp/enterprises/index.html). Tachikawa station.

Customs

The following limits are imposed on travellers coming into Japan: 200 cigarettes or 250g of tobacco; three 750ml bottles of spirits; 57g of perfume; gifts or souvenirs up to ¥200,000.

Penalties are severe for drug importation: deportation is the lenient penalty. Pornography laws are very strict, too; anything showing pubic hair may be confiscated.

There's no limit on bringing Japanese or foreign currency into the country.

Disabled travellers

Tokyo is not easy for those with disabilities, particularly when it comes to public transport, though some stations have wheelchair moving facilities (when lifts aren't available) and raised dots on the ground guide the visually impaired. Train workers will assist those in need. There are often special 'silver seats' near train exits for those requiring them. Pedestrian crossings make a variety of noises to aid the visually impaired.

The best resource in English for travelers with disabilities is an online service, Accessible Tokyo: http://accessible.jp.org.

Club Tourism Division Barrier-free Travel *Centre Kinki Nippon Tourist Co, Shinjuku Island Wing 10F, 6-3-1, Nishi Shinjuku, Shinjuku-ku (5323 6915/www.club-t.com). Shinjuku station, west exit.* **Open** 9.30am-5.30pm.
Some English-speaking staff.

Drinking

The right to drink comes along at age 20, like the right to smoke. Tokyo's licensing laws are virtually non-existent, and many bars in areas such as Shibuya, Shinjuku and Roppongi stay open all night, enabling their drunken customers to stagger home on the first train. Public drunkenness is common, and late Friday-night trains can be an unpleasant experience.

Drugs

Drugs can be found in Tokyo, but penalties for possession are severe. Expect deportation or imprisonment.

Electricity & gas

Electric current in Japan runs like the USA, at 100V AC, rather than the 220-240V European standard. If bringing electrical appliances from Europe, you need to purchase an adapter. Electricity in Tokyo is provided by Tokyo Electric Power Company (TEPCO, 3501 8111); gas by Tokyo Gas (3433 2111).

Embassies

Embassies usually open 9am-5pm Mon-Fri; opening times for visa sections may vary.

Australian Embassy *2-1-14 Mita, Minato-ku (5232 4111/ www.australia.or.jp). Azabu Juban stations, exit 2.*

British Embassy *1 Ichibansho, Chiyoda-ku (5211 1100/www.uknow.or.jp). Hanzomon station, exits 4, 5.*

Canadian Embassy *7-3-38 Akasaka, Minato-ku (5412 6200/ www.canadanet.or.jp). Aoyama-itchome station, exit 4.*

Irish Embassy *2-10-7 Kojimachi, Chiyoda-ku (3263 0695/www.embassy-avenue.jp/ireland/). Hanzomon station, exit 4.*

New Zealand Embassy *20-40 Kamiyamacho, Shibuya-ku (3467 2271/www.nzembassy.com). Yoyogikoen station, exit 2.*

South Africa Embassy *2-7-9 Hirakawacho, Chiyoda-ku (3265 3366/www.rsatk.com). Nagatacho station, exits 4, 5.*

US Embassy *1-10-5 Akasaka, Minato-ku (3224 5000/http://usembassy.state.gov/tokyo). Tameikesanno station, exit 13.*

Emergencies

110 police (keisatsu)
119 ambulance (kyukyu Sha) and fire (Kaji)

The following organisations have an English-speaking service:

Tokyo police *3501 0110.*

TELL (Tokyo English Life Line) *5774 0992/www.telljp.com*

Tokyo Fire Department *(in Japanese) 3212 2323 in the 23 wards of central Tokyo; 042 521 2323 in the outlying cities.* Helps callers find medical centres and provides consultations on emergencies.

Emergency Translation Service *5285 8185/www.jp.from-hanna.com/daily/emergency.* **Open** 5pm-8pm Mon-Fri; 9am-8pm Sat, Sun. Telephone interpretation for communication problems that threaten to stop foreign nationals from getting emergency care. Service available in English, Chinese, Korean, Thai and Spanish.

Metropolitan Health & Medical Information Centre *5285 8181/www.himawari.metro.tokyo.jp/qq/qq13enmnlt.asp.* **Open** 9am-8pm Mon-Fri. The so-called *himawari* service provides medical and health information in English, Spanish, Chinese, Korean and Thai.

Health

Contraception

Condoms reign supreme in terms of contraception in Japan, largely because until 1999 the pill was available only to women with menstrual problems, and taking it is still generally considered risky. Condom vending machines can be found on many street corners, often near pharmacies.

Hospitals & insurance

Japanese are covered by medical insurance, provided by their employers or the state, covering 70 per cent of the cost of treatment. People over 70 pay 10 per cent of the cost of treatment. Visitors will be expected to pay the full amount of any medical treatment received so should take out medical insurance before leaving their own country. Calls (except those to Tokyo Medical Clinic) are answered in Japanese, but say '*Eigo de hanashte yoroshi dess ka?*' ('May I speak English?') and you'll be transferred to an English-speaker.

Dentists

All have English-speaking staff.

BIS Dental Clinic
8F 1-32-14 Ebisu-Nishi, Shibuya-ku (5458 4618). Ebisu station, east exit. **Open** 10am-1.30pm; 3-6.30pm Mon-Fri.

Tokyo Clinic Dental Office
Mori Bldg 32 2F, 3-4-30 Shiba-Koen, Minato-ku (3431 4225). Shiba Koen station (Toei Mita Line), exit A2. **Open** Mon-Sat, by appointment only. Japanese insurance accepted.

Dr J S Wong
1-22-3 Kami-Osaki, Shinagawa-ku (3473 2901). Meguro JR station, east exit. **Open** Mon-Wed, Fri, Sat, by appointment only.

Hospitals

All have English-speaking staff.

Japan Red Cross Medical Centre (Nihon Sekijuji-sha Iryo Centre/Nittseki Byouin)
4-1-22 Hiroo, Shibuya-ku (3400 1311/www.med.jrc.or.jp). Hiroo station, exit 3. **Open** 8.30am-11am Mon-Fri. **Emergencies** 24hrs daily.

St Luke's International Hospital (Seiroka Kokusai Byouin)
9-1 Akashicho, Chuo-ku (3541 5151/www.luke.or.jp). Tsukiji station, exit 3, 4. **Open** 8.30-11am Mon-Fri. Appointments only from noon Mon-Fri. **Emergencies** 24hrs daily.

Seibo International Catholic Hospital (Seibo Byouin)
2-5-1 Naka-Ochiai, Shinjuku-ku (3951 1111/www.seibokai.or.jp). Shimo-Ochiai station (Seibu Shinjuku Line). **Open** 8-11am for consultation, appointments from 12.30pm until last appointment Mon-Sat. Closed 3rd Sat of mth. **Emergencies** 24hrs daily.

Understanding addresses

In a city with no street names, how does one find one's way around? The answer, even for Japanese people, is 'with difficulty'. The Japanese system of writing addresses is based on numbers, rather than street names. Central Tokyo is divided into 23 wards, or *ku*. Within each *ku*, there are many smaller districts, or *cho*, which also have their own names. Most *cho* are further subdivided into into numbered areas, or *chome*, then into blocks, and finally into individual buildings, which sometimes have names of their own. Japan uses the continental system of floor numbering. The abbreviation 1F is the ground floor, English style; 2F means the second floor, or first floor English style.

Thus, the address of the bar Office – Yamazaki Bldg 5F, 2-7-18 Kita-Aoyama, Minato-ku – means that it's on the fifth floor of the Yamazaki Building, which is the 18th building of the seventh block of the second area of Kita-Aoyama, in Minato ward.

To track down an address, first invest in a detailed bilingual atlas, such as Shobunsha's *Tokyo Metropolitan Atlas*, which contains numbered *cho* and *chome*. Then follow your progress towards your destination by monitoring the metal plaques affixed to lampposts or the front of some buildings. Alternatively, ask a policeman. It's what the locals do, and it's one of the main functions of the local *koban*, or police box, all of which have detailed maps of their area.

Alternatively, most station exits in the Tokyo metropolitan area have detailed street plans of the vicinity posted, and maps can often be found on the streets themselves, though these are usually in Japanese only.

If you have access to a fax machine, it's common practice to call up your destination and ask them to fax you a map of how to get there. Most hotels allow guests to receive faxes for this purpose. Alternatively, if you have internet access, type in the home page of the destination, if it has one, and look for the map of how to get there. Japanese websites always have such maps. How else would their customers ever find them?

Tokyo Adventist Hospital (Tokyo Eisei Byouin)

3-17-3 Amanuma, Suginami-ku (3392 6151/www.tokyoeisei.com/). Ogikubo station, west exit. **Open** 8.30am-11am Mon-Fri. Afternoons by appointment Mon-Thur. No emergencies.

Tokyo British Clinic

Daikanyama Y Bldg 2F,2-13-7 Ebisu-Nishi, Shibuya-ku (5458 6099). Ebisu station, west exit. **Open** 9am-5.30pm Mon-Fri; 9am-12.30pm Sat.

This clinic is run by a British doctor. It caters for most aspects of general practice including paediatrics. Twenty-four-hour cover is provided.

Tokyo Medical Clinic & Surgical Clinic

Mori Bldg 32 2F, 3-4-30 Shiba-koen, Minato-ku (3436 3028/www.tmsc.jp). Shiba Koen station (Toei Mita Line), exit A2. **Open** 8.30am-5.30pm Mon-Fri; 8.30am-noon Sat. **Emergencies** 24hrs daily.

Doctors at his clinic hail from the UK, America, Germany or Japan and all of them speak English. The clinic also has a pharmacy on the first floor.

Optician

Fuji Optical

Otemachi Bldg 1F, 1-6-1 Otemachi, Chiyoda-ku (3214 4751/www.fujimegane.co.jp/index2.html). **Open** 10am-7pm Mon-Fri; 10am-6pm Sat.

An appointment may be required for a consultation with an English-speaking optician.

Pharmacies

For English-speaking pharmacies, *see p192.* Some pharmacies in major centres or near busy stations are open till midnight. Some branches of the 24-hour convenience store chain AM-PM have in-store pharmacies.

Basic items, such as sanitary towels, condoms or sticking plasters, can be purchased at any convenience store, but these are forbidden by law from selling pharmaceuticals. Most convenience stores are open 24 hours daily.

Helplines

The following offer advice or information in English.

AIDS Hotline *0120 461995.* **Open** 24hrs daily.

Alcoholics Anonymous *3971 1471* (taped message).

Immigration Information Centre *5796 7112.* **Open** 9am-5pm Mon-Fri.

Tokyo Foreign Residents' Advisory Centre *5320 7744.* **Open** 9.30am-noon, 1-4pm Mon-Fri.

HELP Asian Women's Shelter *3368 8855.* **Open** 10am-5pm Mon-Sat; in Japanese and English.

Japan Help Line *0120 46 1997/ http://jhelp.com.* **Open** 24hrs daily. Jhelp.com is a non-profit worldwide assistance service. Among other services, it produces the Japan Help Line Card, which contains useful telephone numbers and essential information for non-Japanese speakers, as well as a numbered phrase list in English and Japanese for use in emergencies.

Internet & email

Many of Tokyo's venerable 24-hour *manga* (comic-book) coffee shops also offer cheap internet services, but the cheapest of the lot is the chain of cafés run by Yahoo! Japan in collaboration with Starbucks, which are free. Proof of ID and registration are required, and you will be issued with a free loyalty card that can eventually be exchanged for gifts. There are branches inside both Narita and Haneda airports.

i-tea *Nakaya Bldg 5F, 1-9-8 Kichijoji-Honcho, Musashino-shi (0422 20 3337/www.arcadia-ent.co.jp/i-tea/). Kichijoji station, north exit.* **Open** 11am-11.30pm daily. Closed 1st Tue of mth.

GaiaX Café *Kagaya Bldg 2F, 7-10-7 Nishi-Shinjuku, Shinjuku-ku (5332 9201). Shinjuku station, west exit.* **Open** 10am-midnight daily.

Virgin Café *3-1-13 Shinjuku, Shinjuku-ku (3353 0056/www.virginmegastore.co.jp). Shinjuku-Sanchome station, Exit C1.* **Open** 10am-11pm daily.
Free internet access if you buy a drink.

Yahoo! Café *Garden Square, 5-11-2 Jingumae, Shibuya-ku (3797 6821).* **Open** 8am-10pm daily.
For information on the four other branches in Tokyo, see http://café.yahoo.co.jp

Wireless internet hotspots

Personal computers fitted with wireless LAN cards that meet the 802.11b wifi standard (such as Apple Computer's Airport card) can access the internet in the following locations. An up-to-date list of wireless hotspots in Tokyo can be found at www.freehotspot.jp/en/tokyo01.html.

Makena *Seibu Shinjuku PePe 3F, 1-30-1 Kabuki-cho, Shinjuku-ku (3205 1111). Shinjuku JR station, east or west exits.* **Open** 10am-9pm daily.

Starbucks Shimo-Kitazawa *Shimo-Kitazawa UC Bldg 1F, 2-30-6 Kitazawa, Setagaya-ku (3467 0266). Shimo-Kitazawa station, north exit.* **Open** 8am-10pm daily.

Language

For information on Japanese language and pronunciation, and a list of useful words and phrases, *see p296*. Hundreds of schools in Tokyo run courses in Japanese. Most offer intensive studies for those who want to learn Japanese as quickly as possible or need Japanese for work or school. They may offer longer courses, too. Private schools tend to be expensive, so check out lessons run by your ward office. Ward lessons cost from ¥100 a month to ¥500 every two months – a bargain compared to ¥3,000 an hour for group lessons.

Arc Academy *1-9-1 Shibuya, Shibuya-ku (3409 0391/www.arc.ac.jp).*
The Arc academy offers a wide variety of courses.

Meguro Language Centre *NT Bldg 3F, 1-4-11 Meguru, Meguro-ku (3493 3727/www.mlcjapanese.co.jp).*
A wide range of courses is available, from private lessons to group lessons.

Temple University *2-8-12 Minami Azabu, Minato-ku (0120 861 026/www.tuj.ac.jp).*
Temple University offers fairly cheap evening classes, as part of its continuing education programme.

Legal advice

Legal Counselling Centre

Bar Association Bldg, 1-1-3 Kasumigaseki, Chiyoda-ku (3581 1511/www.dntba.web.sh.cwidc.net/english/index.html). Kasumigaseki station, exit B1-b. **Open** 1-4pm Mon-Fri (by appointment only).
Consultations in English for ¥5,000/half-hour, over 30 minutes ¥2,500. Free for the impoverished on Thursday afternoon. A range of issues, including crime, immigration matters and labour problems, are covered. Appointments on a first-come, first-served basis.

Tokyo Human Rights Counselling Centre

Otemachi Joint Government Building No.3 6F, 1-3-3 Otemachi, Chiyoda-ku (3214 6697). Otemachi station, exit C2. **Open** 1-3pm Tue, Thur.
Free counselling in English.

Libraries

Each ward has a central lending library with a limited number of English-language books. You need an Alien Registration Card to borrow books. The following reference libraries have a healthy number of books in English. All libraries close for Japanese national holidays.

British Council Library & Information Centre

1-2 Kagurazaka, Shinjuku-ku (3235 8031/www1.britishcouncil.org/japan.htm). Iidabashi station, exit B2a, B3, west exit. **Open** 9am-9pm Mon-Fri; 9.30am-5.30pm Sat.
There's information on the UK, plus internet access, and BBC World is always on. For ¥500 a day you can use all the facilities. People under 18 not admitted. Library loans for members only.

Japan Foundation Library

Ark Mori Bldg, West Wing 20F, 1-12-32 Akasaka, Minato-ku (5562 3527/www.jpf.go.jp/e/learn/library/libindex.html). Roppongi Ichome station, exit 3. **Open** 10am-5pm Mon-Fri. Closed last Mon of mth.
Books, mags, reference material and doctoral works on all aspects of Japan. Specialises in humanities and social sciences, and has translations of Japanese novels. Houses about 25,000 books and 300 magazine titles. Lending as well as reference. People under 18 not admitted.

JETRO Library

Kyodo Tsushin Bldg 6F, 2-2-5 Toranomon, Minato-ku (3582 1775/www.jetro.go.jp/top-j/index.html). Tameikesanno station, exit 9. **Open** 9am-4.30pm Mon-Fri; closed 3rd Tue of mth.
Houses information about trade, the economy and investment for just about any country in the world. Lots of statistics as well as basic business directories. People under 18 not admitted.

National Diet Library

1-10-1 Nagatacho, Chiyoda-ku (3581 2331/www.ndl.go.jp). Nagatacho station, exit 2, 3. **Open** 9.30am-5pm Mon-Fri; closed occasional Mon & Sat.
Japan's main library, with the largest number of foreign-language books and materials. Over two million books, 50,000 mags and 1,500 newspapers and periodicals. People under 20 not admitted.

Tokyo Metropolitan Central Library

5-7-13 Minami-Azabu, Minato-ku (3442 8451/www.library.metro.tokyo.jp/). Hiroo station, exit 1. **Open** 1-8pm Mon; 9.30am-8pm Tue-Fri; 9.30am-5pm Sat, Sun.

This is the main library for the Tokyo government, with the largest collection of books about Tokyo. Over 150,000 titles in foreign languages. People under 16 not admitted.

Lost property

If you happen to leave a bag or package somewhere, just go back: it will probably still be there. If you left it in a train station or other public area, go either to the stationmaster's office or nearest *koban* (policebox) and ask for English-language assistance. Items handed in at the station are logged in a book. You will have to sign in order to receive your item. If you leave something in a taxi on the way to or from the hotel, try the hotel reception – taxi drivers often bring the lost item straight back to your hotel.

JR *3423 0111.*
English-speaking service.

Metropolitan Police 3501 0110 English-speaking service.

The following numbers will all be answered in Japanese, so be sure to ask a Japanese person to call for you.

Eidan subway *3834 5577.*
JR Shinjuku station *3354 4019.*
JR Tokyo station *1880.*
JR Ueno station *3841 8069.*
Metropolitan Police *3814 4151.*
Narita Airport *0476 322802.*
Toei subway & buses *3812 2011.*
Taxi *3648 0300.*

Media

Newspapers

The Japanese are among the keenest newspaper readers in the world, with daily sales of over 70 million copies, and *Yomiuri Shimbun* is the world's largest circulation newspaper, with daily sales of 14.5 million. For English readers the choice is limited to three newspapers, the *Daily Yomiuri*, the *Japan Times* and the *International Herald Tribune*, which incorporates the English version of the *Asahi Shimbun*. All cost ¥120-¥150 and are available at most central Tokyo station kiosks.

Daily Yomiuri

www.yomiuri.co.jp/index-e.htm.
Produces supplements in collaboration with other newspapers around the world, including the *Independent* (Sunday) and the *Washington Post* (Friday). There's a what's-on supplement published on Thursday.

IHT/Asahi

Launched in April 2001 as a joint venture between the *International Herald Tribune* and the *Asahi Shinbun*. The only English-language paper in Tokyo to read like English is its first language.

Japan Times

www.japantimes.co.jp.
The longest-established English-language newspaper in Japan. Consists mainly of agency reports. Heavy on business. Motto 'All the news without fear or favour' could read 'All the news without fear or flavour'.

Nikkei Weekly

www.nni.nikkei.co.jp.
The Japanese equivalent of the *Financial Times* produces this weekly digest from the world of finance.

Free reads

Metropolis

www.metropolis.co.jp.
Formerly known as *Tokyo Classified*, this is Tokyo's biggest and best weekly free magazine, with listings and adverts galore. It's distributed at foreigner-friendly bars, clubs, shops and hotels every Friday.

Tokyo Notice Board

www.tokyonoticeboard.co.jp.
The most visible rival to *Metropolis*, although *Tokyo Notice Board* is smaller and more amateurish.

Tokyo Weekender

www.weekender.co.jp.
This one can be tricky to find. Contains bland ex-pat community gossip and news.

World Magazine Gallery

3-13-10 Ginza, Chuo-ku (3545 7227). Ginza station, exit A7.
Open 11am-7pm Mon-Fri.
A reference-only magazine library, with over 800 titles from all over the world; read them at a table or take them to the coffee shop on the second floor. Also a distribution point for Tokyo's free publications, some of which appear only sporadically.

Magazines

If you read Japanese there's a wealth of what's on information available in weekly publications such as *Pia* and *Tokyo Walker* (both ¥320). If not, there's Tokyo's only paid-for English-language listings monthly, *Tokyo Journal.*

Tokyo Journal

www.tokyo.to.
Long-established monthly English-language listings magazine.

Radio

InterFM

www.interfm.co.jp.
Broadcasting on 76.1MHz, this is Tokyo's main bilingual station. Plays rock and pop.

NHK Radio Japan

www.nhk.or.jp/rj/index_e.html.
News on the internet.

Television

Japanese state broadcaster NHK runs two commercial-free terrestrial channels – NHK General (channel 1) and NHK Educational (channel 3) – and two satellite channels, BS1 and BS2. The five remaining terrestrial channels in Tokyo – Nihon TV (channel 4), Tokyo Broadcasting System (channel 6), Fuji Television (channel 8), Television Asahi (channel 10) and TV Tokyo (channel 12) – have too many advertisements and show a constant stream of unimaginative pap, illuminated occasionally by a worthwhile documentary or drama series. NHK1 news at 7pm and 9pm daily is broadcast simultaneously in both English and Japanese: to access the English sound channel push a button on the remote to a bilingual TV set (most big hotels have them). Many non-Japanese TV series and films are also broadcast bilingually. Japan's main satellite broadcaster is Rupert Murdoch's SkyPerfect! TV, which offers a multitude of familiar channels, including CNN, BBC World and Sky Sports.

Money

The yen is not divided into smaller units, and comes in denominations of ¥1, ¥5, ¥10, ¥50, ¥100 and ¥500 (coins) and ¥1,000, ¥2,000, ¥5,000 and ¥10,000 (notes). Prices on display do not usually include the five per cent purchase tax.

Banks

Opening a bank account is quite easy if you have an Alien Registration Card. With savings accounts you will be issued a book and card. Getting a card can take up to two weeks. It's generally delivered to your address; you have to be home to sign for it. Or get the bank to inform you when it arrives and pick it up. Banks are open 9am-3pm Mon-Fri. Do not go to a bank if you're in a hurry – queues are long, especially on Fridays, and the procedure involves taking a number and waiting.

You can also open an account at a post office and withdraw money from any other post office branch.

Changing money

You can cash travellers' cheques or change foreign currency at any authorised foreign exchange bank (look for the signs). If you want to exchange money outside regular banking hours, most large hotels exchange travellers' cheques and currency, as do large department stores, which are open until about 8pm. Narita Airport has several bureaux de change staffed by English speakers, open daily from 7am to 10pm.

Credit cards & cash machines

Japan is a cash-based society, and restaurants and bars may refuse cards. Larger shops, restaurants and hotels accept major cards, but you should always keep some cash on you. ATMs are rarely open after 7pm and often close at 5pm on Saturdays. Many banks also charge for withdrawals made after 6pm, and on Sundays and public holidays. Still, there is a growing number of 24-hour ATMs in Tokyo, mostly around major train stations. All ATMs have stickers or logos showing which cards are accepted. Some will not accept foreign-issued cards; **Citibank** is your best bet, with 24-hour ATMs all over Tokyo (information 0120 50 4189). **Mitsui-Sumitomo Bank** (head office 3282 5111) has a good reputation for dealing with foreigners. Post Office ATMs also accept foreign-issued cards.

Although there are ATMs at Narita Airport, the machines only work during banking hours. Make sure you have some Japanese cash if arriving early in the morning or late at night.

To report lost or stolen credit cards, dial one of the following 24-hour numbers.

American Express 3220 6100/0120 020 120 (freephone). Be patient, the English message follows the Japanese one.
Diners' Club 3570 1555/ 0120 074 024 (freephone).
MasterCard 00531 11 3886 (freephone).
Visa 00531 44 0022.

Money transfers

When you're having money sent to a Japanese bank account, you will need to give your bank account number, bank, branch and location. Mail transfers are cheaper than telex/telegraphic but they may take longer.

Opening hours

Larger stores in Tokyo are open daily from 9.30am or 10am to around 8pm. Smaller shops are open the same hours six days a week. Monday and Wednesday are the commonest closing days.

Most restaurants open at around 11am and close around 11pm, though some *izakaya* and bars are open till 5am. Some remain open till they're empty.

Office hours are 9am to 5pm. On national holidays, most places keep Sunday holidays, but on 1 and 2 January most are closed.

Convenience stores offer 24-hour shopping at slightly higher prices than supermarkets, and they're found all over the city. The major chains are 7-Eleven, AM-PM, Family Mart and Lawson's.

Police & security

Japan is one of the safest places to visit. *Koban* (police boxes) are everywhere, though officers don't usually speak English (and may not be overly friendly). Theft is still amazingly uncommon, so it's not unusual to walk around with the equivalent of hundreds of pounds in your wallet without giving it a second thought.

Of course, crime does occur from time to time and it's best to take the usual precautions to keep your money and valuables safe. There are certain areas, such as Roppongi or Shinjuku's Kabuki-cho, as well as at airports and on crowded trains, where one should be particularly cautious.

Postal services

www.post.japanpost.jp.
A red-and-white sign like a letter 'T' with a line over it marks a post office. Most big streets have one. Postcards overseas cost ¥70; aerograms cost ¥90; letters under 25g cost ¥90 (Asian countries), ¥110

A fair cop?

Japanese police are seen as the glue that keeps society harmonious – keeping things in their proper place, smoothing over irregularities before they become a problem. That means that the police here still do things the old-fashioned way. It's normal when first moving into a Tokyo apartment to receive a courtesy call from a local policeman, who will tell tenants to avail themselves of his services at any time.

The downside of this community-based approach is that actual detection suffers. Forensic science in Japan lags far behind that in other nations. What's more, Japanese law states that a suspect can be held for 23 days without charge, and there's a tendency to rely on confessions to convict. Which means that the Japanese police appear regularly on Amnesty International's hate list.

As a foreign visitor or resident, the most frequent contact with the police is usually made through the *koban* – the police boxes dotted around every neighbourhood, from which the officers patrol the area by car and bicycle. Each major *koban* has four officers on duty at any one time to deal with all enquiries and complaints from the public. It's estimated that the *koban* outside Shibuya station's Hachiko exit receives around 3,000 visitors a day.

Common causes of friction between Japanese police and foreign nationals are being drunk and aggressive, having noisy parties at home, traffic violations, and bicycle theft (if you buy a bike here, please take careful note of the registration number – you'll need it).

If you are stopped by police officers in Tokyo, present your passport or Alien Registration Card (you're legally required to carry it with you at all times). If detained at a police station, ask to speak to someone from your embassy. Claim you speak no Japanese, even if you do, and don't sign anything you can't read.

Don't forget to compliment the officers who detained you on their skilful use of English; turnabout is fair play.

(North America, Europe, Oceania) or ¥130 (Africa, South America).

Local post offices are open from 9am to 5pm on weekdays, and are closed on public holidays.

For poste restante, contact the Central Tokyo Post Office (3284 9539/www.tokyo.japanpost.jp/dpo/tcpo/). You can also receive mail at the main International Post Office (3241 4891/www.pluto.dti.ne.jp/~tokyoipo/), near exit A2 of the Otemachi subway. Mail is held for up to 30 days. The post office is open from 9am to 7pm Monday to Friday; 9am-5pm Saturday; 9am-noon Sunday and public holidays. A 24-hour service is available at a counter to the rear of the main building.

When writing addresses, English script is acceptable, as long as it's clearly written. You can get more information in English on the Japanese postal system from the Postal Services Information line (5472 5852). It's open 9.30am to 4.30pm Monday to Friday.

Sending parcels by surface mail is cheaper than by air, but items take longer to arrive. Larger department stores can arrange postage if you purchase major items.

Religion

According to the *Religion Yearbook* issued by the Agency for Cultural Affairs, 208 million Japanese are members of religious organisations – that's almost twice the population of the country. Bear in mind that it's not unusual for a family to celebrate birth with Shinto rites, have a Christian marriage, and pay last respects at a Buddhist ceremony. Freedom of worship is a constitutional right.

Rubbish

After the subway sarin gas attack in March 1995, most bins were removed from subway stations. All JR stations, however, have rubbish bins near the exits. They are divided into three sections: cans, newspapers and magazines, and other rubbish. If you can't find a bin, carry your rubbish home with you.

All domestic rubbish should be divided into four categories: burnable, unburnable, recyclable and large items. For more information, contact the relevant section of your local ward office.

Smoking

Around 40 per cent of the adult population in Japan smoke cigarettes, more than in any other similarly industrialised nation, and cigarettes are relatively cheap, at around

¥280 per packet, and readily available from street vending machines and convenience stores. The age at which it is legal to start smoking is 20. Smoking is therefore common in the city's restaurants and cafés, although in recent years a growing number of venues have started to offer the option of no-smoking areas. Very few restaurants are entirely smoke-free. In October 2002, central Tokyo's Chiyoda-ku became the first area in Japan to ban smoking on the streets, although in typical Japanese fashion the rationale behind the move had nothing to do with health: it seems that burning cigarettes pose a danger to clothes and babies' heads in the area. As of 1 May 2003, smoking has been banned on the platforms of all private train lines in Tokyo, although JR stations still have platform smoking areas.

Telephones

The area code for Tokyo is 03. If you're calling from outside Japan, dial the international access code plus 81-3, followed by the main number. For domestic calls from outside Tokyo, dial 03 followed by the number.

Throughout this guide, we have omitted the 03 from the beginning of Tokyo telephone numbers.

The virtual monopoly enjoyed by NTT on domestic telephone services was broken in April 2001 with the introduction of the Myline system, which allows customers to choose domestic providers for local and long-distance calls.

If you have your own phone line in Tokyo, call the Myline Information Centre (0120 000 406/www.myline.org) to register your choice of phone service provider (English-speaking operators are available).

NTT still controls nearly all **telephone boxes** in Tokyo. Calls from call boxes cost ¥10 for the first three minutes, then ¥10 for every minute after that. There are two types of NTT telephone boxes. One, the older type, contains a grey phone that accepts flexible phonecards. The other, the IC Card phone, has a brownish phone with an open slot for the card. This is an integrated circuit card; its corner must be snapped off before it can be used. Both types of public phone have sockets for PCs, but international calls from old-style phoneboxes can only be made with cash, and only from those boxes with 'ISDN' or 'International' written on the side. Both types of phone display instructions in English as well as Japanese.

Several companies offer **international call services**, at roughly the same rates. To make an international call, dial 010 (KDDI), 0041 (Japan Telecom), 0033 (NTT Communications) or 0061 (Cable & Wireless IDC), followed by your country's access code and the telephone number.

NTT phonecards cannot be used to make international calls, so you need to buy a prepaid card (*see below*) or have a lot of change handy. Rates between the three companies differ, but only slightly. The cheapest time to call is between 11pm and 8am, when a 40 per cent off-peak discount applies.

The 'home country direct' service conveniently allows you to charge the call to your home telephone bill, provided you have set up the service in your home country in the first place.

Numbers starting with 0120 are **freephone** (receiver-paid or toll-free) numbers.

NTT East Information
0120 364463.
English-speaking operators are available.

Mobile phones

You can get a mobile phone at outlets operated directly by mobile phone companies or at electronics stores. Japanese mobile phones can be used to surf the internet, send email and photos and movies. Oh, and you can talk on them too. To buy a phone, you have to show your Alien Registration Card and passport. Applications will not be accepted if the applicant's visa is due to expire within 90 days. If you're here on a tourist visa or if you're about to renew your visa, you should get a pre-paid mobile phone. You can purchase a phone for ¥5,000-¥10,000 and a prepaid card for about ¥3,000 or ¥5,000. Proof of ID is required at the time of purchase.

NTT DoCoMo
0120 005 250/www.nttdocomo.com.
NTT DoCoMo is Japan's biggest mobile phone operator.

Prepaid phone cards

Three kinds of telephone card can be bought in Tokyo. KDDI (www.kddi.com/english) produces a 'Super World' prepaid card for international phone calls, which is sold at most major convenience stores. They come in four different values – ¥1,000, ¥3,000, ¥5,000 and ¥7,000 – and can be used with any push-button telephone.

NTT EAST (www.ntt-east.co.jp/ptd_e/index.html) produces two cards, one primarily for the domestic market, the other – an IC card – can be used for both national and international calls. Both cards sell for ¥1,000 and contain 105 ¥10 units. These cards are available from most convenience stores as well as from vending machines inside some phoneboxes.

Telephone directories

Unless you're fluent, using a Japanese phonebook is out of the question. NTT publishes an English-language phonebook, 'Town Page'. You can get it free from English Townpage Centre (0120 460815). It's also available on the internet at http://english.itp.ne.jp.

Useful numbers

Repair Service *113.*
Moving & Relocating *116.*
Directory Assistance *104.*
KDDI Information service *0057.*
Japan Telecom *0088 41/www.japan-telecom.co.jp/english.*
NTT Communications *0120 506506/www.ntt.com.*
Be patient. English information follows Japanese information.
Domestic Telegrams (in Japanese) *115.*
International Telegrams 005 3519/0120 445124.

Time

All of Japan is in the same time zone, nine hours ahead of Greenwich Mean Time (GMT). Daylight Saving Time is not used, but is a recurring topic of debate.

Tipping

Tipping is not expected in Japan and people will generally be embarrassed if you try to tip them. If you leave money on a restaurant table, for example, you will probably be pursued down the street by a member of staff trying to return it. At upmarket establishments, a service charge is often factored into the bill.

Toilets

Public toilets can be found in and around most train stations. If there's not one in the station, there probably is one near the entrance or just outside the exit.

Station toilets usually offer Japanese-style commodes. The way to use them is to squat over them, facing the back wall. Many public toilets do not have toilet tissue. You can buy tissue from machines outside the doors, or keep an eye out for part-time workers handing out free tissues on the street. The packets are ads for companies and services around Tokyo.

If you don't fancy squatting Japanese-style, you should head for a large shop or department store, where western-style toilets are the norm. In some women's toilets there might be a small box with a button on the wall: pushing it produces the sound of flushing. Many Japanese women flush the toilet two or three times to cover the sounds they make, and the fake flush was designed to save water.

If you happen to be staying in a Japanese home or good hotel, you may find that your toilet looks like the command seat on the *Starship Enterprise* (*see p18*). The controls to the right of the seat usually operate its heating and in-built bidet controls.

Tourist Information

The **Odakyu Sightseeing Service Centre** provides services to tourists. The staff speak English, Chinese and Korean. **Tourist Information Centres** (TIC) are affiliated with the Japan National Tourist Organisation (JNTO/www.jnto.go.jp).

Odakyu Sightseeing Service Centre *Ground floor concourse, Shinjuku station, west exit (5321 7887).* **Open** 8am-6pm daily.

TIC Tokyo Office *Tokyo Kotsu Kaikan 10F, 2-10-1 Yurakucho, Chiyoda-ku (3201 3331/fax 3201 3347).* **Open** 9am-5pm Mon-Fri; 9am-noon Sat.
Friendly multilingual staff and a wealth of information: maps, event booklets, books on Japanese customs, even NTT English phonebooks.

TIC Narita Office *Arrival floor, Terminal 2, New Tokyo International Airport (0476 34 6251).* **Open** 9am-8pm daily.

TIC Narita Office *Arrival floor, Terminal 1, New Tokyo International Airport (0476 30 3383).* **Open** 9am-8pm daily.

Japan Railways East Infoline *3423 0111.* **Open** 10am-6pm Mon-Fri.

Japan Travel Phone *3201 3331 0088 22 4800.* **Open** 9am-5pm daily.
A free nationwide service for those in need of English-language assistance and travel information on places outside Tokyo and Kyoto.

Tokyo Tourist Information Centre *Tokyo Metropolitan Government Bldg 1F, 2-8-1 Nishi-Shinjuku, Shinjuku-ku (5321 3077/www.kanko.metro.tokyo.jp/public/center.html). Tochomae station (Toei Oedo Line), exit 4.* **Open** 9.30am-6.30pm daily. **Branches**: 1-60 Ueno-Koen, Taito-ku (3836 3471).

Yes! Tokyo *www.tcvb.or.jp.*
This well-organised web page, masterminded by the Tokyo Convention and Visitors Bureau, is packed with lots of useful travel information.

Visas

By August 1998, Japan had concluded general visa-exemption arrangements with the USA, Canada, the UK and the Republic of Ireland. Citizens of these countries may stay in Japan for up to 90 days. Japan also has working holiday visa arrangements with Australia, New Zealand and Canada for people aged from 18 to 30. At the time of going to press, a similar agreement was due to be concluded between Japan and the UK.

The following types of visa are available. For more information, contact Tokyo **Regional Immigration Bureau** (5-5-30 Konan, Minato-ku; 5796 7112, open 9am-noon; 1-4pm Mon-Fri) or the **Immigration Information Centre** (3213 8523).

Tourist visa A 'short-term stay' visa, good for anyone not intending to work in Japan.

Working visa It's illegal to work here without a visa. If you arrive as a tourist and work, your company has to sponsor you for a work visa. You generally must then go abroad to make the application (South Korea is the cheapest option). If you plan to stay in Japan for more than 90 days, you need an Alien Registration Card. For this, you need to provide two passport-sized photographs, a passport, an address and a signature.

When to go

In Tokyo, winter is marked by clear skies, cold days and the occasional snowstorm. Spring begins with winds and cherry-blossom viewing (*see p196*). The rainy season for Honshu (the main island) begins in June. This is followed by summer, with its hot and humid days. Finally, autumn is marked by the changing of the leaves.

Temperatures range from around 3°C in January to 35°C in July and August. The summer months can be unbearable for those not used to humidity. It's advisable to travel with a small hand-held fan, a bottle of water and a wet cotton cloth or small washcloth. Fans are often handed out in the street as of ad campaigns.

Public holidays

Japan has 14 public holidays: New Year's Day (Ganjitsu) **1 January**; Coming of Age Day (Seijin no Hi) **second Monday in January**; National Foundation Day (Kenkoku Kinen no Hi) **11 February**; Vernal Equinox Day (Shumbun no Hi) **around 21 March**; Greenery Day (Midori no Hi) **29 April**; Constitution Day (Kempo Kinenbi) **3 May**; Children's Day (Kodomo no Hi) **5 May**; Marine Day (Umi no Hi) **20 July**; Respect for the Aged Day (Keiro no Hi) **15 September**; Autumnal Equinox Day (Shubun no Hi) **around 23 September**; Sports Day (Taiiku no Hi) **second Monday in October**; Culture Day (Bunka no Hi) **3 November**; Labour Thanksgiving Day (Kinro Kansha no Hi) **23 November**; Emperor's Birthday (Tenno Tanjobi) **23 December**.

Saturday remains an official workday, but holidays falling on a Sunday shift to Monday. If both 3 May and 5 May fall on weekdays, then 4 May also becomes a holiday.

Weather report

Average daytime temperatures, rainfall and hours of sunshine in Tokyo.

	Temp (C/F)	**Rainfall** (mm/in)	**Sunshine** (hrs/dy)
Jan	6/42.8	50/2.0	6
Feb	7/44.6	60/2.4	5.7
Mar	9/48.2	100/3.9	5.1
Apr	14/57.2	130/5.1	5.5
May	18/64.4	135/5.3	5.8
June	21/69.8	165/6.5	4.0
July	26/78.8	160/6.3	4.7
Aug	28/82.4	155/6.1	5.7
Sept	23/73.4	200/7.9	3.8
Oct	18/64.4	165/6.5	4.2
Nov	13/55.4	90/3.5	4.7
Dec	7/44.6	40/1.6	5.5

Women travellers

The crime rate in Japan is very low compared to that in many countries. Women should exercise standard precautions, but the risk of rape or assault is not high, and women can ride the subways at night or wander the streets with little concern. A woman alone might be harassed by drunken, staggering salarymen, but they are rarely serious; ignoring them generally does the trick.

This said, Tokyo is not immune from urban dangers, and boys will be boys even in Japan. The low incidence of rape is often attributed by some to under-reporting rather than respect for women. Don't let fear spoil your holiday, but do exercise a little caution at night, particularly in areas such as Roppongi and Shinjuku's Kabuki-cho.

A less serious type of assault occurs every day on packed rush-hour trains, where women are sometimes groped (or worse). Many Japanese women ignore the offence, hesitant to draw attention to themselves. It's pointless to vocalise anyway, as rarely will anyone step in to assist. This doesn't mean you have to stand there and take it: the best recourse is quiet retaliation; dig your nails into the offending hand or, if you're certain of the perpetrator, a swift kick to the shins or a jab in the gut should do the trick. But before taking action, be sure that something really is going on. What might feel like a hand between your legs often turns out to be just a briefcase – or a handbag. Avoiding rush hour is the best strategy.

Some public toilets are not segregated. This may not pose any danger, but some women (and men) find it disconcerting to do their business in mixed company. If this is a concern, look for toilets marked with 'male' and 'female' symbols.

Further Reference

Books

Fiction

Abe, Kobe *The Woman in the Dunes*
Weird classic about a lost village of sand.
Birnbaum, Alfred (ed) *Monkey Brain Sushi*
Decent selection of 'younger' Japanese writers.
Erickson, Steve *The Sea Came in at Midnight*
American novel set partly in a Tokyo 'memory hotel'.
Howell, Brian *Head of a Girl & others*
Elegantly weird short story by expat English writer based close to Tokyo.
Kawabata, Yasuwari *Snow Country*
Japan's first Nobel prize winner for literature.
Mishima, Yukio *Confessions of a Mask & others*
Japan's most famous novelist, 20 years after his suicide.
Mitchell, David *Ghostwritten & Number9dream*
Ambitious novels by expat UK writer teaching English in Hiroshima.
Murakami, Haruki *Norwegian Wood & others*
Most of Murakami's books are set in Tokyo.
Murakami, Ryu *Coin Locker Babies & others*
Hip modern novelist, unrelated to Haruki.
Oe, Kenzoburo *A Personal Matter & others*
Japan's second winner of the Nobel prize.
Yoshimoto, Banana *Kitchen & others*
Modern writer who's made a splash in the west.

Non-fiction

Birchall, Jonathan *Ultra Nippon*
British journo follows Japanese soccer team, and fans, for a year.
Bird, Isabella *Unbeaten Tracks in Japan*
Amazing memoirs of intrepid Victorian explorer.
Bix, Herbert P *Hirohito and the Making of Modern Japan*
Post-war Japan under the wartime Emperor.
Bornoff, Nicholas *Pink Samurai: Love, Marriage and Sex in Contemporary Japan*
All you ever wanted to know about the subjects, but were perhaps too confused to ask.
Chang, Iris *The Rape of Nanking: The Forgotten Holocaust of World War II*
The Japanese Imperial Army's atrocities in China revealed in all their horror.
Dower, John W *Embracing Defeat: Japan in the Wake of World War II*
Award-winning account of the American-led post-war reconstruction of Japan.
Ferguson, Will *Hokkaido Highway Blues*
One man's manic mission to hitchhike through Japan following the progress of the cherry blossom from the south to the north.
Galbraith, Stuart *Giant Monsters Are Attacking Tokyo: Incredible World of Japanese Fantasy Films*
The ultimate guide to the weird and wacky world of the city-stomping giants of Japanese cinema.
Harper, Philip *The Insider's Guide to Sake*
Readable introduction to Japan's national libation.
Kaplan, David & Marshall, Andrew *The Cult At The End of The World*
Terrifying story of Aum and the subway gas attacks.
Kaplan, David & Dubro, Alec *Yakuza: Japan's Criminal Underworld*
Inside look at the gangs who control Japan's underworld.
Kawakami, Kenji & Don Papia *101 Unuseless Japanese Inventions: The Art of Chindogu*
Everything you never knew you needed.
Kennedy, Rick *Little Adventures in Tokyo*
Entertaining trips through the off-beat side of the city.
Martin, John H & Phyllis G *Tokyo: A Cultural Guide to Japan's Capital City*
Enjoyable ramble through Tokyo with two amiable authors.
Okakura, Kazuko *The Book of Tea*
Tea as the answer to life, the universe and everything. Which, as every Japanese knows, it is.
Ototake, Hirotada *No One's Perfect*
True story of a boy who overcome handicaps and prejudice. A record-breaking best-seller.
Pompian, Susan *Tokyo For Free*
Good but dated guide for skinflints.
Richie, Donald *Public People, Private People and Tokyo: A View of the City*
Acclaimed writer and long-time Japan resident on the Japanese and their capital.
Richie, Donald *Tokyo*
That man again, with a beautifully produced work from Reaktion Books.
Satterwhite, Robb *What's What in Japanese Restaurants*
An invaluable guide to navigating the menu maze.
Schilling, Mark *Enyclopedia of Japanese Pop Culture*
From karaoke to Hello Kitty, ramen to Doraemon.
Schilling, Mark *The Yakuza Movie Book : A Guide to Japanese Gangster Films*
A testament to the enduring appeal of the gangster in Japanese movies.
Schlesinger, Jacob M *Shadow Shoguns: The Rise and Fall of Japan's Postwar Political Machine*
Pretty good non-academic read.
Schodt, Fredrick L *Dreamland Japan: Writings on Modern Manga*
Leading western authority on publishing phenomenon.
Schreiber, Mark *Tokyo Confidential: Titillating Tales from Japan's Wild Weeklies*
Japan laid bare through translated magazine stories.
Seidensticker, Edward *Tokyo Rising & Low City, High City*
Eminently readable histories of the city.
Sharnoff, Lora *Grand Sumo*
Exhaustive account, if a little on the dry side.
Tajima, Noriyuki *Tokyo: Guide to Recent Architecture*
Pocket-sized guide with outstanding pictures.
Tajima, Noriyuki & Powell, Catherine *Tokyo: Labyrinth City*
LP-sized guide to more recent projects.
Takemoto, Tadao & Ohara, Yasuo *The Alleged 'Nanking Massacre': Japan's Rebuttal to China's Forged Claims*
The right-wing Japanese take on the Imperial Army's actions in China.
Twigger, Robert *Angry White Pyjamas*
Scrawny Oxford poet trains with Japanese riot police.
Walters, Gary *Day Walks Near Tokyo & More Day Walks Near Tokyo*
Detailed routes for escaping the city's crowds.
Whitting, Robert *You Gotta Have Wa*
US baseball stars + Japan = culture clash. The template for many sports book written since.
Whitting, Robert *Tokyo Underworld: The Fast Life and Times of an American Gangster in Japan*
Enthralling story of underworld life in the bowels of modern Japan.

Language

Three A Network/Minna no Nihongo Shokyuu
Book 1 for beginners, 2 for pre-intermediate.
Integrated Approach to Intermediate Japanese
Well balanced in grammar, reading and conversation.
A Dictionary of Basic Japanese Grammar
Standard reference book from the *Japan Times*.
The Modern Reader's Japanese-English Dictionary
Known affectionately as Nelson, this is the definitive tool for students of the written language.

Maps & guides

Shobunsha Tokyo Metropolitan Atlas
Negotiate those tricky addresses with confidence.
Japan As It Is
Eccentric explanations of all things Japanese.
Asahi Shinbun's Japan Almanac
The ultimate book of lists, published annually.

Films

Akira
(Otomo Katsuhiro, 1988)
The film that started the anime craze in the west – the story of freewheeling youth gangs trying to stay alive in Neo-Tokyo.
Audition
(Takashi Miike, 1999)
A lonely widower, a beautiful actress: another Japanese shocker.
Diary of a Shinjuku Thief
(Oshima Nagisa, 1968)
A picaresque trip through 1960s Tokyo with a Japanese master of the movies.
The Eel
(Imamura Shohei, 1996)
Yakusho Koji in a bizarre tale of love in the aftermath of murder.
Gamera 3
(Shusuke Kaneko, 1999)
Countless Tokyo dwellers' dreams are realised when the turbo-powered turtle demolishes Shibuya.
Ghost in the Shell (Kokaku Kidotai)
(Mamoru Oshii, 1995)
A complex and thought-provoking animated look at a future society where computers are the home of human minds – and vice versa.
Godzilla, King of the Monsters
(Honda Inoshiro, 1954)
The big green guy makes his debut following an atomic accident, and promptly smashes up Ginza. Subtext: Japan recovers from the blast of Hiroshima.
Hana-Bi
(Kitano Takeshi, 1997)
Kitano's best film won him a Venice prize, but in his native country he is still better known as a TV comedian.
House of Bamboo
(Samuel Fuller, 1955)
A gang led by an American pulls off raids in Tokyo and Yokohama.
Mononoke Hime (Princess Mononoke)
(Miyazaki Hiyao, 1997)
Record-breaking animated fable of man's butchery of the environment.
The Ring
(Nakata Hideo, 1998)
Chilling urban ghost story, which has spawned a seemingly endless boom of psycho-horror movies.
Spirited Away
(Miyazaki Hayao, 2001)
Oscar-winning animated feature from the same studio as *Princess Mononoke*.
Rashomon
(Kurosawa Akira, 1951)
Influential tale of robbery from Japan's most famous film-maker.
Tampopo
(Itami Juzo, 1986)
The idiosyncratic and sadly missed director's trawl through the Japanese obsession for food, with particular reference to ramen noodles.
Tokyo Pop
(Fran Rubel Kazui, 1988)
Aspiring artiste can't make it in New York, so heads off to Tokyo.
Tokyo Story
(Ozu Yasujiro, 1953)
Life in the metropolis and the generation gap it produces are explored in Ozu's masterpiece.
Une avenue à Tokyo
(Tsunekichi Shibata, 1898)
One of the earliest short films showing life in Japan during the Meiji era.
Until the End of the World
(Wim Wenders, 1991)
William Hurt and Sam Neill lurk briefly around Shinjuku in Wenders' worthy but dull SF epic.
The Yakuza
(Sydney Pollack, 1974)
Robert Mitchum stars in writer Paul Schrader's tribute to the Japanese gangster movie.
You Only Live Twice
(Lewis Gilbert, 1967)
Connery's 007 comes to Tokyo. Look out for the New Otani hotel doubling as the HQ of the malevolent Osato Corporation.

Music

Denki Groove *A*
A multi-faceted band that does pop, dance music and techno. One member, Takkyu Ishino, has toured in Europe as a DJ.
Dragon Ash *Morrow*
One of the most popular rap groups in Japan.
Hajime Chitose *Konomachi*
Born on Amami Oshima island. She sings poppy versions of traditional local songs in unique warble.
Hamasaki Ayumi *A Ballads*
Top selling female vocalist in Japan.
Misia *Misia Greatest Hits*
The Japanese queen of ballards.
Quruli *The World is Mine*
One of Japan's most talented bands.
Rovo *Flage*
Heavy, progressive rock, with pronouced jazz influence. Great live.
Sheena Ringo *Karuki Zamen Kuri no Hana*
Top female rocker.
SMAP *Sekaini Hitotsudake no Hana*
Only in Japan would a group of pop stars host their own cookery show.
Tokyo SKA Paradise Orchestra *A Quick Drunkard*
The name says it all: innovative music bases on SKA beats.
Yoshida Brothers *Soulful*
Two young *shamisen* players play traditional music to modern backing tracks.
Utada Hikaru *Colors*
Japan's answer to Sade.

Websites

Getting around

Japan Travel Updates
www.jnto.go.jp
Site of the Japan National Tourist Organisation (JNTO), featuring a selection of useful travel information, tips, an online booking service and several sketchy reference city maps.
Japanese Guest Houses
www.japaneseguesthouses.com
Guide to traditional *ryokan* accommodation in Tokyo, Kyoto and other cities, with online booking facility.
NTT Townpage
english.itp.ne.jp
NTT's English-language phone book online.
Shauwecker's Japan Guide
www.japan-guide.com
Shauwecker's guide to Japan online. Practical information covering the whole of the country.
Subway Navigator
www.subwaynavigator.com
Interactive subway route planner. Enter your departure and destination stations and it'll provide the route as well as how much time to allow for your journey.
Tokyo Life Navigator
www.ima-chan.co.jp/guide/index.htm
The place to start if you know nothing Tokyo and want to swot up before you get here.

Tokyo Subway Maps
www.tokyometro.go.jp/e/index.html
Up-to-date maps of the sometimes baffling subway system.

Lesbian & Gay

Cruising
www.cruisingforsex.com/elsewherelistings.html
Long list of recommendations plus good information on saunas.
Film Festival
www.tokyo-lgff.org/
Homepage of the queer film festival staged annually in July.
Gay Net Japan
www.gnj.or.jp
English and Japanese forums, classifieds and support groups. Especially good for making short-term friendships.
Utopia
www.utopia-asia.com/tipsjapn.htm
Useful, fun and informative page of listings, links and more from this Asian gay portal site.

Media

Daily Yomiuri
www.yomiuri.co.jp/index-e.htm
Tokyo's second English-language newspaper's site (after the *Japan Times*) is smaller but prettier.
Debito's Home Page
www.debito.org
Amusing and informative home page of one Arudou Debito, a former US citizen once called David Aldwinkle (Debito is David in Japanese) now a Japanese national and crusader for foreigners' rights and chronicler of many of the curiosities of life in Japan for non Japanese.
i-mode Links
www.imodelinks.com
Definitive guide to all that is i-mode and the English-language sites available on this phenomenally successful Japanese mobile internet system.
Japan Inc
www.japaninc.com
Online version of the monthly magazine tracking Japan's progress in the so-called 'New Economy'.
Japan Times
www.japantimes.com
The most comprehensive news about Japan available on the web. The events section of the site is only sporadically updated.
Japan Today
www.japantoday.com
Tabloid news about Japan.
J-Port
www.j-port.com
This is an online free classifieds site with zero editorial and very few classifieds.
Mainichi Daily News
mdn.mainichi.co.jp/index.html
Formerly a printed English-language newspaper, now internet only. Great for quirky stories.
Radio On
www.radioonactive.com
One of Tokyo's best alternative radio stations, on the net.
Weekly Post
www.weeklypost.com
The home page of one of the country's biggest-selling magazines contains English-language news and the occasional bit of gossip.

Music & clubs

CIA (Club Information Agency)
www.ciajapan.com
Online version of this monthly guide to club events in Tokyo has listings and party pictures.
CyberJapan
www.so-net.ne.jp/CYBERJAPAN
Stylish youth-culture site has fashion reports, news and streaming videos from Tokyo clubland.
Smash
www.smash-jpn.com
Homepage in Japanese and English of one of Tokyo's biggest concert promoters.
Tokyo Record Stores
www.bento.com/rekodoya.html
Where to get your hands on the vinyl you've been hunting for, be it techno, bebop, hip-hop, ambient house, Latin jazz, rockabilly, easy listening, jungle or any other genre you'd care to think of. The larger Tokyo Meltdown site (www.bento.com)is also worth checking out.

Offbeat

Engrish
www.engrish.com
Hundreds of prime examples of the Japanese mutilation of the English language.
Quirky Japan
www3.tky.3web.ne.jp/~edjacob/index.html
Off-beat home page 'dedicated to digression, kitsch, eccentricity and originality' with alternative things to do in Tokyo when you're 'tired of shrines and temples'.
Ramen
www.worldramen.net
All the best ramen noodle restaurants in the world, rated and reviewed in English. Particularly good Tokyo section.
Tokyo DV
www.tokyodv.com
One for broadband users, with full-length films to download. Check out the penis-worshipping festival. Also features gossip from the world of Japanese showbiz.

Portal sites

Insite
www.insite-tokyo.com
An upper-end portal that carries lots of interesting articles on controversial topics.
Japan Tips
www.japantips.com
A whole library of information on everything in Japan.
Tokyodoko
www.tokyodoko.com
Portal with an easy-to-use and relatively in-depth reference search facility.
Tokyo Pop
www.tokyopop.com
Cute site covering Japanese pop culture from every angle.
Yahoo Japan
www.yahoo.co.jp
Yahoo is a big success in Japan: the nation's most popular search engine and information provider.
Zigzag Asia
www.zigzagasia.com
Has some original sections and also includes an impressive list of Japan-related sites.

What's on

Cool Girls Japan
www.coolgirlsjapan.com
Fun page revealing the finer details of fashion and fads among Tokyo's hippest chicks.
Metropolis
www.metropolis.co.jp
Metropolis is the most reliably updated English-language source for what's-on listings for clubs, concerts and art galleries as well as feature articles and classified ads.
Ski Japan
www.skijapanguide.com
During the winter, it's more than possible to head off to the mountains for a day's skiing and be back in Tokyo by nightfall. This page tells you exactly how to go about it.
Superfuture
www.superfuture.com
Hyper-stylish site mapping out all the coolest shops and bars, and the best restaurants.
Tokyo Food Page
www.bento.com
An awe-inspiring restaurant guide to the city searchable by cuisine, location or both. Also has recipes, beer news and so much more.
Tokyo Q
www.tokyoq.com
Tokyo's best-known online mag, it's crammed with details on restaurants, hotels, clubs, what's on in Tokyo and more.

Getting By in Japanese

JAPANESE LANGUAGE

Pronunciation

Japanese pronunciation presents few problems for native English speakers, the most difficult trick to master being the doubling of vowels or consonants (see below).

Vowels

a as in bad
e as in bed
i as in feet
o as in long
u as in look

Long vowels

aa as in father
ee as in fair
ii as in feet, but longer
oo as in fought
uu as in chute

Consonants

Consonants in Japanese are pronounced the same as in English, but are always hard ('g' as in 'girl', rather than 'gyrate', for example). The only exceptions are the 'l/r' sound, which is one sound in Japanese, and falls halfway between the English pronunciation of the two letters, and 'v', which is pronounced as a 'b'. When consonants are doubled, they are pronounced as such: a 'tt' as in 'matte' (wait) is pronounced more like the 't' sound in 'get to' than in 'getting'.

Reading the phrases

When reading the phrases given below, remember to separate the syllables. Despite the amusing way it looks in English, the common name Takeshita is pronounced Ta-ke-shi-ta. Similarly, made (until) is 'ma-de', not the English word 'made', and shite (doing) is 'shi-te', rather than anything else. When a 'u' falls at the end of the word, it is barely pronounced: 'desu' is closer to 'dess' than to 'de-su'.

Reading & writing

The Japanese writing system is fiendishly complicated and is the main deterrent to learning the language. Japanese uses two syllabaries (not alphabets, because the letters represent complete sounds), hiragana and katakana, in conjunction with kanji, characters imported from China many centuries ago. The average Japanese person will be able to read over 6,000 kanji. For all but the most determined visitor, learning to read before you go is out of the question. However, learning katakana is relatively simple and will yield quick results, since it is used mainly to spell out foreign words (many imported from English). For books on learning Japanese, *see* **Further Reference**, *page 293*.

Numbers

1	***ichi***	2	***ni***	3	***san***
4	***yon***	5	***go***	6	***roku***
7	***nana***	8	***hachi***	9	***kyuu***
10	***juu***	11	***juu-ichi***	12	***juu-ni***
100	***hyaku***	1,000	***sen***	10,000	***man***

Days

Monday ***getsu-yoobi***
Tuesday ***ka-yoobi***
Wednesday ***sui-yoobi***
Thursday ***moku-yoobi***
Friday ***kin-yoobi***
Saturday ***do-yoobi***
Sunday ***nichi-yoobi***

Time

It's at ...o'clock. ***...ji desu***

Excuse me, do you have the time?
sumimasen, ima nan-ji desu ka

Months

January ***ichi-gatsu***
February ***ni-gatsu***
March ***san-gatsu***
April ***shi-gatsu***
May ***go-gatsu***
June ***roku-gatsu***
July ***shichi-gatsu***
August ***hachi-gatsu***
September ***ku-gatsu***
October ***juu-gatsu***
November ***juu-ichi-gatsu***
December ***juu-ni-gatsu***

Dates

yesterday/today/tomorrow
kinoo/kyoo/ashita

last week/this week/next week
sen-shuu/kon-shuu/rai-shuu

the weekend ***shuumatsu***

Directory

Basic expressions

Yes/no ***hai/iie***

Okay ***ookee***

Please (asking for a favour) ***onegai shimasu***

Please (offering a favour) ***doozo***

Thank you (very much) ***(doomo) arigatoo***

Hello/hi ***kon nichiwa***

Good morning ***ohayoo gozaimasu***

Good afternoon ***kon nichi wa***

Good evening ***kon ban wa***

Goodnight ***oyasumi nasai***

Goodbye ***sayonara***

Excuse me (getting attention) ***sumimasen***

Excuse me (may I get past?) ***shitsurei shimasu***

Excuse me/sorry ***gomen nasai***

Don't mention it/never mind
ki ni shinai de kudasai

It's okay ***daijyoobu desu***

Communication

Do you speak English?
Eigo o hanashi masu ka

I don't speak (much) Japanese
Nihongo o (amari) hanashi masen

Could you speak more slowly?
yukkuri itte kudasai

Could you repeat that? ***moo ichido itte kudasai***

I understand ***wakari mashita***

I don't understand ***wakari masen***

Do you understand? ***wakari masu ka?***

Where is it? ***doko desu ka***

When is it? ***itsu desu ka***

What is it? ***nan desu ka***

SIGNS

General

左 *hidari* left

右 *migi* right

入口 *iriguchi* entrance

出口 *deguchi* exit

トイレ/お手洗い *toire/o-tearai* toilets

男/男性 *otoko/dansei* men

女/女性 *onna/jyosei* women

禁煙 *kin-en* no smoking

危険 *kiken* danger

立ち入り禁止 *tachiiri kinshi* no entry

引く/押す *hiku/osu* pull/push

遺失物取扱所 *ishitsu butsu toriatsukai jo*
lost property

水泳禁止 *suiei kinshi* no swimming

飲料水 *inryoosui* drinking water

関係者以外立ち入り禁止
kankeisha igai tachiiri kinshi private

地下道 *chikadoo* underpass (subway)

足元注意 *ashimoto chuui* mind the step

ペンキ塗り立て *penki nuritate* wet paint

頭上注意 *zujoo chuui* mind your head

Road signs

止まれ *tomare* stop

徐行 *jokoo* slow

一方通行 *ippoo tsuukoo* one way

駐車禁止 *chuusha kinshi* no parking

高速道路 *koosoku dooro* motorway

料金 *ryookin* toll

信号 *shingoo* traffic lights

交差点 *koosaten* junction

Airport/station

案内 *an-nai* information

免税 *menzee* duty free

入国管理 *nyuukoku kanri* immigration

到着 *touchaku* arrivals

出発 *shuppatsu* departures

コインロッカー *koin rokkaa* luggage lockers

荷物引き渡し所 *nimotsu hikiwatashi jo*
luggage reclaim

手荷物カート *tenimotsu kaato* trolleys

バス/鉄道 *basu/tetsudoo* bus/train

レンタカー *rentakaa* car rental

地下鉄 *chikatetsu* underground

Hotels/restaurants

フロント *furonto* reception

予約 *yoyaku* reservation

非常口 *hijyooguchi* emergency/fire exit

湯 *yu* hot (water)

冷 *ree* cold (water)

バー *baa* bar

Shops

営業中 *eegyoo chuu* open

閉店 *heeten* closed

階 *kai* floor

地下 *chika* basement

エレベーター *erebeetaa* lift

エスカレーター *esukareetaa* escalator

会計 *kaikee* cashier

Sightseeing

入場無料 *nyuujoo muryoo* free admission

大人/子供 小人 *otona/kodomo* adults/children

割引 (学生/高齢者) *waribiki (gakusei/koureisha)* reduction (students/senior citizens)

お土産 *o-miyage* souvenirs

手を触れないでください
te o furenai de kudasai do not touch

撮影禁止 *satsuei kinshi* no photography

Public buildings

病院 *byooin* hospital

交番 *kouban* police box

銀行 *ginkoo* bank

郵便局 *yuubin kyoku* post office

プール *puuru* swimming pool

博物館 *hakubutsu-kan* museum

ESSENTIAL WORDS & PHRASES

Hotels

Do you have a room?
heya wa arimasu ka

I'd like a single/double room
shinguru/daburu no heya o onegai shimasu

I'd like a room with...
...tsuki no heya o onegai shimasu

a bath/shower **furo/shawa**

Reception

I have a reservation
yoyaku shite arimasu

My name is...
(watashi no namae wa)...desu

Is there...in the room?
heya ni...wa arimasu ka

air-conditioning ***eakon***

TV/telephone ***terebi/denwa***

We'll be staying... ***...tomari masu***

one night only ***ippaku dake***

a week ***isshuu-kan***

I don't know yet ***mada wakari masen***

I'd like to stay an extra night
moo ippaku sasete kudasai

How much is it...? ***...ikura desu ka***

including/excluding breakfast
chooshoku komi/nuki de

Does the price include...?
kono nedan wa...komi desu ka

sales tax (VAT) ***shoohi zee***

breakfast/meal ***chooshoku/shokuji***

Is there a reduction for children?
kodomo no waribiki wa arimasu ka

What time is breakfast served?
chooshoku wa nan-ji desu ka

Is there room service?
ruumu saabisu wa arimasu ka

The key to room..., please.
...goo-shitsu no kagi o kudasai

I've lost my key **kagi o nakushi mashita**

Could you wake me up at...?
...ji ni okoshite kudasai

bath towel/blanket/pillow
basu taoru/moofu/makura

Are there any messages for me?
messeeji wa arimasu ka

What time do we have to checkout by?
chekkuauto wa nan-ji made desu ka

Could I have my bill, please?
kaikei o onegai shimasu

Could I have a receipt please?
reshiito o onegai shimasu

Could you order me a taxi, please?
takushii o yonde kudasai

Shops & services

pharmacy ***yakkyoku/doraggu sutoaa***

off-licence/liquor store ***saka-ya***

newsstand ***kiosuku***

department store ***depaato***

bookshop ***hon-ya***

supermarket ***supaa***

camera store ***kamera-ya***

I'd like... ***...o kudasai***

Do you have...? ***...wa arimasu ka***

How much is that? ***ikura desu ka***

Could you help me? ***onegai shimasu***

I'm looking for... ***...o sagashite imasu***

larger/smaller ***motto ookii/motto chiisai***

I'll take it ***sore ni shimasu***

That's all, thank you ***sore de zenbu desu***

Bank/currency exchange

dollars ***doru***

pounds ***pondo***

yen ***en***

currency exchange ***ryoogae-jo***

I'd like to change some pounds into yen
pondo o en ni kaetain desu ga

Could I have some small change, please?
kozeni o kudasai

Health

Where can I find a hospital/dental surgery?
byooin/hai-sha wa doko desu ka

Is there a doctor/dentist who speaks English?
eego ga dekiru isha/ha-isha wa imasu ka

What are the surgery hours?
shinryoo jikan wa nan-zi desu ka

Could the doctor come to see me here?
ooshin shite kuremasu ka

Could I make an appointment for...?
...yoyaku shitain desu ga

as soon as possible ***dekirudake hayaku***

It's urgent ***shikyuu onegai shimasu***

Symptoms

I feel faint ***memai ga shimasu***

I have a fever ***netsu ga arimasu***

I've been vomiting ***modoshi mashita***

I've got diarrhoea ***geri shitemasu***

It hurts here ***koko ga itai desu***

I have a headache ***zutsu ga shimasu***

I have a sore throat ***nodo ga itai desu***

I have a stomach ache ***onaka ga itai***

I have toothache ***ha ga itai desu***

I've lost a filling/tooth
tsumemono/ha ga toremashita

I don't want it extracted ***nukanaide kudasai***

Sightseeing

Where's the tourist office?
kankoo annai-jo wa doko desu ka

Do you have any information on...?
...no annai wa arimasu ka

sightseeing tour ***kankoo tsuaa***

Are there any trips to...?
...e no tsuaa wa arimasu ka

On tour

We'd like to have a look at the...
...o mitain desu ga

to take photographs ***shasin o toritain desu ga***

to buy souvenirs ***omiyage o kaitain desu ga***

to use the toilets ***toire ni ikitain desu ga***

Can we stop here? ***koko de tomare masu ka***

Could you take a photo of us, please?
shasin o totte kudasai

Travel

To..., please. ***...made onegai shimasu***

Single/return tickets ***katamichi/oofuku kippu***

How much...? ***...wa ikura desu ka?***

I'm here on holiday/business
kankoo/shigoto de kimashita

I'm going to... ***...ni ikimasu***

on my own ***hitori***

with my family ***kazoku to issho***

I'm with a group ***guruupu de kimashita***

ticket office ***kippu-uriba***

ticket gate ***kaisatsu-guchi***

ticket vending machines ***kenbai-ki***

shinkansen ***bullet train***

Where's the nearest underground station?
chikatetsu no eki wa doko desu ka

Where can I buy a ticket?
kippu wa doko de kaemasu ka

Could I have a map of the underground?
chikatetsu no rosenzu o kudasai

Index

Numbers in **bold** indicate the key entry for the topic; numbers in *italics* indicate photographs.

t

u

Gay & lesbian bars

Coffee shops

Restaurants

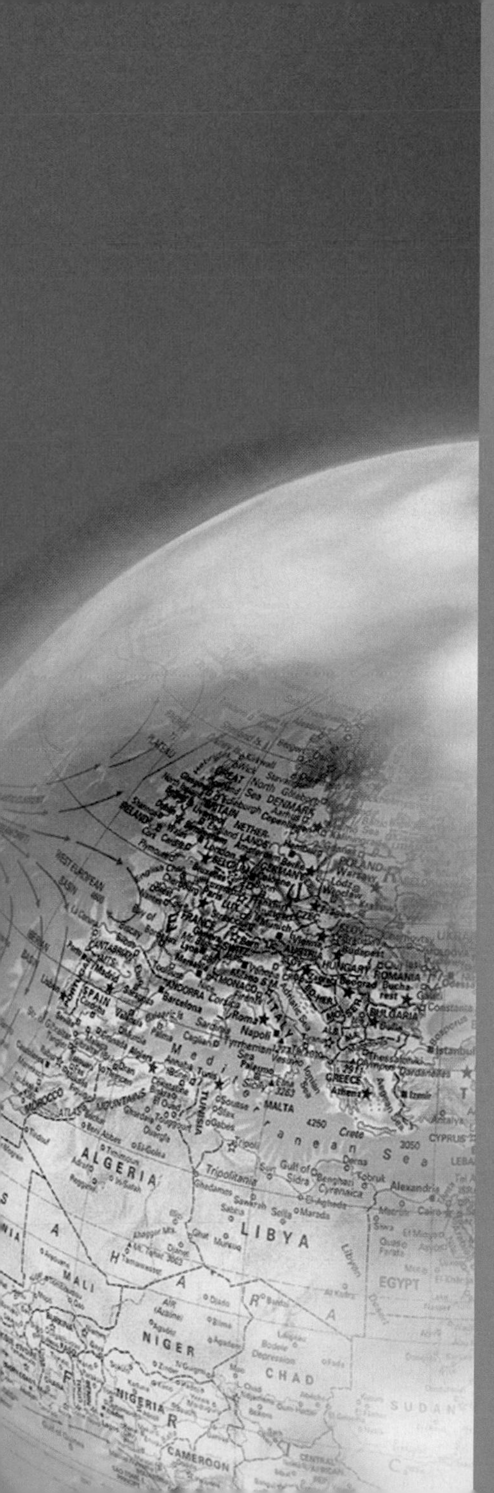

Place of interest and/or entertainment	
Railway station	
Park	
Hospital/university	
Post Office	✉
Temple	
Shrine	⛩
Tram Route	
Area	GINZA

Maps

Yamanote Line Connections

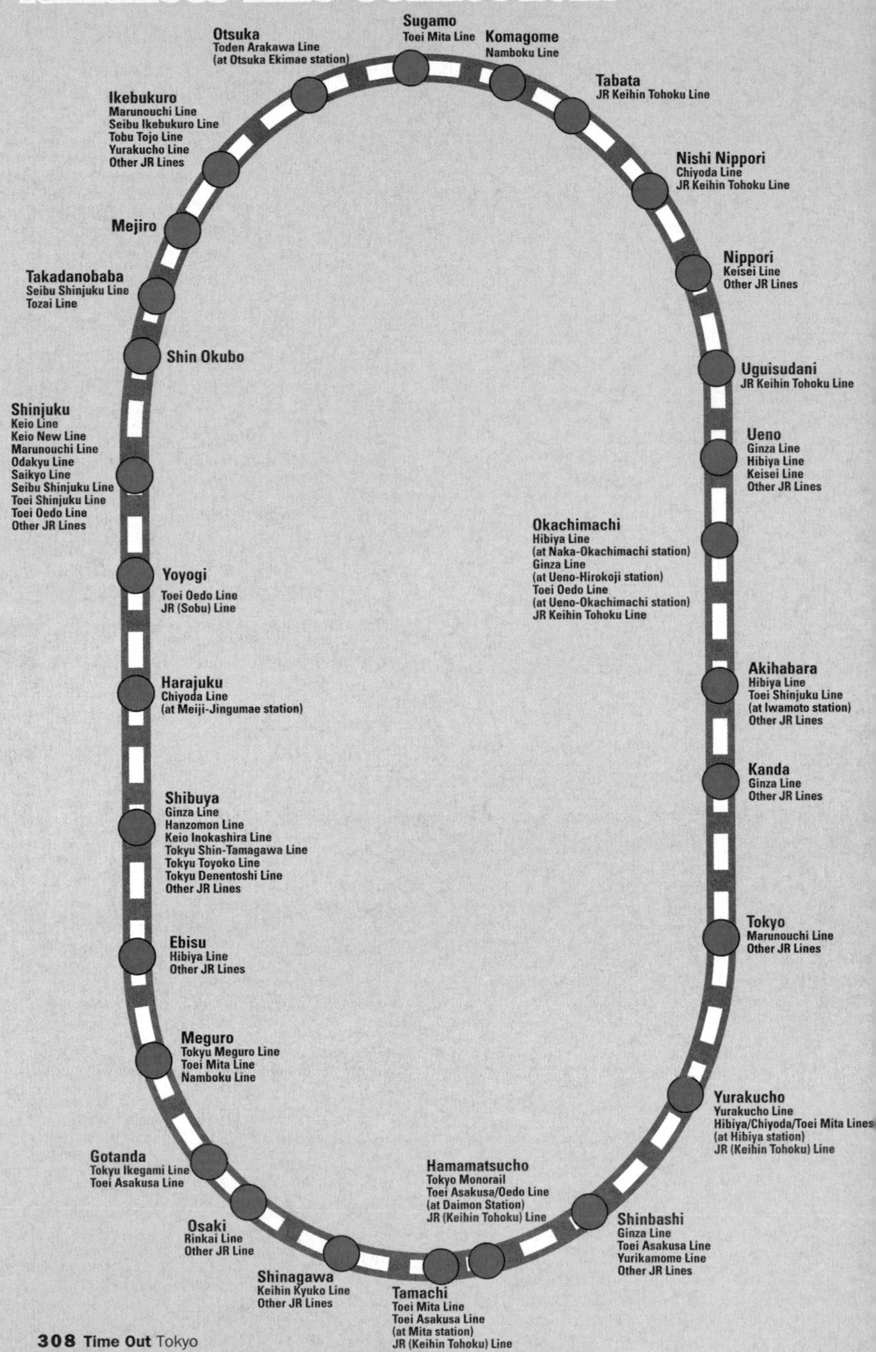

Mainland Japan

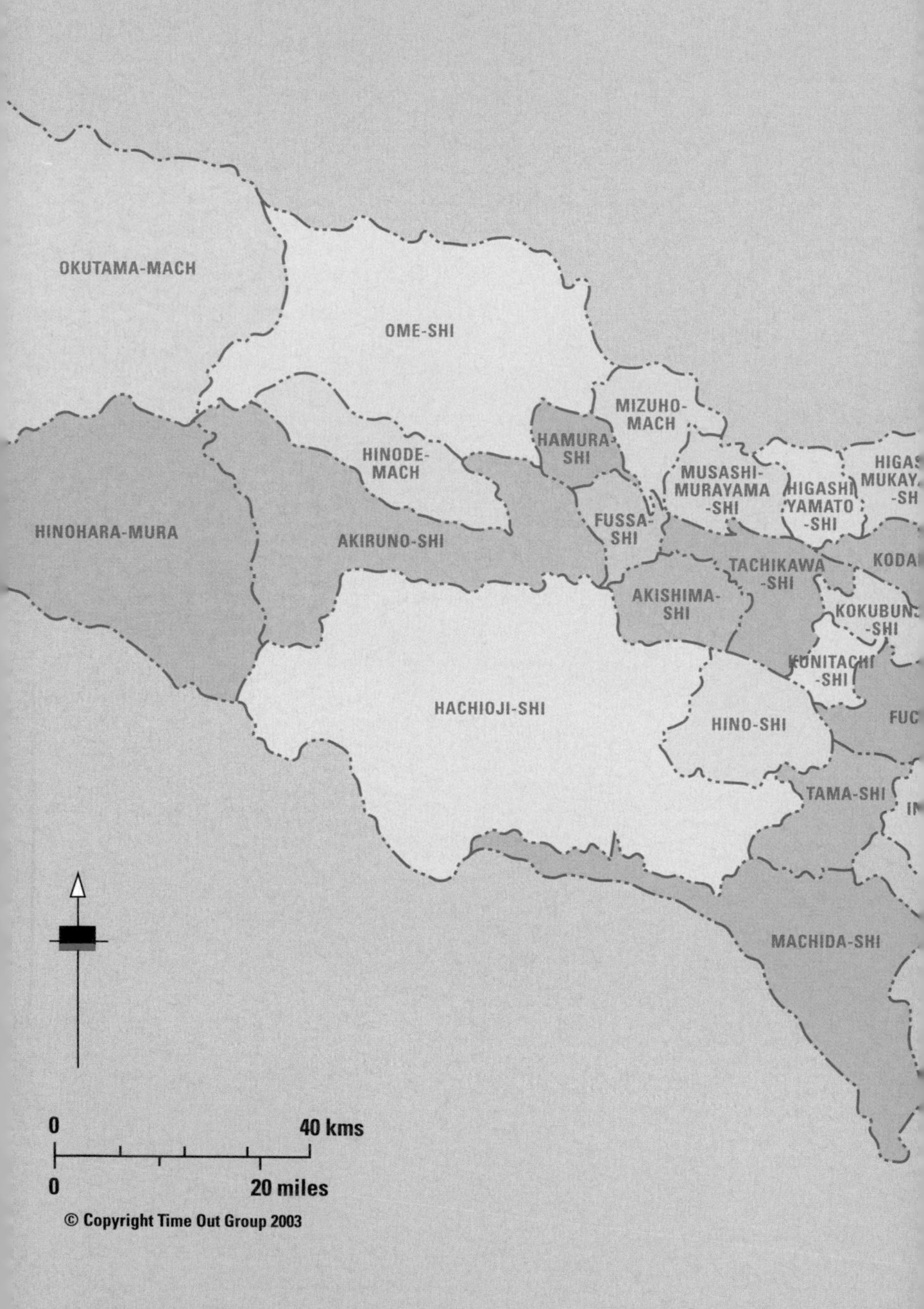
OKUTAMA-MACH
OME-SHI
MIZUHO-
MACH
HAMURA-
SHI
HINODE-
MACH
MUSASHI-
MURAYAMA
-SHI
HIGASHI
YAMATO
-SHI
HINOHARA-MURA
AKIRUNO-SHI
FUSSA-
SHI
TACHIKAWA
-SHI
AKISHIMA-
SHI
KOKUBUNJI
-SHI
KUNITACHI
-SHI
HACHIOJI-SHI
HINO-SHI
TAMA-SHI
MACHIDA-SHI
0
40 kms
0
20 miles

Greater Tokyo

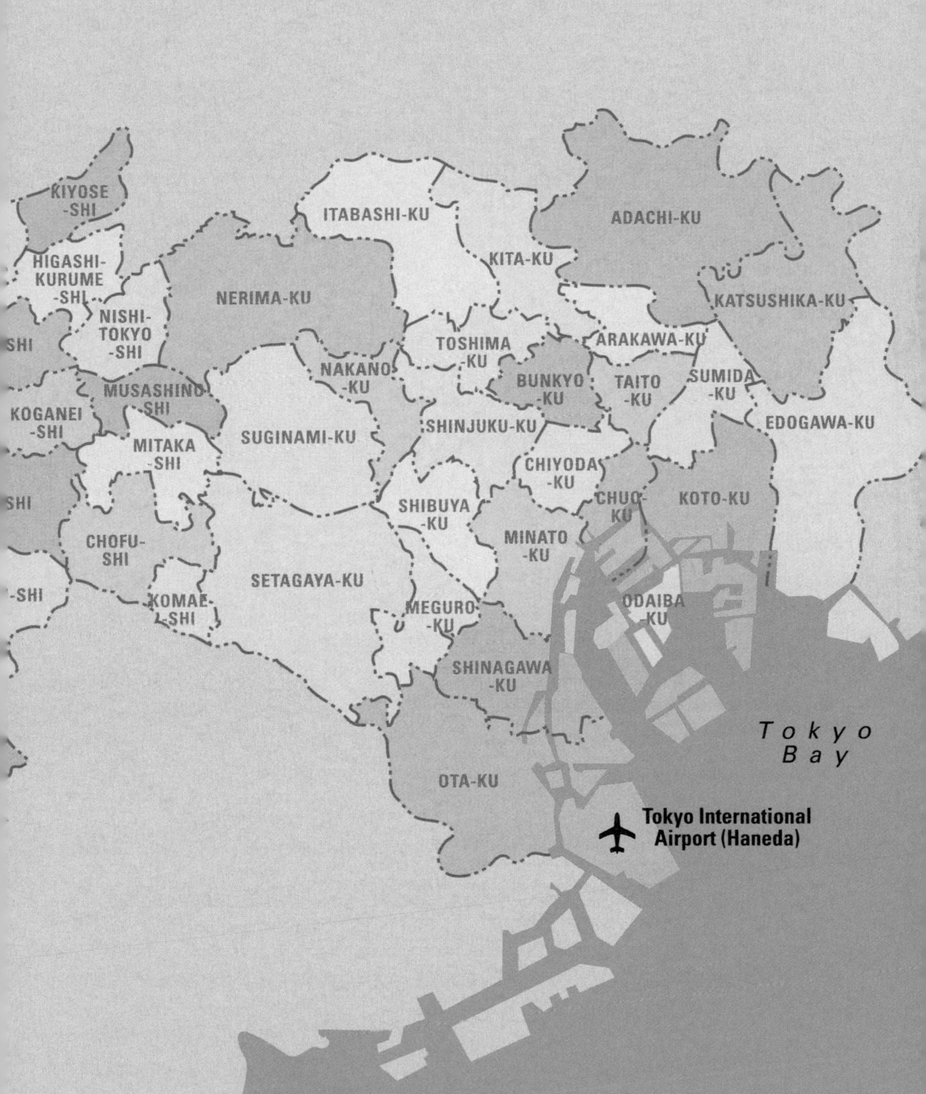

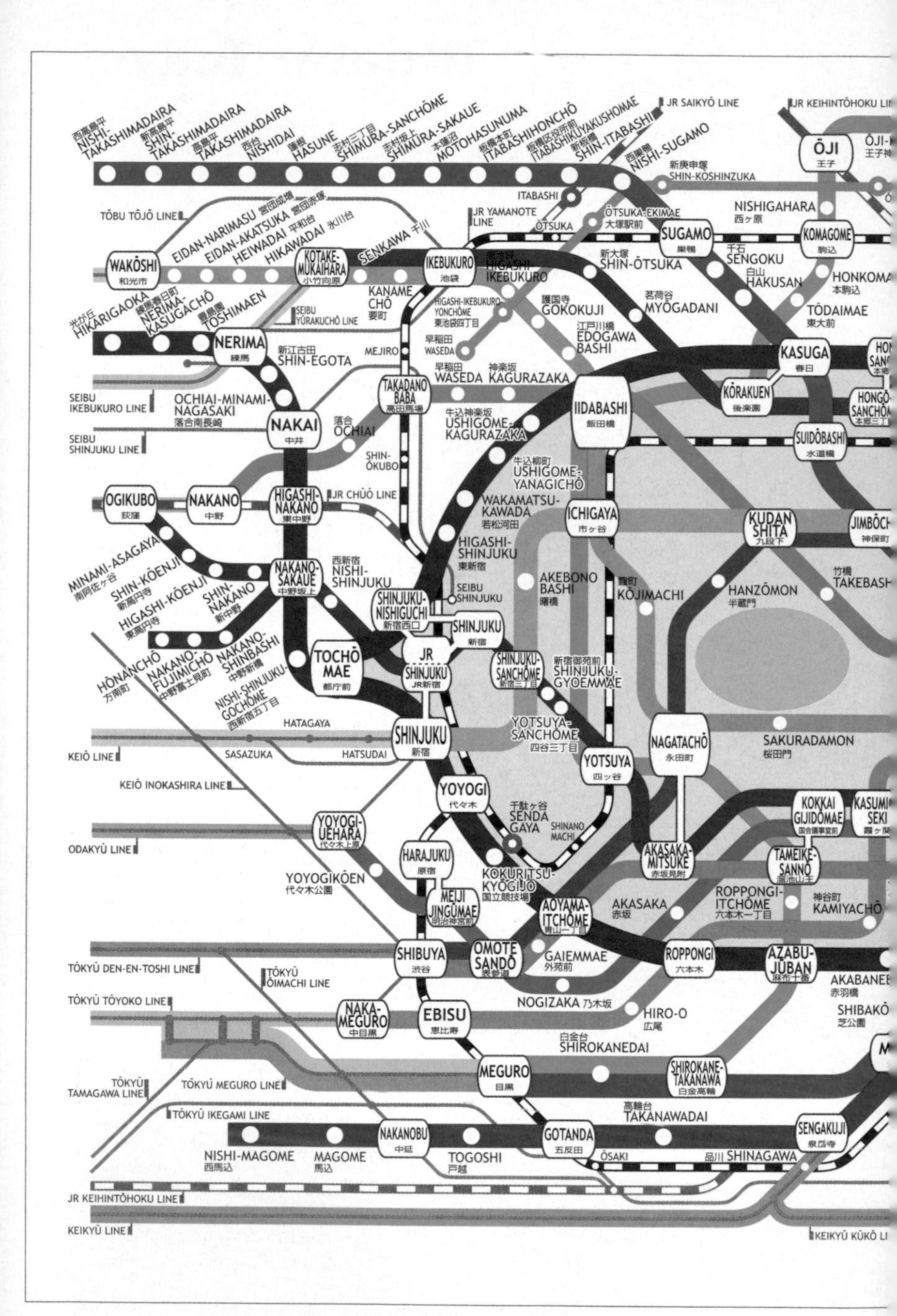

JR SAIKYŌ LINE
JR KEIHINTŌHOKU LINE
NISHI-TAKASHIMADAIRA 西高島平
SHIN-TAKASHIMADAIRA 新高島平
TAKASHIMADAIRA 高島平
NISHIDAI 西台
HASUNE 蓮根
SHIMURA-SANCHŌME 志村三丁目
SHIMURA-SAKAUE 志村坂上
MOTOHASUNUMA 本蓮沼
ITABASHIHONCHŌ 板橋本町
ITABASHIKUYAKUSHOMAE 板橋区役所前
SHIN-ITABASHI 新板橋
NISHI-SUGAMO 西巣鴨
ŌJI 王子
SHIN-KOSHINZUKA 新庚申塚
ITABASHI
NISHIGAHARA 西ヶ原
TŌBU TŌJŌ LINE
EIDAN-NARIMASU 営団成増
EIDAN-AKATSUKA 営団赤塚
HEIWADAI 平和台
HIKAWADAI 氷川台
JR YAMANOTE LINE
ŌTSUKA
ŌTSUKA-EKIMAE 大塚駅前
SUGAMO 巣鴨
KOMAGOME 駒込
SENKAWA 千川
WAKŌSHI 和光市
KOTAKE-MUKAIHARA 小竹向原
IKEBUKURO 池袋
HIGASHI-IKEBUKURO 東池袋
SHIN-ŌTSUKA 新大塚
SENGOKU 千石
HAKUSAN 白山
HONKOMAGOME 本駒込
HIKARIGAOKA 光が丘
NERIMA-KASUGACHŌ 練馬春日町
TOSHIMAEN 豊島園
KANAME CHŌ 要町
HIGASHI-IKEBUKURO YONCHŌME 東池袋四丁目
GOKOKUJI 護国寺
MYŌGADANI 茗荷谷
TŌDAIMAE 東大前
SEIBU YŪRAKUCHŌ LINE
WASEDA 早稲田
EDOGAWA BASHI 江戸川橋
NERIMA 練馬
SHIN-EGOTA 新江古田
MEJIRO
KASUGA 春日
HONGŌ-SANCHŌME 本郷三丁目
SEIBU IKEBUKURO LINE
OCHIAI-MINAMI-NAGASAKI 落合南長崎
TAKADANOBABA 高田馬場
WASEDA 早稲田
KAGURAZAKA 神楽坂
IIDABASHI 飯田橋
KŌRAKUEN 後楽園
SEIBU SHINJUKU LINE
NAKAI 中井
OCHIAI 落合
USHIGOME-KAGURAZAKA 牛込神楽坂
SUIDŌBASHI 水道橋
SHIN-ŌKUBO
USHIGOME-YANAGICHŌ 牛込柳町
OGIKUBO 荻窪
NAKANO 中野
HIGASHI-NAKANO 東中野
JR CHŪŌ LINE
WAKAMATSU-KAWADA 若松河田
ICHIGAYA 市ヶ谷
KUDANSHITA 九段下
JIMBŌCHŌ 神保町
MINAMI-ASAGAYA 南阿佐ヶ谷
SHIN-KŌENJI 新高円寺
HIGASHI-KŌENJI 東高円寺
SHIN-NAKANO 新中野
NAKANO-SAKAUE 中野坂上
NISHI-SHINJUKU 西新宿
HIGASHI-SHINJUKU 東新宿
AKEBONOBASHI 曙橋
KŌJIMACHI 麹町
HANZŌMON 半蔵門
TAKEBASHI 竹橋
SEIBU SHINJUKU
SHINJUKU-NISHIGUCHI 新宿西口
SHINJUKU 新宿
HŌNANCHŌ 方南町
NAKANO-FUJIMICHŌ 中野富士見町
NAKANO-SHINBASHI 中野新橋
TOCHŌMAE 都庁前
JR SHINJUKU JR新宿
SHINJUKU-SANCHŌME 新宿三丁目
SHINJUKU-GYOEMMAE 新宿御苑前
NISHI-SHINJUKU-GOCHŌME 西新宿五丁目
HATAGAYA
SHINJUKU 新宿
YOTSUYA-SANCHŌME 四谷三丁目
NAGATACHŌ 永田町
SAKURADAMON 桜田門
KEIŌ LINE
SASAZUKA
HATSUDAI
YOTSUYA 四ッ谷
KEIŌ INOKASHIRA LINE
YOYOGI 代々木
KOKKAI GIJIDŌMAE 国会議事堂前
KASUMIGASEKI 霞ヶ関
YOYOGI-UEHARA 代々木上原
SENDAGAYA 千駄ヶ谷
SHINANOMACHI
ODAKYŪ LINE
HARAJUKU 原宿
AKASAKA-MITSUKE 赤坂見附
TAMEIKE-SANNŌ 溜池山王
YOYOGIKŌEN 代々木公園
KOKURITSU-KYŌGIJŌ 国立競技場
MEIJI JINGŪMAE 明治神宮前
AOYAMA-ITCHŌME 青山一丁目
AKASAKA 赤坂
ROPPONGI-ITCHŌME 六本木一丁目
KAMIYACHŌ 神谷町
TŌKYŪ DEN-EN-TOSHI LINE
SHIBUYA 渋谷
OMOTESANDŌ 表参道
GAIEMMAE 外苑前
ROPPONGI 六本木
AZABU-JŪBAN 麻布十番
AKABANEBASHI 赤羽橋
TŌKYŪ ŌIMACHI LINE
TŌKYŪ TŌYOKO LINE
NAKA-MEGURO 中目黒
EBISU 恵比寿
NOGIZAKA 乃木坂
HIRO-O 広尾
SHIBAKŌEN 芝公園
SHIROKANEDAI 白金台
TŌKYŪ TAMAGAWA LINE
TŌKYŪ MEGURO LINE
MEGURO 目黒
SHIROKANE-TAKANAWA 白金高輪
TŌKYŪ IKEGAMI LINE
TAKANAWADAI 高輪台
NAKANOBU 中延
GOTANDA 五反田
SENGAKUJI 泉岳寺
NISHI-MAGOME 西馬込
MAGOME 馬込
TOGOSHI 戸越
ŌSAKI
SHINAGAWA 品川
JR KEIHINTŌHOKU LINE
KEIKYŪ LINE
KEIKYŪ KŪKŌ LINE

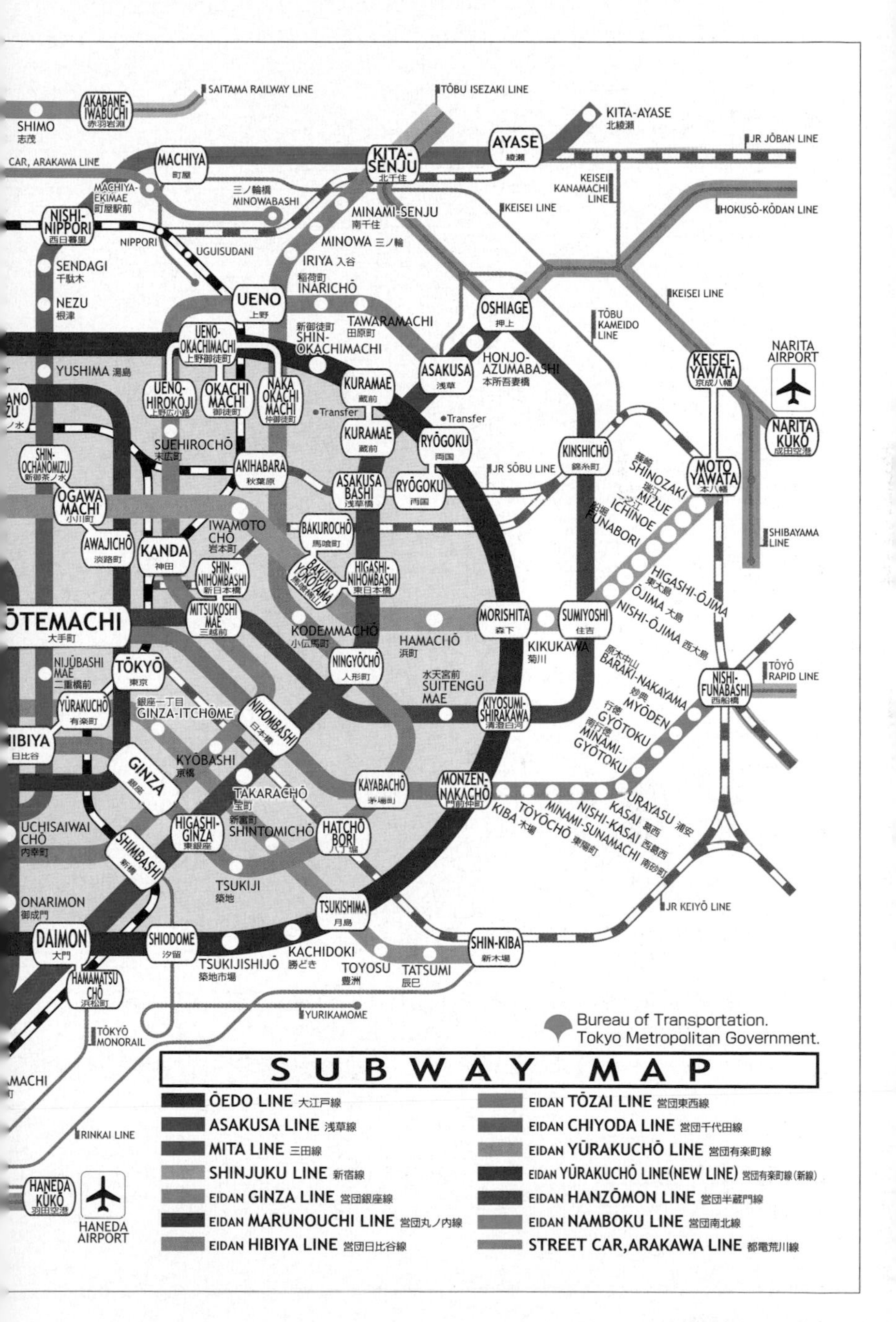
SUBWAY MAP
Bureau of Transportation.
Tokyo Metropolitan Government.
ŌEDO LINE 大江戸線
ASAKUSA LINE 浅草線
MITA LINE 三田線
SHINJUKU LINE 新宿線
EIDAN GINZA LINE 営団銀座線
EIDAN MARUNOUCHI LINE 営団丸ノ内線
EIDAN HIBIYA LINE 営団日比谷線
EIDAN TŌZAI LINE 営団東西線
EIDAN CHIYODA LINE 営団千代田線
EIDAN YŪRAKUCHŌ LINE 営団有楽町線
EIDAN YŪRAKUCHŌ LINE(NEW LINE) 営団有楽町線(新線)
EIDAN HANZŌMON LINE 営団半蔵門線
EIDAN NAMBOKU LINE 営団南北線
STREET CAR,ARAKAWA LINE 都電荒川線
SAITAMA RAILWAY LINE
TŌBU ISEZAKI LINE
JR JŌBAN LINE
KEISEI KANAMACHI LINE
KEISEI LINE
HOKUSŌ-KŌDAN LINE
TŌBU KAMEIDO LINE
JR SŌBU LINE
SHIBAYAMA LINE
TŌYŌ RAPID LINE
JR KEIYŌ LINE
YURIKAMOME
TŌKYŌ MONORAIL
RINKAI LINE
NARITA AIRPORT
HANEDA AIRPORT
AKABANE-IWABUCHI 赤羽岩淵
SHIMO 志茂
KITA-AYASE 北綾瀬
AYASE 綾瀬
KITA-SENJU 北千住
MACHIYA 町屋
MACHIYA-EKIMAE 町屋駅前
三ノ輪橋 MINOWABASHI
NISHI-NIPPORI 西日暮里
NIPPORI
UGUISUDANI
MINAMI-SENJU 南千住
MINOWA 三ノ輪
IRIYA 入谷
稲荷町 INARICHŌ
SENDAGI 千駄木
NEZU 根津
UENO 上野
OSHIAGE 押上
新御徒町 SHIN-OKACHIMACHI
TAWARAMACHI 田原町
UENO-OKACHIMACHI 上野御徒町
YUSHIMA 湯島
UENO-HIROKŌJI 上野広小路
OKACHIMACHI 御徒町
NAKA OKACHIMACHI 仲御徒町
ASAKUSA 浅草
HONJO-AZUMABASHI 本所吾妻橋
KURAMAE 蔵前
Transfer
RYŌGOKU 両国
KEISEI-YAWATA 京成八幡
NARITA KŪKŌ 成田空港
KINSHICHŌ 錦糸町
MOTO YAWATA 本八幡
SHIN-OCHANOMIZU 新御茶ノ水
SUEHIROCHŌ 末広町
AKIHABARA 秋葉原
ASAKUSA BASHI 浅草橋
OGAWA MACHI 小川町
篠崎 SHINOZAKI
瑞江 MIZUE
一之江 ICHINOE
船堀 FUNABORI
IWAMOTO CHŌ 岩本町
BAKUROCHŌ 馬喰町
AWAJICHŌ 淡路町
KANDA 神田
SHIN-NIHOMBASHI 新日本橋
BAKURO YOKOYAMA 馬喰横山
HIGASHI-NIHOMBASHI 東日本橋
HIGASHI-ŌJIMA 東大島
ŌJIMA 大島
NISHI-ŌJIMA 西大島
ŌTEMACHI 大手町
MITSUKOSHI MAE 三越前
KODEMMACHŌ 小伝馬町
HAMACHŌ 浜町
MORISHITA 森下
SUMIYOSHI 住吉
KIKUKAWA 菊川
NIJŪBASHI MAE 二重橋前
TŌKYŌ 東京
NINGYŌCHŌ 人形町
水天宮前 SUITENGŪ MAE
原木中山 BARAKI-NAKAYAMA
妙典 MYŌDEN
行徳 GYŌTOKU
南行徳 MINAMI-GYŌTOKU
NISHI-FUNABASHI 西船橋
YŪRAKUCHŌ 有楽町
銀座一丁目 GINZA-ITCHŌME
KIYOSUMI-SHIRAKAWA 清澄白河
HIBIYA 日比谷
NIHOMBASHI 日本橋
KYŌBASHI 京橋
GINZA 銀座
TAKARACHŌ 宝町
KAYABACHŌ 茅場町
MONZEN-NAKACHŌ 門前仲町
URAYASU 浦安
KASAI 葛西
NISHI-KASAI 西葛西
MINAMI-SUNAMACHI 南砂町
TŌYŌCHŌ 東陽町
KIBA 木場
UCHISAIWAI CHŌ 内幸町
HIGASHI-GINZA 東銀座
新富町 SHINTOMICHŌ
HATCHŌ BORI 八丁堀
SHIMBASHI 新橋
TSUKIJI 築地
ONARIMON 御成門
TSUKISHIMA 月島
DAIMON 大門
SHIODOME 汐留
KACHIDOKI 勝どき
TSUKIJISHIJŌ 築地市場
TOYOSU 豊洲
TATSUMI 辰巳
SHIN-KIBA 新木場
HAMAMATSU CHŌ 浜松町
HANEDA KŪKŌ 羽田空港

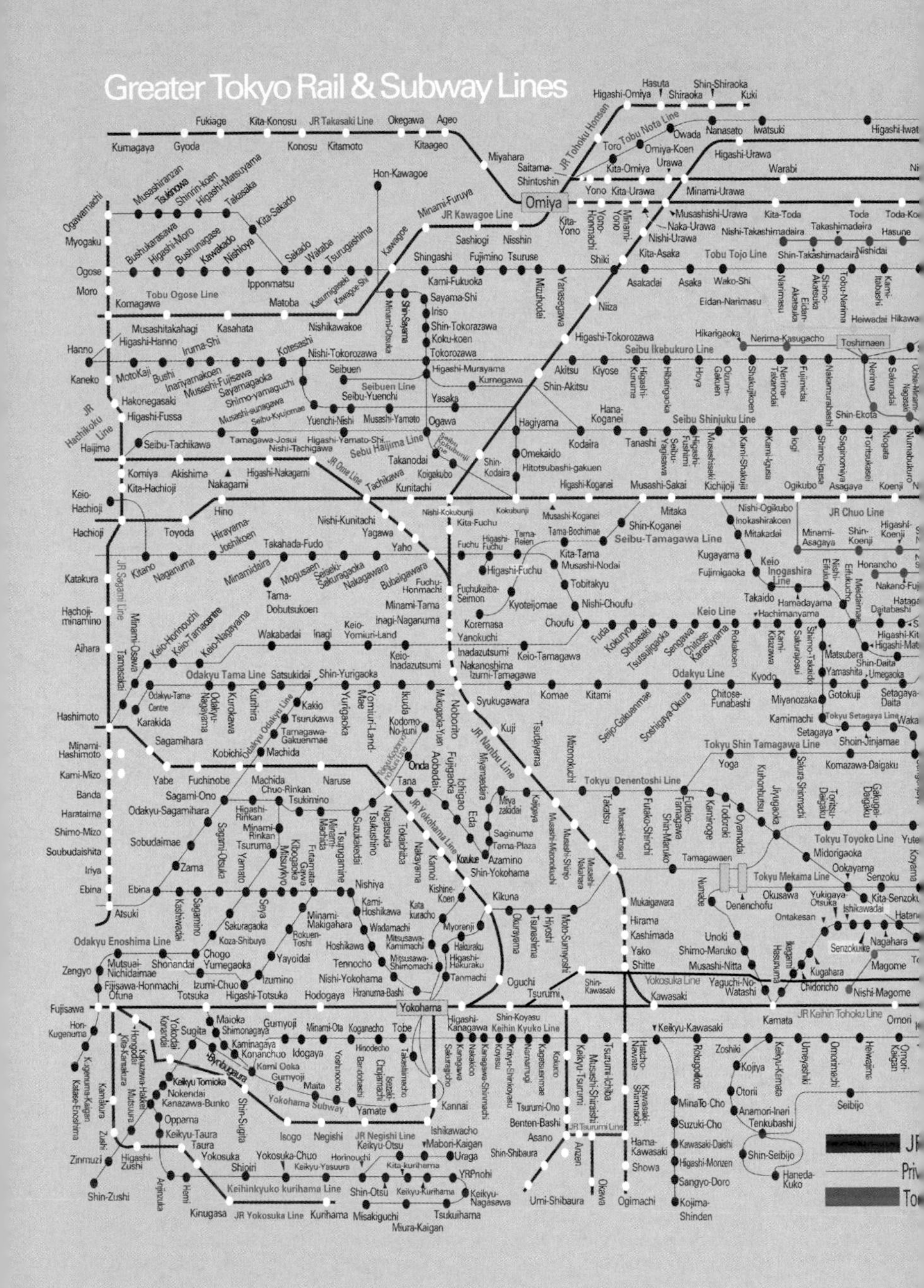
Greater Tokyo Rail & Subway Lines
JR Takasaki Line
Fukiage
Kita-Konosu
Okegawa
Ageo
Kumagaya
Gyoda
Konosu
Kitamoto
Kitaageo
Miyahara
Saitama-Shintoshin
JR Tohoku Honsen
Omiya
Hasuta
Shin-Shiraoka
Higashi-Omiya
Shiraoka
Kuki
Tobu Noda Line
Owada
Nanasato
Iwatsuki
Toro
Omiya-Koen
Kita-Omiya
Urawa
Higashi-Urawa
Warabi
Yono
Kita-Urawa
Minami-Urawa
Musashi-Urawa
Naka-Urawa
Nishi-Urawa
Kita-Toda
Toda
Toda-Koen
Nishi-Takashimadaira
Takashimadaira
Hasune
Shin-Takashimadaira
Nishidai
Hon-Kawagoe
Minami-Furuya
JR Kawagoe Line
Sashiogi
Nisshin
Shingashi
Fujimino
Tsuruse
Kami-Fukuoka
Mizuhodai
Yanasegawa
Shiki
Kita-Asaka
Tobu Tojo Line
Asakadai
Asaka
Wako-Shi
Eidan-Narimasu
Niiza
Narimasu
Heiwadai
Hikawadai
Ogawamachi
Myogaku
Ogose
Moro
Komagawa
Tobu Ogose Line
Musashiranzan
Tsukinowa
Shinrin-koen
Higashi-Matsuyama
Takasaka
Kita-Sakado
Bushukarasawa
Higashi-Moro
Bushunagase
Kawakado
Nishiiriya
Sakado
Wakaba
Tsurugashima
Kawagoe
Kawagoe-Shi
Kasumigaseki
Ipponmatsu
Matoba
Shin-Sayama
Minami-Otsuka
Sayama-Shi
Iriso
Shin-Tokorozawa
Koku-koen
Tokorozawa
Higashi-Murayama
Kumegawa
Nishikawakoe
Musashitakahagi
Kasahata
Higashi-Hanno
Hanno
Kaneko
Iruma-Shi
Kotesashi
Nishi-Tokorozawa
Seibuen
Seibuen Line
Seibu-Yuenchi
Yasaka
Ogawa
Yuenchi-Nishi
Musashi-Yamato
MotoKaji
Bushi
Inariyamakoen
Musashi-Fujisawa
Sayamagaoka
Shimo-yamaguchi
Musashi-sunagawa
Seibu-Kyujomae
Hakonegasaki
Higashi-Fussa
JR Hachikoku Line
Haijima
Seibu-Tachikawa
Tamagawa-Josui
Higashi-Yamato-Shi
Nishi-Tachigawa
Seibu Haijima Line
JR Ome Line
Takanodai
Tachikawa
Koigakubo
Kunitachi
Komiya
Akishima
Kita-Hachioji
Higashi-Nakagami
Nakagami
Hagiyama
Omekaido
Hitotsubashi-gakuen
Shin-Kodaira
Higashi-Koganei
Higashi-Tokorozawa
Akitsu
Kiyose
Shin-Akitsu
Hana-Koganei
Kodaira
Tanashi
Seibu Ikebukuro Line
Seibu Shinjuku Line
Hikarigaoka
Nerima-Kasugacho
Toshimaen
Nerima
Hoya
Hibarigaoka
Shakujiikoen
Fujimidai
Nakamurabashi
Sakuradai
Shin-Ekota
Musashi-Sakai
Kichijoji
Ogikubo
Asagaya
Koenji
Musashiseki
Kami-Shakujii
Kami-Igusa
Iogi
Shimo-Igusa
Saginomiya
Toritsukasei
Nogata
Numabukuro
Keio-Hachioji
Hachioji
Hino
Toyoda
Nishi-Kunitachi
Yagawa
Yaho
Nishi-Kokubunji
Kokubunji
Musashi-Koganei
Mitaka
Shin-Koganei
Seibu-Tamagawa Line
Nishi-Ogikubo
Inokashirakoen
Mitakadai
JR Chuo Line
Minami-Asagaya
Shin-Koenji
Higashi-Koenji
Kita-Fuchu
Fuchu
Higashi-Fuchu
Tama-Reien
Tama-Bochimae
Kita-Tama
Musashi-Nodai
Tobitakyu
Nishi-Choufu
Choufu
Kugayama
Fujimigaoka
Keio Inogashira Line
Takaido
Hamadayama
Honancho
Hirayama-Joshikoen
Takahata-Fudo
Kitano
Naganuma
Minamidaira
Mogusaen
Seiseki-Sakuragaoka
Nakagawara
Bubaigawara
Fuchu-Honmachi
Fuchukeiba-Seimon
Kyoteijomae
Minami-Tama
Inagi-Naganuma
Tama-Dobutsukoen
Katakura
JR Sagami Line
Hachoji-minamino
Minami-Osawa
Keio-Horinouchi
Keio-Tamacentre
Keio-Nagayama
Wakabadai
Inagi
Keio-Yomiuri-Land
Koremasa
Yanokuchi
Keio Line
Hachimanyama
Aihara
Tamasakai
Keio-Inadazutsumi
Inadazutsumi
Nakanoshima
Keio-Tamagawa
Fuda
Kokuryo
Shibasaki
Tsutsujigaoka
Sengawa
Chitose-Karasuyama
Roka-koen
Kami-Kitazawa
Sakurajosui
Shimo-Takaido
Matsubara
Yamashita
Umegaoka
Shin-Daita
Odakyu Tama Line
Satsukidai
Shin-Yurigaoka
Izumi-Tamagawa
Odakyu Line
Kyodo
Karakida
Odakyu-Tama-Centre
Odakyu-Nagayama
Kurokawa
Kurihira
Kakio
Tsurukawa
Yurigaoka
Yomiuri-Land-Mae
Ikuta
Mukogaoka-Yuen
Noborito
Syukugawara
Komae
Kitami
Chitose-Funabashi
Miyanozaka
Gotokuji
Setagaya-Daita
Hashimoto
Sagamihara
Tamagawa-Gakuenmae
Kodomo-No-kuni
JR Nambu Line
Kuji
Tsudayama
Mizonokuchi
Seijo-Gakuenmae
Soshigaya-Okura
Kamimachi
Tokyu Setagaya Line
Setagaya
Minami-Hashimoto
Kami-Mizo
Kobichi
Machida
Onda
Tokyu Shin Tamagawa Line
Shoin-Jinjamae
Yoga
Komazawa-Daigaku
Banda
Yabe
Fuchinobe
Naruse
Tana
Tokyu Denentoshi Line
Haratoima
Sagami-Ono
Chuo-Rinkan
Tsukimino
Aobadai
Fujigaoka
Ichigao
Miyamaedaira
Miyazakidai
Kajigaya
Takatsu
Futako-Shinchi
Futako-Tamagawa
Kaminoge
Todoroki
Oyamadai
Kuhonbutsu
Jiyugaoka
Sakura-Shinmachi
Gakugei-Daigaku
Odakyu-Sagamihara
Higashi-Rinkan
Minami-Rinkan
Shimo-Mizo
Sagami-Otsuka
Tsuruma
Yamato
Eda
Saginuma
Tama-Plaza
Azamino
Tokyu Toyoko Line
Midorigaoka
Sobudaimae
Soubudaishita
Iriya
Zama
Kozukue
Shin-Yokohama
Tamagawaen
Ookayama
Yutenji
Tokyu Mekama Line
Senzoku
Ebina
Kashiwadai
Sagamino
Seya
Nishiya
Kami-Hoshikawa
Kishine-Koen
Kikuna
Okurayama
Tsunashima
Hiyoshi
Moto-Sumiyoshi
Mukaigawara
Hirama
Kashimada
Yako
Shitte
Numabe
Denenchofu
Okusawa
Yukigaya-Otsuka
Kita-Senzoku
Ishikawadai
Ontakesan
Hatanodai
Atsuki
Sakuragaoka
Koza-Shibuya
Minami-Makigahara
Wadamachi
Myorenji
Hakuraku
Higashi-Hakuraku
Tanmachi
Unoki
Shimo-Maruko
Musashi-Nitta
Nagahara
Senzokuike
Magome
Odakyu Enoshima Line
Chogo
Yumegaoka
Yayoidai
Hoshikawa
Tennocho
Nishi-Yokohama
Oguchi
Tsurumi
Shin-Kawasaki
Yokosuka Line
Kawasaki
Yaguchi-No-Watashi
Hasunuma
Ikegami
Kugahara
Chidoricho
Nishi-Magome
Zengyo
Mutsuai-Nichidaimae
Shonandai
Izumi-Chuo
Izumino
Fujisawa-Honmachi
Ofuna
Totsuka
Higashi-Totsuka
Hodogaya
Hiranuma-Bashi
Yokohama
Higashi-Kanagawa
Shin-Koyasu
Keihin Kyuko Line
Kamata
JR Keihin Tohoku Line
Omori
Fujisawa
Hon-Kugenuma
Maioka
Gumyoji
Minami-Ota
Koganecho
Tobe
Keikyu-Kawasaki
Kugenuma
Yokodai
Konandai
Sugita
Shimonagaya
Kaminagaya
Konanchuo
Idogaya
Kami Ooka
Yoshinocho
Bandobashi
Isezakichojamachi
Hinodecho
Takashimacho
Kanagawa
Kanagawa-Shinmachi
Namamugi
Kagetsuenmae
Kokudo
Keikyu-Tsurumi
Tsurumi-Ichiba
Hatcho-Nawate
Kawasaki-Shinmachi
Rokugodote
Zoshiki
Kojiya
Otorii
Keikyu-Kamata
Umeyashiki
Omorimachi
Heiwajima
Kanazawa-Hakkei
Kanazawa-Bunko
Keikyu Tomioka
Nokendai
Kamakura
Zushi
Shin-Sugita
Maita
Yokohama Subway
Yamate
Kannai
Tsurumi-Ono
Benten-Bashi
Asano
Shin-Shibaura
JR Tsurumi Line
Hama-Kawasaki
Showa
MinaTo-Cho
Suzuki-Cho
Kawasaki-Daishi
Higashi-Monzen
Sangyo-Doro
Kojima-Shinden
Anamori-Inari
Tenkubashi
Shin-Seibijo
Seibijo
Haneda-Kuko
Oppama
Keikyu-Taura
Taura
Isogo
Negishi
JR Negishi Line
Keikyu-Otsu
Ishikawacho
Mabori-Kaigan
Uraga
Zinmuzi
Higashi-Zushi
Yokosuka
Yokosuka-Chuo
Horinouchi
Shioiri
Keikyu-Yasuura
Kita-kurihama
YRPnobi
Shin-Zushi
Anjinzuka
Hemi
Keihinkyuko kurihama Line
Shin-Otsu
Keikyu-Kurihama
Keikyu-Nagasawa
Umi-Shibaura
Anzen
Okawa
Ogimachi
Kinugasa
JR Yokosuka Line
Kurihama
Misakiguchi
Tsukuihama
Miura-Kaigan

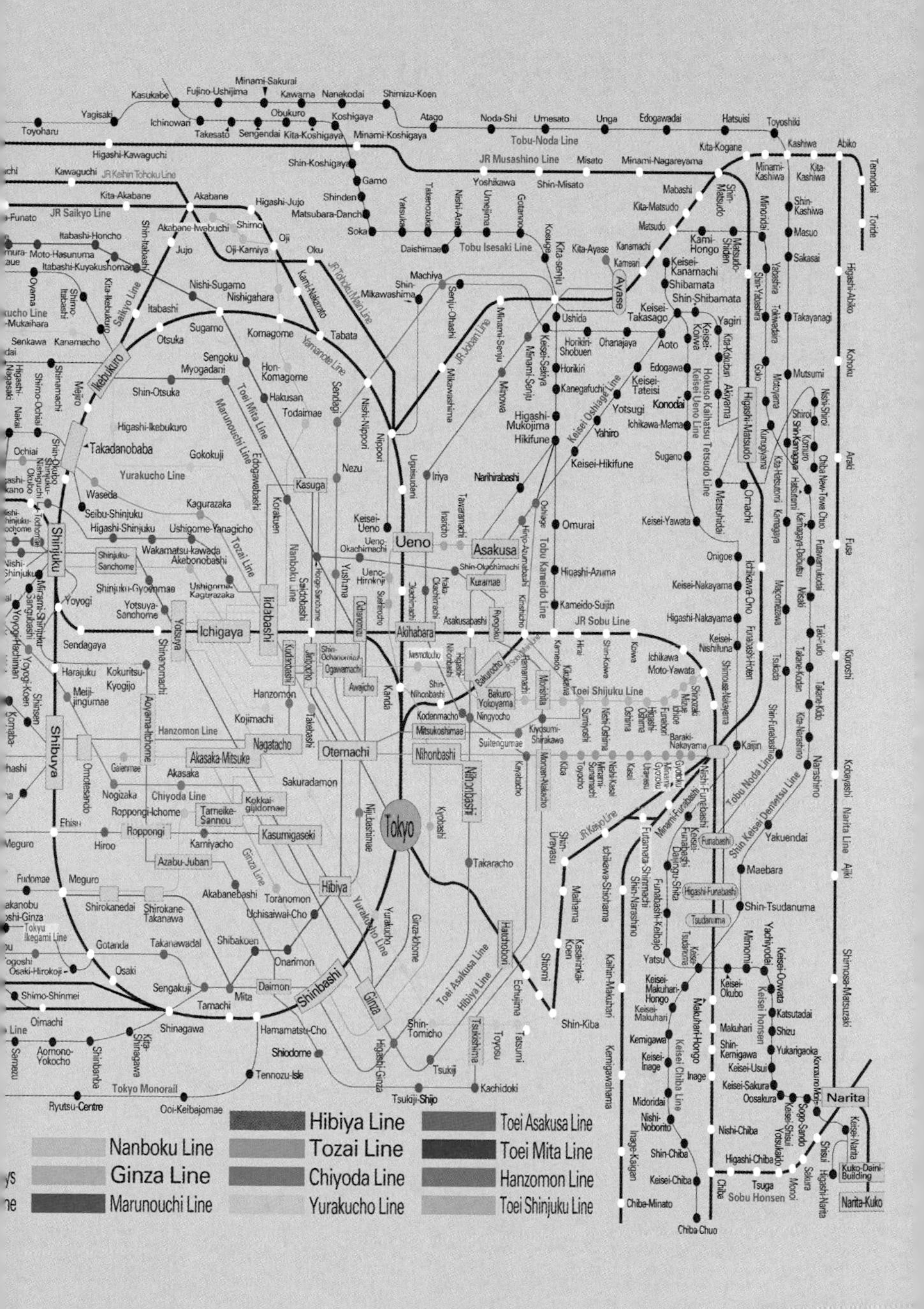

Nanboku Line
Ginza Line
Marunouchi Line
Hibiya Line
Tozai Line
Chiyoda Line
Yurakucho Line
Toei Asakusa Line
Toei Mita Line
Hanzomon Line
Toei Shinjuku Line
Tokyo
Ueno
Asakusa
Akihabara
Shinjuku
Shibuya
Ikebukuro
Takadanobaba
Ichigaya
Iidabashi
Yotsuya
Otemachi
Nihonbashi
Kasumigaseki
Hibiya
Shinbashi
Ginza
Nagatacho
Akasaka-Mitsuke
Roppongi
Hatchobori
Narita
Narita-Kuko
Kuko-Daini-Building
Tobu-Noda Line
JR Musashino Line
JR Saikyo Line
JR Keihin Tohoku Line
JR Tohoku Main Line
Yamanote Line
JR Joban Line
Tobu Isesaki Line
Keisei Oshiage Line
Hokuso Kaihatsu Tetsudo Line
Tobu Kameido Line
JR Sobu Line
JR Keiyo Line
Tobu Noda Line
Shin Keisei Dentetsu Line
Keisei Chiba Line
Keisei honsen
Narita Line
Sobu Honsen
Tokyo Monorail
Toei Asakusa Line
Hibiya Line
Marunouchi Line
Toei Mita Line
Yurakucho Line
Nanboku Line
Hanzomon Line
Chiyoda Line
Tozai Line
Toei Shijuku Line
Shinagawa
Tamachi
Hamamatsu-Cho
Yurakucho
Kanda
Ochanomizu
Nippori
Tabata
Komagome
Sugamo
Otsuka
Mejiro
Yoyogi
Harajuku
Ebisu
Meguro
Gotanda
Osaki
Sendagaya
Akabane
Oji
Kasukabe
Kashiwa
Abiko
Matsudo
Funabashi
Tsudanuma
Chiba
Chiba-Chuo
Shin-Kiba
Tsukiji
Kachidoki
Tennozu-Isle
Ryutsu-Centre

Advertisers' Index

Please refer to relevant sections for addresses and telephone numbers